The Man Who Was Rip Van Winkle

BENJAMIN McARTHUR

The Man Who Was Rip Van Winkle

JOSEPH JEFFERSON AND
NINETEENTH-CENTURY
AMERICAN THEATRE

Yale University Press
New Haven &
London

Published with assistance from the Kingsley Trust Association Publication Fund
established by the Scroll and Key Society of Yale College.

Set in Sabon type by Keystone Typesetting, Inc.
Printed in the United States of America by Thomson-Shore, Inc.

Library of Congress Cataloging-in-Publication Data
McArthur, Benjamin.
The man who was Rip Van Winkle : Joseph Jefferson and nineteenth-century
American theatre / Benjamin McArthur.
p. cm.
Includes bibliographical references and index.
ISBN 978-0-300-12232-9 (cloth : alk. paper)
1. Jefferson, Joseph, 1829–1905. 2. Actors—United States—Biography. I. Title.
PN2287.J4M33 2007
792.02′8092—dc22
[B]   2007012620

A catalogue record for this book is available from the British Library.

10 9 8 7 6 5 4 3 2 1

To Callie, Emily, and Mills

Are we so soon forgot when we are gone?
— *Rip Van Winkle*

Contents

Acknowledgments   ix

Introduction   xiii

1. Cradled in the Profession   1

2. Marking the Progress of Civilization   29

3. Behind the Cart of Thespis   54

4. An Actor Prepares   85

5. Echoing the Public Voice   107

6. Triumphs in Comedy and Melodrama   134

7. Nibbling at Stardom   163

8. A Mighty Nimrod of Theatrical Touring   184

9. Mr. Jefferson and Rip Van Winkle   213

10. Bringing the "Sleepy Piece" Home   241

11. A Fellow of Infinite Jest, of Most Excellent Fancy   269

12.   Are We So Soon Forgot?   305

Epilogue: A Shy Thing Is Comedy   350

·   Notes   357

Index   423

Acknowledgments

During my decade-and-a-half pursuit of Joseph Jefferson I have incurred many debts to librarians, scholars, and other individuals who kept Joe's trail fresh for me. It is a pleasure to recount my obligations.

I regret that the individual perhaps most interested in my project did not live to see its completion. Gervase Farjeon, Joe Jefferson's great-grandson, offered enthusiastic support from the moment he learned of my efforts. A man of the theatre in his own right, Gervase provided a link to the English branch of the Jefferson family. I have also appreciated the ongoing generosity of his friend Ann Harvey.

Two Jefferson scholars preceded me, and I have profited greatly from their scholarship and assistance. Douglas McKenzie was the pioneer scholar of the great comedian. His dissertation offered insights and bibliographical leads. Even in retirement Doug generously provided source material available no-where else. Arthur Bloom, author of the first critical study of Jefferson, per-sonifies the ideal of scholarly collaboration. He shared much research material with me and critiqued my chapters.

Joe Jefferson in his later years was affectionately styled the "dean of the American theatre." In a similar vein Don Wilmeth has earned the title "dean of American theatre history" for his tireless efforts on behalf of the field. I've been the beneficiary of his broad knowledge of the theatre, his close reading of my manuscript, and his general encouragement for my project. Likewise, Michael Morrison's impressive mastery of American theatre history and his generosity with his collection of illustrations served me well. All the above did their best to warn me off factual and interpretive errors. Any failure to heed their advice remains mine alone.

My research of Jefferson's Australian sojourn was greatly aided by two Australian theatre scholars — Harold Love, who shared his unmatched knowledge of the Australian stage, and Mimi Colligan, who proved to be an indefatigable sleuth of Joe's antipodean journeys. John and Edna Leywood, descendants of Joe's Australian offspring, have shown ongoing interest and support for my project. Other scholars from a variety of fields deserve mention for help on very particular issues: Jon Carstens, Veronica Kelly, Tice Miller, Ronald Numbers, Gary Pennell, David Rinear, and Shauna Vey. I also am beholden to Jean-Christophe Agnew for his generous assessment of my manuscript and useful suggestions for revision.

My research ranged from London across North America to Melbourne. As all scholars know, debts to librarians are never adequately paid. I must mention here the staffs of the British Library; the New York Public Library (and in particular the Billy Rose Theatre Collection); Annette Fern and staff of the Harvard Theatre Collection; the Boston Public Library; Martha Hassell of the Bourne Archives, Bourne, Massachusetts; Jill Taylor of the Historic Hudson Valley Manuscript Collections (located at the Rockefeller Archive Center); the Shelburne Museum in Shelburne, Vermont; the Strong Museum in Rochester, New York; Ray Wemmlinger of the Hampden-Booth Library at The Players in New York City; the archives of the American Academy of Arts and Letters also in New York; the William Seymour Theatre Collection at the Princeton University Library; the Folger Shakespeare Library; Bowen King, curator of the Live Oak Gardens Foundation, New Iberia, Louisiana; Louisiana State University Library Special Collections; Harry Ransom Humanities Center at the University of Texas; John Lupton of the Lincoln Legal Papers project in Springfield, Illinois; the Lilly Library at Indiana University; the Family History Center in Chattanooga; the Special Collections of the University of Tennessee Library; the Arts Centre, Melbourne, Australia; the Missouri Historical Society; the J. Porter Shaw Library of San Francisco Maritime National Historic Park; the Bancroft Library of the University of California–Berkeley; and the Huntington Library. My thanks go as well to librarians at many other special collections for providing specific documents through the mail.

In addition to these I offer special thanks to Christina Bowersox and Ann Thublin of the Joe Jefferson Players, Mobile, Alabama, for making the Sonneborn Collection of Jefferson letters available to me. Eric Anderson and the History Department at Pacific Union College, in Angwin, California, through the benefaction of the Walter Utt Foundation, provided hospitality and valued leisure to forward my research and writing during my time in California. Southern Adventist University, Collegedale, Tennessee, supported my endeavors through many years with research leaves and generous financial assistance. The staff of McKee Library modeled diligence in attending to my research requests, Melody Ferguson and Jennifer Huck of the interlibrary loan department in particular.

At Yale University Press I am indebted to Keith Condon for seeing my manuscript through the acquisitions process. Jessie Hunnicutt then shepherded my project to completion with steadiness and grace. Eliza Childs gave my manuscript the thorough copyediting scrubbing it needed.

Introduction

Actors, according to a melancholy and self-pitying theatrical proverb of the nineteenth century, "carve figures in snow." Joseph Jefferson understood this unhappy truism, belonging as he did to the generation of performers whose careers preceded the transforming impact of recorded drama. He shared the experience of earlier stage actors, for whom any success was temporary since their art died with them. Perhaps Jefferson felt the stab of drama's ephemerality as he neared the end of his career. Perhaps he welcomed the opportunity to achieve a measure of artistic permanence through the inchoate tools of a mass media, which in 1900 could only tantalize performers with promises of immortality.

In any event, the sole remnants of Jefferson's art available to us today are bleached artifacts from the dawn of recorded sound and motion. One must listen carefully and with considerable imagination to the faint, crackled renderings of scenes from *Rip Van Winkle* that he made for Columbia's acoustic cylinders at the turn of the century. "Hi old fellow. Sit down. What's the matter vit ya?" intones Jefferson to the ghosts of Henry Hudson's crew, speaking in the Dutch dialect of an actor who, now in his seventies, was already considerably older than Rip after his twenty-year nap. One senses a performer reciting lines as comfortably familiar as the tattered coat he wore in the mountain scene. There is a sing-song cadence to his speech — not unpleasant, but a locution that modern theatergoers would find affected. His is clearly the dramatic parlance of another era. To view the Library of Congress's copy of Jefferson's mountain scene, done for Mutoscope in 1896, is to encounter similarly ghost-like images. The acting appears stilted and conventionalized in the manner of most early films, but Jefferson, then sixty-seven, looks surprisingly spry in a scene that requires a fall.

Except to the scholar, these bits of film and phonographic archaism are only of antiquarian or novelty interest. They do little to suggest the magic that Joe Jefferson possessed in casting his spell over an American theatrical public. "Fifty years from now," drama critic William Winter wrote in the 1890s, "the historian of the American stage, if he should be asked the name of the actor of this period who was most beloved by the people of this generation, will answer that it was Joseph Jefferson." No other comic actor of the nineteenth century matched Jefferson's combination of longevity, prosperity, and acclaim. Yet the mention of his name today to virtually any educated American invites a blank stare. One might even wonder how many of Chicago's theatrical community know for whom their Jefferson awards (Chicago's Obies) are named. Not memorialized by his connection to an infamous brother (as was Edwin Booth), by a noteworthy urban riot (Edwin Forrest), or by a celebrated and auto-biographical playwright son (as was James O'Neill), Jefferson has suffered near effacement from the American historical memory.[1]

Why should modern readers care about an unfamiliar name whose greatest role came in a tired melodrama? For several reasons. Most obviously because so many people were moved by his art. Understanding why requires stretching our imagination and rethinking our prejudices. We reconnect rather easily with the flickering images of early motion pictures or the patter of vaudeville's frenzied pace. Likewise, recent historians have struggled to recreate the working-class world of storefront entertainments and the culturally transgres-sive challenges of female impersonators. But the more sedate confines of Vic-torian middle-class theatre have attracted less attention, being seemingly too obvious in its meaning, too predictable, too smug perhaps for modern sen-sibilities to merit extensive comment. If one's goal, however, is to glimpse the lineaments of Victorian culture (meaning the organizing set of values by which the middle class and those aspiring to such station defined themselves), then the legitimate theatre becomes an obligatory stop. Not only the drama per-formed on stage but also the social dramas played out within the audience, among actors themselves, and between actors and society provide a window to the age.

This is not to claim for popular theatre of that age a compelling artistic virtue. As Alan Downer, the eminent Princeton theatre scholar wrote many years ago, "The nineteenth century is primarily a century of great actors rather than great plays." For good reason few of the comedies and melodramas remain in our modern repertory. Formulaic, overwrought, and to our taste, inexcusably silly or dull, the productions of the age (with some notable exceptions) are as properly consigned to the dustbin of history as is most of 1950s television. But as a means of revealing, say, a gentle resistance to the antebellum American obeisance to English customs, Anna Cora Mowatt's *Fashion* cannot be improved upon. Or to glimpse the Civil War in popular memory shortly after its end, Bronson Howard's potboiler *Shenandoah* becomes essential. Understanding a past generation requires grasping why it was moved to outrage, delight, or sorrow by a particular bit of stage business. The sensibility of a culture is put on display along with its performers.[2]

Joseph Jefferson's career, spanning eight decades, offers an unparalleled occasion to chronicle and evaluate the nineteenth-century theatre. No other actor of equal consequence enjoyed a career of such duration. Nor did any other player witness — or actively participate in — more of the changes in theatrical styles and business organization than did he. Carried on stage as a child by the daddy of minstrelsy, Thomas Rice, Joe accompanied his parents in itinerant theatricals throughout the Midwestern frontier. With his mother and sister he helped entertain American troops in Mexico. As an adult he crafted Tom Taylor's *Our American Cousin* into the comic phenomenon it became. He performed a leading role in the premier of Dion Boucicault's racially charged melodrama *The Octoroon* (as well as acting in revivals of the most popular play of the century, *Uncle Tom's Cabin*). He breathed life into Washington Irving's beloved folk tale *Rip Van Winkle,* making it his signature piece and an obligatory stop of American theatergoers for decades. When Jefferson began his career, stock companies formed the basis of theatrical organization. But in his early days of stardom he helped forge the traveling combination company — the road show — which persists to the present. Finally, Jefferson's career mirrored the transformation of acting styles through the century; indeed, theatre critics credited him as auguring the more realistic style that came into vogue.

In this book I recount the life of this remarkable comedian even as I seek to restore to public memory the "mere players who strutted and fretted upon the stage and then were no more." Recapturing on paper the magic of stage performance is notoriously difficult. The surviving descriptions of critics or fellow players rarely give an adequate sense of dramatic art, especially the physicality of comedy. Effort and imagination can, however, provide the lineaments of a past performance. Easier is retrieving the texture of a life. But readers expecting to find in Jefferson's story the angst or outré behavior often associated with performers' lives will be disappointed. He was a person of remarkable equanimity. Free from the melancholy and brooding introspection that character-ized the great tragedian Edwin Booth, Jefferson enjoyed a life that to all ap-pearances was emotionally rewarding. Conversely, this good fortune may have contributed to his limitations in undertaking heavier dramatic roles. Jefferson recognized his gift for comedy and stayed within his talents.

Joseph Jefferson (1829–1905) was in many respects the perfect American Victorian. (His career from childhood to retirement was nearly coincident with the reign of Queen Victoria.) Although part of a profession that most guardians of culture defined as disreputable, Jefferson embodied the values of integrity, hard work, career, and family so dear to his age. His stardom — burnished by these marks of respectability — provided him entrée into the highest reaches of American society. His association with such literary nota-bles as William Dean Howells and Richard Watson Gilder reveals the pecu-liarly tight network of artists and men of letters in the late nineteenth century. In this sense, his life becomes a means of recapturing the singular ampleness of leisured late Victorianism. American novelists of his time and later found Jefferson's acclaim a useful emblem of the age. Theodore Dreiser's Hurstwood regaled Carrie with his merits: " 'Did you ever see Jefferson?' he questioned as he leaned toward Carrie in the box. . . . 'He's delightful, delightful.' " The sybaritic Hurstwood likewise took great pleasure in patronizing a restaurant that Jefferson was known to frequent. Wallace Stegner, in his 1971 novel *Angle of Repose,* describes a cultured New England pair whose "days and nights were filled with art, literature, theatre, music, good talk. Saint-Gaudens and Joseph Jefferson were their intimates, Whitman had visited their studio."[3]

Jefferson will always be known first as an actor, but his talents extended beyond the stage. An accomplished painter, he was also a connoisseur of art, who lost one collection to fire only to rebuild another of considerable distinc-tion. He was in demand as a lecturer later in his life before prominent au-diences. And as a writer he produced the classic work of autobiography in American theatre annals. Although filtered through an imperfect and some-times creative memory, *The Autobiography of Joseph Jefferson* provides a spritely account not only of his singular career, but also of an American theatre as it once was. His memoir, so lacking in affectation and so full of affection for the American stage, should be read as a companion to my study.

Most clearly, though, Jefferson's career is an opportunity to revisit the the-atre of the nineteenth century, the golden age of the American stage. It was peopled with fascinating personalities — Charlotte Cushman, Augustin Daly, Edwin Forrest, Clara Morris, Richard Mansfield — to mention only a few of the more eminent. It was also a cultural institution whose devotees often pursued their craft in difficult settings and always in economic uncertainty.

Joseph Jefferson's career touched on theatre at many points, and my account will frequently digress from his life to explore other theatrical avenues. I seek to explain an institution as well as a life. This requires a deliberate pacing and a greater attention to his long rise than to his bountiful years of stardom. In addition to biographical and broader cultural interpretations, I seek to provide a vivid sense of how both the theatrical community and its public experienced the stage. Such an understanding just might provide a chastening brake on our quick dismissal of the era's drama and performance.

"Are we so soon forgot when we are gone?" Rip sadly asks, after returning to his village, "No one remembers Rip Van Winkle." That lament could serve as the epitaph for Joseph Jefferson and most of his theatrical contemporaries. Given their importance for their age, Jefferson and his generation deserve better.

A life, an aesthetic, an institution, a culture: The contemplation of an exceptional individual and his art can reawaken appreciation for a theatre and its age which have long needed sympathetic evaluation.

The Man Who Was Rip Van Winkle

Cradled in the Profession

"I may almost say that I was born in a theatre," Joseph Jefferson confides at the opening of his *Autobiography*. "At all events, my earliest recollections are entirely connected with one." In an age when the socially conscious considered such origins déclassé, Jefferson embraced his thespian pedigree without a hint of self-consciousness or embarrassment. Nor was the man who had delivered the famous paean to the "Little Church Around the Corner" for its kindness to a deceased and outcast fellow actor one to apologize for his own theatrical roots.[1]

Those roots reached down as far as anyone's in the American theatre. He was Joseph Jefferson III, but he was actually part of the fourth generation of performing Jeffersons. Such family connections constituted the core of early theatre. Recall the Crummles family of *Nicholas Nickleby*, whose playbill "in very large letters" announced "Mr. Vincent Crummles, Mrs. Vincent Crummles, Master Crummles, Master P. Crummles, and Miss Crummles." The kinship basis of theatricals predated Dickens, reaching back to small itinerant troupes earlier in European history. It had been a family, the Hallams, which first brought professional theatricals to the British colonies in the 1750s. And the American frontier's westward march across the continent was accompanied by such barnstorming stage families as the Drakes and Chapmans.[2]

Acting constituted a way of life. Wives acted alongside their husbands in this less patriarchal vocation. Indeed, they were among the few married women who could pursue a livelihood. Stage children performed among cousins, aunts, uncles, and grandparents. A multigenerational theatrical family could cast parts for the entire age range found in many melodramas. Even if they had wanted to, children might find it difficult to move outside the theatre, for the theatrical world was tightly bound, with few occasions for regular outside contacts. Parents' frequent travel denied children the usual clutch of permanent childhood friends. Grammar school education often gave way to the informal tutorials of the road. Their pertinent education occurred in the theatre. Children grew up poking around dressing rooms and wings, eavesdropping on the endless anecdotes of veteran players, literally and figuratively inhaling the greasepaint. It was an intoxicating environment. Add to this — less pleasantly — the ever-present drone of antitheatricality in Anglo-American culture, which drove actors to close ranks. This powerful sense of community seemed to hold children within its orb, even as some actor fathers (Junius Brutus Booth, for instance) pointedly advised their children to seek careers outside the theatre. More often, an acting career was an unstated assumption. "I can't even tell you when it was first decided that I was to go on the stage," Ellen Terry, the storied English beauty of the later Victorian stage recalled, "but I expect it was when I was born, for in those days theatrical folk did not imagine that their children could do anything but follow their parents' professions."[3]

The Jefferson clan of Joe's childhood vividly illustrated the family basis of theatre. Fathers, mothers, and children acted, often from cradle to grave (in some cases a very early grave). Although members ventured forth periodically to work for other managers, most returned to the Jefferson troupe. Even after Joe had become a star in the 1860s and after the New York–centered theatre business no longer operated on kinship, he dutifully placed nearly all of his children at one time or another in his *Rip Van Winkle* productions.

Altogether, seven generations of Jeffersons labored in the theatre, reaching well into the twentieth century. Exact numbers are elusive, complicated by such questions as whether to include the branches of the various families the Jeffersons married into and those who acted for only a short time. The family genealogy tracing five generations indicates thirty-five members went on stage (not including their theatrical cousins, the Warrens).

Joe's great-grandfather, Thomas Jefferson (1728–1807), birthed the theatrical tradition. Family legend holds that as a young man he encountered the great David Garrick, who impressed by his rustic dash offered him a position. Jefferson performed with Garrick's Drury Lane Company in the 1750s, playing supporting roles in the Shakespearean productions Garrick so notably revived. Jefferson arrived during an efflorescence of English theatre, when the comedies of manners of Goldsmith and Sheridan graced the Georgian stage.

Jefferson, admittedly, played a secondary role in this new Augustan age. His strengths lay in his versatility, strong declamation, and a superficial resemblance to Garrick (sufficient to allow him to be sometimes accepted as a substitute for the master). Most of his career, however, was spent away from the theatrical center of London, traveling with itinerant troupes in the provinces, and, increasingly, in managing his own theatre in Plymouth. Thomas Jefferson possessed the "docile amiability and droll humour" that would characterize many of his progeny. And as with his more famous descendants, only the imminence of death would drag him from the stage.[4]

It was to Jefferson's second wife, a "Miss May," that Joseph Jefferson I (1774–1832) was born. After appearing on his father's Plymouth stage as a boy, Joseph headed to America in 1795. Charles Powell of the Boston Theatre, who had put Jefferson under contract and paid his way to America, was out of business by the time he arrived. Fortunately, Jefferson received an invitation to join the John Street Theatre Company in New York; in 1798 he moved to its successor, the Park. The Park's managers, William Dunlap and John Hodgkinson, were among the most important figures in early American theatre. Hodgkinson, the American stage's foremost player, was contentious and unscrupled, but he provided Jefferson an opportunity to advance in his line of low comedy. Jefferson spent five years at the Park, after which he was invited to join Philadelphia's Chestnut Street Theatre, where he stayed for many years. Jefferson debated the move, cautious about risking the popularity he enjoyed in New York and uncertain whether he could win the hearts of Philadelphians. In the end he "plucked up a manly spirit" and accepted.[5]

It was a good move. The Philadelphia he found was then the second-largest city in the country, with some 200,000 residents who enjoyed living in perhaps the most beautiful and well-planned major town in the nation. Moreover, the Chestnut Street Theatre was then in the process of becoming one of the country's venerated houses under managers William Warren and William B. Wood. Indeed, Philadelphia during the 1820s temporarily surpassed New York as the theatrical center of the nation. The new theatre that replaced the one which burned in 1820 offered theatergoers a convenient location less than a block from Independence Hall and an elegant marble-columned front. Here, out from the shadow of Hodgkinson, Jefferson earned his greatest acclaim. Part of a company finely fashioned for comedy (though presenting the usual range of plays), Jefferson possessed the versatility necessary for the diverse repertoire of stock. Chestnut Street manager William Wood recalled that in just one season Jefferson performed three characters in Sheridan's *School for Scandal,* an unusual flexibility for a low comedian. Further, as a machinist Jefferson constructed intricate bits of stage wizardry from English models.[6]

Joe's grandfather, Joseph Jefferson I. From Joseph Jefferson,
Autobiography (1890).

"Old Jefferson," as he was called (for his frequent and celebrated portrayal of old men), was the "reigning favourite of the Philadelphia theatre for a longer period than any other actor ever attached to the city," claimed later Chestnut Street manager and theatre chronicler Frederick Wemyss. Of slight build, Joseph Jefferson I was more handsome than his grandson. An illustration of him in his role as Solus in *Every One Has His Faults* shows a magisterial figure with a Grecian nose and somewhat imperious gaze. An actor "formed in Nature's merriest mood — a genuine son of Momus," Jefferson knew all the stage tricks. Antebellum novelist John Pendleton Kennedy recalled Jefferson's habit of declaiming his opening line from behind the curtain "to herald his appearance, and instantly the whole audience set up a shout." Jefferson's popularity and name led to an acquaintanceship with the Sage of Monticello; the two men speculated on possible family ties in the distant past.[7]

Beloved by actors and audiences alike, Jefferson enjoyed the double fortune of a constant wife and bountiful children. Jefferson wed Euphemia Fortune, who adopted the stage and became part of the Chestnut Street Company. Of their nine children, seven followed their parents on stage. Although he was acclaimed in his career and content at home for much of his life, his final few years brought professional decline and private heartache, which were only too typical of the vagaries of theatrical life at that time. The Chestnut Street Theatre fell victim to the common afflictions of stock companies: fire, a fickle public, constant pressure of bills and creditors, the expenses of touring to Baltimore and Washington, and personal bickering among management. Jefferson's deepest wound came from being elbowed aside in the public's affection by the younger players of the company. When his final two benefit performances of the season—which produced a significant portion of a player's yearly income— earned scarcely enough to cover expenses, Jefferson, formerly the people's choice, had had enough. Devastated and demoralized, he viewed the indifference as a personal affront from the entire Philadelphia community. "I am not wanted here any longer," Jefferson declared, and he quit Philadelphia never to return.[8]

Between the two most acclaimed Jeffersons, Josephs I and III, came the Jefferson noted more for affability than dramatic genius. Joseph Jefferson II (1804–1842), like most of his siblings, mounted the stage as a youngster and moved on to dramatic apprenticeships. But his attraction to acting was subordinate to his love of drawing and architecture, and his modest place in theatre history comes as a talented scenic artist. At the Walnut Street Theatre the middle Jefferson accomplished some spectacular effects. For the forgettable melodrama *Undine* he contrived "a huge flying fish and a bridge that changed into a 'car drawn by horses' amid atmospheric displays of water and moonlight." As a performer he, like his father, was most accomplished at playing old men. This curiosity—repeated again in his son's portrayal of Rip Van Winkle and Caleb Plummer—bespoke the essential strength of the Jeffersons as character actors.[9]

In 1826 Joseph Jefferson II married Cornelia Thomás Burke, a widow eight years his senior. Cornelia's background was entwined with the revolutionary history of the Caribbean, her family having narrowly escaped the St. Domingue slave uprising of 1804. After landing in Charleston, Cornelia found an early talent as a vocalist, and a career on stage was launched. Her portrait reveals a dark-featured woman, heavy browed and large-boned. Portraits can deceive, but hers leaves an impression of a formidable woman, perhaps deficient in warmth, but if so, it was the excusable by-product of a life where survival itself remained the paramount goal.

Cornelia's first husband, Irish comedian Thomas Burke, died a wastrel's

Joe's mother, Cornelia Burke Jefferson. From Joseph Jefferson,
Autobiography (1890).

death in the mid-1820s, leaving her with a young son — Charles Burke — to
raise. She married Jefferson II in 1826. Joe Jefferson III, their first and only
son, was born in Philadelphia on 20 February 1829.[10]

Imagining a Childhood

Born less than a year before his grandfather broke with the Chestnut
Street Company, Joe, along with his parents, joined other family members in
following the patriarch to Baltimore and Washington. While just a toddler, Joe
discovered the footloose nature of theatre life.[11]

Scattered playbills, newspaper accounts, and a few stage annals offer
glimpses into Joe's childhood career, but his remarkable *Autobiography* remains our chief witness. Jefferson's description of his childhood trails the sort
of wispy nostalgia common to Victorian memoirs. No storm clouds threaten
his juvenile idyll. Only when baby sister Cornelia stole some of the previously

undivided attention of doting adults does Joe recall any childish dismay, a lapse into jealousy at which he later pokes fun. The modern reader's skepticism about such roseate recollections (what of parents' irregular income? exhausting travel? social snubs?) is apt to be misplaced — at least in Jefferson's case. Jefferson lived the dream of most children. The backstage was his playhouse. Stage props loomed magically around him: "In a dark corner stood a robbers' cave with an opening through which old Ali Baba used to lug the bags of gold he had stolen from the Forty Thieves." The backstage warren's nest of wings and flats lay beneath an even more intriguing clutter of suspended artifacts, "boats and baskets, tubs and chandeliers, and those sure tokens of bad weather, the thunder-drum and rain-box."[12]

Nor, despite his parents' downward mobility, can one say that Joe was the son of privation. His birthplace was a (rented) substantial three-story brick Georgian structure at Sixth and Spruce streets in central Philadelphia. His father, a yeoman of the theatre, was capable of providing a housekeeper/nurse for his children, Mary, whom Joe considered a beloved second mother (a more kindred spirit, his autobiography suggests, than his real mother). And it is doubtful that young Joe ever felt the sting of social disapproval. He belonged, after all, to the Jeffersons of Philadelphia, a boy whose grandfather once knew few equals on stage and lived an unstained personal life. The remarkable equanimity and emotional maturity Jefferson displayed throughout his life must be attributed at least in part to this gift of youthful security.

Joe attempted to balance this recitation of childhood bliss with a generally self-effacing depiction of his juvenile acting career and a not-very-convincing attempt to portray himself as something of a Huck Finn miscreant. "I was one of those restless, peevish children who, no matter what they have, always want something else," he tells us. "The last new toy was always dissected to see what made it go, and the anticipated one kept me awake all night." As an eight-year-old he managed to get some grammar school experience while in New York, perhaps the longest stretch of formal education in his life. More proudly he describes falling in with a group of rowdies whose pastime was painting gravestones. He softens this vandalism by admitting fears of ghosts lurking about the cemetery at night. The childhood persona Jefferson claimed as an adult was not so different from that of his stage Rip: mischievous, undisciplined, but essentially good-hearted. Moreover, when his autobiography appeared in 1889 Jefferson's public would have immediately recognized its Twainsian qualities and delighted in Joe's wholesome deviltry.[13]

It would have been surprising had Jefferson chosen any career but the theatre. The gravitational tug toward the stage within acting families was nearly inescapable. Joe knew little else. He was, simply put, stage struck at the most tender of ages. Perhaps the affliction had its subliminal roots in having been

Joe's first billing: "Master J. Jefferson," age three. Used by permission of the Harvard Theatre Collection, The Houghton Library.

carried before the footlights as the dressing-room baby, an infant prop. It may have been nurtured in the moments stolen from his nurse's supervision when he peered through the greenroom door at figures splendidly costumed — performers. The earliest surviving playbill listing young Joe dates from a 23 November 1832 production of *The Legion of Honor* at the Washington Theatre. The next documented appearance was the following January, when still shy of age four he was Julio in the "celebrated Melo-drama" *The Hunter of the Alps.*[14]

Early Infatuations

The tragedies and melodramas in which young Joe was most often paraded were standard stage fare. But he also crossed paths with two novelties of the American stage: tableaux vivants and minstrelsy, the first of which remains an intriguing footnotes to American theatre while the second quickly moved into the theatrical mainstream.

At about age three, Jefferson became smitten with a mute drama, the tableaux vivants, or "living statues," of English showman John Fletcher. Not to be confused with the dramatic tableaux of actors that frequently concluded an act in melodrama, these human posings of classical works of art became a minor theatrical genre that waxed and waned in popularity throughout the nineteenth century. Young Joe became "statue-struck," modeling before mirrors as "Ajax Defying the Lightning" or the "Dying Gladiator." His family, always ready to thrust their infant prodigy before the public, let him strike these poses to a paying audience. We have one eyewitness to this quaint art; stock actor Edmond Connor recalled decades later seeing "little Joe" in "white fleshings, white wig, and chalked face" standing upon a small table giving his own imitations of Fletcher's statuary to an audience "charmed with the graceful, lovely boy." Although Jefferson's early attempt at this art occasioned no comment in the press, the larger phenomena of tableaux vivants certainly did.[15]

An unlikely marriage of high art and popular theatre, living pictures had some eighteenth-century precedents on European stages. In one sense they were a theatrical extension of the heroic portrayals of historical and classical themes produced by popular artists. "Realizations," as they were known, embodied the urge to bring still pictures to life. Their vogue seems to have followed publication of Goethe's novel *Elective Affinities* (1809), which narrated efforts at domestic tableaux. In the drawing rooms of the rich, elegant tableaux were mounted. The fad moved onto American stages by the 1830s, where audiences in New York enjoyed such spectacles as *Raphael's Dream* at the Park Theatre. Billed as a "classical, historical, mythological Drama," it offered a series of tableaux tied together by a minimal mimed dramatic plot about the Florentine artist. By the end of the 1840s living pictures had become a mainstay of New York's variety entertainments, commonly seen alongside panoramas, dioramas, and wax museums.[16]

What was it about living pictures that enticed audiences? Part of their attraction, no doubt, was their novelty. Tableaux vivants enjoyed several revivals of interest through the end of the century, as new generations of theatre patrons appeared. More to the point, for an American middle class hungry for the accoutrements of culture, these three-dimensional renderings of classic art were both more accessible and more interesting than the originals. They also appealed to a public desire for visual spectacle, a hunger that grew more intense as the century wore on and as the means for staging ever more elaborate productions increased.[17]

During the 1850s several theatres — the Wallhalla, the Franklin Museum, and the Temple of the Muses among them — made tableaux their primary bill (alongside acrobats, minstrels, dancers, and the like). But in their living statues the "edification" of high art had surrendered to the "symmetry" of the female form. These thinly veiled precursors of burlesque sought a veneer of legitimacy by replicating such works as Hiram Powers's statue "Greek Slave." A better opportunity for joining culture to prurient desire could hardly have been imagined by tableaux managers. The Walhalla trumpeted its artists as "the most beautiful women in the world," displaying them as "Suzanna in the Bath" and "Venus Rising from the Sea," as well as the "Greek Slave."

For a time during and after the 1850s the respectable and raffish traditions of tableaux coexisted. Marquee language often keyed the public about what to expect inside the theatre: reference to "model artists" suggested voyeuristic fare; tableaux vivants, or "pose plastique," implied more demure art. Increasingly after the Civil War, tableaux were incorporated into legitimate drama. Nearly every play, it seemed, brought down the final curtain with a dramatic pose, effectively usurping not only the form but the very term. The "model artists" variety also met competition from a diversifying American theatre, where the female limb was showcased in stage spectaculars, notably *The Black Crook* (1866).[18]

Still, tableaux vivants made a comeback in the last half of the 1870s and then again in the later 1890s. Some were continued attempts at cultured artistic novelty, faux art though they may seem to later sensibilities. Mary Anderson, for example, widely considered the classic beauty of the American stage, incorporated a striking tableau of the statue "Galatea" in her major starring vehicle, a retelling of the myth of Pygmalion and Galatea. And the new sensation of vaudeville, with its insatiable appetite for acts to fill its continuous format, found there was still a public for tableaux portraits of masterpieces, historical scenes, or — with a bow to the vogue of physical culture — the muscular poses of Eugene Sandow. But the guardians of morality suspicioned most tableaux entertainment to be an excuse for dressing up young women in flesh-toned body stockings under sheer robes. Anthony Comstock and his Society for the Prevention of Vice hounded many tableaux producers in the later decades for their "debauching and corrupting influences." Ultimately, it was not Comstock or other crusaders for purity who finally drove tableaux from the stage, but rather more aggressive competition — burlesque, theatrical revues, and of course motion pictures, which provided more effective titillation.[19]

In 1833, just shy of age four but already displaying the instincts of a seasoned trouper, Joe witnessed the hit of the season on the Washington stage: the novelty act of Thomas D. Rice, which would become the sensation of the country — and of Europe — and evolve into one of America's most distinctive theatrical forms. Blackfaced and affecting the lame shuffle he had reportedly copied from a stable hand in Louisville, Rice's star turn brought down the house:

> Wheel about, turn about,
> do jis so,
> An' ebery time I wheel about
> I jump Jim Crow

Enthralled by the "knight of the burnt cork," Joe endlessly rehearsed his own Jim Crow steps. Rice saw his young shadow and insisted that the boy — scarcely more than a toddler — appear at his benefit. That evening Rice toted a bag on stage, which he shouldered mysteriously as he began his routine. His second stanza ran:

> O Ladies and Gentlemen, I'd have you for to know
> That I've got a little darky here that jumps Jim Crow

Rice emptied the bag of its juvenile contents — a "tiny comic *Doppelgänger*," Constance Rourke called him — corked and attired identically to himself. The two launched into an antiphonal song and dance duet that brought down the house. Showered by coins that he frantically retrieved, Joe learned an early lesson about the tangible rewards of stardom. He also had been present, if not quite at the creation, at the formative youth of minstrelsy.[20]

It is unclear how often young Joe was blacked up. His success with Rice would suggest that his family revisited the act often, though Jefferson made only two specific allusions to such in his autobiography. Yet even late in his life Jefferson's prodigious memory could recall the lyrics and gestures of his long-ago routines:

> Sing, sing, darkies, sing!
> Don't you hear de banjo ring?
> Sing, sing, darkies, sing!
> Sing fo' de white folks, sing![21]

No account of mid-nineteenth century popular culture can ignore minstrelsy. The minstrel clown, whether styled as plantation slave Jim Crow or northern urban dandy Zip Coon, capered and cut up before enthusiastic audiences and seems, in retrospect, to say something important about our national culture. Blackfaced entertainers had been seen on American stages since before the Revolution and by the 1820s were common features. By one count some five thousand stage performances included blackface representations before 1843. But it was Thomas Danforth Rice, an angular, sharp-nosed figure with a deep-dimpled chin, who most shaped the genre through his "Ethiopian operas."[22]

In the 1840s and 1850s groups such as the Virginia Minstrels and the Christy Minstrels elaborated his formula into its familiar format. On stage sat a semi-circle of usually four to six dandified blackfaced entertainers, with the interlocutor emcee in the middle and Messrs. Tambo and Bones on the ends. The two-part program opened with a series of songs interspersed by raucous exchanges between the clownish end men and the pompous "straight man" interlocutor. The second half featured individual minstrels in their specialty musical or dance number along with short skits, the "stump" speech (a travesty on Jacksonian political oratory), closing with an afterpiece. The latter, a brief, one-act bit of theatre, epitomized the minstrel experience: song, dance, and tomfoolery with a cobbled-together plot, often laced with current political commentary, or perhaps a shameless burlesque of Shakespeare, as in "Desdemonum," a send-up of *Othello:*

> JUDGE. Brabantium, what's de matter, dat you look so blue?
> BRABANTIUM. Dat darky's stole my darter, but de act I'll make him rue.
> JUDGE. To this what says Oteller?
> OTELLER. Judge, de fact am so;
>   de gal, you see, got struck wid me, and would to parson go,
>   I ain't much on de talk, but when fightin's found I'm dere,
>   Knock de chip from off my shoulder, and for bloody work prepare![23]

A hugely popular form of theatre in the middle decades of the century, minstrelsy might properly be seen as the first truly native entertainment form to achieve preeminence. Minstrel songs enriched popular music (one thinks of Stephen Foster) and the fast-paced variety format would influence later vaudeville, radio, and television programming. The sort of simple word play and low humor that have since become the staple of any seven-year-old's first attempts at wit (Why did the chicken cross the road?) seeped down from the minstrel stage. If its verbal nonsense seems harmless enough, minstrelsy has nevertheless occupied an uncomfortable position in the pantheon of American theatricals. It stands as the entertainment field's monument to political incorrectness, its leering black masks and mangled diction seemingly a perpetual reminder of a corrosive racism afflicting our culture. Indeed, in the last half of the twentieth century interpretations of blackface minstrelsy became bound up with wider debates about race and folk culture. Did minstrelsy accurately reflect its putative black origins? Was it guilty of unremitting racist stereotyping? Scholars have worried these questions in recent decades in some of the most innovative scholarship of American cultural history.[24]

For all the complexity of minstrelsy's roots, it is clear that it bore an intimate relation to America's broader native humor tradition. The characteristic American stage figures — the laconic, shrewd, and nationalistic Yankee, Brother Jonathan, Jack Downing, or Adam Trueman; the imperfectly civilized, yarn-spinning, larger-than-life backwoodsman, Davy Crockett or Mike Fink — constituted an indigenous repertoire of stock comic figures that Jim Crow both resembled (in the latter two cases) and surpassed as national icon. "Western myth-making was woven deep in early minstrelsy," wrote Constance Rourke, "so deep that it can hardly be counted an alien strain." The grotesque tall tales of the southwestern tradition were echoed on the minstrel stage:

> My mammy was a wolf, my daddy was a tiger
> I'm what you call de ole Virginia nigger;
> half fire, half smoke, a little touch of thunder
> I'm what dey call de eighth wonder

Rourke argues that minstrelsy added to the Yankee and backwoodsman caricature an element of nonsense, an "unreasonable headlong triumph launching into the realm of the preposterous" that became the signature of the afterpieces (and a comic tradition that would persist in the anarchy of Marx Brothers comedies). The images were warped and distended in many ways, but the point was less to present faithful likenesses of urban Irish or western keelboaters than to create compelling types or, especially in the case of blackface, to offer distanced comic commentary on marriage, politics, woman's rights, or any of a host of current concerns. The legacy of troubled race relations makes it nearly impossible to see stage caricatures as anything other than cruel parody. But minstrel shows played the entire keyboard of emotions, "moods and meanings tumbled after one another with incredible quickness." Sympathy, subversion, even hints at resistance, appeared under the age-old protective guise of humor.[25]

All of this lay in the future the night young Joe tumbled out of Daddy Rice's valise onto the Washington stage. A mature Jefferson would remember the incident in matter-of-fact terms. He displayed no sense of regret about participating in an arguably racist entertainment. Nor should he have. The interpretative burdens later placed upon minstrelsy were not a part of his experience. For Jefferson and his contemporaries, blackface was outlandish and foolish fun laced with sentimentality. If as perceptive a social observer as Mark Twain could find in minstrelsy essentially "happy and accurate representations" of black culture, the less culturally astute Jefferson would hardly manage better. Sanguine by temperament, he would feel no urge to lift the minstrel mask and contemplate any disturbing meaning it hid.[26]

Family Trials

The evolving dramatic form of tableaux vivants and minstrelsy touched Joe's young life but failed to enrich it materially. His mid-childhood, emotionally secure though it was, was spent after his grandfather's death in an acting family of hardscrabble existence. The tenuousness of life in the Jacksonian age haunted the Jeffersons and brought to a premature end a potentially synergistic merger of leading stage families. Joe's aunt, Elizabeth Jefferson (b. 1810), married Samuel Chapman in 1828, a union of promise for the American theatre. "No actress who ever preceded or followed her on the Park stage," wrote Joseph Ireland, chronicler of Gotham theatre, "excelled her in general ability." As for Chapman, despite suspicions among some wise heads in the theatre that his ambitions were inordinate, there was wide agreement that "had he lived he would have produced an entire revolution in the minor drama of America." However, a fall from a horse killed him in 1830.[27]

When the family clan headed to Baltimore in early 1830, the elder Jefferson no doubt hoped to recapture happier days of family touring. Initially this band of self-exiles attached itself to manager John Purdy Brown, who operated theatres in Baltimore and Washington was surely delighted to feature on his playbill "the first comedian of our country," as he puffed Jefferson. By this time, second-youngest daughter, Mary-Anne, and Jefferson II's stepson, Charles Burke, only eight years old, were likewise receiving notices.[28]

Late that year the family head, perhaps out of pride, perhaps out of financial aspirations, decided to form an independent troupe, eighteen members in all, the nucleus of which was seven of his immediate family. The *National Intelligencer* announced their debut at the Washington Theatre on 1 December 1830 with the three-act comedy *Animal Magnetism,* an entr'acte of comic songs by John Jefferson and Cornelia Jefferson, and a concluding farce, *The*

Comet. Between then and the following March the company presented 178 performances of 90 different plays on a six-night-a-week schedule, a dramatic fecundity that modern ensembles would deem as impossible to imagine as the multiple children of many Victorian families.[29]

Things got no easier in early 1831. By the end of the Washington season, the elder Jefferson was clearly wearing out. His wife Euphemia had died that January, and further dispirited by his chronic gout, he could no longer serve as the troupe's head, a task he passed on to son John. The company undertook a half-month run at Alexandria, Virginia, largely repeating the repertoire of Washington, then on the road to a small-town circuit in Pennsylvania from April to October of 1831. York, Lancaster, Reading, Pottsville, Harrisburg, and back to Lancaster: the Jefferson company produced revivals of their productions in such spaces as the Red Lion Tavern in Lancaster, Mr. Boyer's Ball Room in a Reading tavern, and a Masonic hall in Harrisburg. Although still touring near Philadelphia, the elder Jefferson had figuratively traveled far south from his exalted position at the Chestnut Street Theatre.[30]

In December of 1831 the troupe returned to Washington for an extended stay. The city the Jeffersons encountered that winter was substantially the town that Alexis de Tocqueville and Gustave de Beaumont would visit in January 1833. A national capital for scarcely three decades, Washington with its 20,000 residents was smaller than a number of other American cities and only a tenth the size of New York and Philadelphia. Yet it was spacious, which made it all the more odd to European eyes — the way houses were littered across the landscape "with little order or symmetry." The scattered houses lent a rural air to the middle of town and complicated the social obligations of visitation. Thomas Jefferson's dream of a cosmopolitan capital that might rival London or Paris still seemed laughably absurd. Indeed, condescended Count Francesco Arese on a visit from Italy, "one might strain in vain to find a city there." Washington was, in short, an ugly town, with a landscape of dirt roads, cedar bushes, and sand bisected by the malodorous Washington Canal. "Washington altogether struck me," English actress Fanny Kemble noted, "as a rambling, red-brick image of futurity, where nothing *is,* but all things *are to be.*"[31]

The Jefferson company sought to make its own contribution to Washington's cultural "futurity" with a remodeling of the Washington Theatre. The theatre was small by the day's standards, seating perhaps seven hundred. Fanny Kemble, who performed there with the Jefferson company, called it "the tiniest little box that ever was seen," not much larger than the "baby's playhouse at Versailles." In preparation for the fall-winter season, extensive interior remodeling was accomplished: the whole theatre painted, boxes extended, pit enlarged, and greater warmth promised via a new furnace. The theatre would be, enthused a reporter for the *National Intelligencer,* "resuscitated in a manner worthy of the enlightened audience of the Metropolis." Unfortunately, more was promised than could be delivered. A new system of "patent portable gas" stage lighting, installed shortly before the second night's performance on 5 December, proved so feeble that the drastic step of stopping the performance and dismissing the audience was required. By the protocol of the day, such an act dictated a published apology to the public.[32]

Although their experiment failed, the Jefferson company commendably had attempted to bring the lighting of the Washington Theatre to the new standard. The tallow candle chandeliers and newer oil lamp footlights shed little light and decreed that stars stand "in the focus" to benefit even from that. As gas began to be manufactured from coal, new possibilities for theatre illumination became apparent. No longer would candle wax drip on patrons nor would the task of trimming scores of candles require hiring extra labor. Gas offered convenience, control, and a modest increase in warm, yellow light. Covent Garden adopted gas in 1815; other London theatres followed shortly after. American theatres lagged slightly in their adoption of gas (the balky anthracite coal of Pennsylvania's mines posed a technical difficulty). Philadelphia's Chestnut Street Theatre introduced gas lines in 1816 only to have the theatre burn down a few years later. A similar early experiment at a Baltimore theatre thrust cast and audience into plutonian darkness one night when the lights suddenly failed. Not until the 1820s did gas make much headway.[33]

Despite the hitch in their lighting plans, the Jefferson company had some success in the 1831–32 season, hosting stars of such magnitude as Charles Kean and Edwin Forrest. Within the company, the elder Jefferson now limited himself to benefit performances of roles he had known most of his professional life, notably Polonius, Dogberry, and Sir Peter Teazle. His decline meant the company's performances shifted noticeably away from comedy, Jefferson I's forte, and toward tragedy, the usual vehicle of a traveling star. The company member now featured most often was daughter Elizabeth — the widowed Mrs. Chapman — who was gearing up for her conquest of the New York stage two years later.[34]

But the ill luck that had plagued Jefferson I since his unceremonious departure from Philadelphia was never far away. "Life is short, but its ills make it seem long," a Roman proverb runs, and for Jefferson the final few years of life must have seemed endless. Professional humiliation was compounded by domestic tragedy. In 1824 his eldest son, Thomas, died in a freak stage accident. Substituting in a stunt for another actor who (perhaps wisely) begged off, Thomas leapt from a stage precipice, landed awkwardly, and apparently punctured a lung. Now, as Jefferson was reduced to theatrical itinerancy he suffered a quartet of deaths in 1831. His wife and his eldest daughter — both named Euphemia — and then daughter Jane, still a teenager, all succumbed to illnesses. Son John, only twenty-seven, fell down a flight of stairs at a hotel and died of a skull fracture, never having realized his considerable promise. The apple of the elder Jefferson's eye — tall (by Jefferson standards), congenial, and considered the most talented of the offspring in the family's specialty of low comedy roles — John Jefferson had wandered down the road of "conviviality" (a Victorian delicacy for hard drinking and riotous living). For the prematurely old fifty-seven-year-old father, the end came in Harrisburg in August 1832. He died a broken man, lacking even the redeeming knowledge that his grandson would restore the Jefferson name to the pinnacle of the American stage.[35]

After John's death, company leadership had passed to his older brother, Joseph Jefferson II. This Jefferson lacked the fire and raw talent of his sibling, but he possessed an even-keeled disposition that served his family well. He would not have to shoulder the burden alone. Alexander MacKenzie, a Scotsman who came to American in 1829 and married his sister Hester in 1831, provided able support. Although he rarely acted himself, MacKenzie served as company treasurer, house manager, and later that year as the young Jefferson's partner.[36]

The theatrical cycle of life began once more that October back in the nation's capital. Despite the loss of Jefferson I and other family members, the family's remarkable regenerative powers left the troupe bigger than ever. Two Jefferson granddaughters, Elizabeth and Jane Anderson, were ready to debut. Daughters of Jefferson's eldest and favorite (and now deceased) daughter, Euphemia, the two girls — not yet teenagers — had grown up in unhappy circumstances. Their mother had made a disastrous marriage to William Anderson, a capable performer of heavies (i.e., villains) but whose "irregularity of habits" finally embittered his wife and led to separation. More happily, the youngest surviving daughter, Mary-Anne Jefferson, wed David Ingersoll, a former equestrian who had traded his boots for the buskin. Though barely more than a novice on the dramatic stage, he was the company's featured performer by 1832. Endowed with a commanding physical presence, a silver tongue, and according to Charles Durang, a "remarkably dazzling white eye . . . that often electrified the spectator," Ingersoll had the potential to become "the first of American actors," judged Joseph Ireland, "had discretion guided his career."[37]

During the years of Andrew Jackson's presidency, the Jefferson family troupe learned just how bumptious Jacksonian Democracy might be. One evening

South Carolina congressman James Blair, intoxicated and "on a spree," took offense at an actor's line. He pulled out his pistol and fired toward the stage, narrowly missing "Miss Jefferson." The troupe fled the stage "without ceremony." David Ingersoll (serving as stage manager) reappeared to remind the audience — in a classic of understatement — that "if there is to be shooting at the actors on stage, it will be impossible for the performance to go on."[38]

In fall 1832 the expanded company made an ambitious decision to divide their troupe into two parts. The main company remained in Washington while a satellite group revisited the Pennsylvania circuit before moving to Baltimore. In retrospect, the reasoning behind this decision seems flawed, succumbing as it were to the usually fatal decision in battle to divide one's troops and thus weaken forces everywhere. Perhaps it was a move of desperation to generate additional income. In any event, the experiment only served to further reduce the dwindling resources of the company, preventing it, for example, from affording vital newspaper advertising during much of the season.[39]

The Baltimore the touring company visited in the early 1830s was an important seaport and commercial center. A town of more than 80,000, it was the nation's third largest city and easily the biggest south of Philadelphia. Given its history, its class structure, its economic advance, its dockyard muscularity, and its self-promotional manner, one might presume Baltimore to have been something of a theatrical center. It had been, after all, the site of the very first attempt at a permanent acting troupe in America, the Maryland Company of Comedians, organized in 1781 as the American Revolution neared its climax. And Maryland's elite maintained a self-consciously aristocratic spirit, as Tocqueville attests in his account of being fêted nightly by Baltimore society. The links between the privileged order and theatre were longstanding in England, but drama in Baltimore had languished. The town was reputed to be among the worst in America for supporting theatricals. Anglo-American actor Joseph Cowell blamed local standoffishness on the indifferent quality of Warren's and Wood's regular visits, whose "jog-trotting company" and "same old pieces" had "actually taught the audience to stay away." A more likely culprit was the prolonged economic slump Baltimore had endured after the Panic of 1819, which was especially devastating to the city's mercantile elite. Maybe too, as Count Arese claimed, Baltimore's culture was too provincial, at least compared to that of Philadelphia or New York.[40]

Still, MacKenzie, who oversaw the Baltimore venture, attempted to put his troupe's best foot forward. Elizabeth Chapman and David Ingersoll commuted between Washington and Baltimore, enduring the bone-jarring thirty-seven-mile journey by coach in order to perform with both groups. But MacKenzie was also reduced to utilizing Harry Isherwood in the cast. One of the fine scenic artists in the profession, Isherwood, alas, had thespian ambitions that could not be realized. If "anything better than his scene painting was rarely seen," actor Walter Leman bluntly wrote, "nothing could be much worse than his acting." Only spotty dramatic criticism of the company's performances appeared in the Baltimore or Washington newspapers. Fortunately, we have the testimony of Fanny Kemble, whose starring tour was supported by the Jefferson company in these two cities in early 1833.[41]

Frances Anne (Fanny) Kemble (1809–1893) was a progeny of arguably the most distinguished acting family of the early nineteenth-century Anglo-American stage. Her uncle, John Philip Kemble, a towering dramatic figure of the previous few decades, strode across the English stage with an unmatched dignity, declamatory precision, and a "gait of royalty." "If he had not the unexpected bursts of nature and genius," Hazlitt judged in an unstated comparison to the mercurial Edmund Kean, "he had all the regularity of art." Fanny's aunt, Sarah Kemble Siddons ("Mrs. Siddons," as she was normally styled in contemporary accounts), dignified, even forbidding, was the undisputed leading lady of the London stage. Their younger brother Charles, if not quite in their constellation, still attained a commanding position among players. He enjoyed sufficient acclaim to mount a starring tour of the States with his daughter Fanny (a tour they hoped would replenish dwindling family coffers), who was herself entering into that nebulous realm of recognition that allowed one to claim a star billing. Their appearance in 1832 met great acclaim, bolstering theatre attendance wherever they played. At New York's Park Theatre, perhaps the most illustrious in the nation, Fanny headlined for sixty nights in the 1832–33 season, bestowing record receipts on the local stock company.[42]

The Kembles encountered the Jefferson troupe during their southward swing from Philadelphia. The sometimes tatterdemalion quality of American theatricals impressed the Kembles right from the start. Their initial appointment at the Front Street Theatre was canceled because its manager could not provide a supporting cast. Instead they moved to the Holliday Street Theatre, a "very large, handsome house," bigger than the Park Theatre, Kemble thought, "but dirty, dilapidated, and looking as if there had been eleven executions in it that morning." But they had no alternative if they were to perform in Baltimore, so cinching up their resolve the Kembles prepared to make the best of the situation.[43]

Like most stars, the Kembles rotated a limited repertory of plays that supporting companies were expected to know — or to learn quickly. In Baltimore, Fanny would star in *Romeo and Juliet,* supported by aspiring tragedian Augustus Addams as Romeo and the Jefferson company. The results, detailed in subtly comic terms by Kemble, describe a Keystone Cops operation at the theatre, from her leading man, accoutred in a ridiculous-looking costume (like a "strange-coloured melon"), who at the play's crucial moment lost his dagger, to the stage hands, who "broke one man's collar-bone and nearly dislocated a woman's shoulder by flinging the scenery about."[44]

From Baltimore, Kemble journeyed by stage to Washington, the driver scarcely slowing as he plunged through the ravines and watercourses that cut across the road. She was chagrined to discover that here the Jeffersons would again support her. She tried unsuccessfully to beg off further rehearsals with them. "The proprietors are poor, the actors poorer," she pouted, "and the grotesque mixture of misery, vulgarity, stage-finery, and real raggedness, is beyond every thing strange, and sad, and revolting, — it reminds me constantly of some of Hogarth's pictures." One might suspect Kemble of exaggerated ill humor except that the exemplary diarist Philip Hone, taking in the theatre while visiting Washington, concurred with her judgment. Fanny in the Washington Theatre, Hone fretted, "is like a canarybird in a mousetrap." Whatever shortcomings existed in the production, however, official Washington in the persona of Supreme Court justices John Marshall and Joseph Story attended and relished the tragic power of Kemble. Their enthusiasm reflects one of the truisms of the nineteenth-century theatre: audiences attended the theatre to enjoy the star's performance. They normally forgave shabby scenery or indifferent supporting casts if the star fulfilled their expectations.[45]

Mazeppa

We cannot know the degree to which the Jefferson company perceived its shortcomings. No doubt members would have done better if they could. The troupe limped along through the remainder of 1833 and into 1834 dividing time between Baltimore and Washington. Yet the extended family continued to grow. Young cousin William Warren had begun his periodic association with the family troupe previous to his distinguished career as comedian at the Boston Museum. The highlight of the fall 1833 season was clearly the production of the equestrian melodrama *Mazeppa*. Preparations for the spectacle exceeded anything the troupe had attempted. An equestrian trainer was hired to prepare the "poetical steed." New costumes, decorations, equipment and furbishings so filled the stage that no other production could be mounted in the interim — altogether a production of "unremitted exertion and great expense." Their efforts produced a dramatic spectacle compelling enough to justify twelve consecutive nights, unusual longevity, especially so in a small theatre market like Washington. Once again young Joe found himself witness to a distinctive theatrical genre.[46]

That *Mazeppa* had premiered in America only the previous April speaks of the Jefferson company's attempt to transcend provincial limitations and stay current of theatrical trends. In mounting *Mazeppa; or, The Wild Horse of Tartary,* the Jeffersons caught the early wave of equestrian drama, whose popularity reoccurred throughout the century. "Hippodrama," as it was styled, evolved from circus and horsemanship exhibitions of late eighteenth-century France and England. Spacious ampitheaters — hippodromes — such as the Cirque Olympique, where thirty-six horses could perform simultaneously, were constructed in London and Paris for the pantomimed horse dramas. The theatres combined a traditional proscenium stage with a large dirt-floored arena (where the pit seating had traditionally been) separated by an area for the orchestra. Part circus and part theatre, this novelty had productions written expressly for it. Such plays as *The Blood Red Knight* or *Ferdinand of Spain* were essentially melodramas (accompanying the birth of that genre) with the twist that horses rather than heroines were the true stars. Shakespearean dramas, particularly *Richard III,* found itself a staple of hippodrama. The nobility of the steeds in one production, a critic wrote, would cause an audience to judge as a fair trade Richard's cry, "My kingdom for a horse."[47]

Like virtually all new theatrical fashions, hippodrama rapidly crossed the Atlantic and began pleasing crowds in America. The form bespoke a newly democratized audience, heterogeneous and less refined, enchanted by the immediacy of equestrian action and unbothered by a de-emphasis on formal declamation. New York's Lafayette Ampitheater beginning in 1826 and then Philadelphia's Ampitheater and Baltimore's Roman Ampitheater staged horse dramas.[48]

Mazeppa, the greatest equestrian crowd-pleaser of them all, combined the sappy twists of melodramatic plot with the unique challenges horse drama presented to stage logistics. Loosely based on Byron's poem of the same name, *Mazeppa* was first staged in England in 1823, though it did not attain its cultic status until produced at Astley's in 1831. The story concerned a Tartar prince, Mazeppa, raised in Poland under the name Casimar, whose romantic adventures resulted in his being bound to a horse that was then driven east across the steppes. "Bring forth the fiery, untamed steed," was the villainous order, "and send him galloping over the burning plains of Tartary!" This command provided the play's great spectacle. Huge ramps constructed on stage, angled first downstage, then doubled back and up, which the horse bearing Casimar (in less daring productions, a dummy was strapped on the beast) would furiously dash, ultimately climbing toward the theatre's flies. The inherent danger of this stage business was manifest in maimings and even fatalities of horses or actors during the several decades of its popularity. Harry Watkins witnessed this firsthand in

Cincinnati when a horse fell from the third ramp some twenty-five to thirty feet, miraculously with no serious injury to horse or rider.[49]

Mazeppa will be linked forever with the name Adah Isaacs Menken (1835–68), whose meteoric career primarily rested on her breeches role on the back of the Tartar pony. Limited in the finer graces of the stage, Menken nonetheless possessed a pretty face and a figure utterly seductive. With the ensuing fame of *Mazeppa* during the early 1860s she toured the country, enjoying especial enthusiasm in San Francisco and the Nevada silver frontier, where she hobnobbed with such literary luminaries as Mark Twain, Bret Harte, and Joaquin Miller.[50]

The attraction of casting a female Mazeppa followed the twin allures of sex and danger. Barnumesque advertising surrounding her appearances promised an unprecedented display of flesh. Menken's costume, flesh-colored leggings and tight linen tunic, moved well beyond merely suggestive to overtly seductive (this at a time when trousers on women violated basic Victorian proprieties). "Not an actress," the *Sacramento Union* described Menken, "she is an exhibition — a voluptuous experiment." The thrill of danger and possible catastrophe also hung about *Mazeppa* productions, doubly so when it was a women who would be imperiled. Menken's clever blending of androgyny and Orientalism infused new life into the tired horse drama and made herself the theatrical sensation of the day.[51]

True to the Marxian epigram, what began in tragedy ended in farce — or, more properly, burlesque. The success of *Mazeppa* predictably inspired theatrical send-ups on both English and American stages. In one case Mazeppa was strapped onto a rocking horse on wheels; another, minstrel-inspired American version, was done entirely in blackface. But perhaps more to the point, Menken's provocative display changed the future of equestrian drama. In short order, a host of females imitated Menken in the role, and audience admiration of horsemanship bowed before an unrestrained ogling of the skimpily clad form on the beast's back. *Mazeppa* itself became a burlesque in the modern sense of the term, a tantalizing leg show abetted by Menken's abbreviated costume.[52]

For all of its heroics in staging *Mazeppa*, the Jefferson company continued to struggle. The decision to divide into two parts plagued the talent-starved troupe. A Washington reviewer urged the company to get "a sufficient number of talented and respected performers," gently pointing out that despite Isherwood's talents as scene painter he was "not calculated to shine in the higher walks of the Drama." To compound problems, David Ingersoll, perhaps its most gifted member, decided to pursue stardom in Philadelphia and New York. Thus the apparent decision to recombine forces in Washington in November of 1833 seems wise.[53]

Wise but insufficient. Despite mounting 123 different plays in a five-month season and bringing in stars where possible, patronage sagged. Fewer new plays meant less novelty to offer the public. And continued complaints about the inadequate theatre were voiced in the *National Intelligencer:* smoking and chronic rowdiness, nails sticking out of the benches, delays between acts. "A most miserable-looking place, the worst I met with in the country," visiting English star Tyrone Power commented. With columns obstructing sight lines, an inadequate stage, a seating capacity too small to offer the compensation major stars desired on benefit night, and theatre stockholders entitled to complimentary seats on all nights (save benefit performances) and passes they could give their friends, both aesthetics and economics were compromised. Moreover, the theatre, on Louisiana Avenue, was not in a convenient location, a vexatious problem during cold or rainy weather when patrons balked at the ten-dollar hack fare. And though many members of Congress frequented the theatre, the capital's ladies seemed reluctant to attend. MacKenzie and Jefferson responded with an aggressive program of improvement: more stoves installed, music added between acts, police officers stationed inside to combat horseplay, lower ticket prices.[54]

To no avail. When Elizabeth Jefferson Chapman decamped for New York's Park Theatre in August 1834, the company lost its leading lady. By the middle of November, Jefferson II announced that his company, several members of which were "in a very delicate situation so far as regards pecuniary matters," was forced to disband. Company members scattered. MacKenzie opened a bookstore in Washington while Jefferson and his family moved briefly back to Philadelphia. This sad though not permanent end of the Jefferson-MacKenzie company sounds like a cautionary tale for much nineteenth-century theatre. Its struggles were typical rather than exceptional for all but a handful of the most established acting companies. The company faced exceptional pressures to mount fresh dramas, despite presenting a repertory of at least 271 plays over three years.[55]

Did company members sense their artistic failure? It is hard to imagine that they did not. But without the stabilizing and artistically demanding presence of Jefferson the elder, the remaining company members lacked a firm grasp of performance tradition. Tyrone Power, who, like Fanny Kemble, helped the company draw strong houses when he starred with them, nevertheless considered the plays "ill-mounted" and the Jefferson company as "unworthy the capital." Whatever discouragement may have afflicted individual members, the ethic of the stage commanded perseverance. Circumstances required that they seek their acting fortunes apart for a time.[56]

After Jefferson II and Cornelia endured an indifferent spring of touring about the Washington-Philadelphia region in 1835 (a season notable only for young Joe's earning newspaper notice for the first time), MacKenzie reunited several members of the Jefferson family that fall for one more go at the Washington theatre market. MacKenzie tried every thing he could think of to attract elusive audiences, even submitting his company to the indignity of supporting such circus-like novelties as Blanchard the "unrivalled contortionist" and a troupe of trained dogs. The *National Intelligencer* unkindly asked that as company members learned their lines they would also "study a proper disposition of their hands and feet, in the acting of their parts." By November, MacKenzie's band on the Potomac had had enough.[57]

To Gotham

The prolific Jefferson clan scattered once again, the road for many of them leading to New York. Of course, two of the most talented had already moved there. Elizabeth Jefferson Chapman, widowed since 1830 (yet only in her midtwenties), had made herself indispensable at the Park. "Her personal charm," noted stage chronicler George C. D. Odell, "her intellect (common to the Jeffersons), her instinct for acting, and her ability as a songstress" marked her as among that theatre's most versatile performers ever. The gifted but troubled David Ingersoll (along with wife Mary-Anne Jefferson) had a more checkered career and for a time returned south. But by early 1836 he too was back in New York, holding a position at the Franklin Theatre, a connection that opened a door for Jefferson, wife Cornelia, Charles Burke, and other members of the family to join him.[58]

The Jeffersons entered a New York that had for several decades been the preeminent city in America but whose stage had just recently regained primacy from Philadelphia. The change resulted partly from the disastrous competition among theatres in the City of Brotherly Love, a competition that brought about the near collapse of theatricals in that city. More significantly, though, New York's advance followed the economic boom spurred by the opening of the Erie Canal in 1825. The canal compounded New York's inherent geographic advantage of being a day's sail closer to Europe than Philadelphia, giving it a vital edge in transatlantic business information and making it the major point of entry for imports — including stage stars and recent dramas. The idiosyncracies of New York urban culture also nurtured theatricals. Scottish phrenologist George Combe's observation of the city during a visit caught the spirit of its people. The city was filled with strangers, many of them young men, "whose evenings are at their own disposal . . . who live in boarding houses and hotels, who have plenty of money, and no domestic ties." These bachelors, along with the merchants and similarly prosperous families, provided theatre managers with "a solid phalanx of play-going people."[59]

The Jeffersons could hardly have been prepared for what they found. Philadelphia, sedate and charming by comparison, and Washington, still a sleepy southern town, gave no hint of the dynamism of New York. Its steady march up Manhattan Island was well underway. Visually, the city offended more than it appealed. It was continually remaking itself, with buildings going up and coming down. Public services were slack. Streets were dirt — if dry — and if wet, "a realm of mud . . . a slimy alluvial deposit, of the consistency of batter, of bean soup, ankle-deep." Even Broadway, putative showpiece avenue, was uncrossable for weeks in the early winter of 1836 "except by such desperadoes as durst wade through the stagnant, universal pool." But such conditions only underscored the brawny Jacksonianism of the city, where deference to rank was being challenged by working-class mechanics and artisans, abetted by a working-class theatre. A capitalism exuberant in its prosperity nurtured a lively theatrical scene (that is, at least before the Panic of 1837).[60]

Elite theatergoing in 1836 meant a trip to the Park, where manager Edward Simpson was at the peak of his career. The Park presented top foreign stars — Fanny Kemble, Tyrone Power, Charles Kean, Charles Mathews — supported by an adept company. Over at the American Theatre, better known by the name of its location, the Bowery, Thomas Hamblin provided Simpson his stoutest competition. But in truth, Hamblin catered to a different clientele and put on a distinct product. Dedicated to democratic, working-class taste, the "Bowery Slaughterhouse" (so termed for its menu of sanguinary spectacles) was housed in a huge 3,500-capacity hall with a facade of Doric columns that was, according to Mrs. Trollope, "infinitely superior [to the Park] in beauty."[61]

By contrast, the new Franklin Theatre, where the Jeffersons now congregated, lacked the cachet of either. Off the beaten path at 175 Chatham Street and small by prevailing standards — holding about 600 — the Franklin found its "niche in the temple of farce." Joe's father worked primarily as a scene painter, his greater talent, supplemented by some acting. By the first of June he had earned the right to his own benefit performance, for which the wider Jefferson clan banded together. His sister, the accomplished Elizabeth, starred as Julia in one of the day's great potboilers, Sheridan Knowles's *The Hunchback*. To her brother's pleasure she attracted an "overcrowded house." Less happily, "silver-voiced" wife Cornelia, making her first appearance on a New York stage in a decade, revealed that her "voice and person [have] in the interim suffered sadly from the ravages of time." Adding further familial insult, a reviewer suggested that Mary-Anne "had but little of the far-flung Jefferson ability; indeed," the writer drolly continued, "so had the beneficiary of this occasion."[62]

The year spent at the Franklin provided sustenance if not fame for the Jeffersons. But for son Joe, who turned eight in early 1837, his first New York turn marked the serious beginning of his career as a child actor. As a juvenile performer, Joe Jefferson was not famous in the manner of a Master Betty, Clara Fisher, or other prodigies of the late eighteenth and early nineteenth century. No matter. He belonged to an established theatrical family, had considerable stage exposure, and if family testimonies are to be taken at face value, was a "wonderfully precocious boy." "Precocity" did not prevent childish stage panic from causing disaster, as when several years earlier scripted gunfire frightened the very young Joe so badly that he yanked the wig off the head of noble Inca chief Rolla at a climactic moment in Sheridan's *Pizarro*. But audiences dismissed such episodes as easily as they occurred. They expected little more. Professional standards of the antebellum stage — particularly in the provincial theatres — were unexacting. Stars frequently breezed into town, ran through the play once with the local supporting cast, then hoped for the best that night.[63]

This professional nonchalance allowed — perhaps encouraged — the novelty of substituting child actors in adult roles. Beginning in the 1790s and extending well into the 1830s, a juvenile fashion swept the transatlantic stage. Underlying this odd exercise was the Romantic era's reverence for naturalness, which found apparent embodiment in the simple lispings of the child. Master William Betty, at thirteen, so captivated the British theatre world that his Covent Garden premiere threatened to become a mob scene, requiring guards to secure theatre entrances. Pitt the Younger later adjourned Parliament to see him act, and Cambridge sponsored a prize medal in his honor. John Howard Payne, who would become one of America's premier early playwrights, enjoyed a mercurial rise and fall as a teenage tragedian. Joseph Burke, the "Irish Roscius," was the sensation of the 1830 season at Philadelphia's Arch Street Theatre as Young Norval in *Douglas,* charming both in his declamation and in his accomplished musicianship on the violin.[64]

The most eminent American child actors were Kate and Ellen Bateman. Their parents displayed a variety of show business skills, not the least of which was a Barnumesque eye for promotion. In 1846, at ages two and four, Ellen and Kate debuted on the Louisville stage. Drilled relentlessly by their parents, the girls proved to be quick studies, learning not only a repertoire of children's parts but also characters from Shakespearean tragedy. In *Merchant of Venice* Kate played Portia "with amazing skill and propriety." The final act of *Richard III* became their signature piece, with them first barnstorming it by steamboat along the Ohio and Mississippi rivers, then returning east to triumph in Boston and New York before P.T. Barnum himself arranged an English tour and performance to royalty. A portrait from the day shows a diminutive, mustachioed Ellen Bateman dressed in the ermined cape and crown of Richard, wearing also a sneer that suggests either the character of the English king or her own discomfort with the situation.[65]

With the exception of the Bateman sisters, the juvenile tragedian largely disappeared after the 1830s. The theatre public increasingly understood "the absurdities of a little boy's squeaking out the sorrow of a frantic lover." Even in the height of enthusiasm for Joseph Burke, experienced theatergoer Benjamin Brown French found it impossible "to get rid of the idea that he was a mere boy." Dickens concurred, offering a wicked description in *Nicholas Nickleby* (1839) of the "infant phenomenon," whose talent, according to her manager-father, " 'must be seen, sir — seen — to be ever so faintly appreciated.' " We know little about how adult players viewed sharing the stage with juveniles. One suspects that playing second banana to those who would "hector, and combat, and conquer what [they] could hardly reach" must have been a travail for any one with an ounce of professional pride. During this "reign of infant actors," as William Wood wryly phrased it, the venerable Jefferson I found his dignity at risk when he was theatrically slain by the swordplay of eleven-year-old Master George Frederic Smith. Likewise, the clever Bateman sisters seemed to a veteran trouper like Henry Watkins "too much like what it is — child's play." Such critics were pleased to see the novelty of child actors finally surrender to an enhanced professionalism, which invigorated the American stage after midcentury, when the casting of children in adult roles nearly disappeared.[66]

At the Franklin in the fall of 1837 Joe found his name on the playbill in support, interestingly enough, of one of those aspiring prodigies afflicting the Jacksonian stages. Master Titus, son of a city official, was apparently clever enough to be accorded a benefit performance. If his attempts at *Richard II* have passed into oblivion, his brief afterpiece, a mock heroic battle grandiloquently titled *A Terrific Combat Featuring Master Titus and Master Jefferson*, gained favor in part through its historical reference to America's travails with the Barbary pirates a few decades earlier. These military encounters were fresh enough in viewers' historical memory to evoke a patriotic response yet far enough removed to become the stuff of stage travesty. Joe, garbed as a Mediterranean pirate, squared off against Master Titus's Jack Tar. Spirited sword play resulted — inevitably — in Jack Tar's victory. The curtain tableau, with Titus's foot planted on Joe's chest "waving a star-spangled banner" was a certain crowd pleaser, and the curtain calls finally resulted in an encore fight and second death.[67]

Young Joe Jefferson may have lost that battle, but his childhood experiences clearly put him on the high rail to a stage career. Nature and nurture conspired to produce an actor. This apparent inevitability must be qualified, for Joe was not the prodigy his mother believed him to be (his name appeared only fitfully on early stage bills). Moreover, the Jefferson tribe's dramatic genius was not bestowed on every member. It skipped a generation from Jefferson I to his grandson. It fell upon Joe's aunt, Elizabeth Chapman, though not on Joe's sister. Giftedness also resided in the Burke side of the family, partially present in Joe's mother Cornelia and fully in half-brother Charles. But the gods recalled these two benefactions prematurely, before reputations could be secured. Cornelia's talents attenuated rapidly in midlife; Charlie, who achieved some measure of acclaim, died in his early thirties. Of the prolific theatrical Jeffersons, only Joe possessed the proper fractions of aptitude, longevity, and luck that added up to stardom.

2

Marking the Progress of Civilization

While Joseph Jefferson II and his family labored in the theatrical vine-yards of New York, Alexander MacKenzie headed west. Through Cleveland and Columbus he trouped with a company, then on to Detroit, where he was joined by Jefferson's sister Mary-Anne and her husband David Ingersoll. After a short summer season in 1837, Ingersoll left the company for good, heading to Nashville, where his downward spiral of alcoholism culminated in death a year later. Taking his place in the troupe was the steady if unspectacular Harry Isherwood, who itched to join "the misery of management." Isherwood scouted out Chicago for MacKenzie in September. Isherwood arrived at night in a driving rain, and was so unimpressed by the raw-edged young town that he nearly advised against the company's visit. But he was persuaded otherwise. City fathers realized that despite its potential greatness Chicago remained "deficient in that essential feature of metropolitanism — an established place of amusement." When Isherwood and MacKenzie presented a proposal for drama, their offer was "hailed with approving demonstration." In such manner during the fall of 1837 did theatricals first come to Chicago.[1]

The company arrived by a Great Lakes steamer in October. One of many European commentators on the American scene, the Count Francesco Arese, happened to share the boat with the troupe. He recalled Mary-Anne Ingersoll as lacking youth or good looks yet pacing the deck "with an air of as much importance as either Semiramis or Cleopatra could have worn." Once ashore, the company encountered a bureaucratic hurdle in the form of a high license fee demanded by the Chicago Common Council. Uncowed, they appealed and got the original $150 tariff halved. Their first venue in Chicago was a dining room of the Sauganash Hotel — then deserted — near Randolph and Market. For three months the troupe performed to good houses until intractable rain and their limited repertoire ended their season.[2]

The MacKenzie-Isherwood foray into the old Northwest continued the work of such theatrical pioneers as the Chapman and the Drake families in the Ohio and Mississippi river valleys. These were America's strolling players, resembling more their poor Elizabethan ancestors than their more prosperous American descendants. Moving from town to hamlet to river landing — in some cases playing in what was scarcely more than a clearing littered with a few cabins — and with little in the way of advance work, these itinerant troupers gave original meaning to the hoariest of show business clichés, "the show must go on."

The lure of the trans-Ohio West for actors was in many respects similar to that felt by other frontiersmen. With the cessation of hostilities between England and America after the battle of New Orleans in early 1815, the area between Cincinnati and New Orleans witnessed an unprecedented migration of settlers. River towns like Pittsburgh, Cincinnati, Louisville, St. Louis, and New Orleans, aided by the transforming presence of the steamboat, promised to be the next great metropolises. The appearance of a "professional" troupe or, even better, the construction of a theatre served, as Noah Ludlow phrased it, "to mark the progress of civilization." The early date of drama's arrival in western towns suggests the imperative of this form of culture: Cincinnati, 1810; Louisville, Lexington, and Frankfort, 1815; Nashville and Natchez, 1817; St. Louis, 1819; Mobile, 1824.[3]

Accounts of pioneer theatricals are alive with adventure and hardship that are by turn sobering and hilarious. The career of John Banvard (1815–91) is one example. Known to posterity primarily as a designer of panoramas and artist of the nineteenth century's largest painting, Banvard also briefly toured the West as actor and manager. He started with the venerable Chapman clan, who launched America's first showboat (fittingly called *Chapman's Ark*). Their floating stage worked its way down the Mississippi bearing a white flag, stopping at any landing promising a ready audience. The Chapmans were an odd bunch, secretive, unconcerned about employee comfort, and none too regular in salary. Banvard left them after a season to attempt his own showboat theatre. He assembled his company in 1834 on the banks of the Wabash, at New Harmony, Indiana. Only nineteen years old himself, Banvard recruited a ragtag assemblage of performers, including "the Great American Fire-Eater" (he ate hot coals and licked a red-hot iron). With a purse enlarged by a gullible recruit's savings, Banvard purchased an apothecary's flatboat and fitted it with a spacious open-air auditorium. Not willing to put all his eggs in one performance basket, Banvard stocked the boat with groceries and tobacco to sell along the river. The future seemed secure.[4]

Times were comfortable for the Banvard troupe as long as they lingered in New Harmony, the former site of Robert Owen's utopian commune, but when the company pushed off to descend the Wabash and Ohio rivers it quickly left Arcadia behind. Low water on the Wabash meant continual groundings. The snail's pace of progress kept the company from earning money and provisions ran desperately short. Compounding these hardships, many of the group came down with malaria. As they drifted down the Ohio River they were reduced to scavenging food. These chronic hardships encouraged bickering among the actors that culminated in a tragic end to the tour. Near Randolph, Tennessee, a member accused the business manager of withholding what little profits had been realized thus far. A fight left the manager severely wounded from a Bowie knife. Worse, when the local constable came on board to investigate, he fell through the stage trapdoor and broke his neck. With its members now fugitives, the company abruptly disbanded.[5]

The Banvard company's experience was more grim than most, to be sure. But what its members endured — insecurity, hunger, illness, physical danger — were common hardships for most pioneer actors. Nineteenth-century life was hard for all, but vagabond players tempted fate to dish out a double portion. Clearly, only an engrossing attraction to the mimic life made such hardships worth the bargain. Some, such as Banvard, stepped off the boards after disillusioning ordeals. There were limits to what people would endure, even for Thespis.

But there were also those actors and managers who permanently cast their lot with the nascent theatre of the West. Noah Ludlow, who with Sol Smith later formed the most important managerial combine in the old Southwest, began his career with theatrical pioneer Samuel Drake. Ludlow's description of Ohio River theatricals is considerably more irenic than Banvard's. Ludlow portrays leisurely days drifting along the sluggish current of the Ohio, reading, sewing, or just enjoying the landscape. The spirit of Ludlow's memories are summed up in his story of sharing a room at a backwoods inn with mule-handlers, who were taking a herd to market. Bothersome and smelly, the herders needed to be moved on. This Ludlow accomplished through an impromptu performance of the ghost scene from *Hamlet,* which suitably frightened the naive and superstitious guests.[6]

Sol Smith, who regales readers with three volumes of theatrical memoirs, tells the ultimate story of dramatic make-do on the frontier. His small company had reached Bean's Station in the hills of east Tennessee. Exhausted and wanting only shelter for the night, they found a populace excited about the novelty of "show folk" in town and demanding a performance. When Smith asked about lighting and was told there was none — not even candles for the tavern — he stipulated any show would have to be in the dark, expecting this hard fact to end discussion. Instead, townsmen enthusiastically agreed. Consequently, an odd medley of songs, recitations, and instrumental numbers were heard, if not seen, from a Stygian stage.[7]

Actors less charmed by the rigors of western theatricals might view a western tour of duty as simply a training ground for the more genteel East. The West, said tragedian James E. Murdoch, was "that professional school for youthful thespians." Dan Rice, circus clown, humorist, and impresario, honed his art as an itinerant in the Ohio River valley. And Joe Jefferson spent much of his early apprenticeship in the old Northwest and Southwest. In a Turnerian sense, the frontier stage could be understood as a dramatic safety valve for actors whose careers had temporarily — they hoped — waned in the East. The sustained economic downturn of the later 1820s and 1830s encouraged many an actor to perk up his ears at rumors of prosperity on the frontier. As a result, these years witnessed a collection of motley troupes traversing the South and West, discovering too late that conditions were rarely better there. Such ambitions, of course, described the McKenzie-Ingersoll-Isherwood-Jefferson company, or as it was grandly fashioned during its midwestern touring phase — the Illinois Theatrical Company.[8]

A Theatrical El Dorado

With the beachhead secured in Chicago, MacKenzie sent word back to New York for reinforcements. By early 1838 Joseph Jefferson II and family were prepared to head west, for their future in New York appeared grim. Theatricals had been affected by the Panic of 1837, the nation's worst financial reversal to that point. In April, Philip Hone grimly recorded, the desperate clouds of recession "have become darker than ever, and no eye can perceive a ray of hope"; by the end of May he reported, "no goods are selling, no business stirring." Yet most New York theatres in fact kept their doors open, bravely mounting productions to dwindling audiences and rising bills.[9]

After finishing his spring season with the Franklin Theatre, Jefferson, with perhaps more daring than discretion, considering the economic climate, joined John Sefton in producing "vaudeville" at Niblo's Garden. Niblo's had originally restricted itself to musical concerts, but Sefton and Jefferson decided to follow the fashions of London and Paris in staging light theatricals, frivolous nonsense to help patrons endure muggy Gotham nights. Jefferson served as scene painter and actor in such productions as *L'Amant Prêté, or Le Prisonnier de la Rochelle* (these pieces, familiar under their English monikers to many theatergoers, were gussied up with French titles to add the exotic flavor so many Americans craved). There is no record of Joe's parents ever again appearing on a New York stage. For the Jefferson family, the hazardous tides of New York fortune were gladly exchanged for the promise of a "theatrical El Dorado" in the West.[10]

In its pursuit they journeyed by water to Chicago. They constituted a small company, six adults and two children, all of them related: Jefferson II, wife Cornelia, and their two children, Joe and Cornelia (often called Connie); Joe's half-brother, Charles Burke; his cousin, Jane Anderson, and her new husband, Greenbury Germon; and another cousin, William Warren. After traveling up the Hudson to Albany, they took a stagecoach to Schenectady, where they boarded a Erie Canal packet. Brightly painted (as canal boats usually were) with a smart red stripe running from bow to stern, the *Pioneer* had the squat though streamlined appearance common to its breed.

An embarrassment complicated the voyage: Jefferson lacked funds to pay the passage. That canal travel had become ridiculously cheap by the 1830s suggests the precariousness of family circumstances. But Jefferson, who rarely encountered a problem that he did not interpret as opportunity, convinced the packet captain that the company could do turns in Utica and Syracuse, remitting to him the profits. Proceeding upon this makeshift indenture, the family enjoyed the four-to-five-day journey across New York. Canal travel was pleasant in its own way. Boats glided along at four miles per hour, the quiet interrupted mainly by the boatman's horn. The enticing weather of late spring would probably have brought the Jefferson entourage out of the stuffy cabin onto the deck. Here, between Rochester and Utica, they passed through endless stretches of forest; between Rome and Syracuse they saw stands of charred trees as land was being cleared. But ventures topside also meant being subject to continual shouts of "low bridge," requiring an immediate prostration on deck. The novelty of this exercise quickly wore off and drove most passengers back inside. But even within the cabin, the easy familiarity between those who had been strangers (a characteristic of Jacksonian America that foreign travelers found either intriguing or off-putting) encouraged a steady flow of conversation, political debate, card playing, or singing.[11]

The promised Utica performance went well, and prospects of retiring the passage debt seemed assured. But at Syracuse rain spoiled attendance, leaving

Jefferson some ten dollars in arrears. The packet captain, a conscientious church member who eschewed theatre attendance, was nevertheless curious about acting and offered that if the Jeffersons "cut up" for him he would forgive the balance. The company, though in little position to object, felt themselves "highly legitimate" and had to decline this affront. Instead, Joe's parents offered the captain an impromptu performance by their talented son. Jefferson later recalled that the captain seemed "suspicious of his genius" but finally relented. With the rest of the company retiring to the upper deck (having been subjected to Joe's juvenile patter too often), Joe launched into a twenty-five stanza comic song, "The Devil and Little Mike." The captain suffered through half of the song's relentless twaddle before saying he had heard enough.[12]

At Buffalo, before heading onto Lake Erie, the troupe joined a fellow pioneer company — one that included Danforth Marble, an early stage Yankee — and performed for a few nights at the Eagle Street Theatre. With a replenished pocketbook the Jeffersons could book passage on a Great Lakes steamer. This was a new order of craft. Some of the finest steamboats in the country plied the thousand-mile run between Buffalo and Chicago. Accommodating up to five hundred in their double-deck cabins, these large boats sought to emulate the ocean-going steamers along the Atlantic coast with their ornamented sleeping berths, staterooms, and saloons. Joe had fond memories of the weeklong journey. Occasional stops along the way to take on wood gave opportunity for him and his sister to wander by the shore and collect agates. Along the shores of Lake Huron they spotted Indian villages, bespeaking the fact that although boats traversed the upper Great Lakes, the region yet to significantly come within the Anglo-American orbit.[13]

Arriving at Chicago in early May, the Jeffersons disembarked from the steamer and were greeted by hugs from the extended family. They then gazed at a stark urban landscape. Chicago's grid of streets, though pleasantly tree-lined, were unpaved and frequently had prairie grasses in their center. The old enclosure of Fort Dearborn stood nearby, a reminder of Indian days not far in the past; indeed, troops had been posted around the area just two years earlier over concern of renewed trouble. Now, however, excitement focused on the rocketing price of city lots.[14]

Chicago had gained incorporation as a city the previous fall, but in truth it was still but a town of less than 4,000 residents. The Panic of 1837 threatened to rain on Chicago's parade of progress. Although the depression continued for several years, there could be no doubt as to the city's final success, propitiously located between Lake Michigan's flat shores and the Illinois River's egress to the Mississippi. It would take but the completion of a hundred-mile connecting canal to fulfill the explorer Joliet's dream of linking French Canada with the Gulf of Mexico by water. Throughout the family's Chicago stay, local newspaper attention never wavered from the great Illinois-Michigan Canal project.

Even before the Jefferson's arrival, MacKenzie had begun planning a more permanent theatre for the augmented company. This required another license from city fathers. Just a few years earlier Tocqueville had noted how Americans, who granted wide legal scope to most forms of expression, subjected drama to the censorship of municipal licensing. MacKenzie's application bespoke the suppliant posture that entertainers had to assume. He asked permission for his company to "strut and fret . . . upon the stage" beginning in May 1838. He further declared their intention to make Chicago their residence and to that end had already incurred much expense in outfitting the theatre in "a manner as to reflect credit upon our infant city." Besides the usual request for as low a license fee as possible, MacKenzie closed by gently asking for an exclusive right of performance. The latter may seem presumptuous, but in an age of state-granted monopolies to canal and steamship companies and when London's patent theatre privileges were yet the law, MacKenzie's bid was not outlandish.[15]

Located on the upper floor of an auction hall-turned-tavern on Dearborn and Water streets, the "Rialto," as it was styled, sat right in the middle of Chicago's congested commercial district. Adjoining it was the Eagle saloon, gathering place for town politicos. Both establishments suggested a problem to early municipal goo-goos, and rumors of the theatre application elicited a petition signed by nineteen staunch citizens objecting to a license. Why? They objected to the inherent fire danger presented by a theatre "surrounded by wooden and combustible buildings." Chicago had experienced a cleansing fire a few years earlier (it would have a more famous brush with fire thirty-five years later), and theatres had become notorious for their propensity to burn.

The resulting flurry of politicking over the license indicated a depth to the issue beyond fear of fire. The Chicago Council referred the matter to a special committee of three. The minority report objected to the license because of the menace a theatre would pose to public morals as "grossly demoralizing, destructive of principle," and the "nurseries of crime." Even though the city treasury could use the boost the license fee promised, the cost in virtue was too high. But toleration finally prevailed. The majority report acknowledged real safety concerns and moral discomfort on the part of some. Yet it seemed "inexpedient . . . to enter into an inquiry of the morality of the drama." The license was granted.[16]

This accomplished, MacKenzie oversaw the refashioning of the eighty-by-thirty-foot hall into a temple to the muse. It was a rough-hewn temple in some respects. Seats were backless planks. And "the gloomy entrance," recalled Chicago resident Benjamin T. Taylor, "could have furnished the scenery for a nightmare." Yet within their means, the company sought to dignify the dramatic venue with elegance. There were two private boxes over which were painted portraits of Beethoven and Handel. The auditorium dome was muraled in classic themes. Whatever its artistic merit, said early city historian A. T. Andreas, the Rialto was the nursery of drama in Chicago, "and from within the walls of that historical pile issued the infant's feeble wails as it struggled for existence."[17]

The company enjoyed a healthy run of more than five months. In October it mounted the Chicago premiere of *The Lady of Lyons,* just eight months after the great William Charles Macready had first performed it in London. This melodramatic romance by the British Liberal M.P., littérateur, and bon vivant Edward Bulwer-Lytton was an immediate success. That a struggling theatre company on the edge of civilization could so quickly produce a recent hit suggests a determination to provide the latest dramatic fashions (it also speaks to the lack of copyright protection at the time).[18]

The Lady of Lyons, though introduced to American audiences only in the late 1830s, holds the distinction of being the most produced play on American stages in the two decades between 1831 and 1851. It attracted audiences by clever stagecraft, by intermittent verse drama that lent a faux Shakespearean authority, and by well-drawn leading characters, whose moral failings at the beginning were refined by the fires of melodramatic situation into exemplary virtues by the end. Audiences would have been particularly attracted to the play's dominant theme — the hollowness of social pretense, and conversely, the nobility of natural goodness even among the humbly born. What might the MacKenzie company have felt about the villain Beauseant's vow in the first act to humble Pauline by seeing her "married to a strolling player!"? The line intended a laugh, but it must have elicited a bittersweet note of recognition from the actors.[19]

Despite providing gratifying audiences, a young Chicago could not support a year-around theatre company. The eternal search for fresh audiences required a complementary circuit among towns of western and central Illinois and Mississippi River towns in Iowa and Missouri. As transitory as it proved to be, this theatrical circuit — with Chicago as its hub — prefigured the economic and cultural command the Windy City would exert over the Midwest in future years. Unwittingly, MacKenzie anticipated the vital symbiosis of metropolis and countryside, which in following decades defined the character of the entire American heartland.[20]

MacKenzie had led his group on a hinterland tour in the winter of 1838, and in late October, the company again headed out of Chicago, nearly straight west some 160 miles to the mining town of Galena. Joe, still not ten, got his first taste of pioneer travel in an open wagon jolting over the low ridges and marshy depressions of the northern Illinois prairie. They could make relatively good time thanks to a terrain, one traveler sardonically noted, bereft of even a "tenth-rate hill." Seated on slick horse-hair trunks, members desperately clung to the leather handles to avoid being pitched out. In the back of the wagon rode the several standard sets of shutters and wings — painted by Jefferson II — that served as backdrops for a myriad of plays. Joe's father, concerned not to overtax his team of horses, frequently walked alongside. With his placid nature he took every contingency in stride. "If it rained he was glad it was not snowing; if it snowed he was thankful it was not raining."[21]

The land in the northwest corner of the state, untouched by glacial scouring, was resplendent in its variegated pattern of hills and valleys. Galena itself, near the juncture of the Fever and Mississippi rivers, was in the midst of an early boom thanks to exploitation of its rich lead deposits nearby. The recession of late 1830s scarcely touched this outpost of capitalism, and as people continued to arrive, the town rivaled Chicago in size and surpassed it in visual appeal. Here the Illinois prairie gave way to steep bluffs rising from the Fever (now Galena) River. Perched upon concentric, ascending terraces were impressive examples of antebellum domestic architecture. Its citizens, particularly in the salad days of the 1840s and 1850s, sought to make Galena an outpost of civilized life. In the 1830s, still rough around the edges, Galena shared with most mining communities a ready appetite for theatricals — or any entertainments for that matter. And as with boomer towns elsewhere, Galena looked proudly on its new theatre (in reality, a second-floor room in a sturdy stone commercial building on Main Street) as a sign of urban progress. Thus when the MacKenzie entourage lumbered into town that October — though not the first troupe to play there — they were welcomed as harbingers of a more cultured future. "A theatre at this time will no doubt amuse and instruct many of our good citizens," the local paper decided. Especially for Galena youth might the acting company provide an alternative to "scenes of turpitude and self-debasement to one more worthy and more in consonance with civilized communities."[22]

The company had taken on a new look by the time it arrived at the western reaches of Illinois. Harry Isherwood had decamped for Detroit, and Jefferson II replaced him as Alexander MacKenzie's partner. Impermanence and fluidity marked most acting companies, not only on the frontier but in the East as well. Ambition, conflict, boredom — the footloose impatience for which Americans were notorious — all tugged at an actor's heart. Too, as various Jefferson widows remarried, their husbands either joined the troupe or took their wives off to new adventures. At Galena the company consisted of ten men, four women, and the children, Joe and young Cornelia. As modest an assemblage as this would appear, it contained a trio of exceptional talents in the making: Joe, of course, not yet ten but already contributing regular comic songs as entr'acte, and half-brother Charles Burke and cousin William Warren, Jr., then aged sixteen and twenty-six, respectively, both of whom soon became acclaimed comedians.

By late October the MacKenzie-Jefferson company was ready for its Galena premiere. It mounted shows four evenings a week at 7:00 P.M. The one dollar ticket price was steep for the 1830s yet tolerable to mining town residents flush with currency but short on places to spend it. If quantity be a fair measure, they received good value, for shows might reach toward midnight. As per the custom of the time, the featured comedy or drama opened the night, followed by a musical or dance interlude (the entr'acte), and with a farce to close. This prodigality of entertainment, driven by audience demand for novelty, meant that theatre groups had to possess huge repertoires. By one reckoning, the company produced sixty-seven full-length plays and thirty afterpieces. They may well have mounted more. It hardly needs saying that this remarkable outpouring of drama could only be accomplished by forgoing extensive rehearsal or reflective study of individual roles. Further, dramas often looked alike, utilizing a handful of props and scenic backdrops and rotating a baker's dozen of actors through the roles. Even so, this dauntless band presented the classics of Shakespeare and Goldsmith — *Hamlet, Othello, Macbeth, She Stoops to Conquer* — as well as the more commonly produced contemporary European and American melodramas like *Pizarro* or *The Lady of Lyons*.[23]

The Galena season ran intermittently through the winter and into April. The company proved themselves "public-spirited friends of town" when they acceded to a request by local firemen to stage a benefit for the Galena Fire Department in February. During the Galena stay Joe had opportunity to briefly attend school and make some chums. Joe's itinerant theatrical childhood, as rich as it was, denied him the usual circle of playmates, and he later recalled fondly playing ball with local boys.[24]

Ever restless, the company departed Galena in February for a twelve- to fifteen-mile jaunt across and up the Mississippi to Dubuque, Iowa. This midwinter excursion occasioned one memorable anecdote in Jefferson's *Autobiography*. The company crossed the frozen river on sleigh, periodically unnerved by ominous rumbles from the ice but arriving safely. The baggage sleigh, however, containing all scenery and props broke through and became thoroughly soaked. Wet costumes festooned the halls of their hotel, Jefferson remembered. These could dry, but more delicate props, like the gilded paste-board helmets, "succumbed to the softening influences of the Mississippi, and were as battered and out of shape as if they had gone through the pass of Thermopylae." Joe's father, ever irenic, counted it luck that a sand bar kept all their belongings from washing away. But they could not avoid postponing their Dubuque opening until possessions were cleaned and dried.[25]

Dubuque, another lead mining center, had been in existence a scant five years when the Jeffersons arrived, but it already possessed a lively theatrical tradi-tion. The Lafayette Circus Company from New York previously had found an enthusiastic reception in the upper Mississippi Valley frontier. And a year before Joe arrived, a group of ambitious Dubuque amateurs had formed a dramatic club to bring the muse to culture-starved residents on a jury-rigged stage in the descriptively named Shakespeare Coffee House and Free Admission News Room. This was a multipurposed establishment, where patrons could indulge in hard cider in the first-floor shop while also edifying themselves by perusing congressional proceedings and general news from an assortment of newspapers. Now, in midwinter 1839, the visit of a professional troupe seemed too good to be true. Not just any company, MacKenzie-Jefferson was heralded as "the first troupe of professional actors with a metropolitan reputation" to visit Iowa territory. It did not disappoint. An eleven-night engagement pre-sented a sort of greatest hits collection of early nineteenth-century theatre: melodramas *Camille, Rob Roy,* and *The Lady of Lyons;* comedies *Honeymoon* and *How to Rule a Wife;* and the two most performed Shakespearean tragedies, *Othello* and *Richard III,* were among the delights staged before crowded and appreciative audiences.[26]

After returning to Galena for another short season, the company left in midspring for a more extended tour of Iowa-Illinois borderland towns. It followed the serpentine route of the Mississippi to Burlington, Iowa, then continued south to the river's opposite bank at Quincy, Illinois. A namesake of the second President Adams, Quincy reached from the river's shore up the bluffs to the wooded ground above. Destined to soon be Illinois's second-largest city, Quincy had no theatrical tradition and no theatre, necessitating the drafting of the local courthouse for use during the two-and-a-half-week run.

Whatever its inadequacies as a dramatic venue, the dignity of a courthouse was no doubt preferred to what they found at Pekin. A modest entrepôt on the Illinois River where prairie farmers might acquire tokens of material pros-perity from the outside world, its eight or nine hundred residents had seen no need for constructing even a basic hall. Thus the Jeffersons were "reduced to the dire necessity of acting in a pork-house," a simple frame building at the edge of town beneath which pigs were penned. With the distinguished troupe in need of their home, the displaced hogs were banished to the local common. Some scouring and a coat of whitewash readied this rustic Drury Lane. The spring-summer touring about the river towns on the Mississippi and Illinois rivers brought indifferent results. This despite the claim of an Alton writer that "there is nothing that a diseased mind can enjoy so much as a good play."[27]

A Lincoln Encounter

After a brief stay in Peoria, the MacKenzie-Jefferson company headed across the eighty miles of rolling prairie to Springfield. For some members it was a return visit. The previous winter, before Joe's family had arrived, the company had presented a monthlong season here. Prospects looked even better now in June of 1839, as the state capital was in the process of being removed from Centralia to Springfield, a transfer fittingly completed on July Fourth. Despite impressive beginnings on the capitol building in the town center, Springfield cut an unprepossessing figure. Hogs roamed freely through the streets. During rain, its black loam metamorphosed into mud the consistency of wet cement. But the crudeness of its environs could not detract from the purposeful activity of its citizens. Modestly populated with 2,000 residents at best, the town was nonetheless gripped with the feverish anticipation (common to city fathers of the day) of future greatness. Perhaps caught up in the spirit of the moment, the acting troupe here adopted the name Illinois Theatrical Company—a title they might with certain justification have felt they earned through hundreds of miles of touring. On July Fourth the company "greatly improved in numbers and talent" (so promised the *Sangomo Journal*) opened their approximately monthlong season in a newly constructed hall.[28]

This Springfield season provided the occasion for Joseph Jefferson's most widely recounted autobiographical anecdote. Joe's father and his partner, Alexander MacKenzie, fully sharing the confidence in the young capital's future, decided to erect a theatre. All went well, Jefferson remembered, until their plans threatened by a religious revival sweeping the town with its attendant antitheatricalism. Beset by cries of the pious, the town's board of trustees jacked up the license fee beyond what the company could afford. In the midst of this crisis, a young lawyer offered to get the license reduced, "declaring that he only desired to see fair play, and he would accept no fee whether he failed or succeeded." This lawyer, lank of frame, regaled the council with stories from the history of drama and prevailed in getting the tax removed. His name, Jefferson melodramatically concluded, "was Abraham Lincoln."[29]

A wonderful tale, distilling the voice of Jefferson the raconteur, whose eye for detail and ear for pace artfully crafted a story. The anecdote was among

Joe's favorites, retold to friends and even recounted to audiences during curtain calls. There must have been pride in linking his family's name with the Great Emancipator.[30]

But is the account too good to be true? Alas, scholars have concluded so. It stands, they maintain, as another unfortunate example of the quaint unreliability of Jefferson's *Autobiography*. There is no record of the company's having built a theatre in Springfield. Nor does Lincoln's name appear on the 23 July 1839 minutes of the council when the license issue was voted. And a few months later, on the troupe's autumnal return to Springfield when the license issue resurfaced and was finally resolved, there is no mention in any record of Lincoln's involvement. Jefferson, it would appear, could not escape the temptation — common to chroniclers of the nineteenth century — of imagining a moment when their lives crossed paths with the immortalized Lincoln.[31]

But scholars have underestimated Jefferson here. Although he clearly embellished his Springfield account, the essential fact of Lincoln's having aided the company now appears true. In a handwritten entry in his fee book, Lincoln records having received $3.50 and his partner John Todd Stuart $1.50 from "theater folk." The notation, by best estimate, dates to March or April 1838, which falls near the end of the earlier visit of the MacKenzie-Isherwood company to Springfield. Religious indignation toward their performing, as Jefferson suggested, seems to have been real. Religious revivals, which struck western towns with some regularity, generally carried explicit theatrical prejudice. Newspaper reassurances prior to its opening that the company would present nothing "that could possibly offend the most fastidious taste" suggests they anticipated difficulty. Sensing this, MacKenzie sought to deflect moral criticism through newspaper puffs about how their company extolled the "beauties of virtue and the hatefulness of vice." The exact character of Lincoln's service for the company is not clear; perhaps he quietly, in a manner never recorded in official records, smoothed the way with the town council. Lincoln ran some type of legal interference for them, but whatever its nature, it occurred before Joe's parents had come west to join the company. Unsurprisingly, as the tale was retold in later years, Lincoln's assistance became conflated with another dispute over the town's license fee the following year.[32]

Despite these obstacles, the company proceeded to enjoy a month or so of profitable service in Springfield in the summer of 1839. "The house is so crowded that the audience is compelled to laugh perpendicularly," the *Sangamo Journal* hyperbolized. By the middle of August, the Illinois company packed its shopworn properties onto wagons and headed toward Chicago, completing the circuit first opened when the company departed for Galena some ten months earlier.[33]

Coming home to Chicago to a familiar and now refurbished theatre may have lifted the spirits of company members, exhausted from months on the road and debilitated by illness. Troupers always, they opened the season on schedule on 1 September with George Colman's operetta *The Review, or, Wag of Windsor* and continued the back-breaking nightly change of repertory. But Chicagoans responded less enthusiastically than had the folks downstate. Women were conspicuously missing from audiences. "Why do not the fair ladies of our city lend the theatre, occasionally, the light of their countenance?" the *Daily American* asked wistfully. As if to shame them by comparison, the paper noted that Springfield's theatre was generally graced "by the beauty and fashion of the fair sex." Not only the ladies but also the various dignitaries of state patronized its theatre (the paper undoubtedly relied on the word of MacKenzie or Jefferson for this claim).[34]

The same paper that bewailed the absence of Chicago's women indirectly provided the explanation, recounting a few days later how drunken rowdies in the audience disrupted the play. Affairs were so bad that MacKenzie took the offenders to court and had them fined, an act the editors applauded as "exemplary punishment." Undeniably, a crude etiquette ruled theatre decorum of the day. Patrons felt free to shout obscene witticisms at opportune moments during the play. Unsurprisingly, ladies of self-conscious breeding found this coarseness off-putting. MacKenzie sought to counter boorishness by stationing privately employed police in the theatre "to preserve strict order and decorum." However, their duty was only "imperfectly performed," and "straggling baccanalias" continued to vex Illinois company performances.[35]

In the ceaseless struggle to attract the public, MacKenzie next turned to the durable strategy of featuring a new face in the cast. This tactic took two forms. One consisted of inviting a stagestruck local, whose dramatic efforts would attract a loyal following to the playhouse. Companies more established than the Illinois would throughout the century shamelessly sacrifice professionalism to the god of commerce when the situation dictated. When a favorite son of Chicago was announced to perform in the farce *Enraged Politician,* the *Chicago Daily American* commented sardonically, "We have many amateurs among us who might act that character well." The more traditional prescription for ailing audiences, however, was to import a visiting star. Local boosters, concerned about attendance at the Rialto, encouraged MacKenzie and Jefferson to bring in a headliner. This they did — though to term their attractions "stars" begs a stretching of the term. Charles Kemble Mason had a Siddons-Kemble pedigree and extensive experience in London and Philadelphia theatres and playing in support of Charlotte Cushman. Mary Ann Meek McClure, acclaimed as a beauty of the stage, had toured the West and South widely with Noah Ludlow (whom she later married), though she enjoyed only a modest reputation in the East. Both performers had worked with the Jeffersons in their Washington days and now rejoined them in America's heartland. For eight nights in the first half of November these two stars lent their modest cachet to a series of perhaps the most ambitious productions the Jefferson-MacKenzie company would ever mount: *The Lady of Lyons, The Wife of Mantua, Katherine and Petruchio* (David Garrick's adaptation of *The Taming of the Shrew*), *Romeo and Juliet, Macbeth,* and *Hamlet* being but a partial listing.[36]

For Joe Jefferson, now a few months shy of eleven, the final two months in Chicago in 1839 summed up much of his youth. He had seen his family struggle with rowdiness, with illness, and with trying to make ends meet. He had noticed his aunt Mary-Anne Ingersoll turn to offering lessons "in the polite and useful accomplishment of dancing" and sponsoring cotillion parties in an effort to keep food on the table. He had been awakened, no doubt, by the middle-of-night clamor when an entire city block went up in flames on 16 October, Chicago's worst fire in several years. And he well knew the routine of packing up the pasteboard props and storing scenery in preparation for yet another move.[37]

The troupe returned to Springfield, a visit timed to take advantage of the first legislative session in the new capital. The town continued showing signs of the new prosperity. The still-unfinished but already imposing State House lent an air of permanence to the otherwise temporary nature of frontier town construction. When the legislature convened in early December, Springfield began to step lively, invigorated by an infusion of citizen-statesmen; their wives hungry for social life; and young, marriageable girls drawn by the prospect of bachelors like Abraham Lincoln, who appeared to have bright careers ahead. The festive atmosphere well suited the Illinois company's purposes. After setting up their stage in Watson's saloon, the twelve-member troupe commenced its season. "A Stranger's" letter to the *Sangamo Journal* provides a flattering snapshot of the band. "From old and sterling stock of actors," the correspondent reassured, its company members had trod the eastern boards "with great eclat." And young Joe was judged "fairly 'a chip off the old block.' "[38]

An Itinerant Spirit

But as always the sturdy band had to move on. Whether experiencing prosperity or failure, they finally exhausted their repertoire and faced the depletion of their public, however supportive it might have been. Western audiences, even in the nascent urban centers, lacked the numbers to support drama for long. If an exception existed to this theatrical calculus it would be in St. Louis. Such hopes may have persuaded the Illinois company to brave a foray into Missouri after finishing the Springfield season in mid-February 1840.

When the company entered the Gateway City in early March, they found a thriving metropolis of more than 16,000 perched on the steep western bank of the Mississippi. Its commercial bustle sounded a modern echo of the similarly mercantile pre-Columbian Mound Builders, whose vandalized monuments still dotted the center of town. Riverfront activity was a continuous procession of arriving and departing steamers and of ferries traversing the river to the Illinois shore. The half decade before and after the Jeffersons arrived witnessed a particularly frantic pace of new arrivals. "One might imagine that the 'world and his family' are coming here," a local paper boasted. Merchants and builders were hard put to provide for this human tide, but they enjoyed trying, as did area farmers. Evenings witnessed a stream of wagons arriving in town from surrounding farms — getting situated for the next morning's market — laden with chickens, eggs, butter, pork, and other edibles.[39]

The St. Louis venture represented a risk in more ways than one. Having established a successful Illinois circuit, the company now chanced becoming overextended. Moreover, the St. Louis theatre scene was dominated by the entrepreneurs of Mississippi Valley drama, Sol Smith and Noah Ludlow. Their popular and better-equipped theatre would be hard to match.[40]

Smith and Ludlow, the odd couple of early American theatre, ruled theatre in the post-Jacksonian Southwest. Solomon Smith (1801–69), a native New Yorker who apprenticed with the Drakes in the Ohio Valley in the 1820s, was inveterately funny on and off stage. Fast talking, a practical joker, and something of a dandy, Smith won friends easily. Ludlow (1795–1886) was also a New Yorker, whose early career in Albany and then in the West resembled Smith's. But personally he could hardly have been more different. Laconic and thin-skinned, Ludlow cut a figure others had difficulty warming to. Although scrupulous in paying his actors no matter what his circumstances, Ludlow lacked Smith's shrewd business head. On stage their contrasts worked well. "Old Sol" specialized in low comedy, and Noah Ludlow as a "light comic." In 1835 they established a partnership that lasted eighteen years.

St. Louis, Mobile, and New Orleans were the lynchpins of their empire, though they toured throughout the region. For all of their success, the men nursed a dislike for one another that originated before their partnership, festered through eighteen contentious if generally profitable years together, finally sundered their business relationship, and persevered until their deaths.[41]

The Ludlow and Smith combine occupied the handsome St. Louis Theatre, opened in 1837. Its builders hoped to make it usable in the pre-air-conditioned summers of the Midwest by including a bank of large windows along each side. Ludlow sought to accommodate thirsty patrons with separate saloons within the theatre. This convenience (not uncommon in theatres of the time) lasted less than a season though, before the distracting noise from the men's saloon forced its closure. Although St. Louis residents were proud of their new theatre, it was the transient population — the rivermen in particular — who formed the heart of the audience. Theatre receipts rose and fell "by the arrival and departure of the boats," said Sol Smith.[42]

When the Jeffersons arrived in March 1840, Ludlow and Smith were already staggering from a double blow. First, the panic and resultant recession of 1837 had by then infected the West with its depressed conditions, and the public was "drawing tight its purse strings." Second, in the previous two years they lost two theatres to fire in Mobile. "No managers need envy us now," Smith ruefully mused, "involved in debt, & sinking as we are." Smith's melancholy was deepened by the arrival of the Jefferson-MacKenzie troupe, announced in the *Daily Missouri Republican* as "MacKenzie's theatrical corpse" (a malapropism, which, given the company's impending demise, carried more appropriateness than the editor could know). "His reign will be short," Smith predicted to Ludlow, "but I fear he will annoy you for a time."[43]

Their short theatrical season of a few weeks in March was booked not in Ludlow's plush St. Louis Theatre but in the more modest Concert Hall. The *Republican* warned patrons to expect neither the scenic splendor nor the personal comforts of the rival theatre. Concert Hall visitors would warm rude benches rather than individual seats.[44]

These limitations notwithstanding, the fourteen-member cast needed to make no apologies about the quality of their drama. The Jefferson name always drew respect from the cultured citizens of the towns they visited, allowing the company to get its foot, so to speak, in the door. The former Illinois Theatrical Company (no indication that they used that name in Missouri) mounted *The Lady of Lyons* opening night. The 7:30 P.M. performance featured William Leicester and Mary-Anne Ingersoll as Melnotte and Pauline. In customary fashion, the opening drama was followed by the entr'acte songs and dances (Joe and Charlie Burke's department) and the concluding farce, in this case *The Midnight Hour,* showcasing Joe's parents. A gratifying audience turned out for the opening, though a veiled newspaper reference to a smoother second night performance suggests some opening night difficulties.[45]

The MacKenzie-Jefferson company's seventeen-night stand typified the unrelenting pace of theatrical life on the road. Staging thirty-five productions (including features and afterpieces) of thirty different plays in less than a month must have required a willingness to "make do," to accept a rather slap-

Joe's father, Joseph Jefferson II. From Joseph Jefferson,
Autobiography (1890).

dash approach to stagecraft. (In fairness, even the finer productions of eastern theatres of the time rarely knew extended rehearsals.) What did the public demand? What would the public accept? These simple calculations, honed through many nights of product testing before the footlights, were the essential considerations of theatre professionals. Audiences as yet unarmed with sophisticated criteria accepted the simple dramatic conventions and recycled stock scenery given them. Modest expectations might even be surpassed. The editor of the *Daily Missouri Republican* commended the company for its scenery in *Lady of the Lake,* which was "superior to anything we expected to see." Essentially a craftsman rather than a performer, Jefferson II probably found this praise as satisfying as any he ever received.[46]

From St. Louis the troupe recrossed the river for a short engagement at nearby Alton. Then the Jefferson-MacKenzie company began to dissolve. Initially the troupe split temporarily to make separate tours of Illinois and Missouri. It was a practice not uncommon among western itinerant troupes, the advantage residing in the economics of small-town theatre. In theory, separately touring small companies could together gross as much or more as a full company in larger towns. But the strategy seemed not to work for the Jeffersons. A brief reunion in May 1840 was quickly followed by a more permanent disintegration. By the end of 1840, the MacKenzies and Jeffersons had only the Germons and William Leicester with them, having lost six other regulars, including Jefferson's sister, now Mary-Anne Ingersoll Wright.[47]

The historical record does not permit a glimpse behind the scenes of these strolling players to inquire why, after three years, they should divide. But there are plausible reasons. For one, the departure of half the troupe continued—if in more concentrated form—a longstanding pattern. Actors had joined and quit all along the tour. Nineteenth-century acting was a speculative endeavor. It was wildcatting, and dry holes outnumbered the gushers. The work demanded a readiness to pick up and try elsewhere. Even family ties, which bound the Mackenzie-Jeffersons to an unusual degree, could not long inhibit independent prospecting. The next two years would see further splintering of the remaining group, as first Charles Burke and then Joseph Jefferson's immediate family would veer off on their own.

But the possibility cannot be dismissed that tensions within the troupe encouraged the split. The inherent stresses of theatrical touring were abundant and unrelenting. Days of group travel and rehearsal were followed by evenings together at the performance. Even the end of the day would not bring relief from one another, as the company normally retired to the same hotel or boarding house. If the intensity of these social confinements created a theatrical culture of great richness, it could also nurture animosities. Even—or perhaps especially—within a family the strain of close living had to have been great. Compounded by chronic financial worries, the Jefferson family's prolonged intimacy may have stretched the bonds of blood beyond its limits. Conversely, the fact that on this occasion most of the departing players (all except Mary-Anne and her new husband) were nonfamily members may suggest that they felt perpetual outsiders. Nothing indicates that the Jeffersons exhibited the cliquishness of the Chapmans, but it would be an unusual family that could extend the support to nonmembers that it did to its own.

The wandering of the Jefferson family over the next year can be traced only imperfectly. From Missouri it headed back to Illinois, revisiting Quincy, Galena, and finally Springfield, where they passed the winter of 1840–41. Tracking up and across the prairie of Illinois then east to Terre Haute, Indiana, the land must have struck the group much as it did Charles Dickens when he visited a year later: as "the great blank." It would be tempting to think that lacking much in the way of advance publicists this undistinguished itinerant troupe must have wandered into a new town virtually unknown to the townsmen. But thanks to a generous provision of Congress, which mandated that a copy of every newspaper in the nation could be sent postage-free to any other publisher who wanted one, local commentary about a theatrical company might become nationally read plugs. Individual stars as well as full companies enjoyed press coverage well before the age of press agents or wire services.[48]

Fall 1841 found the Jeffersons in new territory, Nashville, where they and the MacKenzies had joined John Potter's theatre. After years of carrying the burdens of self-management it would be a relief, at least for a short time, to turn over that thankless task to another. Neither Cornelia nor her husband were featured during the two-month run. Joseph restricted himself to the more comfortable role of scene painter. Cornelia, afflicted with a chronic ailment, took minor supporting roles. But "Master Jefferson" earned billing for his entr'acte songs, and Charlie Burke began to come into his own as dancer, raconteur, and comic actor.

Rising along the shore of the Cumberland River, Nashville served as state capital with a population then of nearly 7,000. The city had a long but undistinguished theatre tradition. Patronage of earlier productions had been so poor that several companies disbanded while there. Locals blamed second-rate talent for their staying away. John Potter hoped to improve the situation with a more elegant theatre, more newspaper advertising, a solid stock company, and the billing of such top stars as Dan Marble and James Henry Hackett — mostly to no avail. Potter, veteran Walter Leman sarcastically observed, "closed twice as many [theatres] as he ever opened."[49]

With the season in Nashville ending, the Jefferson clan splintered yet again. Burke embarked on an independent career, venturing with his recent bride to Jackson, Mississippi. Joseph and Cornelia, lacking attractive alternatives, likewise headed south to Natchez. They boarded a steamer, perhaps the *Ellen Kirkman,* which left from nearby Smithland on 1 December, to begin the circuitous route down the Cumberland, Ohio, and Mississippi rivers. There was little romance or beauty in such voyages. As the Jeffersons passed near New Madrid, Missouri, they may have been struck, as a more famous traveler would be, by the "loneliness of this solemn, stupendous flood," which league after league "pours it chocolate tide along, between its solid forest walls, its almost untenanted shores."[50]

The Jeffersons arrived in a Natchez whose urban spirit had been sorely tested in recent years. This haven of culture and urbane prosperity (by standards of the striving cotton nabobs of the old Southwest) had suffered an outbreak of yellow fever in 1839 that carried away more than 200 (out of some 4,000) residents, followed in May 1840 by a murderous tornado that devastated the town, killing 300. The resiliency to bounce back from these blows was checked by the depths of the financial panic, which took the form in the South of cotton at five cents a pound. Consequently the Natchez theatre, which had flourished just two years earlier, limped through a short and indifferent season during the winter of 1842. Manager James Scott, an ambitious promoter of theatre in antebellum Mississippi, had replaced his original theatre—leveled by the twister—with a leased building, but he could not replace the earlier audiences of better times. Nonetheless, Joseph Jefferson II, modestly billed as "a worthy gentleman, a good actor, and an excellent artist," staged Jerrold's *The Flying Dutchman* on 28 February.[51]

The depressed conditions in Natchez encouraged the Jeffersons to travel upriver seventy miles to Vicksburg, a small city commanding the river from its perch on the bluffs. An entrepôt for cotton from the Yazoo River delta, Vicksburg had surpassed Natchez as a pillar of commerce. James Scott and partner James Thorne had established here a once-thriving theatre, hosting such luminaries as Joshua Silsbee and Dan Marble (who—with an irony later bestowed by Vicksburg's notorious Civil War experience—specialized in "Yankee" roles). But the hammer of recession had also pounded this city. Where a few years earlier a clever dance might evoke a shower of coins, now the finest talent, lamented a Vicksburg paper, "can't draw a house that would support a candle snuffer." The arrival of Scott's company in March led the *Vicksburg Daily Whig* to gently prod its readers to patronize the troupe: "We need something to dispel the blue devils which care and hard times engender."[52]

For the Jeffersons, already accustomed to living on the edge, life became more tenuous. The deterioration of Cornelia's once formidable vocal power was now compounded by the illness that had plagued her for months. Her husband, though respected as a Jefferson and admired for his unassuming ways, lacked the fire to draw steady audiences. Instead, it was the children, Joe and Connie, now aged thirteen and seven, who received featured billing for their comic songs and dances. Set among newspaper ads for "sack corn," "Illinois potatoes," and "Fresh Blue Lick water" were modest announcements of "Miss Jefferson" performing a "Highland fling," and along with "Master Jefferson" singing a comic duet.

But when their troupe disbanded in late April 1842, even this expedient was torn away. The number of theatrical companies in the Mississippi Valley region at any one time during these years was likely not over a half dozen, sometimes fewer. Companies sprang up and then withered like sun-parched prairie flowers. "Hope for the best—expect the worst," a fellow journeyman actor philosophized, a motto that must have tempted even the sanguine Jeffersons. They had few options. An offer came to join a company in the frontier region of Louisiana's Red River, but that seemed too low to stoop. Joe's father fell back on his artistic skills as a sign painter during the summer, sending Joe out to the river wharf to scare up business. On the verge of desperation and presuming upon their old friendship (Ludlow's earlier admiration for her resulted in naming his daughter after her), Cornelia wrote Noah Ludlow pleading for a position for her husband as artist or actor in St. Louis. Here she also hoped to consult the "celebrated Dr. Merriman" about her chronic affliction.[53]

Nothing came of this. Did the MacKenzie-Jefferson company's intrusion onto their St. Louis turf two years earlier poison her friendship with Ludlow? Or, more likely, did the ongoing depression simply forbid his extending a helping hand? Whichever, the family soon headed up the river to Memphis, where they could rejoin Alexander MacKenzie's troupe.

Memphis, another urban monument to the great river's importance for western commerce, lacked the theatrical tradition of its sister cities to the south. Until the late 1830s only those riverine itinerants, the Chapman family, plus a few other forgettable companies had graced Memphis with dramatics. Even when a permanent theatre was built in 1837, it remained a fitful institution in the following years. The visit of MacKenzie in May and June 1842 represented a notable advance for the muse in west Tennessee. His company, reported the *Memphis American Eagle,* had added actors and "a better band of musicians than has ever before visited this section of country." They brought culture to soldiers stationed at nearby Fort Pickering. And most notably, Nashville colleague John Potter opened in mid-June the first true "Dramatic Temple" in Memphis, the New City Theatre. The building had humble origins as a livery stable, a fact so apparent to audiences that the *Eagle* suggested "a barrel of Cologne" be installed to hide the lingering odor. But adorned with roomy boxes and parquette, sporting back supports for its benches, and providing unobstructed sight lines of the stage, the theatre's civilized interior compelled a proud editor to cry, "What city of the West is capable of a more brilliant display?"[54]

Joe's family does not appear in newspaper billings for these performances (though Joe later alludes to his having performed here). Cornelia's illness may explain her absence. Joseph père probably remained backstage as scenic artist. The quiet desperation into which the family was descending was admitted decades later in Jefferson's *Autobiography*. When the Memphis theatre closed, his father, scrounging for work, again took up sign painting. A recent city ordinance requiring drays and other public vehicles to be numbered seemed an opportunity too good to pass by, if not recognized by his father, then at least by Joe. He approached the mayor and requested the job for his father, a bid that succeeded at least partly because the mayor had delighted in Joe's stage antics. Joe returned home triumphantly bearing a contract that provided work for a month.[55]

The incident became an occasion for the mature Joe — normally so reticent about the intimacies of his home — to obliquely reveal family dynamics. He admits that his brashness in approaching the mayor (something his "too sensitive and retiring" father would never do) was driven by his sense of the family's plight. He also concedes "a lovely revenge" on his mother for a scolding she had delivered. Cornelia, always the forceful personality of the family, and now pressured by illness, poverty, and the melancholy of a talent long departed, must have proven a trial to her son. But the victory of the painting contract bestowed lasting confidence on Joe. "I had experienced a ferocious delight in doing battle with the world."[56]

But the boat passage to Mobile, where they had a November engagement, confirmed their financial humiliation. They were reduced to booking steerage rather than a private cabin. Proud Cornelia, incensed that her husband could accept this indignity with such equanimity, became even more upset to learn that a well-heeled Memphis gambler owed him $200 for decorating his home. Cornelia, with young Joe in tow, promptly marched to the stately residence and appealed to the man's wife. She succeeded in collecting the tardy payment. Having her own triumph to present to her husband, Cornelia added a further note of common sense. Instead of following Joseph's impulse to spend the money on the fleeting comfort of a cabin, she insisted that they endure the hard floor of steerage in order to reach Mobile with gold in their pocket.[57]

The down-river journey was nothing new for young Joe. From Galena and Dubuque to St. Louis, Memphis, Natchez, Vicksburg — and now New Orleans — Joe had traveled up and down the Mississippi River valley by steamboat. Did these ungainly, shuddering contraptions belching smoke and steam capture the imagination of young Joe as they would that of five-year-old Samuel Clemens then living along the river in Hannibal? Judging by his *Autobiography,* apparently not, for he passes over these travels with but slight mention. But the human spectacle on board Mississippi steamers likely made an impression on Joe. This "piebald parliament" of fortune seekers, confidence men, and slavers who together represented, in Melville's words, the "dashing and all-fusing spirit of the West," must have contributed a reservoir of accents, mannerisms, and figures of speech to draw on in creating his adult roles.[58]

Having been used to the privacy of cabin accommodations, the Spartan egalitarianism of deck passage was surely something of a jolt. Such public spaces were generally open to the outside with perhaps a single stove to fight the river breezes. The only food would be that packed by the voyager. Although traveling protocol called for single men and women to occupy separate compartments, families generally remained together. Fortunately, going down the river the boat would not have been laden with immigrants to America's interior and thus was probably less crowded.

Such was the situation of the Jeffersons, who despite their straitened circumstances continued to enjoy the services of faithful Mary, who helped make the journey bearable. Joe's father would not be temperamentally disposed (nor would Cornelia allow him) to join the rounds of whist or cribbage played on marble-topped tables in the lounge. Ever unruffled by circumstances, he usefully spent his time studying upcoming parts and fishing off the stern when the ship stopped for wood. His nonchalance may have been misplaced. French engineer and American traveler Michael Chevalier claimed a Mississippi River journey was more dangerous than an Atlantic crossing. A brief perusal of the region's newspapers suggests his remark was no mere canard. Whether from bursting boilers, treacherous river snags, or explosion and fire from hazardous cargo, boats and passengers went down regularly. Trips on the river, then, were adventures as much as journeys, and Joe's family was more fortunate than it realized in a noneventful passage to New Orleans and on to Mobile.[59]

Throughout their careers the Jeffersons could depend on family for support. It was no different now. The opportunity in Mobile was bestowed by sister Elizabeth Chapman Richardson, who parlayed her New York success into box office strength in the provinces. The widow Richardson, still talented and attractive in her early thirties, had caught the eye of Charles Fisher of Mobile. The English-born Fisher was secretary of the local gas company. But this "gentleman of energy" and "highly cultivated intellect" had artistic ambitions as well. A few years earlier he had founded (though soon sold) an influential paper in New York City, the *Spirit of the Times*. Ironically, his editorial pen had then made caustic remarks about Mrs. Richardson's talents. But his opinion of the "lively, handsome widow" had turned. Now employed by entrepreneur James Caldwell and leveraging his theatrical reputation on the strength of being the brother of Clara Fisher, then a reigning vocalist in the East, he was allowed by Royal Street Theatre managers to assemble a stock company. Looking to ingratiate himself with Elizabeth (successfully as it turned out, for they later married), Fisher sent offers to all descendants of old Joseph Jefferson.[60]

Months of bleak itinerancy appeared behind them as they anticipated a stable and prosperous run at the Royal Street Theatre. They were part of an eighteen-person company (six women and twelve men). Joe's father was once again a featured performer, especially in the farcical afterpieces. But the family had arrived in the midst of a late-fall yellow fever outbreak. They had been in town scarcely a month, just settled in their own house (allowing the children one of their infrequent chances to attend school), when Jefferson came down with chills and a fever. He quickly displayed the saffron pallor and mottled skin bespeaking an acute phase. Whether the rapid progress of the contagion allowed the customary administration of purgatives, bloodletting, or quinine is unknown. Just two days after his first symptoms appeared, at midnight on 24 November 1842, the thirty-eight-year-old journeyman actor and artist — the most handsome if not the most talented of the Jeffersons — died.[61]

3

Behind the Cart of Thespis

The embracing arms of kinship were never more evident then when the middle Jefferson died. In addition to Elizabeth Richardson, two other sisters, their husbands, niece Jane Germon, and her spouse — company members all — rallied around Joe and his family. The Mobile theatre closed for two nights to allow its endogamous company a decent period of mourning.

Joe Jefferson's autobiographical treatment of this sudden disaster is purposefully terse. Determined "not to cloud the narrative of my life with the relation of domestic sorrow," he simply notes the distress it brought his family. He and sister Cornelia continued their entr'acte dance and vocal duets. Additionally, thirteen-year-old Joe was given odd jobs about the theatre, such as grinding paints. Their mother, dispirited by her husband's death and her declining theatrical fortunes, decided to open a boarding house for company members in Mobile, a town chronically short of temporary housing.[1]

For the next four years the family would alternate between residence in Mobile and New Orleans during the fall-winter theatrical season and summers of barnstorming through the South. The family was accustomed to both types of life, understanding the seasonal nature of theatre. The instinctual command to "move on" toward fresh audiences seemed, as it were, firmly imprinted on the thespian genetic code, so naturally did the routine of touring come to them.

Theatre in the Deep South

The initial decision to stay in Mobile in part reflected the city's appreciation of theatre. As the smaller commercial rival of New Orleans, Mobile likewise engaged in the export of cotton, and its cosmopolitan culture resembled that of the Crescent City. In the late fall and winter, Mobile's crushed shell streets and walkways teemed with visitors plying the cotton trade. A city where men outnumbered women nearly two to one — augmented by this seasonal business class — would be a place where amusements would be in high demand. The city fathers recognized the value of supporting a thriving drama scene. "Our city is overflowing with strangers," wrote a local attorney, "the Yankees are as thick as Musketoes. . . . They furnish the material for a good theatrical audience." Conversely, townsmen were warned that if visitors could not find an "intense and refined gratification" in the theatre they might seek other "excesses infinitely gross, demoralizing and expensive." Thus, when fire ravaged a theatre (which happened with near-tidal regularity in Mobile), subscription drives succeeded in rebuilding ever more lavish temples. Such willingness added up to what New York's *Spirit of the Times* characterized as "the most liberal community" in the Union for the encouragement of drama (this compliment coming the very fall the Jeffersons arrived).[2]

Noah Ludlow and Sol Smith contended for supremacy in the Mobile theatre market with the other great impresario of the South: James Caldwell. Born in Manchester, England, Caldwell (1793–1863) was a clever light comedian with vaunting ambition. His drive and organizational acumen led him to establish Virginia's first theatrical circuit in the years following the War of 1812. He then set up a thriving New Orleans theatre in 1820, the first English-language theatre in the city, which by the mid-1820s was the heart of a southwestern circuit that included Nashville and Huntsville. Caldwell prided himself on presenting a select repertoire with a first-class company. He brought British and American stars to appreciative New Orleans audiences. An innovator as well as a businessman, Caldwell was the first to introduce gas to southern theatres, in the process establishing the city's first gas company (refining his product from coal tar). In the later 1830s, he determined to extend his empire east to Mobile Bay.[3]

Caldwell was emboldened in his invasion of the Mobile market by Ludlow's and Smith's recent economic distress. In early 1841 he opened the Royal Street Theatre, a handsome structure featuring the classic Doric columns and arched doorways common to playhouses of the time. This would be the theatrical home of Mrs. Richardson and the rest of the Jefferson clan when they arrived in 1842.[4]

(margin handwritten note: Theatre important to Mobile due to large #s of strangers during trade seasons for cotton.)

Caldwell's challenge compounded an already long list of worries for Smith and Ludlow. They had experienced virtually every risk common to theatrical management in their few years in Mobile. Fire heads this unhappy litany. Nineteenth-century Americans knew fire as their most intimate enemy, but Mobilians had particular reason to curse Prometheus. Mobile theatres had burned in 1829, 1830, 1838, and 1839 (the last part of a conflagration that destroyed much of the town). Most theatres were either uninsured or desperately underinsured, making fires financial calamities. Noah Ludlow lost his first Mobile theatre to fire in 1829, regretting no doubt that he had failed to pay his insurance premium. Remarkably, new theatres sprang up quickly in most cases.[5]

Besides the ever-present threat of fire, theatre operators in Mobile and other port cities were haunted by the ugly specter of yellow fever. The "southern scourge" had visited the American South — especially New Orleans — since the 1700s and continued its human devastation throughout the nineteenth century, particularly so in the 1840s and 1850s, bestowing on the region a reputation as the unhealthiest area of the country. Mobile's afflictions were not quite on the magnitude of New Orleans's but nonetheless were serious. First in 1819, then again in 1835, 1837, 1839, 1843, 1853, and 1858, the pestilence descended on the cotton city, smiting hundreds. Even between major epidemics "Yellow Jack" made regular calls during summer and early fall months. Indeed, Joe's father died in a relatively benign year — and in late November at that, when danger normally had passed. The chronic threat of the disease and its association with the "miasmas" of organic decay during the heat of the year encouraged privileged Mobilians to flee the city during the summer. Predictably, observed Dr. Josiah Nott (a scientific chronicler of the pestilence), common folk of the "unwashed democracy" were the principal sufferers. During fever outbreaks a prudent public avoided mass gatherings. This caution encouraged a later-than-normal opening to the theatre season each fall.[6]

The twin plagues of fire and epidemic were the most serious urban hazards, but theatre managers in Mobile and throughout the slave South contended with other day-to-day challenges, notably the stringent demands of race. The absolute prohibition of theatergoing by slaves or free blacks in a city where they constituted roughly a third of the 12,000 residents would have reduced already thin profit margins. So audiences contained both races but under strict ground rules. Playbills, for example, sometimes added the proviso that "slaves will not be admitted without exhibiting passes from their masters." A promiscuous mixing of the races in the audience was out of the question, a contingency easily prevented by confining all blacks to the third gallery, alongside the prostitutes and other social undesirables. But some urban centers like

Mobile and New Orleans had proud mulatto communities that refused to mingle among slaves. Ludlow and Smith accommodated their sensibilities with a partition in the third tier strictly for light-skinned quadroons, locked, they promised patrons, "to keep out interlopers." It apparently worked. Tocqueville recorded the "strange spectacle" he witnessed at a New Orleans theatre: "first stalls white, second grey, coloured women, very pretty, white ones among them, but a remainder of African blood. Third stalls black."[7]

Ludlow took another step unusual for the time. He sought to reform the "guilty third tier," then notorious in theatres across America as the perch of hookers. Unchaperoned women were refused admission, though only through the vigilance of his private security force. But Ludlow was fighting a millennia-old battle. Eighteen hundred years earlier the poet Ovid had recommended the theatre as a place to find women. Not without a fight would prostitutes surrender the prime real estate of their trade.[8]

Racial and sexual divisions were manageable compared to the raucousness of audiences. Theatre managers everywhere in antebellum America struggled not only to attract audiences but to restrain them as well. Certain outbursts spoke of audience desire to impose their notion of elemental fairness. When Mary Stuart, a longtime favorite at the Royal Street Theatre, appeared to be demoted in favor of another actress, a Mobile crowd responded by rushing the theatre, vandalizing some fixtures, and demanding a benefit for Mrs. Stuart plus ten weeks' salary. It took a speech by the mayor and capitulation to every crowd demand by the theatre manager to quiet the crowd. Even so, the incident ruined the opening night of James Henry Hackett's Mobile stand.[9]

If such displays of chivalrous outrage flattered the Jacksonian public's sense of justice, other incidents in and around the theatre bespoke only criminality. Mobile seemed especially unruly. Why? No doubt the city's preponderance of males explained part of the boisterousness. As an active port city it contained dock workers and boatmen not slow to express their minds. Moreover, the simple fact remained that Mobile in 1840 bestrode a region still frontier in its outlook and demeanor. Unsettling acts of violence around theatres are recorded in city newspapers. On one occasion, a man stabbed a ticket taker (though in the process he managed to shoot off his own fingers); on another, when an agent for a performing troupe bravely ventured outside the theatre to quiet a rowdy he was answered by a dirk through his stomach. The most serious incident occurred during Tyrone Power's visit in the mid-1830s. While on stage Power heard a commotion up in the third tier. The stir was short lived and caused scarcely a ripple in the theatre. Only at a postperformance supper did Power learn that a notorious town roughneck had fatally stabbed a fellow patron. Mobile managers and those in many other cities tried to inhibit patron brawling by stationing private police within the theatre. This was particularly important, Caldwell felt, to reassure ladies of a decorous setting.[10]

Theatre managers also had to contend with their aggravating old friends — recession, weekly payroll obligations, and competition for the entertainment dollar. Western cities were small, and their residents had limited discretionary income. Even a little competition was too much. In 1844 conditions required cutting ticket prices in half (a wise and liberal resolve judged the Mobile paper). A more common expedient in attracting an audience was the unending search for novelty. Elizabeth Richardson, who became one of the few female managers of the antebellum West when she briefly managed the Royal Street Theatre in spring 1843, quickly learned these cheerless facts. Her predecessor had, according to Sol Smith, "cooked up the drama in various styles — boiled, fried, roasted, broiled, or on the half shell — involving a loss of whatever ready money he may have been possessed of."[11]

Richardson's troupe, including nephew and niece Joe and Cornelia, was described by the sharp-tongued Joseph Cowell as "half a company, only half paid, consisting of those with small salaries who could afford one-third or one-half of nothing." It did not help that cotton prices hit a new low. Cotton-sensitive Mobilians struggled to find the dollar for admission. On top of this, a rival, the New American Theatre, opened in mid-April. Whatever loyalty Richardson held to the dramatic muse, it could not offset the need to pay the bills. Any paying attraction was welcome. On 13 April, as the extraordinary feats of strength by Monsier Paul were displayed at the American, Richardson countered with the inauguration of a series of lectures by a dispenser of popular science, "Dr." Dionysius Lardner.[12]

Adding the debilitating effects of recession to the chronic risks of management, one has to ask why James Caldwell and Ludlow/Smith would undertake an apparently ruinous rivalry. The three men would have found such a question odd. Risk, to nineteenth-century entrepreneurs, inescapable as it was, held fewer fears. One simply moved ahead in full knowledge that no agency, state or federal — nor often any insurance company — would provide a cushion during a fall. Important, too, was the peculiar temperament of the theatrical animal. The instinct to perform, or to present the performance of others, gripped a chosen few. It was a blessing and a curse, bestowing as it did an imperative for action, a command seeming to override rational calculations of profit or loss.

For two seasons, from 1841 to 1843, Ludlow and Smith evacuated Mobile, leaving the city to Caldwell. But during this hiatus they launched missiles at Caldwell's monopoly of English-language theatre in New Orleans. Their un-originally named New American Theatre turned up the heat on Caldwell's operation with its equestrian shows and burlesques. Caught off guard, Caldwell was forced to resort in kind, bringing in the horses to his dramatic Temple on St. Charles. This robust competition for public favor was abruptly interrupted in March 1842 when the elegant St. Charles burned. But disaster proved it had no favorites: four months later Ludlow's and Smith's house fell victim to arson. Even in misfortune the rivalry continued. Caldwell stole from under their noses the lease on a new theatre. This new "New American" playhouse seemed to seal Caldwell's victory, but the triumph was short-lived. The New American failed to draw, and Caldwell's various financial losses were catching up with him. He left theatre management for good in January 1843. Four days later Ludlow and Smith triumphantly opened their New St. Charles Theatre, a structure erected in forty days. Theirs survived, occasionally flourished, and hosted a stream of theatrical notables in coming years.[13]

From their base at the New St. Charles Theatre, Noah Ludlow and Solomon Smith dominated southwestern theatricals for the next decade. They did so through perseverance, luck, and an innate grasp of what the public wished to see. Theatrical management was about art, but it was even more about business. American impresarios labored in a country that as yet had no dramatic center, had no government regulations (other than city licensing ordinances), and allowed a completely free market of competition for the audience dollar.

These conditions contrasted sharply with those that prevailed in England. In 1843 — as Joe Jefferson's family continued their itinerant ways in the Southwest — England witnessed the repeal of a landmark theatre restriction: Parliament brought the 180-year-old system of patent licensing to an end. The American theatre, which in so many respects mirrored its British progenitor, knew no similar monopoly or precensorship. This was so in part for the obvious reason that American dramatic history largely postdates our allegiance to a monarchy with its royally sanctioned monopolies, but more important, because our nation had no London. That is, it was not until the post–Civil War decades when New York City clearly became a theatrical center for the nation that Americans had a city as dominant and crucial to the stage as London was for the English. Ironically, when protests against a threatened theatrical monopoly were heard in the 1890s, they were not against government creations but against the centralizing tendencies of capitalism. The Syndicate, a "trust" aimed at controlling theatrical bookings, evoked the kind of outrage and calls for reform that Drury Lane and Covent Garden had earned earlier in the century. Americans learned that market forces could be as coercive as any royal letter of patent.[14]

If the American stage never knew a system of national preproduction censorship, it did contend with—especially in the colonial age—provincial and local licensing restrictions such as those the MacKenzie-Jefferson company knew. These were almost always based on religious suspicions. Boston clergy, unsurprisingly, maintained a tight clamp on drama. And the Pennsylvania assembly's restriction on theatricals occasioned a spirited flurry of writings in 1792 over its repeal. These attitudes persisted well into the nineteenth century. A few states retained tight controls on theatre. Massachusetts banned Saturday or Sunday theatricals until the 1850s, and Connecticut forbad *any* play productions until 1854. These were unusually severe. More common were local licensing initiatives, which remained the primary mechanism of control into the twentieth century. Tocqueville, though impressed by America's laws that "allow the utmost freedom, and even license, of language in other respects," saw municipal restrictions on drama as a kind of censorship and a proof that Americans had not fully embraced the drama. The more aggressive restrictions were generally found in young towns, where either civic leadership begrudged distractions from the more serious business of city-building or where local clergy had gained influence. Virtually never did municipal controls include censorship of specific plays.[15]

The relative freedom of American drama from bothersome government censorship would at first glance appear liberating. But what did it mean? Did the politically unencumbered American stage of the early republic and antebellum age nurture political and social criticism? Hardly so, agree theatre historians. We had a drama of national cheer. A young country, insecure and occasionally belligerent, featured a theatre that — when not dishing out the common dollops of melodrama and comedy — served up morsels of patriotic delight. The historical costume dramas that propelled Edwin Forrest to the front ranks of stardom, *Virginius, Metamora, The Gladiator,* and *Jack Cade,* were thinly veiled allegories of republican virtue. The rare stage treatment of political controversy, as in Joseph Field's *G-A-G; or, The Starving System* (staged during the House of Representative gag rule controversy over antislavery petitions in the 1840s), could proceed only through the genre of satire. Likewise, the most famous piece of social commentary of the antebellum era, *Uncle Tom's Cabin,* succeeded more because of its solid grasp of the melodramatic formulas and domestic sentimentality than because of its abolitionist implications.[16]

Indeed, it is hard to see how freedom from formal censorship benefited American drama. Largely consumers of imported drama, American audiences gave little encouragement to our native playwrights to craft politically provocative plays. The redoubtable Tocqueville (who we know attended the theatre in Philadelphia and New Orleans) attributed this neglect to our essentially democratic audience, which desired more that its heart be touched than its mind be stimulated. What great subjects for drama could exist, he asked, "in a country which has seen no great political catastrophes and in which love always leads by a direct and easy road to marriage?" Moreover, though theatrical attendance had improved by the early 1830s, Tocqueville detected a certain begrudging of drama. "People who spend every weekday making money and Sunday in church praying to God give no scope to the Muse of Comedy."[17]

Clearly, many Americans had no aversion to the stage. Yet ambivalence marked broader cultural attitudes. What was to be drama's place in their life of striving? How could it be reconciled with an ever-stronger strain of evangelicalism? Contrarily, what did it mean that American social relations became more theatrical by midcentury? Or that stage productions of all sorts proliferated as the nineteenth century progressed? Drama, both witnessed and lived, inexorably ingratiated itself in American society. But it happened begrudgingly and with much public debate. This discomfited embrace of theatre was one theme of Joe Jefferson's *Autobiography*. The growth of his own public esteem played out against a checkered backdrop of admiration and social disrespect toward his beloved theatre.

Scrambling Days

For the Jeffersons things in Mobile went from bad to worse when Cornelia's boarding house failed. Whether she was victim of the ongoing national recession or her own shortcomings as a businesswoman is not clear. In any event, the family became an object of charity. The first lady of Mobile, Madame Le Vert, arranged a benefit show and prodded her friends to attend. A greater blow than poverty was the death of Mary, "friend, servant, and dear companion" for sixteen years. Joe characterized himself as her "foster-son," and one senses in his lament, which surpassed that expressed over the passing of either his father or his mother, perhaps the most profound emotional tie of his youth.[18]

With the end of the boarding house venture and the Mobile season drawing to its spring close, there was little choice but for the family to hit the sawdust trail. What else did they know? Theatre was their vocation in the explicit meaning of that term: a calling, a life. They understood that their situation was grim. (Jefferson apologized to his readers for tiring them with "the continuous recital of our misfortunes.") They could take meager satisfaction in knowing that their hard times were widely shared. To be sure, actors were more prone to the vagaries of unemployment than most. But that was understood as part of the game. Modest feasts followed by prolonged famine formed the eternal cycle of the player's existence.

They returned to the hinterlands of Mississippi and Tennessee. The modern tracker will periodically lose the their trail during these several summers of the mid-1840s, although Joe details some of their movements. A few performances in Nashville enjoyed newspaper coverage. But at times they disappeared into areas of the Southwest where neither paper nor playbill followed. Decades later, when a stranger returned some family artifacts to Jefferson, Joe reminisced about the clutch of family possessions sold along the way when things were desperate — pieces of silverware here and there, even their hair trunk when there was nothing else left to peddle.[19]

The summer of 1843 brought an encore appearance of the MacKenzie-Jefferson troupe in Tennessee. Their June return to the "thoroughly cleaned" Nashville Theatre was hailed by a local newspaper. The paper admitted that for too long "the Drama has been at a low ebb with us" but trusted that MacKenzie would usher in a new day. By early July, MacKenzie had indeed won Nashville's confidence. Showcasing the talents of the powerful if undependable Augustus Addams, MacKenzie also presented La Belle Oceana, a child *danseuse* "of great spirit and grace." The *Nashville Union* editor commended the company not just for its artistic merit but also for the "extreme respectability of their private deportment." Well-played, "decent" productions (nary a "joke that could call up a blush on the cheek of the most sensitive"), a decorous cast, and an orderly audience encouraged "even the most nervous female" to attend, thus helping rehabilitate the reputation of drama in Nashville. The short summer season at the capital gave way to touring other locales of middle and west Tennessee. But they returned by late summer to Nashville for a run until early November.[20]

With fall engagements in Mobile and New Orleans looming (and Joe's first seasonal contract with Ludlow), it was time to head down the river. Low water stymied river movement on the Cumberland out of Nashville, but the innovative and frugal company fashioned a crude flatboat to float up to the Ohio River and on down to the Mississippi. With a lean-to cabin and sleeping compartments, this ramshackle barge was just the sort of floating playhouse that a child could love. And Joe, though now fourteen, had enough Tom Sawyer about him to later recall the journey as his great adventure. Fall colors burst around them. Ducks abounded and flocks of pigeons were so thick that any number could be brought down from the deck. Once on the Ohio, the troupe decided to help the current with a makeshift rigging. Stretching out a canvas drop-scene on a hickory pole added a few miles per hour of speed. Steamboats were accustomed to seeing an assortment of barges and rafts on the river but perhaps never had deck hands or riverine residents seen sail artistry of this sort. In a kind of floating performance art, the crew would hoist various canvas backdrops for the sport of their viewers: a woodland landscape might be followed by a palace. A Disneyesque note was added by cast members who pulled out their wooden swords for mock combat. "There is no doubt," Joe admitted, "that at times our barge was taken for a floating lunatic asylum."[21]

In the following two summers the Jeffersons' itinerancy was more elemental. The extended family, with the important exception of Charles Burke and his wife, had gone elsewhere, leaving only a rump company. Not the comparative sophistication of Nashville or Memphis but the hinterland of Mississippi was their audience. Few records of their travels survive; indeed, few ever existed. Atop a wagon that jolted across rutted roads, company members endured a heat made more oppressive by mosquito swarms suspended in the muggy amber. Joe recalled that most of the villages where they stopped had no newspaper nor even a printing press, so he was drafted into painting "flaming announcements" and posting them at the post offices, hotels, and barber shops. Plays were performed in costume but sans scenery in whatever empty space came available, usually a hotel dining room. Near Liberty, Mississippi, their barnstorming days passed beyond figurative meaning. A farmer who had enjoyed the previous night's show invited the troupe to perform at his farm, assuring them that his family and neighbors would form a large and appreciative audience. Skeptical but open to any possibility for income, the Jeffersons accepted. Their playhouse was a barn, or more properly, the covered breezeway connecting two log barns (the barns served as dressing rooms and convenient stage wings). True to the farmer's promise, at dusk people on horseback and in wagons began filing into the farmstead. Most had never seen a play. They were treated to two staples of the day: *The Lady of Lyons* and the comic afterpiece, *The Spectre Bridegroom*. First by candles and then — after those were extinguished by wind — by moonlight, the Jeffersons introduced the muse to local yeomen. The open-air setting, penumbral light, and novelty of the event infused the moment with magic. Audience members, unsophisticated in distinguishing performance from life, shouted out advice or prevarications to characters as the story unfolded. No matter how artless the setting, the players' command of the audience's imagination must have been immensely satisfying. If evocation of a desired emotion is the benchmark of the craft, then the wandering Jefferson company had taken itinerancy to heights equaling any Parisian or London stage.[22]

But never far from such moments were rude reminders of actors' marginal status. On another turn about Mississippi, Charles Burke's agreement with a teamster to convey them to Port Gibson ended abruptly when the driver discovered that the family could pay him only out of their anticipated receipts.

He dumped them unceremoniously by the side of the road, and the family waited in a Mississippi downpour for Charlie to seek other arrangements. That his once-celebrated mother should be so reduced was the most bitter pill for young Joe. "This was so far the darkest hour we had passed," Jefferson later admitted. Only the unprejudiced help of a free black and his ox cart saved them.[23]

The teamster's demand for hard coin on the barrel head was not so strange considering the reputation of traveling players. In the eyes of many, people like the Jeffersons scarcely rose above the rank of vagabonds, performing gypsies. Such stereotypes reached deep in popular culture. Mark Twain's twin rogues, the duke and the king, whose Shakespearean palaver covered more sinister aims, exaggerated only slightly the intertwining of art and artful dodging on the Mississippi — and throughout America.

The suspicions under which actors labored were compounded in antebellum America by broader questions of trust. A nation of commercial bearing required high levels of mutual confidence among strangers. But the openness, mobility, and increasing urbanism of the population undermined the easy confidences of locally based social orders. The secure notions of deference and fixed social rank evaporated in the ferment of Jacksonian America. Whom, exactly, could one trust? How did one ensure that another was who he claimed to be? This was determined only through sincerity of presentation. Appropriately, sincerity became a chief sentiment of Victorian America. The social code of middle-class behavior condemned hypocrisy and required persons to exhibit themselves honestly in demeanor and dress. Such demands, of course, meant nothing to those whose trade was deception. Advice manuals universally warned against the presence of confidence men perched to swoop down on the unwary. Such flimflammery could be as benign as P. T. Barnum's ersatz Feejee mermaid. But if Barnum's fleecing the public with his showcased fraud for a few dimes seemed innocent — even appealing — not so the footpads, gamblers, and assorted con artists who inhabited the cities, plied country paths, and infested riverboat decks. Against such the only defense was cautious skepticism toward any request or offer coming from a stranger.[24]

A few years later Joe himself fell victim to a "professional borrower." Having just left his family to begin his independent career in Philadelphia, a stage veteran at age eighteen but still innocent about the world, he encountered a fellow actor whose real talent lay in the hustle. With woeful tales, tears, and the invocation of regard for Joe's celebrated grandfather, the masterful con man cadged "loans" from Joe every payday. This went on for many torturous weeks until Joe detected the game and then mustered the courage to end it. In one of the few didactic moments in the *Autobiography*, Jefferson warns readers of this social evil: "They lie in ambush for the innocent traveler, and suddenly pounce upon him with a well-told tale, so got by rote, and so often rehearsed, that they act the part of injured innocence to the life. If the victim be timid he is lost, for they recognize his nervousness at once, and browbeat him out of his benevolence."[25]

Herman Melville produced the classic fictional treatment of the subject, *The Confidence-Man*, fittingly set on a riverboat steaming south from St. Louis. Melville's protean trickster engages his targets in a series of philosophical dialogues about trust versus cynicism. As presented by Melville, the dilemma offers no resolution; vigilance must always be measured against the need for social trust. " 'I told you, you must have confidence,' " the charlatan herb dealer hectored his victim as he hawked his worthless anodynes, " 'unquestioning confidence, I meant confidence in the genuine medicine, and the genuine *me*.' "[26]

Actors essentially made the same request. "Trust us," performers implored their audience. Although masters of disguise who traded in make-believe, actors professed a sincerity of purpose. They sought not to gull their audience but to service them with amusement and moral uplift. Yet their pleas for confidence were necessarily compromised by their marginality. Actors performed outside the structured norms of life ("playhouse" aptly designates the artifice of their social home). Their creation of alternate realities, their potential for subversion has been recognized for centuries. Ironically, the more successful actors were in constructing their fantasy, the less able they were to claim sincerity. In the face of clever dissembling on stage, no amount of protestation could convince the public of their lack of guile off.

The social suspicion under which players labored had another less direct and more insidious origin. Culture demanded that attire make an immediate statement of one's self. Actors' professional labors violated the canons of dress and manner. They donned one costume after another. Where etiquette prescribed truthful expressions of one's soul, actors were unabashed masters of pretense. Where middle-class status required severe self-control in all situations, actors — particularly so in the day's unrestrained style of acting — embodied abandonment. But even less forgivable was the disturbing reflection of Victorian culture that actors cast on stage. An unconscious theatricality pervaded middle-class culture in fashion and etiquette. Advice manuals may have preached unaffected sincerity, but the elaborate codes of dress and behavior betrayed another impulse: regimented, highly elaborated ritual display. Americans, nervous about their social standing, engaged in constant performance. In a sense, all were actors. The paid performers of theatre unconsciously reminded their audience of this fact. They made manifest in the flesh an insincerity at the core of Victorianism. Even sophisticates who ignored traditional religious scruples about drama could not forgive actors their unmasking of society's deepest secret. Only when middle-class American culture began to openly accept the pervasive theatricality in society (as increasingly occurred after midcentury) could it extend toward players a larger measure of respect.

Shadowing Greatness

Financial distress, barnstorming insecurities, frontier crudeness: hardly the conditions to engender artistic maturity. And yet in the midst of these trials Joe Jefferson had opportunity to act alongside some of the greatest performers of the Anglo-American stage. The galvanizing effect on him must have been great. Joe knew himself to be a Jefferson and understood the pride of craft his name represented. True, his father offered only a mitigated example of dramatic success (late in life Joe characterized his father as gifted "no matter how mistaken"). And his acclaimed grandfather had died before Joe could truly benefit from his example. At a time when the essence of theatre was the virtuosity of the star, learning to act meant studying their techniques of declamation, gesture, and stage movement. Thus Joe looked to other family members and to various actors they supported.[27]

Joe had many chances for such observation during the time he performed with the Ludlow-Smith company in Mobile, New Orleans, and St. Louis. He witnessed a continual procession of stars cross the boards during the 1843–46 seasons, most of them on more than one occasion. Some of these were stars of limited fame, though not by that fact necessarily second-rate: George Farren, E. S. Connor, and others who could draw respectable crowds and send them out amused or ennobled. But modern readers must be impressed with the quantity of outstanding talent Jefferson supported. In one season alone in Mobile he played behind Edwin Forrest, William Macready, John Brougham, Dan Marble, Thomas Placide, James Field, and Joshua Silsbee. Added to this roster in other seasons were Junius Brutus Booth, Charles and Ellen (Tree) Kean, James Wallack, Sr., and Anna Cora Mowatt.

Joe was, so to speak, a bench player. He and his sister came through the wings only intermittently, filling the most minor roles: servants making announcements, aide to a general or a lady-in-waiting, or simply another body to flesh out a crowd. On various occasions Joe (but more often Connie) danced and sang an entr'acte number. Smith and Ludlow rewarded them with a benefit performance near the end of the 1845 season; for this event the *Mobile Register and Journal* appealed to citizens to support the "orphan children of the lamented Jefferson." One might imagine that the Olympians Joe supported never took notice of the thin, unprepossessing young tyro. Only a few lived to see him enter their ranks, and probably none recalled their having shared a stage. But some stars perked up at the mention of the Jefferson name. When Wallack, Sr., a leading light of the Drury Lane and scion of his own theatrical dynasty, learned of Joe's lineage he warmly greeted him "for the sake of my dear old friend." Such moments reinforced Joe's sense of family standing even amidst the ebb of his current life.[28]

Among those who appeared on the Mobile stage were Junius Brutus Booth and William Charles Macready. Booth (1796–1852), surpassed in notoriety by one son and in histrionic fame by another, merits remembrance in his own right. At one time the rival of Edmund Kean for dramatic preeminence in Britain, Booth emigrated to America in 1821 under circumstances better left unexamined. For several decades until his death aboard a Mississippi steamer he bestrode American stages, his thunderous voice "deep, massive, resonant, many-stringed, changeful, vast in volume, of marvelous flexibility and range," delivering "trumpet-tones, bell-tones, tones like the 'sound of many waters,' like the muffled and confluent 'roar of bleak-grown pines.'" In Booth—as in Kean—Romanticism had found its theatrical fulfillment. It was like watching Shakespeare by "flashes of lightning," Coleridge famously said of Kean's acting—a remark equally descriptive of Booth. A careful student of elocution, Booth avoided the sing-song cadences so common in the worst of that training. He invigorated his words. Short but muscular, Booth featured a face of "antique beauty," and a "healthy pallor which is one sign of a magnetic brain." His great roles were the standards of nineteenth-century tragedians: Richard III, Lear, Iago, Sir Giles Overreach, and Shylock among them.[29]

In a sense Booth combined the mad, mercurial temperament he bequeathed to John Wilkes with the melancholy, tragic genius displayed by his older son Edwin. The father's brilliance was never questioned, his sanity often. "The most eccentric of all mad tragedians," judged contemporary Francis Wemyss. It would be Booth, more than anyone, who passed on to future generations the stereotype of the unreliable, slightly batty, alcoholic actor. His avoidance of sobriety was the bane of managers, who never could be sure which Booth would show up for the performance. It might be the artist whom journeyman actor Walter Leman recalled as possessed of a "towering and tempestuous passion, a supernatural energy that re-inspired the muse of Shakespeare." Or it might the one who arrived at a Boston theatre, drunk and so hoarse as to be inaudible to the audience. "In any other man it would not be tolerated," said Harry Watkins, "in him is it called eccentricity."[30]

Much was forgiven Booth. Theatre managers granted clemency because the public clamored for him. Jefferson likewise extended generosity, remembering him as "simple, unostentatious, and benevolent." Booth, in Jefferson's auto-biographical recollection, often arrived at the Mobile theatre moments before curtain, would casually chat with the cast, then move with seeming effortless-ness into his own part. On one occasion, during a performance of Colman's melodrama *The Iron Chest*, Booth stood offstage reminiscing with Joe about his grandfather, with whom he had acted years earlier. Booth launched into a song Jefferson the elder used to sing, paused in the middle to rush on stage and recite one of Edward Mortimer's most powerful scenes, then came again back-stage, where he shed his character and picked up the song where he left off. Such was Booth's ability to move in and out of a role.[31]

William Charles Macready (1793–1873) did not approach art so casually. His career was marked by an intensity and purposefulness that left no room for backstage banter. If Booth exemplified the slightly demented face of stage genius, Macready embodied the stage egoist, toward whom script, cast, and audience were to bow. The Byronesque portrait of Macready created by Henry Inman suggests the tormented intensity of an artist frustrated by the artistic limitations of others. Macready had debuted on the London stage in 1816 and enjoyed his first (and very successful) American tour in 1826. Along with Edmund Kean, he was one of the two greatest performers of the English stage in the first half of the nineteenth century. Macready's résumé included the core of dramatic roles expected of a tragedian: Virginius (which he introduced to the stage), Richard III, Macbeth, Hamlet, and an assortment of forgettable melodramatic leads. He sought the ennoblement of the British theatre, which to him meant recapturing Shakespearean grandeur. With the care of a scholar, Macready looked to restore original Shakespearean texts, freed from the cor-ruptive interpolations of John Dryden, Colley Cibber, and others. He also staged the more current "literary drama," particularly Byron's *Werner*, which became part of his repertoire for more than two decades. Nothing but the best, Macready believed, should appear on stage—and nothing that had not been honed to a fine edge. To this end he transformed rehearsals, which had com-monly been but superficial brushups of cues and stage movements, into serious occasions for study.[32]

As a performer Macready likewise established a new standard. Rather than coming to life for his occasional "points" while perfunctorily walking through the remainder of the script (a common practice among stars), he insisted on a unity of performance. And though it would be grossly misleading to consider his acting naturalistic in any sense recognizable to modern audiences, Mac-ready deserves credit for adding detail of performance and even introducing a kind of proto-Stanislavskian inner reflection and identification with a role. He eschewed the unbridled fire of the Kean-Booth school for a more cadenced albeit idiosyncratic elocution. The "Macready school," some called it. Noah Ludlow found it "affected," but he never objected to the crowds Macready drew to his theatre. Mobilians interpreted his visit as a major cultural event. "He has been received everywhere in this country with the highest manifestations of respect," the *Mobile Register* enthused, "senators, scholars and literary savans, have flocked to witness his masterly deliniations of life and nature."[33]

But the unquestioned greatness of Macready the performer was compromised by an unbridled temper and a pathological jealousy (self-confessed) of any actor who might challenge him for the public's affection. Fellow countryman George Vandenhoff admired Macready's devotion to stagecraft but could not overlook his equal desire "of making himself the one mark for all eyes to look at, the one voice for all ears to listen to, the one name for all mouths to repeat and eulogize." Macready's jealousy extended to politicians. Henry Clay, then at the height of his public career and an expected presidential candidate during the fall elections, visited Mobile in spring 1844. His presence at the theatre one evening was duly noted on the playbill in large print alongside Macready's. "Who is—a—Mr.—a—Mr. Clay?" Macready demanded. The explanation was not satisfying. Macready had been hired to fill the house each night; no other attractions were needed.[34]

Macready's intensity was so great that any misstep by another cast member or stagehand destroyed his concentration. Theatrical annals are filled with stories of Macready's summoning a guilty party to his dressing room after a performance for a tongue-lashing. Jefferson encountered vintage Macready. Unlike Booth, with his tardy arrivals and disregard of protocol, Macready arrived at the theatre and went immediately to his dressing room where he remained undisturbed while assuming his character. If events proceeded smoothly and he could maintain his focus, the audience enjoyed dramatic art at its highest levels. But misfortune smiled upon Joe. Occupying his usual minor role in a performance of *Werner,* he had been schooled by Macready as to the exact place of his stage exit. During the performance, however, Joe was horrified to see "Werner" standing directly in his line of egress. Nothing to do but pass by as best he could, torch in hand. Just off stage with the curtain fallen, Joe sniffed the scorched odor of singed wig. He turned and saw that "the enraged Werner had torn his wig from his head, and stood gazing at it for a moment in helpless wonder. Suddenly he made a rush in my direction; I saw he was on the war-path, and that I was his game." Man and boy tore about the wings and through the set, Macready capturing his prey when Joe ran into a carpenter. Shaken and disgraced, Joe was not allowed on stage again during Macready's engagement.[35]

Macready may have provided one of Joe's most humiliating moments, but Jefferson's last words on the "eminent tragedian" were nonetheless charitable. He regretted having joined in the customary actor sport of ridiculing the "Macready tantrums." With the hindsight of age and the benefit of having read Macready's memoirs — so filled with regrets about his inability to command his temper — Joe wrote with sympathy and admiration for Macready's efforts on behalf of his fellow actors. This tone of conciliation, even admiration, toward nearly all former associates characterizes the *Autobiography.*[36]

In the Crescent City

In fall 1845 Joe moved up, as it were, from class Triple-A Mobile to the theatrical major league of New Orleans. Such an analogy may mislead more than it clarifies. Ludlow and Smith maintained companies at both towns without any sense that one location was more important than the other. Members of the two companies often traveled back and forth during the season (a full day's trip aboard a steamer). Even itinerant stars, who visited not only major cities, such as Mobile or New Orleans, but filled in the geographic interstices by appearing on provincial backwater stages, generally gave little indication that they begrudged their small-town gigs. Nineteenth-century theatre demanded an egalitarian spirit. Wherever audiences would come and managers would pay, there players would act. Nonetheless, Joe and sister Connie must have felt some sense of professional advancement in the call to the Crescent City. It was the great city of the American Southwest, seven or eight times larger than Mobile, with proportionally greater energy and excitement. But even more, it was, after New York and Philadelphia, America's third greatest theatre town, the "emporium of the Southern stage," testified New York's *Spirit of the Times.* A glance at the extensive coverage of local drama given in New Orleans's newspapers suggests the importance of the institution. Theatre was a seven-day-a-week proposition in New Orleans, the town being almost alone among American cities in enjoying Sunday evening theatricals. Ludlow and Smith could count on their New Orleans theatre to turn a profit more often (though not invariably) than the one in inconstant Mobile.[37]

The local appetite for amusement, one contemporary explained, followed naturally from the presence of so many young men attracted to the city for work, especially during the prime theatre months of winter; their boarding house life offered few diversions. And the town had a steady flow of visitors, ready always for a night on the town. But it was not just outsiders. New Orleans residents had more appreciation than most American urbanites for drama. Even by the raucous standards of the day, Orleanians displayed un-

usual enthusiasms for their stage favorites. They massed at the levees to welcome arriving stars and serenaded them at their hotels. The local appearance
of Fanny Ellsler, the European danseuse who electrified American audiences,
set off a street riot. Sober-minded Charles Lyell, the eminent English geologist
who visited New Orleans during the very months Joe appeared there, found
the residents' unabashed embrace of amusement (especially during Mardi
Gras) a welcome relief from the unremitting labor ("from morning till night,
without ever indulging in a holiday") he saw elsewhere in America.[38]

The Jeffersons' midfall trip from Mobile to New Orleans was likely pleasant. Steaming out of beautiful Mobile Bay their vessel proceeded along the
smooth waters of an inland passage to Lake Pontchartrain. From its southern
shore, a point six miles above the city, the party transferred to a train for the
last leg. The cypress swamps soon yielded to a suburban landscape of gardens
and orchards. French inscriptions on tavern signposts signaled their approach
to an old world culture in America.

Joe knew the city slightly from his brief trip through the area with his family
a few years earlier. But even on his return it is doubtful that the sixteen-year-
old could grasp the depth of the city's complex society. The dynamics of the
city's racial hierarchy, its unspoken byzantine rules regarding the interaction
of Creole, black, and mulatto were found nowhere else. Dueling had just been
outlawed by the revised state constitution, but a notorious episode occurred
during Joe's residence. And what might Joe have thought about the public
execution of Pauline, a slave accused of abusing her mistress, an event that
drew a large crowd, including "female spectators" in carriages, who "were
stretching their necks, standing on tip-toe, pushing and jostling each other that
they might get a good sight." If such episodes came to Joe's attention, he never
averred to them later in his *Autobiography*. The fact that he penned his recollections in the late 1880s, as race relations in America were beginning to
deteriorate, might have deterred him from making any derogatory comments
on issues peculiar to the South. More likely, it never occurred to him to question regional policies on race. The locale agreed with him so well that he later
purchased an estate in Cajun Louisiana.[39]

New Orleans boasted a handful of theatres and ballrooms. In the French
Quarter stood the Orleans, the city's oldest and the nation's only theatre devoted to French-language drama. At the Olympia, "red-hot melodramas and
vulgar burlesques appear to be the standing dishes," sniffed one contemporary. "They please the mob." The St. Charles, Ludlow's and Smith's establishment in the uptown district, was Joe's new home Its season began on 18
November. Ludlow and Smith had lined up a substantial company of forty-
eight actors and nineteen actresses (split between New Orleans and Mobile)

and a formidable collection of visiting stars. Booth, James H. Hackett, Joseph Field, Dan Marble, the Keans, and Anna Cora Mowatt, along with a host of secondary stars illumined the St. Charles stage between November and April. The St. Charles managers also attended to audience convenience and comfort. Their box office kept long daytime hours to ease ticket purchase. A private security force made an effort to control rowdies. A ventilation system circulated heated air during chill evenings. Moreover, the lingering clouds of recession were at last receding, and there was no repeat of the previous year's cholera outbreak. All signs pointed to one of the best seasons in years.[40]

Theatrical apprenticeship meant learning by watching and by doing. Every night Joe had occasion to study the tricks of the masters. The Yankee roles of Dan Marble (*Sam Patch in France* and *Sam Patch, the Jumper of Niagara Falls*) and broad comedy of James Henry Hackett (Falstaff and Rip Van Winkle) must have especially invited study because it became apparent during the season that the youngest Jefferson, like father and grandfather, was destined for low comedy. Not that we know many of Joe's roles early in the season. He belonged to the body of support cast who labored anonymously so far as newspaper billing was concerned. His and Connie's names generally appeared only when they performed entr'acte songs or dances. They had taken advantage of the summer's freedom to practice some new steps, which they now showcased. At the season's opening, for example, after the ever-popular Booth headlined *The Iron Chest*, brother and sister danced *La Polka*. Advertised as having been taught them by the "celebrated Mons. Korponay," the dance bespoke the polka craze current at the time.[41]

Two engagements highlighted the St. Charles season: the appearance of Mr. and Mrs. Charles Kean, and Anna Cora Mowatt starring in her new comedy *Fashion*. The Keans, first individually and then collectively among the more celebrated British performers of the mid-nineteenth century, came to New Orleans during their first tour of the American South. Charles Kean (1811–68) was son of Edmund Kean. Following his father on stage was natural, but the younger Kean lacked the forcefulness and presence of the elder. Plagued by an annoying voice (like a "frog in the gutter," Colman sniped), Kean found many critical detractors. His public, though, remained supportive. Kean displayed the virtues of dedication over genius. He compensated for a deficiency of brilliance through sheer grit, becoming a consummate craftsman of the stage. In the history of theatre Kean occupies a notable transitional position between the passionate, ranting style of his father, whom he early unsuccessfully attempted to emulate, and a more nuanced, carefully constructed approach to roles during the final fifteen years of his career. As a champion of contemporary French melodrama and a producer of Shakespearean drama he had no equal in the theatre of his day.

Mrs. Charles Kean (1805–80) was before her marriage already famous as Ellen Tree. Noted as a tragedian and an acclaimed Romeo, she was (according to Ellen Terry) "more formidable than beautiful." Yet illustrations show a delicate, refined face, marred only by a too-prominent nose. The union of such strong and temperamental wills would not suggest marital harmony. But in fact they were utterly devoted through their twenty-six years of marriage. In the best Victorian fashion Ellen Tree refused any billing but "Mrs. Kean."[42]

Both Kean and Tree had known very successful American tours before their marriage in 1842. Their return as a duo promised an even better reception, and they were not disappointed. Their drawing power allowed them to command one-half of each night's gross receipts, a demand some managers considered excessive but nonetheless paid. Charles Kean also elicited some grumbling from certain of his supporting casts, who considered him imperious and overrated. "A pale and ineffectual replica of the father," journeyman player Harry Watkins opined, "cold and formal, he stalked through his Shakespearean presentations with a catarrhal grandeur." Kean, to be sure, tolerated no departure from his notion of how a scene should be played. Yet few stars did. On balance, Kean possessed more amiability than Macready or Forrest, his occasional irascibility being no more than expected from an artist of his rank.[43]

The Keans accepted Smith's and Ludlow's offer of a southern tour despite reservations of its profitability. They were wrong. Buoyed by a strengthening economy, audiences swarmed to the theatre in all three cities where they appeared. They ultimately pocketed $15,000 from their extended tour. "The dress circle of the St. Charles has become the focus of fashion," the *Daily Picayune* noted approvingly. The paper's critic, one less given to abject puffery than many scribes, found Mrs. Kean delectable. "Vivacious, sarcastic, bewitching and bedevilling," he said of her Beatrice, a "creature who was wont to exact the homage of pit, boxes and gallery."[44]

Fashion

Anna Cora Mowatt Ritchie (1819–70) (the last name bespeaking a later and desperately unhappy marriage to the secessionist editor of the *Richmond Enquirer,* William Ritchie) visited in February and again in April. She had a life so full of turns that she may be taken as an apt example of the uncertainties of nineteenth-century America. Born to "Knickerbocracy" privilege, she descended from a signer of the Declaration Independence on her mother's side. Her merchant father helped sponsor expeditions to seek independence for colonial South America. She likewise married well (at age fifteen) to attorney James Mowatt. Indulged and classically educated by her husband-cum-tutor, Anna's adolescence continued well into her marriage. But her husband's ruin during a recession and later invalidism forced Mowatt into the unaccustomed role of breadwinner. As a child Anna loved playing theatre, earnestly staging juvenile Shakespeare. She now turned to the platform, rejecting conventions of gender and class to become a public reader, then a highly popular entertainment form among the public. This was the age of elocution, and men with stentorian voice recited Browning, Shakespeare, Scott, and lesser bards of momentary acclaim among Victorian audiences. Actors, for obvious reasons, found in public reading an alternative stage for their talents, particularly if their theatre career languished. George Vandenhoff, a tragedian of some acclaim, left the stage by choice to give Shakespearean readings, finding in solitary art a control and dignity he missed in the commercial scramble of the theatre. Anna Mowatt was among the first women to mount the elocutionary stage, pioneering a vocation that other actresses subsequently took up as second careers.[45]

But her new career ended abruptly. Never strong physically, Anna endured recurring bouts of the Victorian scourge: tuberculosis. Forced to withdraw from her platform routine but still required to support her family (which later included three adopted children), she took up her pen. With little apparent effort, though fortified by periodic mesmeric hypnotic treatments, she produced a torrent of biographical sketches, magazine articles, poems, works of fiction, and, unlikely as it seems given her cosseted upbringing, practical treatises on domestic chores. Encouraged and aided by close friend and noted playwright Epes Sargent, Mowatt returned to her first love: drama.

Her first and best play, *Fashion; or, Life in New York,* premiered in March 1845 at New York's tony Park Theatre. It ran for twenty nights, by prevailing standards a smash. It also became a staple of parlor theatricals. Moreover, the play marked an important moment in American drama—"America's finest nineteenth-century comedy," one modern critic attests. Indeed, it is one of the century's few American plays to enjoy successful twentieth-century revivals. Part of the play's cachet was bestowed by Edgar Allan Poe, who attended the play not once nor twice but eight nights running. Skeptical of its merits at first, after a week he began to appreciate *Fashion*'s send-up of the well-heeled's slavish obedience of fashion. Poe hoped that public enthusiasm for the play augured a new age for American drama.[46]

With a successful production under her belt but still plagued by financial worries, Mowatt became intrigued with the notion of applying the greasepaint herself. She threw herself into her new career with demonic energy. In her first year she performed some two hundred nights in twenty roles, not just in New York but all about the country. "In the annals of the stage of all countries," Laurence Hutton boldly claimed, "there is no single instance of a mere novice playing so many times before so many different audiences and winning so much merited praise." The pace was murderous but exhilarating, a "nepenthe of inner peace" allowing her to catnap even while on stage. Illustrations of Mowatt show a refined face with expressive gray eyes and a high forehead (exposing, according to the day's phrenologists, the seat of intellect), ringed by lush auburn hair. She had a mellifluous voice, marred only, judged a smitten Poe, by an "occasional Anglicism of accent."[47]

When Mrs. Mowatt arrived in New Orleans in February 1846 for the first of her two engagements, Joe Jefferson and other cast members may have shared the tinge of resentment many veteran players felt toward her: an interloper on the stage, who without paying the dues of apprenticeship used the capital of her social prominence to vault to the top of the profession (where she remained until voluntary retirement at age thirty-five). But they could not fail being impressed by her trouper spirit in persisting each night despite flagging health. They must have been pleased, too, by the unusually complete stage directions offered in the prompt book. Joe, like most players, had been used to the most rudimentary of script promptings—entrances, exits, and stage positions—trusting his familiarity with the customary stage business to see him through a scene. But *Fashion* heralded the future of scripts, providing detailed instruction for stage actions and attitudes. Whatever Joe's feelings toward Mowatt, they were overshadowed by an important moment in his career. At her return engagement in March, when *Fashion* was first staged at the St. Charles, Joe had the pleasure for the first time in his career of seeing his name listed in the newspaper beside a feature role. For five nights to full houses Joe corked up for the blackface part of Zeke, a stereotyped Negro servant in the fashionable New York household of the Tiffanys.[48]

Essentially an American comedy of manners, *Fashion* was often compared with Sheridan's *School for Scandal*. Critics quibbled about the quality of Mowatt's dialogue and characterization but most agreed that Mowatt had created a peculiarly American play. "Are there materials in American society for constructing a successful comedy?" the New York newspaper the *Albion* asked. Yes, and Mrs. Mowatt's "naturally keen powers of observation" and "refined taste" has so proven it. She populated it with types familiar to all theatergoers. Adam Trueman, the rustic, sound-hearted farmer who is the play's moral conscious, continues the Jonathan tradition of stalwart Yankees created by Royall Tyler. Trueman plays foil to the Tiffany family and sophisticated urban residents generally and captives all of French fashion, a foreign influence comically embodied in the maid Millinette and an imposter French count Jolimaitre. A variety of other stock types flesh out the cast: a blackmailing villain, a spinster on the prowl for a mate, a virtuous girl from the country (who in the melodramatic final twist proves to be Trueman's daughter and heiress), and an army officer to serve as romantic match for the daughter.[49]

Not to forget Zeke, the first character seen in act 1. He provides regular comic relief through his impudence and his mangling of the English language. Debriefing the maid about his new employers, the Tiffanys, he asks, "Now, as you've made the acquaintance ob dis here family, and dere you've had a supernumerary advantage ob me — seeing dat I only receibed my appointment dis morning. What I wants to know is your publicated opinion, privately expressed, ob de domestic circle." How did seventeen-year-old Joe handle this dialect? How many laughs did he coax from the audience? The answers would be an early measure of his talent, instruction — and ear. Joe might have modeled Zeke's voice on blacks he encountered along the river or in Mobile, but more likely he drew upon the minstrel stage, which had attained a conventionalized rendering of such dialect by the 1840s. The role also offered him creative opportunities for physical humor. In the first scene he is instructed to move a table, which he does incorrectly but nevertheless with great fanfare, miming immense satisfaction with himself. It was the sort of low comedy stage business that the Jefferson men had been specializing in for generations. Having been exposed to the line of acting since infancy, Joe could practically intuit the shrugs and mugging his part required.[50]

If the black stereotyping now seems off-putting, it must at least be seen as no more than one arm of an entire body of caricatures. As the reviewer in the *Albion* noted, Mowatt's characters represent classes not individuals. And the most biting satire of the play was reserved for that class of socialites who shamelessly aped French manners. Mrs. Tiffany was served up as an American Mrs. Malaprop, hopelessly mauling the French language.[51]

> MRS. TIFFANY: This mode of receiving visitors only upon one specified day of the week is a most convenient custom! It saves the trouble of keeping the house continually in order and of being always dressed. I flatter myself that I was the first to introduce it amongst the New York *ee-light*. You are quite sure that it is strictly a Parisian mode, Millinette?
>
> MILLENETTE: O, *oui*, Madame, entirely *mode de Paris*.
>
> MRS. TIFFANY: (aside) This girl is worth her weight in gold. Millinette, how do you say arm-chair in French?
>
> MILLENETTE: *Fauteuil*, Madame.
>
> MRS. TIFFANY: *Fo-tool!* That has a foreign — an out-of-the wayish sound that is perfectly charming — and so genteel. There is something about our American words decidedly vulgar. *Fowtool!* How refined. *Fowtool!* Arm-chair! What a difference.

Mowatt created in Tiffany the stock figure of the pompous Francophile society matron so often lampooned in Hollywood films of the next century.

The culture mongering of Mrs. Tiffany made her an easy mark for a phony French count. Although played for laughs, the figure of the count reminded audiences yet again of the dangers in placing one's confidence too easily into the hands of strangers. Equally regrettable was the city's pernicious influence on Mr. Tiffany's business ethics. He had allowed himself to begin forging signatures (a favorite plot line of melodramas — the signature being a fitting marker for the demoralizing entanglements of contracts and capitalism). The forgery cast him into the clutches of his blackmailing clerk. In the best Yankee style, Adam Trueman provides an antidote to the foibles of both Tiffanys. He unmasks the dissembler count and betraying clerk. He first excoriates the genuflecting before the god of fashion. "Fashion! And pray what is *fashion*, madam? An agreement between certain persons to live without using their souls! To substitute etiquette for virtue — decorum for purity — manners for morals! To affect a shame for the works of their Creator! And expend all their rapture upon the works of their tailors and dressmakers!" Trueman also lectures his friend Mr. Tiffany on allowing his pursuit of profit to compromise his principles.

The sole remedy for these ills came from imbibing the tonic of country living. The moral of *Fashion* was clear: happiness resided in a return to our agrarian, republican roots. That the elite audiences of New York's Park Theatre presumably found its message of republican simplicity appealing, even while many of their number sought to be à la mode, pointedly illustrates the ability of cultures to contain stark contradictions. American capitalism was a powerful engine of prosperity, yet Jacksonians could not escape a suspicion of businessmen and a longing for simpler times. Thomas Jefferson, the very prophet of agrarian virtues, fondly embraced Parisian culture and pursued a sybaritic life on his Virginia hilltop. His own life apart, Jefferson understood that as long as Americans defined themselves largely in opposition to Europe and its ways, the rhetoric of a homespun nationalism would trump all other appeals. The gentle satire of *Fashion* provided a homeopathic, sugar-coated dose of cultural criticism. The great successes of our mass culture have relied on stock appeals to the simple life — a truism Mrs. Mowatt well understood.[52]

Theatre, to some degree, followed the cycle of nature, and midspring meant the Ludlow-Smith company sidestepped the approaching steam bath of New Orleans for the more tempered springtime of St. Louis. The same entourage of stars — the Keans, Mrs. Mowatt, and Booth — came calling at St. Louis as they had done in Mobile and New Orleans. Smith and Ludlow in effect ran a theatrical circuit, and like all such organizations of scale it offered stars the convenience of a preplanned season. Moreover, the bane of itinerant starring — new supporting companies of widely varying caliber every week — was avoided through a modicum of familiarity.

"A brilliant and densely crowded audience" greeted Mr. and Mrs. Kean at the 25 April opening. "A prompt attendance at the box office," warned the *Daily Missouri Republican,* "offers the only sure guarantee of obtaining seats." The Kean engagement went smoothly, but Junius Brutus Booth, on his best behavior in Mobile and New Orleans, fell off the wagon in St. Louis. At his typical opening piece, in a favored role as the melancholy Sir Edmund Mortimer, Booth seemed in control through two acts. "But suddenly," Ludlow later recalled, "the demon eccentricity laid hold on him, when he dropped his gloominess and became a *leetle* too *spirited.*" Ludlow, who had seen just about everything during his long theatre career, swore that Booth's performance topped all. It was pure camp. He transformed Colman's dour character into something of great energy. And the young men in the audience, by one account, egged on the inebriated star in his travesty. The final death scene came —and came again and again, as Booth rose repeatedly from the stage to acknowledge the applause and then die once more. But Ludlow was not amused. He dispatched a boy to Booth's dressing room with the tart message that his engagement had ended.[53]

Booth was not the only player consigned to the doghouse that summer. Joe also felt the stick of discipline. Now seventeen and possessed by the unruly spirit of youth, he and two other young players were chronically rowdy in the dressing rooms. Such an offense might seem petty, but the backstage pressures before a performance being what they were, no distractions could be tolerated. Joe proved compliant to the verbal rebuke, but his two compatriots required the slap of a fine to quiet them.[54]

Within the following two weeks, though, Joe suffered a more distressing moment. Ludlow and Smith organized a grand extravaganza for their July Fourth performance. The "SPIRIT OF FREEDOM; or, the Fathers of the Revolution," as it was styled, included a "GRAND PROCESSION," and at the emotional pinnacle, the assembled cast's singing of "The Star-Spangled Banner." Joe, a veteran of entr'acte songs, had the honor of a solo for the first stanza. But the words had been changed. Joseph Field (now editor of a local paper) for whatever reason had devised new lyrics to what was not yet the national anthem but already a patriotic favorite. Cornelia tutored her son throughout the day and then stood in the wings to prompt Joe if needed. But that night on stage he got only as far as "Oh, say can you see— " before blanking out. The audience on that muggy St. Louis night, burning with a patriotism white-hot from the expansionist fires of the Mexican War and loosened by Independence Day drink, had no patience with the failings of a gangling teen. They began the dreaded hiss, finally routing Joe off the stage in tears to the waiting arms of his equally stricken mother. Joe's recollection of the event forty years later was vivid and pathetic, suggesting it was the worst stage humiliation he ever suffered. The teen's discomfit was hardly a disgrace. Virtually every star of the era recounted a similar moment early in their career. Anna Cora Mowatt endured regular visits by the "incubus," as she called it, fits of acute stage fright. Not talent nor even genius was exempt from the refining fires of such attacks.[55]

But Joe drew another lesson from the episode. From the perspective of his later life he recalled not so much regret over his stage failure but a salutary contrast of that age's boorishness with later audience's decorum. "The hissing and jeering that were so liberally bestowed upon me will never be vented again in this country for so slight an offense," he judged. "The well-dressed, decorous audience of to-day, when an accident occurs, sit quietly, bearing it with patience and consideration." Jefferson credited this infusion of public mannerliness to free public education. But more was involved. The taming of American audiences remains among the most mysterious and striking developments of nineteenth-century theatre — a story deserving closer attention later.[56]

Off to the Mexican War

When the St. Louis season ended on 7 July 1846, Joe's family and a handful of others headed to Texas and the Mexican-American war zone in the heart of the seasonal heat. The exact reason for this venture will never be known, but perhaps it was for lack of good alternatives. The Mississippi Valley tours of recent summers had been largely futile. Too, the enticements of Texas were on everybody's lips. The American eagle had screamed from local papers for several years, announcing that Texas, Oregon — indeed much of the West — were ripe for annexation and development. News from Galveston told of the "host of strange faces, both European and American," arriving daily in search of their particular El Dorados. And the build-up of troops along the Texas coast meant a fresh market for players willing to relieve soldiers of their tedious routine. With the eternal optimism of the stroller who intuits better days just around the next bend, the Jefferson family decided to test the theatrical waters of Texas. Barnstorming days had returned.[57]

This was their second trip to the Gulf Coast. At the close of their dismal summer itinerancy in 1845 they had played the small Texas theatre circuit of Galveston and Houston. Drama had been to Houston for less than a decade. In a fashion somehow appropriate to the raw-edged nature of the land, the area's first attempt at theatre had been stymied by General Santa Ana's attacks in 1836; the second by the capsizing of the boat along the Gulf Coast with a fated troupe aboard. No major stars had played the stage in Texas before the Jeffersons' arrival, and their coming did not alter that record. After a day and a half's journey by steamer from New Orleans they disembarked at Galveston, a settlement once governed by Jean Lafitte and in 1845 still less than a decade old as an incorporated town. Sitting precariously on the spit of sand guarding the entrance to Galveston Bay, Galveston was Texas's window on the world, the "New York of Texas," as one paper described it. Such a boast could hardly have impressed Joe when he arrived. A dreary settlement set against wind and water, the town battled periodic visits of yellow fever and storm but had burgeoned in the 1840s, nurtured by the cotton trade. Hotels, taverns, banks, a newspaper — and a theatre — were erected. The latter, Sydnor's Theatre, hosted the infrequent itinerants who strayed from the usual circuit, and here Joe and his comrades put in a brief season of no distinction and little reward.[58]

From Galveston the Jeffersons next headed by boat fifty miles up the Buffalo Bayou to Houston. Having risen from the ashes of Santa Ana's depredations, this town exemplified the boosterism of the West, never allowing its rough-hewn exterior or loss of the state capital to Austin to dampen its pretensions to culture. Indeed, the city contained an assortment of intellectually curious people with a taste for drama. And they demanded it well done. When manager John Carlos produced a poorly acted version of *The Dumb Girl of Genoa*, he found his effigy hanging from a tree in front of his theatre. Little is known about the several-week Houston sojourn, but the visit occasioned one of the *Autobiography*'s longest anecdotes: the appearance of an old theatrical warhorse named "Pudding" Stanley.[59]

Stanley had retired from an undistinguished though colorful career as a strolling player to earn greater prominence as saloon keeper in San Antonio. News of a professional company in Texas stirred his old impulses, and he saddled his horse for the three-hundred-mile ride to Houston. Stanley attempted to convince the struggling company that San Antonio was their ticket. His enthusiasm was contagious, but second thoughts quickly followed a realization of the wearisome journey — and particularly the path they would follow through the center of Comanche country. The company could not help remembering the tragic fate of another acting troupe just six years earlier during the Seminole War in Florida, which was set upon by natives while traveling from St. Augustine to a garrison to entertain troops. Two players were murdered. Stanley's reassurances that the company might bluff its way through with prop weapons if confronted by Comanches failed to allay worries. As a concession to the stout-hearted Stanley, Joe's group let him perform his favorite starring vehicle, *Richard III*. The result was less tragedy than tragicomedy: on stage Richard's wig was set ablaze by a candle, while in the audience the star's rowdy friends breached the code of spectator etiquette — lenient as it then was — with impunity.[60]

The story is pure Jefferson. Charmingly told with an eye for the western exoticisms readers cherished, the sketch manages to entertain while at the same time being instructive about theatre life. Out of the yarn of anecdote Joe wove history. His ability to convey the full-grained texture of American theatre sets his *Autobiography* apart from the common run of theatrical memoirs. His account of Stanley tells us two things about frontier theatre. First, itinerants occasionally faced genuine peril. The lighthearted manner of Joe's narrative, while not demeaning the trials of strollers, attempts to render danger less threatening. One does not sense so much a play for public sympathy as a bid for respect: amidst hardship and with good grace actors carried forth their civilizing mission. Second, Jefferson's tale reveals the raucous nature of antebellum audiences. Jefferson's genteel readers of the 1890s, who knew only the restrained manner of modern audiences, were reminded that it was not always so. Once, not so long ago, playhouses could be unsafe for player and patron. But Jefferson, like most of his countrymen, defined national experience in terms of progress, and theatre no less than rail travel or home lighting symbolized the upward march of American life.

If the *Autobiography* resonates with the full-throated spirit of nineteenth-century American life it also on occasions betrays the limitations of Joe's memory. His account of the Jeffersons' visit to Texas in midsummer 1846, during the early stages of the Mexican-American War, suffers serious lapses of accuracy. Jefferson recalled how their intrepid company (managed by a Mr. Hart) attempted to mix patriotism and profit by providing drama for Zachary Taylor's soldiers in the war zone. The expedition seemed a good bet. American soldiers stationed on frontier posts had long found drama a diversion from the humdrum of garrison life; indeed, amateur theatricals flourished among the Stars and Stripes (where necessity dictated restoring the Elizabethan practice of casting males in female lines, as when a young officer named Ulysses Grant on duty in Mexico played Desdamona).[61]

Hart's troupe of seven women and four men first journeyed to Point Isabel, the staging area for American troops along the Texas coast. According to Jefferson they arrived in early May 1846, just in time to witness the opening battles of Palo Alto and Resaca de la Palma. Jefferson gets his battle dates correct but could not be more wrong about his presence there. In May he was safely situated in St. Louis; it was not until July 19 that the company arrived in Matamoros.[62]

How could Joe be so sure—and so mistaken—of what he experienced? In part, distance from the events explains some garbling of memory. Accumulated decades played their pack of tricks on the past, inverting events, juxtaposing moments of wide separation, conferring certitude on vague impressions. In the case of Jefferson's memory, a hierarchy of recollection was at work. When recalling stage experiences his remembrances are nearly flawless (apart from forgivable imprecision on dates); memories of theatre events he witnessed can often be corroborated by contemporary records. But his grasp of historical events is less sure. Joe's comments on the Mexican-American War hint at a later reading about the conflict, probably done while writing his memoirs. He superimposed a secondhand knowledge of the war on top of a modest firsthand experience. Empowered by his reading and encouraged by a storyteller's desire to embellish his encounter with the century's purest embodiment of manifest destiny expansionism, Joe produced an account not fully restrained by the facts.

His actual experience must have been intriguing enough. Joe does not indicate their means of travel, but it is likely that from Point Isabel the small band of strollers boated up the meandering, muddy Rio Grande toward Matamoros, fending off mosquitoes whose nighttime ferocity frustrated sleep. In all of his young travels Joe had never ventured into a region so utterly desolate. Claimed by two governments, the prairie and chaparral landscape sheltered wild horses and cattle, and its wetlands harbored exotic flamingo. No Brownsville, Texas, yet existed on the American side of Rio Grande. The region surrounding Matamoros had fallen to the American army in May, and this town of yellow adobe houses became the staging area for General Zachary Taylor's march on Monterrey.

Never before off United States soil, Joe now encountered a true Spanish town, the second-leading city of northern Mexico. It had substantial, sturdy houses with impressively barred windows clustered about the central plaza. But the troops and the troupe found only a shell; the "respectable class" had fled ahead of the American army. Matamoros was left to Mexican army deserters, brigands, gamblers, and city poor. With the permission of the commanding officer, the company set up theatrical shop in the occupied local theatre. Jefferson and his cohorts were a godsend, the commandant must have believed, a diversion for his troops at the rear, where time hung especially heavy in late summer heat. Volunteer units, who saw the war as a lark, frequently lacked the most elemental restraint. Better that the men expend their energy hissing stage villains.[63]

Hart's company wasted no time in mounting its first production the night following its arrival, despite lacking scenery or wardrobe (which had mistakenly been sent farther up the river). Joe received some complimentary notices, but he took a backseat to his younger sister, whose vivacious dance and song made her a particular favorite of the troops. If audiences in America's most sedate confines occasionally threatened disruption, the atmosphere in this outpost must have been bedlam. "Here we acted to the most motley group that ever filled a theatre," Jefferson wrote without resort to hyperbole, "soldiers, settlers, gamblers, rag-tag and bob-tail crowd": the loose-ends of a moving army of occupation. Hart resorted to stationing a detachment of regulars in his theatre to preserve order, but even so a thief once brazenly reached through the ticket window and made off with the night's receipts. The Hart company knew that their rowdy clientele wanted action. *Richard III* was a natural choice. Not content with the bard's bloodletting, the company portrayed "wholesale murder out and out." "Indiscriminate hacking and cutting and slaying," an amazed observer recorded, "regardless of age, sex, or condition." But life and art were circling one another in the war zone. King Richard was played by Jack Haynes, less an actor than a renowned Texas roustabout. On a Matamoros street the day after the sanguinary *Richard III*, Haynes became involved in gunplay, then an evening later fell victim to a stabbing.[64]

Perhaps with few regrets the Hart company found its audience dwindling by the middle of September as the siege of Monterrey climaxed and more soldiers were brought forward. Hart concluded that demand for drama had departed with the troops and thus disbanded his own troupe. Joe, his mother, and his sister were now out of work.[65]

In this situation—not the grimmest they had known but still daunting, thrown on their own amongst people of an alien tongue—Joe stepped forward as family leader. Just a few months shy of eighteen, he had not fully emerged from the awkward years. But his father's absence (nearly four years now) and his mother's decline as breadwinner inevitably thrust responsibility on him. If acting had separated him from the normal world of work, it nonetheless instilled a large measure of resourcefulness. He and fellow player Edward Badger opened a cigar stand in a Matamoros saloon, sensing that even with the soldiers gone, the human detritus of frontier and war possessed ready cash. "Cigars of the best quality" and "good chewing tobacco always on hand, ready for use," they advertised. Joe had seen a great deal of life by his teenage years, but never had he known the collection of gamblers and cut-purses who wandered into the Grand Spanish Saloon. One new acquaintance, a hardened Comanche fighter, was stabbed to death before Joe's eyes. This brutality climaxed a reign of violence that swept Matamoros, and Joe and his partner were persuaded to sell out and take leave of the border country. In November 1846 the Jeffersons obtained permission to board an army boat returning wounded soldiers to the Gulf Coast, from where a steamer to New Orleans was secured.[66]

But the Matamoros sojourn had a gentler side as well. Here Joe found his first love—Metta, a Mexican girl whom Joe recalled as having brilliant black eyes and aristocratic features. She tutored him in the arts of smoking, guitar music, and conversational Spanish. A youthful infatuation with a lovely girl requires no explanation (and Joe would later show himself prone to such temptations), but why would he extend her such attention in his *Autobiography* while keeping his adult family life safely offstage, mentioning his first marriage only briefly and refusing to name either of his wives? The answer surely must pertain to the Victorian penchant for domestic privacy (more than a penchant — a code — which Joe never breached). The experience with Metta, conversely, merited no such privilege. Joe's fond account is tinged with a condescension unimaginable if his love had been a daughter of northern Europe. He suggests that had he stayed in Matamoros much longer, his mother would have acquired a Mexican daughter-in-law. But this was a throwaway line. Jefferson's very ability to publicly examine his feelings suggests how far outside the tightly held inner circle of his life Metta resided. Her memory existed at the level of good copy, an exotic romance of no seriousness, serving primarily to establish its actor-author as a hale, well-rounded youth.[67]

As Joe stood on the deck of the boat headed to New Orleans he may have assumed his return there foretold more seasons with Ludlow and Smith. In fact it would be a brief stopover, just long enough for Joe to catch a glimpse of his future before journeying east.

An Actor Prepares

Joe Jefferson stepped off the gangplank onto a New Orleans wharf sometime in November 1846. To say he returned as a man rather than a boy may be stretching the truth. For all of Joe's travels and wide-ranging experiences, his life thus far had been spent in the sheltering fold of his immediate and extended family, and it had been a bare few months since his humiliation on the St. Louis stage. But he was approaching his eighteenth birthday in an era when most males had by then assumed the yoke of adulthood. Unlike his father, who when financial misfortune struck could pick up his fishing rod and put worry behind, Joe keenly felt the obligations that the vicissitudes of family fortunes had cast upon him. The experiences of Texas and Mexico, if colorful in retrospect, required a quickened sense of responsibility for the well-being of his mother and sister. He could meet that obligation only one way: by returning to the boards.

Seeking a Stage Home

Joe wasted no time in checking the newspapers to learn if theatres had opened their fall season and was delighted to find Ludlow and Smith's St. Charles — his old haunt — already underway. He went that night to a performance featuring the season's major star, James W. Wallack, Jr. (1818–73).

Wallack hailed from a theatrical family that took a backseat to none in producing pedigreed performers, spawning fourteen across four generations, each
seemingly more urbane and sophisticated than the last. The Wallacks aptly
symbolized the pervasive British presence on the American stage. From the
1850s through the 1870s Wallack's Theatre in New York, operated by two
generations of the family, became famous for its well-wrought comic productions. Joe considered Wallack "the most romantic-looking actor I ever saw."
His dash and brio invigorated tragic roles. Unfortunately, he also had an ego
so large that even Ludlow and Smith — accustomed to demanding stars — lost
patience. When Wallack petulantly refused to act in productions he thought
beneath his talent, Ludlow bought out his contract for the remainder of the
season and sent him and Mrs. Wallack packing.[1]

Jefferson found Wallack less intriguing than he did a young low comedian
who had recently joined the company. John E. Owens (1823–86) enjoyed a
stint with Ludlow and Smith in the Crescent City that would catapult him into
the ranks of comic leads (comedians were generally not "stars" in this age of
tragedy and melodrama). His major roles were staples of low comedy that
likewise marked Jefferson's career: Caleb Plummer, Solon Shingle, Dr. Pangloss, Bob Acres. He also won favor with Bowery audiences for his rendering
of the urban comic bully Mose in the *New York Fireman*. His place in the
history of nineteenth-century American theatre is modest but secure. Owens
was an effortless laugh machine whose standing among some critics was
tainted by a tendency to let his clownishness lapse into tasteless improvisations ("gagging," in the day's vernacular) or running joke lines that wore thin.
His reputation would necessarily be diminished by the shadowing presence of
Jefferson's greater talent.[2]

That night as Owens took the stage at the St. Charles, Jefferson thought him
the "handsomest low comedian I have ever seen," a "neat, dapper little figure"
with a face "full of lively expression." Joe was witnessing a performer's coming of age. Owens won his audience from the first, his style and "great flow of
animal spirits capturing them and myself too." For the only time in his *Autobiography* Joe admitted envy of another performer. He had returned to the St.
Charles Theatre expecting that his adventures in Texas and at the war's front
would give him added cachet; management would surely welcome him back
with an enhanced spot on the company's roster. Instead, he found himself
displaced by a new face. "I am afraid that I had hoped to see something not
quite so good," Jefferson admitted, "and was a little annoyed to find him such
a capital actor."[3]

But Jefferson managed to turn his jealousy to advantage. More than forty
years later Joe singled out this moment as defining his career's ambition. Hav-

ing lived his life entirely within the musty and candle-sooted environs of the stage, only now did he determine that theatrical fame was indeed his goal. In retrospect, one might ask how he could have done anything else. Yet he might have been content with a journeyman's career, as was his father. If one credits heredity as a shaping force in human personality, then the burning ambition so conspicuously lacking in Joe's father was supplied by Cornelia. Not coincidentally did her two sons — by different fathers — both achieve theatrical acclaim. The laconic persona Joe frequently showed the public (as though Rip were his true self) belied a steely determination. Joe's relationships were generally marked by amicability and an admirable freedom from ego, but in the bitter moment of Owens's triumph on the St. Charles stage, his competitive fires raged. "I resolved to equal Owens some day, if I could," he admitted. Characteristically, even this silent vow did not preclude a lifelong friendship with Owens — once Joe had established himself as an equal on the stage. Indeed, they later acted together on the New Orleans stage.[4]

With Joe's stage opportunities foreclosed in New Orleans, a Jefferson family council concluded that he should accept brother Charlie Burke's plea to join him in Philadelphia. For the first time Joe would leave behind his mother and sister. The decision to leave New Orleans in December 1846 was fortuitous. The next year brought the worst plague of yellow fever New Orleans had yet known; nearly three thousand fell under Yellow Jack's scythe. Not quarantine of the afflicted, nor burning barrels of tar in the streets and cemeteries about town, nor the endless rounds of cannon fire to purify pestilential air would slow its course. But Joe had left. His fate would not be that of his father's.[5]

What did he take with him to the City of Brotherly Love? Materially, little more than a valise of personal items and a few standard costumes. Less tangibly, he possessed unusually rich memories of a distinctive childhood growing up in circumstances neither genteel nor — a few months excepted — grinding. He could admit to only an indifferent formal education, probably no more than a scattered handful of weeks when his family took temporary root in a town. But if his education was fitful, it was rich both in experience and in the witness of drama's power to move. His age reverenced the spoken word, and command of Shakespeare was a central definition of literacy. Joe also enjoyed the self-assurance of family name. He had known the nurturance of a large family through most of his childhood and youth (which he would continue to draw on through his connection to Burke). He had inchoate talent. And he had increasing command of an experiential tool chest stocked with the implements of his trade. From constant exposure to the ways of the stage, Joe knew almost instinctually how to take the stage, how to cross, how to avoid upstaging the leads or stepping on others' lines, how to project his voice amid the din of the theatre, and countless other tricks of his craft. He also had a sizable repertoire of comic songs and a handful of dance steps that could be recombined in various ways. Joe had every reason to be confident about returning to his ancestral city.

The early winter trip by boat up the Ohio to Wheeling, Virginia, was interrupted by river ice, and the subsequent leg by stagecoach and train was an education in the rigors of overland winter travel. His companions, who huddled near him on the stage and shared a bed in the inns, would have seen a young man of average height, perhaps five feet eight or five feet nine inches, slender build, wide gray eyes that protruded slightly, and a sharp, jutting chin — nothing remarkable in his appearance, nothing to announce greatness. Only when, in the fashion of Canterbury's pilgrims, the passengers began swapping stories and songs did Joe's gift manifest itself.[6]

The Jeffersons had left Philadelphia when Joe was not yet five, and he had not visited there for over a decade. When he arrived, he found a fast-growing city with nearly 400,000 residents crowding its expanding grid system of streets. Accustomed to the slower paces of Mobile and New Orleans, Joe must have wondered at the buzz of commercial and industrial energy centered on Market Street on weekdays, when some 30,000 people headed to work in the central ward. He probably would not have noticed what to modern eyes would have been so striking: the chaotic mixture of residences, artisan shops, small manufacturing enterprises, retail shops, and other businesses. Rich, poor, and middling lived side by side in the assortment of brick row houses and back-alley shanties, or in modest walk-ups above their shops. Lacking parks, playgrounds, or other later public recreational amenities, and having shed Quaker reservations about the stage, Philadelphians were ready to patronize the city's clutch of theatres.[7]

Joe's choice of Philadelphia to launch his adult career was natural, considering his family's roots there and Charlie Burke's connections with the local theatres. Moreover, the city remained a major theatrical center, trailing only New York. On many evenings three or four playhouses competed for the public dollar. The Arch Street and a rejuvenated Walnut Street Theatre captured the elite market. The Chestnut Street — America's Old Drury — continued to suffer through up and down years. It closed and opened spasmodically as management rented the hall to traveling opera companies and a miscellany of concert singers, German-language companies, and minstrels.[8]

Philadelphians enjoyed the return of flush times to the nation in the mid-1840s by patronizing a legion of theatricals. Over the Christmas holidays in 1848 they could choose from three theatres offering standard melodramas and comic afterpieces, an Italian opera, a band and orchestra concert, two minstrel shows, a lecture on phrenology, a voice recital of popular songs, and a diorama. But city folk took their recreation out of doors just as readily. A swaggering male street culture centered on the volunteer fire units, whose parades assumed a magnitude of preparation and execution equaled by few other community endeavors. Horse-drawn engines were polished to a high luster and garlanded with flowers, and firemen with military aplomb marched behind them in their signature red shirts.[9]

Joe took up his duties at the Arch Street Theatre immediately upon arriving, thrust into the cast of *Beauty and the Beast* on an unseasonably warm New Year's Day in 1847. His new company was housed in a theatre with an impressive facade that sported a double-columned portico topped by a balustrade and large classical sculpture in the pediment. Yet the theatre had struggled to attain the respect accorded its rivals on Chestnut and Walnut streets. The cavernous and poorly located Arch Street Theatre had known some bright moments, particularly when the young Edwin Forrest debuted some of his most popular vehicles there, but more often it seemed a financial sink hole for its managers. Only when William E. Burton took a lease in 1844 did the fortunes of the house (and Burton) turn. Burton also understood the increasing importance of a middle class that desired genteel surroundings when they ventured out on the town; thus he cleared out the denizens of the third tier, closed the in-house saloon, and suffered no rowdyism in the audience. He made it Philadelphia's premier theatre in the later 1840s.[10]

Joe Jefferson's new employer, William Evans Burton (1802–60), was one of the American theatre's more colorful figures. A native of England, Burton decamped for the United States in 1834 to escape the shadow of more established stars and — perhaps more to the point — scandal over his recent bigamous marriage. Philadelphia proved congenial to his ambitions as actor, manager, and editor. He established one of the foremost periodicals of the era in 1837, *The Gentleman's Magazine,* with the editorial collaboration of Edgar Allen Poe. Burton's literary accomplishments, like those of his contemporary Joseph Field and the later autobiographical work of Joe Jefferson, compel us to appreciate actors not simply as interpretive artists but, in some cases, as skilled practitioners of the belles lettres. Further, Burton was the first American actor-manager to take up the cause of restoring full productions of Shakespeare's texts. As dramatist, Burton is best remembered for *The Toodles,* his adaptation of a D. W. Jerrold play. In the character of Timothy Toodles, Burton found the signature role of his career. Burton took an apparently conventional stage sot and managed to imbue him with a bumbling pathos. But his repertoire contained other favorites as well. "What will Burton play tonight?" theatergoers regularly asked. The public found his bluff, hearty manner utterly engaging. "I never laughed so much at a representation," diarist Philip Hone noted, "nor ever felt at times so much inclined to cry."[11]

Joe's relationship with Burton was stormy. It would be easy to assign blame to the thorny manager, but one senses that Joe may have contributed to his own difficulties. Without his tough-minded mother nearby for counsel, Joe, still only seventeen, proved sophomoric in matters of career. After only a short time with the Arch Street Company he began bragging about offers from other quarters. Burton, who had an efficient network of informers within his company, called Joe in for interrogation. A "scene" ensued, during which Joe demanded higher pay and Burton denounced Jefferson's ingratitude, threatening a lawsuit should he dare appear elsewhere. Such confrontations are the stuff of theatre, and this one seems unexceptional. But it does provide another hint that the laconic exterior Jefferson normally displayed (and self-promoted later in life) hid a dynamo of ambition underneath.[12]

Whether Joe could have stayed at the Arch Street house if he had wished is not clear; less than a month later he moved to Peale's Philadelphia Theatre, a dime museum a rung or two down the artistic ladder. Finding work elsewhere was not difficult. Joe had a legendary Philadelphia name, and the city's theatres were enjoying their most prosperous season in years. "Young Joe Jefferson, the grandson of the celebrated comedian of days of yore, who possesses in a great measure the rare humor and genius of that unrivaled actor," had come upon the Arch Street stage "with great and prodigious abilities," Charles Durang wrote a few years later. Over the next nine years Jefferson moved among several Philadelphia companies and appeared in all the major theatres. Such mobility was normal. Actors were footloose, always ready for a better part or two dollars more a month. Moreover, they often had no choice but to find another position. Theatres closed and opened with startling frequency, requiring actors to be nimble if they wished to remain employed. Joe moved with the best of them, alternating turns in Philadelphia with his first adult efforts on the New York stage.[13]

The Age of Stock

Joe's entire life had been a preparation for a stage career. He absorbed its language and culture along with the air he breathed. But the explicit study of his craft took place through his apprenticeships with a variety of stock companies: his family's, Ludlow's and Smith's, Burton's Arch Street and other Philadelphia companies, and finally Chanfrau's National in New York. Apprenticeship had long been the single path to an acting career. Stock companies would decline in the late nineteenth century and provoke endless jeremiads over the "decline of the actor's art." Whether or not such laments were warranted, Joe understood himself fortunate to come of age when the system still thrived.[14]

"Stock" was something of a misnomer, for no example survives of a nineteenth-century company where players took shares in lieu of salary (theatrical families came closer to the spirit of stock, since they shared a common risk). Stock companies, rather, should be understood as a collection of actors employed by a manager for a season. Generally, a company would perform at its home theatre for a portion of the year and then take to the road to visit a regular circuit of theatres in smaller cities. But companies varied so much in size and quality that generalizations are tendered only at risk. A first-class company, such as Warren's and Wood's in Philadelphia or the Boston Museum, employed some thirty actors and produced well over a hundred plays in a season. A second-rank company mounted a similar number of productions but often did so with as few as ten or fifteen players. The MacKenzie-Jefferson family troupe experienced tidal swings in its size, having as many as twenty-one in its salad days in the East, contracting to just eight (including two children) when Joe's family headed west in 1838. During a fifty-two-night season in Nashville, the company, then eleven members (eight men, three women), staged an amazing 112 performances of 91 different plays (including the short afterpieces). Many of these plays belonged to the standard repertoire; still, the demands on players to master several scores of roles was enormous. Not surprisingly, prompters stood by ready to provide a dropped line. Nevertheless, early American actors performed feats of memory that later generations, unschooled in the common culture of the spoken word, cannot fathom. Learning five new roles during a single week was not uncommon, and theatre greenrooms posted rules dictating that actors must be ready to play any role at four hours' notice. Neither Jefferson nor his contemporaries in the theatre considered these efforts heroic. No one denied, though, that the six-night-a-week schedule was anything but grueling. "Such labor," complained Edwin Forrest, whose impressive fitness was unexcelled by any actor of his age, "God and the actor only know the fatigues of it."[15]

Therefore, it must have been a relief when longer runs of popular plays began to replace the nightly change of bill in the larger cities by midcentury. Even a week of the same bill (which with only a few exceptions then constituted a "long run") offered a break from the grind of costume changes and script reviews. This also opened the door to more polished performances, rather than the slap-dash staging unavoidable when each night brought a different look. This point should not be overstressed, as a fresh nightly bill remained common. Joe's experience as he bounced among the Arch Street,

Athanaeum, and Philadelphia Museum in the late 1840s is revealing. During the first week of 1847 at the Arch Street he played the Artful Dodger in *Oliver Twist* for two nights, took a minor role in *Dumb Man of Manchester* for the third night, then portrayed Fatham in *Mrs. Coleman's Pope* for the next two. In a four-night stint at the Athanaeum the next year he handled different roles in farces each night. And in a sixteen-night stretch in spring 1849 he attempted ten different parts, usually repeating a role for two nights and in some cases appearing in two different plays during an evening.

The ten and a half years from the beginning of 1847 until early fall of 1857 marked Joe's adult apprenticeship. He spent more time in Philadelphia, but he also had long stretches in New York and even longer periods touring the Atlantic Coast and the Southeast. He had laughably ambitious forays into management and starring. But for the most part he soldiered along in the utility roles that tyros were expected to endure. These years are the hardest of his career to document. Not yet a star nor often even a featured player, his comings and goings were chronicled fitfully in the spotty coverage of theatre by local newspapers. His utility roles frequently failed to merit even a notice in the theatre bill. A Jefferson he may be, but that did not confer a pass to stardom.

A sense of Joe's hopscotch career can be gleaned from an overview of his Philadelphia appearances. Through the first month and a half of 1847 he played at the Arch Street Theatre. In mid-February he followed his brother to Peale's Philadelphia Museum, staying through most of April. He returned to the Arch later that month, where his mother and sister joined him and Charlie that summer as part of the company. After a stint with Burton's company in Baltimore, Joe disappears from Philadelphia theatre notices until early 1848, when he again took the stage at the Arch Street. That summer he returned to Peale's for several nights in July, before another lacuna appears in the records. In December (1848) he made his first appearance at the Athenaeum and National Museum, staying into mid-January. For the balance of the 1848–49 winter season he moved over to the Circus and National Theatre at Ninth and Arch.

Joe returned to Peale's Philadelphia Museum stage in mid-April, staying until the end of May. The embrace of minstrelsy by Peale's management meant Joe's departure. With the uncanny timing he had displayed in leaving New Orleans, Joe managed to avoid the coming fury of Philadelphia's cholera outbreak of 1849 by taking a two-year leave of the city. After an interlude where he made his adult debut in New York and undertook management in the south Atlantic region, Joe — aided as always by Charlie Burke, who was then stage manager — returned to Philadelphia for a short run at the Arch Street in summer 1851. But this proved to be just a respite from his early touring career, for he soon was organizing another tour of the South before joining the Chestnut Street Company two years later.[16]

Joe's early career was defined by the unique demands of the stock system. "Stock parts," so called, reflected the custom of nineteenth-century companies to typecast their members. Companies could do this conveniently since the plays, whether comedies, tragedies, or melodramas, were constructed within tight conventions of casting. The leading men and ladies took the choice parts (except when a star visited); light comedians assumed the romantic or more refined comic roles; juveniles handled the inevitable subplot of young love; heavies shouldered a variety of parts from villains to middle-aged characters of less menacing hues; singing chambermaids (later styled soubrettes) fit a narrower line as saucy and flirtatious young women; walking gentlemen served as key support figures in many scenes, the Rosencrantzes and Gildern-sterns of a play; finally, utility players helped fill out the stage, delivering occasional lines as needed. These "lines of business" were followed with a resoluteness that modern audiences, expecting that actors "look" the part, would find baffling. Like men on a chessboard, Anna Cora Mowatt wryly observed, "each has his appointed place and fights his battle for distinction in a fixed direction." Actors protectively clung to their lines, resenting managers' occasional attempts to cast a play untraditionally as a sort of guild violation.[17]

Joe's line of business—as was his father's, his grandfather's, and his half brother's—was low comedy. No more varied or demanding line existed. It comprised, said one theatre scholar, "the flesh and bones of comedy." Except for some melodrama, most plays had a low comedy part. And even if the feature lacked a plum role, the afterpiece usually provided a vehicle. A clown in the tradition of *Commedia*'s Harlequin, the low comic expressed silliness and pathos, practiced quick witticisms as well as broad pratfalls. Low comics handled some of the beloved roles in Western theatre: Falstaff, Bottom, Tony Lumpkin, and Lord Dundreary. Sober-minded tragedians considered low comics the bane of existence. "Privileged creatures, these low comedians," said Otis Skinner, himself one of the last of the great matinee idols, "spoiling sentimental scenes and ruining tragedy." Garrick so despised the breed that he cut the Gravedigger scene from *Hamlet*. Each new generation added its own gloss on the classic parts. Joe filled many roles known to one or both of the first two Joseph Jeffersons: Dogberry in *Much Ado About Nothing,* Touchstone in *As You Like It,* Bob Acres in *The Rivals,* and many others (including rather improbably, one of Macbeth's witches). Low comics were also, in twentieth-century terms, character actors. Highly stereotyped ethnic roles—German or Irish most often—supplied bread-and-butter parts for many low comedians (also termed "eccentric" comedians) in the later nineteenth century. But it would be the Yankee who most often graced — if such a verb can be applied to so angular a figure — the antebellum stage. Acid-tongued, impatient of all pretentiousness, citadel of good sense, masterful storyteller: the homespun stage Yankee mixed comedy, rural values, and nationalism in a tart blend audiences relished.[18]

John Owens and William Burton were important models for Jefferson, but neither equaled the influence of Charles Burke (1822–54). No other comic figure of the nineteenth-century stage possessed the same potential as he did in the early stages of his career. In his thirty-two years, Burke helped define the tradition of low comedy and burlesque. He was an actor's actor, remembered by his peers decades later as a consummate and emulated comedian. Burke had been trained for the stage from childhood. His precocity encouraged his blended family to push him into the limelight (candlelight, actually) in the worst manner of stage parents, to the point of offending other members of the company. After following the vagabond trails of the Jefferson-MacKenzie company for several years, he married a young actress and set off on his own career, largely in Philadelphia and New York Although Burke never became a star hallowed in the annals of theatre, he developed a singular style of physical comedy well suited to the broad comic pieces of the day. He cut an odd figure. Homely, with a small, round head and pug-nosed face perched atop a cadaverous, long-armed and bandy-legged body that extended over six feet, Burke in another century might have been cast as Dorothy's Scarecrow. His "emaciated" appearance, said chronicler Joseph Ireland, could be made "almost ludicrously grotesque." In the manner of true clowns, Burke could in a twinkling transform his face from buffoonery to pathos. "He had an eye and a face," Jefferson noted admiringly, "that told their meaning before he spoke."[19]

Supplementing Burke's comic frame were gifts of music and dance that surpassed those of his half brother. In burlesque these were ideal. Among his most remembered travesties was his send-up of Ole Bull, a Norwegian concert violinist of great acclaim, for which Burke played the fiddle with considerable skill. His talents were not simply imitative but also creative. In *The People's Lawyer* he made over the character of Solon Shingle into a shrewd old Yankee (which, in the manner of the theatre, John Owens then adopted as one of his primary vehicles). When William Burton, then still in Philadelphia, sought music for his burlesque of a popular ballet, Burke proceeded to improvise a complete score for the orchestra leader.[20]

For all of his comic display, Charles Burke's short life remained a melancholy affair. His first wife died; he contended with lifelong illness, which in his final few years turned into a debilitating, losing battle with tuberculosis (and

The beloved half-brother, Charles Burke. From Joseph Jefferson,
Autobiography (1890).

by one account, alcoholism); and perhaps most dispiriting, the golden ring
of financial success always remained just out of reach. In part, claims stage
chronicler William Winter, the blame falls on William Burton, whose jealousy
kept Burke off the more prominent New York stages, effectively banishing him
to the boards of the Bowery.

If Burke's career was short and underappreciated, to Joe Jefferson he remained a giant. Alone among Joe's immediate family members, "Charlie"
earned an affecting remembrance in the *Autobiography*. Although just seven
years older, Burke "seemed like a father to me," Joe testified. "There was a
deep and strange affection between us." Rooted in blood, the bond was nurtured by a similar gift for comedy. It would carry beyond the grave, for Burke's
rendering of *Rip Van Winkle* became Joe's initial version of the play. More
immediately, he served as Joe's exemplar and patron, dunning managers in
Philadelphia, New York, and others theatrical centers of the East to hire his

talented younger brother. Joe shadowed Charlie throughout the East in the later 1840s and early 1850s, not yet commanding the parts Charlie could but benefiting from the experience and exposure that secondary roles provided. With Charlie's death in 1854 (family legend states he died in his brother's arms), the Jeffersonian torch of low comedy passed to Joe. By then Joe had the experience and contacts to blaze his own trail.[21]

Joe's metier was comedy. But his career occasionally took odd turns, none more so than when Burton decided to stage *Antigone* during Joe's first season at the Arch Street. Greek drama was rarely seen on antebellum stages. Nonetheless, Burton the scholar was determined to give it a credible try, engaging James Wallack for the lead. Jefferson was part of the chorus, an unruly gang of four that during rehearsals irreverently spouted faux Greek quotations to one another. Costumed in togas and crowned with laurel wreaths, the chorus looked properly Theban, but its assigned task of commenting on the stage action left the audience baffled. Chastened, Burton shelved Sophocles for good.[22]

In farce Joe found purer reward and surer preparation for stardom. The antebellum American stage was awash in farce. These one-act comedies were the afterpieces on the nightly bill of most theatres. Despite the disapproval of such British critics as Leigh Hunt (who found in the form's ubiquity an unhappy displacement of classical comedy), the time-honored genre prospered with the growth of the provincial English theatre in the early nineteenth century. It crossed the Atlantic and found an equally enthusiastic audience during the century's middle decades. The forty- to fifty-minute length of most farces required an unrelenting pace. Its stage business was hectic, filled with running on stage and off, eating and drinking, on occasion nearly devolving into slapstick. These were often cheap laughs. Plots almost always built upon misunderstanding, misidentification, and coincidence. Surprise entrances and the clustering of stage figures in unexpected juxtapositions created zany situations resolved through clever contrivance at the play's end. It was pure fantasy — and audiences eagerly embraced its conventions. Farce could not escape — indeed it glorified — sentimental domesticity. If its collection of stock characters were roguish, they nonetheless reinforced the propriety of home and family. Farces frequently used working-class settings: tailors' or printers' shops or humble lodgings, creating the ambience of an antebellum O. Henry tale. Commonplace physical objects, a tablecloth or leg of mutton, often figured prominently in the comedies ("domestic materiality," Michael Booth characterizes it), bespeaking the rising significance of material things in ordinary life.[23]

Jefferson acted in more than a score of these theatrical tarts. Some became staples of his repertoire during the early and middle years of his career, particularly roles in productions of the leading *farceur* of the age, English playwright John Maddison Morton. *My Precious Betsey, The Spitfire, A Regular Fix, Box and Cox* (whose title characters Jefferson and William Burton introduced to America in 1848), and, most especially, *Lend Me Five Shillings* showcased Joe's abundant talent for low comedy. In the last he portrayed Mr. Golightly, a fashionable dandy who finds himself embarrassingly broke during a fancy dinner party after having gambled away his purse. Compounding Golightly's dismay is his inability to impress a young lady by ordering her a drink or hiring a coach. Events continue to deteriorate for Golightly, as he fails to beg or borrow five shillings from either a friend or a waiter; indeed, new debts continue to accrue to him quite accidentally. Golightly's character is the very model of the comic ineptitude that would be so prevalent in Hollywood's screwball comedies: a figure good-hearted but inept, the victim of circumstances who is saved only by fortuity of events. *Lend Me Five Shillings* offered Joe wonderful verbal humor in the form of Golightly's spoonerisms. In a typical manner, he struggles to save face after having a woman close a door in his face: "I flatter myself I know the difference between a shut and a sham. I mean between a slut and a sham. I say between a shut and a slam."[24]

In *My Neighbor's Wife,* a French farce of love and flirtation, Joe plays Timothy Brown, a character who finds delight in his friend's discomfit over the suspected infidelity of his wife. A rococo plot ensues whereby tests of marital fidelity are devised by husbands and wives. Inevitably, characters find themselves hidden away, overhearing conversations that are intended to provoke jealousy. And subplots intertwine, complicating the original one. The madcap results are best compared to early television's *My Little Margie* or *Honeymooners* sketches. And as in those television farces, *My Neighbor's Wife* ends in a ritualistic affirmation of the marriage bond.[25]

The Spectre Bridegroom; or, A Ghost in Spite of Himself, among the most popular farces, may have given Joe a rare opportunity for a blackface role as an adult. Although the written script of Englishman W. T. Moncrieff's 1826 play gives no indication, the dialogue of Dickory (often rendered Diggory), a liveried servant, and his exaggerated fear of the supposed spector strongly suggests a stereotyped black role. "He be coming—he be coming Squire!" Dickory shouts at the appearance of the presumed ghost. The 1850s were the glory years of minstrelsy, and audiences loved the stereotype. In the affected dialogue, the shuffling steps, and the several ditties he sang, Joe reaped dividends of laughter from the role.

Joe's closest brush with Philadelphia theatre history came not in a misbegotten Sophocles production nor in his procession of farces but as part of the Quaker City's first staging of *Uncle Tom's Cabin* in fall 1853. The immediate success of Harriet Beecher Stowe's sentimental novel prompted inevitable dramatizations. Although Stowe's antitheatrical prejudices led her to refuse early requests for permission to stage her story (she later moderated her stance and even attended some productions), the absence of federal copyright protection rendered her objections moot. Within a few months of the book's appearance in spring 1852, the first of several stage versions was mounted. The most popular adaptation by far was that of George L. Aiken, a young Bostonian who prepared the piece for his cousin George Howard, whose company performed in Troy, New York. Its triumph in Troy set the stage for even greater success in New York City's National Theatre, beginning in midsummer 1853. Two months later it arrived in Philadelphia, where in late September it started a two-month stand. Joe finally experienced the satisfaction of a long run.[26]

Aiken's *Uncle Tom's Cabin* showcased the possibilities and limitations of using drama to address controversial issues. Its reach was unparalleled. Far more Americans saw the play than read the book (though that number was impressive too). And the emotional impact of its signature scenes — Eliza's dash across the ice floes or Little Eva's death — surpassed anything Stowe could accomplish by pen. But for the sake of assured patronage, antebellum theatre also demanded loyalty to its cherished melodramatic conventions. Consequently, some of the most forceful dialogue of Stowe's novel was necessarily cut and humorous byplay added for comic relief. Moreover, the dialogue suffers from the common melodramatic tendency to substitute the explanation of an emotion for its display. And as always in melodrama, action drove the plot. Yet within these constraints, Aiken did a remarkable job of preserving Stowe's antislavery message.[27]

Jefferson played Gumption Cute, one of the figures created by Aiken to interject some raillery into the action. (At least five of the characters were essentially comic, including Ophelia, who in Stowe's rendition was a zealous antislavery New England spinster.) On one level Cute was a comic Yankee figure quite familiar to audiences. But Aiken shaped him into a type particular to that age, the confidence man. Cute makes a career of "speculating." He sought his fortune through a school for the "instruction of youth in the various branches of orthography, geography, and other graphies," then went into "Spiritual Rappings" (modern spiritism had begun only five years previously) until his faulty readings exposed him as a "pesky humbug." Cute behaved true to his character during the action of the play, seeking to win the hand (and means) of Ophelia and suggesting to Topsy (then living in the North) that he publicly display her as the "woolly gal," just as Barnum did the woolly horse. When those proposals failed, Cute considered heading to Latin America as a "fillibusterow," before agreeing — in the penultimate scene of the play — to accompany Marks in blackmailing Legree. Cute is partially redeemed from this litany of misdeeds by his single refusal to engage in slave catching, albeit for reasons of personal safety rather than principle. The comic treatment and the resonance with audiences of these contemporary issues and personalities — spiritism, filibustering, fugitive slave captures, and P. T. Barnum — made more digestible the antislavery message of *Uncle Tom's Cabin.* And in Gumption Cute, Jefferson found a role that anticipated the lovable ne'er-do-well Rip Van Winkle.[28]

Oddly, Jefferson makes no mention in his *Autobiography* of his part in the nation's favorite drama. Like the dog that did not bark, this oversight demands explanation. It strains belief that he simply forgot his part in what was his longest run up that point in his career. Did he deem his role insignificant or unsatisfactory? Hardly. More likely he found his involvement uncomfortable and embarrassing: uncomfortable in that the drama raised the vexing issue of race and slavery, social topics that Jefferson strenuously avoided in his public life; embarrassing, perhaps, by associating him with what by the late 1880s had become lowbrow sensational melodramas, the Tom Shows that continued to attract large audiences with their maudlin, clichéd, and even racist scenes. The play, if incredibly popular, became something of a national joke (capped, surely, by Oscar Wilde's wicked aside that no one could witness the death scene of Little Eva without suppressing the urge to laugh). Joe's productions of *Rip* in the same decades threatened to take on a similarly hackneyed aura. But he continued to play in first-class theatres and thus may have wished to avoid any identification with his poorer theatrical cousins. Indicting Jefferson for artistic snobbery in this matter may be unfair. Joe's lack of pretense and ability to laugh at himself remain among his most endearing traits. Still, for him to pass over such an important association in his theatrical career suggests a repression of memory — conscious or otherwise — that remains intriguing.[29]

Mounting Gotham's Stage

With Philadelphia as a base, Jefferson ventured both north and south for a decade. South meant Baltimore, nearly a second home in the mid-1850s. Beyond Baltimore lay the Atlantic seaboard territory and inland Georgia, hungry for the muse. To the north was New York City, then well established as the nation's theatrical capital. Joe realized, no doubt, that progress in the profession required a presence there. In late summer 1849, now age twenty and with brother Charlie again running interference, Joe made his first adult foray to Gotham.

During the dozen years since his visit as an eight-year-old, New York City had weathered a prolonged recession, followed by an economic expansion that was changing the face of the city. Its wealth lay with the cluttered docks along the East River, where half the nation's imports were unloaded. A few days after Joe began his run at the National Theatre, the *Empire,* laden with California gold dust and coin, entered the harbor, further fueling an already overheated gold rush. The city — approaching 600,000 — exuded a throbbing, palpable energy. "Superb-faced Manhattan!" Whitman rhapsodized. But if New York was a grand stage, its plot occasionally held tragedy. The city suffered its worst cholera outbreak the summer that Joe arrived, recording more than 5,000 deaths between May and August. Bodies lay uncollected in the gutters at the plague's height. Yet again, good fortune smiled on Joe. By 6 September, shortly before his debut on the National's stage, the epidemic had "so far fallen off," reported diarist George Templeton Strong, "that the Board of Health [is] to make no more reports."[30]

When in his spare moments Joe strolled up Broadway from City Hall, he would have experienced the full-throated energies of America's metropolis. The older theatre district in the lower reaches of Manhattan still housed the Chatham Theatre, Burton's Chambers Street Theatre, and others, though the venerable Park had been lost to fire in 1848. But the changing neighborhoods around lower Broadway brought new immigrant and working-class clienteles who inevitably changed the bill those theatres must present if they were to survive. Walking north toward Canal Street, Joe would pass the city's prime shopping district. Although losing its status as the residential address of choice, this stretch of Broadway remained in favor for promenading. The vital nature of New York public life was apparent everywhere. Oyster bars "that you could tumble into at every corner," catered to midcentury Gothamites insatiable appetite. On the bricked streets congested with horse-drawn conveyances, omnibus drivers packed in as many riders as conscience allowed. Pigs, goats, and dogs still roamed freely as the most efficient disposers of refuse. ("Republican pigs," Dickens called them, going where they wished and mingling with the public as equals.) For all of the disorder, however, New York streets were less cluttered than usual, since the summer's cholera plague had finally roused civic authorities to attempt a general cleanup.

Joe would probably have been impressed by the procession of hotels lining Broadway, though the ubiquitous and more economical boarding houses would be his likelier choice. Beyond Canal, Joe would notice the concentration of theatres devoted to minstrel shows. Minstrelsy hit its stride in the 1850s and remained urban America's signature amusement throughout the decade. Bustling Union Square at Fourteenth Street marked the midcentury terminus of tony residential development. New York's burgeoning class of comfortable burghers "had fled by dignified degrees up Broadway" to more sedate and spacious environs. Here Joe might have paused to appreciate the artistry of the plaster molders at work on a Greek Revival structure, sporting their characteristic folded newspaper caps as they perched on scaffolding.[31]

The city's theatrical panorama was spectacular in number and variety. At midcentury New Yorkers, pockets filled with coins from the flush times of the 1850s, could select a different theatrical every night of the week. This rich theatre culture, reflected in the *Herald*'s extensive coverage of entertainments, may have been nurtured by the boardinghouse life of so many city dwellers. Lacking the ties of a home, many New York residents were ready for night life. They could choose, of course, from an assortment of dramas and minstrel shows — and not only in English, for the German National Theatre had taken over Mitchell's Olympic. One could take drama with a dash of education and moralism at Barnum's American Museum, located at the busiest intersection in the city. More salacious tastes would gravitate to the Walhalla or Franklin theatres, the latter featuring a female minstrel company billed as "the Original Arab Girls." There were spectacles, such as the panorama of the Hungarian wars at the Bowery Ampitheater, boasting 80,000 hand-painted figures. And circus and menageries shows, such as "The Revolt of the Harem," at White's Melodeon, promising Arabs, Tartars, Circassians, camels, and horses. On a more sedate level, one could attend any number of concerts. Elevated tastes enjoyed the New York Philharmonic, founded the previous decade, or grand opera, then becoming a signifier of status. A procession of vocal and instrumental concerts by foreign musicians were presented (tempered occasionally by native voices, such as the singing family Hutchinsons).[32]

One might imagine that this grand spectacle of New York street life was compelling to Jefferson, but in truth, we have no idea of Joe's reaction to New York, for in his writings he records neither exhilaration nor disgust with the urban scene. The city as artifact did not register with him; its landscape never captured his imagination. Given his descriptive and narrative powers as writer and the flaneur literature of New York then in such abundance, it is odd that Gotham's vivid human scene so little impressed him. Such apathy seems best explained in reference to his essentially romantic temperament. A child of Philadelphia, whose life was passed amidst the intrinsic urbanism of the theatre, he nonetheless felt at home only in the calm of a pastoral setting. A penchant for quiet, rural environs informed all his art. In his painting he chose the muted landscapes of the French Barbizon school, and on stage he eschewed the clamorous brew of Boucicault's *The Poor of New York* for the rustic provincialism of the Hudson River Valley in *Rip Van Winkle*.

Despite these preferences, in 1849 Jefferson found himself in the very heart of catcalling, masculine urbanism: Frank Chanfrau's company at the New National Theatre, a smallish house parked in the rough and tumble environs of Chatham Street. Chanfrau (1824–84), appropriately born on the Bowery, had apprenticed as canal driver, carpenter, and fireman before beginning his slow rise to stage stardom. His firefighting experience was particularly significant, as it introduced him into the close-knit and sometimes violent world of the volunteer firefighters. During breaks at Mitchell's Theatre, Chanfrau regaled company members with improvisations of the fire b'hoys' swaggering walk and slang. Inspired by this bit of urban Americana, Benjamin Baker sketched *A Glance at New York* as a vehicle for Chanfrau. A theatre phenomenon had been born: Mose the Bowery b'hoy became an urban legend overnight and Chanfrau a star. A series of Mose plays ensued, starring the energetic Mose, who in his plug hat, soaplocks, red shirt, and cuffed trousers embodied the aggressive posturing of democratic male urban culture, a perfect counterpart to Mike Fink and the Southwest river braggert tradition. Despite his urban bluff, Mose's independence, simple tastes, honesty, and loyalty has been seen by some scholars as an affirmation of rural values that some feared the city had destroyed. The Mose craze continued for several years. In the derivative manner of theatre it evoked countless imitations and permutations (e.g., *Mose in China*). Chanfrau was content to serve as manager of the National during most of Joe's time there. But in February Joe got a firsthand look at the Mose mania when Chanfrau reprised his celebrated role in *Mysteries and Miseries of New York*. Joe understood how to work an audience through comedy, but what were his impressions of the "crowding, clamor, squeezing, pushing, clapping, shooting, hurraing [*sic*]" of the audience prompted by Mose's belligerent antics?[33]

The blustering, bullying ways of a Mose bespoke all too aptly an urban population quick to take offense at real or imagined slights. The forthcoming Civil War was foreshadowed in the frequent battles fought on northern city streets. Antebellum civic culture exulted in confrontation. A jealous badge of honor was worn not only by Cavalier but by Yankee males as well. Riots plagued antebellum American cities, often spurred by serious political issues like abolitionism or bank policy but sometimes tripped by delicate issues of class or national pride. In theatres, wounded pride occasionally spilled over into fury. Joe was fortunate to have missed the worst theatre riot America had known, which occurred the previous May outside the Astor Place Theatre.[34]

The Astor Place riot originated in a feud between reigning stars of the British and American stages, William Charles Macready and Edwin Forrest. Vulnerable American egos were quick to detect condescension or disrespect from visiting English players or managers. Even the eminent Edmund Kean was not immune from the long-memoried wrath of Boston mobs when he once declined to perform before a small audience. Such national pride sparked the Astor Place outburst, but class resentment provided the sustaining fuel. The new Astor Place Opera House, situated in the upscale environs of Broadway, with a dress code that made white kid gloves de rigueur and featuring an objectionable Englishman, was an affront to the boys of the Bowery. Premonitions of trouble were realized on 10 May with a full-blown riot that left twenty-three dead.[35]

In the twenty-five or so incidents in and around theatres during the fifteen years before 1850 the Astor Place riot was by far the worst. Perhaps chastened by the human and property cost of the Astor Place riot, the nonchalant acceptance of unruly audiences came to an abrupt halt. Police, rather than in-house security, were now stationed in theatres on a common basis. Further, the angry voice of the theatre mob lost its legitimacy within the theatre and without. In the coming years theatre etiquette slowly stilled the boisterous assertions of its viewers. This civilizing process was aided by a new sorting of audiences, which led working-class clientele to vaudeville and burlesque houses, leaving behind a tamer middle-class patronage in legitimate theatres. The courts also handed managers new legal tools for controlling audiences with a series of rulings beginning in the 1850s stating that patrons had no right to disrupt a performance and may be properly expelled. By 1870 an experienced theatergoer, now accustomed to decorous surroundings, might struggle to recall the bedlam sometimes known in earlier days.[36]

The Astor Place riot (the trial of whose accused leaders dominated the front page of the *Herald*) apparently did not deter Joe in his decision to attempt the New York stage. After all, he had connections. With Charlie as stage manager, Joe was, by his own admission, "put forward more rapidly than my merits deserved." But his talents quickly excused the nepotism. Premiering 10 September in the forgettable role of Jack Rockbottle in the unmemorable *Jonathan Bradford,* Joe won favorable notice for his performance and also for his resemblance to Charlie "in figure, face, [and] gait." Surrounded by a highly competent company, Jefferson could further tune his comic skills, and playing second comedian to his brother reduced the pressure of audience expectations. Joe could not have guessed, supporting Charlie in his new version of *Rip Van Winkle* that January, how important another version of the romance would be to him fifteen years later. This was but one of fifty-eight separate roles he attempted in little over a year. Normally these passed with little critical attention, but by spring 1850 Joe succeeded in drawing the attention of the *Herald* critic, who announced (somewhat prematurely) that he "stands already at the head of comic actors." Jefferson simply needed, the writer perceptively noted, "good pieces to draw out his peculiar talents." What actor ever felt differently?[37]

Marriage

Joe arrived at Chanfrau's New National Theatre in September 1849 determined to seek out more than stage success. He was, he later claimed, an "old young man, and looking upon life perhaps more seriously than one should at my age, I bethought me that it was time to marry and settle down." This businesslike approach to matrimony was not so odd for that age. Joe could now reasonably expect at least modest career success, an essential criterion for considering marriage. In keeping with his customary reticence, Joe never breathes the name of his betrothed in his *Autobiography*. But other sources identify her as Margaret Lockyer, born in Somersetshire, who had immigrated to America as a child with her parents. She had just turned seventeen when Joe encountered her in Chanfrau's production of *The Poor Soldier*. She was a tyro, having first stepped on the boards two years earlier in Troy, New York. We have no idea what "Maggie" looked like and know little of her talent. But she apparently danced creditably enough for Charlie Burke to hire her in supporting roles, and she was attractive enough to encourage the eager Jefferson to pursue her. This he did so diligently that by the following May they were set to marry.[38]

Their spring nuptials were but one of several among company players that year. "The National must have been a rich field for Hymen," stage chronicler George C. D. Odell quipped. In truth, there was nothing terribly unusual about such developments. Actors generally looked to fellow players for prospective mates. No one outside the thespian circle could fully understand or share the uniqueness of their life. And many of the "respectable" classes would not have allowed their daughter to wed an actor. Oddly, Charles Burke tried to thwart the union, thinking Joe too young (he was twenty-one, Margaret still only seventeen). Jefferson attributed it — probably jocularly, since Charlie was recently remarried — to his brother's jealousy. They quarreled, but Joe would not be deterred. He took no chances with the wedding, however. Margaret had insisted on a church ceremony, but Joe, knowing the company members' fondness for practical jokes (a "passion for quizzing which seems to be so deeply planted in the histrionic breast"), determined to foil them. Decked out in a new lavender wedding suit, Joe and his bride plighted their troth on 19 May 1850 (a Sunday, their only day off work), at a nearly empty Oliver Street church. Joe had deviously sent his friends to the wrong church.[39]

The joy of marriage must have been enhanced by a Jefferson family reunion of sorts at the National Theatre that spring: Charlie, his wife, Joe, Margaret, and Joe's sister Connie acted together briefly. Joe's benefit in late May drew a handsome house, made more gratifying by Connie's much-applauded interpretation of "Little Pickle" in *The Spoiled Child*. Although the modestly talented Mrs. Jefferson ("More fire, more fire, Margaret," Charlie would implore from the wings) continued to act, she almost immediately became pregnant. During the span from March 1851 to September 1856 four children would be born. Of the marriage itself we know nothing beyond the procession of children and Margaret's apparent willingness to continue acting well into her pregnancies. One senses a subordination in Margaret quite different from Joe's assertive, hard-driving mother. Margaret seemed amenable to Joe's peripatetic inclinations, willing to follow along or stay behind as situations dictated.[40]

Other events during that busy spring of 1850 reveal the politics of acting. Players, especially those near the top of their game, were ever alert to potential competition. The choice roles went to the first comedian of a company. When Charlie Burke left the company in March to tour the South, Joe moved up a notch. But Barney Williams, the leading Irish stage comedian remained with the company to share the comic leads. Fortunately, he and Jefferson got on well, giving the National a potent one-two punch. "Comic talent reigns now predominant at the National," the *Herald* exclaimed. Burke returned in May to find Chanfrau departed from management and Barney Williams enjoying a great following; thus he decided to leave for the less competitive stage of the Astor Place. Conversely, when Williams withdrew from Chatham Street, Charlie returned, now secure as the house's first comedian and allied with brother Joe in "a constellation of comic genius."[41]

The National's fall season of 1850 blended imperceptibly into its previous summer run. New Yorkers' voracious appetite for entertainments continued even through the summer's heat. In September, the traditional beginning of the fall season, the ominous rumble of sectional strife gave pause to the prosperous pursuit of amusement. The House of Representatives had approved a new fugitive slave bill, which promised to reawaken abolitionist activity. Nor was all theatrical news happy. The *Herald* trumpeted on its front page the newest developments in the notorious divorce of Edwin Forrest and his wife Catherine. America's premier tragedian now suffered the humiliation of arrest and court injunction against any contact with his wife. For New Yorkers, both of those events were overshadowed by the first appearance of Jenny Lind in their city on 11 September. Beyond the crowds, the scramble for tickets, the reaching for adjectives to characterize the Swedish Nightingale, her appearance signified a peculiarly democratic moment for America. It was not the aristocracy filling the seats at Castle Garden, James Gordon Bennett boasted, but the "mechanics and the storekeepers with their wives and daughters. . . . Here the majesty of the people were present."[42]

The nation breathed a collective sigh of relief when the Compromise of

1850 momentarily resolved the disunionist scare. Americans could now return to the business of filling a continent. Joe shared the restlessness afflicting so many Americans. He had been, with a short break in July to join Burke and Chanfrau, across the East River at the Brooklyn Museum, performing at the National nearly continuously from September 1849 to early November of 1850. It had been a grueling if remunerative fourteen months. Actors normally took at least some summer vacation during the traditionally slow theatre period, and the unremitting pace of performance must have been exhausting for Joe. The fatigue of unending work may have affected his normally cautious judgment. Or perhaps it was his vaunting ambition — a personal form of Manifest Destiny. Whatever the cause, in a fit of pique, Joe resigned his job at the National in early November, offended that the name of journeyman player Harry Watkins appeared in larger letters than his. Joe informed the manager of his billing error — to no avail — and then quit. "You are a good fellow, Joe," Watkins generously confided to his diary, "but you are too jealous for your own good."[43]

New York had been good to Joe, and he would return for brief seasons in 1851 and 1852 (he returned to Philadelphia several times as well). For the moment, though, he sought a more independent course — free from Gotham's theatre hierarchies and controlling managers. Full of the dreams and the energies of youth, Joe took his young (and expectant) bride on the road. For the next half decade Jefferson pursued other prizes in the theatrical provinces of the southern Atlantic seaboard.

Echoing the Public Voice

"There is nothing a young actor enjoys more than itinerant theatricals," Joseph Jefferson proclaimed from the safe distance of stardom. "It is so grand to break loose from a big tyrant manager in the city and become a small tyrant manager in the country." With his good-natured hyperbole Joe described himself in his *Autobiography* as a "juvenile theatrical anarchist" stirring up trouble in the greenroom and egging on compatriots to join him on the road. "Let's all be equal, and I'll be king!" His revolutionary credentials are doubtful, yet it is true that for Jefferson, now that he had accrued some capital during recent seasons in Philadelphia and New York, the temptation to form a troupe and hit the hustings during the summer was great.

In 1848 Joe and John Ellsler, a friend from the Arch Street Theatre, had created a circuit of Pennsylvania towns. Soon after, Jefferson teamed up with John Sefton to tour small towns in mid-Atlantic states (their itinerary now largely lost to history). With a budget so small that players had to post their own bills, the company brought earnestness if not sophistication to its small-town patrons.[1]

In the early and middle 1850s Joe's ambitions extended further, and he devoted several of the traditional fall and winter theatrical seasons to the lush pastures of the American South, which shared in the American prosperity of the 1850s. Unexpected developments forced him more deeply into management than he had planned. Still, he had the opportunity to tackle leading roles not entrusted to him in the theatrical centers. Joe must have been drawn to itinerancy by the memories of his youth. The loving detail in which he recounted his childhood of touring in his *Autobiography* suggests an indelible imprinting. The road was in his blood.[2]

His southern travels of the 1850s rotated about two axes. Early in the decade he performed in the coastal towns of Wilmington, Charleston, and Savannah, with inland forays to such smaller centers as Macon, Augusta, and Columbia. Beginning in 1854 he moved a bit north, to the port city of Baltimore, with frequent trips to Washington and Richmond. Throughout these years he often returned, sometimes for extended stretches, to northern theatrical centers, including one trip to Boston. His sojourn in the southern states never meant he had abandoned the hope of one day starring on America's leading stages.

Trouping through Dixie

Jefferson's initial sally into the South came as part of a company headed up by Charles Kemble Mason that played the coastal cities of Savannah, Charleston, and Wilmington. Traveling from New York on the packet *Sullivan*, many of the company landlubbers retired below deck to cope with unsteady legs and stomachs. But not Joe, who, professing saltwater experience, claimed that provisions of cigars and brandy would make the week's journey endurable. After arriving safely, the troupe performed a week in Savannah in early January 1851 before boarding a coastal steamer to head the few leagues north to Charleston for a longer run that lasted until 5 March. This was a well-staffed company of fifteen men and nine women (including Margaret Jefferson) capable of mounting a wide spectrum of theatricals: classic tragedies and comedies of Shakespeare and Sheridan; the comparatively adept melodramas of Knowles and Bulwer-Lytton; more formulaic melodramas; and of course a large array of comic afterpieces. The variety appeared to please Charlestonians, who handsomely patronized what the *Courier* described as "the best [theatricals] we have had for many years."[3]

What started as a routine tour ended abruptly in early March with a serious contretemps between players and management. The issues remain in doubt, each side having its own story. By account of theatre manager H. S. Smith (advantaged by his ability to air his side in the newspaper), the actors had committed serious breaches of decorum. In a tone of injured righteousness Smith alluded to a "prevailing jealousy among Actors," their desire to "control the house," and in particular the efforts of a few "to defeat the objects of the

Managers." Was Jefferson part of the insurgency? Perhaps a ringleader? If one takes seriously his autobiographical statement, he might be counted among the "troublers of Israel." Certainly Joe's increasing confidence based on his successes in New York, his pride in a first-rate theatrical pedigree, and a youthful willfulness (masked in later life by his geniality) suggests that he could have been at the heart of the fracas. But John Ellsler gives a different and more credible spin. By his account, management intended to interrupt the season with performances by a visiting opera company. Worse, the enforced furlough was unremunerated. The actors cried foul, pointing to their contract. Unsurprisingly, Ellsler confirms that he and Jefferson were spokesmen for the disgruntled troupe. To no avail. Smith played hardball with the recalcitrants, refusing to "submit to dictates" of the players. Instead, the theatre closed its doors until the opera company arrived.[4]

Thus checkmated, the unhappy company was forced into the time-honored expedient of troupers cast adrift: they formed their own company. Styled self-importantly as the New York Dramatic Company, it was in fact a collection of adventurers setting off on a wing and a prayer. Through talent and grit they survived—and at times even thrived. Reading the recollections of Jefferson and Ellsler, moreover, one is convinced that they also had fun. Led by Jefferson, Ellsler, and journeyman player William Deering, the company fashioned an ambitious circuit through Georgia and North and South Carolina over the next eight months. Despite the spat, manager Smith was willing to pay off the company by letting them use the theatre to prepare new scenery for their tour. In a furious two-week effort, company members pitched in to plan their circuit, sew costumes, fashion scenery (which Joe painted), and rehearse.[5]

John Ellsler (1822–1903), with whom Jefferson teamed up again in the following fall for a second southern tour, was a player of no special distinction. Early in his career he found his metier in portraying old men (a melodramatic type in strong demand). Thin and hawk-nosed, Ellsler was modest about his own career and generous toward others. He had formed a fast and lasting friendship with Jefferson in Philadelphia, changing theatres to act with him. Their admiration for one another proved the exception to the rule of theatrical partnerships based on convenience rather than comradeship. Being in different lines of business, they did not compete for roles (indeed, Ellsler is credited with teaching Joe the Dutch dialect that served him so famously later). Likewise, they carefully demarcated their respective duties: Ellsler negotiated business matters while Joe oversaw performances. Ellsler recalled Jefferson's disregard for finances, even affecting a sort of careless improvidence. Regardless, Ellsler effused warmth for Joe in his memoirs. "If there is such a thing as one man loving another, Joe Jefferson was a man that might be so loved."[6]

The company headed first to Macon, Georgia, a town of only a few thousand. Considering the town's modest size, the company's four-week engagement was impressive. National politics may have aided their efforts. In the aftermath of the contentious debates over slavery in 1850, a Constitutional Union Party formed. Its state organizational meeting in Macon doubtless brought men to town who by evening were anxious for diversion. "Encouraged by the liberal patronage," as the Macon paper phrased it, Jefferson and Ellsler sought to make the hall friendlier to spectators, particularly by banking the seats of the flat-floored concert hall. They witnessed an ambitious card, including *Othello, Richard III,* and *Macbeth*, complete with visiting stars (though admittedly of the second rank). Provincial as the audiences may have been, they were not incapable of astute dramatic criticism. R. E. Graham, a tragedian with pretensions to stardom, was scored for deficiencies of voice in his role as Othello. "He did not meet the expectations of the audience, the paper tersely reported."[7]

The turn in Macon proved memorable to Joe for personal reasons: the birth of his first child. Joe testified to the affection and influence of his half brother by christening the son Charles Burke Jefferson. When the company pushed on to Savannah in April, Margaret and child stayed behind for a short time in Macon. She soon rejoined the troupe and took up again the minor roles to which she was accustomed.[8]

Buoyed by a nine-hundred-dollar profit, the New York Dramatic Company headed to coastal Savannah via the Central of Georgia Railroad, a railroad that unlike most southern lines was run on a schedule "punctual to a second." Savannah, Georgia's beautiful founding settlement, was dotted by green public squares and tasteful private residences. The town thrived as a cotton entrepôt. The company had high expectations for the stand and leased the Savannah Theatre indefinitely. It proved otherwise. Their lineup of standard hits failed to tempt Savannah audiences. Company coffers emptied. Reflecting on the occasion many years later, Joe was struck by how he and his group would suggest any cause for the failure but themselves. "The mortification of a personal and public slight is so hard to bear that he [the actor] casts about for any excuse rather than lay the blame upon himself."[9]

But in theatrical touring, as in baseball, ill luck might turn when least expected and sometimes from the least likely place. For Ellsler and Jefferson it came in the form of an English baronet-turned-actor, William Don (1826–62), who happened to be "between engagements" in Charleston at this opportune moment. Don bestrode the American stage as a caricatured cross between a true British performing star and the sort of aristocrat Americans seemed unable to resist. He first appeared in New York in 1850 to mixed reviews. He then traveled the country, utilizing his formidable physical presence (six feet six inches), an imposing patrician demeanor, and impressive letters of introduction to enter fine society wherever he stopped. Don was an eccentric and a spendthrift, and gambling and high living kept him in perpetual debt despite resources from England. When Jefferson and Ellsler asked him to join them in April 1851, he readily accepted (although he was unable to join them until they advanced him funds to pay his Charleston hotel bill).[10]

Jefferson and Ellsler banked on Don's aristocratic appeal to bring out the genteel, Anglophilic Savannah residents, and they bet correctly. "One of the largest audiences which we have ever seen in our theatre" came out for the debut of "Sir William Don," marveled the *Savannah Morning News*. A light comedian (meaning he assumed roles of high social rank or with a romantic interest), Don was featured in both farces and longer comedies, such as *Beauty and the Beast*. With his arrival the finances of the New York Dramatic Company took an immediate turn for the better. William Don's presence conferred benefits beyond the curtain and the box office. A bon vivant, Don invigorated the company with his endless stories, mimes, and late suppers, where he insistently treated the company. Jefferson, clearly taken by his "animal spirits," devoted several pages of his *Autobiography* to a character he liked yet never fully trusted. Having saved Savannah for the company, Don was coveted by the two managers for later dates in Wilmington.[11]

The company journeyed next to Columbia, South Carolina. The state capital for sixty years, the town nonetheless retained a rustic manner, which carried over into its theatre culture. The college men, in particular, enjoyed a boisterous time at the theatre. A concerned Ellsler asked if extra constables might be assigned the house. No need to worry, replied a town official, no respectable lady will be present anyway. When the managers were further informed to expect smoking in the audience, they had enough. The night of the performance signs were prominently displayed forbidding smoking, explaining that smoking "impairs the insurance" as well as the performance. College students being what they were, the admonition was ignored as the play began. Jefferson was forced into a hectoring stage lecture, with modest results. Calm came only when the comedy earned the scholars' attention.

From Columbia, the company headed to Wilmington, North Carolina, a thriving port near the mouth of the Cape Fear River. The town's theatre stood forlorn on a sand hill, sturdily bricked but in a sad state of dilapidation: broken windows and doors, precious little scenery. Yet Wilmington audiences more than compensated. Relatively sophisticated in matters of drama (at least Ellsler and Jefferson so chose to believe), they turned out in gratifying numbers mindless of the surroundings. Oddly, though, when Sir William Don starred with the company he failed to excite the admiration he had in Savannah. Lacking the genteel pretensions of Savannah, Wilmington residents judged drama with a different eye.[12]

Evaluating the overall success of the New York Dramatic Company in its few months of life is difficult. Financially, things were up and down. Artistically, we can form an opinion only from a few generally favorable newspaper notices and from (brief) recollections of Jefferson or Ellsler. But the tour fulfilled other more visceral needs of the strolling players: a desire to perform and a camaraderie that few occupations provided — so testify the abundant actor memoirs from the century.

At least one hopes that the esprit de corps provided sufficient reward, because other aspects of the tour must have been acutely unpleasant. The litany of difficulties encountered by Jefferson's troupe — economic uncertainty, unfriendly authorities, suspicious inn keepers, rowdy audiences — reveal a profession standing always at the margins of society. In the constant struggle with solvency actors were not so different from most sectors of society in the boom-and-bust nineteenth century, but in the other regards they stood apart. Actors would retain an aura of cultural suspicion through the entire century and beyond. Certain theatrical practices fed this situation. Actors' clannishness, for example (difficult to avoid given the nature of their life), nurtured outside suspicions. This was doubly true in a democratic society that valued openness. The custom of the benefit performance carried another price. Although a necessary supplement to salaries, it suggested that actors needed to prostrate themselves before the public. Players advertised their benefit, entreating the public to support them as if they were charity cases. Such practices did not engender either professional self-esteem or public respect.[13]

Nor did the rambunctious and frequently boorish behavior of audiences suggest their high regard for players. Audiences treated the theatre as an extension of the street, carrying its informality into the temple of the muse. Hats often stayed on men's heads. Players had to project their lines over not only a buzz of conversation but also the crunching of peanut shells and the rustle of patrons arriving late or moving about the hall. In a southern theatre a visitor heard a "pattering shower" of tobacco hit the floor during a pause in an impassioned address as excited patrons chewed their quid. Most notably, patrons felt at liberty to respond to the drama in any way they chose, frequently by voice. A German visitor was struck by the ongoing and unabashed stage whisper commentary on *Othello* from the boxes when he attended Forrest's production at the Park Theatre. Audience displeasure was voiced firmly and immediately. By midcentury managers often sought to tame the audience beast by domesticating theatre interiors: carpeting floors, upholstering chairs, and renaming the pit (the traditional home of the rowdies) "the parquette," increasing the prices of these seats and banishing the former pittite element to the gallery. If stars became sufficiently annoyed — and if they were sufficiently bold — they took on unruly audience members directly. Junius Brutus Booth once had his dramatic moment interrupted by a drunk in the gallery. Casting his ferocious gaze upward he repeated a pertinent line from his play: "Beware, I am the headsman, I am the executioner," a line that at least momentarily quieted the lout. Charlotte Cushman, who took a backseat to no one in her powers of intimidation, suffered the indignity of a catcall thinly veiled as a sneeze during a tender moment of *Romeo and Juliet*. Tittering in the audience ruined the moment. Cushman (who characteristically took the breeches roles of Romeo) gallantly took her Juliet backstage, then proceeded to march before the audience to seek out the culprit and demand his removal, threatening that if no one else took action, she would. The audience cheered her bravado and ejected the yahoo.[14]

The marvel is that actors so routinely carried on their duties seemingly oblivious to the barely contained pandemonium before them. Indeed, on occasion they seemed to encourage it. At the Bowery (not surprisingly) actors frequently played to the pit, trading confiding remarks: "Isn't that so, boys?" or "Don't you, boys?" Audiences seldom needed prompting to respond to the stage action. They felt licensed to do so — as actors well understood — because of a bond of cultural understanding that joined them. Allardyce Nicoll speaks of a family atmosphere that once surrounded theatre. A performance might occasion a love feast or provoke a squabble, but either bespoke ties of affection.

Here lies the great paradox of theatre. Actors, as abstracted social types represented rootlessness, marginality, threat. Yet as beings experienced in the theatre, they invited intimacy. The stock company system, in which a set of players reappeared nightly, offered local audiences a chance to establish a comfortable familiarity, to learn the endearing or off-putting quirks of players in their roles. Even as a traveling company moved on after only two weeks, a temporary sense of community had been established, a communication that always ran two ways. There was little of the sanctimony of "art" about theatre performance. If some stars indulged self-importance as creative artists, their efforts nonetheless tended to evoke from audiences exuberance and involvement rather than deferential respect. The stage, as Samuel Johnson phrased so memorably for David Garrick, "echoes back the Publick Voice." And the public echoed the stage. Theatre was an emotionally charged event, and actors would probably not have had it any other way.[15]

An Expanded Repertoire

As unpredictable and financially checkered as the early 1851 season proved to be, it still offered Joe an important new showcase for his talents. The tour introduced some roles of great importance. In Charleston he portrayed Bob Acres in Sheridan's *The Rivals,* which after Rip Van Winkle would later become his most acclaimed personation. And in his initial Savannah appearance Joe debuted his Dr. Ollapod in George Colman's *The Poor Gentleman.* Ollapod and Dr. Pangloss, from Colman's other enduring comedy, *The Heir at Law,* which Joe undertook during a turn at Philadelphia's Chestnut Street Theatre in 1852, became much-loved roles in following years. Colman's sentimental comedies, though not distinguished parts of the English dramatic canon, nonetheless had remarkable staying power. Conventional in their assemblage of stock characters and situations, they reflected the growing emphasis on domesticity.[16]

Dr. Pangloss in *The Heir at Law* provided Jefferson with one of his most enduring roles, and one he counted among his personal favorites. Pangloss, a pedantic tutor whose mercenary streak runs deep, provides the comic glue to a set of interlocking plots. *The Heir at Law* (1797) presents a social world gone askew: an heir to a peerage feared dead; his love brought to penury through family misfortune; a noble yeoman displaced from their land; and conversely, a tallow chandler and his linen-starcher wife who are temporarily elevated to a peerage. This is comedy in the classical meaning of the term. Incongruity and anxiety drive the comic action until, in the nature of the genre, the social world is put right again through such contrivances of plot as the winning of the lottery by the sturdy Zekial Homespun (a sort of John Bull Yankee farmer) and the baron's rightful heir surviving a shipwreck.

Colman created Pangloss as caustic satire on those pedestrian and self-serving tutors who peopled the social landscape. Dr. Pangloss, L.L.D., A.S.S., had been a favorite comic role for leading players since his inception. William Burton, John Brougham, William Warren, John E. Owens, and John Sleeper Clarke — all except the latter being slighter older contemporaries of Jefferson — followed Colman's intention in making the tutor an object of scorn. But in a manner that would characterize Jefferson's approach to most of his roles, he recast Pangloss as a sympathetic figure — though not so much in dress, where a ridiculous wig of unruly gray hair sprang out from beneath a tricornered hat, and kneesocks and breeches suggested a clownish figure, nor in the abundant humor of the role, where Pangloss's tireless spouting of Latin or Shakespearean phrases gave ample chance for droll byplay. But he managed to soften the edges of the pandering pedant who played on the social ambitions of his

Dr. Pangloss, L.L.D., A.S.S. Painting by John Singer Sargeant, courtesy of The Players.

clients. At the play's end, turned out by his benefactors, Pangloss faced meager prospects. But rather than a sense of just desserts, Jefferson infused new pathos into his plight. The audience went away sad that one "so genial and so helpless" should be left to such an uncertain future, a later critic said about Jefferson's interpretation.[17]

Jefferson admitted some nervousness about undertaking the role of Pangloss. It did, after all, represent an important addition to his repertoire at a notable theatrical venue, Philadelphia's Chestnut Street Theatre. Unschooled in the classics, Joe, perhaps for the first time in his life, felt his lack of formal education. But he set about to master the part in the methodical fashion that marked his approach to all his significant roles. Enlisting the assistance of stage manager and fellow comedian John Gilbert, Jefferson deciphered the meaning of Latin phrases, then determined their pronunciation. The accompanying stage business would be Jefferson's devising, reciting his meaningless learning with eccentric posturing and ridiculous pomposity. "'*Erectos ad sidera tollere vultus,'* Ovid," ran one of his opaque profundities, which he punctuated — as he did every pronouncement — with a closing "Hem."[18]

The Heir at Law assumed greater importance for Jefferson when he joined Laura Keene's acclaimed troupe in New York in 1857. Pangloss was Jefferson's debut role as lead comedian with this major company, and he immediately raised eyebrows with his novel approach to the part. "A nervous, fidgety young man, by the name of Jefferson, appeared as Dr. Pangloss," wrote one annoyed critic, "into which character he infused a number of curious interpolations, occasionally using the text prepared by the author." This charge disturbed Jefferson enough so that years later he responded to it in his *Autobiography.* The issue, he felt, went to the heart of a popular misconception about theatre. Audiences and critics alike held a profoundly conservative notion of performance. Traditional interpretations of leading parts were cherished; deviations were upsetting (unless innovations were obviously superior). "If an actor," complained Joe, "presumes to leave out any of these respectable antiquities" or if he amplifies any traditional business he is thought "impertinent." To the contrary, Joe argued, "if there is any preference it should be given to the new, which must necessarily be fresh and original, while the old is only a copy." Jefferson's argument goes beyond the matter of Peter Pangloss. The chief criticism of Joseph Jefferson's career was that he refused to take chances. Having found a ready formula, he stuck with it, eschewing artistic risk. But at key moments in his career Jefferson repeatedly broke with tradition. He could sense change in theatre and in audiences, which constitutes one definition of theatrical genius. The occasional critic objected to his novelties, but more often they and audiences recognized — and appreciated — the presence of a gifted actor.[19]

After a short stint in Philadelphia in late summer of 1851, Joe and Ellsler again teamed up for another tour of the South. While the rest of the company headed to Wilmington on a weather-beaten freighter from New York, the partners took the quicker route by train so they could arrange the tour. The American rail system had taken substantial form by midcentury. It was now possible to travel nearly all the way from New York to Wilmington, North Carolina, by rail (with only a short steamship run on the Potomac below Washington), and tickets for the entire journey could be purchased at the point of origin. But train travel remained an ordeal of lurches, sparks, and soot behind locomotives that, in the words of one 1851 observer, were "tearing and wheezing, and panting away." A host of short lines formed the infant American rail system, so a trip of any distance required repeated transfers to new coaches along the way. American rail travel was a profoundly democratic experience: no first- or second-class compartments sorted passengers, and only women were given the option of a car reserved exclusively for them. Democracy extended even to drink: thirsty passengers shared a common water dispenser borne up and down the train by boys. Sensitive travelers had to steel themselves for the ordeal of strangers who would "fidget up and down" the center aisle of the car, inquiring about their destination and business, or worse, loose a Niagara of tobacco juice that splashed about their feet. As Jefferson and Ellsler entered North Carolina railroad conditions worsened, the Weldon to Wilmington stretch being notoriously poor even by lax regional standards.[20]

Arriving at Wilmington they found the theatre had not improved since their visit five months earlier. Further work was needed to prepare the "dusty old rat-trap." Joe's ability with the paint brush remained invaluable in getting up scenery. The company opened on 20 October 1851 and won plaudits from the discriminating local critic. Audiences expected for their twenty-five or fifty cents a full evening of entertainment. They were not disappointed, enjoying the normal mixture of comedies, melodramas, and tragedies, with musical interludes, such as Joe's and Margaret's comic duet "When a Little Farm We Keep," and closing farces. *Romeo and Juliet* pleased exceedingly.[21]

A week and a half into their stay the company was hailed by the *Daily Journal* as the "best [company] which has ever visited Wilmington." Not an unblemished company, to be sure. Certain members had been found wanting "in spirit." And J. H. Allen, in particular, who assumed a lead in *The Hunchback*, fumbled many lines (a fault he apologized for in a curtain speech, blaming the many new parts he had been forced to learn in successive nights). The generous Wilmington audience, however, seemed willing to forgive these failings along with a complete absence of any stars. Jefferson and Ellsler evidently intended a two-week stand, but they were warmly — and profitably received — and remained until 15 November, an impressively long run for a town of just 14,000. An indication of the townfolks' appreciation came when a group of "our most respectable citizens" offered to sponsor a complimentary benefit for the managers.[22]

After Wilmington the company had a short stay in Savannah before heading north to Charleston, where on the first day of 1852 they took over management of the Charleston Theatre. Proud Charleston could no longer boast of being the leading port of the South (New Orleans had long since surpassed it), but it retained a sense of itself as the cultural center of the region. The local theatre had gone through some troubled years, but Charlestonians provided a long and generally profitable reception to Ellsler and Jefferson. The troupe stayed until the end of May, mixing stock performances with the hosting of several notable stars. With four actresses and ten actors, they promised to produce "with great care" "THE STERLING OLD COMEDIES" along with "the new and successful Dramas, &c., now being performed in New York and London." They wasted no time in making good on their promise. The opening night saw Sheridan's classic comedy *The Rivals* (with, presumably, Joe as Bob Acres). Audiences viewed plays in what then passed as comfort, for the 1837 Greek Revival structure sought an environment of elegance. The ladies' restroom was carpeted and fitted with mirrors. In the boxes sofa seats were covered in crimson moreen and walls painted a light peach blossom "best adapted to display the beauty of the fairer part of the audience." The traditionally unruly pit had been civilized into a parquette through individual cushioned seats, which were numbered for reserved seating. Capping the theatre was a great dome with gilt moldings and individual paintings of suitably dramatic themes.[23]

The Charleston stand was highlighted by the guest appearance of first-rank stars. Julia Dean (1830–68) inaugurated a five-week starring turn at the beginning of February, a highly successful run in a city of Charleston's size (about 42,000, a third of whom were slave) by any contemporary standard. Julia Dean had a distinguished theatrical pedigree: her grandfather Samuel Drake had been a pioneer of Ohio Valley theatre, and as a teenager Dean acted with the Jeffersons in Mobile. Joe had great affection for Dean and devoted considerable attention to her in his memoirs. She was entering the peak of her career, the juvenile lead of choice. Photos reveal a pensive, rather pretty dark-haired woman "with a generous Hibernian nose and generous, sensitive mouth." "Tall, stately, graceful, and interesting," critic William Winter said of her. Although a crowd-pleaser, she never escaped faultfinding by critics. Some objected to Dean's frittering away her talents on "a few hackneyed dramas"; others admired her naturally melodious voice but regretted her tendency to strain it in a "melo-dramatic guttural tone." Dean, like Fanny Kemble, found a husband among the southern elite and, like Kemble, found profound unhappiness in the marriage.[24]

Charleston accorded Dean an enthusiastic southern welcome, many of the city's most fashionable seeking personal audiences with her. "All vied in paying homage to her beauty and her virtue," Jefferson recalled. "Julia Dean" hats moved quickly off store shelves. And the *Courier,* in an excusable piece of hyperbole, encouraged citizens to see "one of the brightest stars of histrionic hemisphere." They needed little prodding. She entertained as Julia in *The Hunchback,* as Pauline in *Lady of Lyons,* as Lady Teazle in *School for Scandal,* as Lady Gay Spanker in *London Assurance,* as Juliet in *Romeo and Juliet,* among her eighteen roles in twenty-four nights of acting (including a highly promoted firemen's benefit). After her first week the managing partners had cleared $900 each. Feeling like a "plutocratic comedian," Joe rushed out and bought handsome watches for himself and Margaret.[25]

The next star could hardly have been more different. "The tragic muse has dropped a curtsey to her friends," recorded the *Courier*, "and made way for Momus." Charlie Burke was, like Dean, at the height of his abbreviated career, and his Charleston reception was, if less captivating than Dean's, nonetheless very cordial. He also brought freshness to roles like Solon Shingle in *The People's Lawyer*, Timothy in *The Toodles*, or Dromio in *Comedy of Errors*. Too, Burke lacked the coarseness that clung to other popular comedians, such as Charles Burton. In Charleston, where propriety held sway, Burke's freedom "from vulgarity or anything objectionable" was a clear mark in his favor. In Charleston, as in New York, Joe had the opportunity to perform alongside his brother in Burke's version of *Rip Van Winkle*. Every exposure to the haunting tale of the Catskills must have intrigued Joe further with its dramatic possibilities.[26]

Managerial relations with stars were filled with potential conflict. With Julia Dean, Jefferson shared youthful memories that helped smooth the way; Burke was his beloved brother; but with the appearance of the third star — Junius Brutus Booth — came an unpredictable temperament. Fortunately for the managers, Booth seemed to be on his best behavior, and on the wagon, during his run. His two-week stay made money. Jefferson and Ellsler may simply have been lucky. Perhaps Booth's irenic tone had something to do with the two men's quick acquiescence to his salary demands: $400 per week and $50 for his son Edwin. And perhaps his cooperation spoke of Joe's growing friendship with Edwin. The nineteenth century's greatest American comedian first met its greatest tragedian when sixteen-year-old Edwin (1833–93) accompanied his father to an engagement at New York's National Theatre in September 1850. Joe saw a dark-eyed youth with a prominent nose and small mouth, who reminded Jefferson of "one of Murillo's Italian peasant boys." Raised in the theatre and now hitched to Thespis's cart, the two forged a bond. Their simpatico may also have been rooted in a complementarity of temperaments. To Joe's gregariousness and unflagging good cheer, Edwin's reserved and rather brooding nature stood in sharp relief. However formed, it would prove a consequential friendship in many ways.[27]

Following the long Charleston stand came a quick swing in spring 1852 through Augusta and Columbus, Georgia, before doubling back to Wilmington. The Augusta stand began in late March. Located well up the Savannah River from the coast, Augusta had been branded by local partisans as the "Lowell of Georgia." Its incipient mill industries held promise of a regional industrialization that was never fulfilled. The peripatetic company established itself there with difficulty attended by tragedy. The difficulty came in the form of theatrical prejudice, when neither of the two principal hotels, as Ellsler recalled, could find room for "vagabonds." Accommodations in an "unpretentious house" had to make do. More serious distress came on opening night, when a devastating fire struck an Augusta foundry. Residents had little appetite for theatricals with a fatal fire on their minds. The next evening a spring downpour flooded the streets. Calling off the first week's performances, the company regrouped to try the next week. It devoted Monday's performance to a benefit for the widow of a mill fire victim. The company's kindness netted $1,900 and its "liberality" was much lauded in the press, opening the door for strong business in the balance of its nearly four-week stay.[28]

Once underway, the Augusta visit gained quick momentum with a four-night stand by Junius Brutus Booth in his customary rotation of Sir Giles Overreach, Iago, and Richard III. "High-wrought tragedy," the *Daily Chronicle and Sentinel* correctly labeled it, Booth rendering "all the wildest and darkest passions of human nature with singular power." The Jefferson-Ellsler troupe was thrown back upon its own resources after the mercurial star moved on. It managed on its own handsomely, staging a different bill every night, occasionally remounting an especially popular offering of a few nights previous. Near the end of the run, during the season of benefits, came an occasion worthy of more detail than has survived. The final act of *Richard III* was mounted as the closing piece with Joe as King Richard and Ellsler as Richmond. This tragedy reigned unchallenged as the most produced of the Bard's plays in the nineteenth century. Intended as a testament to villainy, Jefferson turned it into a travesty.[29]

After brief sojourns in Columbia and Wilmington, the Ellsler-Jefferson road show had run its course. This marked the conclusion of Joe's days of stock company touring but not an end to his inveterate traveling; he would appear with many different companies in the next few years, and even as a star he would cover thousands of miles in a typical year. But save for some short summer jaunts while based in Baltimore in the mid-1850s, he never again managed an itinerant repertory company. He could not have known this at the time, and even if he did he probably would not have regretted the fact. "No one who has not passed through the actual experience of country management, combined with acting, can imagine the really hard work and anxiety of it," Jefferson confides. Although he got along famously with Ellsler, such had not been the case with his earlier partner Sefton, from whom he parted less than amicably.[30]

Joe's *Autobiography* devotes disproportionate time to this phase of his life. He understood that his public would covet accounts of an earlier homespun theatre. By the closing decades of the nineteenth century Americans had grown nostalgic for a perceived simpler age. Jefferson's memoir fulfilled that craving with the most compelling portrait of itinerant theatricals ever produced. Up close, the romance of the road betrayed much tattered wear, but in Joe's retelling decades later such inconveniences were covered by a gauzy cloak of remembrance. And to be sure, many players stayed loyal to the muse even in the face of apparent defeat. "There was a fascination about the life so powerful," Joe testifies, "that I have known but few who abandoned it for any other."[31]

A Yeoman of the Stage

Summer and fall of 1852 found Joe back in Philadelphia and New York, moving from Gotham's Niblo Gardens to Philly's Chestnut Street Theatre and then back again. As first comedian with the Chestnut Street company he reclaimed the position — if not quite the renown — of his grandfather. At Niblo's Garden he revisited the stage of his father. The Jefferson name meant comedy, and Jefferson III was beginning to remind the broad public of that fact. In early 1853 he veered north, with a pregnant Margaret in tow, to join Albany's stock company for a short stay. In February it was over to Boston, where he briefly joined William Warren at the Boston Museum.[32]

Jefferson recorded no impressions of his several months' stay in Boston. Perhaps he found little to distinguish among America's largest cities. But surely he sensed a pace of life less frantic and unabashedly competitive than what he knew in New York. Boston's elite made their fortunes in the mill towns north and west of the city, and they preferred to keep their city a quiet domestic retreat. Boston's Back Bay had not yet been filled in, leaving the pinched, peninsular city little room for growth. But the town, ornamented with Charles Bullfinch's elegant architecture, continued confident in its self-declared status as the intellectual hub of the universe.[33]

Whereas on his southern tours Joe had found a region growing testy with the national debate on slavery, in Boston he found a rising nativist movement unsettled by the Irish-Catholic "menace." But if prejudice toward recent immigrants was on the rise, age-old intolerance toward drama had finally been surmounted. In a town where theatricals were officially (and effectively) banned until well into the 1790s, the professional stage had taken firm root. A clutch of theatres presented drama, opera, and minstrelsy to a public apparently unconcerned with their Puritan forbears' reproach.

Joe first went to the Boston Museum on 12 February to join his cousins William Warren and Elizabeth Thomas. Warren and the Boston Museum stock company were in the process of becoming local institutions. Founded in 1843, the Boston Museum began earning critical attention about the time

Warren joined it in 1846. It was the quintessential Boston institution. Demanding standards of production were maintained. And decorum reigned. In the term of the age, it was styled a "deacon's theatre." Prompt books reveal scripts carefully vetted to replace "damns" with "curse," "lusty" became "fat," "cuckolds" turned into "fools." The theatre's very name, of course, betrays the high Victorian penchant for euphemism when referring to the "devil's playhouse." Fittingly, too, although comedy became the company's signature style, it premiered such didactic classics as *The Drunkard* and *The Gambler*. Well-run theatres like the Boston Museum (indeed, all theatres to some extent) were governed backstage by an elaborate set of rules. Fines were handed out for being late for rehearsal. Missing a stage cue, failing to learn one's lines, being drunk at curtain time, or refusing to accept a role meant a stiff penalty of a week's salary. Respect for the greenroom, where actors readied themselves for a performance, demanded that men remove their hats and maintain decorum (again, under threat of fine).[34]

Joe's professional work with Warren (who was seventeen years his senior) appears to have been limited to this short 1852 visit. In a sense, one stage could not hold them both, for they pursued the same line. The heavy-lidded Warren (1812–88) shared the family gift for eccentric comedy (his father was the estimable comedian William Warren, Sr.), and the roles for which he would be remembered paralleled many of Joe's: Bob Acres, Sir Tony Lumpkin, and Dr. Pangloss. Possessing "a quaint and tender genius," Warren remained with the Museum company from 1846 until his retirement thirty-seven years later. He became a fixture in Boston society (a "city that absorbs genius as New York absorbs wealth," a critic admired), the performer visitors to the city wished to see when attending the theatre. Without the brutal demands of travel and established as a pillar of his community, Warren had a career even Jefferson might have envied.[35]

By mid-March Joe had moved over to the Howard Athenaeum. Constructed in 1846 on the site of a Millerite tabernacle, the structure was an excellent facility for viewing drama. Unfortunately, under manager Henry Willard its company proved lackluster. "Thespis and Melpomene," hyperbolized Boston critic Henry Clapp, must be "weeping over the tomb of the legitimate drama." A new season was announced in March 1853 with much fanfare and with a refashioned, presumably stronger company. But many patrons "could not discover the improvement." Joe was among the few singled out by Clapp and other critics as distinguishing themselves. In no sense a star, Joe nonetheless caught the eye of critics with his "wide streak of dry and quaint humor" and a technique "legitimate and free from buffoonery."[36]

In fall 1853 Joe returned to Philadelphia's Chestnut Street and a long run of

Uncle Tom's Cabin. In a season lasting into spring, Joe performed thirty-seven roles. The most intriguing must have been his Artful Dodger in *Oliver Twist.* Dickens's good-humored larcenist provided the stock from which Jefferson made his favorite broth: a swindler that cannot carry off the sting; a charlatan undone by his decent instincts.[37]

The next autumn Jefferson took an extended leave from the dramatic circles of Philadelphia and New York and traveled south to Baltimore, Washington, and Richmond. He accepted an offer from Henry C. Jarrett to become stage manager and lead comedian at the Baltimore Museum and later Holliday Street Theatre. Stage managing was not quite directing in the modern sense (a theatrical position not yet devised), being more concerned with the quotidian details of theatre production. Carrying the responsibility for a smooth performance along with his own acting preparation must have been taxing, yet Joe knew the ins and outs of production intimately. And in his new position Joe was relieved of the worry of finances — at least so far as meeting payroll was concerned.[38]

Baltimore had grown since Joe visited it with his family in the early 1830s, becoming the leading city of the upper South. A thriving seaport with a population approaching 200,000 and with the country's largest free black contingency, Baltimore possessed that odd mixture of nativist parochialism and emergent cosmopolitanism that marked some antebellum cities. With "an air of elegance and refinement," noted diarist Sidney George Fisher in 1848, it also had a "thousand evidences of the influences (good and evil) of slavery and of southern habits." The 1854 season opened early on 28 August. The Baltimore Museum had had a face-lift, and the newspaper celebrated the appearance of the "renowned Jefferson" among the company. For Joe, the season began with a bang. He was featured as Pangloss in *The Heir at Law* and as Bobtail in the ever-popular farce *My Precious Betsy* to an opening night crowd so packed that even standing room was unavailable shortly after the curtain. Joe "filled the measure of his celebrity," according to an observer, as "one of the best comedians on the American stage." Even acknowledging a weakness for hyperbole among the era's newspaper criticism, it is clear that Joe had hit his stride.[39]

In October a Scottish-born beauty who was rapidly becoming one of the most popular young actresses in America took her turn at the Baltimore Museum. Agnes Robertson (1833–1916), known as "the Fairy Star," was the new wife of widower Dion Boucicault (their vows privately exchanged rather than in a church, thus enabling her to keep her stage name). She had essentially run away with him to America the year before, where under his tutelage she blossomed into a popular stage attraction in the 1850s. While Boucicault suffered through one of his periodic financial reverses, Robertson kept the couple afloat with successful tours of New York and Canada. Although limited in range, Robertson maintained a longtime popularity on the Anglo-American stage with her artless charm, frequently portraying the simple Scottish or Irish peasant girls of her husband's creation.[40]

The holiday seasons of Christmas and Easter were a popular time for families to attend theatre, and managers often accommodated their tastes by mounting lavish productions. The early decades of the nineteenth century saw English theatres beginning to stage such fantasies as *Cinderella, Sinbad the Sailor, Bluebeard,* or *The Island of Jewels.* As a genre these are hard to characterize. A mixture of music, comedy, fairy tale, nursery rhyme, ballet, romance, and topical humor, the productions were set against opulent scenery and tied together by a thin plot. They were firmly rooted in the pantomime tradition, which itself reached back to the old Commedia dell'Arte. The pantomime's dumb show conventions had been altered by changing audience tastes into the freer form known as extravaganza or burlesque. English playwright J. R. Planché substantially defined the genre in the second quarter of the nineteenth century with his series of Christmas and Easter extravaganzas. Their conventionalized mixture of fairy tales and spectacle fed the Victorian love of fantasy, while the transformation to the darker harlequinade scenes added an ominous counterpoint. These holiday spectacles were so popular with the public that despite their expense to stage, they accounted for an impressive share of a theatre's yearly profits.[41]

Jarrett's Baltimore Museum, in an early December bow to Christmas tastes, presented *The Naiad Queen, or the Nymphs of the Rhine!* in 1854. More dramatized musical review than dumb show, it was a "gorgeous spectacle," a two-and-a-half-hour pageant that would merit various productions throughout the remainder of the century. All new scenery was prepared and a large cast readied. The challenges in stage managing this "truly magnificent spectacle" (as the newspaper saw it) must have been considerable. Every night Joe had to worry over coordinating the lavish production while handling a leading role himself. It paid to have the energies of youth. It also helped that Joe, by temperament, was obsessive about details. Pulling together a complex production night after night and maintaining its quality required such care. Decades later, Jefferson would exhibit the same strenuous oversight on his *Rip Van Winkle* productions.

All efforts expended in preparing *The Naiad Queen* proved fully justified. The play's reception was "almost without parallel in the annals of this popular place of amusement," effused a local critic, who was particularly complimentary of the casting and stage settings. For his part, Joe earned plaudits for his "inimitable representation of Schnapps," whose "songs, drolleries and humor never fail to elicit rounds of applause." In an age when two to three weeks constituted a long run for a play, the seven-week stand of *The Naiad Queen* was exceptional. "Those who wish to see it," the *Baltimore Advertiser* admonished, "would do well to procure their seats before night, as it will then be impossible to obtain on in the parquette or dress circle." For the first half of its run the play stood by itself, with no need to encourage attendance with an afterpiece. By late December, though crowds continued strong, the usual mix of farces (featuring Joe) were added: *My Precious Betsy, The Spectre Bridegroom,* and *Lend Me Five Shillings* among them.[42]

The overwhelming success of *The Naiad Queen* encouraged Jarrett to risk another fantasy spectacle in April: *Aladdin, or the Wonderful Lamp,* which served up a generous dollop of fairy romance, humor, dance, and music. We might regret that no pictures of Jefferson as the Arabic Kasrac exist (it is highly unlikely that any were taken; in this early era of photography pictures of stage productions are virtually unknown). What endures are descriptions: "From the rising of the curtain in the first act until the 'grand finale,' round after round of applause bore witness to the talent of the artist, the skill of the costumer, the inventions of the machinist, and the liberality of the management." Fittingly, a week into the show the production's scenic artist (our stage designer) received an unusual bow, a benefit performance tacitly recognizing him as the true star. *Aladdin* ran for more than a month and was later reprised.[43]

The long Baltimore Museum season lasted into the beginning of June. Joe had his benefit at the end of May, mounting "four startling pieces" that showcased his versatility in "tragedy, comedy, interlude and farce." His attempt at the last act of *Richard III* is hard to credit, unless it was the burlesque version he had previously shown. Joe then spent a relatively quiet summer with his family in Baltimore, becoming a father for the third time.[44]

Jefferson's peaceful summer gave way to a hectic fall. Members of Jarrett's Baltimore company had the doubtful privilege of working for a man who understood the possibilities of the transportation revolution. The "railroad manager," Jarrett was termed, for his practice of casting a player in a short opening piece in Baltimore, then hiring a special train to carry him that same evening to Washington for his role in the same afterpiece. Jarrett was likely the first theatre man to make the iron horse central to his operations, and it early showed what later generations would learn: improvements in travel or communications tend to add rather than reduce work. Harried company members at least benefited from the most up-to-date passenger comforts: the Baltimore and Ohio line was in the process of upgrading its passenger stock to heighten ceilings, extend leg room, and provide generously cushioned seats with footrests.[45]

Because of the railroad, Jarrett was able to stage parallel productions in Baltimore and Washington beginning in October 1855, when he rented the National Theatre for his troupe. Joe had not been in the capital city since early childhood some twenty years earlier, when his grandfather was still patriarch of the Jefferson family. In the intervening decades Washington had become a grander city, particularly during the 1850s, as a buoyant economy persuaded Congress to appropriate money to beautify public grounds, commission statuary, and begin a monumental new dome for the capitol. The recent installation of gas lamps made evening strolls on major thoroughfares a safer proposition. Too, since 1850 Washington visitors no longer had to endure the spectacle of slave pens near the new Smithsonian building. The only regret Joe might have had as he wandered about the federal district's center was that money shortages and squabbles had halted work on the Washington monument just 150 feet above ground.[46]

These were surely among the most feverish days Jefferson ever knew, stage managing and performing at two theatres, moving back and forth between them on a regular basis, while Margaret stayed in Baltimore with their growing family. Joe had occasion to stage manage nearly every type of dramatic entertainment, including melodramas, comedies, historical plays, Shakespearean tragedy, and even such operatic dramas as *Rob Roy*. Although Joe's future would not lie in management, his command of every aspect of theatrical arts cultivated during these years served him admirably in his years of stardom.[47]

The Washington performances were originally only weekly affairs, but the frequency picked up as autumn progressed. Washington audiences enjoyed a feast of entertainments. Agnes Robertson brought her special allure to the "protean burletta" of *The Young Actress*. The old reliable equestrian melodrama *Mazeppa* was revived in November, with Joe in a featured role (though upstaged by Rocket, the steed whose spirited run up the ramps stole the show). Joe undertook what would appear an unconventional role as the First Witch in a production of *Macbeth* (with James W. Wallack, Jr., as Macbeth). In truth, there was an established tradition of male eccentric comedians assuming the role since they possessed the necessary skills of makeup and voice to attempt the outrè look and incantatory tone the part demanded.[48]

The fall Washington season also brought one of Joe's dearest friends for a star turn, comedian Barney Williams (1823–76). Professional jealousies seemed never to taint their camaraderie, helped perhaps by Williams's staying within a specialized line of work, Irish comedy. This particular variation of low comedy ethnic types (alongside the Yankee, Dutch, Bowery b'hoy, frontiersman, and minstrel) was widely seen on American stages beginning in the 1840s and 1850s. That its popularity corresponded with mass Irish immigration is no coincidence. Americans were having their first encounter with the migration of a peasantry, and the experience had its bumps. Humor, ever a means of coping with prejudice and potential social conflict, served the nation well here. In plays like *Handy Andy, O'Flanaghan* or *The Irish Emigrant*, native-born Americans observed simple, good-natured, and nonthreatening Celts (though roguish, improvident, and given to tippling). Tyrone Power's 1830s tour of America in such plays as *The Irish Ambassador* turned the stage Irishman into a leading figure. John Brougham (who also composed Irish sketches) and John Drew the elder handsomely carried forth the type onto midcentury stages. Williams added a further bit of stage interest when he married the widowed Mrs. Charles Mestayer, herself having carved out a stage niche as a "Yankee gal." This conjugal union of contrasting ethnic types became a popular novelty in the theatre (acceptable only in comedy since hybrid marriages were socially unthinkable). Williams and his wife presented a Thanksgiving evening show, *Irish Assurance and Yankee Modesty*, whose featured character Pat was "gifted with blarney."[49]

The most spectacular event of the holiday season in both Washington and Baltimore was an all-star production of Sheridan's *The School for Scandal*. The idea apparently was Jarrett's (at least Jefferson did not claim credit for it), a daring move to be sure in an age when the expense of a single star was considerable. But the search for novelty to fill theatre seats was endless. Jarrett's expensive gambit was exploited in his newspaper ads, which proclaimed in a Barnumesque puff, the "MOST DISTINGUISHED ARTISTES of the age," a "GALAXY OF STARS far exceeding the amount ever before expended on any single dramatic production." This claim sought to justify ticket prices of fifty cents and a dollar, nearly double the usual rate. Apparently undaunted by the tariff, a "large and brilliant audience" gathered for a major occasion of the Washington social season. Henry and Thomas Placide, James W. Wallack, Jr., James Murdoch, and Edwin Adams headlined the fifteen featured performers (including Joe) in the production. The *National Intelligencer* reviewer, overawed by the assemblage of talent, fell over himself in his appreciation. "We shall not attempt to criticize the acting of the leading performers, who indeed merit only terms of commendation."[50]

And yet Joe Jefferson, who devotes several pages of his *Autobiography* to the star-laden event, found it a flawed artistic moment. Part of his discomfit was surely that as stage manager he had grown accustomed to a measure of authority, but with this collection of notables his position was reduced to little more than a "sinecure." When he did suggest some slight bit of stage business, Joe was quickly rebuffed by one of the stars. Lacking much authority over the production, Joe approached the evening with some foreboding. Sure enough, though the occasion was a financial success, he judged it "an artistic failure." Further, he took wicked satisfaction in observing the scene he sought to influence "virtually go to pieces."[51]

Jefferson's retelling this story provided him a moment of reflection about his art. He fashioned a useful metaphor of theatre as a "fine mechanical contrivance" that works well only with cogwheels of different proportions. But in *The School for Scandal* the stars were "identical in size, highly polished, and well made, but not adapted to the same machinery." Actors accustomed to center stage were unable to subordinate themselves to a group. This seems only commonsensical to modern theatergoers, for whom ensemble performance is axiomatic. Not so on the mid-Victorian stage. Many plays were little more than thinly connected plots linking histrionic moments for the star. But Jefferson was among the early practitioners of his art to grasp a different vision. "A play is like a picture: the actors are the colors, and they must blend with one another if a perfect work is to be produced." These are the words, of course, of a mature Jefferson looking back, not those of the young yeoman comedian he had been. Yet it may well be that even at age twenty-six Joe understood something grasped by few of his seniors. When a decade later he helped create his own starring vehicle, *Rip Van Winkle*, it would be notable for precisely these qualities of balance and cohesion.[52]

When Jarrett's Baltimore-Washington season ended in early March 1856, Joe departed for John T. Ford's company at Washington's National Theatre. Ford (1829–94), forever associated with the notoriety of his eponymous Washington theatre, was a man who deserved much better. A Baltimore native of humble birth, Ford broke into show business as an advance man for a minstrel company. His acquisition of the Holliday Street Theatre in Baltimore launched his career of management. By 1856 he had his first Washington house (he would dominate District theatricals for years), to which he added establishments in Richmond and a circuit of stages further south, all the way to New Orleans. He maintained several acting companies — themselves composed of figures who would later prove important on the stage — to support the day's most eminent stars. Ford's talents extended well beyond the stage. He had a sense of civic duty unusual for people of the theatre. A man of standing in Baltimore, Ford served variously as city councilman, acting mayor, philanthropic trustee, and organizer of various civic improvement projects. Ford also earned a reputation as a man of honor, being the only American manager to pay Gilbert and Sullivan royalties for their shamefully pirated *H.M.S. Pinafore* in 1878. His thirty-nine-day detention following President Lincoln's assassination was a travesty of justice, which Ford, fortunately, was able to surmount.[53]

Jefferson and Ford, nearly the same age, formed a fast friendship during the season. Jefferson's work with Ford included occasions when he stage managed the proverbially difficult Edwin Forrest in his usual assortment of Shakespearean and melodramatic vehicles. Joe may have suffered some anxious moments in calming the temperamental star, but at the least he acquired a pocketful of rehearsal anecdotes, which he artfully retold in his *Autobiography*. He stayed with Ford through the end of May, taking his benefit on the thirty-first in an unlikely production of *Macbeth*. No records of the production remain, but it was almost surely a travesty along the lines of his earlier *Richard III*. He then went on a quick touring jaunt of provincial Maryland and Pennsylvania towns with John Sleeper Clarke before leaving for a few months in Europe.[54]

In the fall Joe returned to John Ford's fold, this time working mostly at the theatre Ford managed in Richmond. Although far inland, Richmond was a port city on the fall line of the James River. It was a lovely setting for a town, visitors agreed, with elegant neighborhoods on its north side, but these graces were insufficient compensation for a slovenly city center. Dickens sensed in Richmond "an aspect of decay and gloom which to the unaccustomed eye is most distressing." Appropriately, the opening of the Richmond theatre in April 1856 coincided with a different sort of gloom in the Far West. Violence and political chicanery in Kansas following the Kansas-Nebraska Act dominated news in Virginia. "Black Republicanism in Virginia" screamed a headline in Thomas Ritchie's Richmond *Enquirer,* condemning any who would suggest excluding slavery from the western territories. News from Kansas and regarding the contentious upcoming fall presidential elections cast an ominous cloud over the newspaper's daily invitations to enjoy the playhouse.[55]

To the apolitical Jefferson, though, Richmond represented further steps forward in his career: successful stage managing, more comic leads, and the opportunity to support established luminaries like Edwin Forrest or E. L. Davenport and rising stars, such as Edwin Booth. Joe won plaudits for his acting, convulsing audiences nightly "by his drollery and rollicking wit." Indeed, the Richmond paper effused at Joe's first appearing: "It appears to be the general opinion, that he is the best comic actor who has for many years visited our city." Joe also oversaw a stock company full of interesting—and portentous—figures, including Edwin Adams, who would become one of America's leading interpreters of Shakespeare.[56]

Also joining the Richmond company in the 1856 season was John Wilkes Booth (1838–65), the melancholy and mercurial youngest Booth, mildly talented but wildly ambitious, with more charm than anyone else in his family. Only eighteen, he acted under an alias, reserving the august family name until the time he felt worthy to assume it on stage. The dashing yet flawed scion of

America's first family of tragedy cut an impressive figure. Yet Jefferson, even as late as 1889 when his *Autobiography* was serialized, never mentions him. Why? It can only be explained by reference to the trauma Booth's assassination of Lincoln wrought on the American theatre community. Latent suspicions of actors surfaced, and the acting fraternity's much-coveted social assimilation was dealt a blow. Too, Edwin still lived. The awkwardness of saying anything about his intimate friend's younger brother was daunting beyond words. Silence was best.[57]

Another company member in Richmond would evoke far sweeter memories from Edwin Booth. Mary Devlin, only sixteen, had been put under the care of Joe and Margaret when she joined the Baltimore Museum a year earlier. From a first-generation Irish family in Troy, New York, Mary had debuted as a danseuse while not yet a teen. She continued to live with the Jeffersons in Richmond, where Joe was both her stage supervisor and an elder-brother figure. Devlin frequently traveled and performed with the Jeffersons over the next several years, even joining them at their summer retreat in the Poconos. Joe introduced her to Booth when the latter came to rehearse Romeo to her Juliet. Strong-jawed and pug-nosed, Devlin possessed blunt Irish good looks and an amiable disposition. She was immediately smitten by her dark-eyed Romeo, sentiments Booth reciprocated. Despite Joe's initial reservations about his ingenue's involvement with a volatile Booth, the relationship moved forward to marriage a few years later.[58]

The fall season, accented by a revival of *The Naiad Queen* in Richmond and Washington, was a prosperous one. Good times continued throughout the spring season of 1857. Joe was taking fewer roles now, beginning to specialize in those parts in which he felt most adept. Although not remembered for his singing, Joe handled some comic numbers nimbly enough to be "loudly encored." And he continued to stage manage a range of productions, including, near the end of his spring tenure, Italian opera in the form of Donizetti's *Daughter of the Regiment.* Those who years later dismissed Jefferson as a one-trick actor failed to grasp the terrific variety of his apprenticeship, not simply in the ninety roles he sometimes played in a year but also in his simultaneous activities as manager. He learned the trade from the bottom up.[59]

Melancholy Days

If the early and mid 1850s brought Joe wide exposure and increased confidence as a rising comedian, during this decade he also experienced the vicissitudes of personal life. Romance, marriage, and fatherhood came his way, but also abrupt family losses due to infant mortality and the "white plague" of TB that Victorians knew so intimately.

Joe lost his mother in 1849. She had returned to Philadelphia, the closest thing to home the footloose family had known. Joe and Charlie Burke were out of town when she died and had to be summoned by telegram. Family legend, written down much later by granddaughter Eleanor Farjeon, has them hurrying to Philadelphia for the funeral, later dealing with their grief in a most Jeffersonian way — attending the theatre that evening. It is hard to measure the twenty-year-old Joe's reaction to Cornelia's death. Clearly he had no doubts about his ability to support himself; that had been a necessity for several years. In likelihood he had already been helping to maintain his mother and sister. But his mother's passing cut an important tie with the heroic generation of Jeffersons, those who spanned the glory years from Jefferson I in Philadelphia to the hardscrabble itinerancy of the 1830s and 1840s. Even with a surviving sister and half brother, Joe must have felt the ache of melancholy common to every person who confronts a future devoid of both parents.[60]

His marriage to Margaret in 1850 helped fill the emotional hole. They wasted no time in building a family. Ten months after their May wedding Margaret gave birth to Charles Burke Jefferson, followed in 1853 by daughter Margaret, in 1855 by another daughter, Frances, and in 1856 by a second son, Joseph Jefferson, Jr. The rapid succession of births was unexceptional for the nineteenth century, as was the early death of two of the infants. Frances, born during a Baltimore summer, survived only until December. Becoming pregnant almost immediately, Margaret gave birth to Joseph Jefferson, Jr., in Richmond early the next fall. But Joe's namesake came down with scarlet fever and died the next month. Joe or Margaret rarely had the luxury of extended grief: the night Frances died, Joe had to carry on with the comic lead in *The Heir at Law*. As difficult as the loss of his children was to Joe, Charlie's death, from tuberculosis in 1854, was probably more devastating. When word came of his brother's imminent death, Joe was managing for Jarrett in Baltimore. He rushed to New York by train, arriving in time to say his good-byes. The story of Charlie dying in Joe's arms may be a sentimental fiction, but it was what Joe would have wanted. No other family member or friend would ever be so close.[61]

Neither a string of family losses nor a growing family would prevent Joe from taking a brief trip to Europe in 1856. He had been squirreling away funds for two years with this excursion in mind. Such an undertaking was both arduous and expensive (though less taxing than what faced Margaret — six months pregnant, she had to endure Joe's two-month absence during the heat of a Washington summer). But at age twenty-seven Joe probably felt it time to pay his homage to the temples of European culture. A visit to the shrines across the Atlantic was de rigueur for any American with pretensions to taste, and Joe, for all his plain-style persona, was a man intensely appreciative of European culture. For him it would be a working vacation; he made the rounds of London and Paris theatres, admiring and analyzing the stars of the English and French stage. Moreover, with Barney Williams and his wife then appearing on London's Adelphi stage, Joe had the possibility of introductions and contacts useful to future appearances across the Atlantic.[62]

After an uneventful journey aboard the clipper ship *Neptune,* Jefferson debarked at London. He found a capital city astride the world, its million plus residents basking in the glory of empire even as they endured a city robed in a garb of soot. He spent his evenings making his way along the twisted streets and blind alleys of London's theatre district. "Rich in comedians and poor in tragedians," he judged the London stage. Whether or not the latter verdict is fair, the justness of the former cannot be gainsaid. This was a golden age of English comedy. At the Olympic, Frederick Robson displayed his genius for burlesque in *A Conjugal Lesson* (perhaps offering Joe a model for his popular interpretation of the role). At the Haymarket, veteran performer J. B. Buckstone was spinning his brand of extravagant farce. The master of virtually all contemporary low comedy roles, Buckstone stood as the nearest equivalent to Joseph Jefferson as existed on mid-Victorian stage. Yet Sadler's Wells manager and actor Samuel Phelps left the deepest impression on Joe, who admired his mastery of an impressive range of parts. Phelps had made Sadler's Wells the venue for Shakespearean revivals, and Phelps himself moved among the Bard's tragic and comic roles — from Lear to Falstaff to Bottom — with a versatility rarely seen on the nineteenth-century stage.[63]

But more than London, Paris caught Joe's imagination, and he devoted most of the short chapter in his *Autobiography* to his three-week Paris pilgrimage. His mother's French roots had given him a fascination with the land, and he was prepared to see it in idealized terms. For the first (but not final) time in his *Autobiography* he postures himself as tourist, evoking for his American readers the quotidian Parisian atmosphere. Essentially a storyteller, Joe filled his book with anecdotal descriptions, of common people in situations of comic conflict (in this case, a baker and cook fighting in an alley). He enjoyed painting himself as an American naïf awed by the culture of Europe, anxious to return home to show off his acquired breeding.[64]

In reality, such affectations were impossible for him. Joe was too firmly rooted in the simple persona of the Yankee. But he no doubt enjoyed displaying the treasures he acquired at Parisian theatrical costumers. Having diligently saved for this occasion, he indulged himself in an orgy of purchases of colorful silks and velvets, outfitting himself for upcoming roles before he returned to Richmond.

The European jaunt was the longest trip Joe would make unaccompanied by family member or friend. The unhurried ocean voyage must have occasioned reflection over career and family. Did Joe return with a plan that fall of 1856? At age twenty-seven it might appear that his future offered many years for advancement. Yet he knew that if he were to approach (or surpass) the renown of his grandfather, he must soon ascend the next rung of the theatrical ladder. With that sixth sense that marked his career, Joe stepped up the following year by moving to the most acclaimed stage in America.

6

Triumphs in Comedy and Melodrama

When Joseph Jefferson joined Laura Keene's company in August 1857, he did so by invitation; Keene had never seen him perform. His reputation as an accomplished low comedian had preceded him to New York City, which by now had emerged as the nation's theatrical center. In joining Keene's family-oriented theatre Joe left behind the Bowery environs he had known at the National and Olympic. Scrambling days were over. Joe would never again lack for work. Already a prudent steward of his finances, he quietly began his steady climb toward great wealth.

At age twenty-eight Joe was physically unimposing. Certainly not more than five feet, nine inches in height, small-framed and slender with straight brown hair, he would not command a second look if passed on the sidewalk. He was neither handsome nor homely. One had to look closer, to focus on his face, to catch a hint of the transforming power that occurred on stage. His features were unexceptional — thin lips framing a small mouth, a jutting jaw bisected by a cleft chin, and a slightly hooked nose (the "pure Nut-cracker type," as Joe described his profile). Only his startling eyes would capture one's attention. Joe's slightly protuberant eyes seemed to miss nothing, lending him an air of impish inquisitiveness. They were not the eyes of a tragic actor but those of an engaging confidante ready to swap stories.

It was for those eyes — along with his malleable face, fidgety, riveting stage

Joe at age twenty-eight. Courtesy of Michael A. Morrison Collection

energy, and absolute command of low comedy—that Laura Keene brought him to her theatre. The Astor Place riot notwithstanding, British actors still dominated leading parts in the better houses, and native-born Joe was made to feel an interloper by some colleagues. They would soon have reason to be grateful to the Yankee, though, for Joe helped pull the theatre out of the economic doldrums and keep it going when panic struck that year.[1]

But 1857 would prove fateful for more than economic recession. That year both Edwin Booth and Joseph Jefferson descended on New York to claim the attention for which family pedigree and extended apprenticeship prepared them. During the next four decades the two men would define stardom: Booth in tragedy, Jefferson in comedy. Already friends, their careers ran parallel tracks in many ways. But where Booth's subsequent life would be pocked by melancholy, economic setback, and family tragedy, Jefferson moved steadily forward. Although stalked by the pale rider (who left few homes unvisited in this age), he was blessed with an equanimity that allowed him to quietly absorb whatever life dealt him.[2]

With Laura Keene

Laura Keene (1820?–73) was an actress-manager of a mysterious past and unconventional present. Born in modest circumstances in England and disastrously married to a man later transported to Australia, she was left with two children and dim prospects. She secured a place in the London theatre of Madame Vestris, where she nurtured a latent talent. James W. Wallack spotted her in 1852 and made an offer for her to join his estimable company in New York. Her frenetic energy complemented a clarion voice, luxurious chestnut hair that trailed in curls down her shoulder, and statuesque good looks. She had, as later generations might say, stage presence. Jefferson, whose relationship with Keene was stormy, nonetheless lauded her versatility. She could easily assume the "rustic walk of a milkmaid" or the "dignified grace of a queen." Keene was, above all, ambitious and iconoclastic. She abruptly left Wallack and decamped for Baltimore with notorious gambler John Lutz (with whom she lived openly for years until a proper marriage could be had), where she took on management of the Charles Street Theatre. Keene found her way back to New York in 1855, set on having her own theatre.[3]

Female theatre managers were hardly unknown in antebellum America. Catherine Sinclair, Matilda Vining Wood, and most famously, Mrs. John Drew made similar undertakings during these years. Nevertheless, their lot was a hard one, for the job entailed moving outside Victorian gender expectations in so many ways. Keene's challenge to male prerogative met hostility from the theatrical fraternity. Her theatre was vandalized, she had trouble getting bank credit, and she lost her first theatre on a legal technicality. Highly competitive, headstrong, and acerbic, Keene instigated highly public newspaper brawls with other managers and financed aggressive advertising campaigns. But Keene was more than a provocateur. She envisioned a stage that would be more than a platform for stars to parade their virtuosity. She was among the first generation to seek a theatrical tout ensemble. Keene had no knowledge of small parts nor of the insignificant details of costume or scenery. To that end she assembled a company that rivaled that of trend-setting Wallack. Keene's sponsorship of audience-pleasing drama also merits mention. Her staging of *Our American Cousin* is famous, as is her championing the plays of Dion Boucicault. But Keene also understood perhaps better than her contemporaries the new importance of female theatergoers. She sought to give them a drama that appealed to their Victorian sensibility: stories of fallen

Laura Keene. From Joseph Jefferson, *Autobiography* (1890).

women, such as *Camille,* or women as victims of fraudulent marriage, like *Rachel the Reaper.*[4]

Keene is an important figure in nineteenth-century theatre whose personal legacy is decidedly mixed. "With a native grace at the start, a fresh and delicate inspiration," recalled Henry James, who visited her theatre as a youth, she "was to live to belie her promise, and, becoming hard and raddled, forfeit . . . all claim to the higher distinction." James's assessment may have lacked generosity, but it did grasp a self-destructive pattern that afflicted her career.[5]

After a promising start in 1856, her company faltered the following summer. Her stock company, the *Spirit of the Times* editor suggested, needed a "pretty thorough purgation." In particular, her male performers were "abominable." No doubt with this criticism in mind, Keene went out and hired the hottest young comedian on the circuit, Joe Jefferson. Joe joined a revamped acting company (the sole theatre relying only on its own stock company) for the opening of the fall season on 29 August. Keene needed every edge she could muster, for the *Spirit of the Times* predicted a fall of rugged dramatic competition. Whoever ran a theatre would "have no child's play to encounter."[6]

Joe's debut at Keene's came in his well-practiced role of Pangloss in *The Heir at Law,* followed on succeeding nights by two other standard farces of the afterpiece literature: Mr. Lullaby in *A Conjugal Lesson* and Dickory in *The Spectre Bridegroom.* New York critics were ecstatic. "Of truth, he is a man of genius," wrote the critic for the *Tribune.* "He is a comedian from his nose to his toes. He is as ductile as dough, as facile as gossamer." Both the *Tribune* and *Herald* critics were charmed by Joe's ability to make something new of the old chestnuts of low comedy. He infused a new sophistication into parts that were long the province of the pratfall and the boisterous gesture. Not so much restrained as refined, suitable now for the middle-class female spectator, Pangloss was "racy and laughable, without vulgarity." "To use a seeming paradox," a critic observed, he is a low comedian "who is not the least low." The *Tribune* critic in one of the few surviving detailed descriptions of Joe's early acting admired his stage entrance: before showing his face he extended through a door his leg—a drunken leg waving sinuously at the edge of the stage. By holding himself back, toying with the audience before emerging (ignoring the time-honored convention of a full and immediate entrance on the stage), Joe worked the audience into convulsions. Later, confronting an apparent ghost, Joe's makes his Dickory the epitome of fear, turning "his backbone into the consistence of calf's-foot jelly, the variety of the tints of unutterably forlorn terrors, were received by the audience with enthusiastic applause and laughter." In sum, said the critic, "better acting of the school cannot be found."[7]

September continued the run of good luck. In *A Conjugal Lesson,* Joe played a partying husband whose late night return home is complicated by incriminating evidence in the pocket of a coat he mistakenly wore home. The farce's "irresistible humor" so affected the audience that it "literally screamed with laughter," and Jefferson "established himself in the opinion of all present as the best comic actor in the country." He offered comic relief even in dramas. *Judith of Geneva,* described by a local critic as a "romantic drama of the atrocious school," gave opportunity for Joe to portray a good-natured tippler (a type he would elevate to high art in *Rip Van Winkle*). Connie acted alongside her brother in most productions, winning pleasing notices for modest roles. And on 10 September, Margaret gave birth to their second surviving son, Thomas. Joe now had a family of four to support.[8]

Laura Keene and Joseph Jefferson were off to a promising fall season. Her theatre seemed "a social reunion of friends, male and female, so pleasant and agreeable is everybody and everything." No one anticipated that capitalism's other, more demonic, face would so quickly intrude. A business failure in late

August set off a run on specie in September, which in turn dried up credit. The Panic of 1857 spread from New York across the Atlantic. Locally, business expansion halted and thousands of workers were laid off. By early November the specter of class war seemed at hand (as Karl Marx, following events from London, gleefully expected). Elite New Yorkers debated whether charity, public works, or militia protection was the order of the hour. Under Mayor Fernando Wood some variety of all three were tried. Patrons avoided theatres; even fifty-cent admissions now imperiled household budgets. The traditional Monday payday for actors stretched later in the week — if it ever came. Only the musicians, Joe claimed, had the leverage to demand their wages and get them.[9]

As indomitable as ever, Laura Keene refused to let economics dictate her stage. Jefferson gives Keene high marks for her mettle and her ability to find inexpensive substitutes for settings and costumes that maintained the look she coveted. "The dispiriting nature of the times" could not confound her, noted one paper. She lowered ticket prices and kept right on. Further, she mounted a timely farce, *Splendid Misery,* poking fun at social pretensions of parvenus that helped patrons for a few moments perhaps to forget their own miseries. What carried Keene through the heart of the business depression was the revival of a melodrama Joe had produced in Baltimore a few years earlier, *Sea of Ice, or a Mother's Prayer.* With a plot more implausible than most melodramas, the play achieved success through a combination of scenic tours de force, able casting, and an effective contrast of Old World society with the "wild grace and freedom of the half-savage" of the New World. From early November — when theatre business was said to be at its lowest point ever in New York City — until 19 December, the play defied recession, luring patrons to the theatre.[10]

The Panic of 1857, occurring as it did amidst a fundamentally sound American economy, did not set off as extended a depression such as the nation had experienced from 1837 until 1843. Still, New York's economy struggled into the spring of 1858, and Laura Keene found herself straining to make ends meet. Jefferson later suggested that part of the problem was Keene's selection of plays. "Too much influenced by their literary merit," she subordinated dramatic action to well-turned dialogue. No one would ever accuse Joseph Jefferson of confusing a polished script with compelling drama. No story or play was beyond alteration if a better dramatic effect could be secured. His thoroughly pragmatic approach to dramatic literature was grounded in a lifetime of theatre. Jefferson possessed a highly developed sense of what "works" on a stage, be it the cutting of a scene, the enhancement of a role, or a slightly altered piece of stage business.

In spring 1858 he put this theatrical sixth sense to good use. Along with

Keene's stage manager James G. Burnett, Joe adapted for the stage a well-known Revolutionary War story of George Lepard, *Blanche of Brandywine.* "Battles, marches and countermarches, murders, abductions, hairbreadth escapes, militia trainings, and extravagant Yankee comicalities boiled over in every chapter." Jefferson's and Burnett's effort was hardly the first of its kind. Revolutionary War plays dated back to *Bunker Hill,* a 1797 effort. The topic was a popular one, not only for obvious patriotic reasons but also because it was a subject where American playwrights had the field to themselves. Joe's production was less a drama than a loosely connected series of scenes — from Bunker Hill to the battle of Trenton — heavy with action and scenic effects. The expected assortment of military heroes and villainous Tories were present, but the gravity of the moment was tempered by the inclusion of stock comedy types, the Pennsylvania Dutchman and the Yankee. Something of the tenor of the play (and Jefferson's desire to provide himself a vehicle) can be seen in the generous part Joe penned for himself as Seth the Yankee. Jefferson placed himself "almost continually before the audience," as one critic observed, "whom he keeps in excellent humor." Joe's down-home wit notwithstanding, the play's appeal for New York audiences probably resided in its visual allure. The second act concluded with a stunning tableau based on John Trumbull's epic painting of the battle of Bunker Hill. "This scene alone is worth any price, almost, to witness," opined the *Spirit of the Times.* "Do not neglect to take your wives, daughters, sisters and sweetheart."[11]

When the long season ended in May 1858 Joe had much reason for satisfaction. The panic had not closed Laura Keene's theatre as it had some other prominent houses; indeed, there had been some notable successes. Joe had been granted two benefits, a privilege only Keene herself shared. Moreover, he essayed just thirty-six roles, formidable by modern standards but several steps down from the ninety roles he played during his earlier turn in New York in 1849–50. The advantages of fewer roles and greater repetition are obvious: more time to prepare a part and then perfect it. Joe was cultivating the repertoire on which his reputation was based.[12]

Jefferson returned to Laura Keene's company for the fall season. And why not? He was a featured performer in what was regarded as the leading company of New York. There were tensions, to be sure, in his relationship with Keene. "If the fair Laura kicks up any shindy with me (and we are not on loving terms) you shall hear from me," Joe wrote back to John Ford after Ford had queried him about a stint in Washington. This hedging of bets typified Jefferson's cautious approach to his career (if "cautious" can be used in a profession filled with risk). Stardom now appeared a real possibility, but any temptation he may have felt to hit the starring circuit may have been tempered by his friend Edwin Booth's missive to him the previous April. Booth had left New York to try his hand at itinerant starring. He encouraged Joe to do likewise. But the letter is filled with the ordeals of such a venture, and though comically conveyed, they were surely a reminder to Joe of what life on the road entailed. Those days would return soon enough, but for the immediate future Joe was content to enjoy the relative security of New York's stages.[13]

It was a prudent decision. The 1858 fall season proved to be the most notable of Keene's career. She had assembled a sparkling cast. Keene herself headlined a lineup of fourteen actresses. The eighteen male actors included several who would leave a bright mark on the American stage: Jefferson, comedian Edward A. Sothern, tragedian Charles Couldock, and in a more modest way, supporting actor Frank Bangs. The cast's genius lay in its sense of the ensemble, especially for comedy. "The indefatigable Miss Laura is certainly taking the town by storm," exuded the *Spirit of the Times,* "presenting a succession of sterling comedies which fill the house to overflowing nightly." Keene had no choice but to fill her house. Besides her large company, she had to write weekly checks to an orchestra and musical director, stage manager, treasurer, prompter, ballet master, scenic artist, machinist, costumer, and property man, not to mention the assemblage of dancers and supernumeraries frequently required. The daunting overhead demanded a string of successes.[14]

Our American Cousin

"The history of Laura Keene's for 1858–59," judged the great chronicler of the New York stage, George C. D. Odell, "is, to all intents and purposes, the history of the extraordinary success of *Our American Cousin.* The production set a record for its duration, assured Laura Keene her place in theatrical history, and put not only Joseph Jefferson but also Edward A. Sothern on the theatrical map. It is one of the "events" of American theatre history.[15]

Tom Taylor, English playwright and polymath (barrister, critic, professor, philologist, and editor of *Punch*) had initially submitted the script to James Wallack, an understandable choice given their friendship and the thoroughly British pedigree of Wallack's company. But Wallack demurred, noting that the prominent Yankee part found no adequate performer in his cast. Wallack's son Lester recalled many years later that his father — perhaps with a prescience that casts some suspicion on the memory — recommended that Taylor's agent take the play to Keene, because if the play was to succeed, "Jefferson is the man to make it." Even so, it was not immediately apparent that Keene would take up the offer. She was in the midst of preparations for a sumptuous production of *A Midsummer Night's Dream,* but production delays required a

The "Yankee" Asa Trenchard. From Joseph
Jefferson, *Autobiography* (1890).

stop-gap show to keep the theatre open. At this point her business manager/
lover John Lutz brought the script of *Our American Cousin* to Joe for an
opinion. He saw "little literary merit" but detected a promising theatricality.
And as always in these decisions, Joe considered whether there was a choice
role for him. Encouraged in this, he admitted, "I was quite selfish enough to
recommend the play for production" — and not only to recommend it, but also
to thoroughly vet it, making his character, Asa Trenchard, the cynosure.[16]

Joe was not the only member of Laura Keene's company with an ego. Casting the parts inevitably meant that some players received plums while others
lent distinctly secondary support. Edward A. Sothern, a rising young light
comedian (actors who would take the romantic leads and portray individuals of elegant breeding), forlornly scanned his vagrant lines and in a fit
of pique refused the part. Keene, understanding his discontent, gave him
license to improvise. Neither had any inkling of how Sothern would soon
transform the part into a household word. Indeed, Taylor's entire play was

substantially altered during rehearsal, the title itself being changed several times. (The nature of these alterations became the focus of an extended court battle.)[17]

Our American Cousin takes a melodramatic structure and adds an overlay of comedy. An English baronet, Edward Trenchard, is threatened by loss of property and status. Coyle, his business manager, has cheated him and now holds the mortgage of his largest estate (a variation of the hoariest melodramatic plot of all), threatening to ruin him if refused the hand of daughter Florence. At this moment of crisis, Asa Trenchard, a cousin from America, arrives from Vermont to claim an inheritance. Ungainly and unmannered, Trenchard nonetheless brings Yankee shrewdness and impeccable honesty to the troubled manor house. Meanwhile, in the usual fashion of comedy, other love plots move forward. Florence's desired marriage with a naval officer is stymied unless she can persuade Lord Dundreary (Sothern) to obtain a ship's command for her lover. And cousin Asa falls in love with a distant kinsperson and kindred spirit, dairy maid Mary, whose rightful inheritance he has inadvertently received. With the directness and good sense characteristic of the stage Yankee, Trenchard resolves all problems and ties up all loose ends. Dundreary is gently coerced into obtaining the necessary commission; Coyle is exposed as a swindler and compelled to stop threatening the baronet; and Trenchard restores the inheritance and wins the heart of Mary.

Our American Cousin began strong on 18 October and continued gaining momentum, running for an extraordinary 140 consecutive performances. Only *Uncle Tom's Cabin* and *The Drunkard* had gone longer. Seeing a performance became essential for anyone pretending to fashion. George Templeton Strong, the sober-minded lion of New York society, wrote in his diary of attending in November: "One Jefferson was admirable as the Yankee hero. . . . The fair and sinful Laura, though less fresh and dashing than she was some five years back, is fascinating still."[18]

What made the comedy so appealing? Certainly Taylor had produced a well-crafted piece. "The plot is not especially brilliant," wrote a critic in the *New York Times*, "but it runs smoothly." Comfortably familiar in its plot structure, the comedy had a serviceable script, particularly notable for its dialect. "The dialogue is by no means pretentious," the critic continued. "It is genial and homely rather than epigrammatic and brilliant." Taylor the philologist had a keen ear for language, and his plays contained cockney and other British dialects as well as Americanisms. He has Asa Trenchard and an English servant spar over whether one takes a "bawth" or a "bath," and the dialogue is littered with provincialisms of the day (he will "drop like a smoked possum," ran a typical Trenchardism). This line also suggests how Jefferson played his part as a cross between a Yankee and a backwoodsman. "I'm Asa

Trenchard, born in Vermont, suckled on the banks of Muddy Creek, about the tallest gunner, slickest dancer, and generally the loudest critter in the state," a boast worthy of Mike Fink. There were also wonderfully conceived theatrical moments. The emotional peak of the play comes as Asa Trenchard fabricates the story of how Mary's grandfather changed his will on his deathbed to make her his heir. Trenchard illustrates the grandfather's burning of the original will (making Asa his heir) by setting the paper afire with his cigar. Only the audience realizes that Asa is consuming the document that names him heir to the estate. A contrivance? Of course. But it constituted a brilliant piece of theatre. Taylor's play also appealed to American patriotism, a sentiment of which antebellum audiences seemed never to tire. It was the Yankee cousin full of natural good sense who crossed the ocean, sized up the situation at a glance, and saved the estate of his English cousin.[19]

If *Our American Cousin* had a certain freshness in its script, the production values helped make the play a success. Laura Keene lavished her usual care on the details. Completely new scenery was prepared. The acting company outdid itself in the exquisite harmony of effort. Keene was in the vanguard of the new emphasis on ensemble performance that would eventually sweep across theatre.

The play, the staging, the company all contributed to the comedy's success. But finally it was the two comic leads who put *Our American Cousin* on the map. Initially, Joseph Jefferson did the favor. His Asa Trenchard was in some respects the Yankee figure long familiar to audiences, "an odd, queer, quaint creature," who descended from Jonathan in Royall Tyler's *The Contrast*. But Jefferson recast the conventional type. His Asa Trenchard lacked the long hair, nasal voice, and short trousers of the stage Yankee. Trenchard dressed respectably in a light gray suit with matching hat and talked normally (though in dialect). The stage Yankee would never be the same. In making the figure less idiosyncratic, less of a "type," Jefferson rendered him more believable and thus more sympathetic. The process of remodeling stage characters as realistic beings rather than as stock types — one of the most important developments in nineteenth-century theatre — was underway. On a personal level, Jefferson would testify three decades later that his opening night success firmed up his resolve to become a star.[20]

But as much as *Our American Cousin* did for Jefferson, the play ignited the career of Edward A. Sothern (1826–81) even more. Born in Liverpool, Sothern came to America in 1852, joining Wallack's company two years later, where he remained until departing for Keene's in 1858. An intelligent, workmanlike actor, blessed by fine looks and striking silver hair, Sothern had known modest success as a journeyman, but his past career gave no hint of what was about to transpire. Initially dejected at the inconsequence of Dun-

E. A. Sothern's Dundreary. From Joseph
Jefferson, *Autobiography* (1890).

dreary, Sothern began experimenting with eccentricities. He made him an
affected dandy with a bright red frock coat, plaid pants, outrageous mut-
tonchop whiskers, and a monocle. The whimsical actor introduced a minstrel
shuffle that became the famous Dundreary hop. And he affected a sneeze, a
stammer, and lisp that would influence comedy right down to Mel Blanc's
cartoon voice for Elmer Fudd. "Iwwesistible," as Dundreary would say it, a
lampoon of British aristocracy that left audiences howling. The Dundreary
character evolved nightly over the first month or more of performance. His
unpredictable "gagging" to gain the spotlight would normally have earned the
cast's reproach. But his fellow actors seemed not to mind. It quickly became
clear that Dundreary, that "vapid, languid, vacuous swell," brought another
level of attraction to the play. Anyone who had not seen the play for two
weeks, a reviewer advised, would now find it a "different affair altogether." At
some point during the season Dundreary became the play's star and a cultural

phenomenon. Certainly no other figure would be as remembered. Jefferson, generous in his assessment of Sothern's accomplishment, recalled that by the play's end Sothern was "considerably in advance of us all." Sothern took a melodrama laced with comedy and essentially refashioned it into farce. His career now established, he went on to perform Dundreary and similar types for the next twenty years.[21]

Our American Cousin ran to the end of 1858 and on into the new year with no sign of losing momentum. Advertising for the play became easy: simply count the nights performed, the patrons attracted, and let the figures speak for themselves. "Forty thousand people," an ad trumpeted in mid-November, a figure it revised upward regularly. By February the *Spirit of the Times* mocked, "We have almost despaired of seeing anything but *Our American Cousin* at Laura Keene's for the next year or two." As always, the play's triumph summoned imitators. Burton's Theatre staged a travesty of Keene's hit entitled *Our Female American Cousin*. At the Bowery, George L. Fox, the great miming clown, gave his own send-up, *Our English Cousin*. A group of amateur thespians paid homage by forming the Joseph Jefferson Dramatic Association in early 1859. For Joe's February benefit, the *New York Clipper* urged a liberal turnout, celebrating "the ability and tact with which the character of the hero — Asa Trenchard — is nightly sustained by Joseph Jefferson.[22]

By March the play would be retired temporarily (later revived again and again). Keene was anxious to get back to the *Midsummer Night's Dream* production so long delayed. In the manner of such things, success sowed the seeds of dissension. Blame can be laid at several doors. Laura Keene's for one, whom fortune had not mellowed. As the season progressed the "duchess," basking in the gaslight glow of success, took on an imperious manner. When she and Sothern changed a bit of stage business without informing Joe, he prematurely entered the stage, stepping on their lines. Keene barked at him — fully audible to the audience — "Go off the stage, sir, till you get your cue for entering." Jefferson responded in kind, the most serious breach of theatrical protocol. The resulting row after the curtain fell led to a serious rupture between the two.[23]

But as Jefferson himself admitted in his *Autobiography,* he must field some responsibility for the alienation. His new celebrity nurtured a "confidence in my growing strength" that challenged Keene's control. The heady spirits of stardom made Joe impatient with the necessary subordination to a company and its strong-willed manager. Never one to meekly suffer affronts, he now became even more impatient. It is hard not to conclude that he was seeking reasons to leave the company.

In any event, it did not take Joe long to sense another insult. He had informed Keene that he would not return to her company in the fall. She took the news badly, accusing Joe of disloyalty, sniffing at his intention to attempt starring, and refusing to give permission for him to take *Our American Cousin* on the road. Joe soon seized his revenge. In the upcoming *Midsummer Night's Dream* he had anticipated playing Bottom, the role normally assigned the low comedian. But that left nothing for Rufus Blake, an exceedingly portly low comedian who had joined the company months earlier but had been left without a role during the long run of *Our American Cousin*. Keene implored Joe to undertake Puck instead, but he stood on his customary right of role selection in his line. One struggles to imagine Joe as Oberon's mischievous sprite. But after a few rehearsals, Joe sensed his unsuitability for the part of Bottom and thus offered Keene a compromise: he would step aside if she allowed him the rights to *Our American Cousin* (sharing with her the profits). Finding common ground at last, a very public rift was closed.[24]

Under Boucicault's Spell

Joe's starring turn in midspring of 1859 was short and undistinguished. The *New York Clipper* reported in late April that he had "sloped" to Buffalo for an engagement. He then traveled northeast to Halifax (his only known appearance in Canada) to offer Asa Trenchard to the Haligonians. His starring turn in *Our American Cousin* was under the auspices of the Sothern company (though E. A. Sothern himself remained safely in New York). In later May he turned south to Portland, Maine, in the same play. "My starring adventure," Jefferson frankly admitted, "was attended with what is termed qualified success; not with what could be called positive failure." Not that this dampened his ambitions. He negotiated with Tom Taylor to get the British rights to the play, hectoring (unsuccessfully as it turned out) Benjamin Webster, prominent manager of the Adelphi Theatre, for use of his stage. Newspaper reports in early June had Joe leaving for England, ostensibly to star in *Our American Cousin* at London's Haymarket. The *Clipper* warned him that the Haymarket is "a solemn Church" and feared he may be disappointed to find that "London theatres are not the toys for everybody to make a jingle with on the New York principle." Jefferson, who rarely let his vaunting ambitions trump his streak of realism, determined not to go, instead choosing the shorter and safer route to Boston's Howard Atheneaum for a brief run.[25]

Joe's new prosperity allowed him to "summer" properly. He moved his family (including the unmarried Mary Devlin) from New York to eastern Pennsylvania's Pocono Mountains, an area becoming known as a rustic retreat for actors. The summer's rest had an imperative beyond family bonding. From childhood Joe had, in his words, been "delicate." His family's scourge, tuberculosis, damaged a lung. With a tenacity belied by his laconic persona, Joe had soldiered on during his long apprenticeship, refusing to concede an inch to the cough, fever, spotting of blood, and night sweats that periodically visited. But as soon as he was financially able he sought a routine that provided seasonal relief from an otherwise torturous schedule. His family boarded in a rambling farmhouse in Paradise Valley, with all of the country amenities that the Jefferson children learned to love. In the local stream Joe began his lifelong affair with fly fishing; in the evenings he strummed his guitar for local children on the piazza surrounding the house. It was, for a family unaccustomed to the stability of a home, an idyll.[26]

Joe allowed himself only a few weeks respite. Although he did not yet possess the drawing power of a first-magnitude star, he recognized that his moment was at hand. A half-year beyond his thirtieth birthday now, he dared not miss a opportunity to put himself before the public. By 23 July he returned to New York's Niblo Gardens for a brief engagement. Margaret, five months into her sixth pregnancy, acted alongside him. During this slow part of the theatrical season Joe enjoyed a benefit performance at Niblo's that gave a measure of his soaring popularity. He was still publicly toying with a tour to England, which may have brought out his fans in unusual number. Joe rewarded them with excerpts from four of his popular comic roles. At the end — according to the custom of the day — he went before the crowd to give his thanks and admit that his fall travel plans remained unsettled. Jefferson must be proud at the way "his friends and admirers rallied to his standard," the *Times* admired. "The public mustered at the call of their favorite actor in crowds." The *Clipper* editor approached the event more cynically, suspecting the previously announced departure for England as a pretext for packing the house.[27]

The autumn season of 1859 proved as significant for Jefferson as had that of the previous year. Prompted by restlessness and the hope of escaping the difficult Laura Keene, he signed on at manager William Stuart's Winter Garden. At the Winter Garden he encountered one of the most vital men of the nineteenth-century stage: Dion Boucicault (1822?–90). The Anglo-Irish Boucicault had risen meteorically in the British theatre, having written at age twenty *London Assurance*, a comedy of manners that quickly became a repertory standard. He performed intermittently but with success throughout his fifty-year career on both sides of the Atlantic. His genius lay in stagecraft and an eye for possibility. He translated and adapted French melodramas for the English stage, wrote original dramas, and staged myriad productions. Of the two hundred plays he created or doctored (few of his works were completely original) the great majority were potboilers: *Peg Woffington, The Corsican Brothers, The Poor of New York, Dot, The Colleen Bawn, The Octoroon, The Shaughraun,* and *Arrah-na-Pogue.* These titles, known only to a small circle today, resonated with audiences of his day as few works did. Boucicault brought to the stage current topics—urban life, Mormonism, race relations, even India's Sepoy revolt—cleverly staged with an eye to the sensational effects audiences were learning to crave. He also transformed the highly caricatured stage Irishman into a figure of human warmth. Boucicault's delicate good looks and bald pate bestowed a cherubic demeanor, but his manner was anything but angelic. He was among the most hard-driving—and disliked—men of the theatre, frequently accused of stealing others' ideas while aggressively contesting any intrusion on his own dramatic turf. ("If he steals satin, he embroiders it with silk," Joe once said charitably, typifying the qualified praise that Boucicault earned from those who knew him well.) Whatever his flaws, Dion Boucicault twice played major parts in Jefferson's life. The first in the 1859–60 season; the second in his revision of *Rip Van Winkle* for Joe in 1865.[28]

In early September Joe began rehearsals under Boucicault's direction for *Dot,* an adaptation of Dickens's 1845 Christmas tale, *The Cricket on the Hearth.* The story was not one of Dickens's stronger efforts ("mawkish and maudlin," one reviewer said), lacking both the vivid characters and the evocative power of *A Christmas Carol.* Modern readers will find Boucicault's script no better. Its lachrymose sentimentality is unremitting. All the chestnuts of Victorian melodrama are present: constrained family circumstances that will be relieved if dutiful daughter May will marry the knavish Tackleton; the misplaced jealousy of John toward his faithful wife Dot; the noble, wronged, impoverished Caleb, who patiently waits for his son while mercifully deceiving his blind daughter into thinking they live in beautiful surroundings; and Caleb's son Edward, who ran away to the sea, is presumed dead, but returns to claim his beloved May. In the spirit of a Christmas drama, even the scheming Tackleton redeems himself through an act of charity. Bathos suffuses the drama; yet in different versions the play remained popular among nineteenth-century audiences. How to account for this?[29]

First, there is the obvious fact that Victorian audiences enjoyed being moved to tears, which the play facilitated through several subplots. Authorship must also be considered. Charles Dickens had secured a literary standing among the burgeoning middle classes that guaranteed an audience for his efforts. Moreover, Dickens's works adapted well to theatre; indeed, some scholars see Dickens's fiction as profoundly indebted to the early Victorian stage. But one must also credit the genius of Dion Boucicault. He intuitively grasped how to exploit the theatrical potential of a story. Boucicault understood, for example, the singular effect of using a recurring cricket's chirp as symbol of hearth and home. Home and family, the cherished locus of English and American culture, stirred audiences to anxiety when threatened and to tears of relief when restored.[30]

Boucicault also grasped how particular scenes in drama should be played. Jefferson pays high tribute to Boucicault's shrewd advice on attempting Caleb Plummer. The role represented Joe's first sustained excursion into a more serious part (though Joe had briefly performed in another version of Dickens's story earlier in the 1850s), one that demanded sustained pathos. Like many comedians facing similar attempts, he experienced self-doubt. Boucicault, having "more confidence in my powers than I had," sought to reassure him, but Joe insisted as a condition of the role that he be allowed an afterpiece farce, *Bobtail and Wagtail,* to redeem his reputation. (This lasted only several nights; neither the play nor Jefferson needed help.) Further, during rehearsals Boucicault observed how intensely Joe attacked his first scenes (acting "your last scene first"), leaving no way for the part to build. After a moment's struggle with his actor's ego, Joe took the suggestion to heart. The encounter, by his own testimony, profoundly influenced his approach to role preparation thereafter. Through understated performance he sought to hint at a character's inner emotion, holding back the full display of self until the crucial moment of the drama was at hand.[31]

Dot opened on 14 September and, if not the overwhelming smash of *Our American Cousin,* was by contemporary standards a great hit, running for more than a month. Critical plaudits were passed around like party favors. Agnes Robertson (for whom Boucicault prepared the piece originally) scored marks for her "delicate artistic perception" of the good-hearted peasant wife Dot. Mrs. John Wood, who as the doltish servant Tillie Slowboy had the best comic lines (in an unusual female low comedy role), "kept the audience in a continuous roar." But Joseph Jefferson enjoyed the "triumph of the evening." The writer for *Frank Leslie's* found Joe's Plummer "quaint and beautiful; we have never seen a more careful and evenly balanced conception and execution of character. This gentleman has earned for himself a reputation well deserved." "Mr. Jefferson as the Toy Maker Every Evening," simply stated one ad, suggesting the importance of Joe to the drama's appeal.[32]

The play ran so strongly that for a time ticket scalpers raised premiums on the valued ducats. But the production suffered some degradation as the weeks progressed. By the middle of October the *Times* critic felt it necessary to score certain of the cast for clogging the script with "cheap and worthless emendations and paltry interpolations." Mrs. John Wood, in particular, among the greatest burlesque performers of the age, could not restrain her urge to have Tillie Slowboy steal every scene. Audiences fell off their seats in delight, but at the cost of Wood's stepping on other performers' lines. "The permanent repu-

The toy maker Caleb Plummer. From Joseph
Jefferson, *Autobiography* (1890).

tation of an artist is not plucked from the ready laugh of an astonished parquette," the *Times* scolded. Joe escaped censure. To the contrary, he was commended for his discretion. He was among the few "eminent low comedians
who can command pathos and the only one . . . who perceives the true Dickensian balance." This balance, which might be understood as two parts pathos
mixed with one part folksy humor, became the Jefferson stage formula.[33]

Caleb Plummer entered Joseph Jefferson's repertoire, revisited in future years
of stardom when Rip needed respite. Some considered Caleb his best role, even
after his later triumphs. Laurence Hutton, among the most informed and
articulate of mid to late nineteenth-century critics, described his Plummer as
"simply perfection," "the best things that he ever played." "We saw it often,"
Hutton reminisced, "never wearied of it, and were willing to go to Winter
Garden at least once a week to sympathize with Caleb, to laugh at and rejoice
with him, and to shed over him tears which we could not restrain."[34]

Boucicault and Jefferson teamed up to rework another Dickens story in late

October. *Smike* was the Irish master's title for his loose adaptation of *Nicholas Nickleby.* This most overtly theatrical of Dickens's works is barely recognizable in Boucicault's hands ("without a plot worthy of the name," sniffed one critic). His dramatic pen focused on the novel's minor characters. Jefferson portrayed Newman Noggs, the tippling clerk of Ralph Nickleby, who though not a villain, in the manner of English stage drunkards must die at the end. *Smike* was another popular triumph for Boucicault and Jefferson, running a gratifying nineteen nights. Again Jefferson garnered the most critical attention. "Newman Noggs is — what shall we say? — a surprise," wrote the admiring *Times* reviewer, "such as each new role becomes in the hands of this admirable actor." The unnamed reviewer put his finger on an aspect of Joe's art. In a dramatic age of rigid type casting, where versatility was less highly regarded, Jefferson approached his craft rather differently. Theatergoers were accustomed to actors who put on their role as casually as their costume. But Joe poured himself so completely in his part that audiences were "tempted to believe he can never emerge again to fill any other part. When he was Caleb Plumber [*sic*], who believed that he ever played Asa Trenchard? Now that he is Newman Noggs, who will believe that he was ever Caleb Plumber?"[35]

While Joe's professional career advanced, his domestic life encountered ordeals all too familiar to the age. He and Margaret now had a more permanent home. Its location, though unknown, may have been in Yorkville, on the Upper East Side of Manhattan. During the 1850s this still-rural environ became so favored a residence of players as to be called "Actorsville." Here, in early November 1859, a sixth child, Josephine Duff (better known as Josie), was born. Margaret, whose health was beginning to falter, now had four children under age nine to nurture. Worse, a nurse dropped Josie, damaging her back and leaving her essentially disabled for life. The pathos Joe portrayed so well on stage insinuated itself into his private life.[36]

The Melodramatic Vision

Another production by Boucicault and Jefferson, their most acclaimed and controversial one, had a different sort of subject matter: race relations. Boucicault's *The Octoroon* treated less the issue of slavery than the more nuanced matter of how race should be defined, but it tackled this subject at a volatile moment in American history. *The Octoroon* illustrates both the power of melodrama and its inherent limitations.

The artistic impoverishment of nineteenth-century melodrama, long a truism of both popular and academic perceptions, has given way to a begrudging appreciation. The change was a long time coming. "It is impossible to mention the word drama," wrote English critic Leigh Hunt in the early nineteenth century, "without being struck by the exceeding barrenness which the stage has exhibited of late years." The situation was deemed serious enough in England to merit a parliamentary investigation in the 1830s. American contemporaries understood the condition of their stage to be no better. Managers preferred dramas filled with "pasteboard, tinsel, and trumpery," dramatist James Kirke Paulding complained. The conventional Whig interpretation of American theatre history sees an early domination by melodrama and other inferior forms of theatre that were finally challenged in the late nineteenth century by works of James A. Herne, William Vaughn Moody, and a few other harbingers of realism before Eugene O'Neill put American drama on the map in the 1920s.[37]

It is true that the economics of the theatre, including lack of copyright protection for dramatists, discouraged first-rate drama. But there were aesthetic reasons as well. Michael Booth sees the early nineteenth-century playwrights as captured by a past tradition of dramatic greatness and by a more recent Romantic passion for gothic extravagance, which resulted in a theatrical literature that was cut off from its immediate social context. But melodramas, Booth insists, infused new life into theatre, putting theatre back in touch with its audience. Often charged with being simply escapist entertainment, it in fact roused middle-class passions unlike any other cultural form. *Masaniello* helped spark Belgium's drive for independence in 1850. *Uncle Tom's Cabin* and *Ten Nights in a Bar-room* galvanized social crusades of great importance to America. Further, melodrama became the driving force behind advances in stagecraft during the century. Improvements in scenery, props, and lighting all followed from melodrama's incessant demand for greater realism across the entire range of theatre.[38]

Melodrama was an international phenomenon, born in France and quickly spreading to Germany, England, and America. Why its immediate appeal? George Steiner has provided a partial answer — an enabling condition, one might say — in his much-cited "death of tragedy." The Romantic impulse, in Steiner's view, driven by its willful heroes and a renunciation of innate evil, killed the tragic impulse. Peter Brooks takes the argument a step further, asserting that melodrama replaced a tragic vision with its own sensibility. The mythmaking of an older sacred order no longer found resonance in a democratizing, postrevolutionary society. "The dissolution of an organic and hierarchically cohesive society" undermined such literary forms as tragedy and comedy of manners that required those qualities. The need for venerable sanctions did not disappear but now had to be found elsewhere. Melodrama provided such ritual sanctions in a radically secular, democratic format. Its resolutions did not reconcile humans with a transcendent power — as in tragedy — but with a more mundane social order, which through the action of the play was momentarily purified of evil. The melodramatic mode, claims Brooks, is "the central fact of modern sensibility."[39]

The alienation of American audiences from a tragic vision reflected the hopeful tenor of national life. Melodrama bespoke the prevailing worldview of progress and moral order, promising reward to the virtuous and hard-working, regardless of station in life. The melodramatic hero, historian David Grimsted asserts, was "nature's nobleman," a pure Jeffersonian in rejecting rank and privilege.[40]

In conveying their message of threat and deliverance, melodramas followed a set of stereotypes that became so clichéd as to invite burlesque even in their day. Melodramas were peopled by symbolic figures — heroines whose virtue was at risk; villains who sought to defile chastity or indulge avarice (or both); heroes who confounded evil; an aged father or mother who embodied wisdom and virtue but whose situation was frequently desperate; and a series of low comedy types whose humor and humanity added a dollop of realism. These figures portrayed a world of innocence into which strode villainy. No ambiguity clouded the stage; virtue was apparent at first glance. ("Character is destiny," Joseph Donohue phrased it.) Rarely was change or development of character allowed, although insight into motive was frequently verbalized at the end. Evil resulted from individual malfeasance rather than from social inequity, a notion critical to Americans' faith in the essential goodness of their society.[41]

Melodramatic dialogue, wooden and predictable as it was, took a distinctly second place to action. The genre had originally depended on music and pantomime, and in a sense that never changed. It was not a writer's theatre. It sold spectacle. Gothic melodrama intended to horrify with scenes of graveyards or evoke foreboding with forlorn renderings of wild heaths and moors. When urban melodrama gained popularity toward midcentury, producers sought to convey a palpable sense of city life and its dangers (in particular, catastrophes such as the fire in Boucicault's 1857 production of *The Poor of New York*, considered one of the great effects of the century). The sort of lavish stage spectacle associated with later century had made its appearance well before 1850. Although still working within the day's limitations of lighting (electric illumination would not appear until the 1880s), stage artisans accomplished feats of realism that a less visually sophisticated age found convincing. Indeed, melodrama's most careful student, Michael Booth, asserts that melodrama was a creature of technology. Its true stars were the carpenters, gas men, costume designers, and machinists.[42]

The visual emphasis was appropriate to the externalization of life that melo-drama portrayed. Audiences went to the theatre not to plumb human depths but to gain reconfirmation that the moral law of nature would at last triumph. The suffering of the virtuous, the peril to the family, had a purpose. Menacing villains often served as catalysts to help families resolve chronic problems. These transcendent purposes of melodrama, of course, had to be highly enter-taining and visually arresting, for above all patrons went to the theatre to enjoy themselves. The power of melodrama to deeply move cannot be denied. In modern dress, its enchantment continues unabated.[43]

The Octoroon, a prime example of midcentury melodrama and surrounded by controversy from beginning till end, has several histories. It is notable for its subject matter; it served to advance the cause of copyright protection; and it provided yet another vehicle for the ascending career of Joseph Jefferson.[44]

Boucicault adapted the play from Mayne Reid's novel *The Quadroon* and slated it to premiere at the Winter Garden when *Smike* closed. He created the Yankee part of Salem Scudder specifically for Jefferson. Nonetheless, Joe had a problem with the production. Ever vigilant to guard his prerogatives as a leading player, he was outraged to discover that early announcements of *The Octoroon* failed to mention him. "I felt I was something of a favorite with the public, and naturally became irate at this indignity." Joe sent his part back to management along with his resignation, keeping the door ajar, however, by promising to listen to any reasonable offer they might suggest. His act was carefully contrived. He resigned on Saturday; the play opened Monday. As he expected, management did reconsider and he returned with honor and pub-licity intact.[45]

The Octoroon, or Life in Louisiana partook of the "tragic octoroon" tradi-tion of American letters that dated to the 1830s. In this highly stereotyped story line a beautiful young woman, light-skinned but with African heritage (Boucicault's octoroon being, of course, even more white than Reid's quad-roon), is raised as a cultivated white lady, often possessing a distinguished lineage on her paternal side. To the virtuous ingenue comes threat. Zoe (played by Agnes Robertson) is "the natural Child of the late Judge by a Quadroon Slave." When her father-protector dies, Zoe discovers her true status. Worse, her father's indebted estate is attached by creditors. Slave dealer McCloskey has her in his clutches. The play works its way to its tragic end, the plot aided by ingenious use of a recent invention, the camera.[46]

The role of Salem Scudder gave Joe a chance to return to his comfortable and best-known stage persona. Scudder has the rough-hewn integrity of all Yankees, capable of spotting a knave at a hundred paces. He is onto the villain's game from the beginning, and his camera provides the evidence of the villain's crime, which ultimately leads to the law of frontier justice effecting its awful vengeance. Scudder also serves as Greek chorus, summing up the play's development and commenting on the action. As such, he is given the last word. After Zoe's suicide (by poison), he concludes the play with the pithy irony: "Poor child; she is free."[47]

The Octoroon is an unusually well-constructed melodrama, meriting the enthusiasm it received. The shrewd Boucicault grasped the timeliness of the subject. The play opened just three days after John Brown's execution. The United States Senate was in the midst of — as the *Times* phrased it — a "Violent Discussion of the Slavery Question." Talk of secession in the South was passing beyond idle threat. In this environment *The Octoroon* might seem one more northern attack on the peculiar institution. The *New York Herald* warned its readers about the dire impact of "niggerism" on the stage. Antislavery could only lead to problems, as indeed it already had at the Winter Garden, where (the paper noted with unspoken satisfaction) threats had led to the withdrawal of one of the cast. The *Spirit of the Times* writer was more blunt. *The Octoroon's* effect is "to misrepresent and villify [*sic*] the South." Worse, its "gross libel upon the social relations of the South has been hailed by a part of the press, and a gaping multitude, with 'an unparalleled enthusiasm.' " The reviewer took offense at nearly every aspect of Boucicault's drama. That three white men would "seriously propose to 'marry a nigger' " defied southern conventions. That "the ignorant and degraded beings" — the southern slaves — should have anything in common with the portrayal of Zoe ("dressed in snowy muslin, and overflowing with sentiment and sensitiveness") was ridiculous. And if such a being existed "the taint of her blood would create a gulf between her and the whites that would be wider than the poles. . . . The incendiary author of this piece creates . . . the false idea that there is an equality in the races, an idea that is preposterous, unnatural, and profane." The climactic outrage came with Zoe's being put on the auction block. Such things happened, the reviewer had to admit, but to so characterize southern life "is disgusting," and those holding up such a distorted mirror are "guilty of the worst kind of treason."[48]

In truth, Boucicault almost certainly never intended a slander upon the South. As an Irishman he probably shared his countrymen's typical disdain for the slaves. Further, his eye was firmly fixed on the box office. He fashioned a work safely within the well-established octoroon tradition that would have broad appeal (though there is no evidence that the play was staged in the South before the war). Jefferson concurs. "The truth of the matter is," he judges, "it was non-committal." The story certainly told against slavery's pernicious nature, yet the characters were drawn in a manner to evoke sympathy for the region. At the notorious slave auction scene, for example, the bidders and auctioneer strive to keep families intact. And the southern belle Dora (Zoe's

rival for the affections of George Peyton), as witless and insipid as she sometimes appears, offers her own fortune to buy and release Zoe. During the
performance audiences cheered for nobility on both sides, whether it reflected
well on North or South.[49]

The Octoroon was a sensation. Even standing-room tickets were scarce.
Pre-opening night rumors of a threatened disruption proved unfounded. For
Jefferson, the play was another in a string of triumphs. The *Times* review,
though partial to Joe's "rarer talents" as Newman Noggs or Caleb Plummer,
allowed that in his Yankee specialty he excelled. "In all the broader phases of
the character Mr. Jefferson brought down the house with abundant laughter,
and in the sadder ones achieved the greater triumph of true and earnest pathos." The play ran without interruption from 5 December 1859 until 21 January 1860. For all the controversy it evoked, the most consequential disputes
were purely internal and concerned not slavery but money and ownership.[50]

From Stage to Court

Theatre people could be among the most amiable of folk. Certainly the
nature of their work, reinforced by chronic low-grade social prejudice, encouraged a tight-knit, even parochial, community. But when money was at
stake the gloves came off. Actors showed no reluctance to take their professional kinsmen to court when aggrieved, nor did managers or playwrights. In
the latter case, the issue was clouded by a near total absence of effective copyright protection. Joseph Jefferson (who only once — in mid-career — initiated
theatrical litigation) learned these hard facts firsthand in 1859 and 1860 when
he found himself in the middle of salary disputes and copyright fights.

In early 1860, during the *Octoroon* run, Joe was called to testify on behalf
of George Jordan. Employed by Laura Keene as a "leading man," Jordan was
taking the temperamental manager to court to recover salary withheld when
he refused a role he considered insufficient. Keene argued that the production
suffered poor attendance because of his absence. Jordan summoned Jefferson
to tell the jury about the theatrical custom of not forcing players to act either
outside of their line or below the level for which they had been hired. Joe well
understood the issue, having left Keene's less than a year earlier over this very
complaint. A leading player may not always choose his role, Jefferson conceded (perhaps this was the stage manager in him speaking), but the part
Keene attempted to force on Jordan was clearly not a leading one, certainly
less consequential than another available role. Four other actors supported
Jordan's contention, and a jury subsequently awarded him a hundred dollars
in damages.[51]

This squabble — examples of which could be multiplied — signified the jeal-ous regard actors had for their roles. What may appear simple pettiness — refusing to accept a role even if salary was unaffected — actually bespoke a more serious issue. Professional reputation was at stake. Players marked their standing by their ability to define their line of acting business. Our modern regard for versatility in actors awaited the twentieth century. Nor did the later fashion of stars taking the occasional small part in a play or movie they admired find any resonance among stage luminaries of the nineteenth century. Joe's own demands for proper billing and selection of his roles were little different from what other ambitious players claimed.

Jefferson also figured in battles over copyright ownership of two plays he had helped propel to success: *Our American Cousin* and *The Octoroon*. As in so much of his career, Joe found himself present at telling moments in theatre history. In these cases he witnessed early tests of recently revised American copyright law. Under longstanding common law doctrine, the public produc-tion of a play put the work in the public domain. For playwrights, perfor-mance of their work was the whole point, and practically speaking they la-bored without copyright protection. Thus, they commonly sold outright their literary efforts to stars or managers who had commissioned them (better to get the money up front). Stars, in turn, protected the precious starring vehicle by memorizing their lines and giving the supporting cast their lines and cues only. Despite precautions, play piracy was endemic, becoming more of a problem as printed versions of plays became common at midcentury.[52]

The lack of any international copyright also meant American play pirates could loot European dramas with impunity, opening a wide door for the staging of English plays. America's impoverished dramatic literature was com-monly explained by the ease with which managers could import foreign plays at no cost. Why is there "no standard American drama" asked Joseph Jones, who at midcentury exemplified America's small corps of playwrights. "One of the best answers is, nobody will pay for it," he replied. The cause was taken up by the Copyright Club in 1843 and publicized repeatedly in literary journals and newspapers like the *Spirit of the Times*.[53]

Protracted lobbying, particularly by those most affected, American play-wrights, finally succeeded in effecting change. George Henry Boker, whose *Francesca da Rimini* is generally considered America's finest verse drama of the century, used his political connections to get a bill brought before Congress in 1853. It would take three more years and the support of Philadelphia publisher Henry C. Carey and the irrepressible Dion Boucicault to win pas-sage of an important revision of federal copyright law in 1856. The remedy was incomplete, as the law covered only titles, a gaping loophole that allowed virtually identical plays with different titles to escape sanction. Disputes arose that could only be resolved only judicially.[54]

Laura Keene had purchased *Our American Cousin* from Tom Taylor after he had encountered difficulty in marketing it. Although Keene held a copyright on the piece, its handle proved slippery. Unauthorized versions soon appeared in and out of New York. In Philadelphia, just six weeks after the New York premiere, John Sleeper Clarke and William Wheatley opened a production at the Arch Street Theatre, which enjoyed a long run. Laura Keene instituted legal action. With neither side willing to settle, the case went to court: *Laura Keene vs. Wheatley and Clarke.* The case offers an unusual glimpse into the competitive underside of the theatrical world.[55]

Clarke and Wheatley defended their production on the grounds of having acquired a different version of the play than Keene's. In truth, an unauthorized copy of Taylor's play had been imported from England. But the script they used was not the unauthorized copy, but rather the one Jefferson had shaped into the hit it became. This script, with Joe's penciled emendations, was entered into evidence, crucially compromising Clarke's and Wheatley's claim to having acquired their vehicle independently.[56]

How, then, did the pair imitate the New York version so closely? Two ways. Several of their company attended performances intently noting stage business. Had they been able to recreate the play purely from their firsthand observations, Clarke and Wheatley would have been within the law. But they needed more in order to duplicate her version. Jefferson himself volunteered a copy of his revised script. It was an inside job.

Why would Jefferson abet Clarke and Wheatley in their piracy? It may be that given his part in revising the play, Joe felt free to share it as he wished. Too, Joe and Clarke shared close ties. They had spent part of a previous summer barnstorming together. They both belonged to the Rabelaisian fraternity of low comedians. If jealous toward his own billing and selection of roles, Joe withheld no professional secrets from fellow actors. It may also be that Jefferson considered a Philadelphia production of *Our American Cousin* as no competition to Keene. This was before the age of the touring company, and it was unlikely that Keene would decide to take the play on the road to the City of Brotherly Love. In truth, Joe displayed naivete. He did not consider what he did as — in the court's blunt phrase — "a breach of professional duty." Apparently neither did Keene, or at any rate she readily forgave Joe his indiscretion. This contretemps was well before their much-publicized feud a few months later, and she had reason to be grateful for his part in laying the comedic golden egg. Still, it must have been an embarrassing moment for Joe to suffer a public revelation of his part in aiding the Philadelphia play pirates.[57]

A year later Joe found himself again entangled in litigation. Just as *The Octoroon* had established itself as a Broadway success, Dion Boucicault and wife Agnes Robertson left the production, purportedly because Robertson's racially controversial role had evoked threatening letters. "I felt that I was unconsciously made the instrument to wound the feelings of one part of the public," Robertson confessed, implicitly blaming Winter Garden management. But this was surely a pretext. The heart of the battle between the Boucicaults and manager William Stuart was control of a play that had turned into a bigger hit than anyone anticipated.[58]

Boucicault and his wife had contracted for her to star and him to stage manage and write two dramas during the Winter Garden's fall season. It had been a modestly rewarding arrangement for them if not for the theatre until *The Octoroon*'s unexpected fortune sent profits skyrocketing. Robertson's salary, tied to box office receipts, soared; Boucicault's income remained flat, despite authorship. Renegotiations with management soured, and on 14 December they left. Management sensed the disaffection and was prepared. A copy of the prompter's script had been prepared (Boucicault walked out with the original), and two other members of the cast were moved to fill the vacancies. Louise Allen, herself a beauty, took on the part of Zoe to creditable notices, and the show continued to packed houses. "Everyone talks about *The Octoroon*, goes to see *The Octoroon*, wonders about *The Octoroon*," the *Times* opined.[59]

The inevitable legal battles started soon afterwards. Boucicault initiated proceedings to prevent Stuart from staging the play. Stuart and his partner, anticipating an unfriendly judgment, effected a shrewd maneuver, selling their tenuous rights to other impresarios and closing their production on 21 January 1860. The new defendants took a fresh tack, claiming that Boucicault's *Octoroon* had various authorial origins. At this point Jefferson was deposed. His testimony offered little succor to the man with whom he had just labored. Joe suggested that *The Octoroon* had its roots in Mayne Reid's novel *The Quadroon*. As it happened, the issue of origins was irrelevant to the case, and Boucicault ultimately received a small judgment against the defendants.[60]

The case, as minor as it seems, helped break new copyright ground. It affirmed that a play may receive copyright protection even if it was a reworking of earlier material. More significantly, it established that the public performance of an uncopyrighted play does not constitute an author's loss of such property to either the public or the theatrical profession. The litigation over *Our American Cousin* and *The Octoroon* (and Boucicault, like Keene, defended his intellectual turf against several challengers) were early clashes in recurrent wars against play piracy in the late nineteenth century. *The Black*

Crook, Under the Gaslight, Hazel Kirke, Pirates of Penzance — virtually all of the greatest box office hits of these decades contended with unauthorized productions. Beginning in the early 1880s, under the prompting of *New York Mirror* editor Harrison Grey Fiske, a final major campaign to enlarge both domestic and foreign copyright protection got underway, ultimately achieving that purpose.[61]

These incidents held personal significance for Jefferson. In both cases he found himself awkwardly poised in court against close associates. And yet he managed to later regain cordial — or at least working — relations with Boucicault and patched over more serious differences with Keene. The rapprochement should probably be credited less to human relations gifts on Jefferson's part than to the more general need in the theatre world to quarrel — but then put away the dispute should future work so require. Players and managers could be a litigious fraternity, but the brotherhood, in the end, usually prevailed.[62]

When Boucicault left the Winter Garden the task of stage managing fell to Jefferson. He responded with diligence if not brilliance. He opened in late January with Matilda Heron's *Lesbia*. Exemplifying the "sensation drama" then in its heyday, the style was marked by overblown emotionalism, especially for actresses who generally took the starring roles. *Camille,* which earlier defined the genre, had catapulted Heron to fame. Considered among the most "fascinating and brilliant ladies on the stage," Heron's photo appeared everywhere, and she was feted and serenaded as the object of male devotion. Joe directed a formidable cast, including Heron, George Jordan as her leading man, with James W. Wallack, Jr., and James H. Stoddart among the support. It would appear to have been a moment when star and vehicle came together in perfect synergy. And yet, as the *Clipper* gently phrased it, "though not exactly a failure, it cannot be called a success." Joe apparently did his job creditably; the paper complimented the settings and costumes. But the "points of excellence of the play itself" were comparatively few. Running only a week, *Lesbia* claims its modest place in theatrical history for being among the first to quote favorable reviews in its newspaper ads.[63]

In the midst of *Lesbia*'s short run Joe mounted an unusual Saturday matinee aimed largely at children. The first half of the double bill presented an olio of classical and popular numbers. The Winter Garden orchestra performed Mendelssohn, and an array of soloists sang and played the violin. Joe (who was not performing in *Lesbia*) appeared in his popular vehicle *The Spectre Bridegroom* for the finale. This odd variety show looked both backwards and ahead. In a time when New York theatres had largely abandoned the musical interludes and dances traditionally featured as part of an evening's entertainment, such a format was something of a throwback. On the other hand, the matinee's appeal to a younger audience ("charming and refined entertainment for Ladies and for Children, Children, Children") recognized what became an ever more important market for the American theatre in coming decades: entertainment for the family.[64]

A few days later Joe premiered his own redaction of *Oliver Twist*. The Dickens story had, of course, already proven a popular stage item (Charlotte Cushman had early triumphed as Nancy Sykes). Joe adapted his version to suit the corps of strong personalities he led at the Winter Garden. Heron would play Nancy Sykes; Jordan, Bill Sykes; and Wallack, Fagin. Yet Jefferson makes no mention of *Oliver Twist* (nor of any of his Winter Garden managerial efforts) in his memoirs, reflecting perhaps the artistic judgment of the day. The *Clipper* allowed that his adaptation was well designed but was staged so carelessly as to "entirely deprive it of the merit it might otherwise possess." The scene in the London magistrate's office "is a libel on the intelligence of the audience," condescending to the patrons as if they had no knowledge of Dickens's famous story. Compounding Jefferson's troubles was balky stage machinery, requiring a premature lowering of the final curtain. Moreover, some critics excoriated the cast for its "mediocre rendition." "Jordan could not disguise himself as Bill Sykes," judged one. Yet for all of this, the play persisted a creditable two weeks.[65]

During the *Oliver Twist* run Joe, who was not involved as performer, led a group of troupers to Boston, hoping to "entertain the Athenians." They had a short stay. The company learned firsthand why Boston audiences ("that notional, capricious, and rather uncertain public") had a reputation for frustrating its entertainers. Joe and friends suffered, by one account "a sad and mortifying failure" at the Boston Theatre, returning to New York with "fleas in their ears."[66]

Joseph Jefferson was not beyond failure. No actor is. But even in the chagrin of his train ride back to New York he must have reflected with satisfaction on the several achievements of the past two and a half years. He triumphed in popular melodrama and comedy, if not in management. He could finally spot the small cloud of stardom in the distance.

7

Nibbling at Stardom

By late winter 1860 the fortunes of nation and actor appeared to diverge. The political fallout of Bleeding Kansas, Dred Scott, and John Brown cast a pall over the upcoming national political conventions and subsequent fall elections. The trajectory of Joseph Jefferson's career, however, described a bright arc above the troubled landscape. Now thirty-one (on 20 February), he knew he had far surpassed his father's professional achievements and could realistically expect to equal his grandfather's acclaim. For the moment, Joe was something of a shooting star. Acclaim in early 1860 gave way to box office distress later that year and family tragedy the next. Stardom proved more elusive than he perhaps expected. But if moments of professional disappointment, recurring illness, and profound family heartache intruded, Joe accepted them as part of life's bargain, refusing to allow himself to be thrown off stride.

A Master of Burlesque

Early in 1860 Joe prepared to star in one of his own productions at the Winter Garden. On 22 February he and Mrs. Wood headlined the farce *The Governor's Wife*. New York critics and audiences both proved appreciative: Mrs. Wood was "especially jubilant and ecstatic," and Joe was "confusedly great." The *Times* predicted a healthy run, a forecast that was fulfilled. The play remained on the boards until the second week of March.[1]

Amidst his daunting schedule Joe took an afternoon off to treat his family to Cooke's Royal Amphitheater (circus) at Niblo's. Such leisured moments were rare. Joe maintained his relentless pace of work, driven, one suspects, not only by his professional ambitions but also by the practical imperative of five mouths to feed. When times were good (the Panic of 1857 had already receded) and theatres bustling, actors had to work. But they knew by hard experience that days of bounty were sure to be followed by days of want. In truth, Joe would never again be seriously threatened by lack of work. But he could not know this. What he remembered — indeed could never forget — were his formative years as part of a vagabond family. Those memories may have instilled the nearly obsessive pace of work he displayed during these middle years of life.[2]

Back at the Winter Garden, Jefferson prepared a successor to *The Governor's Wife.* Aided again by Mrs. Wood, he got up a burlesque of *Ivanhoe.* Scott's Highland tale had never known this retelling. It was sheer revelry, "the broadest and most frolicking kind of fun." The broad slapstick (not often a part of Joe's repertoire) burlesque even included a boxing match, where Woods gave Jefferson "sundry sockdolagers, and belly-go-winders." *Ivanhoe* was a hit, and for Joe it was an especially sweet success because Laura Keene and Dion Boucicault had since teamed up at her theatre. His rivals did well, to be sure; yet "although Boucicault and Laura make a clever team," noted *Frank Leslie's Illustrated Newspaper,* "the grand object of the union has not been accomplished — the Winter Garden still flourishes like a 'green bay tree.' " There was no apparent acrimony in this rivalry, just business as usual in the highly competitive world of theatre. The virtues of competition were manifest for the public: New York theatre (and especially comedy) flourished.[3]

But Joe seemed unable to leave well enough alone. He next staged a "sensation melodrama," an adaptation of Longfellow's *Evangeline.* The *Clipper* had warned, "eschew the sensation stuff. Burlesque . . . will prove a better card with him." Why, in the wake of previous successes, did Jefferson ignore the paper's admonition? Perhaps it was the opportunity to star Kate Bateman (1843–1917). Among the most acclaimed child actresses of the century, Bateman now attempted her first adult role in Longfellow's poignant tale of an Acadian refugee. The story would appear to have all the makings of first-class melodrama. Per the demands of the genre, Bateman's mother (who adapted the poem) altered the story by making its melancholy ending a dream, thereby restoring Evangeline to her love. It was not enough. The play "was by no means dramatic, either in construction, characterization, or incident." Nor did Bateman, as popular as she was, escape blame. "Her voice lacks fulness and her manner repose," opined *Leslie's.* Only the staging of Jefferson earned plaudits.[4]

The Winter Garden closed abruptly on 7 April, with its cast receiving only four days' notice. "Rather short, in our opinion," the *Clipper* curtly noted, "and a brief 'season' in comparison with the time for which the company was supposed to have been engaged." The season's premature end was probably orchestrated by manager Stuart, who sought better returns with opera. Not one to sit on his hands, Joe used the furlough to revisit Baltimore and Washington stages. But by the middle of May, Joe had returned to New York. He leased Laura Keene's theatre at Broadway and Bleecker for a summer season (Keene sought rest) that proved an extraordinary success. This time Joe stuck to his knitting. Farce and burlesque every night.[5]

"Our friend and favorite," the *Spirit of the Times* said of Jefferson, opened a season on 16 May with *The Invisible Prince,* a burlesque by the English master of the form, J. R. Planché. "The fun was fast and furious." Joe cobbled together an unusually capable summer company. Always one to take care of his own, he included sister Connie and brother Charlie's stepdaughter, Ione Burke, along with his cousin Hettie Warren. He also profited from players who had known acclaim — former Bowery b'hoy Francis Chanfrau — and those destined to achieve their own renown — James Stoddart and Charles Thorne. Most important, he had Mrs. John Wood.[6]

Matilda Vining Wood (1831–1915) provided Joe a starring partner fully capable of commanding her side of the stage. Born into a Liverpool theatrical family, she came to America with her husband in 1854 under contract at the Boston Theatre. Estranged from her husband, Wood became one of the earliest female theatre managers in the hurly-burly California of the 1850s. She came east to the Winter Garden in 1859. The zenith of her career occurred in the mid-1860s, when she took over Laura Keene's Theatre (renamed the Olympic) and fashioned a great comedy house. Photos show an attractive, doe-eyed woman, whose apparent sedateness gives no hint of the stage high jinks of which she was capable. The comic energy she exuded may best be compared to the antics of Fanny Brice or Lucille Ball. She dared to take on the physical humor of low comedy generally reserved to males. "Gamy and rollicksome" described one critic, "a low comedian in petticoats" who can "do what no other female artist can in this city — make the house roar." Such capering could scandalize. Mrs. Sam Cowell, the prim wife of an English music hall comedian, found Wood's Jenny Lind "clever," but "disgusting" in its "vulgar 'abandon.'" Wood's transgressive disregard of expected gender boundaries (she was also accomplished in breeches roles) particularly suited her for burlesque, which more than any other stage form relied on the confusion of theatrical categories.[7]

Although Joe Jefferson appeared in many standard comedies and some melodramas, his early career consisted more of farces and — especially during

The "incorrigible fun maker," Mrs. John Wood.
Courtesy of Michael A. Morrison Collection

the 1850s — burlesques. The latter were among the greatest crowd-pleasers on the mid-nineteenth-century American stage. Burlesque is as old as Aristophanes, but its ancient pedigree has not secured it the respect bestowed on other dramatic genres. Perhaps its parasitic nature, deriving its material from other putatively more serious works, lent an air of artistic illegitimacy. "A joke," the word meant in its Italian origins. Like connective tissue, burlesque occupies a crucial interstitial space in the theatrical world. If drama was born amidst the noble suffering of tragedy, on the one hand, and the renewal of life implicit in comedy, on the other, burlesque served as a sort of dramatic coda, providing a healthy distancing from the intensity of tragedy (and later melodrama). Burlesques appeared on the English stage during the Shakespearean age. But only with John Poole's 1814 travesty of *Hamlet* did burlesques become permanent features of Anglo-American stages. Not coincidentally, melodrama was emerging as the dominant theatrical form at the same time. The heart-rending emotionalism and byzantine plots practically begged caricature.

Such playwrights as John Brougham, J. Sterling Coyne, and Henry Byron happily obliged. William Mitchell's Olympic Theatre, which opened its doors in 1839, stood at the heart of national burlesque, as Burton's would a few years later. By midcentury burlesques of popular plays and of current politics and fashions filled America's stages.[8]

What does it mean when the habit of theatrical parody becomes so widespread that it forms a genre unto itself? It suggests the existence of a critical mass of dramatic material sufficient to cannibalize. It bespeaks also how theatricals so suffused public consciousness that audiences quickly grasped any comic deviation. Burlesque thrives only in a culture that has embraced theatricals. The intricacies of not only Shakespearian plots but also those now forgettable melodramas like *Black-Eyed Susan* or *Mazeppa* were familiar enough to allow audiences to catch the lampoon. Finally, burlesque's prominence was intimately tied to the cultural power of the penny press, which insistently trumpeted affairs, both consequential and otherwise. Burlesque never lifted its ear far above the cultural terrain, and with the print media now helping shape that landscape, its messages were clearly audible. Plural marriage in Utah or spirit rappings in New York: these found sensationalized treatment in books and journals and inevitably called forth satiric stage treatment. This meant a public increasingly conscious of itself and capable of examining itself in the looking glass of humor.

Burlesque, extravaganza, travesty: the terms were used loosely in the nineteenth-century theatre. But they all implied caricature, outrageous pun, frequent musical number, and nonsense. One might also presume that their good-natured irreverence toward melodrama must necessarily have corroded the latter's credibility. Surprisingly, the deflating barbs had less effect than one might suspect. Audiences seemed capable one moment of genuine outrage at the effrontery of the villain only to enjoy burlesque's caricature of him in the afterpiece. It has been argued that burlesque's subversive humor ultimately undermined the dramatic gravitas that melodrama needed for conviction, and decades of parody must have taken its toll. But the likelier suspect in melodrama's slow death was a more refined public that came to desire greater complexity of characterization.

No one was more parodied than the Bard. The ubiquity of his tragic works, of course, largely explains what made him a fat target. Characters, plots, and dialogue so familiar were a satirist's dream. *Othello* suffered this fate most commonly. Its premise of interracial marriage struck Americans as inherently absurd and deserving of a send-up. America's favorite villain, King Richard III, was also good for a trimming. Joe had burlesqued the tragedy to good effect several years earlier during his southern tours. J. Sterling Coyne's version of

Richard III typifies the genre with its frantic pace and comic songs. "Will you come to the Tower?" Gloucester entreats the young princes in one number:

> Will you come to the Tower?
> I've got there for you
> Nice lollipops, and gingerbread
> and barley sugar too.
> There's a nice little bed
> Where so quietly you'll lie
> And a large feather bolster —
> You will want it bye and bye.

Richard's famously pathetic plea during his final moments at Bosworth Field was travestied by Coyne:

> A horse! A horse! My kingdom for a horse!
> A black horse — brown horse — chestnut horse — or bay horse.
> A horse of any kind, age, even a dray horse.

There were, obviously, no sacred cows in the burlesque universe.[9]

During the summer 1860 season Jefferson and Wood cast burlesque's merry eye toward current infatuations in sports and politics. At the end of May, Joe played the "Benecia Boy," the nickname of boxer John C. Heenan, whose bout with an English rival dominated sporting news. Mrs. Wood, for her part, gently mocked New York society's love affair with its divas, reviving her classic operatic send-up, *Jenny Lind*. The most anticipated political and social event during the summer was the opening of the first Japanese embassy to the United States. Commodore Matthew Perry's demand that Japan open its ports to American ships several years earlier had led to formal relations between the two countries. America began its fascination with the Orient, and the landing of the ten-member Japanese diplomatic mission at Manhattan's Washington Heights in late June was covered with all the detail the print media could then lavish. Anticipation enveloped the amusement industry, and thousands of visitors to New York kept theatres and minstrel halls open well into the traditionally slow summer season. "Everybody expects to make a pile by the advent of the 'outside barbarians,'" noted one paper.[10]

Joe knew an opportunity when he saw one. His staging of *Our Japanese Embassy* (now unfortunately lost) hit pay dirt. Jefferson's and Wood's "irresistibly swell parts," noted the *Spirit of the Times*, "kept the house in a roar." Like most burlesque, the piece "seethed with song and dance," as stage chronicler Odell phrased it. The humor of the play depended as much on caricaturing English manners as Japanese (whose exotic unfamiliarity made them hard to parody). Portraying C. F. Item, a Yankee newspaperman, Joe does a slow burn while a boastful Englishman comically demeans everything American, then delivers a comeback about the Sayers-Heenan bout. Topical wit does not carry far beyond its day, and the humor of that moment is lost to us. But to contemporaries it was as hilarious as 1970s jibes at Watergate. "Mr. Jefferson's heart must rejoice when he counts the money, which his excellent selection of pieces and good acting brings to his coffers," the *Clipper* admired. With a public predisposed to consume anything Oriental, Joe quickly mounted a sequel in early July, *The Tycoon, or, Young America in Japan.*[11]

Joe Jefferson and Mrs. John Wood may have capered through many a farce and burlesque, but the real master of the style was their competitor over at Wallack's Theatre, John Brougham (1810–80). "If America has ever had an Aristophanes," wrote contemporary Laurence Hutton, "John Brougham was his name." The high praise bespoke Brougham's accomplishments as playwright as well as player. Born in Dublin and schooled on the Irish and English stages, he followed the example of so many of his countrymen in 1842, seeking better fortune across the Atlantic, where his career would stretch over the next four decades. His greatest work came when teamed up with William Burton or James W. Wallack at their companies (he was at Wallack's during Joe's tenure at the Winter Garden). A prolific author, he is best remembered for *Met-a-mo-ra; or, The Last of the Pollywogs* (1847), his send-up of John Augustus Stone's popular Indian melodrama, *Metamora*. As performer, Brougham played a convivial, refined Irishman. His good-natured affability carried across the footlights, and audiences seemed never to tire of him. Yet Jefferson, though admiring of his talents, felt him not a "great actor" even if a crowd-pleaser. "He invariably acted a part as though it were a joke," a violation of Jefferson's belief in the dignity of the comic vocation. Even so, "Genial John" reigned as favorite among both audiences and actors. Gifted with Irish blarney, his curtain speeches were sometimes more anticipated than the night's comedy. As dinner companion, after-dinner speaker, and general bon vivant, Brougham had no peer. He, as well as Mrs. Wood, remind us of the melancholy truism that theatrical acclaim was, with very few exceptions, as ephemeral as their echoing words.[12]

Joe's string of successes at Laura Keene's theatre faltered briefly near the end. His benefit in *Paul Pry* (playing a noisome busybody) was judged deficient. "We had something too like Asa Trenchard," complained the *Clipper,* "and, in fact, too like Mr. Joseph Jefferson himself." Maybe Joe had Trenchard on his mind, for he was then preparing to punctuate the summer season by revisiting that fine Yankee gentleman in a revival of *Our American Cousin.* He had been urged to return to legitimate comedy by the *Spirit of the Times* reviewer, who complained "we are growing *ratherish* tired of burlesques." It had been well over a year since Joe had left Keene's original production; now he accomplished something of a managerial tour de force by regrouping several key members of the original cast. He pulled together E. A. Sothern, Sara Stevens, Charles Couldock, and others and inserted the capable Mrs. Wood in the role originally handled by Keene. The same improvisational quality that had invigorated *Our American Cousin*'s initial run marked this production, though not always to the taste of some guardians of propriety. "Putting a tin pan on Lord Dundreary's head, is a liberty which no Yankee, however, impudent, would . . . take," wrote one reviewer. "We are sorry to see such things from gentlemen who know better." A "gross caricature throughout," tutted another, yet it was unarguably funny. The comedy's ability to attract audiences — even in the dog days of August — seemed endless. "We dropped in," wrote a *Times* critic at the end of August, "there was scarcely standing room, although the play has been performed this season and last near two hundred nights." Joe's ability to sustain a role over a long run was fortunate, for just a few days after *Our American Cousin* closed he would locate the role that would demand from him thousands of performances in coming years.[13]

Encountering Rip

As driven as he was to scramble up the greased pole of success, Joe always sought periodic refuge in the haven of his family. Extended — and even adopted — family remained vital. In early September he returned with his imwmediate family to Paradise Valley in the Poconos for a much-needed rest. Apart from his 1856 trip to Europe, the two-month span in 1860 was his longest respite from the boards since childhood. Daughter Margaret would remember these lazy childhood days as among her happiest. She and her three siblings were able to experience something approaching a normal family life. And Joe, according to his *Autobiography,* experienced the central epiphany of his career.[14]

"On one of those long rainy days that always render the country so dull I had climbed to the loft of the barn, and lying upon the hay was reading that delightful book, *The Life and Letters of Washington Irving*." Reading this early collection of Irving's writings, Jefferson was surprised and gratified to learn that the romantic chronicler of the Hudson Valley had seen him act at Laura Keene's in 1858, noting how much Joe reminded him of his father (Irving certainly meant Joe's grandfather). "I was comparatively obscure," Joe enthused, "and to find myself remembered and written of by such a man gave me a thrill of pleasure I can never forget. I put down the book, and lay there thinking how proud I was, and ought to be, at the revelation of this compliment. What an incentive to a youngster like me to go on!" Joe rushed into his house, retrieved *The Sketch-Book* and read Irving's account of Rip Van

Winkle. Joe's success as Asa Trenchard had gotten him thinking that a similar role melding pathos and humor might be his ticket. He now determined that Rip Van Winkle offered just such a blend. For the balance of his holiday he studied Hackett's and Burke's versions of the play, crafted his own vehicle, and returned to New York to ransack theatrical wardrobes for his Dutch garb.[15]

Jefferson's story has the quaint charm that is the very hallmark of his *Autobiography*. His readers, understanding the significance of Rip, would recognize it as a pivotal moment in his career. The story suffers only from the inconvenience of untruth. Neither his resolve to take on the role nor his preparation during his sojourn at Paradise Valley are in doubt. But the inspiration from reading Irving's testimonial cannot have happened, since the first volume of *Life and Letters* was not published until 1862. Joe's discovery of Irving's regard could only have come after he had begun to act Rip, and more than likely it came after he had returned from London in 1866. Why would Jefferson manufacture such a story? Because he saw a chance to establish a distinguished pedigree for his greatest work. By publicizing Irving's private journal entry Joe implicitly suggested that Geoffrey Crayon himself endorsed his version of Rip. The opportunity to plant his starring vehicle firmly within the tradition of Rip's original creator could not be passed up in his *Autobiography*.

Jefferson's appropriation of Rip Van Winkle has been carefully assessed by Arthur Waterman. He conjectures — with good reason — that Joe found in Rip a re-creation of his own father's character: happy-go-lucky and improvident, a man whose weaknesses were more than offset by his good-heartedness. Jefferson's close friend, critic William Winter, suggested that the insight Joe brought to the role may have been more autobiographical than he could ever admit. As early as age twenty Joe became an admirer of the part when he supported brother Charlie in his version of Rip. So infatuated was Joe with the Dutchman that in private moments he would dress up in the role and act it for his own pleasure. Beyond this intrinsic attraction, making Rip his great work was a tribute to Charlie. Although there was none of Edwin Forrest's brassy Americanism in him, Jefferson clearly viewed himself as an "American" actor. In a theatre dominated by translated dramas and English-born actors, Joe had to covet the chance to make his mark with one of the most beloved stories to come from the pen of a native author. These visceral and probably unconscious motivations abetted Joe's conviction that Rip Van Winkle uniquely fit his talents. Seldom has an actor so well calculated the promise of a role.[16]

Laura Keene had invited Joe to rejoin her for the fall season in September 1860, but Joe had put forever behind him membership in a stock company. He was to star. Resolute in his purpose, he contacted managers in Washington, Baltimore, and Richmond for a short late-fall tour (it is not clear at this point if

Joe had a manager). The nearly two months to prepare a new piece was an unaccustomed luxury in the nineteenth-century theatre. So also was his advance publicity; District of Columbia residents began to read of Joe's appearance two months before he arrived.[17]

Joe opened in *The Heir at Law* and *Robert Macaire* on 5 November, a Monday. It is hard to imagine that Washingtonians' minds were on comedy. The next day was the presidential election. Not only the nation's but in a singular way the capital city's future hung in balance. If southern sympathizing eastern Maryland carried the state out of the Union, Washington's position would become untenable; the seat of national government would have to be moved. Not surprisingly, the editor of the *National Intelligencer* endorsed the Constitutional Union Party ticket in the wan hope of avoiding conflict. Indeed, in the week after the election results (which were not broadcast in the paper until Friday the ninth) became known, the Washington real estate market collapsed and local banks suspended specie payments.[18]

Still, residents turned out for the theatre, needing a tonic of humor to settle the national dyspepsia. Joe's popularity, the *Intelligencer* judged, was not forced but based on a "genuine ability of understanding, catching, and copying the humorous and ludicrous in human character." He produced a string of his favorite farces, burlesques, and comedies, including *The Conjugal Lesson, Lady of the Lions,* and *The Rivals.* On 12 November he premiered his own version of *Rip Van Winkle,* featuring "New Comic Situations, Illustrations, Songs, Choruses, Dances, &c." The last day of his two-week run brought unusual double matinee-evening performances (matinees were not yet part of the theatrical routine): *Our American Cousin* in the afternoon and *Nicholas Nickleby* and *Rip* at night.[19]

After twelve nights on the Potomac, Joe made the short train ride to Baltimore. At Ford's Holliday Street Theatre he presented a similar lineup of feature comedies chased by a farce or burlesque: *The Rivals* and *Lady of the Lions; The Heir at Law* and *Spectre Bridegroom; Rip Van Winkle* and *Lend Me Five Shillings.* Every piece (*Rip* possibly excepted) was known to most of the audience. The entertainment came not in the drama's novelty, but in the originality of Joe's interpretation of the familiar roles of Dr. Pangloss or Mr. Golightly. Expectations were high. Ford puffed "the incomparable Jefferson" in daily broadsides as "without a peer," "THE GREATEST LIVING COMEDIAN."[20]

In early December, Joe retraced his steps through Washington on his way to Richmond for a two-week stint. Virginia did not fully share the secessionist fever then rising in the Deeper South, but concern over the forthcoming "black Republican" president hung about the largest of the slave states. "What Will Lincoln Do?" asked a *Richmond Enquirer* headline. On 2 December, the day after Joe opened, "Junius" sounded a long warning in the same organ: "secession by the whole South, or submission and utter degradation . . . are the only alternatives." From people pondering these immediate, unhappy choices Joe sought to elicit laughter. How little laughter residents of the future Confederate capital had remaining they of course could not know. As for Joe, it proved to be his last visit to the South until long after the war.[21]

Included in Joe's assorted repertoire for the New Richmond Theatre was *The Village Lawyer,* a farce by Englishman Charles Lyons. Its comic lead, Sheepface, was made to order for Joe, and he performed it often in tandem with a featured play. A shepherd and lovable rogue, Sheepface worked for a miser (Mr. Snarl), whose niggardly wages drove him to sell a few of his master's sheep to the butcher ("before they have time to catch it [the rot] ," he explains when caught). Sheepface joins forces with a scamp lawyer to defraud Snarl in court, accusing him of abuse. The play's comic highpoint comes when Sheepface, under instruction of his attorney, responds to the magistrate's questions with a "baa." Whatever was asked, Joe's character could only bleat a response, the result, so the court was informed, of dementia caused by his master's beatings. The ruse successful, Sheepface then turned the animal routine on his lawyer when accosted for his fee. In the fashion of all sentimental comedy and drama of the day, the final scene explained much of the odd behavior. Sheepface was in league with Snarl's son, killing sheep at his instruction in order to obtain money for the son's marriage (to the improvident attorney's daughter) and teach Snarl to mend his mean, miserly ways. This confluence of sentiment and laughter, centering on a lovable rogue, anticipated the formula that would later propel Jefferson to fame. Joe continued to refine his idiosyncratic comic voice.

Joe returned to New York in time for Christmas, determined to give himself a go as Rip Van Winkle. It was a troubled Christmas season. South Carolina had tipped the first domino of secession on the twentieth. Yet judging from patronage of New York theatres, public life seemed to proceed unvexed. "Wars and rumors of wars," said the *Clipper,*" yet "during the holiday season in the metropolis of the Western World, no one would have imagined that our good ship of state was drifting towards breakers." Edwin Forrest presented the old war horse *Richard III* at Niblo's Garden. Wallack had a historical drama. Barnum's revived the melodramatic spectacle *Sea of Ice.* Most other theatres had traditional Christmas shows: a harlequinade at the Bowery; a burletta at Keene's; the *Messiah* at the Academy of Music. The holiday rush of visitors to Gotham invigorated the commerce of diversion. It seemed a propitious moment for Joe, "justly called," in the words of the *Spirit of the Times,* "the 'Great American Comedian," to premiere as a headlined star on a New

York stage. And his chosen vehicle, *Rip Van Winkle,* appeared a stroke of inspiration. "A better holiday piece could not be thought of," considered the *Times*.[22]

Joseph Jefferson and the *Times* were wrong. *Rip* lasted only a week on the Winter Garden stage. After two years of acclaim as first comedian at Laura Keene's and the Winter Garden's stages, Joe fell to earth in his inaugural solo flight on Broadway. The problem lay in both piece and performer. The *Clipper* found "our friend J. J. . . . amusing, but nothing to the extent we have found him to be in parts better suited to his specialty." The *Times* reviewer offered a more penetrating assessment of Joe's failure — and more generally of the difficulty faced by comedians who attempted to star. As a member of Keene's company he shared in the larger group's success. But now "we find him alone and cold, and overwrought, going through the egotisms of a star engagement." Joe, who had been "the spice of an evening's entertainment" at Keene's, strived to be "the solid meat thereof, and is, we are bound to add, a little tough." At *Frank Leslie's Illustrated Newspaper* the critic agreed. "There is no use denying the fact, his name is not sufficiently a tower of strength to warrant his assumption of the star." Did Joe violate the cardinal rule of comedy: balanced ensemble effort? Was he trying to carry the play alone? It seems so. "Comedians seldom succeed as stars," the *Times* reminded readers, because the "situations which cause that fun cannot be piled on one man's shoulders." There is a further possibility that New York audiences, already having typecast Joe as a Yankee, refused to give credence to his Dutch role (a delicious irony given Joe's later imprisonment by the part). In any event, the *Times* regretted his regression from the "enviable position of first stock actor of the Metropolis to the 'lower range of feeling' of a mere comic star." Or, in the blunt colloquialisms of the *Clipper,* Joe's "business has been rather on the 'secession' order, more going out than coming in. Rip Van Winkle put the people to sleep, and it will take something extraordinarily good to wake them again."[23]

Joe's chagrin at having his starring vehicle — a play in which brother Charlie had done so well — rudely dismissed by public and critic alike had to be acute. Only an individual of unusual resilience could rebound so quickly. His trouper's instinct told him to roll out the old comic war horses: *Paul Pry, A Conjugal Lesson, The Spectre Bridegroom,* among others. And even while discouragement hung about nightly performances of *Rip Van Winkle,* Joe led the cast in afternoons devoted to preparing a new offering, this time in the surefire formula of burlesque. He imported Henry J. Byron's travesty on that great equine spectacle *Mazeppa, or, the Fiery, Untamed Rocking Horse,* which had enjoyed tremendous success in London. Joe must have had confidence in the piece because he premiered it for his benefit on 7 January.[24]

As with all successful burlesques, *Mazeppa* entertained because its audiences knew the original so well and appreciated its blatant corruption. The Byronic tale (Lord Byron penned the *Mazeppa* poem) held endless possibilities for satire. One of its outrageous puns went as follows:

> I feel within — oh, think it not a crime!
> Olinksa! Yes, I feel — 'tis breakfast time;
> And though I've heard that lovers cannot be —
> Especially in Poland — Hung-a-ry,

There were also take-offs on other popular melodramas, such as *The Lady of Lyons,* and tortured lyrics from various minstrel songs.[25]

An irreverent, protean genre, burlesques were frequently reshaped as they passed from theatre to theatre. Joe put an American spin on his *Mazeppa* "by the usual references to Jersey and lager beer." Most famously, he travestied the spectacle for which *Mazeppa* gained renown: Cassimer's being tied to a steed and ridden up a huge stage ramp. He performed his "daring act" upon a toy rocking horse, an inspired bit of foolishness that "elicited shouts after shouts of laughter and applause" and demands for encores until Joe begged "to be excused from the overtaxing honor,"

> The brute that even Rarey couldn't tame
> The animal doth kick, and plunge, and gib
> And with one fearful bite hath cracked his crib

Joe's act was twice blessed in the happy chance that John Rarey was that week lecturing New York audiences on horsemanship. Rarey, the greatest horse tamer America has known, had garnered international recognition for his ability to take "unbreakable" horses and subdue them. He returned to New York from a triumphant British tour in November 1860 and proceeded to advance a career that included instructing Union cavalry during the war. Rarey played along with *Mazeppa*'s nonsense, tendering a tongue-in-cheek offer to buy Joe's "untamed steed."[26]

For all of this, *Mazeppa* failed to have "legs." Joe concluded his run at the Winter Garden on 19 January with the unhappy knowledge that his was the only unprofitable week the manager had endured. Although the *Times* considered Jefferson to be "truly excellent," he could not compensate for the weakness of his supporting cast. The absence of Mrs. Wood, in particular, was telling. In the previous summer's triumphs the synergistic comic duo generated palpable excitement. Now, though touched by moments of inspired mirth, the sum of the performance fell short. Receipts were so poor that the Winter Garden manager wanted Jefferson to go after a week. Joe, desperate to avoid the humiliation of leaving after such a short turn, offered to forgo any salary if

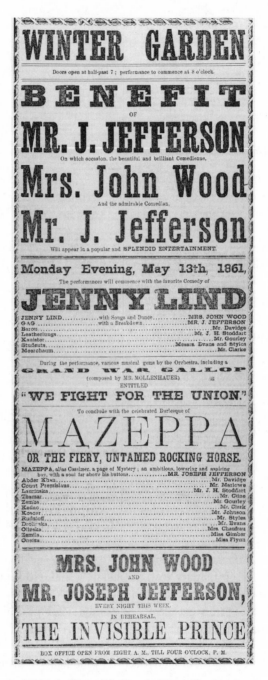

Broadside for "Jenny Lind" at the Winter Garden,
13 May 1861. Used by permission of the Museum of
the City of New York.

he could stay an extra week. Jefferson's failure was taken as a cautionary tale of the theatre. "It is one of the misfortunes of our drama that the moment a good stock actor contributes to the success of a piece," the *Times* moralized, "he assumes entirely to himself all the honors. . . . And, eaten up with a ridiculous self-conceit, sets up at once for 'a star.' " "We have only to hope," the critic concluded, "that out of the evil of Mr. Jefferson's failure may come some good," and that he and others may be disenchanted of the "gay delusion that because an actor shows himself a good stock actor and plays two or three parts excellently well, he is able to carry alone the weight of attraction of a first-class metropolitan theatre."[27]

So it was back to the road for Joe. He returned to Baltimore, where he had traditionally found admirers. The city, a haven of southern sympathizers, was alive with interest in the secession conventions meeting throughout the Deep South. He served up a potpourri of Trenchard, Newman Noggs, Cassimer, Rip, and Caleb Plummer. Audiences were "remarkably large" despite the "depressing influences of the times, and the gloomy weather of the past three or four nights." The Baltimore paper on the eve of Joe's departure after a week's stand expressed its "full appreciation" to the "most finished and competent of comedians now adorning the English stage."[28]

Joe returned to New York in early February. On 19 February 1861 Abraham Lincoln visited New York on his procession to Washington. Manhattan streets were thronged and Barnum's Museum laden with banners for the president-elect's much-publicized breakfast with business leaders and evening visit to the opera. But Joe scarcely noticed. On the eighteenth, two days before his thirty-second birthday, his wife Margaret died.[29]

Whether the young couple (Margaret was twenty-eight) had previous warnings of serious health problems is unknown. A "short illness" is all the papers report. "Asthenia," the official cause of death, says more about the wasting symptoms than the etiology. Their eleven years of marriage had produced six children; the four surviving offspring ranging from nearly ten to a fifteen-month-old. A growing family and Joe's career success had allowed Margaret to leave the stage and become the nurturing mother celebrated in Victorian culture. We know nothing of the emotional interior of the Jeffersons' marriage. Nor does any photograph of Margaret survive (possibly due to the consuming fire at Jefferson's Buzzards Bay home in 1893).[30]

After Margaret's burial in a Long Island cemetery Joe closed down their Twelfth Street house. Raising the children by himself was unthinkable. An actor's life, even if confined to the New York locale, was incompatible with the demands of child nurture. Fortunately, the Lockyers, Margaret's parents, had situated themselves comfortably in Paradise Valley and would be able to help with the children. In later years Joe loved to surround himself with his children and grandchildren at his various estates, an indulgence that may have had its roots in the necessary separation that marked early fatherhood.[31]

A Nation Sundered

For Joe Jefferson the show went on. By mid-March he had picked up the pieces sufficiently to take another engagement in Washington. His last visit there in November had coincided with Lincoln's election. His arrival in March came on the heels of Lincoln's inauguration. The peaceful transition and conciliatory inaugural address had lent some reassurance of normality despite secession; a surface tranquility covered the city. The fashionable set determined to wait out the end of "black Republicanism" and the return of "nice people." But evidence of the nation's slow dissolve could not be ignored. The Washington paper was filled with reports from southern secession conventions, and seething intrigue marked government circles, where important military and Cabinet officials were resigning to join the Confederacy. In the midst of national anxiety Joe's private situation held its own pathos. A new friend recalled seeing Joe seeking to manage his "brood of children" while carrying on his work — the "saddest spectacle I had ever seen."[32]

Jefferson may have struggled to make starring pay in New York, but Washingtonians seemed to have no trouble in embracing him as a headliner. Each day's newspaper notice listed his role above the play title. They came to see Jefferson and in good numbers. "The Theatre during this week looks like itself again," the *National Intelligencer* reported. "It is nightly crowded and will evidently continue to be crowded during Mr. Jefferson's engagement." The success must have been some consolation to Jefferson.[33]

Joe opened on the eighteenth with a double bill of *The Rivals* and *Mazeppa*. The second night he linked *Mazeppa* with the comedy *Paul Pry*, giving Joe a chance to portray the famous busybody. Later in the run, he took a new role for himself in John Maddison Morton's *A Regular Fix*. The farce resembled *Rip Van Winkle* in its central premise. Hugh de Brass falls asleep after a ball and upon being discovered the next day has no idea where he is. His disorientation is compounded by a bevy of problems that descend upon him. To get out of his "fix" he invents a new identity — which only compounds his farcical distress.

Despite its New York failure, *Rip Van Winkle* had become a staple of Joe's repertoire, and it was mounted for two consecutive nights. The character of Rip was pleasing, but casting problems compromised the production. Members of the supporting cast stumbled through their parts. It was no wonder that Rip "did not feel at home on his return to Catskill," a critic sarcastically noted. Moreover, the company was understaffed. The climaxing scene was insufficiently cast. "This deficiency of supernumeraries and minor actors detracts from the effect of Mr. Jefferson's really fine acting," the paper concluded. Jefferson, whose precise attention to detail of each performance later became famous, must have sorely suffered over these inadequacies. The incident pointed out the limitations of almost nightly changes of billing. Players heroically labored to master new scripts and stage business in the briefest time. But this was the fifth different feature the company had attempted during Joe's first week. None had performed it before, and the sorry results were a consequence.[34]

These shortcomings notwithstanding, the Joe Jefferson known to theatre history had substantially emerged. Pursuing comedy occasionally relieved by a more serious Yankee role in *The Octoroon* and the highly sentimentalized part of Caleb Plummer in *Cricket on the Hearth,* Joe had learned how to infuse melancholy touches that effectively humanized his characters. The formula would be his ticket to fame.

The uneasy spring quiet was twice broken. First, by torrential rains on 9 April that washed away portions of the railroad, spilled over the canal banks, and backed up into Pennsylvania Avenue cellars; second, four days later, by war news from Fort Sumter. Crowds gathered on street corners to trade rumors as the city tensed in anticipation of southern reaction to Lincoln's post-Sumter call for troops. They had only a short time to wait. On 17 April Virginia seceded, placing the federal district on an exposed border of the Confederacy. Rumors of imminent attacks by Virginians were rife, and the Long Bridge across the Potomac to Alexandria was guarded by artillerymen. The still-unfinished capitol was fortified with makeshift stone and cement breastworks. The Baltimore and Ohio rail line that Joe traveled from Baltimore formed a slender umbilical connection between Washington and the sustaining North.[35]

In the midst of a "capital ringed by rebellion" Joe carried on his jovial business for another week. It is not clear how profitable the final week was. The *Intelligencer* scarcely paid notice to theatre happenings, filled as it was the reports of Sumter, of renewed secessionist activities in the upper South, and a heartfelt appeal from the mayor of Washington for citizens to forego "violent political discussions and harangues in public places." As if to counter the melancholy news, Joe returned to assorted comedies. His farewell on Friday evening the nineteenth combined three of his favorite roles in the farces *A Regular Fix, Spitfire,* and *My Neighbor's Wife.*[36]

Although Baltimore had been kind on previous southern visits, Joe did not perform there this trip. The Holliday Street Theatre was shuttered from mid-March through April. In any event, the real drama in Baltimore was not on the

stage but in the streets. On the day of Joe's Washington benefit, the first
northern regiment heading to Washington by rail passed through Baltimore
and provoked a riot among Confederate sympathizers. As the train cars were
being shuttled among stations, a mob blocked the rails, tore up paving stones,
and pelted the Massachusetts regiment with them. The ugly scene turned yet
more vicious as the troops returned fire. The way home to New York took Joe
through the city where the war seemed already to have begun. It was a fright-
ening experience, admitted one of Joe's traveling companions. With the railroad in and out of Baltimore now a critical artery for the movement of troops,
Joe and two of his children who accompanied him on the southerly swing
required a "passport" of safe passage to leave Baltimore by rail. Unsurprisingly, Joe was relieved to return to New York's relative calm.[37]

But Joe found New York likewise nervous. Where in the holiday season
residents craved escape, theatres now "felt the depressing effects of the fearful
news daily received from the seat of hostilities." The "play folk" were in a
quandary, reported the *Clipper,* with two Broadway theatres set for closing
because of poor attendance. Edwin Booth had just finished a disastrous run at
the Winter Garden. Yet Joe's irrepressible optimism seemed plausible given the
knowledge that he would be united with Mrs. John Wood. These "incorrigible
fun-makers" would provide a change from "grave to gay." It was burlesque:
Jenny Lind, Hiawatha (Mrs. Wood as Minnehaha and Joe as Hiawatha),
Mazeppa; old comedies: *Robert Macaire* and *The Invisible Prince;* and even an
American premiere of a new comedy: *Bowled Out.* But Joe's positive thinking
was not enough to overcome New Yorkers' war anxieties. "Marching against
[the] tide," they made "but little headway." Business, however, picked up
toward the middle of May, and they became nearly the only New York house
to arouse enthusiasm among Gothamites. Even so, management seemed compelled to resort to extravagant puffery and papering the house. *Spirit of the
Times* editors complained of the "bad taste in which everything and everybody
is beslavered with fulsome panegyrics in the bills and posters." When a bill
featuring "them 'funny fellows' " Wood and Jefferson struggled, one must
conclude the times were indeed worrisome.[38]

By some point in early May, Joseph Jefferson had reached a major decision:
he would leave the familiar environs of the Atlantic Coast cities and test his art
by the Pacific. San Francisco had been hospitable to theatricals since the gold
rush, and most of the stage's headliners had gone to "see the elephant." Thus,
Joe's plans were not in themselves particularly daring. The timing, though, is
striking. A tangled skein of motives appears to have influenced the decision.

There was first his disappointing foray into starring. His categorical triumphs in *Our American Cousin* and *The Octoroon,* along with his summer

stock acclaim at Laura Keene's in 1860 gave every indication of success. But Joe learned the harsh truth that the *Times* critic had driven home: starring in comedy was tough business. It was much easier, it seemed, to remain first comedian of a company. "Art," reflected Jefferson decades later, "reminded me that I had taken too great a liberty, and that if I expected to win her I must press my suit with more patience." Whatever the conventional wisdom (or his own experience) about comedy may have been, Joe was unready to surrender his ambition. He was, said close friend William Winter, one who "compelled fortune" by acting on his resolution. He may have reasoned that the distractions of secession and then war damaged his starring debut. The golden coast was far removed from strife. It had also been kind to comedians, such as effervescent Lotta Crabtree. It might be so to him.[39]

Physical and emotional reasons also recommended a change of scene. Joe's intermittent bouts with TB could be helped by the salutary air of the West. And the lingering pain of Margaret's death surely played its part in his decision to seek new surroundings. Leaving three of the four children at their grandparents in Paradise Valley, Joe chose ten-year-old Charley to accompany him on his adventure. He could not bear to forgo all family.

The most intriguing question of all is whether the crisis of the Union influenced Jefferson's decision to leave. Years later, when fame stirred public interest about his absence during the nation's defining moment, old acquaintances came forward to suggest it did. Henry Watterson, leading voice of the New South as editor of the *Louisville Courier-Journal,* recalled that as a young journalist in Washington, during the days surrounding the Sumter crisis, Joe had told him: "There is going to be a great war of sections. I am not a warrior. I am neither a Northerner nor a Southerner. I cannot bring myself to engage in bloodshed or to take sides. I have near and dear ones North and South. I am going away and I shall stay away until the storm blows over. It may seem unpatriotic, and it is, I know, unheroic. I am not a hero. I am, I hope, an artist. My world is the world of art, and I must be true to that; it is my patriotism, my religion." Theatre manager John T. Ford (whose experience with the war was as dramatic as that of any theatrical figure) corroborated Watterson's account, noting that Joe had prophetically discounted William Seward's assurances of a three-month window to suppress the rebellion. The struggle once mounted would last for years, Joe believed, and he "would have no part or share in it."[40]

It is tempting to credit Jefferson with an intuitive grasp of the coming war that none save a few military figures envisioned. He certainly had been in the storm's eye during the fateful months from fall to spring 1860–61. Sensing reactions in Washington and Richmond to Lincoln's election in the fall and the mob's rage against Union troops in Baltimore the following spring might have

The Jefferson family on the eve of Joe's westward
trek. From Eleanor Farjeon, *Portrait of a Family*
(1936).

persuaded him that serious trouble lay ahead. He not only headed to California, he continued on to an extended tour of Australia, following which he
traveled east to England in early 1865 without stopping in America. He gave
every appearance of avoiding his homeland in turmoil. One is reminded of
another soon-to-be-famous American entertainer who decamped for western
quarters after a cursory bow to military action. Samuel Clemens accompanied
his brother Orion from Missouri to Nevada Territory the month after Joe left
New York (in Clemens's case, taking the overland route). The war had retired
the young pilot from his budding career on the Mississippi, so he looked to
new ventures on the mining frontier. Just as San Francisco—and especially
Australia—would foster Joe's new identity as Rip Van Winkle, Nevada and
California would create for Clemens a whole new persona as Mark Twain. If
the Civil War begat military heroes, it also fostered iconic status among some
who nimbly sidestepped the conflict to pursue individual dreams.

For his part, Joe states only that he broke up his household and left for California after the death of his wife. No explanation, no apology. But Charles Burke Jefferson (Charley), in a long remembrance at the time of his father's death, sought to minimize the war as a factor in his travels, even while acknowledging the general truth of Joe's aversion to the conflict. More significant, he emphasized, were reasons of health. The son probably got it about right. Career, health, emotional healing: these were sufficient to encourage him west. Travel was what ambitious actors did. His distraught talk of war can be taken as the sincere but offhand sort of comment that appears portentous only long after the fact.[41]

Ever popular with his peers, Joe Jefferson embarked in early June with the good wishes of the New York community. "This admirable artist leaves us today in the California steamer," announced the *Times* on 1 June. "We can ill afford to part with Mr. Jefferson. His style is so genial and elegant, so quiet and nervous, so excessively funny, yet free from exaggeration, that we can scarcely hope to find his equal until he returns to us. . . . There are some low comedians who think that they never can be low enough — who vulgarize the profession for the sake of raising a nasty laugh. Mr. Jefferson is not one of these. Good taste is never offended in his performances, but always satisfied." "May prospering gales attend him," intoned the *Clipper*, "and waft him safely to his destined haven."[42]

8

A Mighty Nimrod of Theatrical Touring

Visiting the Golden Coast

As Joseph Jefferson packed his bags for California, Congress was still a year away from voting to underwrite a transcontinental railroad. Six years would pass before the Golden Spike was driven. Consequently, the only "comfortable" means of transportation to California in June 1861 was by sea. What a mass of emotions must have knotted Joe's stomach as he boarded the ship at a Hudson River dock. Pain over his first extended separation from his children contended with excitement regarding the venture. He continued to believe in his destiny as a star and sold himself to San Francisco managers as the "acclaimed Jefferson."

The outbound journey on the iron side-wheel steamer *Champion*, part of Cornelius Vanderbilt's Atlantic and Pacific Steamship Company fleet, took several weeks. Assuming that he and Charley took a first-class fare (and given Joe's professional status they certainly would do so), they would have been spared the worst discomforts of frequent overcrowding. They would have enjoyed a cabin shared at most with two other people and priority seating at meals. But they took the Vanderbilt line (the "Nero of the Sea," as the Commodore was styled), whose vessels were once characterized as "floating pig stys." After one voyage in 1861, *Champion* cabin passengers collectively signed an open letter complaining of the tainted meat, dirty tablecloths and sheets, and lack of bathrooms or spittoons. The reputation of Vanderbilt's line for crowding, filth, and rude service prompted Congress — in an unusual fit of regulatory action — in 1864 to require that inspection certificates be publicly posted on board. As a lifelong trouper intimate with the inconveniences of travel, Joe may have found the nonstop nine or ten day voyage to Panama less taxing than some of the other passengers.[1]

At the port of Aspinall the Jeffersons transferred to train for a daylong sixty-mile crossing of the isthmus to Panama City. It is not clear whether the pair had time to explore the historic Spanish town, now reeling under the impact of hundreds of American travelers. As with most argonauts, Joe and Charley looked to make their Pacific connection as quickly as possible and leave behind the oppressive tropics. They boarded the *St. Louis*, a wooden two-engine side-wheel steamer of the Pacific Mail Company, for the last leg of their journey. The ship had begun service on the Panama-San Francisco run only a few months earlier and was by reputation a step up in comfort from the *Champion*. The Jeffersons apparently avoided an outbreak of "Panama fever," or cholera, that plagued some voyages. Their two-week northerly trip was interrupted by a provisioning stop in Acapulco. This must have been as exotic an experience as Joe had known: natives diving for dimes in the harbor, local fruit markets offering fresh bananas and oranges, and a June tropical heat memorable in its brutality. But the morning routine of coffee served in the cabin at 6:00 A.M. was properly civilized, and the camaraderie on shipboard had to be pleasing to the ever-convivial Jefferson.[2]

Impressive, too, would be the entry into San Francisco in late June, especially if it happened at night, when the massive lighthouse on the Farallones pierced the sky and the ship's multicolored signal lights announced her approach. Passing through the Golden Gate, Joe would see Fort Wood (perched at the site where the southern end of the bridge now reaches land) and Alcatraz Island, still serving as a military fortress. Coming around the point, the *St. Louis* passed docks filled with everything from stinking hide ships to the glorious clippers. Beyond the waterfront lay San Francisco perched on its famous hills.[3]

Long before this point, as the *St. Louis* appeared off the headlands on 26 June, word was sent to the semaphore telegraph atop Telegraph Hill, whose extended arm signaled to the city a steamer's arrival. In a city connected to the East only by the slender filaments of the Pony Express and Butterfield stage line, the coming of a steamer meant much-coveted mail. In the wake of Fort Sumter, political news took on new urgency. Thus, Joe Jefferson would have been disappointed had he thought the crowds milling about the docks gathered because of the presence of "the celebrated American comedian."

Joe might have had reason to think the crowds were for him. His advance man had papered the city with playbills. Moreover, a collection of reviews of Joe's major parts and his place in the theatrical firmament appeared in the *Golden Era* a week before his arrival. "Those fatal documents," Joe sighed, "known as the 'opinions of the press' had been so freely circulated that every one was aware not only of what I could do but what I had done, and must therefore take for granted what I was going to do." Jefferson, having already seen what damage inflated expectations could inflict, braced himself for disappointment. "I felt that I should fail, and I did fail."[4]

Joe judged his San Francisco experience too harshly. By most standards, he enjoyed success there. He was fortunate to arrive in San Francisco as the town was entering a boom period fueled by silver from Nevada. The city of some 60,000 was an odd mixture of precocious sophistication and rough-hewn camp life. A prospering theatre spoke of the city's cultural flourishing in the 1850s. Newspapers, magazines, and libraries supported writers who crafted a colorful Bay area literature. But these accomplishments occurred within a physical environment of unpaved streets, insubstantial structures, a harbor besotted with abandoned ships, and civic lawlessness that a few years earlier had thrice roused civic vigilantes to restore order. Joe also benefited from appearing at the Opera House of the greatest theatre impresario west of the Mississippi, Tom Maguire. In the early 1850s Maguire opened the first of his several Jenny Lind Theatres (three went up in flames). He persevered, opening his opera house in 1856 and coming to so dominate the local stage that he was dubbed the "Napoleon" of San Francisco theatre. His career in the fickle business of theatre management ended in New York, where his throw of the dice came up empty, and he died in the same obscure poverty in which he was born. But in summer 1861 Maguire was at the top of his game. His theatre was packed, and the recently reopened Metropolitan Theatre provided spirited competition (not to mention the variety halls with their cadre of bawds enticing men to the bars). San Franciscans displayed discriminating theatrical taste, and Maguire obliged by importing the leading stars from the East and staging productions that would have proudly graced Wallack's Theatre.[5]

For his initial six-week stand Joe drew on nearly his entire repertoire: Newman Noggs, Asa Trenchard, Caleb Plummer, Dr. Pangloss, Rip Van Winkle, and Bob Acres, not to mention the dozen or so roles in farces he routinely cycled through as afterpieces, and even some melodramatic roles in *Blanche of Brandywine* and *Jonathan Bradford*. The ability of nineteenth-century actors to mentally juggle fistfuls of scripts through nightly rotations should compel the admiration of modern performers. His choice of Simon Lullaby in *A Conjugal Lesson* and Casimar in his burlesqued *Mazeppa* may imply Jefferson's own sense of what would be a sure hit. His grandiloquent advance notices left audiences with expectations. "He comes here with a national reputation," noted the *Bulletin,* "and, of course, every body will make a point of seeing him." Despite strong houses, Joe's choice of roles to open his run did not please one critic, who regretted his selection of two insignificant characters as hints that he "does not merit all that has been so industriously said and puffed about him." Jefferson may have had a method in giving himself initially to audiences in small doses, teasing audiences impatient to see the full measure of his genius.[6]

Nothing is harder to recapture in words than acted comedy. More so than tragedy, where a play's speeches can convey the emotive moment, the timing and physicality essential to producing humor must be seen. But the astute comments of various San Francisco critics provide some insights. They alluded to his "rare instinctive humor," an admittedly elusive quality but one amplified in another's observation that Joe had the knack of turning any small incident in the play into a comic moment. A low comedian, Joe nonetheless possessed a humor that sidestepped vulgarity. Too, observers were impressed by Jefferson's absorption in his role. And he concocted memorable comic moments. Toward the end of *Mazeppa,* for example, he worked audiences into an uproarious lather, culminating in his signature moment from the play: planting himself immediately before the footlights and, as a demented Casamir, going through a routine of mimicking the many postures of circus trick riders. It brought down the house.[7]

From the burlesques Joe moved into his larger roles. As Bob Acres in *The Rivals,* Jefferson, wrote one fawning critic, was "gloriously triumphant"; he "stamped himself" indelibly as a great artist. The reception was even warmer for his trademark Yankee Asa Trenchard. Earlier productions of *Our American Cousin* had not caught the imagination of San Franciscans, but Jefferson's Trenchard "captured the audience at sight." He benefited from a supporting cast of merit. Yet the complaints voiced by some dissident voices in New York sounded again: Joe's Trenchard seemed to hog the stage. "It is to be hoped that there is at least one other character in the piece beside Asa Trenchard," grumped one writer. "Good Mr. Jefferson, please allow Lord Dundreary to remain in the 'American Cousin.'" Oddly perhaps, in the brawny atmosphere of early California, some faulted Jefferson's Trenchard for its coarseness. "His Yankee is offensively vulgar, and a buffoon. He continually plays to the spectators in his conceited meaning looks, and his chuckling grimaces. This may be very funny to the groundlings, yet it is not comedy — it is only farce." Steeped in the broad comedy of farce, Joe fell naturally into mugging his way through a scene, even if the play might be better served by restraint. He may also have considered his western audience to be rustics who needed the broad stroke of humor.[8]

If Joe thought his Golden Coast audiences unschooled in drama he was wrong. The dramatic criticism he received from the several newspapers was among the most trenchant he had known to that time. The *Bulletin* critic, while admiring his Bob Acres, noted some physical features that limited Joe's ability to hide himself in different roles. His "sharp-cut" features are "immediately recognizable in any character." Likewise, his "punch-like nose and that chin cannot be transmogrified." Joe possessed a voice not particularly strong or refined but distinctive. Jefferson was Jefferson, whomever he played. This was not a displeasing fact, the critic agreed. A "naturally dapper figure," he practiced an art that was "neat and finished." He did not take the audience by storm, but he would "grow upon the favor of the public the oftener they see him." Clearly, the journalist sensed one key to Jefferson's enduring success: his acting had great staying power. If mannered in certain respects, his performances seemed always fresh. They avoided being so overbearing in peculiarities that audiences tired of them. While a few found his Yankee roles buffoonish, more often Jefferson's performances were characterized by their polish, grounded in a professionalism in which he took great pride.[9]

Of course, Joe brought his new version of *Rip* to Maguire's Opera House. He staged it only in early August, well after his bona fides had been established with the locals. San Franciscans were more appreciative than New Yorkers. "Admirable as have been all that artist's pervious performances upon our boards," said one local, "Mr. Jefferson certainly gained his greatest triumph in 'Rip Van Winkle.'" The critic's claim that "no grander achievement of histrionic genius have we ever witnessed" must be labeled hyperbolic license, but even admitting only a tenth of his remarks as accurate would hint that Joe had at last found the response he had been seeking. Yet even here he could not escape the observation of others that his Rip was a thinly veiled Asa. "The Yankee showed too clearly through the small disguise of Dutch dialect," reported the *Alta California*. More seriously, the problem of low comedy mannerisms intruding into his part again surfaced. What was intended as a seriocomic role quickly regressed into low comedy. This problem — one of both technique and interpretation — was a challenge Jefferson had to surmount before the play would take wing.[10]

Joe made the arduous trip to California in part to convalesce. The grind of nightly performances (Sunday performances were not uncommon in San Francisco) over six weeks, including a trip up the Sacramento River for a short turn at Maguire's theatre in the state capital, provided small chance for recuperation. Unsurprisingly, Joe's tuberculosis flared up, prompting him to leave the city in August for the therapeutic waters of Geyser Sulphur Springs in the Napa Valley to the north. Joe exhibited a stoicism honestly acquired in a life punctuated by the early death of those close to him. The only complaints one finds in the *Autobiography* are those intended in jest or self-depreciation. Yet the enforced convalescence must have raised a nagging question: was brother Charlie's fate to be his own?[11]

By early October Joe felt well enough to return to Maguire's for a final engagement. Two things were new. Telegraph wires had finally reached San Francisco, at last allowing the Bay City instantaneous news about the war. The other development was the appearance of English comedienne Mrs. W. H. Leighton, who had taken San Francisco by storm during Joe's absence. Joe's return was thus on rather different terms: he was to share billing with her. Whatever he thought of the arrangement, it proved lucrative; they triumphed in the burlesque *Pocahontas,* and farces like *Sketches in India* and *The Governor's Wife.* They returned to the "old school comedies" the following week. Even spectacles like *The Naiad Queen* were dusted off and staged. "Jefferson is immense," the *Clipper*'s correspondent affirmed. If Joe felt disappointed by his San Francisco reception, he had inflated expectations indeed.[12]

On to Australia

At some point during the summer or fall of 1861 Joe decided to push on to Australia. It had been publicly reported that he was considering such a move even before leaving New York. The decision was not quite as audacious as it might seem. American actors had been seeking their own gold fields in Australia for more than a decade. Edwin Booth, for example, had supported Laura Keene in an 1854 tour. Joe was probably helped in his decision by the common assumption that southerly climes were the answer to lung affliction. One could scarcely do better in this regard than Australia. The Civil War may also have played a part in Joe's calculus; by fall 1861 he had likely concluded that no quick end to hostilities was in sight. A return east may have been out of the question for him. Still, the *Clipper*'s report that Joe intended to return in the near future for another California engagement suggests he did not anticipate a four-year sojourn. In any event, he knew that it would be many months before he would again embrace his three youngest children who remained in New Jersey. His only consolation lay in the miniatures of them he had painted in San Francisco. Pocketing them, he embarked for Sydney.[13]

Regular steamship service to Australia was still a half decade off, so Joe and Charley shipped out on the square-rigged sailing ship *Nimroud.* At more than a thousand tons, she was considerably larger than the typical packets working the Atlantic trade. "One of the staunchest and fleetest packets" that plied the waters between California and Australia, claimed a California paper. (This was no idle boast; their voyage lasted but two months, compared to the average journey of some hundred days.) The paper also noted that among the passengers was Joseph Jefferson, who sought both work and recuperation in Australia.[14]

As the ship weighed anchor at two on the afternoon of 5 November, Joe and Charley must have stood on deck along with the nineteen other passengers to bid their farewells to America. A sign of Joe's rising star was his taking along an agent, James Simmonds. Simmonds (or Symonds in Jefferson's retelling) had traveled to Australia with Lola Montez in 1855. He also served as Laura Keene's stage manager during the epic run of *Our American Cousin,* where Joe made his acquaintance and hired him as business manager and publicity agent. Simmonds's ardor for Joe's talents resulted in profuse billings that sometimes exceeded Jefferson's wishes. With austral experience under his belt, Simmonds also brought a reassuring grasp of geography and folkways to the tour. Simmonds's mother completed the party, probably to help watch over Charley.[15]

The passage was blessedly uneventful, the prevailing trade winds providing generally smooth sailing. Yet even a routine voyage was hardly quiet. Ship's timbers moaned and creaked, sailors called out their orders and bustled about the deck, and depending on where the cabins were located, the din of livestock (fresh meat) could be unceasing. Moreover, the still, hot days of the tropics exacerbated the peculiar stench of a ship: reeking bilge water, animal stalls, the rot of the wooden ship itself, and decomposing cargoes of earlier voyages created a rank stew. Discomforts were offset by the camaraderie among cabin passengers. The passengers on the *Nimroud* had abundant time on their hands to chat, enjoy endless card games, check the daily posting of the ship's position, and linger over leisurely dinners.[16]

The approach through Sydney harbor provided one of sailing's great sights. The "finest harbour in the world, in which a thousand sail of the line may ride with the most perfect security," Captain Arthur Phillip had written to Lord Sydney after commanding the British First Fleet to the antipodean continent. Now seventy-four years later, Joe entered under conditions more salutary by far than those known to the hundreds of convicts transported in that first wave of settlement. Jefferson, who had a painter's eye for beauty, remembered nearly thirty years later the effect of that scene. No other passage of his *Autobiography* was more eloquently descriptive.[17]

The *Nimroud* docked early in January of 1852 in the midst of an austral summer. Sydney, capital of the first Australian colony, New South Wales, had advanced from a collection of rude convict dwellings to a flourishing city of nearly 100,000 irregularly spread about the sprawling harbor. More than its sister cities, Sydney managed to convey an Old World flavor. Lovely public gardens graced the city. The most far-flung (save New Zealand) of all British imperial outposts, Sydney's aspirations for respectability required effacing its origins from collective memory. Theatricals became one means of helping natives forget.[18]

Ironically, Australian theatre had its beginnings in the dramatics got up by convicts aboard the first transport ship to Botany Bay. Professional theatre arrived in 1833 with construction of the Theatre Royal in Sydney, and through the rest of the decade houses began to dot Sydney, a barometer of its prosperity and cultural self-awareness. Australia found its great theatrical promoter in George Coppin. He toured throughout the colonies, opened a series of theatres, imported stars and plays, and most important, understood Australian dramatic tastes. In the best tradition of theatrical impresarios, he made and lost fortunes several times. With the gold strikes of the early 1850s, theatricals thrived as never before. New South Wales and Victoria were thronged with bachelors with pockets full and evenings to fill. Coppin recovered one of his last fortunes managing a Geelong theatre during the gold boom. The flush 1850s also brought a flow of performers via California, a number of whom, like Joe, spent several years there. Veteran performers of America's gold strike region naturally felt an affinity to audiences in Australia's. Singly and in groups, American thespians mined the Australian stages.[19]

The brief existence of Australian professional theatre might suggest second-rate performances, but not so. The tradition-bound nature of drama allowed easy transport across thousands of miles of ocean. Thus Joe could arrive — unknown to the Australian public or theatrical community and with only such knowledge of local conditions as Simmonds provided — and reasonably expect to find accomplished supporting companies and audiences alert to the nuances of drama. Moreover, Joe had arrived at a fortuitous moment in Australian theatre history. The acclaimed Gustavus Vaughan Brooke had recently departed, leaving audiences hungry for the next sensation. Too, Australia was less influenced by the strong evangelical tradition with its attendant prejudice against drama that formed an annoying backdrop to American theatre.

Although trusting that his art would transcend oceans, Jefferson had enough savvy to adapt his habits to a new culture. Upon his arrival he hurried to a haberdasher to purchase a new, suitably Aussie wardrobe. This accomplished, he and Simmonds visited the manager of the Royal Victoria Theatre. They found a blunt cockney, skeptical of yet another "blawsted Yankee comic" who arrived with raving reviews. Nor did he want in his theatre that "dismal old guy 'Amlet." Joe's assurances that he would not desecrate his house with Shakespeare only partially alleviated the worry. In the end, Jefferson ended up renting the theatre and managing himself. Two thousand dollars up front for a month's use were the terms — and lucrative they proved to be.[20]

Joe in Australia. Used by permission of the La
Trobe Picture Collection, State Library of
Victoria, Melbourne, Australia.

It took nearly a month before Joe would realize any return on his investment. His Australian debut was delayed not only because a stage had to
become available but also because much had to be done preparing scenery for
Rip Van Winkle, a production new to the continent. Finally on 3 February,
promoted as the "celebrated eccentric comedian," Joe opened in *Rip* and
Mazeppa. The reception was ecstatic. "He is an *artiste of no mean excellence,*"
reported the *Sydney Morning Herald,* "not merely an amusing comedian, but
one as able to draw tears as to excite laughter." Joe had brought an assortment
of other proven vehicles, including some previously unknown to Australians,
such as *Our American Cousin* and *The Octoroon,* which he could rotate. His
redaction of Boucicault's adaptation of Dickens's *Nicholas Nickleby* he styled
Newman Noggs, its new title suggesting the degree to which Joe had made his
character the heart of the play.[21]

The initial two-week stand was a smash. "We had a hog-killing time of it," son Charley later recalled. "Cash was abundant." It was so profitable, in fact, that the Royal Victoria Theatre proprietor would not rent them the hall again. He wanted a larger part of the action as their manager. Under these new arrangements Joe continued for another month to undimmed public ardor. "From the moment of making his *debut* in Sydney, Mr. Jefferson has continued to increase in public favor," the paper exclaimed. He excelled in comedy, naturally, but also in such domestic drama as *Cricket on the Hearth*. Joe's popularity was enhanced by his willingness to stage a farewell benefit for the "All-England" cricket team. This first visit of Britain's all-stars to Australia had been an important moment in Australian sports and a great point of national pride. Joe "generously tendered his services" in staging *Rip* and *Mazeppa*, sealing his approval in local eyes by identifying himself with the national passion for sports. By the time of his closing in mid-March there was little doubt that his benefit (featuring three of his most popular farces) would be a huge success. Joe had been adopted as well by the theatrical sporting set. Invited to a "sheep-bake" at Manly Beach, Joe disappeared just as the main course was ready for carving. Worried friends finally found him comfortably ensconced at an ocean-side hotel, preferring the repose of his room to the "fast and furious" beach party.[22]

The Jefferson entourage left Sydney harbor in late March aboard the steamer *Wonga Wonga* for a two-day passage to Melbourne in the neighboring British colony of Victoria. Although this corner of southeastern Australia had been colonized only since the mid-1830s, the region had already surpassed New South Wales in wealth and population. Sheep grazing originally drove growth, but beginning with the rush of 1851 the prospect of gold lured thousands more. More than half a million people occupied the colony by 1861, 125,000 of whom resided in Melbourne.[23]

The Melbourne Joe encountered lacked the affecting natural beauty of Sydney. Rather, Melbourne's distinctiveness came from its magnificent broad streets built after the manner of Philadelphia's rectangular grid. It also conveyed a fastidiousness in keeping with its unremittingly middle-class aspirations. Victoria inhabitants boasted of their colony's minimal ties to the "transport system," being peopled largely by unassisted immigrants. Like Chicago of a generation later, Melbourne was Australia's "Windy City," shamelessly self-promoting its virtues. This tiresome trumpeting, characteristic of all youthful Australia, was especially loud here. "The Melbourne blast," said Anthony Trollope after his 1871 visit, beats all the other blowing of that proud colony."[24]

As in Sydney, Jefferson and Simmonds rented a theatre for Joe's Melbourne premiere. Their choice seemed unpropitious. Royal Princess's Theatre was an ugly, barnlike structure that clearly bespoke its origins as a hippodrome amphitheater. Its ornate decor could not hide the botched job of remodeling, which had left the house with poor ventilation and lighting. But its deficiencies failed to dampen audience enthusiasm for Jefferson. Announced to the public several days before his opening on 31 March, Joe hit the ground running. He again mounted *Rip Van Winkle* for his premiere, and through the first half of April continued to stage the Dutch historical romance. His performances excited "something like a *furore* in this city," wrote *Argus* critic James Smith. As usual, Joe chased the featured play with an assortment of afterpiece farces.[25]

When *Rip* had spent itself with Melbourne audiences Jefferson moved on to *The Rivals* (only two nights), *Our American Cousin* (twenty-six nights), and *The Octoroon,* which proved the most popular vehicle of all (twenty-seven nights). But these were not all. He followed up with impressive runs of *Cricket on the Hearth, London Assurance, The Yankee Teamster* and *Newman Noggs* (a joint bill), and (somewhat improbably) *A Midsummer Night's Dream.* Sprinkled among these longer-run productions were old chestnuts, such as Colman's *The Poor Gentleman* and *The Heir at Law,* as well as some works new to Joe: *Wives as They Were* and Bulwer-Lytton's comedy, *Money.* Joe and Simmonds had rented the Princess's for three months, but nearly six passed before Joe made his final bow, 164 consecutive nights, as he would later boast. Their coffers bulged. "We just simply coined it," son Charley recalled. "It was like a mint."[26]

What would Jefferson encounter during a performance night? He would arrive at the theatre well before the doors to the public opened at 7:30. Make-up attended to, adjustments to stage business communicated to supporting cast, and other odd details to ensure: Joe had by this point acquired the perfectionist habits that marked his career. Nothing to chance; no detail dismissed. Once on stage his art enveloped him. No cute byplay with audience members sullied his work. He likely never noticed the motley array of hats worn by the patrons in the pit, no two alike. The featured play at 8:00 was followed almost always by an afterpiece. Between the two, while Joe changed roles, members of pit, galleries, and stalls often retired to adjoining bars for "brandies hot," "sherry and bitters," or other colonial favorites. Refreshed and perhaps jolli-fied, the audience was prepared to enjoy Joe's exquisite foolishness until well past 11:00.[27]

We do not know what Joe did in his spare moments, but with the rich theatrical lode he had struck, Jefferson would not allow himself to be long diverted from attention to business. He had come to make money and to make himself a star. *Rip* was a good start. *Our American Cousin* proved even better. Although four years had now passed since its premiere, the popular comedy had not yet appeared on an Australian stage. Fittingly, Joe gave it its first antipodean bow. Melbourne audiences could not get enough of the comic duo of Trenchard and Dundreary. Its run of twenty-eight nights was "unprecedented in this city," according to the *Argus*. Smitten Melbournites returned several times to witness the combination of foppery and Yankee wit.[28]

Dickens's lesser contribution to Victorian yuletide sentimentality, *The Cricket on the Hearth,* was mounted in mid-July (the dead of winter in Australia) and proved good for nearly four weeks. Joe's Caleb Plummer occasioned the most trenchant appraisal he received while in Australia. It came from critic James Smith, who discerned the double nature of Joe's art. Like a holographic image, his face of mirth could, from just a slightly different angle, take on the visage of melancholy. "His pathos," wrote Smith, "is as touching as his humour is quaint and contagious." Moreover, Joe's immersion in each scene was complete. He took a "vigilant interest in whatever is passing on the scene," as attentive to the dialogue of others when he stood in the background as when he took center stage, "thus contributing to sustain the illusion of the piece." That such techniques seem utterly unexceptionable to us now is a mark of how far we have traveled from the great age of nineteenth-century tragic theatre, when only the star's words and actions mattered, and the Jovian eminence would pay little heed to the doings of the supporting cast as long as they did not tread on his lines.[29]

Jefferson also distinguished himself by avoiding exaggerated gestures. His acting lacked, in Smith's words, "over elaboration"; nuance rather than broad stroke characterized his playing, and yet it was expressive enough that "a deaf person could infer the purport of his words from their facial commentary." In so doing, he softened "whatever is coarse in expression or equivocal in sentiment" in the old comedies. He cut anything "that, while affording laughter to the 'barren,' should 'make the judicious grieve.'" The Victorian abhorrence of "vulgarism" (defined in strikingly broad terms) clearly found resonance in Jefferson's art. He shared his audiences' increasingly prim values, not just in language but also in a more general refinement he conveyed through his art. Propriety became such a priority that Joe even sacrificed some time-honored comic "points" (which comedians normally live for) to the god of decorum. It may appear odd that in the rough-and-tumble atmosphere of gold rush Victoria a performer needed to heed the sanctions of refinement. But as in California, the forces of bourgeois respectability sought to tame frontier abandon. Stately homes graced suburban streets in both Sydney and Melbourne, advance outposts in the ineluctable march of British civilization.[30]

In mid-August Joe took on one of Boucicault's earliest successes but one still new to him, *London Assurance*. A model of what would be known as drawing-room comedies, *London Assurance* cleverly reworked the standard comic formula of complicated young love, bumbling parent, misidentification, and intruding eccentrics. The latter type was personified in Meddle, a pettifogging attorney played by Jefferson. The role was an odd choice in a sense because Meddle was not the lead comic character. Joe's decision to stage it probably lay in its being an established popular favorite even if not a vehicle for himself. The fate of Joe's production is unknown since the comedy elicited little comment by the press.[31]

Unlike Sydney, Melbourne's fall-winter season presented considerable theatrical competition for Jefferson. The Marsh troupe of juvenile players from America rented the Lyceum for a fruitful three-month engagement. These prodigies mounted a potpourri of melodrama, burlesque, and farce. Their production of *Uncle Tom's Cabin* (precious, rather than stirring, one would imagine) gave Joe's *Our American Cousin* a decent run for its money. But the novelty of the Marsh troupe paled before the attention given tragedian Barry Sullivan. The Irish-born Sullivan had known steady success as a provincial star but had experienced limited London appeal. And like Brooke, he would be embraced by Australian audiences — if not quite as passionately as the mercurial Brooke — over a four-year visit. In August, as Joe was beginning to wind down his unexpectedly long run, Sullivan provided stiff competition.[32]

If a Shakespearean is attracting the public, Joe reasoned, the answer is to produce Shakespeare. Following this logic, Jefferson decided to mount a non-burlesqued production of the Bard. His choice, *A Midsummer Night's Dream*, was of course the play that had ended his association with Laura Keene several years earlier. Joe controlled casting now, and he awarded himself the lead low comedy role of Bottom. Shakespeare's fantasy with its ethereal, interweaving plots offered novel challenges to Jefferson as director, whose experience with Elizabethan drama was distinctly limited. In the role of Nick Bottom, Jefferson assumed one of Shakespeare's finest comic creations. Jefferson must have suffered some misgivings about the role, recalling his difficulty when he attempted the part for Keene. Still, it was a plum. The interlude performed by Bottom and his artisan friends for Theseus's wedding offered splendid antics, especially when the self-assured Bottom had the head of a jackass affixed by Puck. And the interlude's "play within a play" occasions a self-referencing subplot about the contrivances of theatricality, a distancing increasingly unfamiliar to the realistic-minded nineteenth-century stage.

Joe spared no expense in preparations. Despite a smallish stage at the Princess's, his stage crew produced impressive scenery. Mendelssohn's popular score for the play was given a new arrangement. The resulting two-week run marked success by the standards of the age, even though Joe's performance as Bottom was judged by the normally supportive James Smith as the early brush strokes of a master rather than a finished portrait, "an essay rather than an

Melbourne's Princess's Theatre. Used by permission of the La Trobe Picture Collection, State Library of Victoria, Melbourne, Australia.

achievement." In truth, Joe seemed more journeyman than master as he displayed uncertainty and indecisiveness about how to portray the Shakespearean clown.[33]

A Midsummer Night's Dream could not drive Sullivan from the opposing boards, and so another expedient was tried: the men joined forces. Or more properly, Joe invited Barry Sullivan to the Princess's Theatre, where he condescended to support the popular tragedian. No mention is made of the episode in the *Autobiography*, and we have no picture of the dynamics involved in the transaction. Presumably both stars guessed that a joint effort might become a commercially spectacular event. Perhaps they had met and formed a fast friendship. In any event, on a Saturday evening in early September 1862, Sullivan headlined (with Jefferson's name just beneath) in Bulwer-Lytton's comedy *Money*. They reckoned well. The theatre was "in a state of siege" an hour before curtain. Scores were turned away from the box office, and several hundred more, unable to get a seat, planted themselves at far corners of the theatre in order to glimpse the action. Not just seeing these two stars together but witnessing Sullivan in a comedy was a novel attraction.[34]

For a week the Sullivan-Jefferson duo held forth. *Money* for four nights,

Much Ado About Nothing for two, and *School for Scandal* for the final night. In *Much Ado About Nothing* Joe took on Dogberry, a comic heir of Bottom. A successful week concluded, the two men parted. Joe revived *Our American Cousin* (probably the one play that might mitigate the inevitable box office slump after the special event). His last week at the Princess's was devoted to an old comedy but one new to Joe, *Wives as They Were, and Maids as They Are.*[35]

Closing shop at the Princess's did not mean leaving the Melbourne stage. Joe instead moved to a brand new theatre, the Haymarket, which had opened on 18 September. James Simmonds left Joe's employ to manage the Haymarket, and his first act was to engage his old boss. The Haymarket had the ornate veneer and the accouterments (meaning a bar convenient for intermission breaks) expected of a theatre. It also embodied the new trend in theatre design: instead of a stage apron extending out into the pit, its stage was safely recessed behind the proscenium arch. The arch was painted to give the impression of a picture frame, within which the actors moved. Pictorial values were starting to reshape the theatre. But designers made one large mistake with the Haymarket. The dress circle balcony extended so far over the pit that the groundlings and balcony patrons could not see one another. This inadvertently unbalanced audience chemistry. The pit groundlings normally provided the spark of audience reaction to a drama. Their sense of isolation from the rest of the theatre dampened enthusiasm, which in turn subdued the higher reaches. When Joe brought *Our American Cousin* to the Haymarket, the play that had enlivened the Princess's for a month "seemed solemn as a tragedy." The Haymarket would never overcome its poor reputation during its short ten-year life before fire ended its misery.[36]

Joe wrapped up his six-month Melbourne run on 27 September and headed to the gold fields unaware that his triumph would soon stir up a hornet's nest in Melbourne intellectual circles. In December 1862, James Edward Neild accused fellow critic James Smith of accepting "the handsome sum of one hundred pounds" from a manager in exchange for the "absolute and unconditional puffing of a 'star.'" Neither Simmonds nor Jefferson were mentioned, but the message was clear: they had bribed the *Argus* critic.[37]

Joe had stumbled into a thicket of hard feelings that accompanied the awakening of an intellectual class in Australia. Neild and Smith represented a group of English emigrants who sought to cultivate the arts in previously barren Australian soil. Men of letters in the broad, old-fashioned sense, they shared many ambitions for their new country. Neild was one of those remarkable Victorian figures who drove himself to accomplishment in many fields. Trained as a physician and apothecary in England, he frequented British theatres and began writing reviews. He became an early champion of free trade. And when news of the spectacular gold strikes in Victoria reached England, he struck out for the fields. Finding little reward for his back-breaking efforts, Neild headed to Melbourne where he entered a career in the disputatious world of Australian journalism. As a leading theatre reviewer, Neild championed an avant-garde notion of drama as a force that would one day take over from the church the role of moral educator. Smith arrived in Melbourne a year after Neild. Even more than his counterpart, Smith stood at the center of a group self-consciously striving to bring "culture" to the new continent. The mid-1850s, when self-government was first granted to New South Wales and Victoria, were also years of nurturing cultural nationalism. Smith was a member of nearly two dozen clubs, societies, and public institutions, ranging from the Garrick Club to a public library to the Working Man's College.[38]

Like Neild, Smith was at heart a drama critic. And like his erstwhile colleague at the *Age*, Smith appreciated Joseph Jefferson as an avatar of an emerging stage naturalism. The alienation between the two critics had little to do with philosophical differences and much to do with the combative disposition of journalism and the humorless and contentious ways of Neild. The two men had been lobbing criticisms at one another from their respective perches for several years when Neild picked up a rumor that Simmonds had bought Smith's pen. Clearly Joe benefited from approving reviews. He recalled in his *Autobiography* that audiences were "numerous and fashionable" in Melbourne and that reviews in the *Argus* by "the accomplished critic James Smith, were models in style and strength."[39]

But were they purchased? Did Smith write "theatrical criticism to order" for the *Argus*? Such charges carried weight because in the early days of mass journalism critics were known to accept favors for their words. Moreover, Smith had opened himself to insinuation by consorting with Joe (as well as other members of the theatrical community). Smith, in fact, provides the best portrait of the offstage Joe we have from Australia: "Joseph Jefferson about 36; slight & consumptive, with a small, sharp, eager face; forehead very prominent above eyes, soft brown hair, Napoleonic chin, & a quick bright eye, full of expression. One of the most unassuming men, charming companions and most finished comedians I ever met with; an admirable mimic & a no less admirable story-teller; his Yankee stories being the best. Nothing of the actor about him off the stage; none of the professional envy & jealousy; fond of hunting, fishing and sketching."[40]

This private journal entry suggests that Smith found Jefferson an exceptional person, one who earned his laurels without benefit of bribe. Smith quickly denied Neild's charge and at once sued his publisher at the *Review* for libel. That the publisher was quick to print a public apology suggests that no evidence beyond rumors could be found. The apology included letters from Smith, Jefferson, and Simmonds denying any bribe. A modern assessment of the incident would note that Neild's career was full of immoderate charges. His dislike of Smith — nearly pathological — led him to level charges of plagiarism, as well as accusations that Smith accepted a "consideration" for promoting Irish causes in the colony. His contretemps with other public figures betrayed a rashness that sometimes belied good judgment. The issue is important, of course, for Jefferson's historical reputation. How far would he go to achieve success? Joe vigorously promoted himself as a star, but nothing in his career hints at a willingness to take this next step. It seems probable that in this situation he was a marker in a larger game.[41]

The Melbourne run had exceeded every reasonable expectation Joe could have had. Yet in the midst of triumph, moments of acute loneliness must have plagued this widower, now separated by half a world from most of his family. In this predicament Joe sought consolation in a time-honored fashion: he took a mistress.

No photograph is known to remain of Matilda Aram (or, Tilley Buckland, her stage name — the name by which Joe probably knew her), a twenty-one-year-old soubrette on the Melbourne stages. Nor is it known when Joe first encountered her. We know that she performed with him, likely as part of the cast at the Princess's, where a backstage encounter would be natural. And we know that Joe and Tilley became lovers. Neither expected the relationship to endure. Joe was not prepared to take a new wife, especially in a foreign country, and Tilley was already married. Two and a half years earlier she had wed Henry Canavan, a clerk, in a Melbourne suburb. Either the marriage foundered, or Tilley had a wandering eye. A man of Joe's gentle disposition who also happened to be the hottest theatrical property in Australia would be difficult for an unhappily married utility actress to resist. She became a comfort to Joe ten thousand miles from home. Unsurprisingly, the man whose two wives scarcely grace the pages of his *Autobiography* devotes no space to his mistress. Again, Joe's reticence reflects less his false modesty about what the public would find interesting in his life than it does the era's sanctions. Indeed, such circumspect behavior was the very definition of Victorian hypocrisy: do not flaunt it, do not talk about it, and it did not happen. Like the nineteenth-century Australian penchant for effacing the memory of its convict origins, Joe sought to blot out the fruits of his indiscretion from his public life.[42]

To the Diggings

Besides Sydney and Melbourne, the standard theatrical circuit included trips to the gold towns of inland Victoria, Ballarat, and Benigo. Although Coppin had warned Mr. and Mrs. Charles Kean, for example, that "there is no large amount of money out of Melbourne and Sydney," visiting stars recognized that the acclaim of the metropolises could be translated into box office appeal in "the diggings."|A decade after the start of the gold rush, these rough-hewn centers (along with Geelong, which Joe apparently never visited) had become incipient centers of culture, the Grass Valleys, so to speak, of Australia. Roughly a hundred miles northwest of Melbourne, Ballarat was born in 1851 as an unruly clutch of miners' tents staked on gentle hills sparsely covered with gum trees. It quickly mushroomed into a bustling center that reached 22,000 by 1861. Like a smaller-scale Melbourne, Ballarat strove hard for respectability. City leaders succeeded in turning their pride into a model of civic improvement, boasting schools, libraries, hospitals, public gardens, and workmen's associations — a "peculiarly attractive" town, as Anthony Trollope described it.[43]

On 1 October Joe opened at the Theatre Royal, whose stately classical facade embodied the cultural pretensions of the young city. *Rip's* Australian success encouraged Joe to use it to inaugurate his two-week Ballarat run. A smaller city meant shorter runs. After four nights of *Rip,* he countered with four more of *Our American Cousin,* then finished the run with one-night stands of *The Rivals, Nicholas Nickleby,* and a collection of short farces. He tied off his stay with a benefit featuring three of his favorite faces: *The Quack Doctor, A Conjugal Lesson,* and *The Spectre Bridegroom.* Joe had found a formula that rarely failed. He insinuated his characters in audience hearts the first night. His "dry humor, his chuckle, and his admirable imitation of the broken English of the Dutch residents of Catskill, all won upon the audience." The *Star* critic, like the others who watched Joe perform, was struck by his artless approach to his craft and his seamless blending of the comic and pathetic. "Never did we see an audience whose attention was more stedfastly [*sic*] fixed on a dramatic representation." The small theatre nurtured an unusual intimacy between actor and audience, a quality particularly helpful to Joe's understated approach. Audiences were respectful and intelligently engaged by the drama. As was customary when a performer was well received, Joe was called out after the first act and at the play's end to acknowledge the warmth of his reception.[44]

Following the Ballarat run, Joe made the trip north to Bendigo. With the railroad not quite finished, he had to take the stage, an arduous route, though less jolting now that macadamized roads had been laid. Joe no doubt appreciated the discounted tickets that the line offered actors. Bendigo represented the unwashed face of the gold rush. A bit smaller than Ballarat, its character bespoke the rough-hewn boxer for whom it was named. "It had the appearance," said Anthony Trollope, who visited in 1871, "of having been scratched up violently out of the body of the earth by the rake of some great infernal deity." By the early 1860s Bendigo had become the continent's leading gold producer, inducing a boomer mentality that still pervaded. On its open-air "verandah" hawkers gave tips about promising digs, sold shares, and looked for the gullible. Joe's two weeks there may have seemed longer, with the incessant clamor of the quartz-crushing machines adding aural pollution to an environment already bereft of beauty. But Joe had been a trouper since childhood; he refused to bow to conditions.[45]

He reversed the order of his plays, opening with *Our American Cousin* and following with *Rip Van Winkle*. The variation could have resulted from issues of casting or scenery or simply from serendipity on Jefferson's part. It did not matter. Both comedies scored. The critic for the *Bendigo Advertiser* shrewdly noted that it was not the "hackneyed" plot of Taylor's play that carried the show but rather its smart language and the affecting character of Trenchard. In Jefferson's hands, what might ordinarily "only pass muster, becomes a very fine comedy." By the end of his run, Jefferson was lauded as the only player (save the great contemporary comedian Frederick Robson) "who can so readily change the humor of a large number of persons from grave to gay or from gay to grave."[46]

From the gold fields Joe came back to Melbourne, opening the night after Christmas and playing through the end of January. If he saw Tilley during his return (as surely he did), he learned a disturbing fact: she was pregnant. This development cast the relationship into entirely new light. With son Charley as an ever-present reminder of his familial duties stateside, Joe faced the most agonizing moral dilemma of his life. An honorable man, Joe must have pondered his duty to take her as wife. But such was not possible; Tilley was still wed. Inevitably, in the end she would bear the burden of such situations. Responsibility for the child would fall on her regardless of what help her peripatetic lover or erstwhile husband provided.

In mid-February Joe and the Haymarket Theatre company made a quick midsummer trip to the gold country, this time heading to Castlemaine, which lay between Ballarat and Bendigo. How he (or his audience) endured the blasting heat of interior Victoria cannot be fathomed. Only a craving for amusement by the audience and an appetite for abundant box office receipts by Joe could conspire to force them together in an unventilated structure for several hours. It was *Rip* or *Our American Cousin* each of the nights, supplemented as always by an afterpiece. Indifferent scenery and props notwithstanding, Jefferson's acting was "the most effective ever seen on the Castlemaine stage." Appreciations had by now become ritualized. Audiences called for a curtain speech, and Joe obliged with words of gratitude for their kindness.[47]

Joe was considerably less appreciative of the means of promoting his appearance at Castlemaine's Theatre Royal. Strolling about the town, Joe would later recall, "[my] ears were suddenly saluted by the violent ringing of a bell, and a sonorous bass voice roaring out my name in full." He spied a short fat man in a tall white hat standing on a barrel exhorting the public in the manner of sideshow pitchman to "'see the greatest living wonder of the age, Joseph Jefferson, the great hactor from Amerikee,'" an actor so skilled, the barker went on, that "'he caused the Emperor of Roushia to weep on his weddin' night, and made her gracious Majesty the Queen bu'st out laughin' at the funeral of Prince Albert.'" Joe, his artistic pretensions suddenly roused, was horrified at the pitch and demanded of the manager that the shill be quieted. It was done, but only after a comic-opera struggle.[48]

By late February Joe was ready to step off the stage and become a tourist. The pace of acting through his first year in Australia had been brutal. Perhaps he also needed to think about his responsibilities to Tilley — and to his motherless children, from whom he was so often absent. The chance to spend some time with Charley led Joe to pull him out of Scotch College (Victoria's preeminent preparatory school) for a trip to the outback.

The two Jeffersons were guests of the Winter brothers, who owned a sprawling estate, Murndal, in the west of Victoria. Samuel Pratt Winter had been among the original settlers of the colony, coming from Tasmania to claim space on the vast reaches of the continent. He and his brother represented the Australian version of Horatio Alger, rising from squatters to self-made landed gentry. They found on the back of sheep the golden fleece to finance their climb, turning the remote station on the Wannon River into a manor. For several weeks Joe and Charley enjoyed their hospitality, having the run of their estate and indulging a passion for fishing, hunting, and riding. An interesting symbiosis was at work. For the first time in his life Joe found himself courted by "society." This became customary by the later 1870s, but before leaving America he did he not have the stature to interest the Astor set. Conversely, the Winters found satisfaction in attracting the reigning stage presence to their estate: a validation of their standing.[49]

When Charley returned to school, Joe determined to plunge further into the outback toward the Murray River. The longest descriptive passages of his *Autobiography* concern these adventures. It was travel literature, filtered through the lens of a master storyteller. Joe was so accomplished at this in part because he played to the prejudices of his readership. His account of an aboriginal dance, for example, although evocative, betrays perplexity about the meaning of the ritual and disdain for the "miserable lot of human beings." Joe follows this bit of anthropology with a prolonged tale of his encounter with a shepherd in the far back country. The story is affecting, a morality tale of sorts. But it is also, perhaps unconsciously, an allegory of *Rip Van Winkle*. Like Rip, the shepherd was once reputable, but drink had brought improvidence (only a dog remained faithful). His long removal from civilization mirrored Rip's sleep. The epiphanic moment when the shepherd realizes he has overcome his temptation loosely echoed Rip's moment of recognition when he steps up and foils the plot to defraud his family of its land. Such a reading may be strained, but it is supported by the degree to which Jefferson's public persona had come to be defined by Rip. The Irving legend so infused Joe that even in retelling a personal experience he reshaped it according to the Ur-myth.[50]

After a month and a half's strenuous rest, Jefferson undertook his third turn on the Melbourne stage. He realized that he needed some fresh material. Consequently, alongside his old standards he experimented with a new repertoire during his ten-week run. He opened on Easter Monday with two new numbers, a Tom Taylor play, *Hope of the Family,* followed by Planché's "grand fairy burlesque," *The King of the Peacocks.* He attempted a musical comedy, *The Windmill,* a comic drama by Fanchon, *The Knights of the Round Table* (one could easily imagine Joe as a model for Twain's Connecticut Yankee). To mark Shakespeare's birthday, a series of dramatic tableaux accompanied *Nicholas Nickleby.* Despite the novelties, Joe's appeal was wearing thin. Another comedian headlined at the Haymarket. By late June 1863 it was time to move on.[51]

But before he left Melbourne a very personal event occurred. On 23 May, Tilley gave birth to a boy. The birth registration required the father's name, an awkwardness Tilley handled circumspectly by using that of her maternal grandfather. And she listed the father's occupation as "artist" (a partial truth in that). Although Joe was then performing in Melbourne, it is highly unlikely that he had a presence. It was rare enough for him to be nearby when his legitimate children were born. Did Joe at least visit mother and child? This also seems improbable, given that during her lying-in Tilley must have returned to her family. It was clear that her husband was not the child's father, but for Joe to have presumed himself upon Tilley's family in this situation would have been a shameless trespass upon Victorian sensibilities. Joe was certainly capable of financial assistance, and this he must have given. For her part, Tilley apparently held no feelings of betrayal: she named the boy Joseph.[52]

A child's birth had rarely kept Joe from his appointed comic rounds, and this time would be no different. He had a date in Adelaide, capital of South Australia (a city Coppin scorned as "not worth visiting"). Joe found a colony rooted squarely in the English working-class reform tradition, an experimental effort of the National Colonisation Society to create a classless society on Benthamite principles, including suppression of land speculation and the protection and peaceful assimilation of Aborigines. The reality was considerably less than that, but the colony prospered nonetheless, based on a thriving farm economy and copper mining. Joe settled in for a extended run from early June until mid-July, the heart of theatre season in the Southern Hemisphere. Plays were presented in short initial runs but later revived in true repertory fashion. *Rip Van Winkle,* for example, after opening the stand for four nights, was brought back on five dates in July and August.[53]

From Adelaide Joe made his way back to Sydney by coastal steamer. He appeared at the new Prince of Wales Opera House, opened but a few months in its reconditioned state and hailed as the first theater in Australia to be fully outfitted with the latest mechanical appurtenances. Its huge stage could accommodate elaborate operatic productions, and its spacious flies, with an intricate set of ropes and pulleys, could hoist entire scenes (including actors) above the proscenium arch. The new possibilities were evidenced in *The Octoroon* production, which boasted a "gigantic and correct model of a genuine MISSISSIPPI STEAMBOAT" (so the ad ran). The "grand opera orchestra" supplemented drama with a generous sampling of waltzes, quadrilles, and overtures. Joe's nearly month-and-a-half stay included performances before the governor, on the one hand, and "swarms of bedouins of the streets," on the other. The latter "tramped and raced about all over the seats," complained the *Morning-Herald,* "planted themselves . . . in front of the footlights, . . . shutting out the view of the stage from a least half of the rest of the pit." Joe's second Sydney turn can only be described as a triumph. "There is but one opinion as to the genius of this performer," the *Morning-Herald* postulated. It commended Jefferson for "the unimpeachable good taste which is so conspicuous in all the characters he presents."[54]

November and early December brought a quick swing back through Bendigo and another stint at Symmonds's Haymarket Theatre in Melbourne. While there, Joe had a melancholy encounter with the Keans, now in the twilight of their career. They had recently arrived for an Australian tour (the first stop in a Herculean round-the-world effort, which would later take them to the United States and Canada). An elderly player now, Kean, obviously dejected by nagging ill health and by their lukewarm reception by Australian audiences, solicited Joe's counsel. Jefferson responded as diplomatically as possible that a repertoire reflecting the Keans' age might better serve them. Kean, according to Joe's retelling, saw the wisdom in it. This anecdote, given with considerable detail, may be seen as theatrical name-dropping by Joe. But it also partook of another theme of the *Autobiography:* the transiency of career and fame. Players desperately clung to their youth and their youthful roles. Not just in his book but in his career, Joseph Jefferson made the same point. What is *Rip Van Winkle* but an allegory of humanity's mayfly existence?[55]

By late 1863, nearly the third anniversary of his arrival, Joe prepared to leave the continent for New Zealand. The journey was briefly postponed because of that troublesome lung, which demanded a few weeks' rest before he embarked on the short but rough voyage. The gold rush societies he had seen in California and Australia were in their mature phase, but in the New Zealand province of Otago he witnessed the phenomenon in its precocious early stages. The colony itself was scarcely twenty years old and the gold strike but two years previous. Now Dunedin had become its center. A "town of wooden shacks" housing the great influx (many from Australia), it could only hint at the handsome town it would become in just a few years. Typically, the overwhelmingly male population demanded its amusements. Two theatres sought to slake the thirst of boisterous audiences with nightly regimens of music and fun. Most entertainers came from Australia, but occasionally some ventured from America, such as an offshoot of the Christy Minstrels, whose brand of racial humor translated successfully to the antipodes in 1861.[56]

Joe arrived with an engagement secured, but the local manager was having luck with another draw and put off the American for two weeks. Joe took the news in stride and set off to explore the South Island (then known as the Middle Island). He found a landscape and a society that felt — at least according to another visitor of a few years later — as if it were transplanted directly from England. The Maori War blazed hot while Joe was visiting, but conflict centered on the North Island and thus out of sight. He could not resist some humor at the nation's expense in his memoir. Noting their tradition of cannibalism, he facetiously claimed to feel safe since his "attenuated form . . . presented anything but a tempting morsel to these voracious warriors."[57]

On 11 January 1864, Joe at last began his announced twenty-four-night stand in the "now thoroughly ventilated" Princess Theatre in Dunedin. He was guaranteed six hundred pounds for the run plus half the night's proceeds for two evenings. Joe opened with *Rip,* a performance that evoked in the *Otago Daily Times* a long appreciation. It commended local performers who "have learned to strut . . . and to play a thousand other ridiculous pranks with the power of speech" to study Jefferson, who "is a thoroughly good actor, because he is a perfectly natural one." He "does not do violence to the emotions he depicts" and "does not tear a passion to tatters." If Joe had been able to spend extended time in New Zealand, a modern theatre scholar has suggested, he might have infused a new spirit into a tired performance tradition. Not every production he staged found critical delight. His adaptation of Dickens's *Nicholas Nickleby,* which had been maligned elsewhere, was chided for the "clap-trap" he introduced to score cheap points with the audience.[58]

Joe made an acquaintance in Dunedin who would years later become important to his family. Benjamin Farjeon, an aspiring English writer of Portuguese-

Jewish heritage, had joined New Zealand's prominent journalist Julius Vogel at the *Otago Daily Times*. This pair, the nucleus of the colony's nascent cultured class, provided Joe some intellectual companionship during his stay. As Jefferson shared photos of his brood in America, it could not have occurred to himself or Farjeon that a decade later they would meet again in England or that Farjeon would one day take Joe's daughter Margaret as his wife.[59]

From New Zealand Joe returned to Melbourne, but only briefly, for on 15 February he and a supporting company arrived in Tasmania for his first professional tour of the island colony. To a greater degree than any of the other Australian colonies, Tasmania was colored by the "convict stain." The transportation system had ended just a decade before Joe arrived. The notorious prison on the peninsula of Port Arthur continued in operation, stigmatizing all who served time there. Nonetheless, Tasmanians, whether free emigrants or ticket-of-leave men, compulsively sought to recreate English society in their new homeland. English fruits were grown in abundance across the island to sate the craving for jams. The harsh history of the land was softened by the most delightful climate of any part of Australia. The oceanic breezes and paucity of mosquitoes rendered its summers bearable (the reason, certainly, Joe traveled there in the middle of an austral summer).[60]

Joe was scheduled to appear in Hobart Town, but as at Dunedin, the theatre was not ready for him, so he headed north to Launceston. This was the colony's principal port, located where the Tamar River broadens into an estuary emptying into Bass Strait. On the seventeenth he began a ten-day run of his usual repertoire. He deserved, said the local critic, "the high encomiums passed upon him by the press of the neighboring colonies." He returned to Hobart Town for a longer run beginning on the twenty-ninth of that leap year. The capital city was larger (though still under 20,000) and situated more finely, with Mount Wellington as a backdrop. Its wide streets and well-constructed buildings bore testimony to the coerced diligence of the early convicts. The Tasmanian stand was not among Joe's most lucrative. J. R. Greville, Joe's manager in Adelaide and Tasmania, recalled some years later that when they suffered some poor houses during part of the Hobart Town and Lauanceston stands, Joe insisted on writing a check to cover Greville's losses. "He was the only man I ever met in long experience who acted towards his manager like that," Greville admired. A cynic might credit Joe's generosity to the fat profits he usually pocketed during his Australian tours.[61]

Rip Van Winkle opened the Hobart Town stand to appreciative and unusually insightful reviews. But his Yankee figures of Asa Trenchard and Salem Scudder touched a deeper chord of democratic sympathies within Australian audiences here and elsewhere. The squatter mentality had nurtured a sense of self-reliance and aggressive entitlement. Representative government had come in recent decades to most colonies. There was palpable pride over the relative absence of class distinctions. Americans could recognize themselves down under and vice versa. Jefferson's characters "exhibit in their broadest distinctiveness the salient features of his compatriots' nationality," a reviewer admired. His Asa Trenchard, in particular, showed an "American gentleman, bred in the school of social freedom, whose everyday life and actions have been untrammeled by the ridiculous conventionalities of 'polite society,' but who nevertheless maintains within him the true nobility of nature, — a high sense of honor, and a manly heart."[62]

Joe pushed the envelope of local sentiment by introducing to Hobart Town residents Tom Taylor's *Ticket-of-Leave Man*. This, the fifty-fifth of Taylor's remarkable eighty plays (some, like this, an adaptation of French originals), would be among his most popular, a potboiler with a remarkable opening run that continued to be performed well into the following century. In Hackshaw he created the first modern stage detective and the most famous English sleuth until Sherlock Holmes. Joe had first presented the play in Sydney the previous fall. That it premiered in London less than half a year before Joe mounted his own production illustrates how quickly successful drama circulated around the English-speaking world.[63]

He waited until the night before his benefit to stage the drama. By Joe's account, the play's title elicited much hubbub about town and brought out at least one hundred ticket-of-leave men that night. "Before the curtain rose," Joe wrote, in a passage betraying the physiognomic presuppositions of his day. "I looked through it at this terrible audience; the faces in the pit were a study. Men with low foreheads and small, peering, ferret-looking eyes, some with flat noses, and square, cruel jaws, and sinister expressions, — leering, low, and cunning, — all wearing a sullen, dogged look, as though they would tear the benches from the pit and gut the theatre of it scenery if one of their kind was held up to public scorn upon the stage." By Joe's prejudices, the play's protagonist, Robert Brierly, would have been a lowlife indeed. But in fact Taylor's hero is a noble figure brought to shame by bad choices and companions. He serves four years in England's Portland prison (transportation was winding down by the time Taylor wrote his work; only western Australia still received convicts) before receiving his ticket-of-leave. "When I came upon the stage in the second act," Jefferson recalled, "revealing the emaciated features of a returned convict, with sunken eyes and a closely shaved head, there was a painful stillness in the house. The whole pit seemed to lean forward and strain their eager eyes upon the scene." Seeking a fresh start, Brierly finds a loyal wife and an encouraging employer. But the convict stain hounded him to desperation. "I've tried every road to an honest livelihood, and one after another they are barred in my face. Everywhere that dreadful word, jailbird, seems to be breathed in the air about me . . . and then it is the same story — sorry to part with me — no complaint to make — but can't keep a ticket-of-leave man." Jefferson's famous naturalism must have made the scene a powerful moment to an audience who understand the message so well.[64]

This episode took on increasingly large proportions in the Jefferson family retelling. Joe himself wrote that Brierly's absolution at the play's climax made him a local hero, with "lags" constantly stopping on the street to tell their story of justice gone wrong. "All right, old boy, we know, — you've been there," consoled many he encountered. Years later, Charley embroidered the story further, claiming that the pit showered the stage with hats and coins and that the play went on to become their biggest money maker. In truth, Joe staged *The Ticket-of-Leave Man* just once more in Hobart Town, the next evening for his benefit (with the governor in attendance). Even allowing for hyperbole, the melodrama seems to have capped his stay in grand fashion.[65]

Wrapping Up His Australian Sojourn

Joseph Jefferson remained in Australia for less than a year after the close of his Tasmania swing. He revisited the major cities, reprising earlier productions. Although one senses that Joe was squeezing every shilling of return he could from the market, he permitted himself a slightly easier pace. And perhaps he was marking time, waiting for the right moment to take his stardom to new quarters.

After a few months break, he headed back to Adelaide, fulfilling his promise of return. The bond between actor and audience seemed particularly strong there. When he stepped on stage enthusiastic applause broke forth, "as heartily joined in by the occupants of private boxes as by the less polished but equally sincere admirers of talent in the pit and gallery." Critics struggled to find new adjectives for his work. The vocabulary of stage criticism was limited, and references to "naturalness" wore thin. But the *South Australian Register* critic added some useful detail. Rip's "assumption of indolent good nature, the fitful activity, the profitless pursuits, the drunken gravity, and the playful disregard of domestic duties which make Rip the favourite of boys, and the torment of his irascible frow [sic]," combined to effect a portrait of great verisimilitude. And it was not just Joe. Earlier criticisms of dowdy stage sets gave way to fulsome praise for the drops. The supporting cast — by now well attuned to Joe's desires — also merited notice. The increased synergy of company and theatre artists allowed Joe to mount the proven but demanding melodrama *Sea of Ice*. The reviewer lauded the "mechanical feats seldom attempted and more rarely successful in any theatre," which were "absolute triumphs in their way."[66]

By late 1864 the American Civil War had entered its final phase. The outcome was not in doubt; slavery had been dealt a fatal blow. This context rendered Joe's productions of *The Octoroon* even more pertinent, as issues of race relations loomed ever larger for America. The play's revival in Sydney (where he returned one final time, hoping a year's absence had made the citizens' hearts desire him) occasioned critical reflection on its indirect but unmistakable indictment of the slave system. The drama worked, said the writer, because every facet of the peculiar institution was fairly represented. Like Harriet Beecher Stowe's novel, Boucicault's drama, in the capable hands of Jefferson's company, had placed before the public the "crime of the American nation."[67]

In truth, Australian audiences seemed to find *The Octoroon* even more compelling than *Rip Van Winkle* (at least based on the number of performances). It was not just great theatre but seemed to shed light on the great conflict halfway around the world. Thus, when Joe steamed back to Melbourne for his farewell performances, he opened with the stirring melodrama. Two nights later, on 27 October, he staged a command performance for the governor of New South Wales. Joe went on to make the rounds of his favorite characters: Rip, Asa Trenchard, Caleb Plummer, and the wits from the various farces. In what was pronounced the "positively last appearance in Melbourne," Jefferson again teamed with Barry Sullivan in the Bulwer-Lytton comedy *Money*.[68]

Joe could not resist one last swing through the gold fields in late February 1865, this time to Daylesford. In eight days he performed four different feature plays and three afterpieces, a normal week's outing. His originally scheduled seven-night stand was extended a night—so the public was told—because the departure of his ship was delayed. This offered a chance for some fun. "Master Charles Jefferson" was recruited for a small part in *The Octoroon*. The stand was notable primarily for occasioning the only known critical discussion of a little-known play Joe apparently had had written for him: *The Yankee Teamster*. When or by whom the play was crafted remains a mystery. It, like many dramatic productions of the age, was born, enjoyed a brief half-life, and then quietly faded into oblivion. The piece, a "Yankee comedy" featuring Joe as a garrulous old teamster, was "dramatically meagre," judged the paper, too full of improbabilities and overstatements, but—in the manner of all true vehicles—offered up a bonanza of comic points to exploit.[69]

In Daylesford, too, Joe had the only encounter of his life with non-Western theatre. In the Australian diggings — as in California — Chinese miners tried their luck. Their numbers were sufficient to support a company of troupers, who performed under tent. Joe visited after his own show had ended one evening and discovered that Chinese theatre ran far into the early morning hours. A person of Joseph Jefferson's refined sensibility — broadly appreciative of the written and spoken word, an autodidact of contemporary painting — might be expected to have respected the subtleties of a theatrical tradition so apart from his own. And perhaps he did. But his autobiographical judgments could not rise above a philistine level: poking fun at the Chinese band whose music was inscrutable to his ear and delivering a moralistic yarn about the star's inviting him to share an après-performance opium pipe. Was Joe incapable of transcending his provincialism? Or did he understand that the prejudices of his reading audience (and their firmly held stereotypes about the "Chinee") would brook no sophisticated reinterpretations? Both. Joe never gave evidence of a capacity or desire for holding up other cultural traditions for unbiased scrutiny. He shared the insularity of virtually all his countrymen. But even had he possessed the cultural appreciation of a Lewis Morgan or a Franz Boas, it is doubtful that he would have given it voice in his *Autobiography*, a work intended to offer his readers comfortable anecdotes rather than challenging their prejudices.[70]

Daylesford audiences were told Joe's ship left on 9 March, but on the seventeenth he was back at Melbourne's Haymarket for yet another farewell. This would be his second send-off benefit, and he made sure it would be memorable: *Rip Van Winkle* to open, followed by the second act of *The Ticket-of-Leave Man* (in which Charley made his Melbourne debut as the cheeky teenager Sam), and capped with *The Spitfire*, a bill to take patrons to the far side of midnight. The house struggled to contain the crowd, standing two and three rows deep behind the dress circle. Joe's old friend James Smith gave him a parting bouquet of appreciation for his having revived "the drooping fortune of more than one theatrical manager" and predicted that his name would endure "in the recollections of those who have had the good fortune to witness his acting."[71]

The Melbourne and Sydney newspapers as early as autumn 1864 reported Joe's intentions of traveling to England. He had, of course, been talking of such a trip since 1859, but nothing had come of it before. He told his Australian acquaintances that he worried that the damp Albion climate would aggravate his consumption. They wrongly attributed such talk to a mild hypochondria. But more important than health concerns, one senses, is that he fretted over the need for a reliable starring vehicle before risking a London debut.

Although the public in Adelaide, Dunedin, and Melbourne warmly embraced *Rip Van Winkle*, New York critics and audiences had been cooler. Had Joe improved his approach to the role? Or were Australian audiences less demanding than those in America? We do not know. In any event, Joe was ready to tackle London secure at last that he had been dignified as a star of the first magnitude.[72]

Joe's departure was announced again for 15 April, but it would actually be the twenty-second before he embarked. And not, as reported, directly to London via Panama, but through Callao (the port of Lima, Peru) on a guano boat returning "in ballast." No less than when he set sail from San Francisco three and a half years earlier, Joseph Jefferson could not have left Melbourne without mixed feelings. He must have been delighted by the success and duration of his Australian sojourn. Three years of theatrical touring in a foreign country was nearly unheard of. Further, he was surely confident of his future. But Joe must have had some remorse over forsaking a son he assumed he would never know.[73]

About his professional future he was correct; regarding his son, time held its surprises.

9

Mr. Jefferson and Rip Van Winkle

The fifty-seven-day journey from Australia in a freighter across nearly seven thousand miles of tropical sea gave palpable definition to a condition Joe rarely knew: tedium. When they arrived at the port of Callao in Peru, Joe and Charley encountered a diffident Yankee who gave them news of the Civil War's end and of Lincoln's assassination. The latter news, according to son Charley's recollection some forty years later, jolted his father and threw him into uncharacteristic despondency. Predictably, Joe reveals no reaction in his record of events. In the *Autobiography* he tells of learning about the war's end in a rather jocular anecdote without a hint of the accompanying news of Booth's murder of Lincoln. This selectivity may be partly a desire to avoid weighting down a pretty good story by a tragic ending, but more substantially it reflects a kind of psychological suppression. Joe had connections with many of the parties involved: he had known John Wilkes rather well a decade earlier in Richmond; he counted brother Edwin among his closest friends, as he did theatre owner John Ford. Even Lincoln had long ago served as benefactor of the Jefferson clan. This was all too close and too awful.[1]

With ten days to spare before the next vessel to Panama, father and son headed for Lima and Joe's only exposure to Hispanic culture. His account in the *Autobiography* lapses into travelogue, with images of Peruvian beauty, poverty, and religiosity, but he allowed one very personal moment to intrude. A nonecclesiastical whose career was spent in the arena of profane theatre, Joe seemed unexpectedly affected by the richness of Catholic ritual and the splendor of its churches, the liturgy's ceremony perhaps appealing to his innate theatricality. Like John Adams, who a century earlier had a similar experience, Joe found the lush expression of Roman spirituality disturbingly pleasant. He witnessed a passion play at a local theatre. The dramatized crucifixion obviously struck deep chords with local Peruvians. But, Joe reflected, should a producer in America dare to mount a commercial passion play it would likely strike his countrymen "as merely catchpenny." At such moments Jefferson displayed a capacity for critical distance from his native culture. These occasions were few, however, for his genius lay in embodying — not transcending — American society.[2]

Conquering the London Stage

Arriving at Southampton in midsummer 1865, Joe proceeded to London, where he found an old friend in Kensington, E. A. Sothern, whose Dundreary had been delighting English audiences for several years. Joe soon learned that he had arrived at an inopportune moment. American comedians were then finding little favor in London theatergoers' eyes. John Owens, Joe's early inspiration, had just completed a disastrous stand. Consequently, London managers refused to give Joe a stage without a fresh piece to offer audiences.

Joe had not traveled halfway around the world to grow fainthearted at these obstacles. Despite his Australian success with *Rip,* Joe recognized that the play needed work. He sought help in a familiar quarter, from the peerless play doctor Dion Boucicault. By several accounts Boucicault demurred, opining that *Rip* lacked compelling dramatic interest. But Joe's steadfast confidence in the vehicle (and financial incentives) convinced Boucicault to take up his pen. The Jefferson-Boucicault collaboration on *Rip Van Winkle* was one of the famous joint efforts of nineteenth-century theatre, but it was a contentious collaboration. Joe, having seen various versions of *Rip* since childhood and having a half-decade's experience with his own effort, had firm opinions. The strong-willed Boucicault insisted on his own emendations. In any event, it had to be a quick bit of surgery. Boucicault "worked like a steam engine," taking but a week to modify the starring vehicle for Joe's opening at Benjamin Webster's Adelphi Theatre on 4 September. Boucicault was apologetic in handing his work to Jefferson. "It is a poor thing, Joe," Boucicault recalled saying, a confession rendered comically moot by subsequent events. Joe nonetheless took their joint effort and, understanding the piratical ways of the theatre, immediately mailed it to the southern district of the New York District Court for copyright protection.[3]

A Byronic young Rip in London.

Joe not only had to convince Webster and Boucicault of the play's merit, but he also had to earn the confidence of the Adelphi company. American actors were regarded "in somewhat the same light as a Cherokee Indian or an aboriginal savage," a cast member recalled later with tongue firmly in cheek. Joe's earnest confidence and obvious talent finally won them over to their "transatlantic kid," as he became styled. For his part, Jefferson embraced Boucicault's version of *Rip* as the best yet produced, especially pleased that he could exploit the drawing power of the day's leading dramatist. Joe's confidence in *Rip* (and an ample bank account from his Australian stay) allowed him to send for his other three children and set up proper housekeeping on tony Hanover Square. He also agreed to a profit-sharing arrangement with Webster, riskier than the usual assured star salary. Boucicault nearly derailed the production during a final rehearsal when he harangued the cast about imagined past wrongs at the hands of Webster. Only a direct appeal by Joe to the aggrieved Webster (who had overheard the tirade and declared that no Boucicault play would be put on his stage) saved the production. Jefferson understood how crucial the moment was.[4]

The opening of *Rip Van Winkle* was an "event." Not a turning point in Anglo-American theatre, to be sure, but one of those rare occasions where the indissoluble union of actor and role elicited wonder from critic and public. "No truer, more pathetic, or purely artistic piece of acting, within its limits, has ever been seen upon the English stage than Jefferson's rendering of Washington Irving's vagabond hero," judged a historian of the London stage several decades later. "Without any meretricious effects, without a suspicions of the least pandering to degraded tastes, it crowded the house." Contemporary reviews were just as portentous. "For once, we have a real actor to welcome on our boards," wrote the *Pall Mall Gazette* critic. Jefferson appeared to have himself created Rip, said another, so perfectly did he enter the "loose-lived, lazy, lounging fellow." A third noted that Joe received that "sort of hearty and sustained approbation which the practiced ear can as readily distinguish from spurious applause as the experienced touch can detect the superiority of the silver coin over the imitation in base metal." The spell Joe cast over an indiscriminating audience especially heartened some critics. "The success of Mr. Jefferson is as cheering as it is undoubted. It is cheering because it proves that even a common public, with taste vitiated by a long course of alcoholic stimulants, can relish the delicate moderation of truth, and will applaud heartily whatever is good, in spite of its foolish readiness to applaud what is very bad." For 172 nights, Joe's Rip slept the sleep of unreason on the boards of the Adelphi. When Jefferson finally stepped down on 24 March 1866, he found himself swaddled in the ethereal silks of stardom. It was, he said later, "the important dramatic event of my life."[5]

Word quickly returned to America of its long-absent son's triumph. "Joe Jefferson has made a great hit in London," actress Mary Farren wrote Sol Smith from London just two just two weeks after the premiere. Joe's achievement represented a sort of cultural rapprochement between England and America. The Civil War was but five months past, a struggle marked by tension in Anglo-American relations and a time of much disparagement of the United States by the British ruling class. In embracing an American original, English audiences extended the olive branch. "Not seen Jefferson!" became an indictment of dereliction of one's theatergoing duty. Joe accomplished this despite a general suspicion among London critics that the great stars of the American stage proved to be "very ridiculous mice, when shipped to London." Joe earned the highest form of theatrical flattery when a burlesque version of *Rip Van Winkle* hit the London boards in 1866. As Dion Boucicault succinctly phrased it, "The play and comedian made the success of the season." Taking nothing for granted, Joe soon set a vigilant guard over his new status. When the Adelphi Theatre was set to welcome a new performer (perhaps in an afterpiece) in December, Joe implored Webster to ensure that "no name but my own appear on the bill as 'star.' "[6]

His triumph continued in Manchester and Liverpool that spring and summer. Advertised as the "great attraction of the London season," Joe was given full credit for the hit. Indeed, the *Liverpool Mail* critic found the usually reliable Boucicault "sadly deficient as regards those brilliant bits of dialogue" that normally graced his work. But a stale script did not matter if the interpretation was brilliant. After a month of *Rip*, Joe mounted *The Octoroon* for a few nights. Again, success. "The refined perfectness of his art absolutely disguises his art," the critic pronounced of both his Rip and Salem Scudder. It was as official as such things can be: at age thirty-six Joseph Jefferson was a star.[7]

The Story of a Play

But why *Rip Van Winkle?* What confluence of player and play allowed such synergy to build—and continue building—for so many years? What made audiences respond so warmly to a drama we today find hopelessly contrived? Answering these questions requires stepping back from Joe's 1865 triumph. *Rip Van Winkle* was a story before it was a play. And as a play it was refashioned in the hands of various dramatists and actors (continuing to find new interpreters long after Joseph Jefferson died). Its transference from the charming legend spun by Washington Irving into a commercial hit variously crafted by men of the theatre suggests a great deal about American popular culture. In particular it gives focus to the cultural shift from romanticism to realism in the theatre.

Washington Irving's *The Sketch Book of Geoffrey Crayon, Gent.* gave America the story of Rip Van Winkle in 1819. The misfortunes of Rip insinuated themselves into American folklore as rapidly as any story ever had. It did so, surely, by partaking of almost Jungian archetypes. Legends of protagonists being cast into sleep after witnessing mysterious activity go back at least to the Greek myth of Epimenides. The Chinese had their own hoary tale of Wang Chih, who happened upon elderly men playing chess in a mountain grotto and was then cast into centuries of slumber. Irving probably drew upon a more recent version of an old German folk tale. Peter Klaus, a goatherd, stumbled through a rocky crag and discovered a secluded green upon which a group of silent knights were bowling. Quaffing drink from a never-empty tankard, Peter found himself growing drowsy. Next thing he knew he was awakening back in the grazing area sans flock or dog. Wandering back to his village, he recognizes no one and no one knows him. Only when he encounters a girl resembling his wife — his daughter as it happens — does he discover the passage of twenty years. The parallels with "Rip Van Winkle" are not coincidental. Irving had traveled to England a few years earlier where he steeped himself in German folklore. Although his tale of the Catskills is considered a cornerstone of American national literature, it clearly has its roots in European legend.[8]

"Rip Van Winkle" quickly became among the first American short stories to gain a wide acceptance outside the United States. By the time Joe performed it in Australia, reviewers described it in terms that assumed readers' familiarity with it. Irving's story, as Boucicault had observed, lacks the dramatic tension theatre requires, being rather an atmospheric tone poem. Even Rip himself holds little compelling interest until he finds himself witnessing a bizarre reunion of Henry Hudson's crew, falls profoundly asleep, then seeks to reorient himself to his transformed village. Irving gives Rip a happy ending of sorts, but even so his story has a much harder edge to it than the sentimental turns present in every stage version.

The stage history of *Rip Van Winkle* is long and complex and is not finished yet. Its translation from story to stage, involving a procession of playwrights and actors, has intrigued theatre historians. Their interest partly resides in the mystery of who prepared particular versions but also in the ways the story was altered for dramatic production.[9]

Of the ten known dramatized versions of *Rip Van Winkle* that preceded the Jefferson-Boucicault version, the first in America can be pinpointed to Albany, New York, in 1828 (an appropriate beginning as Rip's village was set not many miles south of this city). The original Rip performer was Thomas Flynn, a modest figure of the American stage. It is unknown who adapted the play for him. This early rendering appears to have enjoyed a short life, though it seems to have been carried to the Ohio Valley, where it found a place in the itinerant theatricals of Noah Ludlow. The first attributed version of *Rip Van Winkle* is credited to John Kerr in 1828. An accomplished adapter of French plays for the English stage, Kerr had probably completed his version of *Rip* for the London stage before coming to America. Published in 1830 as the Lenfestey edition, Kerr's text formed the basis of later versions. Indeed, Kerr himself (though some scholars claim otherwise) prepared a later edition, the English Lacy edition of the late 1840s, which differed markedly from his earlier one. Two other playwrights contributed to Rip's life on the stage: W. Bayle Bernard and of course Dion Boucicault. But the issue of original authorship is largely beside the point. *Rip Van Winkle* is an actor's play, and its changing shape owed more to the players who performed Rip. Three actors stand above the others as Rip interpreters: James H. Hackett, Charles Burke, and Joseph Jefferson.

James H. Hackett (1800–1871) was the first of the three most significant Rip interpreters. An innovative actor and scholar of the theatre who actively championed an American drama, a performer equally at home in low comedy and tragedy and whose starring career spanned five decades, Hackett deserves greater remembrance than he has received. He premiered a revised version of Kerr's script at New York's Park Theatre in 1830. Two years later he traveled to England and contracted with Bernard to reconstruct the drama. Bernard, a young, popular playsmith, had already created a completely original version of *Rip* for English actor Frederick Henry Yates. With the commission from Hackett, he proceeded to broadly revise the Kerr edition, and produced the version Hackett performed for decades. Hackett made the play — if not his signature piece — at least an important part of his repertoire. "One of the most artistic and finished performances that the American theatre ever produced," judged the practiced eye of George Vandenhoff. Like its other interpreters, Hackett continually fiddled with the play, even trying Charles Burke's version later in his career.[10]

Burke was the second great Rip. He refashioned Kerr's edition into something distinctively his own, premiering it in 1850 and continuing to mount it until his death several years later. Burke conceived the lines that tore at viewers' hearts: "Are we so soon forgot when we are gone?" His approach to the role would be profoundly influential on his brother's efforts.[11]

It is some exaggeration, then, to say that Joseph Jefferson put *Rip Van Winkle* on the theatrical map. He stood on some broad shoulders. Joe had observed Burke firsthand while supporting him in several productions; moreover, he may have had earlier memories of his father's acting Rip during their days of touring. It does not appear that Joe ever saw Hackett's Rip. But while Hackett, Burke, and a handful of other minor interpreters (including a German-language production at New York's Stadt Theatre in 1856) had succeeded in transforming a literary character into flesh and blood, there is no doubt that Jefferson cast him into the form that would endure. His own contrived account of how during a sleepy afternoon in the Poconos he became inspired to take up the role has already been discussed (see chapter 7), as has his search for the just-right script. But the play itself and Jefferson's particular genius in making it an American institution requires more attention.

Rip Van Winkle belongs to the tradition of American comic folk heroes. The New York Dutchman joined such figures as the Yankee Jonathan, the frontiersman Davy Crockett, and the minstrel character "long-tail'd blue" dandy Zip Coon. No other romanticized stage figures of the colonial Dutch past attained such prominence, the others serving largely as straight-man foils for Yankee wit.[12]

Rip, as every school child knows, was a lovable ne'er-do-well who chafed under the rule of his termagant wife. He found solace among his convivial town friends and in walks through the Catskills, accompanied by his dog and his fowling piece. During one of these jaunts he was summoned by an invisible voice and further surprised to see a grizzled figure in antique dress toiling with a keg. Summoned to help, Rip followed the stranger through a hollow in the rock into a hidden amphitheater. There Rip encountered Henry Hudson's crew silently at play, helped himself to some drink, and lapsed into his fateful slumber. He later roused, returned to his village, which he recognized with difficulty, and only gradually comprehended the profound passage of time. Disoriented by the change, Rip sought and ultimately claimed recognition by his home folk. Freed from the British flag and from the yoke of matrimony, Rip could look forward to happy years in the household of his daughter.

It is a simple story but so affecting that it haunts the imagination of a child from the moment of its hearing. How did a procession of theatre men attempt to adapt Irving's story for the stage? For all their differences all shared a basic strategy: they made it into melodrama. To say this is not to indict Kerr, Hackett, and others for philistinism but to acknowledge an axiom of theatre: audiences demanded the conventions of melodrama. The haunting atmosphere of Irving's story was not easily transferable to the stage, but his figures trimmed in period garb, served in a rich stew of melodramatic situations, and garnished with witty songs and comic banter would serve American tastes well enough.

Within the variety of *Rip*'s stage treatments several common twists of plot emerge. First, melodrama dictated that a villain be inserted. Rip's property was put at risk in part because of his own negligence but more so because (variously named) Deidrich Van Slous or Derrick Van Beeckman, the town burgomaster and his son (or nephew) connive to defraud Rip of his property. The twenty years' sleep comes to an end just in time for Rip to prevent the consummation of their plot. In the Kerr version, a trial is underway for the final transfer of property, whereat Rip proves his identity by revealing a scar on his forehead received when he saved Derrick's son Herman from certain death years earlier. Burke's ending has Rip appearing twenty years and a day after signing an agreement — the exact period of time the contract allowed him to repudiate the pact. Boucicault eschews the courtroom for an assembled village, before which Rip produces a document showing that he never signed away his land.

Not only was Rip's land threatened but in some versions his daughter was also at risk. Early stage productions intertwine the grasp for land with a coerced arranged marriage between Lorenna and the oily Herman, this too being averted by Rip's timely reappearance. One also finds in the Kerr-Hackett-Bernard-Burke versions a love plot rather clumsily inserted. Rip is given a sister,

Alice, who carries on a coy romance with Knickerbocker, the tavern keeper. The byplay has no purpose save fulfilling a melodramatic convention that a soubrette must be wooed.

Rip Van Winkle, as even a brief glimpse at the several plots suggests, was hardly a comedy in the usual sense. Nor was it called such. "A Romantic Drama" is the label on the title pages of the Kerr and Burke versions, "A Romantic and Domestic Drama" on Bernard's prompt scripts ("romance" in this sense implying a tale of imaginary wonder). Theatre historian Allardyce Nicoll categorizes early nineteenth-century melodrama in three divisions: romantic, supernatural, and domestic. The genius of *Rip Van Winkle* lies in its combining all three. Its offbeat exoticism is essentially romantic; the encounter with the phantoms of Hudson's crew is supernatural; and the conflict between Rip and his wife and the threats to property are domestic. Dion Boucicault, who understood contemporary audience desires better than anyone, told actress Marie Bancroft that an audience "might pretend it wanted pure comedy," but it really wanted "*domestic drama,* treated with broad comic character." *Rip Van Winkle* filled the bill handsomely.[13]

Rip Van Winkle had villainy and pathos, but where did the humor reside? In the person of Rip himself, first of all. Ethnic roles were prima facie figures of mirth to Anglo-American audiences. Rip's dialect, his good-natured indolence, his easy surrender to the bottle, his irreverent witticisms, all brought a light touch to the play. There was, too, Rip's affliction with his wife. "Let go my head, won't you?" Rip implores his wife, who has grabbed his hair. "No, not a hair," Gretchen snaps, seething over Rip's latest malefaction. "Hold on to it then, what do I care," Rip rejoins with characteristic insouciance. The Maggie and Jigs banter between Dame Van Winkle and Rip might have caught the biggest laughs. And liberally sprinkled throughout the early stage productions were comic songs that cheered the plot.[14]

If *Rip Van Winkle* was in many respects warmed-over melodrama, in other regards its comedy was planted firmly in the classical tradition. Rip personified the harmless ridiculousness that Aristotle saw as core to the comic persona. Further, Rip was, according to one London critic, "fortune's fool," the "type of all of Shakespeare's drolls. Slippery, airy, the very ideal of Robin goodfellow." Moreover, a disordered, conflicted, yet vital world was restored to its proper sphere when a series of recognitions had been achieved. Rip at last recognized his former home and accepted the passage of time; the villagers acknowledged the sleeper's identity; and the conniving Derrick acknowledged his impending ruin.[15]

Rip Van Winkle thus displayed to its patrons a range of emotional colors drawn from the entire melodramatic and comic palette. For all of this, the play never moved to the front rank of popularity under the tutelage of its earliest creators. Not until Dion Boucicault reframed it and Joseph Jefferson breathed life into the tired figure of Rip did the drama earn its place in theatre history.

The Jefferson Touch

Joseph Jefferson's success in developing *Rip Van Winkle* into a landmark of Anglo-American theatre elicited comment by seemingly every actor and critic of the age. There was little debate that for all of Boucicault's efforts this was Joe Jefferson's triumph. Its genius lay in the acting rather than in the script. Boucicault never quarreled with this assessment; he handed his bit of play carpentry to Joe with apology and never ceased to be amazed at what Jefferson did with it. Naturally, in the *Autobiography* Joe gives considerable attention to the play, though perhaps less than one might imagine. Joe's desire to be remembered as more than a one-horse actor kept him from making it the pivot of his life story. In any event, Jefferson's Rip was amply documented by contemporary written sources, if only partially so by the late-coming media of film and phonograph.

What did Jefferson keep, what did he change, what did he excise from earlier productions of *Rip*? Theatre is a collaborative and an accumulative art, and Joe's determination to make *Rip* his own built on the efforts of earlier players. Joe cherished theatrical tradition and acknowledged his debt to Burke and the other progenitors of the role (at least eight of whom we know). He likewise never stinted in his praise for Dion Boucicault's help. What emerged by the 1870s as the "definitive" *Rip Van Winkle* was clearly a product of many voices.[16]

Joe started making changes long before he handed the script over to Boucicault in 1865. He considered all previous dramatizations as poor efforts but groped to find the means of perfecting them. He never challenged the essential assumption that the play would continue as comic melodrama. Dastardly villains and nefarious schemes would drive the action. Rip's wife would still nag him and his daughter quail before the prospect of an obnoxious marriage. *Rip Van Winkle* remained a strange amalgam of melodramatic convention imposed on Irving's haunting tone poem. Rip, too, would be as endearingly tippling and shiftless as ever. Individual bits of stage business and interpretation, especially Charlie Burke's, would also be maintained Beyond these important continuities, Jefferson reshaped the play in ways that bespoke shrewd theatrical insight.

Most significantly, Jefferson recast Rip's fateful encounter with Hudson's crew. He took lifelong pride in how he refashioned the mountain scene, mentioning it whenever discussion of his contribution to the play came up. The meeting with the mysterious strangers in the Catskills—clearly the focal point of Irving's story—had been oddly diminished by Kerr and his followers. It constituted but a brief final scene of the first act (all *Rips* before Jefferson's were two acts), an almost begrudging interruption before the play could return to its melodramatic twists. At this point in the play Jefferson had one of those insights that would separate him from more conventional actors. He intensified the impact of Rip's being driven into the night by his wife and then meeting the Dutch explorers by putting these incidents into a separate act. Though short, the middle act's power was manifold, rooted in an effective minimalism. (In acting Rip, Joe claimed, to find what *to do* was simple, "but what not to do was the important and difficult point to determine.") Burke had the Dutch phantoms debate Rip's fate in verse (a distancing devise):

> Twenty years in slumber's chain
> Is the fate that we ordain.
> Yet, if merry wight he prove,
> Pleasing dreams his sleep shall move.

But Joe perceived that once in the sacred precincts of the mountain "all colloquial dialogue and commonplace pantomime should cease." These were not men but ghosts, and ghosts are mute. Like Washington Irving, Jefferson understood that dumbshow constituted a foreboding eloquence far beyond the impact of any speech. In one sense, Joe's monopoly of dialogue in the second act (in the 1880s the second became the third of four acts) simply made the play more of a star vehicle. But Joe's innovation was a bold one; few plays of his day attempted this sort of extended monologue.[17]

The mountain scene was Joe's major departure from Burke's 1850 edition. Otherwise, he kept the same cast of characters, same plot, same ending. Significantly, Joe adopted Charlie's signature line from the piece: "Are we so soon forgot." The utter desolation in Burke's voice, testified John Sleeper Clarke, "fell on the senses like the culmination of all mortal despair." Pathos, of course, would be Jefferson's stock-in-trade with the piece, and he delivered the line with similar effect. Indeed, the initial imprint Jefferson put on *Rip* had less to do with the story than with his inspired interpretation of the main character.

How to explain Jefferson's creation of Rip Van Winkle? The conception of a work by an artist remains high mystery. Even Jefferson, whose ability to reflect on his art surpassed most players, could only hint at the process. Rather, the characterization should be seen as a summation of his life's work to that point. Actors sought the "great role" that they could make their own. Joe had discovered with Asa Trenchard that humor mingled with pathos produced a potent blend. Further, he had worked out the technical aspects of portraying an old man in his portrayal of Caleb Plummer. The poignancy of this, his most popular serious role, schooled him for Rip's decrepitude. What other memories he might have drawn on—Charlie Burke certainly, John Owens, perhaps, even distant recollections of his father's example—we cannot discern fully. His visit to Paris may have been instrumental. He makes no mention of seeing Bouffé or other devotees of the new quietism during his stay, but a critic's reference to his being "as quiet as a French actor" raises the possibility. From whatever sources he utilized, Rip had clearly become a compelling stage figure during his Australian tour.[18]

Joe's conception of Rip, then, had matured long before he commissioned Boucicault. But the Irish master, Jefferson confessed, added the "human touch I had so long sought in Rip Van Winkle." Boucicault took over certain changes Joe had already made: reducing the number of main characters by one (young Rip was eliminated) and renaming all the characters save Rip and innkeeper Nick Vedder (another character from the original story). But even Rip did not escape alteration. Over Joe's protests, Boucicault insisted that the Rip of the first act must be a young man, "thoughtless, gay, just such a curly-head, good-humoured fellow as all the village girls would love, and the children and dogs would run after," as Boucicault put it. (This meant that even with twenty years on him Rip would be but in early middle age, a problem of chronology for portraying a frosty-bearded old man and only answered by appeal to dramatic license.) The alterations announced a fundamental break with the Kerr-Hackett-Burke tradition. Such cavalier treatment of Irving's story—or even of earlier dramatic treatments—may offend defenders of artistic integrity and authorial control. But of course Irving's story had been preyed upon for decades already, with no protest from him, and the play's continuing evolution made it easier for Jefferson and Boucicault to countenance yet another and even more thoroughgoing set of revisions. Not that Boucicault was bothered by fine points of authorial ethics. "I am an emperor and take what I think best for Art," he boasted. "I despoil genius to make the mob worship it."[19]

In truth, Boucicault helped restore Irving's story by eliminating some of the byzantine plot lines, such as the romance of Rip's sister Alice (she is gone altogether). He kept Joe's vivid second act with the silent dwarfs. Irving's tone of regional romance was further enhanced by cutting most of the comic songs that had been sprinkled throughout all earlier versions. However, orchestral background music would always be a part of *Rip Van Winkle* productions, and in some productions fiddlers accompanied a town revel at the end of the first act. But music was carefully chosen to heighten emotion, not provide comic relief. Moreover, as in the original story, Rip was now center stage in most scenes. In a play of more than two hours Jefferson was offstage scarcely fifteen minutes. *Rip Van Winkle,* whatever else it may have been, was first a star vehicle.[20]

The melodrama, of course, stayed, streamlined a bit and with some new twists. No longer was there a courtroom climax. Rather, the document Rip had carefully left unsigned (even while in a fog of liquor) stood unenforced for twenty years. When Derrick and his nephew Cockles attempt to execute the document transferring Rip's property by coercing Rip's daughter to sign, not one but two given-up-for-dead protagonists suddenly reappear. Hendrick, Meenie's beloved, returns from the sea, and Rip returns to the village. The true state of affairs was revealed, and the villainous uncle-nephew duo, foiled as always, slink off to financial ruin while Rip is restored to property and respect in his community. In this final act, "all the delicacies of the rest of the story are smothered in the garlic and onions of the melodramatist," London critic Henry Morley wrote with uncharitable honesty. Why not, in the spirit of Irving's story, return Rip to the bench where he will regale the tavern regulars rather than the "claptrap effects of a wife who has been borrowed and improved during his absence, and a magnificent collection of town lots to make him happy ever after"? The only part of the script to find critical approval was Meenie's belated recognition of Rip in the final scene. The reunion provided a moment of affecting drama. But critics saw more here. Boucicault's closing was taken to be an inspired reversal of the blind Lear's recognition of Cordelia. The comparison was flattering, an attempt to elevate the play through association with the Bard. But in truth, the dramatic moment has more in common with other tired melodramatic clichés than tragic epiphanies.[21]

On one level *Rip Van Winkle* remained the most conventional of domestic melodramas: the family beset by malevolent forces. Middle-class life was filled with risk, and mid-nineteenth-century capitalism offered no safety nets. Dangers were cast in highly personal terms; knaves like Derrick Von Beekman sought to steal others' lands and daughters. Some modern interpreters see such roguish figures as human markers for the impersonal forces of capitalism that with apparent capriciousness wrought financial ruin. The play lends some support to this reading. Rip leaves a sleepy village and returns to find a bustling town, whose rapacious financier represents the now dominant economic order. Yet melodramas rarely intended serious social criticism. In this world no fundamental reforms were required for goodness to triumph. Rip, like all melodramatic heroes, was restored once the villain was defeated. Character, not social structure, determined the quality of existence.[22]

But the Boucicault-Jefferson version lacks the sharp patriotism and political comment so evident in earlier productions. Irving's tale has Rip returning to

Falling Waters to find that the rendering of King George on the sign above the tavern had given way to a General Washington. His confused paean to King George evokes angry charges of disloyalty from the crowd. In place of the congenial banter among the tavern regulars he had known, Rip witnessed the contentiousness of electioneering. It was not a flattering change. Kerr's stage version, however, exchanged Irving's Federalist disdain of popular politics for a more sanguine view of democratic ways. "Th' elective franchise claims our voice, nor courtly power directs our choice," a tavern song boasted. This sort of patriotism abounded in Kerr's *Rip* (not unusual for the theatre of that spread-eagle age). Burke toned down the jingoism, and all flag waving is missing from Joe's version, save the unremarked displacement of King George by Washington. The generation of the mid-1860s resonated with new heroes from the recent war, and Federalist-Republican distinctions were out-of-date. Moreover, Joe saw such political allusions as distractions from the poetic tone he wished to sustain. Where an earlier American theatre was untroubled by a potpourri of themes, Jefferson represented a growing impulse to refine the theatrical message, even in melodrama.[23]

This refinement took a literal turn in places. Burke's script was replete with the saltier language of antebellum theatre. When Rip is tempted with a glass of spirits (to which he gives in) he toasts, "Rory, here is your go-to-hell, unt your family's go-to-hell, un may you all live long unt prosper." But Joe removed all profanity. Victorian propriety had bitten deep in both British and American culture by the 1860s, and with a growing interest in attracting families to the theatre, any tinge of disrepute had to be expunged. Far gone, too, was the lechery at which some early scripts hinted. A favorite of local wives for his willingness to do odd jobs, by Irving's account, Rip in initial dramatic retellings was given a roving eye. Jefferson's Rip, by contrast, seemed a safely asexual creature. Jefferson even subdued the broad comic physicality that marked his half brother's efforts. Of course Joe was growing into middle age with Rip. But even apart from issues of agility, he sensed that *Rip Van Winkle*'s new audiences desired less a pratfalling clown than a comi-tragic hero.[24]

Another change, minor in itself, speaks volumes about Boucicault's and Jefferson's ability to make the play pertinent to the day's audience. Rip reappears to find wife Gretchen alive, now unhappily married to Derrick (on the assumption that Rip had died). Gretchen welcomes the chance to throw over her tyrannical spouse. She vows never to "speak an unkind word" to Rip again, and the two reconcile. In Irving's tale, Dame Van Winkle had, to Rip's relief, long since died ("there was a drop of comfort at least in this intelligence"). In Kerr's version, Rip hails similar news with a "Lord be praised." Burke's version, though, begins to show the influence of an encroaching senti-

A moment of Victorian sentiment: Gretchen drives
out Rip. From *Rip Van Winkle, as Played by Joseph
Jefferson* (1895).

mentalism in popular culture. Rip first greets the news of his wife's demise
matter-of-factly — "So de old woman is dead; well, she led me a hard life" —
but then, conscience ridden, follows with a note of affection — "she was de
wife of my bosom, she was mine frow for all dat." Jefferson's complete recon-
ciliation of Rip and Gretchen illustrates how sentimental domesticity had
come to permeate American life. The hard-edged comic treatment of Dame
Van Winkle as an unremitting shrew bowed to a softer, repentant, subservient
wife. Throughout the play, audiences caught hints of her latent devotion. In
the famous scene where Gretchen drives him out into the storm, she immediately repents and tries to beckon him back. Failing, she faints [curtain ending
second act]. At the play's end Gretchen restores Rip to the head of the family,
accepting, even encouraging ("you can get tight as often as you like"), his
indulgence. She may have been a scold, but her quarrelsomeness resided in a
genuine love for Rip and desire to reform him.[25]

Reform Rip from what? Well, idleness for one. In Irving's original telling it is

Rip's "aversion to all kinds of profitable labour" that drives his wife into nagging fits. Only the barest reference is made to his being "naturally a thirsty soul." But from the first staging of the story Rip became a sot. Why this weakness should come to define the stage persona is not clear. Perhaps it presented greater comic possibilities than simple indolence. A tippler offers the low comedian innumerable opportunities for befuddlement, excusable insolence, and pratfalls. The image of Rip the drunkard became so pronounced in the stage version as to permanently alter Irving's original conception.

This emphasis is all the more striking when one considers that temperance plays became such a staple of stage entertainment beginning in the 1840s. *The Drunkard* (1844) and *Ten Nights in a Barroom* (1858) were only the most successful of the many cautionary tales. Audiences were regaled not only with the graphic horrors of delirium tremens but also with the ravages of alcoholism on wife and child. Such plays were occasions for overt proselytizing; when the show was over men were often asked to sign the pledge of abstinence. Amidst this drama of uplift, the tippling of good-natured Rip seemed oddly out of place. He reversed theatrical conventions of blameworthiness. True, Rip rues his habit and the ruin it rained upon his family. "You are too good for a drunken, lazy fellow like me," Rip confesses sadly to his beloved young daughter. Yet audiences sympathized with him rather than with his long-suffering wife. Rip made continual vows to surrender his vice — but he never meant it. And Rip was unrepentant to the end. Even after finding a new beginning, Rip could not resist when his wife offered him the dram. "I'll drink your good health, and your families,'" Rip famously closes the play, "and may they all live long and prosper!"[26]

Nothing about *Rip Van Winkle* aroused more distressed Victorian tut-tutting than its good-natured tolerance of drink. The final recidivist scene evoked particular complaint. Temperance leaders were distressed. Could not Rip swear off drink (and *mean* it) after his redemption? How could a play and its star, both favorites of respectable families (the "Sunday-school comedian" an *Appleton's* writer put it, "because he never says on the stage what he would not say in the family circle") endorse so destructive a social vice? "Those who remember . . . the old story cannot be . . . pleased at seeing their Rip Van Winkle transformed into a drunken loafer," a young liberal magazine called the *Nation* opined. The play's moral seemed to be "the advisability of drinking to excess inasmuch as the hero, after a life of . . . dissipation . . . triumphs over his enemies, retrieves the ruin [his] intemperate habits had . . . induced" and "attributes to his old ways his final success." Even so ardent a champion of Jefferson as critic William Winter was reluctant to defend Rip's weakness. "The element of inebriety might be left out," he frankly judged, and Rip would "still act in the same way."[27]

Rip and his keg of schnapps. Courtesy of Michael A.
Morrison Collection.

These criticisms were not drumbeats but sufficiently persistent so that Jefferson felt compelled to address the issue in his *Autobiography*. His priority was art, not politics, he wrote. "Should Rip refuse the cup the drama would become at once a temperance play." To make a "statement" by embracing teetotalism would replace contemporary relevance for universal appeal. "I should as soon expect to hear of Cinderella striking for high wages or of a speech on woman's rights from old Mother Hubbard as to listen to a temperance lecture from *Rip Van Winkle*." Joe's instincts were unerring here. He sought a theatrical event that would transcend the vagaries of social reform. Let others carry on the good fight. He would entertain.[28]

The themes in *Rip Van Winkle* may seem confused — virtue triumphing over vice, on the one hand; indulgence and indolence carrying the day, on the other — but that is precisely the point. The play cleverly sent a double message. Family, home, wealth, and respectability are always safer in the path of social discipline; but indolence — and even intemperance — may be forgiven those with a large heart. The play ends, true to theatrical convention, with the Van

Winkle family intact again. Yet Rip's toast bespeaks his unremedied irresolu-
tion. Unlike most contemporary melodrama, whose embedded message of
virtue and hard work encouraged their hearers to believe in the rewards of
capitalist endeavor, *Rip* imparted an alternative vision. The play appealed to
middle-class fantasies of escape from routine and responsibility, both of which
weighed heavily on dutiful Victorians. Rip should be seen as the stage counterpart of Huckleberry Finn. Huck was sketched more compellingly and had the
added attraction of a juvenile protagonist. But his famous escape to the West
at the story's end parallels Rip's tipping of the cup at the play's close. Both
characters refused the confinements of respectability or progress. If the history
of America is largely a story of resolute striving, our imaginative history has
instead dreamed of release.[29]

A Begrudging Realist

The conflicted message of *Rip Van Winkle* appropriately reflects its
place in the larger history of American theatre. Jefferson triumphed in a production squarely within the melodramatic tradition, yet it also hinted at a
realistic idiom that in a few decades would dominate the stage. As with any
art, theatre continually stands between a commitment to its traditions and its
periodic outbursts of creative rebellion. To be sure, *Rip Van Winkle* owes
much more to the romantic thrust of early nineteenth-century theatre than to
what would follow. It would be more than a decade before Ibsen would sound
the tocsin of realism with *The Pillars of Society* and two decades after that
before David Belasco brought a thoroughgoing realism to the staging of American plays. Still, it is worth asking in what sense Jefferson's production may
have reflected the most important new impulse in the American theatre of late
century.[30]

"Realism" is a slippery term, one that must be approached from several
angles if it is to be trapped. At its heart it sought to minimize theatricality.
Stagecraft intended to attain an illusion of life, as if settings and action were
driven by nature herself. A realistic idiom generally meant that playwrights
produced scripts peopled by middle-class figures in surroundings familiar to
their audiences. And it bespoke a more restrained acting as well as an appreciation of ensemble values. Realism came earlier to stagecraft and acting than
it did to written drama (and clearly *Rip Van Winkle* as a play did little to
advance realism). Jefferson's 1865 London debut of his new version of *Rip
Van Winkle* came amidst a gradual but pronounced revolution in stage design,
settings, and lighting.

The proscenium stage, for example, had nearly displaced the traditional stage, which frequently raked upward toward the back and was always fronted by a large apron. Whereas actors had formerly strutted and declaimed in intimate contact with the audience, they now retreated behind the proscenium arch. The box set, which cocooned actors in a three-sided, ceilinged set, had begun appearing on a few Anglo-American stages by 1865. The reconfigured stage carried clear trade-offs. It separated audience and actor, reducing lines of communication between the two and nurturing a more passive response among patrons. Members of the audience witnessed, as it were, a living picture. Dion Boucicault verbalized the metaphor: "The stage is a picture frame, in which is exhibited that kind of panorama where the picture being unrolled is made to move, passing before the spectator with scenic continuity." But if a robust engagement between actor and audience was relinquished, several benefits accrued. With house lights now dimmed during the performance and the stage better illuminated by battens of gas jets, the company of players took on clearer focus. Audiences grew tamer and more mannerly. The energetic and frequently disruptive displays of Jacksonian audiences gave way to the decorum and controlled applause of the late Victorian public. By the early 1880s hissing was rare in New York theatres — and when the goose was heard, guilty patrons might find themselves ejected from the house. Players, for the first time in theatre history, began to achieve control over their stage environment commensurate with a rising professional self-consciousness. They dispensed entertainment to a public that politely consumed their offerings.[31]

Advances in scenic realism can be gauged by what came before. Wonderful accomplishments in scene painting and clever diorama backdrops that provided a passable illusion of movement were part of early nineteenth-century theatre. Still, most antebellum theatergoers saw a set of painted backdrop and wings that looked suspiciously familiar from one play to the next. Hamlet, Lear, and both Richards apparently lived in the same palace. Much scene changing was done in full view of the audience, with paper-hatted stage carpenters pushing apart the two halves of a shutter to reveal another behind it. Players entered and exited through proscenium doors on either side of the stage or from among the grooved wings (as if they had walked through a wall). Stage props were few and sadly contrived. Theatre in such conditions was only possible because actor and audience implicitly conspired to accept a wide array of stage conventions. The physical trappings were conceived as but settings against which the excitement of word and action cast their spell.[32]

Theatre of any kind, of course, requires us to suspend everyday perceptions of reality. But Victorian audiences grew less patient with casual stagecraft that demanded too great a license on reality. The variety — even opulence — that urban architecture increasingly provided during the century found its counter-

part in the theatre's quickened emphasis on theatrical illusion. As visual excitement marked the cultures of England and America, theatrical managers
showed again the genius of their calling. Dioramas, panoramas, the exhibition
of great canvasses of epic events: these bespoke a people for whom the consumption of images filled a need.[33]

Although by no means groundbreaking, Jefferson's staging of *Rip Van
Winkle* reflected the ineluctable march of visual realism. He followed the trend
toward more prolific stage properties, though his eye was attuned more to their
effect than to their authenticity. Three-dimensional pieces supplemented the
traditional painted flats, furniture notably, but also stepped platforms backing
the painted rocky crags over which Hudson's dwarfs clambered. Machinery to
maneuver scenery and produce special effects was becoming common in the
leading theatres where Jefferson performed. Thunder in the Catskills scene, for
example, was rendered by rattling a large piece of tin suspended from the flies.
Lightning was flashed (in later years) by powerful carbon arc lights. Joe's
original London productions received favorable notice, even though the Adelphi had a reputation for shoddiness. There "audiences saw more 'flies,'
'grooves,' dead wall, dirty scenery, and unsatisfactory 'supers' than they would
in any theatre in Whitechapel," librettist W. S. Gilbert complained in 1865. *Rip*
was spared such catty remarks, possibly because Jefferson the perfectionist
would not stand for slipshod staging. And yet, as the century progressed and
scenic realism became ever more pronounced, Joe was criticized for continuing
to use dog-eared scenery. Clearly, his attention to stagecraft diminished compared to his regard for performance.[34]

Jefferson responded indirectly to such criticisms during his frequent interviews and public addresses and while preparing to write his *Autobiography* in
the late 1880s. Realism then bestrode all the arts in Western civilization.
Although upheld as an exemplar of acting realism, Joe was a vocal critic of
what he viewed as its excesses. By excesses he meant allowing scenic elements
to trump the artistic purposes of the play (this at a time when stages were
increasingly cluttered with bric-a-brac). He flatly rejected suggestions in his
later years that he spruce up the set of *Rip* with windmills and working sails,
milkmaids and cows, and fancy stage machinery to facilitate Hudson's crew's
comings and goings. He even deflected requests to use a real dog for Schneider
with the retort that realism in art was bad enough but to animate realism
"with a tail to wag at the wrong time, would be abominable." Thus, Jefferson
could never embrace A. G. Sedgwick's characterization of him as an "apostle
of reality" (those before him being "apostles of the unreal.") As Rip would
forever find disconcerting the world of postrevolutionary America, so Joe
would never be fully acclimated to the stage realizations of Augustin Daly,

David Belasco, or James A. Herne. He remained more comfortable with a stage dominated by actors rather than objects.[35]

Not only in scenery but also in plot Joe found the self-styled realistic drama deficient. He once complained to Daly that "the plays of our time are full of realism without humanity." Joe was a romantic. He understood that the public had developed a taste for the harder-edged realism. But his sensibility would always prefer a drama rooted in the misty sentiments of human emotions.[36]

No matter that the play was second rate and the staging just above average, Joe's performance as Rip was a triumph. With a single voice, commentators lauded his simple naturalism and pathos. "Nothing else than its intense naturalness," a Tasmanian critic wrote of his performance, can explain the fact that audiences "look back to him rather as an old friend whom they have met some how in real life, long ago, than as the mere mimic representative." A Sydney critic wrote near the end of Joe's run that Rip was his best artistic effort, "for in this he proves more how humour and pathos go hand in hand together." London critics were no less enthusiastic. "I forgot heat and everything else watching the subtle and truthful play of that expressive physiognomy," marveled the *Pall Mall Gazette* critic, "a physiognomy of hands and body no less than of face." The *Times* commended Jefferson for his "extremely refined psychological exhibition" (a remark unusual for an age that lacked the vocabulary of inner experience used in the twentieth century to describe, say, Method actors). Joe had "no exaggeration in anything he does or says," the *Standard* critic remarked, it is "astonishing to observe the effect he produced on an audience who are accustomed to . . . caricature." Late in Jefferson's career — by which time realism was well established — an American reviewer happily remarked that "as usual, each word he uttered seemed to be the expression of that moment's thought."[37]

But what did "natural" mean to this generation of playgoers? If we watch the short scenes Joe acted before the cameras in the late 1890s, we might conclude that he is just another representative of the broad, highly stylized school of acting normally associated with the nineteenth-century stage. He takes a swig of the crew's schnapps and immediately crumples to the ground. He strikes poses as if in tableau. Could this be the same actor who sent reviewers into flights of rhapsody about his "natural" performance? Clearly one must wrestle with definitions here.

Actors always strove to be natural. But well into the nineteenth century "natural" doggedly held its Aristotelian meaning: players were imitating an action rather than recreating the action itself. Thus, they sought to strip away all extraneous qualities of their part in pursuit of its idealization. "Nature to advantage dressed," it was famously said. Natural acting meant a thorough refinement of speech and action to present a stage type — whether heroic, romantic, or villainous — that the actor embodied. This was particularly true of heroes in the great tragedies. "The loftier persons of tragedy," Leigh Hunt declared, "require an elevation of language and manner which they never use in real life."[38]

This stylized approach was perpetuated by the thoroughly tradition-bound nature of theatre. "Rules are scattered about the stage and transmitted, gipsy-like, in our vagrant life from one generation to another," Dion Boucicault said with his characteristic flair. Players relied on a rich tradition of postures, gestures, and vocal inflections associated with the various types. The semiotics of theatre were so widely shared that audiences knew how to read dramatic body language fluently. Leaning toward a character with front leg bent and fist raised denoted a threat. A body inclining backwards with legs unsteady and arms outstretched with fingers spread signaled great fear. Tradition-bound though it was, theatrical art nevertheless evolved as ambitious performers sought to put their own stamp on classic roles, even within the older vocabulary of interpretation. David Garrick departed from the sonorous cadences of James Quin. Edmund Kean's acting of Hamlet by "flashes of Lightening" certainly diverged from the measured classicism of John Kemble.[39]

But for all the variations within traditional acting of the classic or romantic schools, they shared an essentially pantomimed approach to performance. The rant and exaggerated gesturing (to modern ears and eyes) of such stage acting bespoke not just the inevitably broad scale that large theatres required but also a philosophical statement about the relation of drama to society. Theatre presented ritualized renderings of human life, large in scale and immediate in impact. There was to be nothing veiled about it. Not the nuances of individual personality but the expressed values of the broader community were conveyed through drama. The stylized gestures and declamatory speech also articulated important assumptions about human nature, namely, that emotions are signified in uniform manner. Theorists all agreed that vital emotions evoked kindred physical display. Actors, consequently, drew upon the same bank of expressions to depict the passions of their characters. How deeply they conveyed these emotions, what technical virtuosity they could muster, determined the acclaim they received.[40]

Why did the traditional approach fade away? Was it the exhaustion of a style no longer capable of reinventing itself in fresh ways? Perhaps, but this explanation fails to account for the durability of traditional acting through many decades and a series of stars who refashioned their art successfully. The abandonment of the traditional approach to acting, arguably the most notable change in modern theatre, owed more to the evolving intellectual and social context of theatre. George Steiner's case for the "death of tragedy," which he sees as culminating in the nineteenth century, can be usefully employed here. With playwrights no longer appealing to forces beyond normal human experience or invoking a universal power that takes its own vengeance, nor, in the wake of the European Enlightenment, convicted of the "finality of evil," tragedy inevitably shrank to "near-tragedy." Life became melodrama. Verse drama gave way to prose. The language of "invocation, adornment, or remembrance," which sets heroic action apart from the quotidian, surrendered to the utilitarian work-a-day prose suitable to the comedy and drama of everyday life. Parallel downsizing occurred in acting. Melodrama was often acted in broad strokes, to be sure, but contrary to our usual stereotypes about clichéd acting, the genre often lent itself to subtlety. Audiences, in fact, gained greater sophistication in "reading" nuanced performances. Just as the twentieth-century public acquired finely honed skills in deciphering the fast cuts of motion pictures, so the nineteenth century's mastered a more complex set of body language, facial expressions, and intonations by performers. Cultural intelligence, in this sense, advanced.[41]

The triumph of a more restrained acting also owed much to the advance of middle-class mores. The "rise of the middle class," too often the deus ex machina of modern social history, can easily become a shallow explanatory model. But there can be no doubt as to the new importance of the urban middle class, both as subject for dramatists and as patrons of the plays. Fascination with Shakespeare and exotic melodrama did not disappear, but audiences increasingly wished to see images of themselves on stage. They desired less of a heroic presence and more of a life-sized personality in their stars. These audience preferences gradually reshaped performance style. Theatre historians credit such French dramatists as Eugène Scribe and Victorien Sardou for seizing the moment in crafting plays that demanded less artificial, more subtle performance. From them, English and American adapters learned the art of utilizing common speech, of economy of dialog, of vitality of plot. French actors, too, notably Bouffé and Fechter, injected greater delicacy into the player's art, particularly through stage byplay that fastened audience attention on small details of their actions — tugging at their sleeves, picking up an object — even when they were not speaking. Still, a twenty-first-century spectator nurtured in the age of the visual close-up might have difficulty readily distinguishing a proponent of the newer school from that of the traditional. Changes in acting styles were incremental rather than abrupt.[42]

That wider cultural changes were afoot is suggested by the parallels between Mark Twain's stage monologues and Jefferson's acting. Twain's initial acclaim came with the publication of his "Jumping Frog" story in 1865, the same year as Joe's London triumph. The next year Twain began his comic lectures, which were as popular as his writings and an unfailing source of income. His shuffling, stammering, distracted stage persona bore resemblance to Jefferson's good-natured, indolent Rip. Their comedy was indirect, unconscious, affecting a "deadpan" countenance that audiences had to look behind. Both were indebted to earlier stage Yankees for their shtick, but both imbued the type with psychological depth and continuity. Rip, like monologist Twain, ambled about the stage in absentminded conversation with himself (in "beautiful befuddlement," Henry James called it), telling rambling stories that might lose their point in the middle. Where Twain's seemingly pointless accounts finally came around to comic humbuggery on the audience, Jefferson's character worked his artless guile on the play's villain.[43]

Joe Jefferson matured as an artist during the transitional years between the traditional and the realistic. Unsurprisingly, he exhibited aspects of both and never resolved (or sought to resolve) the tension between the two. The realism of "mere commonplace" had its place in stagecraft, Jefferson admitted, but Rip's fanciful experience called for a very different treatment. "I was attracted by the poetic nature of the legend," he stated in his *Autobiography,* "and endeavored to treat it in harmony with that feature." The aura of his Catskills phantasms seemed to require that the production be suggestive rather than literal.[44]

Rip Van Winkle had an oddly bifurcated character. The initial two acts partook of standard melodramatic realism. Rip loafs with his cronies and plays with the children. His intoxicated negligence of family and property invites the connivings of Derrick to steal his wife and estate. The act culminates with Gretchen's loss of patience with her refractory husband and ordering him ungently into the stormy night. To this point the play remains a rather ordinary treatment of a conventional theme, redeemed primarily by Jefferson's thespian skills. Then, suddenly, the mood shifts with the coming of the third act. Rip is on the mountain and meets the ghosts. "I felt that all colloquial dialogue and commonplace pantomime should cease," Joe later wrote, "the supernatural element begins, and henceforth the character must be raised from the domestic plane and lifted into the realms of the ideal." The remaining two acts becomes a masterful study in the creation and maintenance of theatrical illusions: the illusion of an encounter with Hudson's crew, creatively rendered through Rip's monologue and the elves' pantomime; the illusion of his dog Schneider (described so vividly by Rip that years later audience members swore they recalled the animal's features); and finally, the illusion of a young man transformed into a decrepit, white-haired ancient. The pursuit of a magical ambience led Jefferson to resist Boucicault's suggestion that in the final act

Rip dine with the villagers. Rip must not eat, decided Joe, because he had "become a dream, a myth, no longer a mortal." The enchantment of the last two acts was so powerful, it was said, as to sometimes supplant applause with thoughtful silence.[45]

How did *Rip Van Winkle* look and sound? The most detailed descriptions (and even a few photographs) come from Jefferson's late nineteenth-century performances. One would note the simple, even spare scenery and stage props. Incidental props and bits of stage business, like Gretchen's washboard at which she toiled, added notes of realism. The play's four basic sets could easily be accommodated by small provincial theatres. The least realistic set was the mountain scene, where the faux boulders and cobbled carpentry of the hill scarcely did credit to Irving's picturesque depiction. Of course the gas lighting, though a vast improvement over earlier floats and candles, still forgave a great deal of scenic mediocrity. The young Rip appeared in buckskin, leather leggings, and soft hat, clothes conveying the plain homespun of a ne'er-do-well. The post-slumber Rip donned ragged versions of the same.[46]

Reviewing the play one is struck by an incongruity. Although set in a Dutch village in the Catskills, only Rip Van Winkle speaks with an accent. Joe recognized the oddity and justified it simply by the need to set apart his role. He actually tamed down his accent (more German, some said, than Dutch) to distinguish it from the lower "Dutch" comic types then current. The accent never impeded Jefferson's clear diction. "An enunciation of the utmost distinctness," wrote London critic Frederick Wedmore. Lacking a powerful voice, Joe possessed instead a wonderfully expressive one, "capable of what would be called an almost womanly tenderness." Recordings of two famous scenes done in 1903 for Columbia records suggest a cultured, mid-Atlantic accent lying beneath the Dutch inflection. It is a soothing voice, free of rant or affectation, though marked by a lulling cadence. Jefferson's voice was showcased in the mountain scene, where it was the only one heard. Again, one must appreciate the daring experiment of having a single voice carry an entire scene. Only an overweening confidence could allow the attempt. And not just by virtue of his one-sided conversation. With but a handful of lines, Joe fashioned twenty minutes of action. Surrounded by mute dwarfs (their unwieldy long gowns poorly hid the secret that full-legged actors played the roles by crouching), Joe's Rip ran the gamut of emotions. It was, said James Huneker, a "supreme specimen of pantomime, of vocal inflection, of facial expressiveness."[47]

Historians of the stage, who are left groping for words to recapture the magic of distinguished stage actors, must turn to contemporary writers for help. Some critics appealed to the personal warmth that infused Jefferson's acting, establishing an audience rapport that seems to characterize all great performers. Huneker, among the most sophisticated and avant garde critics of his age, testified to the "mellow, homely, sweet humanity" of Joe's final toast, so persuasive that it made each member of the audience feel "as though the wish had been leveled at him." Aiding this camaraderie was his "winning smile" (helped, noted a writer, by a "good set of teeth"), setting off his "kindly eyes [and] gentle manner which win upon the children." Critics also wondered at how Joe "concealed his art," an accomplishment that resulted from pains-taking care. Otis Skinner, who briefly acted with Jefferson, recalled how he built up his role movement by movement, approaching his art with a self-consciousness that mirrored the technical precision of the great French come-dians. (Might this have been the payoff for his visit to Parisian theatres in 1856?) For example, he made a point of not allowing Rip to yawn after his long slumber. "A man yawns," said Jefferson, "after sleeping one hour or twenty hours, not after sleeping twenty years." He also understood the virtue of patience in comedy: "Never rush your comedy points," he once told Skin-ner. "The quieter and more deliberate you are, the better your effect." To help accomplish this effect, Joe devised an effective technique of seeming to seek for his words. He did not finish his speeches with the expected declamatory polish of stars. His sentences sometimes trailed off or would be slightly changed by his notice of an action about him. "It is the perfection of naturalness," wrote Wedmore, "the perfection of seeming spontaneity." Further departing from a stage tradition that encouraged stars to coax applause at every opportunity, Joe gave the illusion of being oblivious to the audience. "His asides are not stage asides," wrote a critic for the *Nation,* "from the moment when he first appears on the stage . . . all is as natural as if there were no footlights, no audience, no orchestra, no scenery, and no prompter. He seems unaware of the audience's presence."[48]

We may find this unremarkable, but its novelty might be better appreciated by contrasting it with the time-honored practice of playing to "points." Sprin-kled about the standard repertoire were those emotional zeniths where players could showcase their dramatic power. These moments were announced with mute flourish so that the audience would be prepared to judge — and reward — the display. After the Civil War, audiences increasingly found the florid bom-bast a noisome intrusion upon the dramatic illusion. Jefferson intuited these changing preferences. Although his performance was laced with what "are technically known as *points,*" said Clarke Davis, his "genius . . . divests them of all 'staginess.' " One critic, in the most portentous observation of them all, found in *Rip* "an indication of the future of the American drama."[49]

But that prediction proved profoundly wrong. For all its hints of an emerg-ing realism, *Rip Van Winkle* had far more to do with the mid-nineteenth-century stage than with the drama of O'Neill or Shaw. It was melodrama of the familiar sort; all the stock characters took their bows. Without the legerdemain of Joe Jefferson, *Rip Van Winkle* would have remained a footnote to the stage, one more example of a second-rate dramatic treatment of native themes. Joe's performance, rather than the play itself, augured more significantly for the future of theatre.[50]

That said, one still must account for the play's enduring appeal. What made it an American institution? To say Joe touched a chord in audiences is merely to repeat the obvious. Why these particular notes found resonance, however, casts interesting light on Anglo-American culture.

Audiences obviously responded to the sentimentality that washed over the entire production. It is easy to caricature misty-eyed Victorians seeking catharsis in mawkish drama, and *Rip* certainly provided ample occasions for tear-jerking ecstasy. But the play's staying power only started there. In the character of Rip Van Winkle, Joseph Jefferson struck that fine balance between humor and pathos that has marked a handful of other great comedians. Rip's return to Falling Water and search for Meenie invited audiences to experience not pity but true pathos, meaning that "luxury of grief" which provides "keen-edged pleasure." Keaton and Chaplin would later accomplish this before the silent movie camera, their anguished humor rendering less threatening the hectoring desiderata of modern life. For the American post–Civil War generation, it was a wistful sense of the price of progress that beckoned comic release. Victorians clearly gloried in progress but nonetheless were tugged by memories of a society unrent by division and unhurried by the machine. Rip Van Winkle's acute sense of loss — of youth and identity — expressed in poignant human terms a vague apprehension stealing over the industrialized world.[51]

Jefferson's success opened the doors of London's artistic elite to him. He seems not to have experienced (or he did not notice) the condescension of the British elite toward American artists, of which James Russell Lowell publicly complained a few years later. Novelist and humanitarian Charles Reade, then at the height of his popularity, playwright J. R. Planché, and novelist Anthony Trollope welcomed him. Most especially, Tom Robertson became his boon companion. The same year that Joe premiered *Rip* at the Adelphi, Robertson began his remarkable five-year run at the Princess's Theatre, transforming British theatre with his social comedies, such as *Society, Caste,* and *The M.P.* As playwright and stage manager, Robertson brought the same qualities of realistic depiction that Joe had made famous as an actor. The kindred spirits sported their way around the London theatrical scene.[52]

But as gratifying as was his reception by arty London, Joe may have found even more satisfaction in making contact with the English side of the Jeffersons. Shortly after *Rip* began its long London run, previously unknown English cousins introduced themselves. Military officers, a clergyman, and other respectable Victorians made their introductions — but no actors. Tom Jefferson and his family, financially well situated, entertained their acclaimed American cousin in fine style. A second, even larger family reunion occurred at Christmas. A great believer in the virtues of family gatherings, Joe treated twenty-five Jeffersons to a dinner at a noted London eatery and then to a traditional Christmas pantomime at Astley's.[53]

With the long London run followed by stands in Manchester and Liverpool at last ended, Joe gathered his children for a return to America. He bypassed the now-standard transatlantic steamer for a clipper ship, the *Sunrise*. A romantic conceit, his friends said. But what could be a more fitting conveyance for Rip Van Winkle than the symbol of a bygone era?[54]

10

Bringing the "Sleepy Piece" Home

The *Sunrise*, with Joe and his children aboard, docked in New York harbor on 12 August 1866. During the sixty-two months he was away, Joe had seen his son and traveling companion Charley, now fifteen, move into adolescence. But his other children—daughter Margaret, just turned thirteen; Thomas, nine; and Josephine, approaching seven—had only recently become reacquainted with their father. Per usual, in his *Autobiography,* Joe tells his readers nothing about his homecoming.[1]

Joe settled comfortably at the Brevoort House on Fifth Avenue between Eighth and Ninth streets. The hotel, cobbled together out of three adjoining houses, had become the hostelry of choice for visiting European dignitaries in the 1860s. It was a sign of Joe's financial security—as well as a latent sybaritic streak—that he chose to indulge himself thus. Did his children stay with him or return to their maternal grandparents? Given their still tender ages and the fact that the Pennsylvania countryside provided the firmest sense of home they had known, probably the latter. Moreover, the comparatively short train trip to the Poconos would allow for easy visits.[2]

Joe returned to an America with its great war a year past but a country still wrestling with knotty problems of peace. A few weeks before his arrival black Republicans in New Orleans had suffered a bloody massacre at the hands of Democrats, and Republican Party leaders had become even more determined to impose a thoroughgoing Reconstruction. Joe would have sensed little outrage against southern racial depredations among the business community of New York City. For those in New York, peace meant a chance to reestablish commercial relations with the South at whatever cost to the freedmen. Indeed, New York City buzzed with the sounds of new construction. Manhattan, still largely confined below Thirty-fourth Street, was galloping toward the one-million mark in population. The city had largely escaped the cholera scourge that had threatened it at summer's start. Nonetheless, abysmally crowded conditions in the tenements had prompted the state legislature to take the unprecedented step of tenement regulation. For the middle classes, the answer to the housing shortage was to escape to Brooklyn.

Escape was what Joseph Jefferson had done five years earlier. He had, inadvertently or not, eluded the onrushing war when he headed to San Francisco and then sailed half a world away. Like Rip, who slept through the American Revolution only to find a new "King George" on the tavern sign, Joe returned from a self-imposed exile to an America revolutionized first by struggle and then by the economic dividends of peace. Unsuited by temperament and cross-sectional loyalties to deal with the internecine struggle, Joe had neatly sidestepped the "irrepressible conflict." He now was free to resume his life in America, unburdened by any emotional scars the war might have inflicted.

Joe's new life centered about the rialto, then lying south of Union Square. Even before he left for the West Coast and Australia in 1861, theatres had begun to cluster along Broadway above Canal Street. Once a fashionable residential address, Broadway was assuming its more permanent identity as the city's pleasure center. Gregarious and ever popular with his peers, Joe was welcomed back to the roundtable luncheons at the oyster bars and chop shops, fortified in health and with a fresh stock of anecdotes to share from his adventures down under. It took only a few days for Joe Jefferson to find his American legs.[3]

Upstaged in New York

On 3 September 1866, Jefferson made his first American appearance in more than five years. A performer who carried a quiet confidence in his art, Joe may yet have wondered in some corner of his mind whether Rip's London magic would similarly win New York audiences. During his absence John E. Owens and John Sleeper Clarke had made themselves America's favorite funny men. Would Joe regain his standing as a preeminent eccentric comedian? Could he set his star securely in the firmament of theatrical luminaries in New York? Fittingly, his return was at the Olympic Theatre. He knew the stage well, for it had been Laura Keene's house during his profitable years with her, the venue of his first great New York impression as Asa Trenchard. The theatre sat on the east side of Broadway just above Houston, an unimposing structure except for its "Olympic Theatre" sign emblazoned in bright four-feet-high lettering above the top floor.[4]

Joe was fortunate in his producer, Leonard Grover, who spared no expense in mounting a first-class production of *Rip Van Winkle*. New scenery and an able cast were secured. Grover had good reason to go all out. Joe's London triumph portended solid box office returns in America. If "half of the good things said of him by those across the water be true," the *Clipper* judged, Jefferson will succeed in New York, "for certainly no American has ever received such encomiums from the British press." Playing it safe, however, Grover originally announced only a two-week run. Better that sold out houses require an extension than a trumpeted long run be prematurely withdrawn.[5]

When the curtain first rose on *Rip Van Winkle* that Monday in early September, the fall season was not yet in full swing, and the well-promoted Dutchman nearly had the field to himself. Rip did not appear until a third of the way through the first act. Only after some foundation for the melodramatic plot had been laid and a lively chorus scene performed ("Mein Herr Van Dunk, he never got drunk") did Jefferson emerge on stage. A muggy late summer night inside the Olympic Theatre was intensified by the crush of patrons squeezed in. But the "vaporic condition" failed to dim the enthusiasm when "the lazy rascal Rip Van Winkle rolled upon the stage." For a full minute the production stopped as the audience "clapped and stamped and shouted and hurrahed and cheered and hi-hied" the appearance of the new transatlantic star. Although he never expressed his reaction to audience acclaim, this moment had to be among the most gratifying of his career. Especially so as the house was filled with his peers. "We do not recollect ever before having seen so many professional people gathered together on any similar occasion," the *Clipper* writer marveled. Dan Bryant, Frank Chanfrau, John Ford, Billy Florence, John Brougham were a few of the host of actors, managers, and writers in the audience. They had come out of curiosity to see their long-absent, highly acclaimed friend, but also out of respect to one of their favorite colleagues. The reception also seemed to rattle Joe, for he fumbled about with his opening lines.[6]

Once Joe collected himself he gave the performance his auditors came to see. True, the *Clipper* reviewer felt compelled to dismiss Jefferson's London pedigree. "This London reputation is all humbug," he sniffed. Jefferson was the same actor who had left New York years earlier. Still, the *Clipper* conceded that his natural performance made it "one of the finest pieces of acting the modern stage has witnessed." Over at the *Daily Tribune,* the new critic, William Winter, was getting his first good look at Joe. His fulsome reaction marked the start of an admiring and close personal relationship that would endure the rest of Jefferson's career. Winter was completely convinced by Joe's Rip, "a sad dog, a weak, vacillating fellow, fond of his bottle and of idleness," but underneath "good to the very core." Jefferson had plumbed the depths of human nature, Winter believed, and found there the essential struggles men endure. Evidently Winter was not the only one so moved. Jefferson was called to the curtain several times during the play and made the obligatory speech at the end expressing his thanks.[7]

Jefferson and company set off on what gave every indication of a long run. "That sleepy piece . . . attracts anything but sleepy audiences," ran a clever *Clipper* notice. "The house has been thronged every night." In fact it did last four weeks: respectable, but hardly the stuff of theatrical legend. Clearly *Rip Van Winkle* had not yet insinuated itself as an American institution. The problem had nothing to do with Jefferson or the play. It rather bespoke the appearance on 12 September of an unexpected rival, a production that would quickly establish itself in American theatrical history: *The Black Crook*.[8]

No event of the American theatre quite matches *The Black Crook's* daring production, which wedded in novel ways melodrama, ballet, and spectacle. It was, in fact, of no discernable genre. The loosely jointed, wildly improbable fairy tale plot was clearly but a vehicle for visual display. It was "the first attempt to put on the stage the wild delirious joy of a sensualist's fancy," wrote William Winter, who despite being a pillar of Victorian rectitude found himself drawn to the alluring spectacle. *The Black Crook's* producer, William Wheatley, endowed the stage of Niblo's Garden with every device then available for staging spectacle. Not only were traps sprinkled about the stage, but a new cellar was dug to allow entire scenes to fall away. The procession of scenes that followed one another in the leisurely five-hour production (the final curtain did not ring down until after 1:00 A.M.) overwhelmed viewers: a grotto adorned with stalactites in one scene; a tranquil lake in another. Castles and dens hosted a bevy of fairies and demons who assisted or bedeviled the young lovers. The *premiere danseuses* of the French ballet troupe were perhaps the stars of the production. Ballet had gained respectability on the American stage some decades earlier, but the public had seen nothing to match the elegance of these performers. Nor, it must be added, their legs. The reputation of *The Black Crook* lay less in its elegance than in its provocative display of female limbs clad in tights. "Everybody is talking of it [*The Black Crook*] and the many beauties it reveals to our bewildered gaze," gasped the *Clipper*. After the acclaimed "demon dance" where the female imps "wear no clothes to speak of," the curtain was rung up three times. A timetable of the entire show was published, allowing young men to drop by especially for this provocative number. If *The Black Crook* was not exactly burlesque (lacking the impertinent humor of that genre), it certainly opened the door for modern burlesque's most identifiable feature. Naturally, the show endured its share of moral reproof from guardians of culture. Yet this failed to stop even genteel women from attending. *The Black Crook* enjoyed the greatest run New York theatre had ever seen, 475 performances, before shuttering in early January of 1868. During 1867, Niblo's receipts were more than twice that of any other theatre.[9]

The "British Bombshells," as Thompson's collection of statuesque actresses would be styled, represented a new type of transgressive spirit for burlesque. Just at the moment when the legitimate theatre had stood on the brink of hard-earned Victorian respectability, when managers seemed in firm control of their houses, having expunged prostitutes from their "guilty third tier" while attracting a decorous family audience, a new breed of brassy, underclad women mounted its stage. They presented themselves as spectacle, a defiant challenge to Victorian womanhood. Olive Logan, a respected if erstwhile actress (she left the stage, which she found distasteful, for a career in writing and woman's rights) made very public attacks on *The Black Crook* and Thompsonian burlesque for their debasing effect on theatre, feminism, and culture. "An army of burlesque women took ship for America," she harangued, "and presently the New York stage presented one disgraceful spectacle of padded legs jigging and wriggling to the insensate follies and indecencies of the hour."[10]

About these debates Joseph Jefferson remains characteristically silent in his *Autobiography*. The social context of theatre never seemed to engage him. Instead, his eminently pragmatic approach to his career demanded a strategy to counteract the overwhelming *Black Crook* (which, the *Clipper* breezily noted, "knocked down the old Rip's business"). His answer was a change in bill. On 4 October he revived his estimable friend Asa Trenchard in *Our American Cousin*. Staged by agreement with Laura Keene, this was a highly redacted version intended to showcase Jefferson. It ran for two weeks to largely indifferent audiences. Joe then tried the sentimental favorite *Dot*. But the venerable and slow-moving Caleb Plummer seemed not to the taste of a public so recently aroused by *The Black Crook*. Jefferson's normally high production standards had slipped in his rush to find the winning formula. He then fell back upon a double feature, John Maddison Morton's farce *Woodcock's Little Game* and an old standard from touring days, *The Spitfire*. But the former "fell like a wet blanket upon the audience," a fate the second half of the bill could not redeem.[11]

His New York return, which had begun with such acclaim and expectation, thus drew to a whimpering close. Was Joe, with a clutch of glowing London press clippings in his pocket, devastated by this turn of events? Unlikely. He could rationalize that he had run up against an unanticipated force in *The Black Crook*. He had seen before how new sensations caught the public's fancy to the neglect of other stage worthies. Moreover, a lifetime of trouping helped him appreciate the peculiarly fragile nature of stardom, especially for one just on its cusp. And as always, Joe's sanguine temperament helped salve any hurt pride. In this situation he knew exactly what to do. He would return to the road.

Taking Rip *on the Road*

The mid-Atlantic cities of Philadelphia, Baltimore, and Washington — theatrical venues for three generations of Jeffersons — stood ready to welcome an old favorite. He started with a month's stand at Philadelphia's Chestnut Street Theatre. The new Chestnut benefited from its location in a neighborhood of upscale shops and hotels. Joe was part of a stellar lineup that manager William Wheatley had scheduled for the 1866–67 season. Joe's thirteen-year absence from his native city and recent acclaim combined to attract appreciative crowds for his 31 October premiere of *Rip*. But though initial turnout was strong for "the scion of a noble stock," it was scarcely a week before Joe had to turn to a variety of farces — sometimes assuming three roles an evening — and a revival of *Our American Cousin* (which proved "a dead stick," said the *Clipper*) to even approach filling the house. Jefferson relearned a hard truth: Philadelphia theatre was uncongenial to long runs. Lacking the transient population of New York, Quaker City theatre depended on its resident population, a minority of whom were ardent theatergoers. Whatever comfort Joe may have taken from this bit of local sociology was compromised by the knowledge that both Edwin Booth's tragedies at the Walnut and Dan Bryant's Irish tomfooleries at the Arch Street earned steadier audiences.[12]

Jefferson's next stop, at Washington's National Theatre in late November, must have been accompanied by at least small seeds of doubt about his American venture. His manager and friend John Ford had recovered from the opprobrium of the Lincoln assassination, but association with that tragedy just a year and a half earlier, continued to hang overhead. The pressure to succeed increased when Joe grasped the public expectations accompanying his appearance. The "proud laurels with which he came back crowned from foreign lands" stirred an interest not seen among Washingtonians for years, the *National Intelligencer* opined. (The public was assured that trains to Alexandria would be held until 11:30, to forestall the frequent noisy egress of patrons during final scenes.) There was no time to rehearse the National's stock company for the new version of *Rip*, so Joe and Ford agreed that he would open his one-week stand as Bob Acres in Sheridan's classic, *The Rivals*. It was a triumph. The audience impatiently stirred through the opening scenes, awaiting Jefferson's appearance. When the rustic Acres finally emerged, the audience erupted in an apparently spontaneous fit of enthusiasm. It was minutes before the scene could proceed. The play's end brought the expected curtain call, an obligation Jefferson willingly met throughout his career.[13]

Jefferson's initial Washington stand was followed by a week at Ford's Holliday Street Theatre in Baltimore. Here he unpacked *Rip Van Winkle* for his entire stand, enabled by his willingness (and an accommodating train schedule) to travel to Baltimore and rehearse the company in the morning while he was performing in the capital in the evening. Joe felt an urgency about getting *Rip* on the boards in Baltimore, anxious perhaps to test the waters for his putative starring vehicle.[14]

Back in Washington for a second stand Joe withheld *Rip* in his first week, as if toying with District audiences. Instead, he tendered a procession of favorite characters — Ollapod, Pangloss, Diggory, Noggs, Trenchard, among others. Washington theatergoers loved comedy, Jefferson recognized, but instead of duplicating the broad comedy of William Warren, John Owens, and John Sleeper Clarke (all of whom had recently played the capital), Joe decided to "go on the other tact" and exploit his own brand of sentimental humor. His stratagem seemed to work with both critic and public. With these preliminary successes proclaimed about Washington, anticipation for *Rip* surged. At the beginning of his second week Joe presented his starring vehicle. The National Theatre that evening was a "solid mass of human faces; rising tier above tier." Joe did not disappoint. "The triumph of Mr. Jefferson last night in *Rip Van Winkle* was so signal and complete as to entirely eclipse every other effort of his life before a Washington audience." If Boucicault's play contained "no remarkable power," a critic judged, it was peculiarly suited to showcase Jefferson's talents, "those indescribably beautiful, tender and touching traits . . . in which he is incomparably above and beyond every other actor in America." Crowds thronged to the National through the balance of his stand. The best seats had to be procured days in advance. "There never was a piece better put upon a stage in this city," the effusive critic finally judged. Jefferson's merits were "above the power of the pen to adequately command."[15]

It was not in New York but on the road that *Rip Van Winkle* first ingratiated itself with America. The momentum Joe gathered in Washington carried forward throughout the rest of his career — though like all stars, he would experience occasional disappointments. Joe's unique marriage of pathos and humor resonated with mid-Victorian sensibilities in a way that later generations would never be able to fully plumb. The play's nostalgic call to simpler days, to a past unburdened by fratricide, was compelling. John Greenleaf Whittier had already fed the American hunger for homespun memory. Six months before Joe brought Irving's slumberer to New York, Whittier published *Snow-bound*, the work that solidified his reputation and his fortune. Whittier's poetic evocation of the rural simplicities in an idealized New England sounded a chord akin to Jefferson's stage figure.

Joe returned to Baltimore for five weeks at the beginning of 1867. His choice of repertory suggests the practical considerations of star touring. First, having staged *Rip Van Winkle* during his short run just a month earlier, Joe felt obligated to start elsewhere. He turned to probably his second most reliable vehicle, the adaptation of Dickens's *The Cricket on the Hearth*, which he mounted for three straight nights. His run also demonstrated the continued need for variety. Over the course of the five weeks he staged ten full-length comedies and melodramas (in order: *Cricket, The Heir at Law, Old Heads and Young Hearts, Nicholas Nickleby, Rip Van Winkle, The Rival, The Poor Gentleman, Our American Cousin, Ours,* and *Ticket-of-Leave Man*) plus an equal assortment of afterpiece burlesques. The bigger attractions, either because they were audience favorites (*Rip Van Winkle*) or because they were new (*Ticket-of-Leave Man* and *Ours*), earned multiple sequential performances. Additionally, *Rip* was dropped into the lineup on two other occasions as Jefferson felt its demand renewing. Scheduling the right bill — meaning the bill apt to entice the largest audience — was a high art nurtured by long experience in the business.[16]

Even more striking was Joe's taking on two new roles during the run. Nothing need be said about a forgettable Boucicault comedy, but Tom Robertson's *Ours* represented an emerging genre of drawing-room comedies that Joe had never essayed. His London friendship with Robertson no doubt encouraged the attempt. The play's characters are surrounded by bric-a-brac stage props, seem constantly to be fiddling with objects, and engage in the sort of smart patter then much admired. One detects a proto-Wildean mocking drollery coloring his dialogue. ("Blanche is much too nice a girl to have a mother," or, "I'm proud to say she wouldn't have me. Ah! She's a sensible girl.") *Ours* had premiered in London just a few months before Joe staged it in Baltimore in January 1867. Set during the Crimean War of a decade earlier, the comedy's production suggested that enough time had elapsed since that dreadful conflict to allow the public to view it as a backdrop for humor.[17]

After his 9 February closing, Joe took a swing through the Gulf Coast, revisiting cities that had been so important to his youth: Mobile and New Orleans. His New Orleans stand at the Varieties Theatre, beginning in late

February, faced a rugged start. Not only was Adelaide Ristori, the "great queen of tragedy," finishing a run, but John E. Owens, a particular favorite of New Orleans audiences, was still appearing at the St. Charles Theatre. Mardi Gras, too, intervened. Early in his second week theatres were given over to grand balls of the "Mistick Krewe of Comus." Moreover, the weather for much of the month's visit was abysmal. Torrential rains across the South inundated Chattanooga and sparked concerns about flooding in New Orleans.[18]

For all of this, Joe enjoyed great success. Residents braved the elements to fill the Varieties. The *Picayune* critic had witnessed Joe's *Rip* in London two years earlier, which gave him a comparative perspective and a fine appreciation of Jefferson's art. "The performance is infused with a light and warmth, a freshness and grace," he proclaimed, and Jefferson "has thrown over it an air of vrai-semblance, altogether beyond the reach of art." Joe was "a perfect master of detail." Only rarely did he "venture a 'hit' [a stage gag], but certainly not to the vicious degree common to so many of our so-called great American tragedians and comedians, whose reputations rests upon such depraved pandering to the 'groundlings.'" Probably never again, the critic concluded, would he see "a more finished piece of character acting."[19]

Joe's last stop during his 1866–67 season was back in Philadelphia. His stand during most of June proved more lucrative than his first, with *Rip* "his strong card." Summer was generally not a peak time for theatre with the oppressive heat, but Jefferson defied the elements to attain what the *Clipper* characterized as among the most successful stands in the history of the city.[20]

By the time he closed in Philadelphia in late June 1867, Joe had been on the boards nearly continuously for ten months. He took a brief needed rest with his children in Paradise Valley. But the compulsive worker could not long stay away from the theatre. He had brought back from London a new burlesque spectacle, *The Woodcutter of Baghdad, and the Lovely Forty Thieves,* which he produced for John Ford in Baltimore. Although no details of the production survive, the title suggests it resembled earlier spectacles he had managed and attests to burlesque's growing affection for the female leg.[21]

Rip *and Shakespeare*

On 9 September 1867 Joe made another bid for the extended loyalty of Gotham's theatergoers at the refurbished Olympic, untroubled this autumn by the competition of a runaway hit. He triumphed from opening night. The "audience was large and critical," wrote the *Herald* critic, enthusiastic about Jefferson's "jolly hero." It quickly became a "foregone conclusion" that *Rip* would have a long run. Seats were at a premium; reserved seats sold early, and at night a long line snaked from the box office to the curb. Demand for tickets was such that what later became known as the "Rip matinee" was instituted. These early Saturday afternoon performances encouraged families to attend. Joe had to overcome some criticisms. His supporting cast was deemed shakier than the year before, and some critics found the play itself irredeemable. "The piece is worse than trash," the *Frank Leslie's Illustrated Magazine* writer judged. He wished "somebody would write a new play for him [Joe] with a leading part to "fit his peculiar powers." Such opinion was in a clear minority, though. William Winter over at the *Tribune* better caught the public mood. He declared Joe's *Rip* to be "one of the gems of the stage," a memorable production that should be attended by all.[22]

Uncertain as to how sturdy *Rip*'s "legs" would be, Joe and his management prepared and announced a new production of *A Midsummer Night's Dream* in late September. But Shakespeare had to wait; *Rip* held the stage until the latter half of October. It was a contract to appear in Chicago in November, not lack of audience enthusiasm, that led to the closing of his Olympic engagement. Theatre management loved the box office receipts. Jefferson may have even been happier, pocketing $15,000 for less than two months labor.[23]

With the Olympic stage cleared of *Rip*, *A Midsummer Night's Dream* could now be mounted. Joseph Jefferson's involvement in this production displays a side of his career easily overlooked, that of regisseur. While in England he had been on the lookout for fresh productions to carry across the Atlantic. *The Woodcutter's Dream* and *A Midsummer Night's Dream* were the fruit of his search. Joe had a painter's eye for visual detail. The centerpiece of the latter play's scenery was a panorama backdrop of Athens painted by an acclaimed London theatrical artist. "Shakespeare's operatic spectacle" (as it was billed) had been tried out in Philadelphia the previous summer, achieving a remarkable seven-week run. This success on the road augured ever greater enthusiasm on Broadway. "We have seen crowded houses, heard immense applause, seen successful first performances . . . but nothing that we have ever seen before in the way of all these things could come up to the scene witnessed every night last week at the Olympic," wrote the *Clipper*'s experienced critic. Shakespeare's beloved text was well served by imaginative production values and extensive rehearsals, helping opening night to come off flawlessly. The timing of the fantasy's production was propitious. New Yorkers loved stage spectacles — *Aladdin* and *The White Crook* (a burlesque of a burlesque) served up similar wares. But these lacked the rich language or appealing characters found in the Bard's effort. *A Midsummer Night's Dream* reminded patrons of the many-layered pleasures in great theatre. Admittedly, the production's appeal relied more on spectacle and broad comedy than poetic language. It was "marred by a coarseness that smacked of the east-side," sniffed one critic. On whatever level, audiences demanded it for a hundred nights, making it one of the most lucrative Shakespearean comic productions of the day.[24]

A Midsummer Night's Dream had been well cast. Joe's sister, Cornelia Jefferson, who played Titania, showed that she had more to recommend her than simply the Jefferson name. The most notable cast member, however, was the age's great clown, George Washington Lafayette Fox (1825–77). Fox was then stage manager at the Olympic (a responsibility that certainly gives him some credit for the show's acclaim), but his fame lay in the particular and troubled niche he carved out for himself as a clown and low comedian. If Joseph Jefferson embodied the possibilities of wealth, professional respect, public respectability — even love — in the day's theatre, Fox exemplified the frustrated, self-destructive opposite. Fox, like Jefferson, grew up in an acting family, albeit one that limited its range to New England. During the 1850s, Fox established himself as a burlesque favorite among the Bowery crowd at the National Theatre, where he offered famous send-ups of Shakespeare. Fox's great gift was for pantomime, an art form identified at its highest levels with European performers, especially the acclaimed Franco-Italian Ravel family. With his characteristic chalk white face, bald head, knickers, and affected look of injured innocence, Fox defined for generations the appearance and demeanor of a clown. His greatest triumph came in the spring of 1868 (just a month after *A Midsummer Night's Dream* closed) in the pantomime *Humpty-Dumpty*. Never before had a pantomime comprised the entire bill of a Broadway theatre. Its madcap, unbridled exuberance excited audiences for nearly 1,300 performances.[25]

Fox came out of the same Yankee comic tradition as Jefferson, but the two traveled different roads. Where Jefferson assumed the more typical comic persona of the laconic but shrewd Yankee, Fox turned the figure toward comic anarchy. Where Jefferson's stage figures ultimately solidified the social order, Fox's destroyed it in a frenzy of violent physical humor or verbal send-ups of New York politics and society. If Jefferson anticipated Will Rogers, Fox foreshadowed the Marx Brothers. His aggressive style of humor matched his temperament. Joe Jefferson won public respect by his unfailing courtesy and earned the admiration of colleagues for his camaraderie and professionalism. But "Laff" Fox could not shake the plebeian dust from his boots. "A flour-smeared Bowery boy, feisty, greedy, pugnacious, bullying, and showing off, yet cowardly and expedient," his biographer Laurence Senelick characterized him. The crudeness of his humor and immoderate self-promotion tainted his reputation. ("Have you seen Fox's Bottom?" leered an ad for *A Midsummer Night's Dream* widely plastered about New York streets.) Further, his disagreeable manner kept him unpopular with other actors. Insecure and easily offended, Fox threatened violence at the drop of a hat. His final years were spent in a scramble for solvency. Against Jefferson's inner peace and equanimity Fox offered emotional turmoil and erratic behavior that devolved finally into insanity. Still, if his art form — pantomime — declined and his reputation receded, the comic genius of this "Grimaldi of America" must be acknowledged. Indeed, the fierce physicality of his humor certainly caught the tumultuous spirit of late nineteenth-century American cities better than the quaint folksiness of Joe's Rip.[26]

A New Mrs. Jefferson

The end of Joe's stand at the Olympic in late October 1867 marked the beginning of a long starring tour throughout the Midwest and South. He opened in Chicago at McVicker's Theatre. James McVicker (1822–96) was nearly synonymous with Chicago theatre for decades. He opened his first Chicago theatre in 1857, prospered during the booming war years, and earned a reputation for high-quality productions. McVicker was to the Chicago stage what Augustin Daly or Lester Wallack was to New York's. Jefferson liked McVicker, feelings no doubt reciprocated given the box office receipts Joe generated.[27]

Oddly, Joe had not performed in Chicago since childhood, when he helped his parents in their westward swing. Joe may not have recognized the city, which had entered its unexampled era of growth. The uniform flatness of the land was now interrupted by massive grain elevators fronting Lake Michigan; an enlarging gossamer web of rails converged on the city. The unremittingly commercial nature of Chicago was omnipresent. Even at McVicker's Theatre Joe would occasionally have caught the pungent odor drifting east and north from the new stockyards. The prefire city was without sophistication but not without a desire for amusement. Thus Joe encountered a populace eager for his art. "We are glad to give Mr. Jefferson a hearty welcome," proclaimed the *Chicago Times*, "he is thoroughly American, as well as a great actor." Why would the paper find Jefferson particularly welcome? Because he offered a refining influence to the stage, which contrasted "so pleasantly with the 'blood and thunder,' the sensation and shallowness, of the modern drama." The opening night Chicago audience, "always chary of its applause," was won over during the first act, calling Jefferson before the curtain at scene's end. Rip's transformation in the final act was especially affecting. His "torn and tattered clothing" and his rusted musket, which fell apart the moment Rip picked it up, mirrored Rip's physical decay. Nineteenth-century audiences had not known such verisimilitude. *Rip Van Winkle* played to strong houses for the full three-week run.[28]

Rip found a warm reception on Lake Michigan's shores, but Joe found even more. He met the teenaged daughter of McVicker's treasurer and was smitten. No known pictures survive of Sarah Isabel Warren (probably a result of the Buzzards Bay fire of 1893), but one can guess she possessed the frail beauty Joe found appealing. Further, she had the family credentials so important in the tight-knit theatrical culture. Her father, a second cousin to Joe, was part of the Warren clan, and Sarah was a niece of the great Boston comedian William Warren. At age seventeen she was not even half of Joe's age (thirty-eight), but such disparity was not unusual for the day. The two had a whirlwind courtship. On 20 December they wed in Chicago. Three days later, Joe inaugurated a two-week run in Cincinnati. "Toney," as Joe called her, learned firsthand the hard facts about touring and theatrical marriage.[29]

Joe's mention of his second marriage in his *Autobiography* was typically succinct. He indirectly apologizes to his readers for lack of expansive detail, justifying his terseness with a desire not to weary them with a tedious "descant upon the wonderful talents of our children." It was left to that garrulous commentator on contemporary theatre, Olive Logan, to publicly comment on the marriage shortly after it occurred. She noted the parallelism between Joseph Jefferson's and Edwin Booth's marriages. Both lost their first wives to illness. More strikingly, both second marriages were to daughters of McVicker theatre management, Booth marrying Mary McVicker just a year and a half after Joe's and Sarah's nuptials. The intimate friendship of Jefferson and Booth extended even to matters of matrimony it seemed. Ultimately, though, their experiences diverged: although Joe had to nurture his wife through chronic bouts of TB, Booth contended with a spouse who not only suffered from the same affliction but whose spiral downward into depression and debilitating mental illness absorbed much of his emotional energy.[30]

Joe's young bride joined him on his tour, accompanied by daughter Margaret who was just a few years younger than her stepmother. Being from a theatrical family, Sarah presumably understood that nothing was going to deter Joe from continuing a lucrative starring tour. Joe did make some bows toward a honeymoon. While in Kentucky the newlyweds visited Mammoth Cave (the "great subterranean monster," Joe styled this new American tourist attraction). Even here, Joe could not put career fully out of mind. He took an artist along to sketch the cave's wonders with an eye to using them for an unrealized stage spectacle. The tour lasted into the summer of 1868 and was far more extensive than that of the previous year. Joe added Nashville and Memphis to his stops in the South, St. Louis in the West, and Pittsburgh,

Louisville, Detroit, and Toledo in the Midwest. In smaller markets the run would last a week. Two-week stands were also common. Larger cities, such as Philadelphia, merited four. The only way such schedules could be met was by the graces of the railroad.[31]

Joe's traveling career had been dependent on the iron horse since at least the late 1840s. He had known the rigors of rail travel in its antebellum formative stage, though even then it must have seemed a large step up from the wagon and riverboat travel of his youth. With the war past, American railroads entered a period of expansion and consolidation. The 30,000 miles of track in 1860 had quadrupled by the early 1880s. Equipment was improving, and the creature comforts of passenger coaches became a concern for competing railroads. Gas jets lit coaches; heating and ventilation improvements made unsteady bows toward rudimentary climate control; and the elevated clerestory window design of coaches beginning in the early 1860s allowed men — even with their hats — to walk through the car without stooping. Nonetheless, the air in an enclosed coach quickly thickened from bodies and clothes that were, as one traveler put it, "more or less in need of purification." Joe found considerable regional variation in the quality of passenger service as he toured the country. The Northeast and Middle West lines generally offered reliable service by the day's standards. but during the late 1860s and into the 1870s on trips through the South he encountered the residuum of war. Lines remained disjointed, each state tending to have its own rail company that tendered limited passenger service on thin road beds and rickety rails. "The Southern railways are terribly rotten & dangerous," Charles Kean bluntly wrote in 1866.[32]

A glance at Jefferson's touring schedule in the 1869–70 season suggests the extent of his dependence on the rails. From New York, Brooklyn, and Newark in late summer, he moved west to Buffalo for a week; farther west to Chicago for a full month; to Indianapolis and St. Louis for a week each; south to Memphis for two weeks, and farther south yet to New Orleans for three; along the Gulf Coast to Mobile for a week; a canceled engagement in Cincinnati (because of illness); back to the Deep South to Macon, Georgia; back north again to Washington and Baltimore for four weeks altogether; up to New England for a stint in Boston; back west to finally play Cincinnati for two weeks; a week at nearby Louisville; and closing the season out in late May with three weeks in Philadelphia. These tight schedules (and they could be even tighter with a series of one-night stands) proved untenable if trouble arose. In the early 1880s, for example, Joe's company missed two connections between Pittsburgh and Nashville and the opening of his next engagement. With hundreds of touring companies on the road such incidents must have been common.[33]

Delays aside, the prosperity Joe knew by the late 1860s allowed him to upgrade his tickets to enjoy the much-improved dual-purpose cars that appeared just before the Civil War. Day coaches were transformed into sleepers by use of folding seats and hinged bunks. Long passenger routes meant an increasing number of passenger trains that traveled through the night, and night travel brought about heightened demand for such sleepers. The end of the 1860s also saw the introduction of dining cars that offered some relief from abysmal depot food. Beginning in the mid-1880s, Joe sometimes leased special cars to carry his company, a luxury his troupe must have relished. Yet even with these advances touring was grueling. The theatrical trade paper complained that despite the modicum of improvement in interior appointments, train travel remained marked by "dirt, discomfort, and danger." The *Traveler's Official Railway Guide* sought to allay concerns of prospective travelers about railroad safety, boasting that one could take 76,000 trips from New York City to Buffalo before expecting death on the rails. Touring actors were not so easily reassured. The *Mirror* chronicled too many wrecks involving players. Articles told, for example, of the harrowing experience of Keene company's in eastern Colorado when its Union Pacific train struck a herd of cattle, casting engine and coaches off the track. Actress Topsy Venn was seriously injured when the "fast Philadelphia" train derailed in 1881 and she was pinned between two seats. Joe was spared railway tragedy; the most serious injury coming when a cast member tripped while alighting from a train in Omaha and broke her nose.[34]

As Joe swayed along the railroad right-of-ways in the post–Civil War decades he had a front row seat to a transforming America. The extent of the rail network and the accouterment of train travel were themselves barometers of progress. Railroad timetables in 1869 announced for the first time through connections from Omaha to Sacramento. With his eye for landscape composition, Joe would have noted the evolving metropolitan railway corridors in the East and Midwest over the following two decades. His 1860s journeys would have passed through a largely rusticated landscape. The railroad right-of-way, demarcated increasingly by parallel fences built by the train companies to keep livestock off the tracks, became havens for ragweed, dewberry briers, and other botanicals that grew tall in their protected habitat. The cuts and fills necessary for gentle grades created novel visual sweeps. Over the course of the next several decades, Joe would have seen clear evidence of an emerging industrial giant. Railway corridors of the East and Midwest became lined with the artifacts of an industrializing nation: sidings, smokestacks, factories, and the sooty detritus of the industrial zone, as well as coal bunkers, power stations, and wires of the early electrical grid.[35]

A New Touring System

The development of the American rail system revolutionized the nation's theatre. Like much else in American life, theatre became specialized and centralized. And, as in so many other emblematic moments of the nineteenth-century stage, Joe Jefferson found himself center stage in this metamorphosis. The change was from a theatre based on local stock companies that produced a repertory of plays, often complemented by stars who traveled the country, to what was termed "combination companies": touring companies, typically consisting of a star and supporting cast, that took a single play on the road. In his *Autobiography* Jefferson readily takes responsibility — credit or blame, depending on one's perspective — for helping pioneer the most significant change in the organization of professional theatre of the nineteenth century ("the industrial revolution in the theatre," historian Alfred Bernheim characterized it). As Joe tells it, while heading to Detroit and the Michigan hinterland on tour during spring 1873 he had difficulty in securing supporting casts in places like Adrian, East Saginaw, and Bay City. Thus, he hired his own for a short season. Jefferson does not claim originality in this expedient; he encountered similar companies around the same time. Dion Boucicault plausibly lays claim to having organized the first road show when he took a group of American actors on a tour of English cities in *The Colleen Bawn* in 1860. Several profitable tours to the expanding California market in the mid-1870s showed the potential of the road, and by 1880 the road show was here to stay.[36]

But this sea change in the organization of professional theatre had nothing to do with the influence of a single or even a few individuals. Rather it bespoke the conflation of large forces: the expansion of the railroads; economic challenges of traditional stock companies, especially with the devastating Panic of 1873; and the evolving preferences of American audiences.

The enabling function of railroads is self-evident, not only in carrying entire companies with dispatch from Mobile to Muskegon but also in transporting crates of scenery, which the combination companies increasingly required. (Joe carted about the country three elaborate sets for *Rip Van Winkle*.) Clearly, without the railroads American theatre would have remained a very different affair, with individual stars and family troupes continuing to itinerate regions by wagon, stagecoach, or boat.

Even apart from the impact of the rails, traditional stock companies were struggling. Ideally, these venerable theatrical institutions needed only a balanced company of players to produce a sizable repertory of plays that would attract and please audiences. But for many years they had required a procession of stars to meet this end. The expense of maintaining a company of actors, especially in a modest urban market, proved daunting. The Panic of 1873 and subsequent depression hugely intensified economic pressures on these precarious theatrical operations. Already operating on thin profit margins, the theatres found the expenses of maintaining a sizable company untenable as audience declined. The numbers tell a melancholy story. Between 1873 and 1876 the number of stock companies in major cities — so-called first-class companies — fell from more than fifty to less than twenty. By 1880, there were fewer than eight. A byproduct of unemployment and shuttered theatres was the rise of variety entertainment (later styled vaudeville). The plethora of actors "at liberty" created a buyers' market. Producers had their pick of talent from which they fashioned a stage potpourri. In 1873–74 a "great epidemic of variety," in the words of dramatic chronicler George C. D. Odell, swept across New York stages. The new, fast-paced theatrical genre quickly caught on and remained a permanent competitor for entertainment dollars.[37]

The increasingly higher expectations of American audiences also contributed to the decline of stock. Combination companies — built around stars, carrying elaborate scenery for the single play they produced, and remaining in various urban markets only as long as deemed profitable — were superior agents for delivering an entertainment package. The five companies that toured in 1872 multiplied to nearly a hundred just a few years later. The numbers continued to rise, peaking at 420 in 1904. The rapid displacement of stock companies by the combination system stirred some hostility. Opponents saw combination companies as a pernicious commercial erosion of artistic standards. If young actors no longer had the exposure to multiple roles, how would they develop their art? And, at least in the early days of the combination system, local theatre managers complained of being defrauded by fly-by-night touring companies ("snaps" they were called) that misrepresented their product. The abuses threatened to discredit the new theatrical structure.[38]

To the many jeremiads lamenting theatrical decline, Joe gently responded (it was not his manner to dissent aggressively) with a Lincolnesque anecdote. He recalled that when his father refitted his old flintlock with a percussion mechanism, his hunting friends scoffed and warned of trouble ahead when he ran out of caps. So it always is, Jefferson concluded, that novelty engenders opposition. But Joe also went on to engage the issue in its particulars. He admitted the disadvantages of constant travel and single parts that prevented young actors from learning the sweep of dramatic literature. But he reminded critics infatuated with the "palmy days of stock" of how ill suited company members often were for their parts. The modern opportunity for touring companies to cast their plays properly more than compensated for the drawbacks. "And further, the vast continent of America . . . seems to have demanded the establishment of this important institution." Vox populi had spoken, and Joe Jefferson, whose terrific success was built on giving the public what it wanted, was certainly not one to demur.[39]

Despite his professed affection for the combination company, Joe was actually a reluctant convert. He continued to perform with local companies through much of the 1870s. Indeed, when he did form temporary *Rip* companies for short tours—as in Michigan—this was more an extension of the traditional custom of brief stock company hinterland tours than a portent of a revolutionary new system. Reluctance to alter his mode of operation was only to be expected of a careful man who was part of a tradition-bound profession. Further, why take a chance on putting together a full company, with the greater financial risk that entailed, when he could demand a substantial guarantee from managers and leave the headaches of promotion and casting to them? Indeed, Jefferson never fully embraced the strict one-play specialization of the combination system (with the brief exception of his *Rivals* tours of the early 1890s). Although he counseled peace with the new dispensation—and even spoke with pride about his role in its inception—Joe was a creature of theatrical convention. He continued to feature a variety of roles on most of his tours. In his 1885 tour, for example, he alternated between *Cricket on the Hearth* and *Rip Van Winkle* with *Lend Me Five Shillings* continuing the old (and increasingly rare) practice of an afterpiece farce. He never lost his sense that audiences needed a change of pace. Certainly the numbers of plays were greatly reduced as *Rip Van Winkle* became his bread, butter, and dessert. The man who, according to biographer Arthur Bloom, had essayed more than three hundred roles in his career, by the early 1870s rotated but a handful of featured plays and farces. Rarely did he unveil a new role. Not only did such constriction make life easier for Jefferson, but it was expected as a badge of stardom.[40]

Joe's early starring tours were confined to major American cities. By his 1871–72 tour, however, he began to visit much more modest communities. Between September and June, to such regular stops at Brooklyn, Buffalo, Cincinnati, Detroit, and Cleveland, he added Albany and Troy, New York; Galveston and Houston, Texas; Terre Haute, Logansport, and Fort Wayne, Indiana; Springfield, Jacksonville, Quincy, Peoria, and Bloomington, Illinois (what childhood memories that swing must have awakened); Toledo and Akron, Ohio; Meadville, Williamsport, Titusville, Wilkes-Barre, and Scranton, Pennsylvania. Thirty-nine stops in all, many for only one night, though more typically for two. Joe could hardly have managed the breakneck pace without the help of two people. Son Charley had matured into his business manager. Joe also retained a personal valet, Sam Phillips, who not only handled luggage and tended costumes but would sometimes be sent ahead to coach the local company on the basics of *Rip Van Winkle*.[41]

The advantage of a combination company, of course, was that such repetitive schooling was not necessary. Joe himself could cast and fine-tune the troupe, refining points of business as he saw fit during the tour. *Rip Van Winkle* presented some unusual casting demands. It called for a dwarf to portray the member of Hudson's crew who entices Rip to the fateful bowling party (a role so difficult for local stock companies to properly cast that a full-size person would often have to carry out the action in a stoop). In 1882 Joe found Dudley McCann, whose credentials included proper stature for the role and a loyalty to Jefferson that endured until Joe stopped playing the role in 1904. *Rip Van Winkle* also required two children for leading parts. Touring with children posed its own kinds of difficulties, though no complicating Actors' Equity regulations about children were yet in place. There was a nearly seasonal turnover of children for the young Hendrick and Meenie. In one case, however, Elsie Leslie, an acclaimed child actress of the day, spent two years with Jefferson and later returned in several ingenue roles. In her second year, when Joe could not find a suitable boy for Hendrick, Elsie was persuaded to don breeches to take the boy's part. Jefferson's companies would finally employ more than two hundred actors in the twenty-five years between 1879 and 1904. For some minor figures, these tours may have been the pinnacle of their careers. Others moved on to distinguished careers in their own right: Maurice Barrymore, Julia Marlowe, James O'Neill, Mary Shaw, Viola Allen, James Stoddart, and Otis Skinner, among others. William Seymour, who may almost be said to have invented the work of the modern stage directory, played the young Hendrick with Joe in 1869. A few joined Joe already having achieved stage renown, such as Mrs. John Drew and William Florence (as part of *The Rivals* cast, rather than for *Rip*).[42]

Given that Jefferson often made separate fall and spring tours (frail health increasingly dictated a measured schedule), he sometimes had to cast his play twice. He did not relish the turnover in support, as he admitted to being "always attacked with a nervous fit" when meeting a new cast. His supporting casts, whether local stock companies or his own combination companies, varied in quality and were occasionally targets of newspaper criticism. But even social luminaries found they were not allowed to meddle in his casting decisions. When acclaimed agnostic Robert Ingersoll sought a place for a young friend in Jefferson's *Rivals* tour, Joe demurred, explaining that English comedy ("the only dish we have to offer") "seems to lose its flavor when not cooked up by experienced actors." Although polite in his responses, at some level Joe must have been irked by the common notion that most anyone—trained or not—might successfully take up a minor stage role. As Joe revisited cities, he learned the predispositions of particular audiences and instructed his casts accordingly. Some cities needed "a little more force," Joe would say, advising a broader style. He once counseled Otis Skinner (a future matinee idol who toured with Joe in *The Rivals*), "This is Pittsburgh, and you must pull things open a little wider." Naturally, Joe found great advantage in those few players who stayed year after year. Charles Waverly, for example, came on board as Cockles in 1878 then proceeded through a variety of roles in *Rip* and other Jefferson productions until his death from typhoid in 1883. Waverly had an intuitive grasp of Joe's artistic taste that the latter knew could not be easily replaced.[43]

If the decline of stock meant the curtailing of traditional apprenticeship, then companies such as Jefferson's took on added import as thespian finishing schools. Young player — and even journeyman actors — benefited from his decades of experience on the boards. Jefferson was a craftsman. He developed firm ideas about the effects he wanted in every scene, and he possessed the ability to articulate his artistic ideals to the cast. By inclination he loved talking about the art of acting, never hesitant to share the tricks of his trade with acolytes. One of the beneficiaries of his accumulated stage wisdom was Mary Shaw, who played Rip's termagant wife for two seasons in the mid-1890s. Shaw (1854–1929) was not only an actress but an early feminist. She helped introduce American audiences to Ibsen and played a brothel keeper in the controversial New York production of Shaw's *Mrs. Warren's Profession*. With her feminist sensibility, Shaw sought to make Gretchen a more sympathetic character, not hard to do considering Rip's sottish irresponsibility. But after one performance Joe took her aside for a gentle lecture. Whatever justice there may be in Gretchen's distress, nothing must detract from audience sympathy for Rip. The more outrageous Rip's behavior, the more lovable he becomes. As counterintuitive as this advice initially seemed to Shaw, she nonetheless heeded it, at first out of respect for Jefferson and later from a grasp of its truth.[44]

The Theatrical Capital

The American theatre — sustained and extended by the railroads and specialized through the combination touring companies — also became, paradoxically enough, centralized. New York City became the organizing locus of the theatrical world. Although Gotham had long been the preeminent theatrical city, in the late nineteenth century it assumed a more direct role in organizing the nation's entertainment. Amidst the bustle of Union Square, actors, agents, and managers hammered out agreements for upcoming tours, costumers and scenic artists outfitted casts and designed backdrops, and trade paper journalists chronicled the careers of players. Union Square, though still in its formative stage as the rialto, was becoming a theatrical environment unlike any Joe had heretofore known.[45]

Over the course of the 1870s and 1880s, Union Square (centering on Fourteenth Street) served as the heart of an American theatrical establishment approaching its pinnacle as an industry. Traditionally, each theatre employed its own craft specialists: carpenters, painters, costumers, pyrotechnicians, bill posters, and so on. But these skills began to spin off to independent shops when theater managers discovered greater efficiency in contracting out work. A bevy of costume houses, for example, contended for the business of the thousands of actors who sought the just-right stage dress and accessories for domestic or exotic dramas. Jefferson patronized Dazian's Theatrical Emporium at 26 Union Square, the oldest and most prominent theatrical supplier of the city, for his costumes. Joe also paid the expected visit to Napoleon Sarony's portrait studio at 37 Union Square. Although only one among many photographers in the district, Sarony's reputation surpassed them all. Napoleonic in height and in imperiousness as well as in name, Sarony cut a dandy's figure. Capitalizing on the public's desire to purchase fine *cartes de visite* or larger cabinet photos of their favorite stars, Sarony offered munificent sums to the most attractive players (he once paid $5,000 to Lilly Langtry for rights to her likeness). Crowds could often be found milling outside his gallery windows when a new exhibit of his work was displayed. Of course, players also wanted portraits of themselves to promote their careers. They knew that Sarony would spare no effort to photograph them to their best advantage, posing them against striking backdrops and novel props.[46]

Theatrical printers and music publishing houses (before "Tin Pan Alley" earned its name up on Twenty-eighth Street) were established on Union Square. Samuel French had for decades been a leading publisher of play scripts, and his dominance in the market only increased, thanks in part to the company's interest in supporting the vast amateur theatricals market with many how-to books for the avocational thespian. Agosto Brentano, a Sicilian immigrant newspaper vendor, opened his famous bookstore at 33 Union Square in 1876, a cultural institution that became a favorite haunt of actors. A conjunction of theatre and journalism also met on the square. Various theatrical publications were produced here, including the *Dramatic News, Leslie's Sporting and Dramatic Times,* and, most significantly, the *New York Mirror* (later *Dramatic Mirror*). The *Mirror* began publication in 1879 under the editorship of Harrison Grey Fiske, a self-proclaimed champion and reformer of the theatre. He promoted a retirement home for indigent actors, improved dressing rooms, and an international copyright law to combat play piracy, and he exposed the abuses of the Theatrical Syndicate in the 1890s. It became the nearest thing to a recognized trade paper of theatre in the pre-*Variety* age, announcing players' whereabouts and availability, offering bits of professional gossip, and surveying the national theatrical scene.[47]

Another set of rialto businessmen foretold the revolutionary changes in the business of the stage: theatrical agents. Before the 1870s theatre agents played a relatively minor part in the theatrical economy, serving mainly to help bring together actors and managers. In this early phase, actors and agents mingled on the benches around Union Square (the "slave market"), and employment agreements could be sealed with a handshake. But the rapid expansion of theatre as a business, along with the advent of the combination system, called for a more sophisticated network of middlemen. With many hundreds of independent theatres nationwide looking for plays to book and several hundred touring companies seeking routes, a more systematic approach was needed. It happened in two stages. First, agents began negotiating the tours of many stars, thus controlling the heart of the dramatic enterprise. Then, in the 1880s, agents began putting together complete seasons of entertainment for theatres. These "booking agents" found themselves with unprecedented power in bringing together actors and management, which in the mid-1890s would culminate in the formation of a "theatrical trust."[48]

True to his barnstorming heritage, Joe Jefferson resisted surrendering control over his tours. He preferred negotiating personally with individual theatre managers, which meant he devoted considerable energy to epistolary business communications. Joe also bore an occasional cost in uncertainty about touring plans. "Mr. DeBar has engaged me but the date is not filed and it may be some time before I come west," Joe wrote Noah Ludlow. "If Mrs. Field has an offer do not delay its acceptance on my account as my movements are so uncertain." Jefferson was not always certain as to the country in which he would be performing the following season. The memory of his English triumphs constantly tugged at him, leading him to quick dissatisfaction with indifferent American audiences. "Buckstone has made me an offer for the Haymarket," Joe continued to Ludlow in 1868, "and if things don't improve commercially in this country I shall again visit Europe." He did not follow through on his threat on that occasion. But when he wrote to Edwin Booth in December 1874, agreeing to appear at Booth's Theatre the following fall (imploring Saturday night off for rest), he seemingly had no inkling that by the time fall arrived, he would have left for a two-year sojourn in Britain. Increasingly, Joe left business arrangements to eldest son Charley, a welcome relief no doubt from the strain of constant detail while maintaining control within the trusted circle of family.[49]

Charley benefited from the nearly no-lose approach to theatrical contracts his father had insisted upon. With his stature as a premier American star, Joe could well-nigh dictate terms. "Can't take any less," a Jefferson telegram bluntly stated to a negotiating manager. Instead of asking a percentage of a night's box office, Jefferson generally sought a guaranteed sum, leaving management to assume the risk. In Boston in 1869, Joe earned $15,000 for a month's effort. Seven weeks at Booth's Theatre brought $25,000. Usually this was lucrative for both parties. James McVicker realized more than $23,000 in the month Joe appeared in 1869, easily the largest gross receipts of any Chicago theatre that season. Obviously, managers agreed to terms because of their belief that Joe would lure patrons, even if it meant raising ticket prices to cover the costs of his salary. It did not always pay off. After Joe's $500 per night, overhead costs, and softer than expected audiences, impresarios in Denver and Salt Lake City came up short. Jefferson, in fact, suffered some public criticism for insisting on his usual fee despite economic hard times. But theatre managers understood that the public expected to see major stars at the local playhouse — and Joe had become one of the biggest.[50]

Some managers may have taken wry satisfaction in knowing that even Jefferson took his lumps from time to time. The lingering effects of the Panic of 1873 were compounded by the widespread violence and near anarchy of a railroad strike in the summer of 1877. Theatres suffered. Nonetheless, when Joe returned stateside from England that fall, he failed to understand the seriousness of the distress. He demanded $700 per night plus half the receipts over $1,800 to change his plans and move from the Fifth Avenue to Booth's Theatre (then operated by Augustin Daly). Throughout the summer Jefferson and Daly had corresponded about the sets for the new production of *Rip*. Joe, who understood that the play's appeal depended not on the set design but on its star, urged Daly "not to go to great expense in the production" (advice Daly ignored). More important to Joe was getting back on the boards as quickly as possible after coming home. "Twelve days to prepare . . . is more than enough," he judged. All signs pointed to a lucrative run: Jefferson's two-year absence, Daly's lavish production, and an enthusiastic opening-night reception of the play. But business bogged down. A projected two-month run shrank to five weeks. Joe determined to quit Gotham and take his beloved *Rip* on tour under Daly's able management. Audiences were even thinner in such midsize cities as Bridgeport, Elmira, Harrisburg, and Providence. In Troy Joe suffered the humiliation of having the sheriff impound his costume over a dispute with a disgruntled patron. After a single month of touring, Joe and Daly agreed to call it off. A year later, in early 1879, Jefferson fell into the middle of a nasty dispute between Stephen Fiske and D. H. Harkins, co-managers of the Fifth Avenue Theatre. The supporting company and orchestra did not get their pay and walked out, and an audience that had braved the chill of a January night was rewarded with a canceled performance. Joe had enough of his father in him to not let events get him down. He "was seemingly jolly over it" and headed off to his Louisiana retreat, Edwin Booth noted.[51]

These aggravations were still in the future when Joe returned to New York

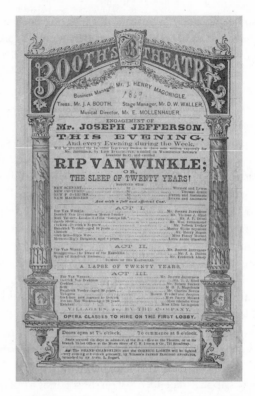

Joe at Booth's Theatre. Used by permission of the
Harry Ransom Humanities Research Center,
University of Texas at Austin.

in 1869 at the end of his extended midwestern tour to perform in Booth's new
theatre at the corner of Twenty-third Street and Sixth Avenue. Joe welcomed
the opportunity to work with a man with whom, though not biological family,
he had so many common bonds. Booth's self-imposed exile after his brother's
vile deed could not outweigh his need to perform, and he had returned to the
stage in 1866. The rest of his career was marked by a series of artistic triumphs
punctuated by personal tragedies — fires, family deaths, and bankruptcies —
that scarred his life. Theatres sprang up like weeds in New York during the
latter half of the nineteenth century, but Booth's held a special place as an
offering to the Shakespearean muse. Never before in American history had a
theatre been so completely the product of a single star's vision about the
possibilities of drama. As a place of amusement it was, testified Jefferson,
"quite perfect." Its lavish appointments and up-to-date design offer a convenient window into the evolving stagecraft of the day.[52]

Most notably, Booth's Theatre displayed the revolution in lighting. Gas remained the primary means of lighting for both stage and house lights until the 1880s, when electricity came into common use. Booth's house lights featured gas jets that were ignited by an electric spark, allowing them to be brought rapidly up and taken down similarly. The ability to easily darken the house (as could also be done in some other theatres) sharpened the contrast with the illuminated stage. Twenty-first-century theatergoers would find the monochromatic gas lighting a rather listless luminescence, but such things are relative. Audiences of the mid-nineteenth century considered gas lighting, especially supplemented by the newer limelight, to be a great boon to drama. The general gloom that had encompassed the traditional theatres lit by candles, whale oil floats, or even early gas footlights demanded a large, stylized — even pantomimed — acting technique. The flickering, undifferentiated light required stars to act downstage center where they could be decently seen. The new age of footlights abetted by battens of gas jets brought other corners of the stage out of twilight and allowed performers to usefully occupy more of the boards. Enhanced lighting was a precondition for the onset of nuanced, "realistic" acting.[53]

Gas was importantly supplemented by the advent of limelight in 1837 (though only widespread in the 1850s), which made feasible the spotlighting of individual actors or of stage locations. Most important, noted David Belasco, the greatest early proponent of improved stage lighting, spotlights solved the ancient problem of illuminating the actor's face. After centuries of exaggeration to convey his visual message, the actor "suddenly found that he no longer had to fight." Spotlights could also be used with filters to bathe a scene in various hues of color. Sunrises, sunsets, moonlight — these could now be approximated and scenes were written expressly to incorporate the effect. Costuming underwent its own revolution in the wake of better lighting. Reflective materials were desirable for their newly dazzling appearance. Real swords and shields replaced the tinseled pasteboard efforts of yesteryear; satins, silks, and brocades gained favor as they showed up with increased brilliance.[54]

Oddly, given his painterly appreciation of light, Jefferson says virtually nothing about the revolution in lighting and stagecraft he witnessed during his career. Comedy, in the theatrical tradition, was played on a brighter stage than tragedy; thus one might infer that the advances in lighting especially aided him. But of the hissing, sputtering limelights and their impact on theatre, Joe writes nothing in his *Autobiography* (nor apparently elsewhere). As with the combination system and most other developments in the theatre, Jefferson seemed content to go along and put the best face on whatever came.

There was absolute unanimity about another aspect of theatre design: the pressing need to reduce risk of fire. Ever since cannon wadding had ignited the Globe Theatre during a performance of *Henry VIII* in 1613, fire had proved the bane of theatres. Few anxieties about public space in the nineteenth century matched those associated with attending a crowded theatre. Stories of horrific theatre fires haunted the public imagination. An 1811 conflagration in Richmond cost more than a hundred lives and elicited extensive religious commentary. In 1820 both Washington's National and Philadelphia's Chestnut Street theatres were consumed. By one count, nearly 50 percent of theatres built worldwide were destroyed by fire within ten years of construction The number of fires did not slow as the century wore on; indeed, the worst theatre fire in American history did not occur until 1906, the Iroquois Theatre fire in Chicago that claimed some six hundred lives. The cost was measured in more than lives, as the disheartening experience of Charlotte Cushman testified. First in 1836 and then in 1841, Cushman lost her entire theatrical wardrobe in New York City fires. Fanny Davenport likewise saw her lavishly exotic wardrobe for *Cleopatra* incinerate (her famous "asp" was rescued) in the flames that reduced the elegant Fifth Avenue Theatre to ashes in 1891.[55]

These tragedies were not the consequence of sheer carelessness. Danger from fire was inherent in the dramatic enterprise. Paint rooms and carpentry shops backstage housed lumber, cordage, glues, oil-based paints, saturated rags, and other inflammables. The open flames of gas, of course, posed constant peril. Lights affixed high above and along the sides of the stage invited contact with scenery or draperies or even performers in gauzy costume flying above the stage in harness for special effects. Limelight required pressurized oxygen and hydrogen, and the heat generated from the crude chemical reaction was intense. Added to this were the discharge of weapons and pyrotechnics often demanded by melodramatic spectacles. As late as the 1860s, foreign visitors remarked on the carelessness of American theatres toward audience safety (part of a more general American cultural predisposition to accept risk as part of the natural order). Only with the terrible Conway Theatre fire in Brooklyn in 1876 did New York authorities become roused to action. Prodded by the *New York Mirror,* which made fire safety a centerpiece of its reforming efforts in the 1880s, state codes and municipal ordinances were rewritten, requiring that theatres add more exits and make the existing one wider. New York theatres were further constrained from having carpentry or paint shops on the premises, and on-site storage of scenery was limited. The revised fire codes helped spur the creation of a new industry of theatrical suppliers for these services. Anxiety about theatre fires even influenced drama, as nervous audiences lost their taste for realistic fire scenes.[56]

Joseph Jefferson's encounter with devastating fire occurred in one of his homes rather than in the theatre. Edwin Booth likewise was spared the con-flagration of his theatre, though not of his precious wardrobe and scenery, which went up with the Winter Garden fire of 1867. Yet the parallel careers of these two bosom friends finally chart contrast rather than resemblance. Both were great successes, of course—the two greatest stars of the last quarter of the nineteenth century. But they departed abruptly in their temperaments and in their business savvy. The tragedian Booth was hapless in his business rela-tionships. Conversely, the pose of naivete struck on stage by the Yankee Jeffer-son in fact masked a calculating mind. Whereas Booth would be reduced to touring late in life to recoup losses, Jefferson possessed the Midas touch in both his career and his investments.

The short history of Booth's Theatre makes the melancholy point. Booth's noble dreams of producing great plays with a first-class company supporting leading stars in newly minted productions proved untenable. Some stars, like Edwin Forrest, would not come; others, like John Owens and James W. Wal-lack, did not draw. Only the great English beauty Adelaide Neilson, who was in the midst of her first American tour, and Joseph Jefferson appear to have brought both artistic merit and financial return. Booth's Theatre, Jefferson once commented approvingly, was conducted "like a church behind the cur-tain and like a counting-house in front of it."[57]

Joe played Booth's stage during three separate seasons. The first, in 1869, was a seven-week stand starting in early August. Here Joe really hit his stride. With new scenery, costumes, and props—indeed, a whole new theatre—behind him, he was rewarded with capacity crowds, who were "made de-lighted," according to the *Tribune* writer, by his "humorous, quaint, tender and lovely presentation of *Rip Van Winkle*." In addition to his 1869 ap-pearance, there were the 1877 stand and a four-week run in 1873, when early box office receipts averaged $1,800 per night and in some cases topped $2,000. Not even the abrupt closing of Jay Cooke's financial institution on 18 September, setting off the Panic of 1873, could stem Joe's momentum. While other theatres struggled to turn a profit, *Rip Van Winkle,* already in the second half of its run, continued strong. "The attraction of Mr. Joseph Jefferson seems unabated . . . notwithstanding the panic," wrote the treasurer of Booth's Theatre. But the depression caught up with Booth's Theatre the next year, and creditors came knocking on the owner's door. Booth's financial woes had started before the panic, but the national recession forced him to declare bankruptcy, give up the theatre, and suffer the indignity of seeing his beloved theatre demolished in 1883, replaced by a department store. Booth's temple of art gave way to a temple of commerce.[58]

Edwin Booth's managerial career may have been fleeting, but his place in the

Edwin Booth. Courtesy of Michael A.
Morrison Collection.

pantheon of American acting was secure well before his death. He possessed
the "unmistakable fire, the electric spark, the god-like quality, which mankind
have agreed to worship," rhapsodized Adam Badeau (Ulysses S. Grant's me-
morialist and, admittedly, a person given to flights of rhetoric). Booth clearly
had a charisma that Jefferson lacked. In part this was a function of the fierier
medium of tragedy and its greater prestige than comedy. But it was also a
product of the public's morbid fascination with the Booth name.[59]

But if the Hamlet of a hundred nights occupied the upper rung on the theatrical ladder, Joe gave no hint of jealousy or resentment. Booth and Jefferson were
hardly rivals for public affection. There were audiences enough for both (the
one criterion that really mattered to Joe). Further, by any measure Joe himself
cut a figure of importance in American society. His renown opened doors to
him that even his ambitious mother Cornelia could have scarcely dreamed of.
In the last several decades of his life, Joe Jefferson became a celebrity.

A Fellow of Infinite Jest, of Most Excellent Fancy

By the late 1860s Joseph Jefferson's star was firmly planted in the theatrical firmament. When Olive Logan identified America's wealthiest actors in 1869, she named Joe along with Edwin Forrest and Edwin Booth. Twenty years later, a Boston paper claimed he was the richest actor in the world. He began collecting houses from Massachusetts to Louisiana, establishing his family in comfort that bordered on opulence.

With the increasing respectability of the acting profession, Joe's theatrical renown was readily translated into more general social prominence. He became the subject of features in magazines — *Appleton's, Harper's*, the *Nation, Lippincott's* (two), the *Atlantic* (two) — and in various literary and theatrical publications. *Kings of Fortune; or, The Triumphs and Achievements of Noble Self-Made Men*, an 1886 paean to American success, included Jefferson alongside capitalists like George Pullman, Charles Goodyear, Eli Whitney, and Marshall Field. In "Histories of Poor Boys Who Have Become Rich, and Other Famous People," a series of miniature biographies packed in cartons of Duke cigarettes, Joe found himself associated with such disparate figures as Buffalo Bill, Andrew Carnegie, William Gladstone, and Mark Twain as part of the new world of celebrity advertising. Jefferson "has a heart which is full to overflowing with all that is best and purest in human nature," the public was told, "and his power over the feelings of his audience is unequaled on the stage today." Joe's Rip assumed a tangible form as well. Sculptor John Rogers, the age's most popular producer of mass-produced Americana statuary, cast three scenes from the play: "Rip Van Winkle at Home," "Rip Van Winkle and the Gnome," and "Rip Van Winkle Returned." It was a rare American home that did not have a copy of Rip adorning a mantle.[1]

The vignettes and artistic renditions of Jefferson and his play were effusive in their praise, with only minor quibbling about his play's artistic merits and virtually none about the performance or the man. Jefferson, in short, had become an American institution.

The Privileges of Stardom

From age forty until his death thirty-six years later, Joe Jefferson was synonymous with Rip Van Winkle. Not that he was the only Rip on the boards. Before Joseph Jefferson, a fistful of actors (eight are known) had staged *Rip Van Winkle.* The most notable of the pre-Jefferson Rips, James Henry Hackett, continued the role occasionally into the 1860s. Hackett finally traded Rip for Falstaff, surrendering the old Dutchman to Jefferson with the comment, "I don't care to play against him." But a number of other players were ready to see if Joe's magic with the play might rub off on them. Chronicler of the New York stage George C. D. Odell identifies at least fifteen other Rips in the New York area alone during the 1860s through 1880s. McKee Rankin, for example, after scrutinizing Jefferson's production, made his own arrangement of the play in 1870 before going on to modest fame with the *The Danites,* a drama effectively exploiting the public's fascination with tales of Mormon secret police. James A. Herne, who later as playwright became a great early exemplar of naturalism, adapted *Rip* for an 1868 San Francisco production. His was notable for its spectacular special effects, including, as the *Alta California* notice enthused, "A SHOWER OF REAL RAIN." There were, too, various operatic versions of *Rip* gracing the late nineteenth-century stage. It is unsurprising that one of the most endearing tales of early American literature (and one which had shown such commercial appeal) should generate a host of interpreters. The stage, like subsequent film and television, emulated winning formulas.[2]

For the most part Joe allowed these theatrical knockoffs to proceed as they would. But an 1869 Chicago production of *Rip* crossed the line, in his eyes, trespassing on his version of Irving. Joe brought suit in a Chicago court in early 1870 against C. D. Hess's and U. H. Crosby's production. In court proceedings it came out that he had paid Boucicault $15,000 for his assistance in writing the play. The work, Joe insisted, had been crafted with him in mind and not for general production. To protect his propriety interest, Joe had both copyrighted and kept the play in manuscript, usually handing out to supporting players just their printed lines. Nonetheless, it was alleged that the Hess Company had "surreptitiously obtained" a script which was used for its production. Joe sought an injunction against the production and damages.[3]

For all of these pretenders, there really was only one Rip Van Winkle. Joe Jefferson caught the imagination of audiences in American and abroad as did no one else in the role. "It is not to be supposed," concluded the *New York Times* in its reception of Joe's 1873 fall season, "that the leading role could be intrusted to any artist but Mr. Jefferson." He owned the persona even more firmly than he held the rights to Boucicault's version.[4]

But did Rip own him? It is tempting to see Jefferson as an early example of role entrapment, a type of victimhood by success that continues to plague actors of both stage and screen. Other, less capable contemporaries of Jefferson found the chains of their starring vehicle even more tightly binding. Denman Thompson created Joshua Whitcomb in *The Old Homestead* to great success. But he had to replicate the homespun New Englander almost exclusively from 1887 until his death in 1911. Frank Mayo had a similar experience with his Davy Crockett (the most popular Crockett until Fess Parker). Of course, the most famous example of role entrapment was suffered by James O'Neill. A young tragedian of promise, he found in *The Count of Monte Cristo* both great reward and artistic repression (at least if we are to believe his playwright son).

O'Neill's regret at wasting a life's talent on a single albeit remunerative role bears only partial resemblance to Jefferson's sense of things. Joe never — at least publicly — rued casting his lot with Rip. To the contrary, he always took pride in the role and enjoyed talking about it. Privately, though, Jefferson did weary of the interminable nights of *Rip*. By the early 1880s he estimated that he had played the old Dutchman some 4,500 times. There were occasions beginning as early as the 1870s when illness or ennui made him restive for new challenges. An 1883 article in the *Atlantic*, "A Good-By to Rip Van Winkle," was premised on the assumption that the play had nearly run its course. But rumors of Rip's death were greatly exaggerated. He neither died nor long slumbered away from the boards. He was simply too lucrative. The acclaim was too great. And further, Joe could proceed without the sort of second-guessing that tormented O'Neill. Jefferson had in fact proven himself a comedian of great versatility and appeal before Rip stumbled along. He had a firm sense of his own accomplishment. The impecunious Dutchman bestowed great wealth on Joe, to be sure, but his role only marginally added to Jefferson's reputation among his peers as a first-rate comedian. Joe frequently set

Rip down for a few weeks or even a season to take on several other roles in which he was also acclaimed by the public. In short, if *Rip Van Winkle* was at times wearisome, it never held Joe hostage.[5]

Nor did his well-honed work ethic impede regular breaks from the stage. As a star who set his own pace, Joe allowed himself rests from his tours. When he moved through the South, he frequently took time at his Louisiana plantation. An avid fisherman, he made occasion for visits to lakes and streams around the country. Debilitating echoes of his youthful bout with TB also demanded at times a moderated pace. By the late 1870s he enjoyed the luxury of playing two seasons a year: a longer September to January season, and a shorter run of perhaps two months in the spring. He could accept "only the plums," as the *Mirror* reported. Joe had earned the right to proceed on his own terms.[6]

The truncated seasons of touring allowed for a richer family life. Unlike Margaret, wife Sarah never performed. She had no career to surrender. If Sarah could not share with Joe the special knowledge available only to the initiates of Melpomene, at least her family's theatrical background schooled her in the peculiar demands of a trouper's life. And where Margaret knew only the unceasing demands of a husband's career in its frantic, formative stage, Sarah reaped the dividends of success. In the first year and a half of marriage she traveled with Joe on his tours, while his younger children remained with their grandfather Lockyer. A doting wife freed from the encumbrances of child care must have been a great pleasure to Joe.

But only a year and a half after their marriage the first child came. On 6 July 1869 a son, Joseph Warren Jefferson, was born. At age forty Joe started another family, one that would see three more sons added: Henry (born in 1874 and died within a year); William Winter (born 1876); and Frank (born in 1885). Three surviving sons (Sarah never got the daughter she desired) joining the two living sons and two daughters from the first marriage added up to a family both large in number and extensive in span. (Joe fathered offspring over a thirty-four-year period). No actor or actress of his age could match Jefferson for his combination of acclaim, wealth, and progeny.[7]

True to Rip Van Winkle's persona, Joe loved nothing better than having his children about him in playful anarchy. Now that the absentee father had returned (at least between tours), there was much lost time to be made up. No doubt the children of the second marriage knew their father more intimately than his first four ever did. But if the children of Joe's first family were largely deprived of him (Charley excepted) during their childhood, they found some compensation in later gifts and sumptuous living. Young Margaret (Tiddie, her affectionate nickname), for example, received an expensive pony when she was fifteen. All the children, further, partook of the special magic of growing up in a theatrical household. None were carried on stage as a baby in the manner of their father, but even at one step removed their father's work of enchantment must have impressed mightily. Theatre was no longer the cradle-to-grave family affair it had been thirty years earlier (a few vestigial family troupes on the sawdust trail of small-town America excepted). Yet Joe sought to maintain some residuum of the great Jefferson family tradition by occasion-ally letting his children take the stage in *Rip*. Moreover, several of his sons would seriously pursue a stage career, and Charley, who quickly learned the limits of his acting talent, become a producer of prominence. Interestingly, neither daughter sought an acting career. It remained risky for a young lady of social pretensions to become an actress. Perhaps Joe's social ambitions for his daughters trumped his pride of profession. Nonetheless, he later encouraged his granddaughters in their stage ambitions (though that may be a case of a grandparent's indulging behavior found unacceptable in his own children).

Despite the death of the family's first mother and the father's frequent ab-sences, by the standards of mid-Victorian America the Jefferson children ap-pear to have had a fulfilling and secure childhood. To be a child of a celebrity in the nineteenth century carried privilege and opportunity without the ac-companying menace and fishbowl existence known to those of the next cen-tury. The Jefferson household was lively, filled with family and visitors, and presided over by a father who could indulge and even foster the merriment of children. The houses he supplied his family from Massachusetts to New Jersey to Louisiana were essentially great, sprawling playhouses.

When his former father-in-law (Margaret's father, who had done so much of the rearing of his first family) sold the inn that he operated near Jefferson's Poconos summer home in Pennsylvania in 1868, Joe understood that it was time to find another residence. Doubtless, a different house, one free from the many associations with his first wife and the Lockyer family, suited Sarah better. For that summer's holiday (a "fishing ramble" as he termed it), Joe rented a cabin in the Poconos, and the next year he became a substantial homeowner, buying not one but two estates within a year.[8]

The first was at Hohokus ("Hokuspokus," Joe would style it in bantering moments) in the Saddlebrook River region of northern New Jersey. Although barely twenty miles removed from Broadway, the region then had a rural ambience that Jefferson found appealing. Its colonial Dutch heritage carried additional appropriateness for the interpreter of Rip Van Winkle. The house, perched on a hill overlooking farm country, was a large rambling structure — half timbered, half stone, with the gambrel roof typical of the area — con-structed years earlier on the fancy of an architect for his own residence. It had the cloistered feel so popular then: low hanging branches brooded over the structure, casting shadows around the windows; tangles of vines and rose bushes climbed the walls and porches. The interior was just as oppressively busy. It was replete with (as a contemporary phrased it) "curiously-carved teak-wood furniture from India, upholstered in rare silk and gold stuffs; embroideries from Turkey, China, and Japan; Oriental rugs; skins of tigers and lions from Indian jungles, and of bears and wolves from the Rocky Mountains; pottery from all lands; bronzes from Italy and France; old cabinets of carved oak and inlaid chairs and tables from Holland and France." Above all, there were pictures. Every room housed prints, oils, engravings, or watercolors. Jefferson was well on his way to amassing a formidable art collection. His need for a small gallery led to plans for an addition, though the Hohokus residence was already a large house (some writers characterized it as a mansion). Helped by an army of laborers and craftsmen that he retained, Jefferson enlarged it even more over the years, placing his stamp firmly upon the home where most of his children grew up (his and Sarah's first child, Joseph, Jr., was born just before the purchase), where two of them wed, and where Joe would spend more time than at any other house in his life. He even became uncharacteristically involved in local affairs, helping to found a private school for his children to attend. Ultimately, several of his sons' families would occupy cabins on the extensive property. Joe's estate became a family village.[9]

The measure of Jefferson's affection for home and family was seen in the efforts he took to commute home when he played Broadway. After an evening performance he would often catch the Twenty-third Street ferry across the Hudson to the Erie Railroad, which took him to within a mile of his house. The 2:00 A. M. arrival seemed not to daunt him. Joe's domestic inclinations caused him to demand an unusual contract stipulation from Augustin Daly when the latter ran Booth's Theatre. Instead of a Saturday night performance, Joe gave only a matinee, freeing up the balance of his weekend but forcing Daly into mounting another (less appealing) drama for the prime Saturday night hour. Few actors of the age could make such a demand. That Joe could inconvenience a powerful theatrical manager this way gives further testimony to his own star power.[10]

The second of Jefferson's new homes was in an unlikely location, the heart of Louisiana's prairie Cajun country, 125 miles west of New Orleans near New Iberia. Orange Island, as it was called (though an island only at unusually high water), was initially more of a winter home. To reach the estate from New Orleans required a trip on a bantam stern wheeler up Bayou Atchafalaya to historic Bayou Têche. The Southern Pacific Railroad would later come within two miles of the estate to the "Bob Acres" station, making the journey easier. The area carried fanciful associations with pirate Jean Lafitte and Longfel-

Orange Island estate. Courtesy of the Joseph Jefferson, Family, and Related Views graphic collection, ca. 1880–1900, in the Archives of American Art, Smithsonian Institution.

low's Evangeline (the Lafitte connection appealed to Joe's romantic streak; he loved to tell visitors about it). Joe had visited the antebellum plantation during a visit to New Orleans some twenty years earlier, enjoying as did another visitor "the lavish hospitality with servants at every hand." The estate was aptly named for its sizable orange grove, but as happened with many such elegances in the South, the Civil War brought decay. The existing house was in ruins, and Joe, with the help of an architect, rebuilt.[11]

Joe sited his ample residence on the crest of a seventy-five-foot hill commanding a fine view. A series of osage, Cherokee rose, and wild guava hedgerows, the first one two miles distant from the house, fenced in a huge lawn. Magnolias and live oaks festooned with Spanish moss lent traditional charm to the setting. Amidst the romantic setting Joe erected an octagonal house, essentially one story, but with a veranda attached and a large square cupola capping it off, the considerable structure looked even larger. "Steamboat gothic," as the style was whimsically known, bespoke the era's penchant for eclectic mixing of designs. There was nothing understated about the home, its dramatic setting and architecture (especially its oddly configured interior) appropriate to a man of the theatre. But Joe also had a business head, and he worked hard to ensure that this retreat turned a profit. His original purchase of twelve hundred acres expanded to nine thousand over the years. The original orange groves remained but were not the heart of the plantation economy.

Rather, his two thousand head of thoroughbred cattle became his pride — and a solid investment, netting as much as $10,000 a year. Oats, sugarcane, pecans, and rice were also raised over several thousand acres. Jefferson's good fortune extended to the management of his estate. Several years earlier, massive salt domes in the area had attracted outside investors, and in 1895 Joe discovered that his property likewise sat atop a salt dome. He sunk a shaft and initiated yet another lucrative operation.[12]

At Orange Island Joe found by turn seclusion and fraternization. It was here that he began to devote himself seriously to painting. The cupola room, with its generous allowance of natural light, housed his atelier, and the luxuriant environment of the bayou provided endless subjects for his canvases. The enforced sociability of theatrical life found welcome relief in the solitary pursuit of art. But Jefferson was by nature a gregarious man, and he welcomed frequent interruptions of children, grandchildren, and the stream of visitors, many of them stage colleagues, who made their way there. Getting there was an adventure in itself during the best of weather, and the rainy season turned the roads into pure gumbo, making the house virtually unreachable. Edwin Booth had wanted to swing by Joe's home during a southern tour, but Joe dissuaded his good friend, frankly admitting the impossibility of the endeavor. Many acquaintances did come and stayed to partake of Jefferson's storied hospitality, good conversation — and if they were of a mind to — fishing in Lake Peigneur or hunting in his three-thousand-acre hunting preserve in the cyprus jungle on the eastern edge of the estate.[13]

Both houses (but particularly Orange Island) became the object of journalistic comment. Although Jefferson lived too early to partake of cinematic immortality, his career bestrode the rise of mass market journalism and its voracious need for celebrity images. The lifestyles of the renowned were a staple of such journalism. The American public coveted a glimpse of private life, and it became part of the implicit contract between star and public that periodic access would be granted. Beginning with James Runnion's 1869 feature in *Lippincott's* and lasting beyond his death in 1905, Jefferson enjoyed his share of such coverage. Invariably, Joe was pictured at repose before his easel, sitting upon his verandah surrounded by family and friends, or with fishing pole in hand. With very few exceptions, newspaper or magazine journalists presented to the public a man simple in his tastes, humble in his wisdom, and unwaveringly faithful to family and friends. This was true of most celebrity journalism of the age (being of a milder disposition than that known later), but it was particularly so of Jefferson, in whom the American public had invested so much emotional belief in the essential goodness of Irving's Rip. Such images, in fact, captured the essential Jefferson. His Louisiana retreat betrayed nothing that spoke of his stage career; some local residents knew nothing of his stage life. An Episcopalian dignitary visiting Jefferson in 1879 confided to his diary that Joe "had nothing of the stage about either his manner or conversation." If a hint of condescension colored the bishop's comment, it nonetheless reflected the respect that Joe's warmth won among those invited into his home.[14]

Joe Jefferson's professional acclaim and personal probity garnered him a social respect unknown to the rank and file of his colleagues. Actors in the mid-nineteenth century continued to labor under the social suspicion that had dogged them for centuries. They typically shared the odd privilege, as David Garrick phrased it a century earlier, of being "petted and pelted." Moments of adulation were interspersed with suspicion, downright hostility, or — perhaps worse for performers — neglect. Their Elizabethan vagabond heritage was hardly improved by the quickened pace of travel brought by railroads and combination companies. A settled home life was more difficult than ever. And actors, with few exceptions, found themselves still excluded from the homes and clubs of the rich and demonized by the majority of American clergy. Although the actor's social status would markedly improve in the last two decades of his life, Jefferson had witnessed an earlier humiliation that burned itself into the collective consciousness of the acting profession: the infamous refusal of a New York minister to conduct the burial of George Holland.[15]

Church and Stage

In life, George Holland (1790–1870) held a respected, though modest, place in theatrical annals. His kind manner and harmless practical jokes endeared him to the profession. Joe came to know Holland when the latter was past his prime and Joe was just coming into his own. Holland's graciousness when Jefferson supplanted him as the stock company's lead comedian earned him Joe's respect. In return, Holland named Joe godfather to his son Joseph Jefferson Holland. Thus, when Holland died in late December 1870, Jefferson willingly accepted the request of his family to arrange services. Along with Holland's twenty-two-year-old son Edward Milton Holland (who would become a distinguished actor in his own right), Joe visited a nearby New York church to discuss funeral plans with Dr. Lorenzo Sabine, an Episcopal minister. All went well until Joe mentioned Holland's profession. Jefferson's hesitant remark that Holland's profession would probably make no difference to the reverend opened the door to the minister's demurrer. Joe's inquiry also suggests a latent fear — almost an expectation — among players that sanctuaries might not welcome them. The clergyman declined to hold the service and suggested that "there was a little church around the corner" that might consent. This turned out to be the Church of the Transfiguration, an Episcopal chapel on Twenty-ninth Street. The Reverend George H. Houghton proved accepting of an actor's funeral, and Holland was properly laid to rest.[16]

The incident quickly agitated the acting profession. When Jefferson told William Winter what had happened, the critic spread the word among the acting community and to the broader public through indignant newspaper comments across the country. Mark Twain saw the affair as yet another example of clerical hypocrisy and penned a scathing piece for the *Galaxy*, colorfully vilifying Sabine as "a crawling, slimy, sanctimonious, self-righteous reptile." The clergyman's slight and Jefferson's response ("God bless the 'little church around the corner.'") instantly became a part of theatrical folklore. By early February, a ballad, "The Little Church Around the Corner," was being heard on variety stages, transforming the insult into bathetic legend. Winter organized one of the most lavish testimonial benefit performances ever in the history of New York theatre. (Holland had died impoverished and left a young family.) On the afternoon and evening of 19 January, eleven theatres hosted a potpourri of entertainments. More benefit performances followed in the next few days and then later in various cities across the country.[17]

In a sense the acting profession now had a martyr. George Holland became a marker for all the exclusion players had experienced for centuries, proof incarnate of the unthinking prejudice aimed at them by the religious establishment. Perhaps at no moment of the nineteenth century did actors gain so immediate a public sympathy. Whereas just five years earlier actors had been excoriated after one of their own had murdered a beloved president, they now earned public sympathy. The *New York Times* encouraged "all who cannot go to buy tickets and present them to others." Public support, the article continued, would "give weight to the moral rebuke" that the occasion intends for "the bigotry that insulted the good old man's remains." Jefferson too garnered praise for his noble response to the sorry affair. Endeared "to the heart of every liberal-minded man and woman" (as a Baltimore theatre critic phrased it), Joe deserved a generous patronage for his production of *Rip*. As for the Church of the Transfiguration — the "little church" — it became an instant shrine in the theatrical landscape, "the church of the profession" as the *Dramatic Mirror* phrased it. Christmas and New Year's found its pews filled with players, and to the present it remains a favorite for actor weddings. After the 1920s, when it was installed, visitors to the church could view a stained-glass window portraying Rip Van Winkle as the Good Samaritan who presents a shrouded George Holland to Christ.[18]

Joe would have found wry irony in such enshrinement. He was not a "churched" individual. He was neither brought up as a churchgoer nor did he inculcate organized religion in his children. Indeed, he maintained a safe distance from the religious establishment. He shared his profession's common distrust of orthodox religion, a suspicion rooted in the latter's traditional antipathy toward stage entertainments.

Social and religious antagonism toward dramatic performance has a long and philosophically distinguished pedigree. Plato banished drama from his imagined republic because of its debased mimesis of reality. Two millennia later, Rousseau considered theatre the embodiment of the overcivilized decadence plaguing French society. But religious arguments would be even more influential. The early church, dismayed by the staged spectacles of the Roman Empire, withheld the sacraments from actors who refused to renounce their calling. Church fathers such as Tertullian articulated a theological underpinning to their antitheatrical posture. Acting was a form of forbidden pretense. Actors, moreover, who impersonated villainous characters were necessarily debased by the experience. Dramatic portrayals were artifices literally inspired by Satan. Puritanism's rise in late sixteenth-century England was accompanied by new levels of church hostility toward theatre, in part certainly because of the Elizabethan stage's popularity. During the English Civil War Puritan leaders would for a time shutter the devil's playhouse.[19]

Similar attitudes informed colonial and antebellum America. John Witherspoon, president of Princeton College, penned an influential treatise in the mid-eighteenth century, *A Serious Inquiry into the Nature and Effects of the Stage,* which recounted the usual litany of Protestant objections. Tragedies such as the horrific Richmond Theatre fire of 1811 occasioned renewed outbursts of moralism (and republication of Witherspoon's sermon). And local pockets of resistance to theatre persisted across America throughout the nineteenth century. Jefferson's recital of the influence of the clerical lobby in Springfield, Illinois, was not a unique circumstance. Such incidences supported Tocqueville's observation of the early 1830s that the American "population still has great reserves about indulging in amusements of this sort."[20]

Evangelical misgivings about the stage persisted during the post–Civil War decades. The Methodist denomination enacted an "amusement ban" in its church discipline in 1877, formally proscribing theatre attendance (removed only in 1920). "The monster of iniquity, the average American theatre," concluded Thomas De Witt Talmage, whose pulpit histrionics attracted mass congregations to his Brooklyn tabernacle. The *New York Mirror* kept a running account of perceived outrages against actors by the clerics. It told, for example, how a member of John McCullough's company was requested to absent herself from a dining table in a Hartford hotel because of a minister's discomfort with her presence.[21]

Yet times were changing. Henry Ward Beecher, eminent divine and bellwether figure of midcentury American religion, suddenly announced his change of heart regarding theatergoing in 1883. Parishioners should consult their own conscience regarding the stage, Beecher suggested, advice that spurred the *Mirror* to encourage actors to attend his Brooklyn congregation. A more liberal clergy, especially in the Unitarian and Episcopal denominations, sought not to suppress drama but to urge upon it a higher task of cultural uplift. The stage "is not merely to be tolerated," claimed Reverend G. W. Shinn, who in 1899 helped organize the Actors Church Alliance, "it has a right to exist because it has a mission that is helpful to society." Such sentiments reflected a quiet, though profound, alteration in the relationship of church and stage. As commercial amusements became legitimized as a necessary component of urban life, actors no longer had to meekly accept clerical aspersions. Conversely, religious spokesmen who counseled tolerance toward drama may have only been bowing to the inevitable. Their pleas that the stage elevate its moral tone represented something of a rearguard effort against an onrushing rival for the public's affection, one that appeared to be outstripping the church's influence.[22]

Joe Jefferson, though chary of traditional ecclesiology — indeed, contemptuous of sectarian creeds — was hardly a skeptic of the supernatural. Described by his daughter-in-law Eugenie Paul as a "seeker after Truth," Joe's spiritual quest wound through the respectably offbeat fields of alternative Victorian religiosity. He was attracted to the teachings of Emanual Swedenborg, the eighteenth-century Swedish naturalist turned mystic, whose persuasive accounts of his communications with the spirit world laid the philosophical and theological basis for modern spiritualism. One can scarcely exaggerate the enthusiasm that Swedenborg, mesmerism, and spiritualism inspired in the American cognoscenti of the 1850s. Henry Wadsworth Longfellow, Thomas Wentworth Higginson, Cornelius Vanderbilt, Harriet Beecher Stowe, and Horace Greeley were among the many litterateurs, businessmen, and politicians who frequented séances. Even complete skeptics, such as Nathaniel Hawthorne, were taken enough by the phenomenon to make it a repeated subject of fiction. The lively debates over the genuineness of the Fox sisters' mysterious rappings in their Hydesville, New York, home paralleled the popular interest P. T. Barnum stirred with his hoaxes and humbugs.[23]

Actors, as masters of make-believe and dissimulation, were predictably attracted to spiritualism's high drama. Joe had no commitment to orthodox Christianity that might inhibit his heterodox leanings; to the contrary, his belief system appears to have been something of a hodgepodge of Swedenborgianism, Theosophy, telepathy, Spiritualism, and later, Christian Science. Was it sheer coincidence or was their a connection between Joe's incipient mysticism and his indulging the eerie phantoms of Hudson's crew in *Rip Van*

Winkle? He made no secret of his interest in the supernatural, and various of his peers enjoyed telling Jefferson stories on the subject. Joe's lack of theological sophistication was compounded by a certain self-admitted credulity not lost on his friends. "Tell it to Jefferson; he'll believe anything," Grover Cleveland once told a friend. Why not entertain the possibility of communicating with the spirit world or even other planets, Joe insisted. Who would have thought a century earlier that New York and Chicago could communicate by telephone? Joe's forays into spiritualism were not solitary; he sometimes invited close friends, such as Winter or Booth, to accompany him to séances, and they discussed the subject in their correspondence.[24]

Jefferson came to the spirit world in early adulthood. He readily accepted the genuineness of the Fox sisters' claims in 1848. As a young man, he and brother Charlie attended a séance where, much to the latter's discomfit, his deceased wife was putatively summoned. Of course, Joe himself would experience the loss of a wife (as well as several children), and his forays into the psychic world were rooted in his grief. A procession of mediums passed through his Paradise Valley home in the late 1850s (housed in terrified daughter Tiddie's bedroom), attempting to help Joe contact his departed Margaret. Joe posed for "spirit photographers," who provided glass images displaying ghostly apparitions standing behind his chair. One medium publicly boasted that Jefferson played Rip under ghostly influence. During trips to Chicago, Joe was invariably invited by friend and Chicago theatre owner J. H. McVicker to enjoy a séance at his mansion. When in the mood, Jefferson would discourse on the subject of spiritualism for an entire evening. Alas, Joe was finally disappointed by the promises of the occult, concluding, as did many others, that the field was rife with charlatans. But Jefferson never abandoned his more general convictions about the reality of man's immortal soul or the role of providence in man's affairs. That he had traveled hundreds of thousands of miles in his career without railway or steamship accident he attributed to a divine protection. One of Jefferson's surviving poems is a clever bit of doggerel pitting two caterpillars in religious debate, quietly resolved when both are transformed into butterflies, "A sign of immortality."[25]

Mortality made itself all too evident in 1872 when Joe had a brush with blindness. The relatively sudden onset of glaucoma must have been unnerving. His left eye was afflicted with a "mist," followed by the intense pain common to the inflammation and intraocular pressure. The seasoned trouper, often slowed but rarely stopped by illness, was forced to end his spring tour prematurely in Philadelphia. Newspapers broadcast the tidings of a stricken Rip Van Winkle, their stories accompanied by encomiums of a Jefferson who might never act again. The great actor had done more than anyone, a columnist in one paper wrote, to restore the stage to its place "as one of the most powerful and elevating influences of civilization." Joe's predicament was serious enough for him to take the unusual step of issuing a public statement regarding the "cheerless intelligence" two doctors gave him: "nothing can save my sight unless I at once give up my profession and submit to an operation."[26]

But even at this bleak moment, the star that seemed to watch over Jefferson shone forth. Joe's career was saved by recent revolutions in the diagnosis and treatment of glaucoma. The ophthalmoscope, devised only in the previous decade, allowed a precise examination of his eye. And a relatively new surgical treatment, an iridectomy, had proven successful in curing the disease. Jefferson's wealth gave him access to the best medical care. George Reuling, a German occulist, performed the surgery at Joe's Hohokus residence. Eyes bandaged and consigned to utter darkness, Joe nonetheless (according to his wife) met the trial with his typical good-natured stoicism. After several weeks of convalescence Joe pronounced himself cured, able to dispense with glasses, and ready to return to the sawdust trail. The return was premature. Just after Joe began a New England swing, the affliction returned and by mid-September he had to cancel the remainder of the fall season. Joe received further treatment, and in January he kicked off a long winter-spring tour that lasted into June.[27]

Still only forty-three, Jefferson resumed his career unimpeded by further threat to vision. Joe, who suffered from a chronic lung affliction and would later endure increasing hearing loss, nonetheless reflected late in life that he was "blest with health." Such serenity reflected the famous Jefferson equanimity, but it also bespoke Joe's realistic understanding that compared to the chronic illnesses that devastated the lives of so many of his nineteenth-century countrymen, he had indeed escaped the worst.[28]

The eyesight incident did change his life in one permanent way: it caused him to swear off hard liquor. Not to the general public, to be sure, but privately Joe attributed the onset of glaucoma to his indulgence in whiskey. Like many actors of the age, Joe had found it enticing, particularly when tired, to invigorate himself before a performance with a shot of whiskey in order to help him "carry the audience." But the one glass, as he put it, was "after a time made two, and even three or four." Such stimulants contributed to his distress, Joe's physician suggested, a diagnosis Jefferson took to heart. This private morality tale (if it can be called such) had an ironic appropriateness to it, since Jefferson faced repeated calls from his loyal teetotaling public to convince Rip to repudiate alcohol. Joe resisted all such carping in the name of art. But if Rip Van Winkle unapologetically raised the tumbler of spirits after his ordeal, a chastened Joe Jefferson would limit himself to an occasional glass of claret.[29]

Travels East and West

Jefferson's career proceeded apace, slowed only slightly by his glaucoma and the recession of the mid-1870s. In a sense things had become too easy, too predictable. The money was too good to stop, but he wanted a new venue. Thus in summer 1875 he made good on his repeated threats to decamp for England. Edwin Booth had scoffed at his earlier desires to head to Britain. "What a silly fellow!" Booth vented to mutual friend William Winter. "Great fortune awaits him here—While the sun is shining, but he obstinately prefers European puffery, and throws away what in a few years he may long in vain for." But Jefferson was not to be dissuaded. His repertoire would be no different, but the audiences would. Although the endorsement of English audiences no longer carried the validating power for American actors that it had a decade or two earlier, the cachet of London theatre remained. Joe could hardly resist the opportunity to return in the manifest glory of his American celebrity. His two-year stay in Great Britain repaid dividends both professionally and personally. It perhaps marked the pinnacle of his career. Likewise, his reception in English society and the luxury in which his family lived must have been immensely gratifying to Joe. The boy whose itinerant childhood was characterized by uncertainty had became the man at the height of his profession, capable of providing his extended household with all the comforts then known.[30]

Joe left New York for England at the end of June 1875, accompanied by Sarah, five children—Margaret, Tom, Josie, Joe, Jr., and baby Henry, a collection ranging in age from twenty-two to under a year—and a nanny. (Eldest son Charley stayed at Orange Island with his new wife.) The entourage made a quick stop in London so Joe could arrange for his November stage opening, then proceeded to Paris for an extended late summer's vacation. In his *Autobiography,* Joe goes into considerable detail about his family's eight-to-ten-week Paris sojourn, lapsing again into a bland mix of anecdote and travelogue. One goal, certainly, of the holiday was to gild his children with an overlay of "culture." A French teacher was retained, and Joe joined his family in intensive—but for him ultimately futile—language study.[31]

By midfall the Jeffersons recrossed the channel and took up residence near Hyde Park. Joe was set to open at the Princess's Theatre on 1 November. Located on Oxford Street, the theatre with its elegant trappings reflected the supreme confidence of an imperial England then in full flower. Befitting an important debut, "new and characteristic scenery" had been prepared. The expenses born by manager F. B. Chatterton proved a sound investment. The return of *Rip Van Winkle* to the London stage in 1875 was an unqualified triumph, surpassing in both longevity and critical attention Joe's 1865 success. Joe would be the cynosure of the London stage until the end of April 1876.

London critics made much of Jefferson's return. They recalled his initial stay with great appreciation. "Of all actors America has sent us," one writer insisted, "Mr. Jefferson is the most widely remembered." A host of newspapers and journals devoted extended columns to his performance, coverage that sometimes approached reverential. *"Rip Van Winkle* is one of the most remarkable exhibitions of the modern stage," printed the *Times*. To try to distill the "superb conception of character, executed with consummate art," said another, is simply "beyond criticism." There was a sense among some that Jefferson's art had gained a delicacy during his absence. "He has an easy way of seeking for his words," a reviewer for *the Academy* decided, "a half-absorbed repetition of part of a phrase, as in our everyday unchosen speech. He does not finish his sentences like an actor." The supporting cast came in for criticism, but in part it bespoke that inescapable fact that "Jefferson's art necessarily dwarfs his fellow players."[32]

Clement Scott, the eminent British critic, added his sanction to Jefferson's art. Editor of the *Theatre*, England's dramatic magazine of record in the last decades of the nineteenth century, Scott used his bully pulpit to attack the dramatic innovations of Ibsen. Conversely, with a sensibility attuned to the sentimentalism Jefferson embodied, Scott could scarcely contain his enthusiasm. Jefferson's was the "rare art which conceals art." He possessed, wrote Scott, a grasp of the value of repose in the midst of the bustle of wife, children, and villainy about him. "Nothing is hurried, nothing is flurried; every look and each hesitation has its proper value." Joe, long an audience favorite, was now securing a loftier critical perch as a paragon of the actor's art.[33]

As with his previous London engagement, news of his triumph crossed the Atlantic (aided by the Atlantic cable, in place now for nearly a decade) and passed about the theatrical community. "Joe J. has grasped the Lion firmly by the jaw with ungloved hand," an admiring Edwin Booth wrote a friend, "& I hope he will shake lots of 'shekels' from old Bull's money bags."[34]

But the sweetness of the moment quickly turned bitter. Little "Harry," born to Sarah barely a year earlier in Chicago, had contracted a brief and fatal illness. He died on 5 November. With a trouper's allegiance to the show business adage, Joe insisted on performing that night. "My little child, look in my face and don't know who I am," the aged Rip laments when reunited with his child, a line whose pathos was unfeigned when spoken that night. "The death of my little boy has thrown us all in to great sorrow," Jefferson wrote an acquaintance some days later. Typical for Jefferson, grief was accomplished in an intensely private manner. No word of the death appeared in newspapers. Instead, Joe looked to the "comforting philosophy" of his own mystical belief. "I have taught myself," he told Winter, "the hard lesson that it is for the best."[35]

The Jeffersons moved from their Hyde Park house, fearing its drainage problems may have contributed to Harry's death. The conditions of the move compounded a process of house hunting the thrifty Jefferson already hated. In his *Autobiography,* Joe complains at length about Paris and London landlords who charged exorbitant damage fees. The family ended up for a time in a residential hotel on Tavistock Square and then later in a house on fashionable elm-lined Belsize Avenue, a recently built suburban development in a historic estate near Hampstead.[36]

Domestic tragedy apart, Joe's career proceeded unimpeded. Fall turned to winter and still the "old Dutchman" continued to pack the Princess's. "Rip seems to have hit the Londoners in a soft place," Jefferson modestly wrote Winter. Even so, he continued, " the critics are clamoring for a new part." But Joe saw no need to change. The public had not yet tired of his signature piece. And it would not. Audiences were strong to the end. *Rip Van Winkle* endured until 29 April 1876, an uninterrupted run of 154 nights, exceeded only by Jefferson's first London appearance. Joe finally had to step down from the London stage because of obligations in the provincial theatres. The newspaper farewells were tender. "We are compelled to put up with the loss of the welcome voice, the merry laugh, and the genial smile of our old friend Rip."[37]

April witnessed not only the jubilant end to Joe's London engagement but the private consolation of a new child. Uncharacteristically, Joe was nearby for the birth. In the flush of theatrical success and in honor of his great friend and champion, Joe named the child William Winter Jefferson. Further, the christening took place at the shrine of English-language drama, the Stratford-on-Avon church where Shakespeare lay. Given the circumstances of his birth, it was not surprising the "Willie" would be a pampered child, the pride of his forty-seven-year-old father.[38]

Family changes were afoot elsewhere as well. When Joe arrived in England he revived a friendship from his days in New Zealand. Benjamin Farjeon, the young newspaperman in Dunedin who befriended Joe during his run there, had moved back to England to launch a career as novelist. Born into a working-class Jewish family, Farjeon, by dint of energy and literary wit, had risen in the world. By the mid-1870s he had published a string of Dickensian novels that enjoyed a measure of acclaim. Jefferson had written him before traveling to England, professing pride in the fact "that I knew and admired you long before you had made your great reputation." Their subsequent reunion a half-world removed from where they first met brought an unexpected development. Margaret, now at age twenty-two in the blossom of womanhood and enjoying the social whirl of London, met Farjeon, who had become a fixture at the Tavistock house. Writer and debutante struck a romance that led to marriage the next year. A middle-aged Jewish novelist with working-class roots might seem an unlikely romantic partner for Joseph Jefferson's privileged daughter, but Farjeon exuded a warmth and a joie de vivre useful for winning an impressionable girl's heart. Joe must have been delighted that his eldest daughter would choose a man who was apparently on his way to a literary success equal to Joe's stage achievement. For her part, Margaret, though not demonstrably talented with voice or pen, possessed an artistic bent that she indulged in the upbringing of her three children.[39]

In late May, Joe began his procession through the other major cities of the United Kingdom, starting in Manchester and then proceeding to Liverpool. Joe encountered not just enthusiastic audiences but critics whose sophisticated grasp of theatre's traditions surpassed most of those who commented on his work at home. "His humour had lost nothing of its freshness," judged the *Manchester Guardian,* and "his pathos had gained in depth without being impaired in its simplicity." A Liverpool critic proclaimed him "one of the few artistes of the day." (Joe probably shuddered at that affectation.) In the same vein, but more sensibly perhaps, another Liverpool writer concluded that Jefferson struck a balance too often lacking in both tragedians and comics. "We have never had before one who had so facile a command over the fountains both of smiles and tears." Humor and pathos blended in "beautiful confusion." The "elephantine" humor of less skilled players paled before Jefferson's comic legerdemain. "It bubbles up like water from a spring. It flows as readily as bad grammar from the mouth of a mob orator."[40]

In early fall Joe continued his provincial tour, first in Edinburgh, where as was often the case when Jefferson came to town, prices were raised, then a stand at the grittier, less scenic Glasgow. Two months previously, another production of *Rip* had hit the Glasgow stage, an obvious attempt to milk Joe's London hit before the real Rip came to town. The Glasgow critic had feared that Jefferson's much-trumpeted fame could only lead to disappointment when he was viewed in the flesh. He was glad to report that the audience "fully endorsed the high estimate of the numerous critics."[41]

In late October 1876 Joe, with his entire London cast in tow, crossed the Irish Sea to test Rip's magic on the Dubliners. By Joe's own telling, the play failed to rouse the patrons at the Gaiety Theatre. In the *Autobiography,* Joe recounts in great detail his meeting with the theatre manager, whose foreboding about the piece led him to suggest that Jefferson play Rip as an Irishman with "the shlight taste of the brogue." Joe would have none of it, but began himself to worry about the twelve-night run. Sure enough, as he later put it, the "attendance was light and the applause delicate." The Dublin papers were rather kinder in their evaluation, though the *Dublin Morning News* did allow that the "strange and exaggerated nature of the plot is rather calculated to repel than to enlist the sympathy of play-goers." His short stay in Belfast found a warmer response.[42]

Joe returned to London in November 1876 ready for a break from the stage. His British sojourn was about more than just acting and box office receipts. It provided opportunity to put his celebrity to work on a bigger social stage. Margaret's marriage to B. L. Farjeon in June 1877 was a type of validation of his artistic prominence (as had been the announcement of their engagement in the tony *London Court Journal* the previous February). And if Joe lost a daughter, his English household enlarged as sister Connie (now Mrs. Jackson) and her son crossed the ocean to join them. Moreover, an unfamiliar family member showed up at Jefferson's Belsize Avenue residence. The Reverend Joseph Jefferson along with his solicitous wife dropped by to meet their "American cousin." Joe, who had a similar experience with another distant cousin during his first English visit, was equally charmed with this new claimant. "His face was like my father's, and reminded me of my own," he said. The importance of family to Joe was displayed again as he readily accepted the credentials of apparently good-hearted individuals who sought an ancestral tie.[43]

In his *Autobiography*, Jefferson lavishes detail on his entree in English society. At a luncheon he tells of being seated next to Robert Browning; even better, he recounts receiving an invitation from Browning a few days later to join him at another luncheon. He likewise enjoyed his visit to London's theatrical club, the Garrick, adorned with portraits of England's storied thespians. But Jefferson unconsciously reveals some unresolved contradictions regarding his own prosperous acclaim. He takes London's artistic and literary community to task for its members' eagerness to build "costly residences, where they entertain their guests most sumptuously. They seemed blind to the fact that they must, now and forever, toil on that they may keep up this generous hospitality." Was Joe really so oblivious to his own obsessive labors to support his family in two landed estates? Jefferson too entertained guests "sumptuously," if in the more casual American style. The good life once tasted was hard to forego. "It is more difficult to retrench than they seem to realize," Joe lectured his readers, advice that at some level he must have understood very personally.[44]

The Jefferson family's extended excursion to the British Isles was going so well that as late as midspring 1877 Joe had fixed no firm time to return to America. He came back to the Royal Princess's stage on Easter for another eight weeks of *Rip*. As a favor to his American colleague and roustabout friend from earlier days, John Sleeper Clarke (who was now managing the Haymarket Theatre), Joe undertook an indeterminate season of double-bill farces in mid-June. His Mr. Golightly and Hugh de Brass (*Lend Me Five Shillings* and *A Regular Fix*, respectively), whose befuddled antics had been part of his repertoire for decades, found new life with English audiences. "Bad air, stale pieces, tired actors," is how Henry James characterized summer theatre. But Joe defied the stereotype. Ticket demand led brokers to advertise ducats on the front page of the *Times*. Playgoers seemed not to have minded the sniffs of a few British players that Joe had a style "too quiet; somewhat lacking in 'point,' in 'life,' or 'go' . . . not 'vivacious' enough, not 'rattling.' " But if a handful of native actors sniped, disgruntled perhaps at an interloper's unbounded success, theatre critics lined up behind patrons in applauding a new style. Rather than the "tumultuous nonsense and inconsequence of pantomime," a babble of words and continual round of backslaps and knowing nudges that comprised the conventional broad humor of the English stage, Jefferson offered a seamless flow of understated fun. "A glance of his eye is worth a hundred jokes," judged critic Mowbray Morris. Joe ultimately performed a full two months at the Haymarket.[45]

While fellow countryman Henry James (who had also come to England in 1875) found himself enduring an unusually hot London August, Joe left the city, heading north to Edinburgh to reprise *Rip Van Winkle*. With a final swing through Manchester in early September, Jefferson brought his English tours to a close. The family stayed by until early October before disembarking from Liverpool. Daughter Margaret and her new husband accompanied the family to New York on board the *Abyssinia*. Although son Willie was but a year and a half old (and another son was yet to follow), Joe would soon be a grandfather. Margaret was already pregnant.[46]

Joe returned to New York in mid-October, 1877 and the unsatisfactory fall season (see chapter 10). After a midwinter break at his New Iberia home, in spring 1878 Jefferson began the first transcontinental tour of his career. A brief swing through Philadelphia, Boston, Rochester, and Buffalo preceded a grueling train trip across the country. From Omaha his destination of San Francisco was reached via the entire length of the transcontinental railroad. Not quite a decade old, the route had already been substantially rebuilt from its original jury-rigged construction. But this mitigated the rigors of the week's journey only slightly.[47]

Joe's only previous appearance in San Francisco had been in 1861, just before he left for Australia. Then he possessed only pretension of stardom; now his credentials were firmly in order. Joe opened 3 June at the California Theatre in a week of *Rip,* spiced with a scattering of his favorite farces. Despite continued hard times, Joe tested the theatre's seating capacity in his successful run. He also tried out a new role, Tracy Coach, in Thomas MacDonough's adaptation of a French farce, *Baby.* Joe played an indulgent tutor to an unruly child, a role with some resemblance to the affable and permissive Rip. That Jefferson would attempt a new role at this point in career suggests that however secure he was in his stardom, he still felt a need to break new ground. But *Baby* was not the flattering vehicle he sought; it met only modest success with Bay area audiences. Edwin Booth, who had been skeptical of the play from the start, exploded to William Winter, "What in the devil's name could he find in *Baby?* Bah."[48]

Because managers in the inland towns could not meet Joe's salary demands, his California excursion was restricted to four weeks in San Francisco. He did take time, though, to visit America's newest national park, Yosemite. "We have seen the big trees and the great valley," he wrote Winter. That respite preceded a brutal mid-July train crossing of the Great Basin. Passengers could choose between being baked in closed coaches or opening windows to admit smoke, cinders, and blasts of thermal air. Enervated by the trip, Joe might be excused for a performance in Salt Lake City that was "somewhat lacking in vim and intenseness." He soldiered on to Denver, where local interest was so high that special fares for local trains were offered during his run, and folks from area towns were assured that if they wished, local individuals would stand in line for them to buy tickets. The highlight of the brief stand in Denver, as far as Joe was concerned, was his several days of trout fishing at nearby Morrison. Acclaim was fine, but a summer's outing with the fishing pole was the preferred release from the strain of touring, a source of restorative therapy for Jefferson.[49]

Thus, in the final year of the 1870s and throughout the 1880s and 1890s, Joseph Jefferson dutifully shared his brand of mirth with American audiences, alternating stands on Broadway with tours of the nation's hinterland. The memory of a midsummer train journey across the desert perhaps lingered, for he did not return to the West Coast until his *Rivals* tour of 1891–92, when he wisely made the trip in February. Some years witnessed extensive tours of the East and Midwest. During three months in the fall of 1884, he made a thirty-seven-city swing through Michigan, Wisconsin, Illinois, Iowa, Indiana, Ohio, New York, New Jersey, Pennsylvania, Delaware, concluding in Washington, D.C. Other spring or fall seasons he took shorter regional tours of New England or the South. On a few occasions he ventured into the Southwest as far as San Antonio, and his Midwestern swings occasionally went as far west as Denver. Secure in his wealth, Joe could afford to make decisions about the upcoming season based on considerations of family life or personal health.[50]

A Man of Affairs

To step back and ask what was most significant about Joseph Jefferson's career invites several responses. Certainly his life demands no greater justification than the pleasure he brought audiences throughout the century. But his place at the head of the comedians' table during the American theatre's great post–Civil War expansion must also be noted, as must his knack of being present at so many important moments of stage history. Alongside these claims to distinction stands another: Jefferson aided his great friend Edwin Booth in his crusade to enhance the social status for actors. Through overt actions, such as founding the Players Club, and through the quiet yet insistent dignity with which each man led his life, they toppled social barriers that had long confined players. Jefferson, in particular, with his recognized gifts as painter and author, made an effective case that actors should no longer be considered the poor cousins of the artistic world.

In modern parlance, Jefferson and Booth were leaders in the movement to professionalize acting. Nineteenth-century players were not given to sociological analysis of their actions, but from a later vantage we see that their efforts paralleled those of engineers, architects, and the academic disciplines in seeking to enhance their occupation. Harrison Grey Fiske's *New York Mirror* lent editorial support to efforts to make dressing rooms healthier, theatrical contracts fairer, and play piracy rarer, among its other reforms. The Actors' Society of America was founded in 1894 as a professional society for actors, for the purpose of elevating standards and monitoring the well-being of players. The call for formalized instruction of acting went forth, and acting schools began to produce young Roscians. Nonetheless, acting remained an imperfect profession (at least when judged by the usual criteria). The Actors' Society never achieved the sort of professional control known by associations of attorneys or physicians. Most players continued to follow the older apprenticeship roads to the stage rather than studying for a certificate or degree. Still, leading actors began to internalize a spirit of professionalism toward century's end. They viewed themselves less as carefree, strolling players and more as purveyors of a fine art, dispensing a product much needed by harried middle-class Americans of the day.[51]

The signal moment in the ennoblement of American actors came in 1888 when Edwin Booth realized his dream in the establishment of The Players. The club's home in a stately four-story townhouse in fashionable Gramercy Park made it a neighbor of Samuel Tilden, Cyrus Field, and Robert Ingersoll. An American Bloomsbury, the neighborhood has been called, home one time to such cultural luminaries as Stanford White, Augustus St. Gaudens, Stephen

Crane, and Edith Wharton. Booth hoped that the club, true to the age's obsession with masculine sociability, would provide a place where the stage's leading men could rub shoulders with New York's elite in business and the arts. He
succeeded. Inducted within the first few years were such playwrights, authors,
and editors as Augustus Thomas, Owen Wister, Samuel Clemens, Thomas
Bailey Aldrich, and Richard Watson Gilder (no drama critics were admitted,
thus sparing everyone potentially awkward encounters); sculptors, painters,
and architects like Augustus Saint-Gaudens, John La Farge, Childe Hassam,
John Singer Sargent, J. Alden Weir, and Stanford White (who remodeled the
building for the club); political notables, Abram Hewitt, Grover Cleveland,
and Elihu Root; and railroad magnates Cornelius Vanderbilt and Chauncey
Depew. Stage stars, among them Joseph Jefferson, Lawrence Barrett, John
Drew, Edward H. Sothern, and William Florence, were invited charter members. Other players included were hardly headliners but met Booth's criterion
of being gentlemen. Most members were not actors, however, which was
precisely Booth's point. This "oasis of quietness," as Henry James styled it
when he visited in 1904, was intended not for show (the club gave no public
entertainments) but for refined conviviality.[52]

Jefferson became the club's second president upon Booth's death in 1893,
his election partly a testament to the friendship of the men but also a sort of
coronation of Joe as titular head of his profession. There was early speculation
that Joe might forego the presidency of The Players, for reasons of health or
because he might incur financial obligations toward the club. But he could
hardly demur. Both from a sense of duty to Booth and from a desire to ascend
the final rung to the head of the profession, he accepted the post when elected
that fall. Joe did not a frequently loiter within club walls. Convivial though he
was, he cherished more his time at home, in his atelier, or with a few friends at
the fishing hole. Moreover, he was in New York rather infrequently. But he
duly presided over business meetings (with a fondness for punctuating meetings with one of his innumerable anecdotes) and made an effort to be present
for the annual Founder's Night commemorations of Booth.[53]

Intermittently at The Players, more often in private homes or by letter, Joe
networked with writers and artists who collectively made up the American
men of letters: Richard Watson Gilder, E. C. Stedman, Laurence Hutton,
Thomas Bailey Aldrich, William Winter. Although history has placed them in
the second rank of American letters, this collection of reviewers, editors, and
critics helped define literary taste for their age. Two slices of this literary pie,
drama critics and playwrights, held obvious importance for Jefferson.[54]

Theatre critics were still a relatively new breed of literary specialists in
Jefferson's day. Antebellum American stage reviews were frequently un-

polished notices in local newspapers written by reviewers who usually remained safely anonymous. The system of reviewing was open to abuses, what
Walt Whitman called the "paid puff system." Reviewers expected free tickets
and paid advertising (and perhaps other gratuities); in return theatre managers
wanted a favorable notice. Predictably, they often got a review "written with
cautious deference to the prospects of the advertising columns." There were
exceptions to this system of hack work journalism. Early in the nineteenth
century a handful of "gentlemen" reviewers, including Washington Irving,
sought an elevated stage. Later, even in the newspapers of smaller provincial
towns, one could find a surprising quantity of insightful criticism that seemed
willing to let the chips fall where they may. In Gotham, two giants of American
letters cast an occasional eye to the stage. Edgar Allan Poe wrote a handful of
theatre reviews for the *Broadway Journal* in 1845 that display a critical grasp
of drama well in advance of his time. Over at the *Brooklyn Eagle* at about the
same time Walt Whitman sounded his lament for American theatre. "Miserable State of the Stage — Why Can't We Have Something Worth the Name of
American Drama!" he demanded, an outcry that typified his jaundiced take on
the contemporary stage.[55]

After the Civil War, as the American theatre expanded and became more
professional, it gained a larger though still uneven body of criticism. Accusations of "bought" newspaper reviews continued to be voiced, and a new tone
of sensationalism was sounded. Charles A. Byrne's *New York Dramatic News*
(founded 1875) revealed private misdeeds and business dealings of actors, a
journalism mild by later standards but intrusive enough to reap a flood of libel
suits and even physical assaults on Byrne. Nonetheless, alongside the puffery,
scabrous attacks, and apparent conflicts of interest, a theatrical criticism
worthy of the name emerged. It came from a new generation of writers, such
as Brander Matthews, professor of dramatic literature at Columbia University, Laurence Hutton, John Ranken Towse, Henry Clapp, and Edward Dithmar, who wrote for major newspapers or for the cultured magazines of the
day — *Harper's, Atlantic, Scribner's, Century, Appleton's*, the *North American
Review*, and others. These men sought to uplift the stage through strictures to
theatre people and by educating the public about the canons of dramatic art.
Realism, then emerging as the dominant force in drama, became the guiding
critical principle, though its definitions were problematic (interpretive battles
were fought over where realism shaded into the harsher hues of naturalism)
and defenders of an established romanticism bitterly carped at its tenets.[56]

If a measured distance between actor and critic would appear the natural
posture, intimacy was in fact the frequent reality. The shared love of drama
and an understanding that both parties benefited from a support of theatre

encouraged amicability. William Winter's weakness for borrowing money from stage figures and forming strong bonds with favored players was so pronounced as to cast doubts on his professional objectivity. Joe Jefferson's relations with the community of drama critics were, as might be expected, cordial. Although not above occasional criticism, his Olympian standing in the fraternity and — more significantly — his professionalism in striving for technically high performance standards kept critics respectful (even the young iconoclast Shaw).[57]

Joe's closest enduring friendship — alongside that with Edwin Booth — was with William Winter (1836–1917). The genteel tradition had no more stalwart champion than Winter. He "spread purple ink like a squid to blot out any playwright who strayed from the path of romanticism," wrote Alan Downer (himself an eminence of theatrical scholarship from a slightly later generation). A highly influential critic through at least the 1880s, Winter took as his task "to instill, to protect, and to maintain purity, sweetness, and refinement in our feelings, our manners, our language, and our national character." Winter's lachrymose prose, bushy moustache, and shock of white hair made him a favorite target of caricaturists, especially as his unbending moralism fell out of favor. (Mencken meanly called him "the greatest bad critic who ever lived.") Jefferson's friendship with Winter was in some ways the quintessential Victorian relationship: an exterior of mannered formality overlay intimacy. Winter came for extended visits to Jefferson's various houses; they occasionally traveled together; and even during the long stretches of separation they carried on a guileless epistolary friendship. We know the relationship best through Jefferson, whose letters suggest that he served as emotional anchor for Winter. "I am sorry to find you in low spirits," Joe sympathized on several occasions. "Tell me all your matters freely," Joe once encouraged, "you know you can talk to me." If Winter failed to drop by after a performance, Joe was quick to make sure he had not been offended in some way. Joe also sent presents to Winter's children and at least once proudly made a gift of oranges from his Louisiana grove. For his part, Joe also confided in Winter. "See me as soon as you can," he wrote. "I have something of importance to tell you." Joe knew that he had an influential friend who loyally championed his career. He even presumed to intervene with Winter on behalf of friends. "I wish you would try and see him [George Vandenhoff] act," Jefferson implored, "and if you can conscientiously say a good word for him pray do." It would be a mistake to see Joe's friendship with the *Tribune* critic as cynical opportunism, however. There was a clear bond of affection that transcended issues of career. They each named sons after one another. Even their wives became fast friends, exchanging gifts and family news.[58]

Drama critics were only one segment of the larger literary world of editors, essayists, poets, playwrights, and novelists that Joe inhabited. Aspirations to respectability predisposed actors to favor the official guardians of the arts, such as fellow club members Gilder, Stedman, and Aldrich, whose Genteel Tradition credentials were impeccable. The poetry of Rimbaud or Baudelaire, fiction of Zola or Crane, or drama of Ibsen or Wilde fell outside their boundaries of cultured taste. Even Walt Whitman's verse, at least to Charlotte Cushman, was deemed vulgar (she preferred the maudlin lines of Sidney Lanier). True, Mark Twain belonged to The Players, where he was frequently found about the pool table. But when in society, the creator of raffish Huck Finn modulated into the eminently respectable Samuel Clemens.[59]

Richard Watson Gilder (1844–1909) was among Jefferson's close literary friends. A trim, thin-faced man with dark, expressive eyes and bushy moustache, Gilder was a poet and editor of *Century* for nearly thirty years, a position of immense influence in the literary world. As a young newspaperman in Newark, Gilder had talked his way into a supernumerary role when Joe appeared locally in *Rip Van Winkle*. His passion for Irving's dramatized legend persisted, and thus when his rising editorial prominence allowed him to seek out Jefferson on more equal terms, he did so. Gilder invited Joe home following his evening's performance. The hour was late, but Joe, animated by the rush of performance, regaled his host with story and opinion until well into the morning. Gilder knew a good storyteller when he heard one, and over time he successfully urged Joe to commit his memories to autobiography.[60]

At Gilder's celebrated salon, Joe had entree to a procession of literary and artistic figures who lived in or passed through New York. It was here in 1882 that Jefferson struck up a quick friendship with George Washington Cable (1844–1925). A New Orleans native who would, after the mid-1880s, become notable for his pioneering attempts to construct an indigenous liberal criticism of his region's racial caste system, Cable at this time was enjoying wide acclaim for his literary portraits of the South in *Old Creole Days* and *The Grandissimes*. Local color was much to the taste of postwar American readers, who reveled in the regional variety of their land. It was a preference that fed the fondness for *Rip Van Winkle*. Cable had come north to take his new seat among the American literati — and perhaps taste the pleasures of Gotham. The latter goal could only be subconscious, for Cable was a southern Puritan. His devout Presbyterianism countenanced no glimpse inside a theatre or truck with actors. But once in Babylon, Cable found the forbidden pleasures enticing. Despite admonitions from his wife and a conscience that plagued him, Cable succumbed. Jefferson contributed to his downfall. Cable found Joe "good and sweet" when they met. Jefferson was engaging and seemed to Cable disarmingly candid about his life and calling. "I-I-I have done things in my life I'm ashamed of — we all do that; but I have no *secret*," Cable records Jefferson confessing. But these admissions made Joe no less attractive to Cable, especially when he discovered an actor who could discourse on many subjects with both authority and modesty and "invariably refuses all kinds of alcoholic drink with gentle firmness."[61]

Such revelations forced Cable to methodically rethink his attitudes toward the stage. For a month, as he struggled with his conscience, he "refused to go & hear Jefferson" perform. But an invitation to see *Cricket on the Hearth* finally persuaded him. Defending his action to his family back home, he wrote, "If it [*Cricket on the Hearth*] isn't as pure & sweet & refreshing & proper a diversion as spending the same length of time over a pretty, sweet, good storybook, then I'm a dunce. . . . I've neither time nor space left to tell you how lovely — how *lovely* — Jefferson is in the play. I feel this morning as if I had had a bath in pure, cool water." Once having crossed the Rubicon of theatre attendance, Cable plunged on, adapting some of his stories for the stage. Cable even became so bold as to write Jefferson and solicit his advice about a dramatization of his 1888 novel *Bonaventure*. Joe, accustomed to these appeals for advice from established writers, knew how to tactfully respond. "It is a charming story," Joe allowed, appealing to his own sense when in Louisiana of being a "Cajun." Nonetheless, the story did not lend itself to dramatization. "The strongest effects are descriptive rather than dramatic." Too, the challenge of casting a story that carried forward gradually the lives of two people from childhood through adulthood would be daunting. Joe softened his unencouraging judgment to the sensitive Cable by concluding that his — or anyone's opinion — must be cautiously received: "For the subtleties of dramatic action are beyond the keenest observer."[62]

Jefferson's friendship with the literati was fitting given the rapprochement between performance and pen in these years. A quickening appreciation of theatre as "drama" was underway. The laments of Whitman and Poe had finally born fruit; literary values were being taken seriously. Augustin Daly found a fistful of reasons why "the prospects of our national drama are bright," including the improving social position of theatre in public life and the ennobled powers of native actors. Not everyone in the theatre agreed. Jeremiads about drama's declension continued, as if an obligatory duty of any self-respecting critic. Dion Boucicault, theatrical genius and contrarian, caused a stir with an 1889 address (and subsequent article) denying that a true American drama existed and blaming its absence largely on the press, charging that critics had usurped public opinion as an influence on theatre. Unsurprisingly, some drama critics (led by William Winter) took umbrage, and a tempest in a teapot ensued in the pages of the *New York Dramatic Mirror*. It was the sort of debate that could only occur when theatre was thriving, which it indisputably was in the late 1880s, with touring companies burgeoning and the various auxiliaries of the stage prospering.[63]

Jefferson avoided these polemical debates over the American drama. He probably understood that *Rip Van Winkle*, though certainly a native American product, held no claim to dramatic distinction. The issue of realism on stage was so persistent, however, that Joe could not avoid addressing it on occasion. Despite compliments for his accomplished realist acting, Joe consistently forswore realism as a guiding principle of stagecraft. He understood that *Rip Van Winkle*'s magic lay not in elaborate stage settings and props. It was fantasy. "So unreal a theme could not have been interwoven with all this realism without marring the play," he judged.[64]

Three of America's leading prose writers held strong views on drama. Henry James was skeptical about the prospects of an ennobled American drama. The trouble with drama, James paradoxically considered, was its connection with the theatre. Where drama was "admirable in its interest and difficulty," theatre was "loathesome in its conditions." Dramatists must attempt to feed an audience "when their taste is at its lowest, flocking out of hideous hotels and restaurants, gorged with food, stultified with buying and selling and with all the other sordid speculations of the day, squeezed together in a sweltering mass, disappointed in their seats, timing the author, timing the actor, wishing to get their money back on the spot, before eleven o'clock." Playwrights necessarily must "make the basest concessions." William Dean Howells and Mark Twain affected a distaste slightly less pointed, but their condescension thinly veiled a fascination — even infatuation — with the stage that prompted ambitious efforts to master its mysteries. Indeed, theatre seemed to keep a diabolical hold on them. "It is strange how the stage can keep on fooling us," Howells abashedly confided to James. All three writers, as well as Bret Harte, worked at one time or another with Augustin Daly, the great regisseur and proponent of stage realism. Aided by these tribunes of American letters, Daly hoped to elevate the literary tone of native drama. If the reach of their collective efforts well exceeded their grasp, it was not for lack of trying. The four above-mentioned writers altogether wrote or collaborated on more than sixty plays. Perhaps this connection is unsurprising when one recalls the melodramatic theatricality implicit in so many nineteenth-century novels.[65]

Neither James nor Howells nor Twain enjoyed substantial success as a playwright. Their inability to make compelling stage figures out of even such promising characters as Twain's Colonel Sellers suggests that the dramatic art was trickier than they suspected. Howells did contribute to the theatre by effectively championing the tenets of realism (upholding Jefferson as a paragon of realism, one who possessed an "art which he has dignified and refined to an ideal delicacy and a beautiful reality never surpassed in our thinking").[66]

Joseph Jefferson understood theatre as these men did not. And although he is not remembered as a playwright, Joe left his mark on American drama. Not with his 1858 dramatization of George Lepard's *Blanche of Brandywine,* but rather in doctoring scripts to conjure up vivid comic characters. His tinkering with Tom Taylor's *Our American Cousin* fostered Laura Keene's great hit. He did the same, even more famously, with *Rip Van Winkle.* And he later performed radical surgery on Sheridan's classic *The Rivals* to make it a more suitable vehicle.

Jefferson was involved in another dramatization, unmentioned in his *Autobiography* and little noticed elsewhere. In the mid-1880s he collaborated with L. B. Shewell in the potboiler *Shadows of a Great City.* The exact nature of Jefferson's contribution remains shadowy itself. Later play credits list Shewell alone, and it appears that he may have done most of the actual composition. But during its run (and it successfully toured for several years) newspaper reviews repeatedly invoked Joe as responsible for the story. It is clear that Shewell (manager of the Boston Theatre) submitted the play for Joe's inspection in spring 1884 and that Joe, having gone over it twice, replied that he found it "admirable in every respect." Jefferson suggested a Chicago opening and offered to supervise its production. "I wish you could spend a fortnight with us here," Joe implored Shewell. "You know how fastidious I am." The play, which opened that fall, proved to be a conventional melodrama in most respects, with turns of plot so byzantine that a coherent synopsis is impossible. It offered the usual cast of heroines fallen from the privileged caste, conniving villains (including that theatrical staple, the venal Jewish pawnbroker), and missing heirs. Its stage settings of New York docks and Blackwell's Island partook of the popular theatrical genre portraying the urban underclass. But if the play was unexceptional in most respects, a Baltimore reviewer noted "its charming absence of anything horrible or shocking — not a shot is fired, nobody draws or brandishes a knife, and no one is killed. This is of itself a novelty." Perhaps Jefferson found an appealing challenge in contriving a melodrama free of the usual overlay of violence. More oddly, given Joe's professed aversion to realism, *Shadows of a Great City* was praised for its special effects. Scenes of boats on the East River had "never been approached in realism by anything" on the Baltimore stage. Another act featured a clever vertical double set, displaying two Blackwell Island cells at the same time. Jefferson kept a proprietary interest in the play into its second season of 1885–86. He also used his interest in the production to further the career of his sons Charley and (especially) Tom, who served as booking agent and producer for some of its road companies. It may well be that Jefferson's primary interest in pursuing the collaboration with Shewell—an undertaking unlike anything else he attempted—was to provide a vehicle for his second son's career. Helping the next generation find their place in the theatre was the Jefferson way. By the mid-1880s Charley was an experienced theatrical businessman, and Joe now used his considerable clout to aid Tom.[67]

An Artist in Oils

Critics, playwrights, and other men of letters were natural associates for Jefferson. He may have felt the most affinity, though, for the painters with whom he rubbed elbows at The Players. Sargent, Hassam, Weir—these were among the commanding figures of nineteenth-century American painting. Jefferson entertained foreign artists visiting New England at his mansion on Cape Cod (and when he owned a piece by a visitor, he would display it prominently). Did Joe solicit painterly tips or submit his own landscapes for his visitors' critique? We do not know. He did not seek out advice on his acting and perhaps was no more willing to do so with his painting. But he clearly enjoyed talking shop with artists. He engaged William Morris Hunt, the landscape artist who helped bring the Barbizon School to America, about the best distance at which to view a painting, drawing parallels with how the size of a theatre dictates the scale of an actor's performance.[68]

One point about Joseph Jefferson is beyond dispute: painting was a life passion that approached, and perhaps exceeded, what he felt for acting. Francis Wilson once directly asked him whether he would surrender the stage for the easel. Jefferson struggled with the answer. In truth, unlike Henry James's Nick Dormer, who gives up a seat in Commons for portraiture, Joe never seriously considered abandoning his beloved vocation. He had the luxury of indulging both. He inherited the Jefferson family talent for art. Indeed, Joe's father was more gifted as scenic artist than actor. His grandfather loved to sketch in his free moments. Acting was the family's lifeblood, to be sure, but for Joe, histrionics were saddled with responsibilities, for providing his livelihood, and were inevitably associated with a hardscrabble youth, years of toil, and ceaseless travel. Joe was proud of his professional accomplishments and manifestly happy in his work, but painting was unencumbered by any vocational baggage. It offered an artistic expression unburdened by public judgment or the need for commercial return. It was the purest sort of joy.[69]

From childhood, Joe dabbled in art, raiding his grandfather's art supplies at will. During his family's hard days in Mobile his talents were forced into use as

The landscape artist. Courtesy of Michael A. Morrison Collection.

paint grinder, and during his journeyman years he sometimes worked on scenic backdrops. But once established as a headliner, Joe could turn his painting into a hobby—a serious hobby, to be sure, one rarely unmentioned in the many articles on him through the years. He loved the solitude of his studio (the perfect counterpoint to his stage work, the most social of the arts). Joe laid out ample studios in all his homes. For a time he painted in a quaint windmill he constructed on the grounds of his Massachusetts estate. Although he coveted his seclusion, Joe could also work while receiving visitors and took pride on how fast he could produce a painting for them. On tour he would set up his easel in an empty baggage car and pass the hours. If he was away from painting for any length of time, his head filled with images struggling to free themselves on canvas. His hobby approached an obsession.

Jefferson was a very fine amateur painter, albeit one with clear limitations. He painted a handful of portraits, two of which (now lost) were homages to his father and grandfather. But his love and true métier was landscape painting. He considered landscapes the highest form of art and in his paintings rendered cottages, falling water, and vagrant terrains. He loved capturing the exotic southern landscapes of Bayou Têche or the Okefenokee Swamp. His painting was of a piece with his theory of drama in that he disdained a slavish realism in favor of more idealized, suggestive art. But rather than the painstaking, detailed layering of expression, gesture, and movement that characterized his acting, Joe approached his painting in an almost slapdash fashion. He often set aside his paint brush and molded his oils with his palette knife, other tools at hand, or even his thumb. He sought an effect, a visual impression, rather than a set of precisely detailed objects. No proto-Impressionist to be sure (lacking any technical understanding of how the eye perceives light), Jefferson nonetheless shared the contemporary notion of many artists that photography allowed painting to explore nature at deeper levels. Even loyal friend Francis Wilson admitted that Jefferson's art was compromised by a failure to master the basics of draftsmanship. Oddly, for one who preferred landscapes, he would not draw from life but only from his imagination (true only to memory, Joe rationalized). He even turned down an invitation from Frederick Remington to join him in sketching a particularly striking southern vista (intimidated, perhaps, by the presence of one so accomplished).[70]

Most of Jefferson's artistic work was for himself or friends. He enjoyed giving his canvases as gifts. When a valued photograph lent to him by Owen Fawcett was destroyed in the house fire of 1893, Joe sought to make amends by offering Fawcett one of his paintings. Joe's work became more public in the late 1870s, when William Winter talked him into providing sketches for a published account of the English travels the two men took at the close of Joe's stay in Britain. Winter's text was a rather tired example of nineteenth-century travel reporting, an Anglophile's sentimental and idealized description of Shakespeare's homeland. But Jefferson's ten sketches (rendered as heliotype in the book) added a note of interest to the text. As a collection, the ten illustrations suggest a pastiche of styles current in nineteenth-century landscape painting, the French Barbizon School as well as Britain's indigenous tradition of Turner and Constable. Joe's idealization of rustic life in some sketches was offset by a brooding gothic presence in others, as in his nighttime view of Victoria Tower at Westminster. The sketches pointedly summarize Jefferson's artistic sensibility. It was, first, utterly derivative. Unlike his original contributions to acting, Joe relied upon earlier vocabularies for his sketchbook and canvases. "Suggestions of Corot and Daubigny [kept] unconsciously intruding themselves" into his work, Joe admitted, "from pure admiration of their work." Second, it was of a piece with his acting, which, as William Dean Howells once wrote, was "exactly a suggestive art," putting "before the spectator only a few facts, and only the most salient points of these facts." And his art bespoke an attraction to a visual style rooted in rural folklore and pastoralism that mirrored *Rip Van Winkle*. No surprises here. Jefferson's art both on the stage and in the atelier reflected his essential self.[71]

Jefferson's passion for collecting art nearly equaled his love for the brush. He possessed an astute eye when it came to judging contemporary art. He built up an impressive collection of European and American works, saw much of it destroyed when his house burned, then proceeded to amass another. The late nineteenth century was of course the great age of the collector, and Joe partook of the American stampede to acquire European masters. Certainly Joe approached the enterprise with far more personal acuity than many of his contemporaries. When his friends reminisced about conversations with Jefferson, they often mentioned his extended and informed discussion of art. Issues of composition and color engaged him with as much ardor as did discussions of stage aesthetics. Apart from dangling his line at a favorite fishing hole, Joe was never happier than when at a dealer's gallery angling for a work by a favorite artist. We do not know when his serious interest in art began, but by his third trip to Europe in the mid-1870s he haunted the art museums. He collected a few works of the venerable European painters, notably a Rembrandt (a well-spent $25,000 investment), three by Reynolds, and a Gainsborough (a portrait of Richard Brinsley Sheridan, author of *The Rivals*). Predictably, he held a fondness for theatrical portraits: Garrick, Macready, Kean, Vestris — all in famous roles.

But Joe's true collecting passion was aroused by the contemporary Dutch and French landscape artists, whose sensibility matched his own. In particular he treasured the work of Camille Corot, a contemporary French artist who was immensely popular during the Second Empire. Joe's collecting essentially started with a Corot, and he proceeded to collect a number of his works. The attraction went beyond sentimentality. Corot's compositions conveyed the subdued and simple tranquility that Jefferson infused into Rip. In Corot, Joe found a kindred spirit.[72]

Jefferson made his several houses showcases of art. In the profuse ornamental style of the day, he furnished his houses with Indian carved teakwood; embroideries from Turkey, China, and Japan; the inevitable Oriental rugs; and skins of tigers, lions, and other exotica collected on his European trips. His walls became a gallery of oils, watercolors, and engravings. As Joe became increasingly wealthy he loved to frequent galleries and network with dealers who tempted him with new art works. If viewed only as an investment (a consideration the shrewd actor-businessman would not spurn), his art purchases were astute. *Return of the Flock* by Mauve purchased for $2,500 fetched $42,000 at his estate sale. His judgment was not flawless. He bought and sold, weeding out canvases he deemed artistically substandard. Nor did he escape the scourge of art fraud that plagued the American connoisseurs. He candidly admitted to having been "bitten" on occasion but claimed to have learned his lesson about dealing only with reputable dealers.[73]

Jefferson never stopped collecting art, nor did he lose his capacity for exploring new visual media. With the advent of the box camera he took up photography. At a more complex level he became intrigued with monotypes, a Renaissance-era type of printmaking rediscovered in the mid-1890s. Joe pursued monotype reproductions at Buzzards Bay, enticing John Singer Sargent into making a print while on a visit. Toward the end of the century Joe also showed greater interest in exhibiting his paintings before the public. Sundry works hung in various galleries and clubs (he made it a point to hang one of his works prominently in The Players), and in 1899 he finally consented to a full showing at the Fisher Galleries in Washington. With great care and not a little trepidation he oversaw the shipping of his paintings, insisting on small details regarding their framing. The exhibit was generously reviewed by the *Washington Times,* so well received in fact (and so lucrative to the dealer) that a year later an even larger showing of other of his creations was mounted.[74]

Joe Jefferson was a subject of portraiture as well as a collector of it. Show business, after all, demands public visibility. Magazines and newspapers, especially after the halftone reproduction advances of the 1880s, carried countless illustrations and photographs of him. Not all were flattering, at least according to "The Usher" (a *Dramatic Mirror* columnist). A portrait of Joe as Rip displayed at New York's Academy of Art (by an unnamed artist) was "among the worst in the whole hideous show." Joe's "red-nosed, mouth-distorted visage" carried little trace of the man. More happily, Joe commissioned eminent portraitists to capture him in his great roles.[75]

His first and arguably most vivid portrait came from the brush of the young John White Alexander (1856–1915). In the fall of 1883 when Joe was in New York he commissioned Alexander, recently returned from studies in Germany and employed as an illustrator at *Harper's,* to render him in the costume of his second greatest role, *The Rivals'* Bob Acres. Alexander embodied the elegant high aestheticism then coming into fashion (mirroring the work of Whistler and Sargent), highlighted by the dramatic lighting characterizing the so-called Munich realism of his European training. Jefferson's Acres, attired in ornate yellow pantaloons and green waistcoat, looms slightly above the viewer, peering out with those merry eyes from the front of the stage. His back is arched as he works at removing a glove. As if in the spotlights' blaze, Jefferson's life-size figure reflects the brightness of a full moon. Exhibited at the National Gallery

Jefferson as Bob Acres. Painting by John Alexander
White, courtesy of Hampden-Booth Theatre Library.

of Design in 1884, the portrait earned immediate plaudits ("one of the most
original and masterly works ever produced in America," a critic applauded).
Jefferson was also delighted. For a time he displayed the painting in the lobbies
of theatres where he performed. It also was reproduced for a *Harper's* magazine feature on Jefferson in 1886. The painting, Alexander's first venture in
theatrical portraiture, proved an important moment in his career, inviting new
commissions and enabling him to distinguish himself in the field over the next
two decades. In a career that paralleled Jefferson's in many respects, Alexander lifted himself from humble origins to becoming both an admired practitioner and also an esteemed figure within the artistic community, respected as
a promoter of American art[76]

Jefferson also had two portraits done by John Singer Sargent (1856–1925).
Sargent's privileged background, European upbringing, formal academic
training, and relatively painless march to fame could hardly have been more
different from Jefferson's, but the two became acquaintances and then friends

through their association at The Players. Sargent had become enthralled with theatre while in London (composing an acclaimed portrait of Ellen Terry), and on a visit to New York in 1889–90, during a frenzy of activity when he painted forty portraits, he produced for The Players a full-length portrait of Edwin Booth and one of Jefferson as Dr. Pangloss. His Pangloss, in frocked sleeves and unruly white wig, gives the characteristically Jefferson wide-eyed stare at the viewer while the mincing play of his left-hand fingers draw the viewer's gaze. Sargent executed another Jefferson painting in 1890, a study rather than a formal portrait. In this rapid sketch (one of Sargent's favorites, which he sent to several exhibitions) of Joe sans makeup, Sargent evokes the unaffected transparency and vitality of America's favorite comedian. Nonetheless, Jefferson later confided that although "Sargent's brushwork is all right," "he doesn't touch me." His favorite portraitist was by a lesser-known figure, N. H. Brewer. Joe visited Brewer's New York studio, donned his Rip Van Winkle costume, and then labored to psychologically assume the persona, not sitting down for the portrait until he was confident he had captured Irving's character. Joe took his role as artistic subject as seriously as his own painting and collecting.[77]

Francis Wilson, Jefferson's younger friend and confidant in later life, wrote that Jefferson considered his painting to be overshadowed by his stage fame but felt that over time his landscapes would gain the recognition they deserved. Such thoughts were not simply a jealous regard for his canvas art. For all of his simplicity and lack of affectation, Joe worried over the fleeting nature of theatrical fame. He wished to leave a tangible legacy of his talent. He would be gratified to know that some of his paintings still hang in museums, are featured in exhibitions, and have gained him a modest place in the art world. Ironically, it would be neither Jefferson's painting nor his acting that would keep his name before the public in future decades. It would be instead a literary accomplishment: the most enduring autobiography ever penned by an American actor.[78]

12

Are We So Soon Forgot?

Telling His Life

"No man should write his autobiography but himself," Joe Jefferson facetiously observes at the opening of his life's story. He wastes no time in setting a tone of good-natured unpretentiousness, an act of self-definition both genuine and contrived. Not that this autobiographical exercise of late middle career was unserious. To the contrary, Jefferson sought to take as firm control of his legacy as he could. Such concerns were not uncommon. In a letter to Henry James, Henry Adams called his *Education* a "shield of protection in the grave," advising his friend to "take your own life in the same way, in order to prevent biographers from taking it in theirs." Unlike Adams, Jefferson felt no need for either apology or defense. He recognized his popularity within the profession and without. His was a more elemental impulse, the urge to be remembered — and remembered on *his* terms. This drive is felt, no doubt, with especial intensity by the celebrated, who grow accustomed to attention and wince before the prospect of its arrest. Joe admitted as much to Francis Wilson: "An actor cannot hope to live after he has made his final exit — an author may."[1]

Unlike his acting or painting, there was little early indication to suggest a talent for writing — except his storytelling. Joe possessed in full measure the actor's gift for vivid anecdote. His life was a treasure chest of family legends and touring adventures. Friends recounted being entertained for hours by his expansive reminiscences. It was a small step, really, from his verbal regaling to putting his stories into printed form, which is not to diminish his accomplishment in crafting an autobiography with such a well-gaited pace and appealing freshness that it has been republished and reread long after companion memoirs molder on library shelves.

The *Autobiography of Joseph Jefferson* first appeared in 1889, but Joe began pulling his thoughts together much earlier. His original recollections were intended as a posthumous legacy for his family, but an 1877 conversation with William Dean Howells convinced him to make it a public work. With the long breaks he typically took between his fall and spring tours and with his leisurely summers, Joe had ample time to assemble his thoughts. The *Mirror* informed the theatrical community of Joe's project in 1886, lending anticipation to what would be an "event" in the tight-knit world of the stage. In the manner of so many works of the time, the *Autobiography* was published first in serial form and then as a book. Jefferson's friendship with Richard Watson Gilder, now editor of the foremost genteel publication of the day, *Century,* predisposed Jefferson to choose this august magazine to publish his work. Gilder considered the project a catch for the *Century,* boasting to Mrs. Grover Cleveland in 1888 that he had secured for his magazine the " 'best thing' . . . available in these present years." Friendship or no, Joe had driven a bargain with the publisher, exacting an advance beyond what had been originally proffered. "These terms are surprisingly good — I mean for J.J.," Gilder confided. In concrete terms, this meant $12,000 for the manuscript plus 10 percent of sales. Joe also demanded that *Century* publish his entire work rather than just excerpts. He had first envisioned his work as an elegant "subscription book" (a common sales approach of the time), with gilt-topped pages and half-morocco back, hawked by door-to-door agents, but he was persuaded to go the serialization route, which brought his memoirs to a "literary audience" and subsequent speaking invitations. The fall season of 1889 did not begin until the middle of October, allowing Joe time to put final touches on his manuscript before the twelve-month serialization began in the November issue.[2]

The *Autobiography* appeared at an auspicious time in American publishing. Century Publishing Company had recently scored something of a coup with its two series "Life of Lincoln" and "The War Series." These serial-to-book publications were major events in late nineteenth-century biography and history. The former, by John Nicolay and John Hay, represented the first authoritative biography of Lincoln, written by men close to him; the latter, an exhaustive and heroic revisiting of the Civil War, now two decades in the past, a heroic age the public was anxious to revisit. Two further landmarks in Civil War publishing, the memoirs of Grant and Sherman, had been commercially successful, establishing the genre on firm ground in publishers' eyes. Moreover, the initial volumes of Henry Adams's monumental *History of the United States during the Administrations of Thomas Jefferson and James Madison* were issued the same year Joe's serialization began. Clearly, the *Autobiography*'s appearance must be seen as part of a remarkable outpouring of Americana.

The genre of actor memoirs first appeared in England with Colley Cibber's *Apology* (1740), which in many respects remained the most enduring example of the type. (An important new edition of the *Apology* appeared the same year Joe's serialization began.) In the following century and a half, both biographies and autobiographies of players picked up in number, accelerating as the nineteenth century progressed and celebrity culture dawned. One might expect stars like Mrs. John Drew, Otis Skinner, Helena Modjeska, Edward H. Sothern, and Mary Anderson to produce a life's story. But journeymen players also told their story: Walter Leman, Dora Ranous, and Kate Ryan offered useful testimony of stage life for the supporting cast. Some actresses, such as Fanny Kemble and Clara Morris, could not confine their memories to a single work (in the case of Morris, authoring three versions).[3]

If prolific, theatrical memoirs were too often barren of enduring significance. "In general [they are] dreary compilations, abounding in dates and trivialities," indicted William Winter in his preface to James Stoddart's (unremarkable) *Recollections*. They were testimonies, Winter continued, to "overweening egotism." They were also formulaic, more committed, as one historian phrases it, "to vocational narration than introspection." Life narratives were also heavily larded with stage anecdotes, tales of touring, and tributes to fellow players — not to mention a healthy dollop of name-dropping. There were exceptions. Anna Cora Mowatt's autobiography remains one of the best treatments of the antebellum stage. Sol Smith produced a trio of memoirs vividly anecdotal and redolent of the southwestern tradition of native humor. Olive Logan used her reminiscences as a protofeminist reflection on the valued independence a stage career offers women (though, oddly, also decrying the immorality of stage life).[4]

Jefferson's *Autobiography* in many respects resembled other theatrical memoirs. Tales of life on the road abound, as do the inimitable Jefferson stories. Its pages are populated with stage luminaries whose paths he crossed. And (fundamental to the genre) it is a story of his rise from common player to stardom, a "narrative of transformation," as scholars term such works. But Joe's memoir departs from those of his fellow actors in its pace, powers of description, and characterization. He wrote as he painted, with a rapid, extemporaneous execution of his prose undergirded by a measured control of his

art. His art balanced a freshness of expression with a satisfying literary structure. This disciplined balance was achieved by trial and error. Not a diarist,
Joe had only his formidable (though not infallible) memory to draw upon. He
approached his task unsystematically, often awaking in the middle of the night
to record a somnolent memory stirred to consciousness. He read the work-in-
progress to visitors and recounted other tales of his life, happily heeding their
demand that a new story be included. The finished product rambled on rather
too much. When Joe saw his work in galleys, he realized the need for a firm
editorial pen. In acting, be suggestive rather than definitive, Joe always admonished, a lesson he learned applied to literary compositions as well.[5]

The *Autobiography* was in no sense a valedictory. The serialized form appeared when he was sixty years old and with nearly fifteen years of performing
ahead of him. Still, it did represent a final statement of sorts. He understood
that he had reached his definitive growth as a performer. Having made the
important addition of *The Rivals* to his touring repertoire in 1880, Joe knew
there were no more new plays. His career had assumed the shape it would
hold. Joe now held the high ground from whence he could assess his life. What
was worth telling — apart from late-career accolades — had probably already
transpired.

And what did Joe tell? He told a story so purely American and in so natural
an idiom as to reaffirm the national mythos. It was Lincolnesque in its account
of a young man's rise from regional itinerancy to national influence and acclaim. Its voice was singular. If less vernacular than Twain's, it nonetheless
spoke with a spare, unaffected language that managed to avoid the stilted
conventional prose of genteel tradition authors. True, some descriptions of his
travels in Australia, South America, or Europe lapsed into prosaic travel literature, but the accounts of his native journeys possess quiet charm. They are
typically set-piece vignettes several pages in length. A selection from his account of winter travels through western Virginia exemplifies his eloquent
Americana:

> It was rather late in the night when we arrived at the supper station, as in
> consequence of the slippery state of the roads we were fully three hours
> behind time; but the cheerful look of the dining-room, with its huge blazing
> fire of logs, repaid us for all the suffering we had endured. We found that a
> large pile of bricks was being heated for us in front of the fireplace; these
> comforting articles were intended for our feet in the coach, and nothing, not
> even the supper, could have been more welcome.
>
> The horses changed and the passengers aboard, we were again ready for
> our journey — more perilous now than ever, for as we reached the summit of
> the mountain the storm increased in its fury. At times we thought the stage

would blow over; the icy roads caused the horses to slip, and several times the leaders went down. It was a night to be remembered. A little after daylight we rolled into the town of Cumberland, the terminus of the stage line and the beginning of the railroad. Shivering and benumbed with cold, we alighted and sought the hotels for warmth and shelter. The driver of the coach was frozen stiff and had to be assisted down from the box. Another hour on the road would have been fatal to him.[6]

Is Jefferson's *Autobiography* a reliable guide to his life? Is any such work? Victorian literati worried less about veracity than about whether confessional candor was ever desirable. In recent years, literary scholars and psychologists have attacked the question of autobiographical reliability head-on. They conclude that autobiographical memory is less the replaying of an internal memory tape than the constructing of a personal identity. Autobiographers unconsciously devise a "script" to serve as a framework for their narrative. This "self-schema" aids in selection of pertinent life incidents and — inevitably — distorts some memories to fit the script. Writers have always grasped what scholars now seek to precisely define. "Autobiography inevitably shirks the truth," Twain once wrote to Howells, although the "remorseless truth is there, between the lines."[7]

How much between-the-lines reading must one do with Jefferson? Rather less than one would expect. The *Autobiography* is a generally transparent document, bespeaking a man largely unmarked by internal struggles and with few skeletons to hide, scores to settle, or unachieved ambitions to explain. Still, Joe had his script. He had led a life of great fortune (in every sense of the word); he was blessed in family and friends; he had traversed the nation and crossed the seas; he had achieved artistic acclaim. All of this he accepted with a Senecan calm (perhaps not a difficult feat considering his generally favored life). As frequently noted in previous chapters, Jefferson was not an always dependable guide to his life. He had kept no journal, and his grasp of personal chronology was tenuous. But the conclusions of memory research suggest generosity toward his failures. It is clear that the ability to recall the time or sequence of events from a distance of even a few years is almost universally deficient. Jefferson's hit-and-miss approach to gathering memories only compounded the problem, inviting holes in his account. He readily accepted William Winter's accusation that he was a "heedless historian." Still, he did share his manuscript with at least one close friend. In the early stages of his writing, Joe called upon Edwin Booth to help him sort through and confirm the recollections he had of Booth's famous tragedian father, Junius Brutus Booth.[8]

The most egregious violence against the truth occurs in two places: his account of his family's brush with a Mexican-American War battle and the story of his first interest in *Rip Van Winkle*. The former seems a product of an innocent desire to place himself closer to a great moment of American history than the facts warranted. The latter clearly demonstrates the power of a cherished life narrative in shaping autobiography. Jefferson understood that *Rip Van Winkle,* the central event of his career, needed to have an auspicious beginning. Instead of admitting his youthful history with the play, he concocts a quiet moment in the Poconos, a scene much as Irving might have painted, for the magical epiphany. "Tell the truth but tell it slant," Emily Dickinson remarked. Joe would probably not admit to any obliqueness in his memoir. But tilt, however slight, there is.[9]

Joe resisted using the *Autobiography* as an occasion for settling scores. Indeed, one has to read carefully to find criticisms of fellow players. His feuds with Laura Keene are betrayed, albeit in tones massaged by the passage of time and the benevolent perch of stardom. He faults William Burton for nurturing a distrustful atmosphere in his New York stock company thirty years earlier. Joe even directs some good-natured zingers at his friend and English counterpart Charles Mathews. Mathews had goaded Joe with the common charge that he was a one-part star, able to "carry all your wardrobe in a gripsack." Sensitive to the accusation, Joe fired his own comic barb: "My dear Charlie, . . . you are confounding wardrobe with talent. What is the value of a long bill of fare if the stuff is badly cooked? You change your hat, and fancy you are playing another character. Believe me, it requires more skill to act one part fifty different ways than to act fifty parts all the same way." The gentle chiding of others by Joe was more than counterbalanced by occasional self-censure (again gently — no tone of severity being allowed into the *Autobiography*). The mellow public voice reflected a sense of private serenity. "I don't think I am so bitter as I used to be," he confided to William Winter in early 1889, "for I have learned to scan my own faults more clearly, and to look with forbearance upon the shortcomings of others." With few exceptions, actors discussed in the *Autobiography* were deceased; Joe refrained from flattering the living just as he avoided disparaging the dead. One oversight caused him embarrassment. Actress Fanny Davenport wrote him a note complaining that he omitted any mention of his friend (and her father) E. L. Davenport. Joe quickly penned a letter of apology on the inadvertence, pledging its correction in future editions (no other editions appeared).[10]

Joe wanted his work to be handsomely packaged, a desire met by the splendid edition Century supplied. "A more chaste and substantial specimen of book-making has not been produced this season," noted one reviewer, "rich typography, excellent illustrations, and embossed parchment covers cannot fail to give a thrill of joy to the lover of fine books." It appeared in late 1890, just in time for the Christmas book rush. Agosto Brentano, proprietor of New York's esteemed bookstore, testified that the *Autobiography* "had the best holiday sale of all the books of the year." Jefferson's work was, in modern marketing parlance, a crossover. Where most theatrical books found only a limited audience of collectors, Brentano continued, Joe's memoirs were sought out by the general reading public.[11]

The book's reviews matched its sales. It was noted in the major literary reviews of the day. "Jefferson has proved that mediocrity is not always the penalty attached to versatility," commended the *Dial*. Its reviewer noticed that Joe's "simple straightforward style" resembled that of Grant. The *Nation* counted Joe among those select few "who know something and who also can write." "There are no purple patches anywhere," the reviewer exuded, but "much quiet and playful humor." It embodied what English critic Walter Bagehot called "one of the rarest of artistic charms, that of magnanimous autobiography." The *Critic* put a decisive point on the judgment of reviewers: "the best book of its kind the century has produced."[12]

An acclaimed memoir added further luster to an already charmed career. His prominence on the cultural landscape hardly needed enhancing by 1890, but here it was. Jefferson further insinuated himself in contemporary American consciousness with a life story homespun and sincere, by turn self-deflating and celebratory, the prototypical American success story. Although America was rapidly urbanizing, its city dwellers found reassurance in the local color of the past, be it Buffalo Bill's caricatures of the Wild West or Jefferson's quieter recollections of the colonial Hudson Valley. Such evocations were put in the service of commercialized entertainment. Indeed, Theodore Dreiser made Jefferson the very symbol of the new power of celebrity and the commodification of desire. In *Sister Carrie*, Hurstwood is smitten with him. When seeking to impress Carrie he could think of nothing better than taking her to watch him. The sybaritic Hurstwood also found great satisfaction in dining at Rector's, the restaurant where "Jefferson was wont to come."[13]

Jefferson was pleased by his book's reception. It served his purposes. Once, when Francis Wilson fawningly sought to reassure him that he would be long remembered, Joe gave his usual skeptical response: "Don't you believe it." But then he let down his shield of self-depreciation long enough to expose his true feelings. "Well, yes, perhaps because of my book, which will rescue me from total oblivion." In fact, Jefferson understood that he had produced a work that would stand at the head of writings about the American stage. Nonetheless, a poignant moment intruded into the celebration. Just as the book appeared,

Elizabeth Jefferson Fisher, Joe's aunt, his last tie with the barnstorming generation of his youth, died at the age of 80. As he reached back to record his life
history, connections to his past faded.[14]

Family Far and Near

But at almost the same moment another connection to the long-ago past
was revived. In early December 1889, a letter carrying the return address of a
Joseph Sefton arrived at Joe's Buzzards Bay mansion. The Melbourne post-
mark must have puzzled Joe, for he had not been there for nearly twenty-five
years. "My Dear Sir or Father," the letter began, "I approach you with mingled
feelings of doubt and pleasure, doubt as I am uncertain that what I have heard
is true and pleasure that one so celebrated as yourself may stand in the relation
of father to me." Was it with relief or consternation that Joe continued to read,
"If I am misinformed in this matter pray dismiss from your mind any thought
of me." The possibilities for blackmail always existed for the celebrated and
rich. But Joe must have quickly realized this was no crank or gold digger.
Sefton's story was too compelling, and the photographs he included of Joe
alongside Tilly (and Charley, for good measure) could not be gainsaid. The
young man (he was then twenty-six) briefly related his life story. His mother,
Matilda Aram, had married a "provider" named Sefton, who subsequently
died in 1884. Matilda herself passed away two years later. Sefton's mother had
given strict orders that he never be apprized of his true father. But his grandmother, in failing health, decided he should know his parentage. Conceivably,
issues of *Century* carrying the earliest serialization of Jefferson's life story may
have reached Australia, prompting the old women's revelation. In any event,
Sefton waited only ten days before he posted his letter to Joe. "Will you kindly
vouchsafe me an answer?" Sefton pleaded. "Whatever your reply is, Yea or
Nay, it will be accepted by me as a final disposition of the matter."[15]

Joe put the letter away for five months. His self-told life story unfolding
month by month to American readers was already being rendered obsolete by
a new set of facts. Finally, an answer was sent. "My Dear Son," Joe began, "all
that your grandmother has told you is true." Joe insisted he would have inquired about him long ago, "but I was not aware of your mother's wishes in
the matter." The social issues were sticky; the Victorian code was remorseless.
"If the world connects any shame with such matters, and it usually does, the
blot should fall upon me rather than on you." Joe refused to dodge the obvious
questions: Should his son make known his paternity? Should he assume a
famous name? Joe counseled caution. "You are a man and have a right to act
as you please. I would however advise you for the present at least to retain the

name you now have." To do otherwise "will only cause those of your friends who live in your vicinity to talk and perhaps treat you with a disregard that you do not deserve." But, Joe went on, "I place the matter unreservedly in your own hands, and I would not have you think that my advice is given to shield myself from the responsibility that it would be cowardly in me to shirk."[16]

What of Mrs. Jefferson? Did she have previous knowledge of the liaison or the son? If not before, she learned of her new stepson now. "My wife is fully aware of what I have written and entirely approves of it in the kindness of her heart." Joe returned the photos Sefton had sent, save the one of his son Charley, which he wanted to keep. He solicited future communications and even a meeting. "You are a bright manly honest fellow — as such I should be proud of you. When we meet . . . you will find that neither me or mine will receive you with anything but affection."[17]

The encounter of father and son never took place, but over the final sixteen years of Jefferson's life they established an annual exchange of letters (brief though they were). Joe offered up fatherly advice on getting along in life ("virtue and truth make for a man an armour that no worldly affliction can beat down"); he sent presents for Sefton, his wife, and their son, and regular drafts for money; he let him know that his neighbor Grover Cleveland had just been called back to the White House; he complained of the foolish intervention of America overseas in the Spanish-American War; and he informed him that he was remembered in his will. But never did Joe say that he informed anyone (beyond his wife) about the son's existence. Every indication suggests not (although good friends like William Winter and Francis Wilson were unlikely to include the impropriety in their accounts of his life). After the initial letter to Sefton giving his Buzzards Bay address, Joe made a point of instructing his newfound son to direct future correspondence to The Players, as if this part of Joe's life was to be sealed off from his family abode. The "Sunday School comedian's" reputation could not be enhanced by such news. Jefferson understood how illegitimacy could tarnish a name. Grover Cleveland had survived the scandal of fathering an illegitimate child — but barely. What Cleveland may have shared with him in private moments about the agony of such public embarrassment would have given Joe pause. Happily, Jefferson's indiscretion had occurred on the far side of the Pacific, and prying tabloid journalism had not yet hit its stride. Would the American public, had it known, been as forgiving as it apparently was to Cleveland? Although actors had long been granted license to suspend the social mores binding others, their striving for legitimation was based on their promise to embrace the middle-class code. Jefferson, the epitome of stage respectability, thus had much to lose for himself but more particularly for his profession. Willingly or not, Joe carried the aspirations of his fellow players and the admiring scrutiny of the public. It was to the good fortune of all that Jefferson's secret would be safe in his lifetime and far beyond.[18]

His Australian son added, if distantly, another member to an already proliferating Jefferson household. By 1890 Joe counted seven surviving children of the ten born to his two wives. They ranged from a five-year-old at home (Frank) to Charley, now aged thirty-nine, who had presented Joe with four granddaughters. Alter ego Rip would have appreciated how Joe kept the extended family near even while he remained on the road a good bit of the year. *Rip Van Winkle* was the family industry, and just as he had enabled the careers of Charley and Tom, Jefferson now found roles for other children and even grandchildren, which allowed them to accompany him in his leased railcars. Daughter-in-law Blanche Bender, for example, took on the role of Meenie for a time in the 1890s; grandson Warren Jefferson was carried on stage as a baby. It was the Jefferson way.

In 1885 the *New York Times* reported that Joe was about to sell his New Jersey estate—fishing ponds notwithstanding—in favor of his New Iberia home. Earlier that year it was publicly announced that Joe was preparing for permanent retirement. Both reports were premature. Needless to say, he did not step down; his fall 1886 tour was among his most ambitious in years. And he would not sell his Hohokus estate for another decade. But he increasingly made the southern home his preferred residence. If indeed he was seriously entertaining retirement, he may have concluded he did not need the New Jersey retreat within hailing distance of Broadway. The expense of two large estates must have been daunting even for a man of Jefferson's resources. And yet he would soon build another summer mansion, the above-mentioned residence at Buzzards Bay on Cape Cod.[19]

In the mid-1880's Joe had begun to take summer fishing vacations in New England and Canada with his sons. During one of these jaunts he discovered the still-isolated beauty of the Buzzards Bay region. In typical Jefferson fashion, once he found a new homestead he began aggressively purchasing real estate, eventually amassing 156 acres near the village of Bourne. "Crow's Nest," Joe would call his first massive home on Buttermilk Bay (an inlet of Buzzards Bay), constructed in 1889. Reached only by boat or strenuous carriage drive, the site offered the seclusion Jefferson appeared to crave. The house was more than substantial; it was elegant, including life-sized stained-glass windows portraying Edwin Booth as Hamlet and William Warren (Jefferson's cousin) as Falstaff. It was originally intended as a summer home; Joe still enjoyed the subtropical climes of Louisiana during the winter. But during the 1890s it increasingly became as permanent an address as a man with Joe's touring schedule could have.[20]

Crow's Nest at Buzzard's Bay.

Homes of the Jefferson children began sprouting up about the estate, another Jefferson signature: Charles and Thomas, the two eldest sons, erected houses, as well as Joseph Warren, the oldest child of his second marriage. Ultimately, six cottages went up for various family members (including sister Connie), housing twenty-six people during summer gatherings. These family occasions gave definition to the term "gay nineties." Afternoon costume parties were devised; on other occasions evening pantomimes were got up. A procession of literary and stage luminaries passed through, enjoying Jefferson hospitality. The Barrymores were frequent guests; young Lionel, especially, would spend weeks at the estate playing with Willie and handling the oars on fishing trips of Joe and his companions.[21]

Joe's most regular fishing companion was Grover Cleveland, whom Jefferson had briefly met in Chicago in 1887. Their paths crossed again when mutual friend Richard Watson Gilder brought the Clevelands to his retreat at Sippicon Harbor. Jefferson and Cleveland discovered their mutual passion for fishing, and a fast friendship was born. Joe helped convince Cleveland to build his own retreat, Gray Gables, nearby. The two men and son Charley took daily excursions on the bay in search of bluefish. The physiognomic contrast of the beefy Cleveland and the slight Jefferson veiled a kindred temperament. They shared a belief in the essential rightness of their America. Moderate in their habits (though linked, paradoxically, by the haunting knowledge of imprudent affairs), congenial in their bearings, they understood how good it was to be part of well-heeled America. Cleveland's essential conservatism was rooted in a principled, though severely limited, grasp of the changing society he presided over. Joe, for all of his artistic gifts, had a similar tin ear for social issues. If, as historian Richard Hofstadter long ago observed, Grover Cleveland was "the ideal bourgeois statesman for his time," then Joseph Jefferson was the perfect bourgeois actor, whose rise to prominence, balanced by a modest, well-mannered offstage persona, embodied accepted canons of middle-class decorum. Further, Joe's well-publicized friendship with an American president served perhaps as the single greatest example of the heightened respectability of actors. The last time actor and president were linked was in April 1865; this later connection bespoke happier times for players.[22]

Although Cape Cod was as bucolic a setting as could be imagined, here struck one of the worst disasters of Jefferson's life. On April Fools' Day 1893, a container holding fuel for the house generator first overflowed, then exploded in the cellar. A catastrophic fire ensued, injuring several people and killing the family's longtime cook. Sarah Jefferson, bedfast from one of her many illnesses, was saved only by the efforts of her servants. Just two days before the tragedy Joe had finished installing his extensive art collection (fussing over the placement of each canvas) in the gallery he appended on the side of his house. He was in New York when he received a telegram about the fire. His art collection was gone, so far as he knew. He learned later of locals struggling to save a large but unworthy piano while a few steps away a Reynolds portrait of Mrs. Siddons languished. Gone, too, were paintings of his mother and father, a lifetime of collectibles, and a unique extra-illustrated edition of the *Autobiography*. It turned out that some treasures were preserved: his three most valuable paintings, a Mauve, Daubigny, and Corot, recently returned from a New York gallery, had been stacked near the front door and thus easily saved. Heartened by this news (though desperately under-insured), Jefferson immediately set out to acquire his second collection.[23]

Jefferson also determined to rebuild. More than on any of his earlier homes, he put his stamp squarely on the new Crow's Nest. It reflected the ponderous Richardsonian look so favored in New England during that time. The first story was veneered with large "rubble stone," the second floor by dark brick. A huge veranda ambled around the structure's rear, offering leisured views across the bay. The interior boasted the massive, ornate furniture still favored. It would soon fill with bric-a-brac Joe acquired from about the world, including a moose's head to adorn the upper hall, proof that Joe's generally good taste was not immune to the decorative clichés of the day.[24]

One Jefferson was no longer a part of the congenial web of extended family life. Eldest daughter Margaret, married to Benjamin Farjeon since 1877, returned to England after an initial visit to America and did not see her father again for twenty-five years. Why Joe made so little effort to see his adoring daughter remains a mystery. Of course trips across the Atlantic were not taken lightly, and he had his regular fall and spring tours. But something unsettling seems at work, an unnamed family tension. Did Sarah get along with a stepdaughter so near her own age? Did Joe approve of his old friend Farjeon as a son-in-law, especially as he proved increasingly unable to support a family? Farjeon's career as novelist took a severe nosedive in the 1880s, and with that decline came a personality change for the worse. Margaret and children had to behave carefully about an increasingly volatile man, and their financial straits were such that Joe regularly subsidized their living expenses. There may be unspoken meaning in Joe's sending for Margaret and his grandchildren only after Farjeon had died. A talented literary and theatrical family the younger Farjeons would prove to be, extending the Jefferson magic to England during the next century.[25]

The Costs of Stardom

There was no shortage of praise for Joe Jefferson in the final twenty years of his life, most of it apparently heartfelt, some of it no doubt obligatory. O. B. Stebbins suggested as much in an 1895 essay. "By common consent Mr. Jefferson is almost universally considered to be the best comedian now speaking the English language. . . . For fine, delicate treatment and keen insight of many of the characters of old English comedy he is unequaled and thoroughly charming. . . . But there has lately arisen a disposition in the gilt-edged classes of so-called 'society' people to deify him, to make him a 'fashionable celebrity' as they have Irving, Patti and Rehan, to consider him perfect and far removed from all other meaner actors so called, to invest him with the divine right of kings who could do no wrong, and finally to pay extravagant prices to see him." Stebbins respected Jefferson but wanted him off the pedestal. In truth, Joe's esteem within the profession and among the general public did not exempt him from criticism. Jefferson was a large target, and some found it impossible to resist a few pot shots. Nat Goodwin (1857–1919), actor, musical comedy performer, and amorous bon vivant, who toured with Jefferson's all-star *Rivals* production, broke with the unwritten code of gracious restraint toward fellow players in his iconoclastic memoirs (published well after Jefferson's death). Goodwin sought to unmask humbuggery and pretension, which he detected in the Jefferson camp. Clearly troubled by the abundant adulation that came Joe's way, Goodwin sought to provide a corrective by one "in the know." A satirical (sarcastic really) account of the all-star *Rivals* tour set up his larger critique: that Joe Jefferson, despite living in an age of substantial theatrical accomplishment, left an insubstantial artistic legacy.[26]

Occasionally critics suggested that Joe might be coasting on his reputation. A Chicago reviewer sternly judged in 1882 that Jefferson "has ceased to be an actor in his presentations," simply going through the motions and picking up his guarantee. Audiences, for their part, were doing much the same, laughing and applauding "the frame which once held the fine old picture and are not conscious their imaginations are filling in from memory the cherished canvas." If harsh, the critic's words no doubt captured a truth that on certain nights Joe may indeed have been acting more from memory than inspiration.[27]

Issues of versatility also arose. As early as 1872, Laura Keene publicly worried that "Jefferson's most brilliant gift, versatility, is lost, merged in one part." Joe's portrayal of Dickens's good-hearted Caleb Plummer in *Cricket on the Hearth* (which he returned to his repertoire in the 1880s and 1890s) was an audience pleaser. Still, some critics harrumphed that Caleb was little more than a warmed-over Rip and that Joe's characteristic mannerisms were transparent in the old toymaker. By the mid-1890s, with Joe clearly aging, a *New York Times* reviewer sadly concluded that "this Caleb was surely not the one we used to cry over and then laugh with before our tears were dry."[28]

Some remarks were clearly the fruit of unbridled ego. Dion Boucicault, whose reputation for self-serving bluster was well deserved, repeated in a book a favorite story of how he taught Joe to act the part of Rip. "I saw at once he had struck the wrong key," Boucicault tutted. "He mistook the character. He made it a weary, dreary, sentimental old bore. Rising from my managerial chair, I stopped the rehearsal." Privately to Winter, Joe claimed to be unbothered by Boucicault's boast. "The public have long since learned how heavily they must discount his assertions. . . . If I chose I would be revenged on him in my book." Joe wisely chose not to press the issue in his *Autobiography*, and the matter died. There was also the aforementioned grumbling among temperance advocates about Rip's irrevocably sottish ways. In the face of the play's redeeming themes, however, such remarks rarely rose to the level of censure.[29]

The professional trade paper, the *New York Dramatic Mirror*, occasionally faulted Joe for failing to maintain the expected standard of a star. It scolded his agent for finding it necessary to puff the day's richest player as a "money-maker" and a "money-winner." "Mr. Jefferson is too great an artist to be worked in that fashion." More seriously, an 1890 report by a Boston paper that Jefferson was indeed the wealthiest actor in the world prompted hard questions by "The Usher" on Joe's failure to return a fair share of his good fortune to his profession. Edwin Forrest established an actors' home; Edwin Booth founded The Players; Henry Irving boasted many benefactions. But Jefferson, their equal in repute and superior in wealth, The Usher noted, could if he chose do even more. "He can attest his love for his art and his desire to benefit the players of posterity in many a fitting way. The question is, does that love and does that desire exist?" This challenge, broadcast to his colleagues, must have stung. But Joe seems to have been slow to embrace the assumption lying behind these comments, to wit, that a leading actor ought to repay his success with public benefactions, an injunction reflecting how professionalization heightened obligations expected from stars. There is little indication that Jefferson ever caught a vision of a tangible philanthropic legacy he might leave his profession or the public. For a man who seemed preternaturally worried about being remembered after death and who possessed abundant artistic gifts, this was an odd deficiency.[30]

The question of what players owed their profession came insistently forward in early 1894, when the impact of the previous year's economic downturn had degraded into outright depression. An "army of unemployed actors" walked the streets of New York; touring companies on the road disbanded, stranding players far from home. Fiske's *New York Dramatic Mirror* championed a self-help effort, dunning still-employed actors and managers to contribute to a relief fund. Louis Aldrich, a premier tragedian of the time, chaired the Actors' Relief Committee, which doled out thousands of dollars to "proper and worthy cases." The *Dramatic Mirror* published names and contribution figures. But Jefferson's was nowhere on the list. He apparently had no notion that as the recently elected president of The Players, he might usefully be seen at the head of the donor list. Like Grover Cleveland, another decent man who presided over the national distress with blissful disregard, Joe's creed of individualism encouraged individualistic solutions.[31]

Yet such judgments threaten to efface both Joe's generosity and his earlier contributions to the profession. He was certainly generous toward fellow actors; his philanthropies are well documented in his correspondence and by the testimony of others. Most of these efforts were private and unheralded. He interceded on behalf of an elderly and indigent actress with Augustin Daly, head of the Actors' Fund, encouraging the fund to extend charity, and even donating his own funds anonymously for the lady's assistance. Throughout his life, Joe supported professional eleemosynary efforts. Before he was twenty he took part in the 1849 founding of the Actor's Order of Friendship, the first effort within the profession to forge fraternal bonds for actors' relief. Although he could not attend the 1882 organization of the Actors' Fund—a much more ambitious effort at collective self-help—Joe was on the original board of directors and made a contribution to the home that was planned for indigent players. And through the years, Joe was generally first in line to offer his services at the many benefit performances that littered the stages of the late nineteenth century. Veteran performer Charles Couldock, to name just one of many examples, profited from a benefit Joe organized at Wallack's Theatre in 1887.[32]

The greatest and most festive moment of professional altruism, the Actors' Fund Fair in May 1892, served to publicly display Jefferson's benevolence as well as his leadership within the profession. The fair was a weeklong grand theatrical spectacle, an architectural augury of Chicago's grand White City, which would open a year later. Madison Square Garden was transformed by Stanford White into an ornately colonnaded city (entered through a triumphal arch) containing scores of booths filled with exotica. Among the many eclectic structures stood a replica of the Globe Theatre, a shrine to drama's Zeus. The fair was also a triumph of organization on the part of theatre managers and players (or more properly, mangers' wives and actresses). They solicited a farrago of objects to be offered to the public, including a cobweb shirt reputed to have been Montezuma's and a pair of embroidered silk stockings worn by the Empress Josephine (looted, it was said, during the Revolution of 1830). The atmosphere was carnival, with barkers enticing patrons to sideshow attractions; concerts and circus and vaudeville acts; and plenty to eat and drink ("dusky maidens" dispensing "cool and innocuous liquid refreshments" from Rebecca's Well). Cash donations, sales, and auctions over the six days netted the spectacular sum of $163,000, an amount more than eightfold the Actors' Fund's previous year's budget for its various relief efforts.[33]

Jefferson supported the fair with a five-hundred-dollar donation (publicly announced, as were all gifts). But along with Edwin Booth he also lent his presence. The two men, titans of the American theatre, opened the festivities by together mounting the stairs into the box of honor. Booth, unwell and never comfortable with formal public speaking, left it to Joe to deliver the inaugural address. The occasion called for little more than ceremonial boilerplate, a need Joe met handsomely, concluding with timely verses of his own creation on Shakespeare.[34]

Certainly the most consistent chiding directed at Jefferson concerned his limited repertoire. Charles Mathews's and Laura Keene's were not the only voices to nettle Joe with the question: Why would such a great talent limit itself to a second-rate piece, no matter how lucrative? "Why has he not made artistic productions?" a newspaper critic asked very late in Jefferson's career, "Why has he stagnated for more than a quarter of a century; contributing nothing new to the contemporary stage; lending no encouragement to native dramatists; maintaining no high standards of acting in his companies?" In part, Jefferson confessed in later years, because he was fearful of failure in a new role. A faltering memory abetted his misgivings of taking on a fresh challenge. Moreover, Joe understood something fundamental about himself: he was not a risk taker, at least no more than necessary in an occupation inextricably tied to uncertainty. A large family, multiple homes and servants, supporting cast salaries: these all demanded regular income. Joe's view of himself was eminently practical, rooted in a childhood of financial insecurity. He had witnessed Edwin Booth's misbegotten journey on the high road of "art." His elegant theatre was the pride of the American dramatic world—and it bankrupted Booth. To Joe, theatre was a livelihood. Art, yes, but first and foremost a means of support. The calculus of the bottom line remained axiomatic.[35]

Thus, Joe quietly endured these admonishments. He even told a story on himself. Approaching the Pearly Gates, the joke ran, he asked St. Peter for admission. Peter complied, but implored: "For Heaven's sake, Joe, get a new play!" In truth, Jefferson continued to stage several plays in the final decades of his career. Besides *Rip Van Winkle,* he frequently presented *Lend Me Five Shillings, The Heir at Law, Cricket on the Hearth,* and especially, *The Rivals.*[36]

The Rivals

The Rivals, a part of Joe's repertoire since 1880, constituted an important legacy in itself. Joe felt compelled to undertake the play, according to William Winter, for several reasons. Criticisms for his lack of variety were already being heard, and in 1880, with Joe still in his prime, such voices could not be ignored. Joe wanted to "revive a just sense of the breadth of his scope as a comedian." A legacy, he realized, was at stake. Moreover, *Rip* had gotten tedious. He needed a new challenge.[37]

Richard Brinsley Sheridan's satiric comedy of manners filled the bill nicely. On one level *The Rivals* embodies the conventionalities of plot and characterization reaching back through Congreve to Ben Jonson. Yet its unlikely plot was actually rooted in Sheridan's flamboyant youth. The romantic comedy's setting in Bath mirrored his life and romance there. This first dramatic effort of a love-stricken but struggling twenty-three-year-old Sheridan met a distinctly cool reception when it was staged at Covent Garden in early 1775. Rambling, poorly acted, and confusing to many patrons, the play was pulled after one performance. Sheridan proved a good doctor to his own work, compressing it, toning down some characters, and removing the more offensive double entendres. Thus scrubbed, the play quickly entered the standard repertoire of Anglo-American comic theatre.[38]

Joe as Bob Acres. Used by permission of the
Don B. Wilmeth Collection.

The Rivals contains lively comic action that mocks traditional sentimental
drama and introduces in Mrs. Malaprop one of the memorable characters of
the stage. A comedy of romantic intrigue, innocent duplicity, and mistaken
identification, *The Rivals* bore all the marks of its breed. The byzantine plot
defies a quick synopsis. At its heart are a pair of troubled courtships. Captain
Absolute seeks the hand of Lydia Languish. Since she clings to the sentimental
twaddle of requiring an impoverished beau (to ensure "true love"), Absolute
must woo her in the contrived form of the modest Ensign Beverly. Further
complicating their conjoining is the determination of Lydia's aunt, Mrs. Malaprop, to disinherit her if she marries the low-born Beverly, not to mention the
conniving of Absolute's father and Malaprop to unite the Captain and Lydia.
A secondary plot concerns Faulkland's courtship of Lydia's cousin Julia, a
story line marked by Faulkland's sulking over Julia's insufficient distress during his absence. Bob Acres and Lucius O'Trigger add eccentric comedy. Acres
is a sort of country cousin friend of Absolute who thinks to win the heart of

Lydia; O'Trigger is an Irish Lothario (with his own designs on an imaginary Delia) who urges on the clueless Acres in his romantic efforts. The play ends with an averted duel between the cowardly Acres and the fictitious Beverly.

Jefferson had of course known the play much of his life; it was a staple of the comedy repertoire. His grandfather portrayed bumpkinish Bob Acres, as had Charlie Burke. In his youth, Joe had taken supporting roles in it, and through the 1850s it frequently appeared in his traveling repertoire. His Bob Acres entertained New York audiences at Laura Keene's Theatre in 1858. But he was not content with Sheridan's original product. *Rip Van Winkle* had required years of fine-tuning to become an acceptable vehicle. By Joe's own telling, *The Rivals* exacted similar years of reflection. "I would often think of him in the middle of the night. At odd times, when there was apparently no reason for him to call, he would pop up before me like an old acquaintance, — for I had acted him years before, — but always with a new expression on his face."[39]

The product of this meditation was the most severe refashioning of a theatrical classic his age had witnessed. Joe did so unabashedly. And he did so secure in the knowledge that the appropriation and emendation of existing dramatic material was a hoary tradition of the stage. (Joe enjoyed pointing out that Sheridan in another work had himself pilfered a Vanbrugh comedy.) Every dramatist was fair game. Indeed, no playwright suffered more well-intentioned intrusions into his text than Shakespeare. This was done not out of disrespect but from affection. Americans felt as comfortable and as free with his characters as with figures from native folklore. His tragedies were widely revised — speeches and scenes shortened or omitted, characters dropped — not so much to stress their melodramatic features or make them more comprehensible to unlettered audiences as to enhance the forcefulness of individual roles.[40]

The well-inked pen Jefferson took to Sheridan's classic produced something recognizable yet distinctly new. His primary goal, certainly, was to fashion a starring vehicle, and this he accomplished handsomely. *Rip Van Winkle* lent itself rather easily to this task, but refitting a classical comedy like *The Rivals* proved tricky. For one thing, Bob Acres was not the play's dominant character. Moreover, a successful production of comedy demanded a strong ensemble performance rather than the indifferent support that melodrama (and in truth, some tragedy) often presented. Late nineteenth-century audiences would have less patience with Sheridan's interwoven comic plots and extended dialogue. Thus, Joe abbreviated the five-act comedy into three, cut perhaps 15 to 20 percent of the dialogue, dropped entire scenes, rearranged others, and updated some language. Although he never published his redaction (Joe had a proprietorial interest in keeping the text to himself), a typescript of the promptbook survives. Comparing his version to Sheridan's gives insight into the creative working of Jefferson and suggests how comedic tastes changed from the eighteenth to the nineteenth century.[41]

Joe radically cut early scenes of act one, eliminating dialogue that had given explanatory background to the story. Gone too are most of Lydia's lines, an augury of her diminished role. Julia disappears completely. Conversely, her suitor Faulkland earns greater prominence through his comic exchanges with Acres. (A character's standing generally rose or fell depending on his ability to serve up fat lines to Acres.) Act two, which in Sheridan's rendering moves the complex love triangles forward, is in Jefferson's telling focused squarely on Acres, setting the stage for the duel. The third act accomplishes the obligatory romantic reconciliations. But again, not Lydia nor Captain Absolute but the bumbling antics of Bob Acres steal the scene. Not even the verse epilogue (which Jefferson composed out of whole cloth) escapes him.

Jefferson knew better than to downsize Mrs. Malaprop, the most famous character of *The Rivals*. Malaprop's mangled diction gave the play legs, the English language a new word, and herself dramatic "immorality." "Make no delusions to the past," she commanded. Her troublesome niece Lydia she considered "as headstrong as an allegory on the banks of the Nile." Captain Absolute she viewed as "the very pineapple of politeness." But not even Malaprop was a sacred cow to play doctor Joe. He tinkered with her lines, constructing howlers with a contemporary twist. Her original quip — "Then he's so well bred; so full of alacrity and adulation" — became in Joe's rendering, "Then he's so well bred, so full of poligamy [*sic*] and adulation," a line pandering to Americans' fascination with Mormonism.

Such topical humor characterized the burlesque sheen Joe placed on Sheridan. He broadened the humor, though he also made it less coarse by eliminating some double entendres. The changes were predictable given that he viewed the play as a vehicle for his low comedy. He added visual humor through the ridiculous paper curls in his hair (to add style to his coiffure) and extended tomfoolery in a scene with his servant David. Too, where *Rip Van Winkle* was cut from the folksy storytelling tradition of American letters, Jefferson's Bob Acres bespoke the faster paced, sharper (and often silly) verbal humor that characterized the burlesque and new variety stages. An example comes in Joe's modified version of the scene with Sir Lucius Trigger, where Acres's characteristic (and hollow) bluster is displayed while composing a challenge to a duel:

> ACRES: "Come, come, indict the challenge while I write — This ought to be written with red ink. Blood red ink. Now, how shall we begin — 'Damme' — "
> SIR LUCIUS: "No, no!"

ACRES: "Well, I'd like to frighten him a little."

SIR LUCIUS: "Now begin as I tell you — 'Sir' "

ACRES: " 'Sir,' no, that's too polite, entirely. 'Damme, Sir' "

SIR LUCIUS: "No, no, now as I tell you — plain 'Sir' "

ACRES: "That's better." (writing) " 'Plain Sir' "

SIR LUCIUS: " 'To prevent the confusion that might arise' " (Acres writes)

ACRES: (writing) "well — 'that might arise' "

SIR LUCIUS: " 'From our both addressing the same lady' "

ACRES: "That's it, that's it. Now let me give it to him."

SIR LUCIUS: "No, no"

ACRES: "Just one little damme right in there"

SIR LUCIUS: " 'I shall expect the honor of your company.' "

ACRES: (throws down in his pen in disgust) "I am not going to invite him to dinner."

One could imagine this banter between Dick and Tommy Smothers eighty years later. In fact, Jefferson and William Florence, who played O'Trigger during the early 1890s, did constitute one of the early stage comedy teams.

Jefferson's Bob Acres, bumptious in the manner of a Tony Lumpkin or other comic figures from the age of King George III, took on a brassier voice, redolent of an urban sensibility. And unlike traditional comedy, where a set of interlocking comic plots are finally resolved, Joe's version expressed the more compressed comedy that would characterize vaudeville sketches. It was a less patient humor, seeking quick laughs. The modern "Fighting Bob" surfaced in another exchange with O'Trigger, when Sir Lucius attempts to buck up Acres's courage before the aborted duel. He reminds him that "there's no going out to get shot at without a little risk," to which Acres retorts (in a line Jefferson contrived), "No, no! I know that — I can't mind a little risk — I don't care how little." One hears the tag line and immediately envisions Groucho's wagging eyebrows and flicking cigar. The series of "dammes," coming as they do from the Sunday School comedian may surprise, but they reveal Joe's openness to a grainier humor.[42]

Still, for all the low comic buffoonery of Acres, what struck some contemporaries was Joe's infusion of sympathy and gentility into the role. William Winter, predictably, marveled at how his friend took an essentially clownish role and made it "fine and sweet," evoking sympathy and affection. The less partial *New York Times* critic, in the initial 1881 review of Joe's new version, found Acres "humane, interesting, and droll." If Jefferson understood anything about comedy, it was that a fine balance of pathos and purposeful nonsense was a sure recipe for success. It was, indeed, his signature.[43]

However much they may have loved and admired Joe, certain actors and critics could not easily forgive his alterations. In some quarters of late nineteenth-century legitimate theatre, respect for dramatic literature was growing. Texts of Shakespeare and other revered dramatists were not to be altered. Not surprisingly, such opinions were particularly strong among Boston's guardians of culture. *The Opera Glass,* a Boston publication, found Joe's Bob Acres too alien to Sheridan's character for its taste. Even Joe's cousin, the estimable Boston Museum comedian William Warren, sarcastically remarked (borrowing a line from a popular contemporary poem about General Philip Sheridan) that Jefferson played Acres "with Sheridan twenty miles away."[44]

When Joe gave an address in 1897 to New York's American Academy of Dramatic Arts, the leading American acting school, a student slyly inquired if it was permissible for an actor to refashion a traditional role. Joe became neither defensive nor evasive at this obvious allusion to *The Rivals.* "I want to vindicate myself before you for the liberties I took," he retorted, and he proceeded, first with his favored story about Sheridan's similar efforts, and then with the rationale that classic pieces might be saved for contemporary audiences "by a little pruning." Before a distinguished assemblage of the National Academy of Arts and Letters he drew a finer distinction. His changes, he said, were not intended as cheap gags—by which he meant jokes and byplay foreign to the subject—but rather as "amplifications of a part." He claimed to add only such lines as "Sheridan would have put in if he thought of them." Utterly pragmatic, the test of dramatic literature for Joe lay not in its textual purity but in its ability to move an audience.[45]

Jefferson's reworked version of *The Rivals* premiered at Philadelphia's Arch Street Theatre in September 1880. Fittingly there, his ancestral home and the home theatre of Mrs. John Drew, who across the years would make Mrs. Malaprop perhaps her most famous role. Maurice Barrymore, progenitor (along with Georgiana Drew) of the illustrious Barrymore stage line, was Joe's original Captain Absolute. (He was "the best Captain Absolute—and the worst," Joe cryptically remarked.) Much of the fall and spring seasons were devoted to the play, and in succeeding years the comedy entered the Jefferson company repertoire alongside *Rip Van Winkle, Cricket on the Hearth, Heir at Law,* and a small collection of farces. The *New York Mirror,* distressed that "Jefferson has so long mouldered in the vagabondage of Rip," welcomed his "return to the old comedies." Stage Chronicler George C. D. Odell enthused that the 1888 production at the Fifth Avenue Theatre featured the "three finest comedians I ever saw together—Jefferson, Gilbert and Mrs. John Drew." The interaction between Gilbert and Mrs. Drew "were like lacework of delicacy and finish." Odell was referring to John Gilbert (1810–89), who from the age of nineteen specialized in older parts. Gilbert ("one of the most respected institutions in the life of Manhattan," Odell said of him) had just finished a storied thirty-year stint with Wallack's recently closed stock company, and had a new freedom, which allowed him to take on the role of Sir Anthony Absolute in Joe's company.[46]

The Rivals proved such a popular and lucrative play for Jefferson that in 1889 he allied with comedian William Florence to form a touring company devoted to its production. Billy Florence (1831–91) had enjoyed a forty-year comedy career that was only slightly less accomplished than Joe's. Frequently specializing in Irish and other eccentric comedy roles, he was adept at burlesque as well as legitimate comedy and melodrama. Florence was bigger than Jefferson, with a large, distinguished head. By every account, Billy Florence was among the most popular — and beloved — figures on the post–Civil War stage. Genial and gentlemanly, one whose success seemed never to threaten those a rung below, he negotiated a long career seemingly without a bad word against him.[47]

Joe shared the general regard for Florence based on decades of friendship and suspected that together they might form a potent comedy team. "He is a good fellow . . . and will be a pleasant companion," Joe confided to Winter. He was inspired, no doubt, by Edwin Booth's and Lawrence Barrett's highly successful partnership in 1888, which took Shakespearean tragedy around the country. One thing blocked a Jefferson-Florence union, however; Florence already had a partner. Like Joe, Florence married into the profession. But far more than Margaret Jefferson ever had, Malvina Florence became her husband's stage partner. Along with Mr. and Mrs. Barney Williams (Mrs. Williams was Malvina's sister), the Florences pioneered husband and wife stage duos, Irish farces for both the early variety and the legitimate stages. A devoted husband, Florence wrote plays for the two of them. Only in midlife, when his wife was prepared to step off the boards, did Florence seriously consider Joe's offer. He may have viewed it as a final venture before his retirement, an opportunity to earn enough in a few seasons to retire in style. Even so, hurdles remained. Florence was displeased with the terms Joe originally proposed. A star in his own right, Florence wanted more — and got it.[48]

Still, this was billed as the Jefferson-Florence company. No one questioned that Joe Jefferson was the headliner. Florence left all managerial decisions to Joe, limiting himself to developing the roles of Lucius O'Trigger and Zekiel Homespun (in *The Heir at Law*). He worked for the princely sum of $1,000 a week (at a time when laboring men might be fortunate to earn $30 per week) while Joe demanded large guarantees from local managers.[49]

The Jefferson-Florence company began rehearsals in September 1889 in preparation for a mid-October Broadway opening. Since assuming the mantle of stardom, Joe had never needed to accommodate another star on his stage. But the transition appeared smooth, eased no doubt by Florence's admirable lack of ego. The two maintained a cordial, bantering relationship. Offstage Florence effused over Joe's humor, plying his friend with compliments that pleased Joe no end. For his part, Joe recognized that he could not steal all the scenes. In the climactic duel scene, Joe had been used to milking his fear for all he could — shaking knees, tremulous voice, and so on — before sneaking off stage. He brought down the house even as he stepped all over Lucius O'Trigger's lines. But Joe held back for Florence's sake, the sort of small compromises necessary with a costar.[50]

Over the next three years, 1889–91, the Jefferson-Florence company toured without break from midfall until May (until March in the third season). This was not an unusually long season for most touring combination companies, but for Joe it marked a departure from his more leisurely practice of discrete fall and spring seasons divided by a long winter break. In the final season, the company traveled 27,000 miles. Indeed, after *The Rivals* tours ended, the sixty-two-year-old veteran would never again submit to such a pace. He did so now only because he recognized the lucrative prize in his clutch.[51]

The company visited forty cities the first year, most of them major urban centers — Philadelphia, Detroit, Chicago, Denver, New Orleans, Atlanta, among them — with secondary cities, such as New Bedford, Wilkes-Barre, and Chattanooga, interspersed. A finely calibrated estimation of audience and demand set the run. New York City earned three-week stands in the fall and spring; Chicago two weeks; a few others a single week; most stops were but for one or two nights. Only a vital rail system made such a schedule possible. A special railcar devoted to the company simplified travel plans. After a performance, the car would attach to the next train heading the proper direction while members retired to their compartment. Enforced familiarity during travel must have engendered group cohesiveness and a certain bonhomie. Joe was putting the final touches on his *Autobiography,* parts of which he read to the company. But frictions inevitably arose. Mrs. Drew left the company after the first year, unhappy with the accommodations. While the two stars had staterooms, the rest of the company slept in ordinary berths, "huddled in like so many sheep." (She returned for the third season.) Jefferson also considered the theatres where they would perform. If possible, he avoided the larger houses for *The Rivals,* believing that, more than *Rip Van Winkle,* its nuanced ensemble comedy required greater intimacy with the audience.[52]

His fame in *Rip Van Winkle* notwithstanding, *The Rivals* tours represented the artistic pinnacle of Jefferson's career. *The Rivals,* first of all, was simply a better play than *Rip Van Winkle,* and his emended version provided Acres better comic possibilities than had Rip. Joe also surrounded himself with an outstanding cast that lifted the play above the usual starring vehicle. An aura of refinement hung about the play; audiences could enjoy themselves even as they basked in the glow of "culture." *The Rivals* was "the greatest dramatic event of the season," exclaimed a correspondent from Topeka, a sentiment echoed frequently even in larger cities. The privilege of attending the "event" sometimes cost patrons double the normal ticket price. Dear prices lent a further cachet to the production, encouraging the crush that met the performers at most towns. Detroit residents greeted Jefferson and Florence with "the largest and finest audience ever assembled at any one time in any theatre in this city."[53]

The acclaim was not untempered by a few notes of criticism, particularly in the beginning, before Jefferson and Florence had hit their stride. Florence came in for some jibing. His O'Trigger was a more refined and subdued character than normally portrayed — perhaps an attempt to mirror Jefferson's less loutish Acres. Florence was the straight man of the duo, feeding lines to Joe. Even so, some critics found his performance lacking in fire and hoped he would "limber his legs and thaw out the frigidity of his mobile countenance." Oddly enough, given Florence's pedigree in Irish comedy, several critics complained that his brogue "would puzzle an Irishman." In contrast, Joe earned almost unanimous plaudits. Otis Skinner, one of the next generation's eminent tragedians and a keen observer of the theatrical art, admired the meticulous manner in which Jefferson constructed his role of Bob Acres: nothing left to chance, every line and effect measured for its comedic potential. In this, Skinner asserted, he was the best American embodiment of the technically precise French school of comedy.[54]

From the standpoint of more than a century later, it is difficult to plumb the chemistry between Florence, Jefferson, and their public that gave such staying power to *The Rivals* production. Even the third season showed no sign of a slacking demand. Part of the attraction must certainly have been the novelty of two prominent comedians sharing a stage. A sense that this was one of those theatrical "occasions" not to be missed seemed to hover about the tour, enticing patrons.[55]

The partnership came to an abrupt halt in mid-November 1891. What appeared to be a common cold on Florence's part turned to pneumonia. A trouper always, he forced himself to go on with a performance of *The Heir at Law* and a testimonial dinner thereafter. Florence, bedfast at Philadelphia's Continental Hotel, was left behind as the tour (with Louis James, a prominent comedian and more than adequate substitute O'Trigger) made its westward swing. The sanguine Jefferson predicted Florence would rejoin the company soon. But it would not be. In six days Florence was dead. The theatrical profession turned out en masse for his memorial service in New York (reported in great detail by the *Dramatic Mirror*). But Jefferson did not attend. The man who went on with the show during the birth of his children and after a disastrous house fire was not one to close down his tour and return to New York for his friend's funeral. Not that he was untouched by the sudden loss. When the news reached him in Detroit, he was clearly shaken and canceled that night's performance.[56]

The success of the Jefferson-Florence *Rivals* tours, of course, depended on more than the two stars. The comedy demanded careful casting, and Jefferson obliged, but not to the exclusion of family members. For eight seasons son Thomas had creditably played the minor role of Fag. With him and older brother Charles now serving as business managers for the tour (Joe most trusted his own sons with the money), younger brother Joseph Warren Jefferson became (as the *Times* phrased it) "an acceptable Fag." Beyond family, the various cast members who supported Jefferson in *The Rivals* (both before, after, and during the Florence partnership) constituted a veritable who's who of the stage. Many of these were in the early stages of their career, such as Otis Skinner, Maurice Barrymore, Elsie Leslie (who actually was returning to the stage as a young woman after a notable career as child star), and Viola Allen (1867–1948), a nineteen-year-old, dark-haired beauty. Already a trouper with several years' experience, she would follow her *Rivals* stint with a prolonged stay with Charles Frohman's notable Empire Theatre stock company and later as a Shakespearean leading lady in the early twentieth century.

Other cast members were already veterans. Charles Couldock, in his mid-seventies, bucked himself up for the rigors of touring. The most notable veteran, of course, was Mrs. John Drew (1820–97), now approaching the end of her illustrious career. Among the many English-born players who made their careers in America, Louisa Lane Drew (John Drew, an Irish comedian, was her third husband) became a venerated comedienne and theatre manager. Closely identified with Philadelphia's Arch Street Theatre, which she managed for thirty-one years, she made her company synonymous with stock company excellence. Plain spoken and lacking pretension, Mrs. Drew had an eye for developing talent and earned a reputation as one of the century's most accomplished stage directors. She was not a beauty, but her formidable appearance lent a commanding stage presence.[57]

Drew understood the need for a chain of command in the theatre. A company member recalled her requesting permission of Joe to add some bit of stage business to her scene. She acted it "with infinite art and charm" to an admiring Jefferson, who readily assented. How could he refuse, Jefferson recalled later, "after the liberties I had myself taken with the comedy." The significance of Drew's Mrs. Malaprop for the success of *The Rivals* tour can hardly be overstated. The imperious dowager whose diction did not match her dignity provided the best running gag in the history of stage comedy. Drew played her superbly.[58]

Seeking an Angle of Repose

When *The Rivals* company wound up its six-month tour in late March 1892, Jefferson rang down a final curtain on marathon touring. He was sixty-three years old, wealthy, and possessing a host of interests he might indulge in his leisure. For the remaining twelve years of his career Joe restricted himself to roughly two months of touring in the fall (usually mid-October into December) and one month in the spring. He took pains to care for his health, even transporting a padded, portable dressing room with him on tour to combat drafts. After three years of staging *The Rivals* almost exclusively, he felt he had succeeded in showing his critics that he could play "with finish and effect" roles other than Rip. To Rip he now returned, predicting that he would play nothing else for the rest of his career. In fact, the improvident Dutchman, supplemented by *Cricket on the Hearth,* the farce *Lend Me Five Shillings,* and occasional revivals of *The Rivals,* constituted his bill of fare thereafter. Joe no longer had anything to prove; the public expected — indeed desired — nothing apart from these chestnuts. "The public's old friend was welcome with affectionate enthusiasm," noted the *Dramatic Mirror* when Joe restored *Rip Van Winkle* to the Star Theatre stage in fall 1892, "the house was crowded and Rip evoked laughter and tears through the magic of Jefferson's art." *Rip* continued to attract New York patrons despite a "French invasion" that fall. "We are deluged with kickers and wrigglers, with mummers and caricaturists, with duettists and *chanteuses* of every description, and New York is catching its breath after the first shock of this novel invasion." Fads of popular entertainment were nothing new, and the "vivacious apostles of folly," as the *Dramatic Mirror* characterized them, soon ran their course.[59]

The greatest cultural event of the 1890s, Chicago's Columbian Exposition of 1893, attracted nearly every individual of note in the country. But Joe did not attend. How did he miss the excitement? Perhaps for lack of interest but certainly from personal trials. At the beginning of April his house burned. He anticipated a summer of rebuilding, but supervision of this project was delayed when at the end of his spring tour he became ill in Cincinnati. At first it appeared no worse than dyspepsia. He canceled his last performance and headed for New York, seemingly fit. But an attack of severe gastritis felled him again. More ominously, a swelling of his neck was feared related to a lump recently removed from his nose. The specter of cancer hovered. Joe's wife (herself recovering from pneumonia and the shock of the fire) hurried down from Massachusetts to be with him. Not until the end of June was he able to head back to Buzzards Bay, to their temporary cottage on the estate, via steamboat and private railcar.[60]

But the irrepressible Jefferson bounced back with a summer's rest. His life had always been an odd mixture of chronic illness and resiliency. The early bout with TB and loss of a lung compromised his constitution but failed to enfeeble his resolve. As with the great female religious leaders of his time, Mary Baker Eddy and Ellen G. White, nagging ill health seemed to call forth compensatory reservoirs of energy. Joe, at age sixty-four, had eleven years of touring ahead of him.

Such was not the case with his bosom friend Edwin Booth. His two years of deteriorating health and suffering came to an end on 7 June 1893 in his bedroom at his beloved Players. Jefferson, also laid low in New York just then, must have wondered if America's two leading actors, each a child of theatrical itinerants, whose acquaintance reached back to their early years and who just months earlier had ascended the grand staircase arm in arm at the Actors' Fund Fair, would both take their final bow that summer.

After Booth's death. Joe took his place as dean of the American theatre. That position was further ratified when Jefferson, along with Henry Irving and Tomasso Salvini, the commanding figures of the American, British, and Continental stages, respectively, spoke at Booth's memorial held in Madison Square Garden in November.[61]

Popular acclaim was Jefferson's constant companion during his final decade: he had transcended stardom and become an icon, a Mount Rushmore of the stage. The crowds — and income — came perhaps too easily. The actor formerly so careful about stage details lapsed into apathy toward his production. The shabby scenery of *Rip Van Winkle,* the *Dramatic Mirror* critic scolded in the fall of 1893, "might have been bought at a sheriff's sale of the contents of a jaytown 'opera house.'" Joe no longer held his supporting casts to the sharp standard he had demanded earlier.

If the career of a great performer was winding down — obligatory praise and gushing box office receipts befogging a creeping artistic mediocrity — he nonetheless had one more trick up his sleeve. In 1896 Joe assembled an all-star *Rivals* tour. With as sure a sense of public taste as P. T. Barnum, Jefferson blended the blandishments of culture with the celebrity appeal of a bevy of stage stars.

The idea sprang from a benefit performance of *The Rivals* Jefferson organized for Charles Couldock in spring 1895. Encouraged by son Charley and a fellow producer, Joe determined to gather many of *The Rivals* cast together for a short one-month tour. It was, without question, an all-star cast. Mrs. Drew, of course, returned as Malaprop. William H. Crane, who in the previous five years had won acclaim portraying a comically arriviste western statesman in *The Senator,* played Sir Anthony Absolute. Nat Goodwin, just coming into his own as a premier comedian, brought to the role of Lucius O'Trigger his seemingly effortless gift of broad comedy. The husband and wife team of Robert Taber and Julia Marlowe took the roles of Captain Absolute and Lydia Languish, respectively. Taber was a leading man whose star would soon fade, but Marlowe (1866–1950), a dark-eyed beauty, had established herself as the leading American Shakespearean actress of her day. Her joining with — and eventual second marriage to — Edward H. Sothern ("Lord Dundreary's" son) would form the greatest Shakespearean acting team our nation has produced.[62]

Another cast member, Francis Wilson (1854–1935), not only took up the role of Acres's insolent servant David but went on to become Jefferson's Boswell. Wilson, like Jefferson from Philadelphia, had carved out a place for himself as comedian and singer in operettas and legitimate comedies. Wilson's greatest hit came in 1909 when he both wrote and starred in *The Bachelor's Baby* (which anticipated a favored Hollywood plot of awkward men confronting the care of a child). Wilson was both an activist and something of an intellectual. In the late 1890s he fought a bitter (and losing) battle with the Theatrical Syndicate over the right of independent actor-managers to book their own tours. In the early twentieth century he became a moving force behind the formation of Actors' Equity, served as its first president, and used his considerable rhetorical skills to energize the first actors' strike in 1919. But the private Wilson was also an avid book collector and author. He penned several works on actors, including a memoir of his friendship with Joseph Jefferson.[63]

As an aspiring comedian, Wilson held Jefferson in distant, worshipful awe, a veneration he never lost even as the two became intimate friends. They met in 1889 when Joe and his *Rivals* cohorts came to see Wilson perform while they were in Boston. Jefferson sensed a kindred spirit in Wilson; they shared a love of collecting and an appreciation for the history and traditions of the stage. In late life, during the 1920s, Wilson would portray both Bob Acres and Rip Van Winkle in special Players and Equity productions, final tributes to the departed comedian. For his part, Jefferson advanced Wilson's name as a director of The Players. And when casting the all-star *Rivals,* Joe immediately sought him out.[64]

Wilson approached *The Rivals* tour with an idea. Populated by one of the finest collections of talent ever assembled on one stage, presided over by the greatest comedian America had produced, the tour promised to be a theatrical event of the first order. During rehearsals and offhand moments he took copious notes of the banterings—especially of Joe's remarks—and then wrote them up. Would Jefferson be willing to allow him to record for posterity the inner history of the tour? He submitted his journal to Joe, who raised no objections (seeing the project perhaps as a kind of appendix to his *Autobiography*) save one: careful as always to preserve his reputation for personal amicability, he did not want any remarks remotely critical of fellow actors to be published. Less seriously, Joe warned Wilson that the tone of the account set Wilson "in the light of a hero-worshipper, and me on a theatrical throne chair with an assumed air of modesty, but slyly acquiescing in the praise." Recognizing this was not exactly the persona he wished to cultivate, Joe nonetheless allowed Wilson to proceed.[65]

Jefferson played an abbreviated spring season in April in order to prepare for the all-star *Rivals* premiere on 4 May 1896. The cast gathered in a Springfield, Massachusetts, hotel the day before for a run-through. So casual an approach to a production so highly ballyhooed may seem remarkable, even irresponsible. How could anything approaching ensemble acting be accomplished in a day's rehearsal? Perhaps it harkened back to a tradition of performance where all players were assumed to have ready command of the standard literature. Rehearsal was primarily a matter of coordinating stage movements. Like all-star baseball games, the unspoken expectation seemed to be in part that the stage's best talent need little preparation to play together and in part that the tour was really a kind of exhibition, about which some looseness should be expected, even excused—which is not to suggest a lack of anxiety on the part of all involved. As Joe conducted the rehearsal (with Mrs. Drew's help) there was palpable nervousness all around, confessed even by Jefferson. To falter before a jury of one's distinguished peers was an unnerving thought.[66]

That the tour opened in Springfield rather than a major urban center suggests that Joe understood the desirability of working out the bugs in the provinces. From Springfield the procession wound about New England to New York and Brooklyn, down to Washington, then out to the Midwest before circling back to upstate New York, New England again, and ending with a second engagement in New York. Twenty-six cities in twenty-seven days; one performance a day, except where geography allowed a matinee and evening performance (e.g., Syracuse and Utica). Joe leased a trio of railroad cars to convey the accomplished assemblage, their baggage, and stage scenery. The stars each had a stateroom in a Pullman; understudies and support staff occupied another car. It was a summer tour—unusual for the age—so Joe took particular care to provide fans and cold treats for the dressing rooms. There

All-Star Rivals cast. Courtesy of Michael A. Morrison Collection.

was, by all accounts, an exuberant camaraderie among the cast during the travel and backstage after a performance. As always, it was a family affair. For so important a tour, Joe brought along four adult sons, Charley, Tom, Joe Jr., and Willie, to share the moment.[67]

The all-star *Rivals* tour was an event, a happening, a prefigurement of the blockbuster complex that would later become so much a part of the American musical and museum landscape. In Washington, both a current and future president (Cleveland and McKinley) attended — likely a unique event in American theatrical history. Ticket scalpers were out in force despite theatre managers' efforts to thwart them. The crush for tickets in St. Louis required a special matinee; the performance was such a fashion event that "full dress prevailed even in the gallery." Public interest translated into gold at the box office, especially with ticket prices jacked up to $3.50 ($5.00 in New York). Overall profits can only be guessed (partly because the only statement regarding financial arrangements comes from the unreliable Nat Goodwin), but best estimates put average gross at $7,000 per performance. Half of this was divided among the company, with Joe taking half of that amount, a share for the short season of roughly $50,000 (easily over a million dollars in twenty-first-century valuation). The proceeds were good for everyone. Julia Marlowe and Robert Taber earned a summer's vacation in Florence through their efforts.[68]

But like many films featuring stellar casts, *The Rivals* production showed that a clutch of headliners do not always memorable theatre make. Even amidst the hype, more dispassionate critics bravely noted artistic flaws. Though most individuals earned plaudits, the overall result, noted the usually upbeat *Dramatic Mirror,* was "incongruous and unsatisfying. The ripe method of Mrs. Drew glaringly contrasted with Mr. Crane's modern sense of art. The finesse and equipoise of Joseph Jefferson were jarringly offset by the grotesquery of Francis Wilson." Another observer judged that "from any point of view of art it was negligible." Nat Goodwin's O'Trigger suffered especial censure. He was "amazingly and intricately bad," wrote one witness; another thought his Irish brogue "hard and forced." Those close to the production recognized that Goodwin labored under a unique difficulty. In his scenes with the comic, Joe would ad lib, step all over Goodwin's lines, or change his stage business without warning. Goodwin was left gasping for his lines. Joe later apologetically recognized what he was doing — but did not stop. Goodwin had his revenge in his famously embroidered memoirs published well after Joe's death. By his account the all-stars tour was little more than commercial opportunism on a grand scale, with a rush to the train car by Joe and his sons after each performance to count receipts and divide the plunder. In truth, there was a bit of stylistic generational disjunction within the cast. Joe and Mrs. Drew, in the grand tradition of theatre, took full advantage of their position as the comedy's two leading characters to return to the stage after an exit to take repeated bows, leaving the other actors frozen in their tracks. Too, as Julia Marlowe complained, despite the presence of electric stage lighting, Jefferson and Drew would move their chairs directly down to the footlights for their conversations, as if the dim candles of former decades were still in place. Younger performers found these ancient customs detracted from the group effort. Joe would agree with them in principle; he publicly exhorted actors to avoid destroying the stage illusion they work so hard to create. But this was his show. And at this point in his career, Joe had little interest in unlearning old tricks[69]

The Uses of Stardom

In 1895 a large gathering of luminaries of the American theatre feted Joe at New York's Garden Theatre. The climax of the evening came when a huge loving cup was presented, inscribed, "The Dean of the Dramatic Profession."[70]

What did it mean to say that Joseph Jefferson was the acknowledged "dean" of the American stage? That he was a master of the comic arts? That he drew the largest audiences? That he commanded the highest ticket prices? That he was universally respected within and without the profession? Certainly all the above. But he also became the unofficial spokesman for the theatrical profession. It was a duty that Edwin Booth, painfully shy as a public speaker, could never undertake. As with so many other roles in Jefferson's life, this one seemed to come easily to him. He was well spoken. He gave an impression of frankness. He was willing to comment on many subjects, and if he punted on some questions, he did so with disarming charm. Newspapers and magazines from the late nineteenth century are filled with interviews with the renowned actor. Jefferson encouraged his publicity agent, Jerome Eddy, to ply newspapers with accounts of his activities. This was, after all, celebrity culture in the making, and Joe was prepared to accept its blandishments for his benefit.[71]

That actors ought to comment on current affairs or be involved in social or political efforts was not a belief of long standing. British players, imprinted by several centuries of licensing laws and stage censorship, instinctively avoided controversies. In America, the impetuous Edwin Forrest had trumpeted his preferences for Jacksonian Democracy in antebellum days. Still, as late as 1880 the *New York Mirror* admitted that "it is one of the unwritten laws of the profession that actors shall take no part in political movements and display no partisanship on or off the stage." Such prominent theatrical producers as Charles Frohman or Augustin Daly discouraged their stars from weighing in on controversial issues, worrying that there was indeed such a thing as bad publicity. Unsurprisingly, given that they were models of female independence, the most widespread political involvement came from actresses, such as Olive Logan, Julia Marlowe, Minnie Maddern Fiske, and Lillian Russell, who championed women's suffrage. Among men, the most vigorous theatrical reformer was actor-playwright James A. Herne. He embraced Henry George's Single Tax reform, believing that it offered a panacea for the economic ills

The "Dean of the Profession." Used
by permission of the Billy Rose
Theatre Division, The New York
Public Library for the Performing
Arts, Astor, Lenox and Tilden
Foundations.

afflicting some of his profession. But actors were no potential fifth column.
With few exceptions they reflected the staid, even smug opinions of comfortable society. As the *Mirror* reminded actors, they had a "property interest . . .
in good government and prosperity." Joe Jefferson fit the general mold of
political quietism. He was adamantly nonpolitical, apparently never having
voted until his friend Grover Cleveland stood for re-election. But he supported
a few carefully chosen causes, such as the incipient kindergarten movement.[72]

Joe found a more professional interest in children — and a more overtly
political one — in the issue of child actors, more precisely, the efforts by the
theatrical leaders to moderate new legislation regulating the use of child actors. The relatively unfettered use of juveniles on stage by parents or guardians

(witness Joe's own upbringing) was challenged in the mid-1870s by an emerging sensibility of concern for children's well-being. A crusade — a term hardly too strong to characterize its intensity — to save New York's exploited children was headed by the eccentric Elbridge Gerry, whose New York Society for the Prevention of Cruelty to Children became a thorn in the side of theatrical producers who sought to cast children's roles. Led (as always) by Fiske's *New York Dramatic Mirror,* the theatre began a legislative and public relations campaign in the early 1890s to roll back some of the more restrictive measures. Joe Jefferson, whose celebrated *Autobiography* cast a mellow glow over a childhood in the theatre and whose starring vehicle required children, could hardly sit out this campaign. In 1893 he was elected president of an ad hoc body to lobby the Albany legislature to allow children to sing and dance on stage. His appearance before the solons was pure Jeffersoniana. His address, widely covered by newspapers, attacked the notion that the stage was unhealthy for children.[73]

If Joe approached the issue of child actors untaxed by ambivalence, such was not the case regarding one of the most emotional issues vexing the theatre of the 1890s: the specter of monopoly. In retrospect, the theatre's march toward centralization seems as inexorable as it did in other fields. Such technologies as railroads and the telegraph allowed national touring companies to dominate the theatrical landscape. In the early years of the 1870s, theatre managers or their agents would descend on Union Square to arrange with touring companies to visit their theatre the following season. This was a chaotic approach, compounded by the uncivil practice of some companies to book several theatres for the same week and then stiff the least lucrative. Predictably, theatre managers began to band together to organize circuits. In the 1880s an ever-more-efficient system of centralized booking offices centered in New York brought rationality to the national theatre. But as in so many fields, the temptation to take the final step toward complete control was great. In 1896 a group of six men pooled their considerable resources in an overt attempt to monopolize theatrical bookings. They controlled most of the first-class theatres in major cities, and if a star wished to appear in a particular city, he or she had to appear *only* in syndicate houses. Its hegemony was quickly won and thoroughly exercised, not breached until the Shuberts attained counterveiling power by 1910.[74]

In an age filled with ominous journalistic images of monopolies and trusts in oil, steel, tobacco, sugar, and many other commodities, reactions to the Theatrical Syndicate's attempts to dominate national bookings carried a high valence of meaning. "A hateful, corrupt and dangerous institution," Fiske's *Dramatic Mirror* sputtered, a "Shylock combination." Most everyone, even the syndicate's opponents, conceded the need for centralized booking and allowed that the syndicate was fair in its prices and fostered prosperity all around. Inevitably, though, some strong-minded and independent stars resented having choice removed. There was also an undercurrent of Luddite resentment that "art" was being sullied by commercialism. Consequently, such notable figures as Mrs. Fiske, Richard Mansfield, Nat Goodwin, James O'Neill—and especially Francis Wilson—stubbornly fought to retain the right to book their own companies. One by one they fell, the syndicate's pocketbook and powers of coercion being too great. Francis Wilson nearly lost his career (he would subsequently have his revenge as the prime organizer of Actors' Equity) before coming to terms. Only the intrepid champion of Ibsen, Minnie Maddern Fiske, held out, buoyed by the support of her husband's paper.

Where did Jefferson stand amidst all the contention? Squarely astraddle the fence. He suffered unusual complications. For one thing, a prime mover in the syndicate, Abraham Erlanger, had been Joe's well-remunerated business manager for five years. That Jefferson could work with someone so imperious and abrasive as Erlanger testifies to his willingness to overlook such traits in one so useful. Also, son Charley was for many years a partner of Erlanger and Marc Klaw. Add to this his naturally conciliatory nature, a desire to avoid a controversial legacy toward the close of his career, and one would predict a tempered reaction.[75]

In fact, that was exactly Joe's response. He failed to join the young Actors' Society of America in its bid to combat the trust, and he refused to join its nativist efforts to restrict English players from American stages (he recalled from whence his grandfather had hailed). But his efforts at temporizing were undercut by demands of activists that he make a stand. Jefferson was "cradled in the theatre," Actors' Society leader James A. Herne publicly stated, "the theatre made him famous. The actors loved and honored him. I can well wish he had espoused their cause." Joe finally did. In a March 1897 telegram to the editor of the *New York Herald* he went on record opposing the syndicate. It was a resolutely fair-minded epistle. He acknowledged the abuses of "double dealing" by some troupes, which centralized booking resolved. Even so, the power of the combine could "crowd some of the companies off of the entire list of houses by refusing their terms." Joe went on to establish his bona fides with fellow actors by relating how he turned down the offer of a syndicate manager out of loyalty to an antisyndicate manager who begged Joe not to desert him. He closed his letter to the profession by protesting that he no longer kept close tabs on movements in the theatre, that he was "conservative and old-fashioned," and that his opinion may be "of little value." Nonetheless, he concluded, because of the syndicate's ability to "dictate" its terms to actors and managers, "I do not approve of it."[76]

As far as possible, Jefferson determined not to let these complicating tensions of late century, by-products of a rapidly changing theatrical business, intrude on the serenity of his final years. The theatre he had known — though never a simple institution — proceeded along less formal and complex business lines. Just as he felt no compulsion to bow to contemporary definitions of realism, he felt no need to fret over the evolving economics of the stage.

More enjoyable to Joe, certainly, than embroilment in rankling issues was his second career as public speaker. It would seem an easy, even obvious, step to move from the stage to the lectern, and yet few actors had actually accomplished it. Fanny Kemble and James Murdoch most notably did so, though they were more properly readers of Shakespeare and other literary texts than lecturers. Jefferson may have first been attracted to the podium from his experience of giving hundreds of brief curtain speeches at the conclusion of his plays. These were set pieces, rarely varying in intonation or gesture, expressing humility, gratitude, and delight for the chance to appear before his audience. Stardom brought multiplying invitations to speak to different types of groups. His formal lecturing began in the early 1880s, but it was only after he finished his intensive *Rivals* tours in 1892 that he assumed a more ambitious lecture schedule. His celebrated *Autobiography* had by that point nurtured a broad public interest in his life, adding to his appeal. He hardly needed the money; indeed, there is no record of his ever charging for a lecture.[77]

Joe, attired in dandyish finery, appeared at fund raising events, such as the Kindergarten Association or Actors' Fund. More typically he spoke at dinners or before various clubs and organizations, such as the Contemporary Club of Bridgeport, or the Buffalo Women's Union, or the Arena Club of New Orleans, or the opening of a new theatre in Portland, Maine (named in his honor), or a Lake Chautauqua assembly (the largest gathering he ever appeared before), or the Massachusetts state prison. He lectured about the stage exclusively. Never one to "wing it," Joe compiled a standard set of anecdotes, observations, and theatrical topics that he drew upon in various combinations for all of his lectures. His popularity as a lecturer no doubt resided in his understanding that audiences much prefer stories with a point than abstract theorizing. He developed lectures on "Starring," "The Drama," and "The Art of Acting." He frequently commented on the Bard and was willing to jump into the fray with good-natured skepticism toward the then-fashionable theory that Francis Bacon rather than Shakespeare authored the great Elizabethan dramas. Joe even penned a satiric poem in rhymed couplet on this literary cause célèbre, which he recited on occasion. The most anticipated feature of his lectures came at the end when he solicited questions. He was not above priming the interrogatory pump by having lecture organizers plant some questioners among the audience.[78]

Joe gave memorable lectures to student groups. He enjoyed a reputation of something of an intellectual among players and thus was invited to give several talks at Yale, and he also spoke at Harvard, the University of Pennsylvania, Johns Hopkins, Princeton, Brown, and the University of Chicago, among other institutions. These occasions were so entertaining because students mixed their adoration of Joe with youthful irreverence. Yale's students formed a particular bond with Joe, but that did not preclude tweaking their hero with some pedantry. One young scholar asked Joe to compare the modern drama with that of Aeschylus. Jefferson outwitted the clever undergraduate, protesting (unconvincingly) that he had never heard of the Greek playwright and thus avoided being drawn into a technical discussion. He also administered a gentle spanking by criticizing the undergraduate penchant for performing burlesques and farces rather than more substantial dramas. At New York's American Academy of Dramatic Arts, the leading acting school of the day, Joe faced close scrutiny since word of his skepticism about the usefulness of acting schools had preceded him. Joe displayed proper deference to the school's purposes, though that did not prevent one tyro from making a pointed allusion to his surgery on Sheridan's *The Rivals*. He handled such moments with aplomb. Still, the first time he spoke at Yale, Joe was visibly nervous. The academic setting, a reminder of his nearly complete lack of formal education, may have compounded the anxiety. If so, it must have been especially gratifying when during the 1890s both Yale and Harvard bestowed honorary degrees on him.[79]

Given Jefferson's distant relations with American clergy, he unsurprisingly said little about religion on the lecture circuit. But religion (or rather religious prejudice) intruded at a Lotos Club dinner in 1896, where three hundred members honored Joe with the sort of decadent, multicourse dinner (striped bass, filet of beef, oysters, roast squab) peculiar to male culture of the age. During the testimonials, a local clergyman, attempting ill-considered flattery, complimented Joe for keeping himself unsullied from the temptations of stage life. Joe's normally congenial demeanor darkened a bit as he rose afterward and pointedly objected to being singled out among his colleagues as "respectable." A tribute that reproached his friends must be declined.[80]

On a few occasions, such as before the National Institute of Arts and Letters in 1901, in some interviews, and in his *Autobiography*, Jefferson spoke of his theory of acting. He would have been uncomfortable with a word as lofty as "theory"; he was simply expressing distilled experience. He generally focused on two things: the requisite qualities for an aspiring actor and principles of effective performance. Regarding the first, he acknowledged that aspiring actors must possess several gifts, which he listed as "sensibility," "imagination," "industry," and "personal magnetism." Joe was not given to encouraging stage aspirants who lacked these essential ingredients. On the second, Joe struggled to convey his disquiet with modern realism. Less is more on the stage, he believed. Avoid overelaboration of scenery, costume, or acting. One of Jefferson's few iron rules of the stage was that no one distract the audience's attention away from the one speaking. "The eye is a great tyrant," Joe loved to say, appreciating that audiences would track trivial activities while neglecting the plot's advance. Joe (speaking now to players) reminded them that they not only acted a role, but they must reproduce it nightly. Speak one's lines and listen to others speaking theirs as if for the first time. Keep the play fresh, in other words. Actors have accepted the public's money and asked for two hours of their time. They must ensure a fair return on that exchange. This means they must neglect no one in the theatre, extending gesture and voice "with unerring aim [to] the boy in the gallery and the statesman in the stalls."[81]

Joe's admonishments did not constitute a lament. Unlike many of his colleagues who bewailed the irretrievable "palmy days" of yore, Joe trumpeted his faith in the current theatre as the finest in America's history. He was very much a nineteenth-century Whig, convinced that progress was the hallmark of the age. The stage "has not been idle . . . in the march of improvement," Jefferson exhorted, "but has kept pace foot by foot with every social advance." A prophet of progress, Joe accepted the proposition that his was a great age in which to live.[82]

Winding Down

The calendar marched inexorably toward a new century. The 1900s would mark the eighth decade in which Joe had performed. Despite increasing newspaper speculations about each season being his last, Joe kept plugging away spring season after fall season, artfully dodging questions about retirement plans. His jesting about premature reports of his impending retirement masked a deeper resentment and hurt that he felt. He wished to "die in harness." Consequently, he showed ambivalence toward the farewell engagements actors conventionally used to draw some last standing room crowds. As early as 1898 his press releases for an upcoming stand at the Fifth Avenue Theatre announced his "farewell to the stage," but on other occasions Joe stopped managers from making such claims. A serious illness in fall 1898, which cut short his Fifth Avenue Theatre appearance and cost the Jefferson family thousands (Joe rented the theatre and assumed all the risks), naturally engendered more talk of a career's end.[83]

It was hard to retire, even for someone whose beloved hobbies could usefully occupy him. The money was too good. And Joe, for all his parsimony, had mounting expenses. Two estates and many children, who though mostly grown appear to have been largely supported (Charley and perhaps Tom excepted) by their father. Daughter Josie, partially crippled, needed perpetual care. He regularly sent money to Margaret in England and frequently to his Australian progeny. The family socialism described by Jefferson required the semiannual tours so that when his boys got "cramped for money" he could refill the coffers — "and there we are, a happy family again." Nonetheless, something more fundamental to his nature than money kept him on stage. He confided to a young acolyte that he was genuinely refreshed from an evening on the stage, that a week without performing left a void. Joe Jefferson continued to act because, like Bob Hope, that was what he did.[84]

He made some concessions to his age. His fall touring seasons fell from ten to seven weeks by the early 1900s. Before evening performances he took long naps to rest himself and took a nip to calm his nerves. Nonetheless, bouts of illness slowed him down, occasionally interrupting a tour. Further, by the mid-1890s deafness was taking its toll (his "deafness was improving," Joe joked). He had to look for visual cues during a performance because he could scarcely hear other actors, a trick rendered rather simple by his intimate knowledge of his plays.[85]

Even more than earlier, the tours of his final years were family affairs, as if Joe was recreating the Jefferson-MacKenzie troupe of his youth. His wife, sister Connie (until her death in 1899), and three of his sons frequently accompanied him on the abbreviated itinerancies. At times as many as four family members supported him in the cast. An easygoing atmosphere surrounded these final tours. Joe knew his part so well that he bothered with only superficial rehearsals with his company before each season. His boys, high spirited by all accounts, ran a loose ship. Young Joe, for example, typically gave cursory instructions to the actors picked up locally to play the dwarfs in the mountain scene, which in one case resulted in an inadvertent speaking part for one of the mute, ghostly crew.[86]

He last played Broadway in spring 1900, at the Fifth Avenue Theatre. Thereafter, the closest he got to the center of American theatricals was the Harlem Opera House. It certainly was not that Broadway had turned him out; he was warmly received at his last stand at the Fifth Avenue. But that house was converted to vaudeville shortly after his last appearance there (an apt symbol of the triumphant new amusement), and Joe may have had difficulty securing a Broadway stage. In any event, his bread and butter continued to be family audiences across Middle America: Toledo, Bridgeport, Roanoke, or Utica.[87]

In a sense, Joe hoped *Rip Van Winkle* would never retire from the stage. Joe had spent the second half of his life making Irving's ne'er-do-well a national institution. One sort of immortality would be gained by having Rip live on in the persona of his son. Thomas, having shown the greatest aptitude, was the anointed Rip. With Joe's increasingly tenuous health, Thomas found himself by 1895 in an active understudy role. Joe groomed Tom with all the care that sixty years of performing bestowed. He stressed time and again that Tom not slavishly replicate his expressions or gestures but instead seek his own empathetic grasp of the role. The father's illness in 1897 required the son for the first time to assume Rip's part. Subsequently, Tom was sent with his own *Rip Van Winkle* road company into the hinterland terrain where Joe no longer traveled on his short tours. Joe arranged to have his own scenery, properties, and costumes given to Tom when he concluded touring. In Joe's final stage appearances, he openly requested audiences to embrace Tom, "to whom he would resign the mantle that was about to fall from his shoulders." Less heavily burdened by his father's legacy was William Winter Jefferson (Willie), a much-indulged offspring who of the five surviving sons most resembled his father. At age twenty he stepped into the Bob Acres role in Pittsburgh when his father took ill. He did a passable job and was able to keep the tour alive until Joe returned. But fewer expectations were upon Willie.[88]

A shortened touring season meant increased leisure at his various homes. Joe continued wintering at his Louisiana plantation (he invited Cleveland to relax with him there when he stepped down from the presidency in March 1897). But by the mid-1890s, Orange Island winters began to be shared with long vacations on the Florida coast at Palm Beach. The change may have been prompted by attractions of the more reliable Florida sun, but it was also probably encouraged by Joe's new acquaintance, Henry Flagler, Rockefeller partner, railroad entrepreneur, and the greatest force in the development of the state's eastern coast. Joe enjoyed the hospitality of Flagler's sumptuous hotels, the Ponce de Leon at St. Augustine and the Breakers at Palm Beach. Joe, himself possessing an entrepreneurial streak, intensely enjoyed the spectacle of land development during this heroic age of Florida. He also took up cycling, a "convert to the all-conquering wheel," as a paper phrased it. He loved being on the waters of the area and delighted in the wildlife (even serving as officer of the Florida Audubon Society). The fishing, too, was good, always an important consideration for Joe.[89]

The social whirl of Palm Beach inevitably drew in Joe. His celebrity made him an ornament to Palm Beach society. On one occasion he served as a judge for a cakewalk at the Breakers. "The negroes had plenty of room for their fancy steps," the newspaper reported of the Palm Beach display of the national dance craze, "and marched around with considerable grace," entertaining the well-heeled gathering at the posh hotel. The moment may have evoked memories of Joe's mincing Jim Crow dance with Daddy Rice. That moment was pure innocence; but seventy years later, with Jim Crow carrying ominous meanings for American blacks, the cakewalk bespoke pure subservience. This was lost on Joe (as, in fairness, it would be on the entire privileged gathering). Jefferson, even at the end of his life, had no more sense of the hard social realities of America than he did in his youth.[90]

Through his final decades of life, Joe's marriage to Sarah appears to have been solid and fulfilling. Toney, as Joe called her, remains a shadowy figure to history, apparently seeing her function as quietly supporting her husband and rearing their four children. Joe's friends became hers as well. There is some indication that she occasionally mounted the stage in very amateur benefit productions. But Sarah endured chronic illness. Joe's letters in later years are filled with allusions to her indispositions.[91]

Joe's clan grew in number and generations. Grandchildren proliferated. By his death he knew of fourteen grandchildren and two great-grandchildren. Stately weddings were hosted at Buzzards Bay for son William and for Charley's daughters, one of whose marriage into a prominent Harvard family suggested just how far the Jefferson clan (and actors in general) had traveled socially. Joe was able to play the patriarch through all of this, not only footing the bills but also dispensing advice to future sons-in-law. Such occasions surely offset the inevitable losses that accompany a long life. Joe had buried a wife and three children and had survived most of his closest colleagues in the theatre, yet he seemed able to meet all eventualities with equanimity. Writer Gamaliel Bradford suggested that Jefferson's proverbial optimism was more a matter of will than of temperament, that his cheerfulness coexisted with a strain of melancholy. Bradford's observation finds support in a confession Joe himself once made when being charged yet again as an inveterate optimist: "No — no, he is mistaken. I am not an optimist, I too often let things sadden me." The advance of old age exacted its price in a way besides faltering health: "The saddest thing in old age is the absence of expectation," Jefferson remarked, an observation reflecting the unavoidable truth that life for him now engendered more contemplation than anticipation.[92]

After having complained much in his late career about the impermanence of the actor's art, Joe Jefferson determined to commit at least a portion of his greatest role to recorded memory. He was fortunate in the final two decades of his life to have the opportunity to use two revolutionary devices of Thomas Edison's invention: the phonograph and the motion picture,

Edison contrived the world's first acoustical recorder in 1877. Originally envisioned primarily as a dictation device, its commercial applications turned instead toward entertainment. We do not know any details, but at some point in 1890 Joe sat in front of a large recording horn and recited lines (presumably from *Rip Van Winkle*). Guests in hotel lobbies could insert their nickels, send the tracking needle along its path around the cylinder, and hear the celebrated comedian. But Edison's cylinders proved not to be the future of the phonograph. In the early 1890s Emile Berliner developed the gramophone, which recorded sound on a disc. In 1898 his Berliner Gramophone Company sought in Jefferson a high-profile star to recite monologues from *Rip*. Again, little is known about these arrangements, although the recordings have survived. A few years later the young Columbia Record Company approached Joe with a similar request. Joe readily agreed, and in some spare moments traveled to the company's laboratory on Sixth Avenue where he recited two speeches from *Rip* into the cylinder. A few days later a cylinder graphophone was taken to Jefferson's quarters at the Fifth Avenue Hotel, where he cut another recording. Columbia officials were amazed — and pleased — when he refused any remuneration, this at a time when the company was paying top dollar for the voice of other celebrities. Two scenes were recorded: one, Rip's famous monologue at Sleepy Hollow; and second, his reunion with Meenie. These emblematic speeches, moments of humor and pathos, were well suited for American fans of Jefferson, who could now own an audio legacy of the stage icon.[93]

The motion picture began its quick rise to commercial viability in the early 1890s. First the kinetoscope (the "peep show") in 1893 and then projected motion pictures in 1896 showed the commercial potential of the medium. What better subjects for the embryonic movies than celebrated natural wonders or personalities of popular culture, from Niagara Falls to Sandow the Strongman to Rip Van Winkle? William K. L. Dickson, a former Edison employee whose Biograph Company was now an Edison competitor, approached Jefferson in early 1896 and asked him to enact eight scenes of the old Dutchman. In the fall, Charley Jefferson, who was then organizing a vaudeville tour, arranged to use these "clear-cut and distinct" images at the close of the shows. These novelty items were also displayed at Hammerstein's Olympia Music Hall. In 1902, Biograph edited the eight pieces together into a three-minute "feature," which it marketed as an abbreviated but faithful reproduction of the famous play.[94]

The scenes were shot outdoors at Joe's Buzzards Bay estate. The action took place in front of and upon a large boulder, with a line of trees as the backdrop.

The limits of cinematic technology were severe; a single stationary camera recorded the action over a narrow frame of activity. At one point Rip, overcome by the dwarfs' brew, unwittingly staggers off camera for a few seconds leaving an empty set. On only one occasion did the Biograph camera move forward to catch a close-up of Rip's face. The eight short vignettes (averaging less than fifteen seconds each) depict Joe's encounter with Henry Hudson's dwarfs at Sleepy Hollow (dwarfs apparently only by virtue of stooping over). This action, the heart of *Rip Van Winkle,* was also the portion of the melodrama best suited for cinematic pantomime. Audiences knew the story so well that the brief captions were superfluous. Jefferson's interest in motion pictures took a pecuniary turn, as Joe not only performed for but also invested in one of the earliest capitalized film companies. Nonetheless, his work before the camera and behind the recording cylinder was clearly less for financial gain than for artistic immortality.[95]

Joe may have gradually slowed down as a performer, but he showed no loss of interest in advancing his personal fortune. We have no good figures as to what he earned as an actor. A contemporary estimated that Jefferson garnered well over a million dollars (at least twenty million in twenty-first-century dollars) on *Rip Van Winkle* alone. But Joe displayed a capitalist streak that went beyond the theatre. With his healthy cash flow and increasing leisure to oversee his ventures (aided by a business agent), he aggressively pursued a series of investments. He had long toyed profitably with various enterprises at his Orange Island estate, producing oranges, pecans, and sugar cane and raising cattle. The region's most famous natural resource, great salt domes beneath the landscape, opened another venue of opportunity when in 1895 it was discovered his property sat atop a rich vein of the mineral. Joe, Charley, and other partners combined to invest in its development. In this case, the world of big business proved more complex than perhaps Joe anticipated. This was the age of great combinations and trusts, and Joe's group encountered the resistance of the established salt trust. But Joe seemed to thrive on the challenge. He optimistically confided to his agent that the coming of the meat packing industry to the South would give a strong local market for his salt.[96]

Joe also invested heavily in Palm Beach real estate. He built himself a comfortable house, he purchased an entire block of buildings in West Palm Beach, and he acquired twenty acres south of town to develop as building lots. Joe was ecstatic about the full tenancy of his hotel, "the Jefferson," and the 14 percent return on investment. "If this keep[s] on I shall begin to think that I am a good business man," he boasted. Besides his investments, Jefferson benefited in late life from income off loans he had made (one of which was to Chicago theatre owner James McVicker). As with so much of his life, Joe's touch appeared golden to the very end.[97]

Joe's final year of life revealed the struggles of age. His 1904 five-week spring tour proceeded uneventfully, concluding in Paterson, New Jersey. Jefferson did not then know it would be his final curtain. Intimations of the end came in late May, when he could sense himself weakening. He called for daughter Margaret Farjeon, now widowed, to visit him at long last with her four children. The ensuing months at Buzzards Bay proved to be an Indian summer of sorts for the entire clan. Cousins made acquaintance. There were parlor theatricals, table games, clam bakes, and outings on the bay for the reunited family. Joe ("the youngest old man I have ever known," according to granddaughter Eleanor Farjeon) benevolently presided over the merriment, spending much of the time in his rose garden, a place "so full of hope." That summer, too, Joe spent a lazy evening with Cleveland and banker E. C. Benedict on board the latter's yacht in Buzzards Bay. It was an occasion reminiscent of the opening of Conrad's *Heart of Darkness:* privileged men in a dusky, languid setting, where talk turned to life's meaning. Joe was inveigled to recite his poem "Immortality." Its message, bereft of either philosophical rigor or theological warrant, nonetheless bespoke the ill-defined hopes of the era's cultured elite for whom Christian orthodoxy seemed unpersuasive.[98]

Joe began hiring players in August for the usual fall tour set to open in Allentown. But his lungs, so long damaged by early tubercular bouts, could not resist a pulmonary infection. It quickly became clear that the fall tour was off. Instead, in midfall he returned to Florida's healing warmth. It was apparent that retirement had at last overtaken him. The announcement, made during his train journey from Boston to Florida, appeared in newspapers across the country. There would be no farewell tour. The end came too abruptly, though as always he put the best face on things with bright descriptions of future gardening and fishing. His illness did not prevent him from scrutinizing his investments, questioning what he deemed excessive charges on a mortgage and — just a month before his death — inquiring whether a battle between the city of Chicago and its traction company might degrade the municipal bonds he held.[99]

Newspapers carried anxious reports of his final month, April 1905. Joe's doctor, perhaps seeking some small final pleasure for his patient, ordered him to get his "mind off himself and on to the fish and tackle." Joe gladly obeyed. Visits were made with son Charley (who had a house nearby), Grover Cleveland (fittingly to fish), and Henry Flagler. The visit to Cleveland occasioned another illness that could not be shaken. Joe rallied briefly. Still the consummate master of the dramatic exit, he held on until 23 April — Easter Sunday, as well as the traditional date of Shakespeare's birth and death. Then, Joseph Jefferson III, now decades older than Irving's Rip at the end of his twenty-year slumber, fell into a sleep from which there would be no awakening.[100]

Epilogue

A Shy Thing Is Comedy

Not all members of the Jefferson clan had gathered about Joe when the end came. In truest family tradition, the show went on throughout his final illness. Only at their father's death did Tom, on tour with *Rip,* and Willie and Joe Jr., touring *The Rivals,* leave their respective companies to return to Buzzards Bay. A special train was chartered to carry Joe's body from Florida back to Massachusetts, his chosen site of rest. Henry Flagler, who owned the Florida East Coast Railroad, put his private car at the disposal of the Jeffersons. The northward journey was a true funeral procession. Stops in Baltimore and Jersey City gave opportunity for crowds to bestow tokens of respect. The train passed through New York City, leading to requests that Joe's body lie in state at the Church of the Transfiguration (the Little Church Around the Corner). It seemed too fitting a gesture to refuse, yet Charley was determined to honor his father's wish for only a simple family memorial service at Crow's Nest.[1]

Such it was. The family — four generations strong — gathered at the rambling Buzzards Bay home on 30 April. By the social conventions of the day, the Jefferson men occupied the chairs at the service while the women retired to nearby rooms for private mourning. Bright sunshine attended the burial at a nearby Sandwich cemetery. Joe wanted to rest near the water, and this hillside spot above the sparkling waters of the bay fulfilled that desire. A large rough-hewn boulder, several tons in weight, was imported as a grave marker, upon which was affixed a bas-relief profile of Jefferson. The boulder, recalling the rocks Rip clambered over while toting a keg of schnapps for Hudson's crew, struck an appropriate final stage setting. The graveside service (Unitarian, in deference to Joe's heterodox views) was just concluding when two visitors pulled up in a carriage. New York Governor Blake and John Singer Sargent alighted and stood respectfully for a few minutes: the worlds of politics and the arts giving their final tribute.[2]

The private service was paralleled by a public memorial at the same hour in New York for stage professionals. The Little Church Around the Corner was jammed and hundreds stood outside. Scarcely a notable of the American stage was missing. Edwin Booth's daughter represented Joe's old friend. Reverend George Houghton, who more than thirty years earlier had endeared himself to theatre folk everywhere by pronouncing benediction over George Holland, spoke affectionately of Joe

Jefferson's death, journey north, and funeral were given detailed coverage by America's press. A theatrical star of the first magnitude was gone, a man clasped more closely by his countrymen than probably any other native actor. His passing was long expected, and the theatrical community had been readied to deliver its various appreciations of dear old Joe. Some of the encomiums were eulogistic conventionalities, to be sure. The durable nature of Joe's career, his having graced the stage since Jackson's presidency, were constant themes. Some writers recalled with delight their childhood trips to see *Rip Van Winkle*. But one is also struck by the willingness of many commentators to engage in frank assessment of his career, his limitations as well as his accomplishments. Something close to a consensus about Jefferson's career emerged from the many voices.

All agreed that the creation of Rip Van Winkle was a work of genius and that Bob Acres, if not the persona of Sheridan, nonetheless represented comedic achievement of the highest order. Jefferson's Caleb Plummer and Major Golightly, too, were triumphs of their kind. "Joseph Jefferson was the greatest low comedian and the greatest technician of our time," judged the *Herald* critic, proclaiming that he had no peer on the English stage and stood with the great French comic master Coquelin. Still, his art had its limits. His great parts all carried some resemblance, and he would never think to attempt poetic drama. Even Jefferson's friend William Winter acknowledged he did not possess the intellectual power of a Henry Irving.[3]

But the limitations troubled only a few critics and the public evidently not at all, for Joe was, above all, beloved. Writers strained to define the root of his appeal, often invoking unhelpfully vague concepts of his "intensely human quality," or the technical proficiency of his hidden art. In simpler terms the public sensed that it had lost a friend. The profession knew it had lost one of its finest public ambassadors. If Jefferson "left no endowed or subscription theater, no stock company . . . nothing to develop a school of American dramatists," as common criticisms ran, "he did more than any other single actor," claimed Clayton Hamilton, "to end the old social prejudices against actors." He did this in part through an exemplary life. "I never knew a man whose moral sensibilities were more acute," testified newspaper publisher Henry Watterson, a comment resembling those of too many other Jefferson acquaintances to dismiss lightly. And he mitigated prejudice through association with political and social notables of his age. "Choosing his associates from among the best of those with whom he came in contact," said James Metcalfe, "he did much to show the world that the actor might be a man among men, a gentleman among gentlemen, even in times when the stage had not entirely escaped from the stigma of vagabondage." The social elevation of the stage, a preoccupation of the age, found an unintended champion in the ne'er-do-well Rip. If Joe took the easier (and more lucrative) artistic career path, he nonetheless "dignified his profession," wrote the *Evening Post*, "He showed his fellow actors how to respect themselves and their calling, and how to make that profession honored."[4]

These tributes would have gratified Joe's desire for appreciation and remembrance. He would have been further pleased to know that future authors would attempt to keep his memory alive. Francis Wilson published his appreciation in 1906 and daughter-in-law Eugenie Paul Jefferson wrote her remembrances in 1909. In the 1920s, Jefferson's career was revisited in sympathetic essays by knowledgeable critics. His *Autobiography* was reissued twice from Century, once in 1917 and again on the sixtieth anniversary of its publication in 1950, followed by a scholarly edition from Harvard University Press in 1964. Interest in Jefferson's life extended even internationally, with a biography published in Russia in the 1980s and a Chinese language edition of his *Rip Van Winkle* a decade earlier. But if the world of theatrical scholarship esteemed his legacy, Joe was sadly prophetic in foreseeing his disappearance from public memory. The ephemeral quality of performing arts before the twentieth century almost guaranteed this. Although his life formed the subject of two historical novels (one for juveniles) in the 1940s and 1950s, the name Joseph Jefferson inexorably sank beneath the surface of public consciousness.[5]

More tangibly, he could appreciate his family legacy of fourteen grandchildren, two great-grandchildren, some of whom he had carried on stage in their infancy. It appeared that the Jefferson name via three sons would continue to grace the American stage. But the mantle fell too heavily on Thomas (d. 1931). The momentum of *Rip Van Winkle* was great enough that he could faithfully soldier on with the play for a number of years. In 1914 he starred in a fifty-eight-minute film version of the tale. But as Montrose Moses gently put it, "a standard was left behind that will be difficult to emulate." Other writers were more blunt in noting that Joe's genius was not hereditary. "A shy thing is comedy," Jefferson once pronounced, an observation prophetic of how Thalia hid her face from the younger Jeffersons.[6]

It would instead be across the Atlantic that the theatrical tradition would thrive. Neither of Joe's two daughters ever took a bow, but Joe would have been delighted to know that the distaff branch of his family continued a sparkling stage tradition. Margaret and husband Ben Farjeon reared their children in an atmosphere rich in the arts. Although far from America, Margaret steeped her children in the grand theatrical tradition of their grandfather. Nurtured thus, all four surviving children found careers in theatre, music, and literature. Herbert Farjeon (1887–1945), who got his professional start with Thomas Jefferson's *Rip* company, made significant contributions to the British stage as producer, playwright, and critic. More well known to the general public was his sister Eleanor (1881–1965), whose children's verses, stories, and plays enchanted a generation of English youth. Theatre remained in the blood of the next Farjeon generation as well. Over much of the twentieth century, Jefferson descendants enriched the British stage.[7]

Across the Atlantic, too, another actor of acclaim died six months after Joe. Tragedian Henry Irving commanded the English stage even more thoroughly than Jefferson did the American. The trajectory of his career resembled Joe's in many respects: working his way up through provincial companies until finding a melodramatic vehicle that propelled him to stardom. But Irving ultimately attempted what Jefferson's American supporters regretted Joe did not. Irving acquired the Lyceum Theatre, assembled a strong stock company, and mounted a series of celebrated productions over the next two decades. He further procured a leading lady of surpassing merit—Ellen Terry—whose stage presence complemented his own, establishing one of the greatest stage partnerships. The Lyceum attracted English society. Irving achieved a more distinguished place in theatre history than Jefferson. He became the first of his profession to be knighted, a distinction Joe could never know. But Irving's life ended less satisfactorily, a catastrophic fire and the financial demands of the Lyceum draining him before he died virtually penniless.[8]

Joe Jefferson, in contrast, died rich, with an estate valued at more than $600,000. He made generous benefactions to servants, theatrical charities, friends, grandchildren, and extended family (including $5,000 to Joseph Sefton in Australia). Widow Sarah, who at age fifty-five would live two more decades, and legitimate children would divide the proceeds from the sale of his estate. Whether his immediate family was able to maintain themselves at the comfortable level to which they had grown accustomed is not clear. Within a few years Crow's Nest and the Orange Island estates were both sold. Joe's beloved art collection was auctioned off, bringing less than his heirs had hoped. With the patriarch gone, the family, so long clustered at Buzzards Bay, scattered, Sarah moving to New York City. The Jefferson clan, which had traveled and performed together off and on since the 1820s, closed shop.[9]

It closed for Joe after nearly seventy-four years on stage. During his many decades, the American theatre grew from a culturally marginalized and economically insecure enterprise to a confident, commercially expansive institution. Americans in the decades after the Civil War demonstrated a hearty appetite for amusements. Joe Jefferson was part of the burgeoning entertainment industry that satisfied these cravings; indeed, Jefferson was a captain of that industry. In the fashion of Carnegie, Joe's rise manifested the proverbial American trajectory of success. A career begun modestly, by being carried on stage as a "property baby," flourished through years of apprenticeship and journeyman effort. The rise was steady, though punctuated by moments of disappointment and heartache. The public frequently heard the story of how Joe discovered Irving's tale, dramatized it, refashioned it with Boucicault's help, and finally triumphed. Happily, as writers also reiterated, success left him unaffected. His considerable ambition was properly cloaked in a seemly robe of humility and bonhomie.

"Has it ever been pointed out how thoroughly Jefferson's genius was in sympathy with the peculiar genius of the American people?" journalist John Corbin asked after Joe's death. His "gentleness and refinement, [his] quaintness and whimsicality" set him apart — possibly excepting the plays of J. M. Barrie — from anything on the English stage. The mention of Barrie was apt, for in the year of Jefferson's death, Maude Adams debuted *Peter Pan* on the American stage. Adams's whimsical, ungendered Peter Pan — the boy who refused to grow up — held the same sort of fantastical appeal to audiences as did Rip. Rip's story, a darker one for all its humor, presents a man who in his own improvident way refused to accept adulthood. He must atone for his stubborn adolescence by the slumbering loss of his prime manhood. The charms of *Peter Pan* are more innocent and without apparent cost. But both plays suggest a theatrical public — English and American — that sought a temporary respite from a complex and swirling fin de siècle reality in an imagined retreat from adult responsibilities.[10]

Even before Jefferson's passing, theatre had taken a turn. The change was more apparent on European stages, where new notions of drama and stagecraft found fertile soil. Joe's life was almost exactly coterminous with Henrik

Ibsen's (1828–1906), yet it would be difficult to imagine two men of the theatre whose personal and dramatic sensibilities veered further apart. A work from Ibsen's early mature period, the fantasy verse drama *Peer Gynt,* bore some familiarity to *Rip Van Winkle.* (*Peer Gynt* was published in 1867, just two years after Jefferson's London triumph in *Rip Van Winkle.*) Peer, a figure from Norwegian folklore, might be understood as Rip's evil twin: an improvident, philandering, dreaming rapscallion. But Ibsen took his famous turn toward theatrical realism in the 1870s. His subsequent career gave dramatic voice to the impetus for personal revolt against all sorts of parochialism and prejudice. He championed a theatre of ideas. This was the crusade of an embittered and profoundly insecure man. By contrast, Jefferson was unsuited for such theatrical assault by virtue of his constitutional good nature and the sentimental, optimistic tenor of American culture. Where Ibsen sought to destroy human illusions, Jefferson fostered them. Where Ibsen savaged provincialism, Jefferson fondly indulged it. Where Ibsen transformed Western theatre but paid a high price in personal unhappiness, Jefferson enjoyed a life of great reward but left an evanescent imprint on future drama.[11]

Americans were slow to embrace the new theatrical sensibility. Audiences as well as the theatrical establishment, for example, long remained cool toward Ibsen. Minnie Maddern Fiske's aggressive staging of his plays in the mid-1890s advanced his American reputation, but the Norwegian master found an enthusiastic reception only in the years surrounding Jefferson's death in 1905. But native playwrights also augured a changing theatre. James A. Herne sought an American drama of greater social and psychological complexity, as did William Vaughn Moody in his abbreviated dramatic career.

Changes in American drama foretold a larger evolution in the theatre. Joe died just months after the legitimate theatre had reached its peak (in terms of numbers of national touring companies). But more popular entertainments were already displacing traditional drama, notably vaudeville and the emerging motion pictures. Legitimate drama was gradually assuming an air of "high culture," another indication of the sacralization of culture Lawrence Levine has so well described. In truth, the final years of *Rip Van Winkle* bespoke the same point. The play became a compulsory cultural event for parents and children, a part of the native landscape that, like Niagara, must not be missed. "[Rip] was a piece of acting to brag about as a national glory," the *New York Times* reported. Joe had become an ennobling American institution, memorialized in statuary, carefully preserved theatre programs, and other collectibles.[12]

Such artifacts may have reassured Joe that he would not be forgotten. But one suspects that in his final days he dwelt less on his material legacy than on his memories. An adventuresome childhood, a doughty youth, an exemplary rise to fame, an extended run of stardom — four lifetimes of experiences in his seventy-six years. Joe had witnessed the transformation of the American stage. Admittedly, that era's acting now appears affected and its plays jejune. But theatre, a social art seeking immediate appreciation, is fashioned for its own day. Joseph Jefferson must then be remembered precisely because he so well captured the mix of aspiration and nostalgia that marked nineteenth-century America. If Rip Van Winkle invited audiences back to their mythic pastoral roots, Joe's celebrated personal life betokened the promise of modernity's rewards. In his geniality, Americans cherished past and present.

Notes

Introduction

1. William Winter, *Shadows of the Stage* (New York: Macmillan, 1892), 151.

2. Alan Downer, "Players and Painted Stage: Nineteenth Century Acting," *PLMA* 61 (1946): 522.

3. Theodore Dreiser, *Sister Carrie* (New York: Library of America, 1987), 101, 40; Wallace Stegner, *Angle of Repose* (New York: Penguin Books, 1971), 173.

Chapter One. Cradled in the Profession

1. Joseph Jefferson, *The Autobiography of Joseph Jefferson* (1890; reprint Cambridge: Harvard University Press, 1964), 5. All citations to this work are from the Harvard edition.

2. Charles Dickens, *The Life and Adventures of Nicholas Nickleby,* facsimile edition (Philadelphia: University of Pennsylvania Press, 1982), 216.

3. Quoted in Nina Auerbach, *Ellen Terry: Player in Her Time* (New York: W. W. Norton, 1987), 30.

4. The main source on Thomas Jefferson is William Winter, *The Life and Art of Joseph Jefferson* (New York: Macmillan, 1894), 1–46. Perhaps the first biographical sketch on Jefferson appeared in the *Monthly Mirror,* July 1804 (typescript copy in possession of Gervase Farjeon). On Garrick and the Georgian stage, see J. L. Styan, *The English Stage: A History of Drama and Performance* (Cambridge: Cambridge University Press, 1996); Claire Tomalin, *Mrs. Jordan's Profession* (New York: Alfred A. Knopf, 1995);

Allardyce Nicoll, *The Garrick Stage: Theatres and Audienes in the Eighteenth Century* (Athens: University of Georgia Press, 1980).

5. "The most complete figure, in beauty of countenance and symmetry of form, I ever beheld," an early biographer of Garrick remarked of the new Mrs. Jefferson. Her death was among the more bizarre recorded on the stage. While watching the rehearsal of a comic dance some item struck her as funny, and "in the midst of a hearty laugh she was seized with a sudden pain and expired in the arms of Mr. Moody." But even this tragedy, according to the later Victorian chronicler of the Jefferson family, "bore witness to the sunshine of her nature; for she died of laughter." Quotes from Winter, *Life of Jefferson*, 15. Winter's *Life of Jefferson* is likewise the best source on Jefferson I. Montrose Moses's chapter on the Jeffersons in his well-known *Famous Actor-Families in America* (1906, reprint Westport, Conn.: Greenwood Press, 1968) is almost entirely dependent on Winter. For a discussion of Dunlop and the arrival of melodrama to America, see David Grimsted, *Melodrama Unveiled: American Theater and Culture, 1800–1850* (Chicago: University of Chicago Press, 1968), chap. 1. On Hodgkinson, see *American National Biography*, s.v. "John Hodgkinson," by Jared Brown. On Jefferson's move, see William B. Wood, *Personal Recollections of the Stage* (Philadelphia: Henry Carey Baird, 1855), 97.

6. Arthur Hobson Quinn, *History of the American Drama*, 2 vols. (New York: Harper and Brothers, 1927), 1:290–91; description of the theatre found in Weldon Durham, ed., *American Theatre Companies, 1749–1887* (Westport, Conn.: Greenwood Press, 1986), 193–94; Wood, *Personal Recollections*, 119, 205.

7. Both quotes in Winter, *Life of Jefferson*, 90–91.

8. Reese D. James, *Old Drury of Philadelphia: A History of the Philadelphia Stage, 1800–1835* (1932; reprint, Westport, Conn.: Greenwood Press, 1968), 59. Jefferson quote in Winter, *Life of Jefferson*, 87; Charles Durang, *History of Philadelphia Stage between the Years 1749 and 1855* (Philadelphia: Pennsylvania Historical Society, 1858–61), series 2, 278. Jefferson may have been too quick to perceive personal rejection by Philadelphia audiences. William Warren also, despite many years of providing quality theatricals to Philadelphians, had a final benefit that failed to reach expenses. James, *Old Drury of Philadelphia*, 62. In any event, the depth of Jefferson's alienation became clear when in 1830 his recently widowed daughter Elizabeth Chapman was arranging her badly needed benefit at the Walnut Street Theatre. She implored him to appear with her. He at first agreed but then couldn't bring himself to return to a Philadelphia stage. Durang, *History of Philadelphia Stage*, series 3, 36.

9. Quoted in Durham, ed., *American Theatre Companies*, 522. Given the severe limitations of lighting and equipment at that time, the florid descriptions of such effects must be understood by the modern reader as more impressive to contemporaries than perhaps for the present day.

10. B. O. Flower, *Lessons Learned from Other Lives* (Boston: Spectator, 1889), 75; Arthur Bloom, *Joseph Jefferson: Dean of the American Theatre* (Savannah: Frederic C. Beil, 2000), 1.

11. Information on the Jefferson company in the earliest years of Jefferson's life is found in an exhaustively researched article by Arthur W. Bloom, "The Jefferson Company, 1830–1845," *Theatre Survey* 27 (May 1986): 89–153.

12. Jefferson, *Autobiography*, chap. 1.

13. Ibid., 14.

14. Ibid., 7–81; playbills in Brander Matthews and Laurence Hutton, eds., *Actors and Actresses of Great Britain and the United States: Joseph Jefferson* (New York: Cassell, 1886), Extra-illustrated Edition, vol. 5, pt. 2, Harvard Theatre Collection, Houghton Library, Harvard University.

15. Jefferson, *Autobiography,* 9; Connor interview, *New York Times,* 5 June 1881, quoted in Winter, *Life of Jefferson,* 104–5.

16. My discussion of tableaux vivants relies heavily on Jack W. McCullough's *Living Pictures on the New York Stage* (Ann Arbor: UMI Research Press, 1981), passim. The phenomenon of amateur tableaux is described in Karen Halttunen, *Confidence Men and Painted Women: A Study of Middle-Class Culture in America, 1830–1870* (New Haven: Yale University Press, 1982), 176–77. A sense of contemporary moral objection to the living statues theatres is found in George G. Foster, *New York by Gas Light and Other Urban Sketches* (New York: M. J. Ivers, 1850), 12–15. Martin Meisel offers useful context to tableaux vivants in his *Realizations: Narrataive, Pictorial, and Theatrical Arts in Nineteenth-Century England* (Princeton: Princeton University Press, 1983), 30, 47.

17. Neil Harris discusses the growing taste for spectacle in his *Humbug: The Art of P. T. Barnum* (Boston: Little, Brown, 1979), 245.

18. *Uncle Tom's Cabin* made famous use of tableaux, as in the apotheosis of Eva, whose stage directions calls for this final scene: "Gorgeous clouds, tinted with sunlight. Eva, robed in white, is discovered on the back of a milk-white dove, with expanded wings, as if just soaring upward. Her hands are extended in benediction over St. Clare and Uncle Tom, who are kneeling and gazing up to her. Impressive music. — Slow curtain." Quoted in McCullough, *Living Pictures,* 64.

19. Quotes are from McCullough, *Living Pictures,* 76. Tableaux never entirely disappeared. They continued as a theatrical device to highlight concluding moments of high drama and as showpieces in the extravagant revues of the early twentieth century. An occasional pageant or museum will still mount a tableau for patriotic reasons or as an artistic curiosity.

20. Jefferson, *Autobiography,* 9–10. Mrs. John Drew added her witness to the event (see the *Autobiographical Sketch of Mrs. John Drew* [New York: Charles Scribner's Sons, 1899]). The playbill from that night's performance can be found in the Harvard Theatre Collection, where it is noted that Rice did his Jim Crow turn as an entr'acte for the Jefferson company's theatricals. Constance Rourke, *American Humor: A Study of the National Character* (New York: Harcourt, Brace, Jovanovich, 1931), 81.

21. Douglas Charles McKenzie, "Acting of Joseph Jefferson" (Ph.D. diss., University of Illinois, 1973), 60; song quoted in Francis Wilson, *Joseph Jefferson: Reminiscences of a Fellow Player* (New York: Charles Scribner's Sons, 1906), 77–78.

22. Carl Wittke's *Tambo and Bones: A History of the American Minstrel Stage* (1930; reprint, Westport, Conn.: Greenwood Press, 1968) remains the best general history of minstrelsy, though lacking the interpretive sophistication of many recent works; Robert Toll's *Blacking Up: The Minstrel Show in Nineteenth-Century America* (New York: Oxford University Press, 1974) was among the first modern works to attempt a broader cultural reading. Eric Lott's *Love and Theft: Blackface Minstrelsy and the American Working Class* (New York: Oxford University Press, 1993) attempts with mixed success

to link the minstrel phenomenon with the formation of a working-class culture. See also Gary Engle's helpful preface and introduction to various minstrel sketches in his *This Grotesque Essence: Plays from the American Minstrel Stage* (Baton Rouge: Louisiana University Press, 1978); W. T. Lhamon, *Raising Cain: Blackface Performance from Jim Crow to Hip Hop* (Cambridge: Harvard University Press, 1998); Rice description quoted in Dale Cockrell, *Demons of Disorder: Early Blackface Minstrels and Their World* (Cambridge: Cambridge University Press, 1997), 15, 63.

23. Minstrel line quoted in Engle, *This Grotesque Experience*, 65.

24. Quoted in Lott, *Love and Theft*, 15; Toll, *Blacking Up*, 66. Minstrelsy's fidelity to African-American culture has long been debated. Constance Rourke, the pathbreaking maven of American folk culture studies in the 1930s, celebrated blackface as an insurgence of black culture into American life, ritualized though it became on the stage. "The Negro minstrel was deeply grounded in reality," she wrote, "even though the impersonators were white, even though the figure was a myth." The confidence of Rourke and historian Carl Wittke in the black folk contribution to minstrelsy sprang in part from the testimony of many early minstrels as to their firsthand observation of slaves in the West and South. Stephen Foster visited black camp meetings and took away rhythms and melodies; E. P. Christy acknowledged the influence of New Orleans slaves' "queer words and simple but expressive melodies." The peculiar shuffles of some slaves influenced minstrel (and later soft-shoe) dance, and the animal fables and other folklore provided fodder for blackface shows.

Carl Wittke tells a morality tale of minstrel folk art corrupted by success. Such an approach veils a more complex story. The music, dance, and humor of commercial minstrelsy emerged out of a process of selection and adaptation, with white entertainers fusing black cultural traditions to older European and contemporary vernacular styles. The essential instrument of the minstrel stage—the banjo—and some of the songs and folk stories clearly originated in the African or African-American experience. But the tambourine and bones (a type of castanet) were of European lineage, and even such a defender of minstrelsy's black roots as Carl Wittke admits that most minstrel songs were ethnically veneered versions of white parlor ballads. Burlesque afterpieces were also part of a long European popular stage tradition. And even the comic exchanges between interlocutor and end men partook of a European circus convention.

Likewise, William J. Mahar in his *Behind the Burnt Cork Mask: Early Blackface Minstrelsy and Antebellum American Popular Culture* (Urbana: University of Illinois Press, 1999) finds a broader set of roots. Not only American influences but the popular musical and dramatic tradition of Europe shaped minstrel shows. The minstrel sensibility, Mahar argues persuasively, was at heart a sort of burlesque, reinterpreting European musical theatre through the lens of topical American events and attitudes. Some might call the minstrel form a sort of debasement or bastardization of European operatic and dramatic culture; but inventive borrowing has always been the case with theatricals. Mahar concurs with the previous two works in saying that minstrelsy frequently conveyed an irreverent attitude toward class relations. Likewise, he sees minstrelsy's relation with antebellum black culture as complex rather than essentially exploitive or derogatory.

Regarding the second question—Was racism at the core of minstrelsy?—an interesting revisionist school has emerged. Recent scholarship, especially Cockrell's *Demons of Dis-*

order and Lott's *Love and Theft,* emphasize the influence of urban working-class tradition of street theatre. Across American cities charivaris, mumming, callithumpian bands — in a word, carnival — sanctioned a public exuberance that frequently passed over into lawlessness. Performers, some of them urban blacks, in impromptu out-of-door theatre often utilized blackface not, says Cockrell, in a fashion demeaning to blacks, but as a mask for challenging their social betters. George Washington Dixon, pioneer minstrel performer (most famous for introducing to the stage the northern black dandy "Zip Coon") was himself a tabloid journalist whose newspaper impudence toward the New York establishment brought him several jail terms. It is intriguing to think that minstrelsy, usually characterized as racially debasing, had at least part of its roots in a socially subversive activity.

25. Rourke, *American Humor,* 91, 94; tall tale quoted in Toll, *Blacking Up,* 41; William F. Stowe and David Grimsted, "White-Black Humor," *Journal of Ethnic Studies* 3 (1975): 95. This study, along with Lott's and Maher's, is the best treatment of minstrelsy's social nuances.

26. Mark Twain *Autobiography* quoted in Lott, *Love and Theft,* 20.

27. Observation on Elizabeth Jefferson quoted in Winter, *Life of Jefferson,* 126–27; Noah Ludlow, *Dramatic Life as I Found It* (1880; reprint New York: Benjamin Blom, 1966), 568–69; Wood, *Personal Recollections,* 349–52; Francis Courtney Wemyss, *Theatrical Biography; or, The Life of an Actor and Manager* (Glasgow: R. Griffin, 1848), 138–39. Durang, *History of the Philadelphia Stage,* series 3, 243. Chapman's surviving four siblings, who had followed him to America, became, under the leadership of William Chapman, barnstormers of the Ohio and Mississippi river valleys, part of the great epic of hinterland theatre. Elizabeth herself remarried twice, always outliving her spouse. She retired from the stage then returned as her personal life allowed or demanded. She knew more than a fair share of grief with both husbands and children, though one of her daughters, Clara Fisher Maeder, achieved some renown as a vocalist. Her checkered life impeded her from realizing the promise so many held for her. The best sketch of her life is found in Winter, *Life of Jefferson,* 124–30.

28. My account of the Jefferson-MacKenzie years relies heavily upon the exhaustive research efforts of Bloom, "Jefferson Company." Arthur Hobson Quinn also mentions that Philadelphia managers returned to Baltimore for a spring season as well as a summer turn in Washington, D.C., and Alexandria, Virginia, thus patching together a year-round schedule. *History of the American Drama,* 1:201; Joseph Cowell, *Thirty Years Passed among the Players in England and America* (New York: Harper and Brothers, 1844), 82; *National Intelligencer,* 4 March 1830, 3.

29. *National Intelligencer,* 1 December 1830, 3; Bloom, "Jefferson Company," 96.

30. Bloom, "Jefferson Company," 98.

31. George Wilson Pierson, *Tocqueville in America* (Baltimore: Johns Hopkins University Press, 1996), 664–67; Count Francesco Arese, *A Trip to the Prairies and in the Interior of North America* (New York: Harbor Press, 1934), 16; Frances Anne Butler [Kemble], *The Journal of Frances Anne Butler,* 2 vols. (1835; reprint, New York: Benjamin Blom, 1970), 2:117, 138.

32. Butler, *Journal,* 2:119. *Daily National Intelligencer,* 29 November 1831, 3; 3 December 1831, 3; 5 December 1831, 3.

33. In a number of cities, theatres had to wait until local gas works were established, though some stage entrepreneurs, such as New Orleans' James Caldwell, ran their own works. Frederick Penzel, *Theatre Lighting before Electricity* (Middletown, Conn.: Wesleyan University Press, 1978), 45–52; James, *Old Drury of Philadelphia,* 27–28; Lawrence. E. Barsness, "The Relationship of Stage Lighting Sources and Methods to Acting Styles in Theatres, 1850–1915" (master's thesis, University of Oregon, 1950).

34. Bloom, "Jefferson Company," 99–102.

35. Durang, *History of the Philadelphia Stage,* series 3, 36. Two accounts of John's fall exist. One, repeated by William Winter, which might be considered the official family story, has John slipping on an orange peel. This account has a certain implausibility, bearing the earmarks of a tale whereby the family protected a favored son's reputation. Another version, told by Charles Durang, has him falling from an apoplectic fit. Winter, *Life of Jefferson,* 80; Durang, *History of the Philadelphia Stage,* series 3, 52.

36. Bloom, "Jefferson Company," 99.

37. Ludlow, *Dramatic Life,* 279; Winter, *Life of Jefferson,* 80–81. Jane and Elizabeth lived with the family of Jefferson II after their mother's death; thus Joe grew up with his young cousins; Durang, *History of the Philadelphia Stage,* series 3, 2; Joseph Ireland, *Records of New York Stage,* 2 vols. (1866; reprint, New York: Benjamin Blom, 1966), 2:88–89; Bloom, "Jefferson Company," 102–3.

38. Benjamin Poore, "Reminiscences of Washington," *Atlantic Monthly* 45 (June 1880): 816.

39. Bloom, "Jefferson Company," 105.

40. On the Maryland Company, see Durham, ed., *American Theatre Companies,* 334; Pierson, *Tocqueville in America,* 489–94; Bloom, "Jefferson Company," 105; Cowell, *Thirty Years,* 82; Gary Lawson Browne, *Baltimore in the Nation, 1789–1861* (Chapel Hill: University of North Carolina Press, 1980), 69–76; Arese, *Trip to the Prairies,* 13.

41. Bloom, "Jefferson Company," 108; Walter Leman, *Memories of an Old Actor* (San Francisco: A. Roman, 1886), 50.

42. William Hazlitt, *Complete Works* (London: J. M. Dent, 1931), vol. 5, p. 379; Durham, ed., *American Theatre Companies,* 399, 486.

43. Butler, *Journal,* 2:104; 1:104–5.

44. A. A. Addams represented another of that too-common type on the American stage: the young man of promise whose career never achieved its potential because of alcohol. Addams went from this early engagement to modest acclaim before starting his long slide. Harry Watkins noted in his diary Addams's death as a pauper in Cincinnati. "Had his great talent been coupled with prudence he might still be living and occupying the very front rank in the Profession. It is the oft-repeated tale: too long an association with John Barleycorn." Maud and Otis Skinner, ed., *One Man in His Time: The Adventures of H. Watkins Strolling Player, 1845–1863* (Philadelphia: University of Pennsylvania Press, 1938), 99; Butler, *Journal,* 2:112–13.

45. Raphael Semmes, *Baltimore as Seen by Visitors, 1783-1860* (Baltimore: Maryland Historical Society, 1953), 112; Butler, *Journal,* 2:136; Philip Hone, *The Diary of Philip Hone, 1828-1851* ((New York: Arno Press, 1970), 116. J. C. Furnas, Fanny *Kemble: Leading Lady of the Nineteenth-Century Stage* (New York: Dial Press, 1982), 119.

46. *National Intelligencer,* 23 October 1833, 3; *National Intelligencer,* 9 November 1833, 3; Bloom, "Jefferson Company," 108.

47. On the history of hippodrama, see A. H. Saxon's fine history, *Enter Foot and Horse: A History of Hippodrama in England and France* (New Haven: Yale University Press, 1968), esp. 140–61.

48. Ibid., 161.

49. Bloom, "Jefferson Company," 108; Walter Meserve, *Heralds of Promise: The Drama of the American People During the Age of Jackson, 1829–1849* (Westport, Conn.: Greenwood Press, 1986), 139; Grimsted, *Melodrama Unveiled,* 80–81. Grimsted notes that *Mazeppa* was the twelfth most performed play in America between 1831 and 1851 (252); Saxon, *Foot and Horse,* 173–90, 7. In the Jefferson company's 1833 Washington production, the original Mazeppa was seriously injured and had to be replaced. *National Intelligencer,* 9 November 1833, 3; Skinner, *One Man in His Time,* 57–58.

50. *Dictionary of American Biography,* s.v. "Adah Isaacs Menken," by Allen F. Lesser; *Notable American Women,* s.v. "Adah Isaacs Menken," by Thurman Wilkins; Robert Allen, *Horrible Prettiness: Burlesque and American Culture* (Chapel Hill: University of North Carolina Press, 1991), 97–99; Saxon, *Foot and Horse,* 195.

51. Allen, *Horrible Prettiness,* 97–99; Saxon, *Foot and Horse,* 190–91; *Sacramento Union* review quoted in Jere Dueffort Wade, "The San Francisco Stage, 1859–1869" (Ph.D. diss., University of Oregon, 1972), 179. Renee M. Sentilles has insightful things to say about Menken's Mazeppa as well as other aspects of her ingenious self-promotions and self-creations in *Performing Menken: Adah Isaacs Menken and the Birth of American Celebrity* (Cambridge: Cambridge University Press, 2003), esp. chap. 3.

52. Saxon, *Foot and Horse,* 188–89; the blackfaced *Mazeppa* featured such characters as Abder Khan, "cream of Tartar, and boss white-washer of Jamaica, Long Island." Instead of Europe it is set in the exotic reaches of New Jersey and displays the foolishness and irreverent send-up of the original melodrama common to the burlesque genre. C. White, *Mazeppa: An Equestrian Burlesque,* Brady's Ethiopian Drama No. 3 (New York: Frederic A. Brady, c. 1854) Saxon, *Foot and Horse,* 201–4; Robert Allen's, *Horrible Prettiness,* 96–101, credits Menken as being an important antecedent of modern burlesque.

Joe Jefferson's later adult experience at the Philadelphia Ampitheater left him scornful of equestrian drama. The frequently absurd juxtaposition of heroic star with recalcitrant horse compromised the dramatic moment (though appealing to Jefferson's comic sensibility). The fearsome tyrant of *Timour the Tartar* who roared about the stage, suddenly "with a lamb-like submission" allowed himself to be boosted up into the saddle, "where he would sit unsteadily, looking the picture of misery." Jefferson recalled how in *St. George and the Dragon* two of the knights — fatally timid around horses — were unable to mount during a scene. One ended up sprawled crosswise across the saddle; the other got the wrong foot in the stirrup and found himself facing backwards. Dismounting, he caught his foot in the stirrup and was dragged across the stage before disentangling himself and taking refuge in the nearest audience box. Meanwhile, the frenzied, rearing animal caused a panic among the orchestra members, who fled.

That *Mazeppa* actually went off well compared to some other productions, no doubt because the title role was ably handled by the manager's son, Charles Foster, an accomplished horseman. In the midst of this horse opera, Jefferson observed a moment of true pathos. J. G. Cartlitch, who played Mazeppa in the original Milner production at Astley's in 1823 and who now, in the late 1840s, resided in Philadelphia, was devastated to the point of tears on learning that he would not have the lead role. Jefferson recalled the incident more than thirty years later in his *Autobiography,* when at the height of his own career he perhaps envisioned himself likewise superannuated: "No deposed emperor feels the force of compulsory abdication more than the stage king who has outlived the liking of the people." Jefferson, *Autobiography,* 95–97.

53. Quoted in Bloom, "Jefferson Company," 108.

54. It is not clear whether the Jeffersons emulated Thomas Hamblin's Bowery Theatre production, unique for its four-room stage set that allowed the audience to see the murder being planned and then carried out. This novelty represented a breakthrough of stage verisimilitude, helping establish new conventions of performance. George C. D. Odell, *Annals of the New York Stage,* 15 vols. (New York: Columbia University Press, 1927–49), 3:676; *National Intelligencer,* 26 November 1833, 2; Bloom, "Jefferson Company," 108–12; Power, *Impressions,* 1:210; Constance McLaughlin Green, *Washington: Village and Capital, 1800–1878* (Princeton: Princeton University Press, 1962), 150–51; *Spirit of the Times,* 12 December 1835, 4. On the history of Washington theatres, see also A. J. Mudd, "The Theatre of Washington City from 1835 to 1850," *Columbia Historical Society Records* 5 (1902) and 6 (1903). For a fine collection of sources on these and other American theatres, see William C. Young, *Documents of American Theater History,* vol. 1, *Famous American Playhouses, 1716–1899* (Chicago: American Library Association, 1973). The older Washington Theatre continued in service, taken over by the Walnut Street Theatre manager Francis Wemyss. *National Intelligencer,* 8 January 1834, 2.

55. *National Intelligencer,* 24 November 1834, 3; Bloom, "Jefferson Company," 111.

56. Bloom, "Jefferson Company," 210

57. In a Wilmington theatre that July, he was billed as "Master Jefferson" in *The Snow Storm.* Bloom, "Jefferson Company," 112–15.

58. Odell, *Annals of the New York Stage,* 4:2. Elizabeth married a second time in 1835 to Augustus Richardson of Baltimore, at which time she left the stage. But like Chapman, he died from an accident (suffered in a fall from the upper story of a store), and she, now as "Mrs. Richardson," returned to the Park stage before joining her brother and his family in the South. Winter, *Life of Jefferson,*

59. Arthur Quinn has a good discussion of Philadelphia and New York theatricals in his *History of the American Drama,* 1:201–2; Combe quoted in Bloom, "Jefferson Company," 112.

60. *New York Mirror,* quoted in "Conditions of the Streets in 1836," in Henry Collins Brown, ed., *Valentine's Manual of Old New York,* no. 6, n.s. (1922): 266.

61. Useful recent overviews of New York theatre culture in these years are found in Grimsted, *Melodrama Unveiled;* Bruce McConachie, *Melodramatic Formations: American Theatre and Society, 1820–1870* (Iowa City: University of Iowa Press, 1992), and Rosemarie K. Bank, *Theatre Culture in America, 1825–1860* (Cambridge: Cambridge University Press, 1997). Trollope quoted in Bank, 116. It should be noted that the second Bowery Theatre, constructed in 1828, was intended for a more elite patronage than it came to serve in the 1830s.

62. Odell, *Annals of the New York Stage,* 4:89; Ireland, *Records of the New York Stage,* 2:171; Odell, *Annals of the New York Stage,* 4:100.

63. This according to Joe's aunt Elizabeth Jefferson, quoted in Winter, *Life of Jefferson,* 104; Jefferson, *Autobiography,* 8.

64. Grimsted, *Melodrama Unveiled,* 103–4; Francis Courtney Wemyss, *Theatrical Biography; or the Life of an Actor and Manager* (Glasgow: R. Griffin, 1848), 128; On the Paris stage, see F. W. J. Hemmings, "Child Actors on the Paris Stage in the Eighteenth and Nineteenth Centuries," *Theatre Research International* 12:1 (1987):9–22. On the British stage, see William L. Slout and Sue Rudisill, "The Enigma of the Master Betty Mania," *Journal of Popular Culture* 8:1 (1974):81–90; Barton H. Baker, *History of the London Stage and Its Famous Players* (1904; reprint New York: Benjamin Blom, 1969), 124–25.

65. John Hanners, *"It Was Play or Starve": Acting in the Nineteenth-Century American Popular Theatre* (Bowling Green, Ohio: Bowling Green University Popular Press, 1993), 59–63; quotation from Laurence Hutton, *Curiosities of the American Stage* (New York: Harper and Bros, 1891), 242.

66. Donald B. Cole and John J. McDonough, *Witness to the Young Republic: A Yankee's Journal, 1828–1870* (Hanover, N.H.: University Press of New England, 1989), 32; Skinner, *One Player in His Time,* 162; Dickens, *Nicholas Nickleby,* 216; Wood, *Recollections,* 221–22. There were occasional exceptions to the cessation of children in adult roles, such as the rage for juvenile *H. M S. Pinafore* companies in the 1880s.

67. Recorded in one of the basic theatrical sources of the age, Joseph Ireland's *Records of the New York Stage from 1750 to 1860;* Jefferson, *Autobiography,* 14–15. A tragic irony later clouded this brief and inconsequential moment of theatre, one that underscores — if bizarrely — the frequently mercurial trajectory of child stars. While the vanquished supporting actor Joe Jefferson would ultimately achieve theatrical acclaim, Master Titus was soon after blinded when a gun exploded on stage, cutting short his career. He was not the only adolescent to suffer a serious stage accident; Mary Marsh, the main attraction of the Marsh Juvenile Troupe, was performing with her company in a southern town when her dress caught fire from a footlight and consumed her. William Winter tells of Master Titus in his *Life of Jefferson,* 162; the Marsh incident recounted in Peter Hay, *Theatrical Anecdotes* (New York: Oxford University Press, 1987), 333.

Chapter Two. Marking the Progress of Civilization

1. A. T. Andreas, *History of Chicago from the Earliest Period to the Present Time,* 3 vols. (Chicago: A. T. Andreas, 1884), 1:474–75. Bloom's "Jefferson Company," 116–18, offers general information on the company during the Chicago years. James McVicker, a prominent Chicago theatre owner of several decades later, notes that previously this entertainment had been limited to such novelties as a Mr. Barnes, who combined "feats of the Fire King" with ventriloquism and slight of hand. McVicker, *Theatre: Its Early Days in Chicago* (Chicago: Chicago Historical Society, 1884).

2. Bloom, "Jefferson Company," 119–21; quote on p. 119.

3. Dates taken from Ludlow, *Dramatic Life,* 405; Wittke, *Tambo and Bones,* 22–23. Joe Cowell claimed that some towns improvised theatres before they built a church. *Thirty Years,* 87. The best general overview of theatre in these years is James H. Dormon, Jr., *Theater in the Ante Bellum South, 1815–1861* (Chapel Hill: University of North Carolina Press, 1967), chap. 3.

4. Anticipating tactics of later Mississippi River casinos, the Chapmans discovered that if they performed on the river they could avoid bothersome licensing fees. The

Chapmans hosted audiences on their ark, a practice that nearly led to disaster on one occasion when local wags at a river town in Indiana cut the craft loose. It floated down river a half dozen miles before it could be moored, forcing the audience to walk home. Accounts of western theatricals include Noah Ludlow, *Dramatic Life as I Found It;* Solomon Smith, *The Theatrical Apprenticeship of Sol Smith* (Philadelphia: Carey and Hart, 1847). Glimpses into this bit of early Americana can also be found in many actors' memoirs and secondary histories of regional theatre. A fine secondary account of John Banvard's career is found in John Hanners, *"It Was Play or Starve,"* chap. 1. Power, *Impressions of America,* 2:208.

5. The low water may have been preferable to the alternative. Sol Smith tells of his tour with the Drakes at a town along the Wabash where bathing meant wrapping in sheets from the hotel and making late-night trips to the river. The day after one visit they discovered a fellow actor missing. A search resulted in the feared conclusion: his body washed ashore a few miles below town. Smith, *Theatrical Apprenticeship,* 39. Sketch of Banvard's career taken from Hanners, *"It Was Play or Starve."*

6. Ludlow, *Dramatic Life,* 17–56 passim.

7. Solomon Smith, *The Theatrical Journey — Work and Anecdotal Recollections of Sol. Smith* (Philadelphia: T. B. Peterson, c. 1854), 122–23.

8. Dormon, *Theatre in Ante Bellum South,* 102–3; David Carlyon provides a full biography of Rice in his *Dan Rice: The Most Famous Man You've Never Heard Of* (New York: Public Affairs, 2001).

9. Quoted in Odell, *Annals of the New York Stage,* 4:130–31.

10. Ibid., 4:237–39, 180–83. Niblo's Garden would endure under many future managers and a different name until 1854.

11. Details of this trip are found in Jefferson's *Autobiography,* 17–19; Ronald E. Shaw, *Erie Water West: A History of the Erie Canal, 1792–1854* (Lexington: University of Kentucky Press, 1964), 198–214;

12. Jefferson, *Autobiography,* 19–20.

13. Bloom, "Jefferson Company," 122; Bessie Louise Pierce, ed., *As Others See Chicago: Impressions of Visitors, 1673–1933* (Chicago: University of Chicago Press, 1933), 93; Jefferson, *Autobiography,* 20–21.

14. Observations of English travelers James Buckingham and Harriet Martineau in Pierce, *As Others See Chicago,* 81–89.

15. Alexis de Tocqueville, *Democracy in America,* ed. J. P. Mayer (New York: Anchor Books, 1969), 493; MacKenzie's license request found in Andreas, *History of Chicago,* 1:476. There is no indication that a monopoly was granted.

16. Various documents pertaining to licensing debate are found in Andreas, *History of Chicago,* 1:476–77.

17. Joe Jefferson's memory of the theatre building directly contradicts itself. In his *Autobiography* he recalls the seats of the dress circle being "stuffed." But in an earlier letter (1882) to James McVicker he says he does not think they were stuffed but "am almost sure that they were planed." This is not an issue of consequence. But it does give further warning to weigh carefully the details he provides from his early life. (He would have been nine years of age at this time.) Andreas, *History of Chicago,* 1:476; Jefferson, *Autobiography,* 22–23.

18. Bloom, "Jefferson Company," 124. To some scholars, Bulwer-Lytton's prose epitomizes the overwrought style of his age. "It was a dark and stormy night," the opening of *Paul Clifford,* has become a much-travestied line, even inspiring a tongue-in-cheek Bulwer-Lytton contest sponsored by the English Department at San Jose State University each year to write the most hackneyed opening line for a story.

19. David Grimsted's *Melodrama Unveiled,* 254, provides a chart of the most produced plays in antebellum America. Actress and playwright Anna Cora Mowatt chose the role of Pauline for her stage debut in 1845; Leonard R. N. Ashley, ed., *Nineteenth-Century British Drama* (Glenview, Ill.: Scott, Foresman, 1967), *The Lady of Lyons,* 1.2., 150.

20. The relation of Chicago to hinterland is tenderly described in William Cronon's, *Nature's Metropolis: Chicago and the Great West* (New York: W. W. Norton, 1991).

21. Quote of George Borrett in M. H. Dunlop, *Sixty Miles From Contentment: Traveling the Nineteenth-Century American Interior* (New York: Basic Book, 1995), 60; Jefferson, *Autobiography,* 24.

22. Descriptions of Galena found in *The WPA Guide to Illinois* (1939, reprint, New York: Pantheon Books, 1983), 333–37; Robert Dale Farrell, "Illinois Theatrical Company, 1837–1840" (master's thesis, University of Illinois, 1964), 28–29, 520; Augustus Chetlain, *Recollections of Seventy Years* (Galena: Gazette Publishers, 1899), 26–27. The most thorough study of Jefferson's Galena experience is given by Don B. Wilmeth, "The MacKenzie-Jefferson Theatrical Company in Galena, 1838–1839," *Journal of the Illinois State Historical Society* 40 (spring 1967): 23–36. Quote from Wilmeth, 25.

23. These figures compiled from listing of plays found in Farrell, "Illinois Theatrical Company." Arthur Bloom's study of the Jefferson Company during the early 1830s documents an even more ambitious repertoire, 123 plays over 116 evenings of performance. "Jefferson Company," 99; Wilmeth, "MacKenzie-Jefferson Theatrical Company," 29–32.

24. Chetlain, *Recollections,* 176; Farrell, "Illinois Theatrical Company," 36–37.

25. Given the unreliable nature of other stories from his early life, one is tempted to look hard at this one. But his account is at least partially verified by newspaper reports of unseasonably warm weather in the area in February 1839. Farrell, "Illinois Theatrical Company," 38; Jefferson, *Autobiography,* 24.

26. The story of Dubuque theatricals told by Harold and Ernestine Briggs in "The Early Theatre in the Upper Mississippi Valley," *Mid-America* 20 (July 1949): 133–36; even more detail on Iowa theatricals is provided by J. S. Schick, *Early Theatre in Eastern Iowa, 1836–1863* (Chicago: University of Chicago Press, 1939).

27. Jefferson, *Autobiography,* 25; Eliza R. Steele, *A Summer's Journey to the West* (1841) quoted in Paul M. Angle, *Prairie State: Impressions of Illinois, 1863–1967, by Travelers and Other Observers* (Chicago: University of Chicago Press, 1968), 186; *Alton Commercial Gazette,* 28 May 1839, 4 June 1839, all quoted in Farrell, "Illinois Theatrical Company," 40–44. The absence of Nauvoo, Illinois, from the MacKenzie-Jefferson itinerary in 1839 and 1840 deserves comment. Nauvoo is located on the Mississippi just a few miles from Burlington. Joseph Smith's Mormon disciples arrived in spring of 1839 and proceeded over the next few years to make it the largest city in Illinois. But Nauvoo's rise and the Jefferson's tour slid by each other unnoticed. Mormons did, however, actively embrace amateur theatricals once they established their new Zion in Utah.

28. *Sangamo Journal,* 21 June 1839, 2.

29. Jefferson, *Autobiography,* 27

30. An example is recounted in *Billboard,* 7 November 1903, reprinted in *American Entertainment: A Unique History of Popular Show Business,* ed. Joseph Csida and June Bundy Csida (New York: Watson-Guptill, 1978), 38. The measure of how deeply Jefferson's story has penetrated American folklore can be taken in two places. The *Autobiography* account was excerpted by Henry Steele Commager and Allan Nevins in their *Witness to America* (1939) and kept intact when Stephen Ambrose and Douglas Brinkley brought out a new edition in 2000. Further, in the mid-1970s WNET produced for public television as part of its American Forum series a half-hour dramatization of the Springfield-Lincoln incident called "The Devil's Work."

31. Paul Angle was the first to call the incident into question in his history of Springfield, *Here I Lived, a History of Lincoln's Springfield, 1821–1861* (New Brunswick: Rutgers University Press, 1935). Ruth Hardin picked up the thread and examined the evidence available to her and reached similar conclusions in "Lincoln and the Jefferson Players," *Journal of the Illinois State Historical Society* 40 (1947): 444–45. Arthur Bloom accepts her version in his "Jefferson Company," 126.

32. *Sangamo Journal,* 24 February 1838, 2. I am indebted to John Lupton of the Lincoln Legal Papers project for a copy of Lincoln's fee book and estimated date of "theatre folk" entry. There is little doubt that the "folk" mentioned are the MacKenzie-Isherwood company. Jefferson's mistaken notion that Lincoln refused to accept a fee for his service partakes of another convention of nineteenth-century reminiscences: the myth that Lincoln served selflessly as legal tribune. In fact, many such stories have been contradicted by the research of the Lincoln Legal Papers project, which finds generous fees that Lincoln charged and collected for his work. Phone conversation with John Lupton, 20 August 1998.

Jefferson's garbled facts might be partially explained by the probable genesis of his "recollection." In 1838 Abraham Lincoln was not famous, nor would he be widely known outside of Illinois for another twenty years. There would be no reason for any of the Illinois Theatrical Company members to think twice about attorney Lincoln. Mention of the Lincoln episode to Joe Jefferson must have come from a surviving company member at some point after Lincoln attained national prominence. Thus Joe was telling an account of an incident that occurred when he was only nine years old, that occurred when he was not present, that was told to him decades later with whatever elaborations one might imagine, and that was then further enhanced through Jefferson's own considerable storytelling prowess.

The verification of Jefferson's account, at least in its essentials, enhances the credibility of his *Autobiography.* Jefferson's memory was frequently faulty, especially regarding chronology in his earlier life. But scholars must resist imputing willful fabrication to his life. For a more complete examination of this incident see my "Joseph Jefferson's Lincoln: Vindication of an Autobiographical Legend," *Journal of the Illinois State Historical Society* (July 2000), 155–66.

33. *Sangamo Journal,* 12 July 1839, quoted in Farrell, "Illinois Theatrical Company," 50; *Daily Chicago American,* 19 August 1839, 2.

34. *Daily Chicago American,* 19 August 1839, 2; 17 August 1839, 2; 31 August 1839, 2; 5 September 1839, 2.

35. *Daily Chicago American,* 5 September 1839, 2; 6 September 1839, 2; 19 September 1839, 2.

36. Robert L. Sherman, *Chicago Stage: Its Record and Achievements,* vol. 1, 1833–1871 (published by Robert L. Sherman, [n.d.]), 46–47; Bloom, "Jefferson Company," 127–28; *Chicago Daily American,* 1 October 1839, 2.

37. *Chicago Daily American,* 19 September 1839, 2; 16 October 1839, 1.

38. See John Mack Faragher, *Sugar Creek: Life on the Illinois Prairie* (New Haven: Yale University Press, 1986), 74; Angle, *Here I Lived,* 83–87; Arthur Bloom suggests that Greenbury Germon had also left, but according to a 6 December account in the *Sangamo Journal,* he remained with the company. *Sangamo Journal,* 6 December 1839, 2. This anonymous letter reveals a highly detailed knowledge of Illinois Theatrical Company members. Its flattering description of each player and the brief it makes for the legitimacy of theatricals opens the possibility that it was in fact penned by MacKenzie or Jefferson. Such veiled self-promotion, in an age of journalistic puffery, was hardly unknown.

39. James Neal Primm, *Lion of the Valley: St. Louis, Missouri* (Boulder: Pruett Publishers, 1981), 147–54; William Oliver, *Eight Months in Illinois with Information to Emigrants* (1843; reprint, Ann Arbor: University Microfilms, 1966), 88–90; St. Louis would double its population to 35,000 by 1845 and surpass 77,000 by 1850.

40. Farrell, "Illinois Company," 69–70.

41. Solomon Smith, *The Theatrical Apprenticeship and Anecdotal Recollections* (Philadelphia: Carey and Hart, 1842), 204–6. The rift is sometimes blamed on Ludlow's prickly personality and his paranoid fear that Smith was cheating him. For his part, Smith had resented Ludlow's cutting him out of co-management of the Mobile theatre before their partnership began, to which was added his conviction that Ludlow had failed to repay a large loan late in their partnership. Smith managed to write three autobiographies without a single mention of their collaboration. Ludlow retaliated in his memoirs with pointed comments on Smith's mendacity. Francis Hodge provides sensible commentary on this feud in his introduction to Ludlow, *Dramatic Life.*

42. William C. Young, *Famous American Playhouses: Documents of American Theater History,* 2 vols. (Chicago: American Library Association, 1973), 1:142–32; Smith quote in Dormon, *Theater in Ante Bellum South,* 181.

43. Dormon, *Theater in Ante Bellum South,* 182; quotes from William G. B. Carson, *Managers in Distress: The St. Louis Stage, 1840–1844* (St. Louis: St. Louis Historical Document Foundation, 1949), 19–20.

44. Carson, *Managers in Distress,* 28; *Daily Missouri Republican,* 9 March 1840, 2.

45. *Daily Missouri Republican,* 9 March 1840, 2; 11 March 1840, 2.

46. Bloom, "Jefferson Company," 129; *Daily Missouri Republican,* 21 March 1840, 2.

47. Bloom, "Jefferson Company," 130.

48. Arthur Bloom has done a yeoman's job in seeking to establish the footsteps of the troupe. "Jefferson Company," 130–31; see also Farrell, "Illinois Company," 71–77; Dickens quote in Dunlop, *Sixty Miles,* 60; Richard R. John, *Spreading the News: The American Postal System from Franklin to Morse* (Cambridge: Harvard University Press, 1995), 37–38.

49. *Daily Republican Banner,* 23 September 1841, 2; 9 October 1841, 2; Bloom, "Jefferson Company," 130–31; Winter, *Life of Jefferson,* 145; comment on Potter from nineteenth-century actor Walter Leman, quoted in Claude Ahmed Arnold, "The De-

velopment of the Stage in Nashville, Tennessee, 1807–1870," (master's thesis, University of Iowa, 1933), 55. Potter also had a reputation for unreliability in paying actors' salaries or repaying loans, according to Douglas McDermott's fine short sketch in Don Wilmeth and Christopher Bigsby, eds., *The Cambridge History of the American Theatre*, vol. 1, *Beginnings to 1870* (New York: Cambridge University Press, 1998), 197–200; Leman quote in Arnold, "Stage in Nashville," 55.

50. Bloom, "Jefferson Company," 131; *Nashville Daily Republican Banner*, 20 November 1841, 2; Mark Twain, *Life on the Mississippi* (New York: Library of America, 1982), 391.

51. Guy Herbert Keeton, "The Theatre in Mississippi from 1840 to 1870" (Ph.D. diss., Louisiana State University, 1979), 18–21, 39–40, 243–51.

52. Ibid., 54–58; *Vicksburg Daily Whig*, 11 April 1842, 4.

53. Cornelia Jefferson to Noah Ludlow, 2 May 1842, Ludlow Field Maury Collection, Missouri Historical Society, St. Louis, Mo.; Bloom, "Jefferson Family," 131; Carson, *Managers in Distress*, 22; Jefferson, *Autobiography*, 44.

54. Raymond S. Hill, "Memphis Theatre, 1836–1846," *West Tennessee Historical Society Papers* 9 (1955): 48–53; Dormon, *Theater in Ante Bellum South*, 211; *Memphis American Eagle*, 6 May 1842, 2; 3 June 1842, 2; 17 June 1842, 2; Bloom, "Jefferson Company," 131–32.

55. Jefferson, *Autobiography*, 28.

56. Ibid., 28–29.

57. Ibid., 29–31.

58. Herman Melville, *The Confidence-Man* (New York: Grove Press, 1949), 18.

59. Jefferson, *Autobiography*, 31; a vivid picture of steamboat travel in this era is given by Dunlap in *Sixty Miles from Contentment*, 161–65; *New Orleans Daily Picayune*, 23 December 1845, 2; E. W. Gould's, *Fifty Years on the Mississippi; or, Gould's History of River Navigation* (St. Louis: Nixon-Jones Printing, 1889) gives numerous and graphic descriptions of steamboat accidents.

60. Cowell, *Thirty Years*, 97; Durang, *History of the Philadelphia Stage*, series 3, 37; Mary Duggar Toulmin, "Annals of the Mobile Theatre, 1808–1861," 2 vols., unpub. MS, Alabama Department of Archives and History, Montgomery, Ala., 2:387–88.

61. Cowell, *Thirty Years*, 97; Toulmin, "Annals of the Mobile Theatre," 2:388–92; yellow fever descriptions found in Jo Ann Carrigan, *The Saffron Scourge: A History of Yellow Fever in Louisiana, 1796–1905* (Lafayette, La.: Center for Louisiana Studies), 8.

Chapter Three. Behind the Cart of Thespis

1. Jefferson, *Autobiography*, 32–33.

2. First and third quotations from Dormon, *Theater in the Ante Bellum South*, 119–20, 183; second quotation from Harriet E. Amos Doss, *Cotton City: Urban Development in Antebellum Mobile* (University: University of Alabama Press, 1985), 46.

3. Dormon, *Theater in Ante Bellum South*, 33, 39, 47, 85–94; Durham, ed., *American Theatre Companies*, 29–32.

4. Dorman, *Theater in Ante Bellum South*, 186–87; Cowell, *Thirty Years*, 27.

5. Durham, ed., *American Theatre Companies*, 306–8, 332–33.

6. Outbreaks were not confined to the South; serious epidemics occurred in northern port cities like Philadelphia, New York, and Boston. But these had largely ended by early in the century. For a detailed history of yellow fever in the gulf region, see Carrigan, *Saffron Scourge*. Margaret H. Warner provides a detailed account of contemporary searches for the disease's cause in her essay "Public Health in the Old South," in Ronald L. Numbers and Todd L. Savitt, eds., *Science and Medicine in the Old South* (Baton Rouge: Louisiana State University Press, 1989), 226–55. During the 1839 outbreak, Mobile also suffered a fire that devastated one-third of the city. Suspicions of arson were further fueled by later testimony by escaped slaves that blacks had set the fire as part of a conspiracy to take over the city during the epidemic. Carrigan, *Saffron Scourge*, 434; Josiah C. Nott, *Sketch of the Epidemic of Yellow Fever of 1847 in Mobile* (1848; reprinted in *Yellow Fever Studies* [n.a.] New York: Arno Press, 1977), 4. Nott also shrewdly noted that the disease had stopped one fall before heavy frost had tempered the decomposition normally considered to be the yellow fever culprit, "thus showing a strong analogy with the habits of insect life" (5). Nott's early suggestion, though unpersuasive to his contemporaries, antedated Walter Reed's discovery by half a century.

7. Dormon, *Theater in Ante Bellum South*, 233–36; Pierson, *Tocqueville in America*, 628. Northern theatres practiced a segregation as thorough as those of the South. Tocqueville's companion, Gustave de Beaumont, was so struck by the relegation of a beautiful white-skinned (but mulatto) woman to the gallery in Philadelphia that he was moved to pen a novel on the subject, *Marie, or Slavery in the United States; a Novel of Jacksonian America*. An odd mixture of fiction and social commentary, the work is essentially an Enlightenment critique of democracy's failure to extend freedom to people of color. The heroine, Marie, to all appearances a white woman, was tainted by a "drop of black blood," which dooms her to second-class status and tragedy. The story includes a telling scene at a theatre where a stirring play about Napoleon (the very play Beaumont had witnessed in Philadelphia) roused the audience from its "accustomed indifference" to what occurred on stage. More important, Marie's mulatto brother is spotted among the white patrons and a cry sent up, "Throw him out! He is a colored man!" A near riot ensues, as George stands his ground until the police came and dragged him away. Although a popular success in France, the work's criticism of a sensitive American practice kept it from appearing in translation until 1958, and only in 1999 did a full English translation bespeak a growing scholarly appreciation of Beaumont's incisive look at America. *Marie*, trans. Barbara Chapman (Baltimore: Johns Hopkins University Press, 1999).

8. Ludlow, *Dramatic Life*, 478–79; Claudia Johnson, "That Guilty Third Tier: Prostitution in Nineteenth-Century American Theatre," *American Quarterly* 27 (December 1975): 575–84.

9. Toulmin, "Annals of Mobile Theatre," 2:396–97.

10. Taylor, "Mobile, 1818–1859," 78–79; Power, *Impressions of America*, 2:219–20; Dormon, *Theater in Ante Bellum South*, 242–43.

11. *Mobile Register and Journal*, 27 December 1844, 2; Smith quote in Toulmin, "Annals of the Mobile Theatre," 2:391; Arthur Bloom compiled the statistics on Richardson's dramas in his "Jefferson Company," 134.

12. *Mobile Register and Journal*, 13 April 1843, 3.

13. Dormon, *Theater in Ante Bellum South,* chap. 8; Ludlow, *Dramatic Life,* 531–63;

14. I am indebted to Dewey Ganzel's fine study for my discussion of Parliament and patent theatres: "Patent Wrongs and Patent Theatres: Drama and the Law in the Nineteenth Century" *PMLA* 76 (1961): 385–96; Ernest Bradlee Watson, *Sheridan to Robertson* (1926; reprint, New York: Benjamin Blom, 1963), 24–25. By the later eighteenth century, various dodges, particularly the burlettas, reduced the bite of censorship. Further, the era of Adam Smith was dawning, and unfettered trade was in the air, making eventual challenges to the monopoly of the patent houses almost inevitable. In 1832 a major parliamentary report by a select committee concluded that the decline of English drama was attributable in part to the official monopoly and called for its end — something that would happen eleven years later. House of Commons Select Committee on Dramatic Literature, *Report from the Select Committee on Dramatic Literature with the Minutes of Evidence,* 2 August 1832. See also L. W. Connolly, *The Censorship of the English Drama, 1737–1824* (San Marino: Huntington Library, 1976). The Continental Congress's vote to discourage theatricals during the American Revolution hardly qualifies as an act of censorship. Its motivation involved maintaining public focus on the immediate task of war. Nor do the voluntary film review boards set up for the movie industry in the twentieth century truly parallel an official government censor.

15. Edmund Morgan, "Puritan Hostility to the Theatre," *Proceedings of the American Philosophical Society* 110 (27 October 1966): 340–47; Jürgen C. Wolter, ed., *The Dawning of American Drama: American Dramatic Criticism, 1746–1915* (Westport, Conn.: Greenwood Press, 1993), 9–11, 29–32; Tocqueville, *Democracy in America,* 493.

16. Major surveys or interpretive studies of American drama of the time include Arthur Hobson Quinn, *A History of the American Drama from the Beginning to the Civil War* (New York: S. F. Crofts, 1943); Grimsted, *Melodrama Unveiled;* Meserve, *Heralds of Promise;* McConachie, *Melodramatic Formations;* Jeffrey D. Mason, *Melodrama and the Myth of America* (Bloomington: Indiana University Press, 1993).

17. Tocqueville, *Democracy in America,* 492–93. Tocqueville's exposure to the American theatre appears to have been limited. We know he and Beaumont attended in Philadelphia and New Orleans but beyond these occasions it is not certain. See George Pierson's *Tocqueville in America* for their reactions.

18. Jefferson, *Autobiography,* 34–35.

19. Mary Shaw, "The Human Side of Joseph Jefferson," *Century* 85 (January 1913): 379.

20. *Nashville Union,* 16 June 1843, 2; 19 June 1843, 3; 4 July 1843, 2; 4 August 1843, 2.

21. Jefferson, *Autobiography,* 39–40.

22. Ibid., 45–47.

23. Ibid., 44–45.

24. On the culture of sincerity and fraud, see Halttunen, *Confidence Men and Painted Women,* and Harris, *Humbug,* esp. chap. 8.

25. Jefferson, *Autobiography,* 73–75.

26. Herman Melville, *The Confidence-Man* (New York: Grove Press, 1955), 102.

27. Comment on his father quoted by Mary Shaw in "Human Side of Joseph Jefferson," 380.

28. *Mobile Register and Journal,* 21 April 1845, 2; Jefferson, *Autobiography,* 35.

29. Quotations taken from Lael J. Woodbury, "Styles of Acting in Serious Drama on the Nineteenth Century Stage" (Ph.D. diss., University of Illinois, 1954), 60–71.

30. Wemyss, *Theatrical Biography,* 37; Stephen M. Archer, *Junius Brutus Booth: Theatrical Prometheus* (Carbondale: Southern Illinois University Press, 1992), 183; Leman quote in Woodbury, "Styles of Acting," 64; Skinner, *One Man in His Time,* 55.

31. Jefferson, *Autobiography,* 37–38. Booth's approach to rehearsals was even more casual than toward performances. George Vandenhoff, when supporting Booth, said he stopped attending run-throughs, knowing how fruitless they were given the star's irregular ways. *Leaves from an Actor's Note-book; with Reminiscences and Chit-chat of the Green Room and the Stage, in England and America* (New York: Appleton, 1860), 234.

32. The standard work on Macready is Alan S. Downer's *Eminent Tragedian: William Charles Macready* (Cambridge: Harvard University Press, 1966), an outstanding example of theatrical biography. See also Ernest Bradlee Watson's fine sketch of Macready's art in his *Sheridan to Robertson,* 298–307, 178–79.

33. Downer, *Eminent Tragedian,* 75–80; *Mobile Register and Journal,* 4 March 1844, 2; Ludlow, *Dramatic Life,* 592.

34. Vandenhoff, *Leaves From an Actor's Note-book,* 221.

35. Jefferson, *Autobiography,* 36–37. Theatrical annals are filled with stories of Macready's summoning a guilty party to his room after a performance where the tongue-lashing commenced. So redoubtable a figure as Charlotte Cushman incurred the tragedian's wrath when her necklace broke during a scene scattering pearls across the stage. Walter M. Leman, *Memories of an Old Actor* (San Francisco: A. Roman, 1886), 171; Leach, *Bright, Particular Star,* 115.

36. In truth, a similar magnanimity marks most actor memoirs. It is a literature that with a few exceptions sets forth an aggressive defense of their profession, that closes ranks and puts aside jealousies, difficult personalities, and wranglings. To publicly air the dirty linen of their calling would have been counterproductive to the aim of professional advance. Macready's memoirs, in contrast, express regret over his career in the theatre, an institution that never lived up to his demanding expectations. Junius Brutus Booth shared at least this with Macready, for he actively discouraged his sons from an acting career.

37. Quoted in Dormon, *Theater in Ante Bellum South,* 174.

38. Harnett T. Kane, *Queen New Orleans: City by the River* (New York: William Morrow, 1949), 163–64, 176; John Gaisford, *The Drama in New Orleans* (New Orleans: J. B. Steel, 1849), 7–8. Charles Lyell, *A Second Visit to the United States of North America,* vol. 2, in Allan Nevins, ed., *American Social History as Reported by British Travellers* (New York: Augustus Kelley, 1969), 333.

39. *New Orleans Daily Picayune,* 7 February 1846, 2; 29 March 1846, 2.

40. Gaisford, *Drama in New Orleans,* 15; *New Orleans Daily Picayune,* 9 November 1845, 2; 18 November 1845, 2; 21 November 1845, 3; Ludlow, *Dramatic Life,* 640–41; John Smith Kendall, *The Golden Age of the New Orleans Theater* (Baton Rouge: Louisiana State University Press, 1952), 260. The following season Ludlow and Smith traded out unsparing wooden benches for cushioned chairs in the preferred seating of the theatre.

41. *Spirit of the Times,* 23 August 1845, 308; *New Orleans Daily Picayune,* 18 November 1845, 3.

42. Background information on the Keans from W. G. B. Carson, ed., *Letters of Mr. and Mrs. Charles Kean Relating to Their American Tour* (St. Louis: Washington University Publications in Language and Literature, 1945). On Charles Kean's place in theatre, see Watson, *Sheridan to Robertson*, 222–31, 362–70.

43. Skinner, *One Man in His Time*, 24; Sol Smith likewise had kind words about the Keans, finding them unassuming and agreeable to deal with, *Theatrical Management*, 199.

44. Ludlow's *Dramatic Life* recounts the performances of the entire season. Dormon's *Theater in Ante Bellum South* adds further detail. The Keans' second run was billed as their "farewell" engagement, a common managerial ploy to get out the crowds. The Keans, however, took this a step further, repeatedly announcing plans to retire only to return yet again to the boards. William Carson interpreted this as more than a transparent gambit for self-gain; rather he believes Charles Kean was truly conflicted about remaining an active performer; *New Orleans Daily Picayune*, 5 March 1846, 2.

45. Information on Mowatt's life can be found in her *Autobiography of an Actress* (Boston: Ticknor and Fields, 1854), *American National Biography*, s.v. "Anna Cora Mowatt," by Mary C. Kalfatovic; Claudia Johnson's *American Actress: Perspective in the Nineteenth Century* (Chicago: Nelson-Hall, 1984) contains a useful chapter on Mowatt. Also Meserve, *Heralds of Promise*, 127–33, has critical comment on Mowatt and her play.

46. Myron Matlow, ed., *Nineteenth-Century American Plays* (New York: Applause Books, 1967), 27; Poe's reviews are reprinted in Montrose Moses and John Mason Brown, eds., *The American Theatre as Seen by Its Critics, 1752–1934* (New York: W. W. Norton, 1934), 59–66.

47. Mowatt, *Autobiography*, 234; Hutton quoted in Johnson, *American Actress*, 126; Edgar Allan Poe, *Essays and Reviews* (New York: Library of America, 1984), 1140.

48. Harold Brehm Obee, "A Prompt Script Study of Nineteenth-Century Legitimate Stage Versions of *Rip Van Winkle*" (Ph.D. diss., Ohio State University, 1961), 247.

49. Wolter, ed., *Dawning of American Drama*, 114.

50. *Fashion* excerpts taken from Matlow, *Nineteenth-Century American Plays*, passim.

51. In Wolter, ed., *Dawning of American Drama*, 15. This quality was hardly different from any other drama of the age. The *Albion* reviewer was answering a concern that Mowatt had sought to deride certain individuals in her play.

52. David Grimsted's introduction to his collection of sources, *Notions of the Americans, 1820–1860* (New York: George Braziller, 1970) discusses Jacksonian unease over social trends. Joseph Ellis points out Jefferson's contradictions of prescription and lifestyle in his *American Sphinx: The Character of Thomas Jefferson* (New York: Random House, 1996). The ongoing cultural appeal of simplicity is the theme of David Shi's *The Simple Life: Plain Living and High Thinking in American Culture* (New York: Oxford University Press, 1985).

53. *Daily Missouri Republican*, 27 April 1846, 3. Actually Booth returned two nights later. The St. Louis public made it known that it forgave Booth his failings, and Smith and Ludlow brought him back to a successful conclusion of his run. Accounts vary about the

audience's initial response to Booth. Ludlow's *Dramatic Life* (644–45) gives the story as I have told it here. But the prompter's book, closer in time to the event than Ludlow's later account, states that the audience hissed Booth. Kendall, *Golden Age of New Orleans Theater*, 261.

54. Kendall, *Golden Age of New Orleans Theater*, 260–61. Kendall mistakenly places this incident in New Orleans.

55. *Daily Missouri Republican*, 4 July 1846, 3; Jefferson, *Autobiography*, 41; John T. Ford recounted his recollection of Joe's story in a letter to William Winter, 15 August 1876, John T. Ford Papers, Manuscript Division, Library of Congress; Mowatt, *Autobiography*, 266.

56. Jefferson, *Autobiography*, 41–42.

57. *New Orleans Daily Picayune*, 27 November 1845, 2.

58. The beginnings of Texas theatre are documented in Clyde Richard King, "A History of the Theatre in Texas, 1722–1900" (Ph.D. diss., Baylor University, 1963), and Edward G. Fletcher, "The Beginnings of the Professional Theatre in Texas," *University of Texas Bulletin*, no. 3621 (1 June 1936). Information on early Galveston can be found in Gary Cartwright, *Galveston: A History of the Island* (New York: Atheneum, 1991); Charles W. Hayes, *Galveston: History of the Island and the City*, 2 vols. (1879; reprint, Austin: Jenkins Garrett Press, 1974); David G. McComb, *Galveston: A History* (Austin: University of Texas Press, 1986). On theatre there, see Dormon, *Theater in Ante Bellum South*, 218–19; and, in particular, Joseph Gallegly, *Footlights on the Border: The Galveston and Houston Stage before 1900* (The Hauge: Mouton, 1962); Jefferson, *Autobiography*, 47.

59. Marguerite Johnston, *Houston: The Unknown City, 1836–1946* (College Station: Texas A&M University Press, 1991), 33.

60. Dormon confirms Jefferson's story in his *Theater in Ante Bellum South*, 142. According to some accounts, the felonious Indians were identified by their theatrical costuming, including the garments of Othello and Hamlet; Jefferson, *Autobiography*, 38–53.

61. Information on theatre in the Mexican-American War from Richard Bruce Winders, *Mr. Polk's Army: The American Military Experience in the Mexican War* (College Station: Texas A&M University Press, 1997), 132–34; John Porter Bloom, "With the American Army into Mexico, 1846–1848" (Ph.D. diss., Emory University, 1956), 232–34.

62. By far the best description of the Hart company's appearance in Mexico is provided by LeRoy P. Graf, "Soldier Entertainment a Hundred Years Ago," *Theatre Annual* 5 (1946): 47–61.

63. Firsthand description of Matamoros provided by a volunteer soldier, John R. Kenly, *Memoirs of a Maryland Volunteer in the Years, 1846-7-8* (Philadelphia: Lippincott, 1873), 45–6,51–2; *Spirit of the Times*, 13 June 1846, 187; Jefferson, *Autobiography*, 55; George Gordon Meade, *The Life and Letters of George Gordon Meade* (New York: Charles Scribner's Sons, 1913), 1:91.

64. Jefferson, *Autobiography*, 55. The eyewitness description of the Matamoros theatre was published in the *New Orleans Daily Picayune*, 16 August 1846, 2. Other detail of the performances found in Graf, "Soldier Entertainment," 51–56.

65. On the Mexican-American War, see Otis A. Singletary, *The Mexican War* (Chicago: University of Chicago Press, 1960); John S. D. Eisenhower, *So Far from God: The U. S. War with Mexico, 1846–1848* (New York: Random House, 1989).

66. The eyewitness description of the Matamoros theatre was published in the *New Orleans Daily Picayune*, 16 August 1846, 2; other detail of the performance in Graf, "Soldier Entertainment," 51–56. In his *Autobiography*, Jefferson describes his commercial venture in loving detail as a "coffee and cake stand." Why this alteration of history? Perhaps he suspected that readers would take a dim view of a seventeen-year-old boy operating a tobacco shop. Although tobacco lacked the stigma in the 1880s that it carries today, Joe may have feared a certain diminution of his reputation. LeRoy Graf in his "Soldier Entertainment," 56–57, provides the true story based on his research in the *American Flag* newspaper published during the American occupation.

67. On the issue of Victorian privacy, see Rochelle Gurstein, *The Repeal of Reticence: A History of America's Cultural and Legal Struggles over Free Speech, Obscenity, Sexual Liberation, and Modern Art* (New York: Hill and Wang, 1996). The story of the coffee shop and Metta appear in Jefferson's *Autobiography*, 55–62; attitudes of American soldiers toward Mexican women are explored in James M. McCaffrey, *Army of Manifest Destiny: The American Soldier in the Mexican War, 1846–1848* (New York: New York University Press, 1992), 77–79.

Chapter Four. An Actor Prepares

1. Jefferson, *Autobiography*, 63–65; Ludlow, *Dramatic Life*, 648–55.

2. Information on Owens's life found in Mary Owens, *Memoirs of the Professional and Social Life of John E. Owens and His Wife* (Baltimore: J. Murphy, 1892), passim; and L. Clarke Davis, "Among the Comedians," *Atlantic Monthly* 19 (June 1867): 755–58.

3. Jefferson, *Autobiography*, 65.

4. Ibid., 65.

5. Carrigan, *Saffron Scourge*, 55, 67.

6. Jefferson, *Autobiography*, 66–70.

7. Information on Philadelphia found in Sam Bass Warner, Jr., *The Private City: Philadelphia in Three Periods of Its Growth* (Philadelphia: University of Pennsylvania Press, 1968), 49–60; Edwin Wolf, *Philadelphia: Portrait of an American City* (Harrisburg: Stackpole Books, 1975), 176–204; Eliza Cope Harrison, ed., *Philadelphia Merchant: The Diary of Thomas P. Cope, 1800–1851* (South Bend: Gateway Editions, 1978), 524–604.

8. Durham, ed., *American Theatre Companies*, 198–99.

9. *Philadelphia Public-Ledger*, 28 December 1848, 3; 2 May 1849, 2.

10. Durham, ed. *American Theatre Companies*, 53–54. Beginning in 1861, the Arch Street would attain even great eminence under Mrs. John Drew, who sustained for nearly two decades an unexcelled standard of stock company excellence. David L. Rinear, *Stage, Page, Scandals, and Vandals: William E. Burton and Nineteenth-Century American Theatre* (Carbondale: Southern Illinois University Press, 2004), chap. 5.

11. The need for a modern critical biography of Burton was handsomely filled by Rinear's *Stage, Page, Scandals, and Vandals*. Randall Knoper has a fine discussion of

Burton in his *Acting Naturally: Mark Twain in the Culture of Performance* (Berkeley: University of California Press, 1995), 61. See also Charles H. Shattuck, *Shakespeare on the American Stage* (Washington, D.C.: Folger.Shakespeare Library, 1976), 103–11; "What will Burton play," quote in Keese, *William Burton*, 43; Allan Nevins, ed., *The Diary of Philip Hone, 1828–1851* (New York: Arno Press, 1970), 855.

12. Jefferson, *Autobiography*, 76–78.

13. Durang, *History of the Philadelphia Stage*, series 3, 279, 276.

14. The classic work on stock company training is Edward William Mammen's *The Old Stock Company School of Acting: A Study of the Boston Museum* (Boston: Trustees of the Public Library, 1945).

15. Bloom, "Jefferson Company," 103, 122, 130–31; Bloom, *Joseph Jefferson*, chap. 3; Forrest quoted in Grimsted, *Melodrama Unveiled*, 88.

16. Stage appearances compiled from theatre notices in *Philadelphia Public-Ledger*, 1847–53. It is possible, perhaps even likely, that Joe made additional appearances in such minor roles that his name did not appear in print.

17. Mammen, *Old Stock Company*, 20–21; Mowatt quoted in Grimsted, *Melodrama Unveiled*, 89.

18. Skinner, *One Man in His Time*, 105; Watson gives a fine portrait of the low comedian in his *Sheridan to Robertson*, 318–19. There are many studies of the stage Yankee. Francis Hodge's *The Stage Yankee: The Image of America on the Stage, 1825–1860* (Austin: University of Texas Press, 1964) remains a standard. See also Meserve, *Heralds of Promise*, 84–108; Rosemarie K. Bank, *Theatre Culture in America, 1825–1860* (Cambridge: Cambridge University Press, 1997), 39–42.

19. Information on Burke must be pieced together from stray comments of various actors. The two most complete sources are William Winter's *Life of Jefferson*, 142–52, and Jefferson's *Autobiography*, passim. Other useful sources include Hutton's *Curiosities of the Stage*, 40, 199–200; F. C. Bangs, "Recollections of Players," *New York Dramatic Mirror*, 5 February 1898, 24; Durang, *History of the Philadelphia Stage*, series 3, 265–66; Ellsler, *Stage Memories*, 40–41; Ludlow, *Dramatic Life*, 708; Ireland, *Records of New York Stage* (New York: T. H. Morrell, 1866–67), 2:194.

20. Burke's widely acclaimed performance on the violin has caused theatre historians to frequently confuse him with Joseph Burke, a violin prodigy of the day.

21. Jefferson, *Autobiography*, 86. Arthur Bloom has usefully reconstructed the interaction of the half brothers during these years in his *Joseph Jefferson*.

22. Jefferson, *Autobiography*, 103–4; Rinear, *Stage, Page, Scandals*, 90–91.

23. Michael Booth, *Prefaces to English Nineteenth-Century Theatre* (Manchester: Manchester University Press, 1976), 111–32; Leigh Hunt, *Dramatic Essays* (London: Walter Scott, 1894), 131.

24. John Maddison Morton, *Lend Me Five Shillings* (1846; reprint, New York: De Witt Pub., n.d.).

25. Alfred Bunn Sergel (adapted from the original French) *My Neighbor's Wife* (Chicago: Dramatic Publishing, n.d.).

26. Thomas F. Gossett, *Uncle Tom's Cabin and American Culture* (Dallas: Southern Methodist University Press, 1985), 260–69; *Philadelphia Public Ledger*, 26 June 1853, 3.

27. The best treatment of the novel's transition to drama is done by David Grimsted,

"*Uncle Tom* from Page to Stage: Limitations of Nineteenth-Century Drama," *Quarterly Journal of Speech* 56 (October 1970): 235–44. Other adaptations of the novel, notably Henry J. Conroy's (which was elaborately staged by Barnum), tempered the antislavery message. In Conroy's version, Uncle Tom does not die at Simon Lagree's hands but contentedly returns to slavery on his old Kentucky plantation. Gossett, *Uncle Tom's Cabin*, 274–75.

28. George L. Aiken, *Uncle Tom's Cabin*, in Don B. Wilmeth, ed., *Staging the Nation: Plays from the American Theater, 1787–1909* (Boston: Bedford Books, 1998), 181–246.

29. The later Tom shows sometimes descended into a decadent phase, relying on elaborate staging, packs of bloodhounds for the river scene, multiple Little Evas, etc. In some cases the script was overhauled to feature a particular character, as in the improbable expansion of Gumption Cute's role from its normal sixteen lines to eight hundred. Grimsted, "*Uncle Tom*," 244.

30. Edwin G. Burrows and Mike Wallace, *Gotham: A History of New York City to 1898* (New York: Oxford University Press, 1999), 651–53; Arthur Hobson Quinn makes the point about New York's port bestowing theatrical primacy in *History of the American Drama*, 1:202. Allan Nevins and Milton Halsey Thomas, eds., *The Diary of George Templeton Strong* (New York: Macmillan, 1952), 1:362; on the cholera epidemic, see Charles E. Rosenberg, *The Cholera Years* (Chicago: University of Chicago Press, 1962), 104–14.

31. Descriptions of midcentury New York are found in Burrows and Wallace, *Gotham*, 714–15; Mary C. Henderson, *The City and the Theatre* (Clifton, N.J.: James T. White, 1973), 35–111; Cowell, *Thirty Years*, 56; Henry James, *A Small Boy and Others* (New York: Charles Scribner's Sons, 1913).

32. The survey of New York theatricals in 1850 comes from Odell's *Annals of the New York Stage*, 6: passim; see also Henderson, *City and the Theatre*, chaps. 2 and 3; David S. Reynolds, *Walt Whitman's America* (New York: Alfred A. Knopf, 1995), chap. 6.

33. *American National Biography*, s.v. "Frank Chanfrau," by John Bush Jones. Walter Meserve's *Heralds of Promise*, 120–27 has a fine discussion of the theatrical phenomenon. An example of Mose in popular urban sociology is found in Foster, *New York by Gas Light*, 105–7; Stuart Blumin argues for Moses' traditional values in "Exploring the New Metropolis," *Journal of Urban History* 11 (1984): 22; *New York Herald*, 20 February 1850, 1.

34. See Mary P. Ryan, *Civic Wars: Democracy and Public Life in the American City during the Nineteenth Century* (Berkeley: University of California Press, 1997).

35. The most complete study of the Astor Place riot is Peter George Buckley's, "To the Opera House: Culture and Society in New York City, 1820–1860" (Ph.D. diss.: State University of New York at Stony Brook, 1984); see also "The Astor Place Riot," exhibit at the Museum of the City of New York (opened 27 March 1999).

36. James R. Anderson, *An Actor's Life* (London: Walter Scott, 1902), 74–75; Buckley, "To the Opera House," 79–83; Robert C. Allen, *Horrible Prettiness: Burlesque and American Culture* (Chapel Hill: University of North Carolina Press, 1991), 71–72.

37. *New York Herald*, 10 September 1849, 2; quotes in Odell, *Annals of the New York Stage*, 5:548.

38. Accounts of the courtship and marriage are given in Jefferson's *Autobiography*, 99–

100. A romanticized account is provided by Joe's granddaughter Eleanor Farjeon in her *Portrait of a Family* (New York: Frederick A. Stokes, 1936), 58–59.

39. Odell, *Annals of the New York Stage,* 6:550; Jefferson, *Autobiography,* 127–28; *New York Herald,* 20 May 1850, 4.

40. *New York Herald,* 22 May 1850, 3; Winter, *Life of Jefferson,* 192–93; L. Clarke Davis, "At and After the Play," *Lippincott's Magazine* 24 (July 1879): 62.

41, *New York Herald,* 30 April 1850, 1; Bloom, *Joseph Jefferson,* 49.

42. *New York Herald,* 13 September 1850, 1; 12 September 1850, 1.

43. Skinner, *One Man in His Time,* 92–93.

Chapter Five. Echoing the Public Voice

1. Jefferson, *Autobiography,* 87–89

2. Bloom, *Joseph Jefferson,* 60.

3. John Ellsler, *Stage Memories,* 45–48; *Charleston Courier,* 8 February 1851, 2.

4. *Charleston Courier,* 5 March 1851, 3; William Stanley Hoole, *The Antebellum Charleston Theatre* (Tuscaloosa: University of Alabama Press, 1946), 57, 130; Ellsler, *Stage Memories,* 49–50. Ellsler confuses the Charleston manager of this episode in 1851 with F. C. Adams, who the following December brought Joe and Ellsler back to Charleston.

5. Ellsler, *Stage Memories,* 50.

6. "Dutch" is an ambiguous term, often used as an English corruption of "Deutsch." It is not clear whether Ellsler instructed Joe in the accent of Hollanders or Germans. The partners' stint as itinerant managers launched Ellsler on a highly successful career in theatre management, notably as longtime operator of the Cleveland Academy of Music, a post from which he dominated the Erie city's theatricals for two decades. Odell, *Annals of the New York Stage,* 6:34–35; Durham, ed., *American Theatre Companies,* 2–3; Douglas McDermatt, "Structure and Management in the American Theatre from the Beginnings to 1870," in Wilmeth and Bigsby, eds. *Cambridge History of American Theatre,* 1:201; Jefferson, *Autobiography,* 102; Ellsler, *Stage Memories,* 76. Jefferson's casual approach to money described by Ellsler does not comport with the careful and even shrewd financial face Joe displayed later in his life.

7. Both Jefferson and Ellsler attest to the success of the Macon stand, as does Harry Watkins in his journal, Skinner, ed., *One Man in His Time,* 119; *Macon Journal and Messenger,* 19 March 1851, 2; 26 March 1851, 2.

8. "Charles Jefferson Talks of His Famous Father," newspaper clipping (1906), Bourne Historical Center, Bourne, Mass.; Bloom, *Joseph Jefferson,* 61–62.

9. Railroad observation made by Frederick Law Olmsted, quoted in Eugene Alvarez, *Travel on Southern Antebellum Railroads, 1838–1860* (Tuscaloosa: University of Alabama Press, 1974), 156; Jefferson, *Autobiography,* 102–3.

10. Odell, *Annals of the New York Stage,* 6:5 Jefferson, Autobiography, 103–5; Ellsler, *Stage Memories,* 54–59.

11. Ellsler, *Stage Memories,* 54-59; *Savannah Morning News,* 24 April 1851, 2; 25 April 1851, 2; Jefferson, *Autobiography,* 106–9.

12. Ellsler, *Stage Memories,* 70–71; Jefferson, *Autobiography,* 107.

13. Theatrical benefits, at least those intended as salary enhancements for actors,

disappeared by the later decades of the nineteenth century. The new combination system of touring shows altered older practices in many ways, one of which was the benefit. But it is important also to note that actors' self-conscious striving for professional standing correlated with the end of this practice.

14. Ben Graf Henneke, *Laura Keene: A Biography* (Tulsa: Council Oaks Books, 1990), 26–27; Buckley, "To the Opera House," 118–25; John J. Jennings, *Theatrical and Circus Life* (St. Louis: Sun Publishers, 1882), 58–59; Eugene Alvarez, *Travel on Southern Antebellum Railroads*, 131; Cowell, *Thirty Years*, 57; Ellsler, *Stage Memories*, 25–26; Francis Grund, ed., *Aristocracy in America: From the Sketch-Book of a German Nobleman* (London: Richard Bentley, 1839), 1:180–82; Montrose Moses, *Famous Actor-Families in America* (1906; reprint, New York: Benjamin Blom, 1968), 25; Joseph Leach, *Bright, Particular Star: The Life and Times of Charlotte Cushman* (New Haven: Yale University Press, 1970), 241.

15. Quoted in Bank, *Theatre Culture in America*, 85; Nicoll, *Garrick Stage*, 91; Buckley, "To the Opera House," 109.

16. Michael Booth, *Prefaces to English Nineteenth-Century Theatre* (Manchester: Manchester University Press, 1976), 55–68.

17. *New York Times*, 25 March 1890, 5; William Winter discusses Jefferson's Pangloss at some length in his *Life and Art of Joseph Jefferson*, 227–32. Joe's grandfather had performed Zekial Homespun in one of the earliest American productions of the play in 1799.

18. Jefferson, *Autobiography*, 115–16; George Colman (the Younger), *The Heir at Law* (London: Longman, Hurst, Rees, and Orms, 1808), 5.

19. Jefferson, *Autobiography*, 139–40.

20. Howard D. Dozier, *A History of the Atlantic Coast Line Railroad* (1920; reprint, New York: August M. Kelley, 1971), passim; Alvarez, *Travel on Southern Antebellum Railroad*, 32, 81, 126–30, 152; John H. White, Jr., *The American Railroad Passenger Car* (Baltimore: Johns Hopkins University Press, 1978), 433.

21. Jefferson, *Autobiography*, 109–12; *Wilmington Daily Journal*, 31 October 1851, 2; 7 November 1851, 2.

22. *Wilmington Daily Journal*, 21 October 1851, 2; 11 November 1851, 2; 3 November 1851, 2.

23. *Charleston Courier*, 1 January 1852, 3; quoted in William C. Young, *Famous American Playhouses: Documents of American Theater History*, 2 vols. (Chicago: American Library Association, 1973), 2:94–96. Joe says nothing about national politics in his *Autobiography*, although his travels to the South during an age troubled by the slavery issue might have prompted comment. The timing of his book, appearing in 1889, may have reinforced his resolutely apolitical nature. The age reacted to Reconstruction with a blind eye to southern intransigence over the matter of race. Sympathy with freedmen or their advocates was out of fashion; rebuilding social and political bridges with southern leaders was current. In such an atmosphere, Joe, even if he had misgivings about issues of slavery, would be highly unlikely to express them.

24. Winter, quoted in *American National Biography*, s.v. "Julia Dean," by Susan S. Cole; *New York Daily Times*, 10 April 1854, 4; 2 June 1853, 4.

25. Jefferson, *Autobiography*, 114–15; *Charleston Courier*, 6 March 1852, 1; 10 February 1852, 2; 28 February 1852, 2; Hoole, *Antebellum Charleston Theatre*, 132–33.

26. *Charleston Courier,* 8 March 1852, 2; 6 March 1852, 2; Hoole, *Antebellum Charleston Theatre,* 133.

27. Ellsler, *Stage Memories,* 79–80; quote in Eleanor Ruggles, *Prince of Players: Edwin Booth* (New York: W. W. Norton, 1953), 33; Francis Wilson, *Joseph Jefferson: Reminiscences of a Fellow Player* (New York: Charles Scribner's Sons, 1906), 144.

28. Ellsler, *Stage Memories,* 60–63; *Augusta Daily Chronicle and Sentinel,* 24 March 1852, 2.

29. *Augusta Daily Chronicle and Sentinel,* 31 March 1852, 2; 24 April 1852, 2.

30. Joe's itinerant days were not quite over. In summer 1856 he joined comedian John Sleeper Clarke in touring small towns of Maryland and West Virginia, and in 1857 he briefly toured hinterland Pennsylvania. Not much is known about this postscript to Joe's touring days except that they must have been very modest productions. Attendance was compromised at times by the summer heat. Jefferson to MC [?], 5 July 1857 [from Pottsville, Pa.], in Hutton and Mathews, eds., *Actors and Actresses of Great Britain and the United States,* Extra-illustrated Edition, vol. 5, no. 9, pt. 1, Harvard Theatre Collection; Bloom, *Joseph Jefferson,* 70; Davis, "At and After the Play," 67; Jefferson, *Autobiography,* 90. Joe refused to lay blame on Sefton for their parting. But Sefton, who was nearly twenty-five years older than Jefferson, had a notorious reputation. He had once been jailed for threatening the life of a member of his company. A "very disagreeable man," Harry Watkins recalled. Skinner, *One Man in His Time,* 159–60.

31. Jefferson, *Autobiography,* 89–90.

32. Bloom, *Joseph Jefferson,* 64–65.

33. Mona Domosh, *Invented Cities: The Creation of Landscape in Nineteenth-Century New York and Boston* (New Haven: Yale University Press, 1996), 100–101.

34. As in other such "museums," founder Moses Kimball included an array of stuffed animals, fossils, paintings, and sculpture. Mammen, *Old Stock Company,* 11–12; Meserve, *Heralds of Promise,* 147, 152. Actress Olive Logan provides a review of theatrical rules and fines in her *Before the Footlights and Behind the Scenes* (San Francisco: Parmalee, 1869), 64–65.

35. Winter, *Life of Jefferson,* 298; *Dictionary of American Biography,* s.v. "William Warren," by E. F. E.; Davis, "Among the Comedians," 759.

36. Richard Foster Stoddard, "The Architecture and Technology of Boston Theatres, 1794–1854" (Ph.D. diss., Yale University, 1971), 182–95; William W. Clapp, Jr., *A Record of the Boston Stage* (Boston: James Munroe, 1853), 463–44; *Spirit of the Times,* 2 April 1853, 74.

37. Durang, *History of the Philadelphia Stage,* series 3, 367–69; *Philadelphia Public Ledger,* 26 September 1853, 3.

38. Jefferson, *Autobiography,* 116–17.

39. Sidney George Fisher, *A Philadelphia Perspective: The Diary of Sidney George Fisher Covering the Years, 1834–1871* (Philadelphia: Historical Society of Pennsylvania, 1967), 211; Patricia C. Click, *The Spirit of the Times: Amusements in Nineteenth-Century Baltimore, Norfolk, and Richmond* (Charlottesville: University of Virginia Press, 1989), 42; *Baltimore American and Commercial Advertiser,* 28 August 1854, 3; 29 August 1854, 2.

40. *Baltimore American and Commercial Advertiser,* 9 October 1854, 2; 20 November 1854, 3; 21 November 1854, 2; 25 November 1854, 3; *American National Biography,*

s.v. "Dion Boucicault," by Joseph Donohue. Robertson's life with Boucicault was a trial. Congenitally unfaithful and unerringly poor in his business judgments, Boucicault saddled her with six children while expecting that she maintain her acting career. Agnes endured the infidelities into the middle 1870s, when she finally had had enough and sued for divorce. (Characteristically, Boucicault, before the divorce was even final, had remarried a girl forty-four years his junior.)

41. Michael Booth, *Victorian Spectacular Theatre, 1850–1950* (London: Routledge Kegan Paul, 1981), 74–75. On the history of pantomime and extravaganza, see Michael Booth, *Prefaces to English Nineteenth-Century Theatre,* chap. 5; A. E. Wilson, *King Panto: The Story of Pantomime* (New York: E. P. Dutton, 1935); Tracy C. Davis, *The Economics of the British Stage* (Cambridge: Cambridge University Press, 2000), 342–46.

42. *Baltimore American and Commercial Advertiser,* 3 December 1854, 2; 8 December 1854, 2.

43. Ibid., 11 April 1855, 2; 17 April 1855, 2; 2 May 1855, 3; Ellsler, *Stage Memories,* 134–35.

44. *Baltimore American and Commercial Advertiser,* 29 May 1855, 2; Bloom, *Joseph Jefferson,* 69.

45. Jefferson, *Autobiography,* 116; White, *American Railroad Passenger Car,* 70.

46. Green, *Washington,* 180, 200–4, 209.

47. Bloom, *Joseph Jefferson,* 59; *Baltimore American and Commercial Advertiser,* 3 September 1855, 3; 2 November 1855, 2; 7 November 1855, 3.

48. *Baltimore American and Commercial Advertiser,* 17 October, 1; 24 October, 1; 10 November, 1; 19 November 1855, 3.

49. Jefferson, *Autobiography,* 167–68, 304–6; *National Intelligencer,* 15 November 1855, 1.

50. *National Intelligencer,* 28 December 1855, 1; 2 January 1856, 3.

51. Jefferson, *Autobiography,* 116–20.

52. Ibid., 120–21.

53. *American National Biography,* s.v. "John Thomson Ford," by William Stephenson. Information on Ford also found in John Ford Sollers, "The Theatrical Career of John T. Ford" (Ph.D. diss., Stanford University, 1962). See page 54 on Joe's and Ford's meeting.

54. Jefferson, *Autobiography,* 123–29.

55. Charles Dickens letter, 21 March 1842, quoted in John Forster, *The Life of Charles Dickens,* 3 vols. (London: Chapman and Hall, 1879), 1:333; *Richmond Enquirer,* 4 April 1856, 1.

56. Jefferson was chagrined to discover after his *Autobiography* appeared that he neglected to mention his eminent friend E. L. Davenport. He wrote a letter to his friend's daughter, the estimable actress Fanny Davenport, apologizing for the oversight. Francis Wilson, *Joseph Jefferson,* 231–33. *Richmond Enquirer,* 15 April 1856, 4.

57. Jefferson's avoidance of any public memory of John Wilkes Booth ran to nearly the end of his life, even after Edwin died. When his son-in-law Benjamin Farjeon came into possession of Asia Booth Clarke's unpublished memoir of her notorious brother, he sought Jefferson's advice on publishing it. Joe firmly responded that he would not approach a publisher with such a proposition, an unsubtle hint that he was uncomfortable in having such material brought before the public. Only decades later, with all the princi-

pals gone, would the memoir appear. Asia Booth Clarke, *The Locked Box* (London: Faber and Faber, 1938), 23–25.

58. Ruggles, *Prince of Players*, 82; "Letters From Old Trunks," *Virginia Magazine of History and Biography* 46 (January 1938): 142–43; Daniel J. Watermeier's *Between Actor and Critic; Selected Letters of Edwin Booth and William Winter* (Princeton: Princeton University Press, 1971), provides wonderfully annotated letters that includes much on Booth's personal life.

59. *Richmond Enquirer*, 8 December 1856, 2; February 27 1857, 1; *Spirit of the Times*, 27 December 1856, 552; Bloom, *Joseph Jefferson*, 61.

60. Farjeon, *Portrait of a Family*, 59.

61. Winter, *Life of Jefferson*, 193; Bloom, *Joseph Jefferson*, 45–61; "Letters from Old Trunks," 142–43.

62. Bloom, *Joseph Jefferson*, 60.

63. Jefferson, *Autobiography*, 131; *Illustrated London News*, 12 July 1856, 34; "John Baldwin Buckstone," in Charles Pascoe, ed., *The Dramatic List, A Record of the Performances of Living Actors and Actresses of the British Stage* (London: D. Bogue, 1880), 52–59; "Samuel Phelps," ibid., 258–65.

64. Jefferson, *Autobiography*, 132–38.

Chapter Six. Triumphs in Comedy and Melodrama

1. Jefferson, *Autobiography*, 139.

2. George C. D. Odell points out that during the two seasons, 1856–57 and 1857–58, a host of major stars made New York debuts, including Lawrence Barrett, William Florence, and E. A. Sothern. *Annals of the New York Stage*, 7:30; the *Spirit of the Times*, 9 May 1857, 156, felt that the "advent of Edwin Booth will be looked upon as an epoch in the dramatic history of New York."

3. Interesting perspectives on Keene can be found in Faye E. Dudden, *Women in the American Theatre* (New Haven: Yale University Press, 1994), chap. 6; *American National Biography*, s.v. "Laura Keene," by Claudia Durst Johnson; Jefferson, *Autobiography*, 155–56.

4. Dudden, *Women in American Theatre*, 132–35.

5. James, *Small Boy and Others*, 113.

6. *Spirit of the Times*, 27 June 1957, 240; 29 August 1857, 348; 14 August 1857, 324.

7. Newspaper comments quoted in Odell, *Annals of New York Stage*, 7:30–31.

8. *Frank Leslie's Illustrated Newspaper*, 12 September 1857, 233; Judith critic quoted in Bloom, *Joseph Jefferson*, 66.

9. *Spirit of the Times*, 17 October 1857, 432; Burrows and Wallace, *Gotham*, chap. 47.

10. *Spirit of the Times*, 24 October 1857, 444; Jefferson, *Autobiography*, 142–43; *Frank Leslie's Illustrated Newspaper*, 24 October 1857, 326; Odell, *Annals of New York Stage*, 7:33–34; *Spirit of the Times*, 7 November 1857, 468; 14 November 1857, 480; 21 November 1857, 492.

11. Hutton, *Curiosities of the American Stage*, 19; Frank Rahill, *World of Melodrama* (University Park: Pennsylvania State University Press, 1967), 227–28; *Spirit of the Times*, 1 May 1858, 144; Arthur Hobson Quinn, *History of the American Drama*, 1:281.

12. Bloom, *Joseph Jefferson*, 71.

13. Jefferson to Ford, 28 July 1858, quoted in Sollers, "The Theatrical Career of John Ford"; Edwin Booth to Joseph Jefferson, reproduced in Bloom, *Joseph Jefferson*, 67–69.

14. *Spirit of the Times*, 18 September 1858, 384; 28 August 1858, 348.

15. Odell, *Annals of New York Stage*, 7:126.

16. Lester Wallack, *Memories of Fifty Years* (New York: Charles Scribners's Sons, 1889), 160; Jefferson, *Autobiography*, 146–47.

17. Henneke, *Laura Keene*, 90; John Bouve Clapp and Edwin Francis Edgett, *Players of the Present*, pt. 3 (New York: Dunlap Society, 1901), 346–47. Sothern's son, E. H. Sothern, claims that one reason Jefferson was so anxious to keep his father in the company is that the two of them had hired a stable and purchased two horses to go riding regularly (a treatment for Joe's consumption). Joe recognized that he could not alone afford the cost of maintaining the stable. Thus he proceeded to enhance Sothern's Dundreary role scene by scene. Edward H. Sothern, *The Melancholy Tale of "Me": My Remembrances* (New York: Charles Scribner's Sons, 1916), 172–74.

18. *Our American Cousin* was hailed as the longest running play ever in a so-call first-class theatre. *The Drunkard* had been staged first at the Boston Museum and later at Barnum's Museum. In London in 1861 *Our American Cousin* would enjoy an incredible 396-night run. Nevins and Thomas, eds. *Diary of George Templeton Strong*, 2:422.

19. *New York Times*, 19 October 1858, 4; Trenchard quote in Rourke, *American Humor*, 146–47.

20. *New York Tribune*, 21 October 1858, 3; Bloom, *Joseph Jefferson*, 73–74; Davis, "At and After the Play," 68; Jefferson, *Autobiography*, 168.

21. *American National Biography*, s.v. "Edward Askew Sothern," by Maarten Reilingh; William Winter, *Other Days* (New York: Moffat, Yard, 1908), 178; James Osler Bailey, *British Plays of the Nineteenth Century* (New York: Odyssey Press,1966), 194–95; Percy Fitzgerald, *Principles of Comedy and Dramatic Effect* (London: Tinsley, 1870), 74–75; critic's quote in Henneke, *Laura Keene*, 95; Jefferson, *Autobiography*, 150; Sothern's Dundreary was in the tradition of light comedy, albeit more mannered than many such roles. Typically, these were "young patricians, volatile lovers, voluble swindlers, well-dressed captains, swells, in and out of luck," testified Tom Robertson, a leading practitioner of the new drawing room comedies of midcentury Dutton Cook described the light comedian as one "wont to run or trip lightly on to the stage, waving his hat, or flourishing his cane, laughing and chattering in a breathless way. Robertson and Cook quoted in Michael Booth, ed., *English Plays of the Nineteenth Century*, vol. 4, *Farces* (Oxford: Clarendon Press, 1972), 150–51.

22. *New York Times*, 15 November 1858, 3; *Spirit of the Times*, 19 February 1859, 24; 26 February 1859, 48; 12 March 1859, 60; Jefferson, *Autobiography*, 147; *New York Clipper*, 19 February 1859, 350.

23. Jefferson, *Autobiography*, 150–51.

24. Ibid., 154–55.

25. *New York Clipper*, 23 April 1859, 6; 30 April 1859, 14; 21 May 1859, 39; 11 June 1859, 62; 9 July 1859, 94; Jefferson to Benjamin Webster, 19 May 1859 (from Halifax, N.S.), Harvard Theatre Collection; Niels Erik Enkvist, "Caricatures of Americans on the English Stage Prior to 1870," *Societas Scientiarum Fennica Commentationes Human-*

arum Litterarum XVIII 1 (Helsingfors, Finland, 1951), 128; playbill, Howard Athenaeum, 27, 28 June 1859, in Hutton and Matthews, eds., *Actors and Actresses of Great Britain and the United States,* Extra-illustrated Edition, vol. 5, pt. 1, Harvard Theatre Collection.

26. Eugénie Paul Jefferson, *Intimate Recollections of Joseph Jefferson* (New York: Dodd, Mead, 1909), 261–62; Farjeon, *Portrait of a Family,* 60; Bloom, *Joseph Jefferson,* 71–72.

27. Bloom, *Joseph Jefferson,* 79; *New York Times,* 25 July 1859, 4; *New York Clipper,* 6 August 1859, 126.

28. *New York Times,* 29 August 1859, 4; Odell, *Annals of New York Stage,* 7:210–11. On Boucicault's personality and influence, see Richard Fawkes, *Dion Boucicault,* and George Taylor, *Players and Performances in the Victorian Theatre* (Manchester: Manchester University Press, 1989), 20; Jefferson quote from William Winter, *Other Days,* 74.

29. Dion Boucicault, *Dot* (1867[?]; reprint, New York: Readex Microprint, 1971, English and American Drama of the Nineteenth Century).

30. Deborah Vlock, *Dickens, Novel Reading, and the Victorian Popular Theatre* (Cambridge: Cambridge University Press, 1998).

31. Jefferson, *Autobiography,* 159–60.

32. Quoted in Odell, *Annals of the New York Stage,* 7:211; *Frank Leslie's Illustrated Newspaper,* 24 September 1959, 265; advertisement quoted in Bloom, *Joseph Jefferson,* 83–84.

33. *New York Times,* 17 October 1859, 4.

34. Jefferson devised his own version of *The Cricket on the Hearth* (as always, he was prepared to alter a play to suit his needs). The plot was changed slightly but significantly. Where Boucicault let the audience in on Edward's disguise very early, Joe kept it a secret until near the end, an effective bit of added suspense. Joe also altered the nature of the cricket (whose cheerful chirps symbolized the bliss of hearth and home). Boucicault opened his version with a sort of Shakespearean fantasy scene, where the cricket joined Oberon, Titania, Ariel, and Puck in setting the plot. In place of this somewhat stilted distancing convention, Jefferson restored Dickens's concept: a fairy cricket who appears to John at the moment of his gravest marital doubt and renews his faith in Dot. (Dickens's talking cricket was surely the inspiration for Disney's Jiminy Cricket, Pinocchio's conscience.) The role of Caleb, with which Joe would likewise tinker, proved critical to forming his essential stage persona of Rip Van Winkle. Even the matter of costuming anticipated Rip. Caleb Plummer, old and impoverished, presented a challenge of makeup. A bald pate with fringes of gray hair, a ragged sack coat, and beat-up slouch hat, though clearly distinct from Rip's disguise, imparted experience with fleshing out aging ne'er-do-wells. Joe was finding his starring voice. The prompt book for Jefferson's production of Boucicault's *Cricket on the Hearth* is held in the Folger Shakespeare Library.
   In the 1880s his sister Connie, whose career had been nearly ended by a mysterious, disfiguring accident, found professional resurgence in the role of dull-witted Tillie Slowboy. Laurence Hutton, *Plays and Players* (New York: Hurd and Houghton, 1875), 40, 198.

35. *New York Times,* 2 November 1859, 4. John W. Frick in his *Theatre, Culture and Temperance Reform in Nineteenth-Century America* (Cambridge: Cambridge University Press, 2003), 109–11, makes the interesting point that English temperance drama was

more deterministic regarding the results of drink than the American tradition, seeming to offer less opportunity for redemption from the bottle.

36. Stoddart, *Recollections,* 132–37.

37. Hunt quoted in George Steiner, *The Death of Tragedy* (New Haven: Yale University Press, 1996), 110; James Kirke Paulding, "American Drama," *American Quarterly* 1.2 (June 1827), and 8.15 (September 1830), both reprinted in Wolter, *Dawning of American Drama;* Thomas Postlewait and Elaine Hadley represent the new academic seriousness bestowed on melodrama. Postlewait's "From Melodrama to Realism: The Suspect History of American Drama," in Michael Hays and Anastasia Nikolopoulou, eds., *Melodrama: The Cultural Emergence of a Genre* (New York: St. Martin's, 1996), believes the pervasive Whig bias in American dramatic criticism — dismissing melodrama as but a necessary forerunner of realism's authenticity in the twentieth century — distorts our dramatic history by failing to appreciate either melodrama's stylistic integrity or the melodramatic features that pervade realism. Hadley's *Melodramatic Tactics: Theatricalized Dissent in the English Martekplace, 1800–1885* (Stanford: Stanford University Press, 1995) argues that fundamental economic and social changes in the nineteenth century evoked antagonistic reactions. Consequently, many people found in melodramatic categories of oppressors and victims, and especially in melodrama's continued championing of traditional deferential and paternalistic values, a useful means of response. She writes of English society, but the social dynamics might well apply to America.

38. Michael Booth, *Prefaces to English Nineteenth-Century Theatre,* 1–11.

39. Steiner, *Death of Tragedy,* 128–35; Peter Brooks, *The Melodramatic Imagination: Balzac, Henry James, Melodrama and the Mode of Excess* (New Haven: Yale University Press, 1976), 11–21, 205–6.

40. David Grimsted, "Melodrama as Echo of the Historically Voiceless," in Tamara K. Haraven, ed., *Anonymous Americans: Explorations in Nineteenth-Century Social History* (Englewood Cliffs, N.J.: Prentice Hall, 1971), 82–84; Grimsted, *Melodrama Unveiled,* 204–10; McConachie's *Melodramatic Formations,* 117, 154–55, sees more complexity to melodrama. On the one hand he sees some great stage heroes, such as Edwin Forrest, conveying — ironically — a message of passivity before authoritarian figures to his audiences. Yet other Bowery productions stressed working-class solidarity and apocalyptic carnage in their class struggle.

41. Brooks, *Melodramatic Imagination,* 28–29; Joseph Donohue, *Theatre in the Age of Kean* (Totawa, N.J.: Rowman and Littlefield, 1975), 112; Grimsted, *Melodrama Unveiled,* chap. 8.

42. Michael Booth, *Victorian Spectacular Theatre,* 60–64; Rahill, *World of Melodrama,* 297–98.

43. Martha Vicinus, " 'Helpless and Unfriended': Nineteenth-Century Domestic Melodrama," in Judith Law Fisher and Stephen Watt, eds., *When They Weren't Doing Shakespeare* (Athens: University of Georgia Press, 1989), 181–82.

44. Less consequentially, George C. D. Odell asserts that *The Octoroon* had one of the first casts printed with men's and women's names intermingled, rather than the traditional fashion of listing men on the left and women on the right. *Annals of New York Stage,* 7:213

45. Wilson, *Joseph Jefferson,* 268; Jefferson, *Autobiography,* 160. Jefferson tells an affecting story of how in the midst of this dispute he had been taking boxing lessons from

an old prize fighter. While he was taking a lesson, Boucicault and Stuart arrived to make peace. Joe suspected that they believed he planned to settle the quarrel with gloves. *Autobiography,* 160–61.

46. Jules Zanger, "The 'Tragic Octoroon' in Pre–Civil War Fiction," *American Quarterly* 18 (spring 1966): 63–70.

47. *The Octoroon* in Myron Matlaw, ed., *Nineteenth-Century American Plays* (New York: Applause Theatre Books, 1967), 97–150.

48. *New York Times,* 8 December 1859, 1; *New York Herald,* 17 December 1859, 5; *Spirit of the Times,* 17 December 1859, 529, quoted in Wolter, *Dawning of American Drama,* 159–63. The reviewer went on to contrast the concern seen for slaves with the apparent unconcern for "pure-blooded whites," who were "poor victims of Northern society." Some of these were "doomed to inevitable servitude and degradation." This argument, a favorite of southern apologists, found occasional echoes in the North.

49. Jefferson, *Autobiography,* 162–63.

50. *New York Times,* 8 December 1859, 1.

51. *New York Times,* 6 January 1860, 2; 7 January 1860, 3; Jordan took Keene to court a second time in later January. Again, Joe testified. This time Keene prevailed before a jury. *New York Clipper,* 28 January 1860, 326.

52. William Charles Teufel, "Playwright in the United States Prior to the Act of 1909" (Ph.D. diss., University of Michigan, 1960) is the best study of this issue. Behind American copyright principles lay the foundation of all modern copyright, the Statute of Anne of 1710, which recognized the author's right to protection as well as the principle of prescribed duration of protection for published works. The dilemma of the French and English playwright is ably discussed by Frank Rahill in *World of Melodrama,* 171–181; Teufel, "Playwright in the United States," 31.

53. Meserve, *Heralds of Promise,* 34–36.

54. Ibid., 35. It is no small irony that Boucicault should champion the playwrights' cause since he was among the most notorious for "borrowing" themes and plots in toto from the French theatre. Might it have been the career of Dion Boucicault that inspired the proverbial English school boy to define a plagiarist as a "writer of plays"? See Rahill, *World of Melodrama,* chap. 23; Teufel, "Playwright in the United States," 39–47; Meserve, *Heralds of Promise,* 58–65.

55. Information on this incident is drawn largely from records of the suit, "Laura Keene vs. Wheatley and Clarke," in Asa I. Fish and Henry Wharton, eds., *American Law Register,* vol. 9, pt. 2 (Philadelphia: Canfield, 1861), 33–103.

56. The story of the play's acquisition is recounted in Thomas Edgar Pemberton's *A Memoir of Edward Askew Sothern* (London: Richard Bentley, 1890), 158–59; see also Henneke, *Laura Keene,* 105–6.

57. Although litigation dragged on for several years, Keene ultimately prevailed in the Pennsylvania court and earned $500 in damages. Judge Cadwallader's opinion (which would hugely influence future cases) was based on what must seem to modern sensibilities a piece of tortured logic from the day's primitive law of intellectual property. The decision was rooted less in the 1856 statute than in much older common law doctrine. Laura Keene's application for copyright was uncompleted because *Our American Cousin* had not been printed. Thus, though she had a "literary proprietorship" because of the assignment from Tom Taylor, she had no statutory right to exclusive presentation of the play.

Further, if Clarke and Wheatley had managed to stage the play solely from viewing Keene's production, their actions would have been legally proper. (At the Boston Museum, Moses Kimball found protection in the prevailing doctrine of "piracy by memorization" and owed Keene no royalties.) Again, a play once performed for the public entered the general domain. Keene prevailed only because the men relied on "a breach of confidence committed by Mr. Jefferson." Without his revisions ("histrionic talent with a matured experience in the production of comic effect," as the court complimented Jefferson), the value of the play would be greatly diminished. And since Jefferson was an employee of Keene, she rightfully expected that his efforts belonged to her. Clarke and Wheatley retorted that what Joe provided was relatively inconsequential, a series of "gags" and stage actions. But in an extended discussion of the role of improvisation in comic drama, Cadwallader maintained that the "judicious introduction . . . of gags happily adapted for the production or improvement of stage effect, may have prevented the failure, or greatly promoted the success of the play." And Jefferson's gags belonged to Keene. Tom Taylor is credited with *Our American Cousin,* but clearly his rather conventional play served only as the chassis for a livelier vehicle based on the improvisational genius of Jefferson first and then Sothern. Laura Keene and John Sleeper Clarke were not through with their contest. In 1866 they revisited the same issue in New York state courts. Keene again prevailed with a two-thousand-dollar verdict. Clarke contended that the damages of his Philadelphia suit essentially rendered him a license to perform the play in the future. The court demurred. *New York Clipper,* 20 October 1866, 220; Teufel, "Playwright in the United States," 67–79.

58. *Spirit of the Times,* 24 December 1859, 552.

59. Quoted in Seldon Faulkner, "The Octoroon War," *Educational Theatre Journal* 15 (March 1963): 36.

60. Faulkner, "Octoroon War," 33–37.

61. Ibid., 37; See Teufel, "Playwright in the United States," passim. The copyright problem would not be substantially corrected until 1891.

62. Despite their well-known feud, Jefferson and Keene in later years "talked and laughed over our rows and reconciliations, and had continued to get as much amusement out of the recollections as we had created trouble out of the realities." Jefferson, *Autobiography,* 155.

63. Hutton, *Plays and Players,* 161; *New York Clipper,* 28 January 1860, 328; *New York Times,* 25 January 1860, 7.

64. *New York Times,* 28 January 1860, 7.

65. *New York Clipper,* 11 February 1860, 243–43; Odell, *Annals of the New York Stage,* 7:214; *Frank Leslie's Illustrated Newspaper,* 11 February 1860, 163.

66. George Vandenhoff, *Lessons From an Actor's Note-book,* 201–2; *New York Clipper,* 25 February 1860, 359.

Chapter Seven. Nibbling at Stardom

1. *New York Times,* 22 February 1860, 4.

2. Terry L. Oggel, *The Letters and Notebooks of Mary Devlin Booth* (New York: Greenwood Press, 1987), 44.

3. *New York Clipper,* 17 March 1860, 382; *Frank Leslie's Illustrated Newspaper,* 17 March 1860, 241.

4. *Frank Leslie's Illustrated Newspaper,* 31 March 1860, 273.

5. *New York Clipper,* 14 April 1860, 414; Bloom, *Joseph Jefferson,* 88.

6. Odell, *Annals of New York Stage,* 7:222; *New York Clipper,* 26 May 1860, 192.

7. *American National Biography,* s.v. "Mrs. John Wood," by Cynthia. M. Gendrich; Stoddart, *Recollections,* 138–39; Anne H. Gilbert, *Stage Reminiscences of Mrs. Anne H. Gilbert* (New York, 1901); *Spirit of the Times,* 23 June 1860, 240; M. Willson Disher, ed., *The Cowells in America, Being the Diary of Mrs. Sam Cowell* (London: Oxford University Press, 1934), 116.

8. My discussion of burlesque owes much to Michael Booth, *Prefaces to English Nineteenth-Century Theatre,* 175–82.

9. *Othello* was a particular favorite on the minstrel circuit. *Dars de Money, Old Fellow, or the Boor of Vengeance* was the title of one such travesty; *Desdemonium* another. Tilden G. Edelstein; "Othello in America: The Drama of Racial Intermarriage," in Morgan Kousser and James M. McPherson, eds., *Region, Race, and Reconstruction* (New York: Oxford University Press, 1982), 187. It goes without saying that burlesque was at the very heart of minstrelsy. Minstrel performers dealt out parody on nearly every aspect of American life through the safely distancing technique black face. *Richard III A Burlesque* (London: William Barth, n.d.; first performed 1844).

10. *Spirit of the Times,* 23 June 1860, 229; *New York Clipper,* 16 June 1860, 70.

11. Odell, *Annals of New York Stage,* 7:223; *Spirit of the Times,* 9 June 1860, 216; 23 June 1860, 229, 240; 30 June 1860, 241; *New York Clipper,* 16 June 1860, 70.

12. *American National Biography,* s.v. "John Brougham," by Dana Sutton; Hutton, *Plays and Players,* 50–51; Hutton, *Curiosities of the American Stage,* 165. William Winter, *Other Days,* 98–123; Jefferson, *Autobiography,* 234; Stoddart, *Recollections,* 81–82; Skinner, *One Man in His Time,* 85.

13. Odell, *Annals of New York Stage,* 7:223–24; quotes from Bloom, *Joseph Jefferson,* 88, 424.

14. Bloom, *Joseph Jefferson,* 89; Eleanor Farjeon discusses her mother's fond recollections of Paradise Valley in her *Portrait of a Family.*

15. Jefferson, *Autobiography,* 169–71; Irving's entry noted: "In the evening went to Laura Keene's theatre to see young Jefferson. . . . Thought Jefferson the father, one of the best actors he had ever seen; and the son reminded him, in look, gesture, size and make of the father. Had never seen the father in Goldfinch but was delighted with the son." Pierre M. Irving, *The Life and Letters of Washington Irving* (New York: Putnam, 1864), 4:253.

16. Arthur E. Waterman, "Joseph Jefferson as Rip Van Winkle," *Journal of Popular Culture* 1 (1968): 373; William Winter, *Other Days,* 76.

17. Bloom, *Joseph Jefferson,* 91, 426.

18. Green, *Washington,* 231–32.

19. *National Intelligencer,* 5 November 1860, 3; 12 November 1860, 3; 17 November 1860, 3.

20. Playbills in William Seymour Theatre Collection, Princeton University Library.

21. *Richmond Enquirer,* 20 November 1860, 1; 4 December 1860, 1.

22. *New York Clipper,* 12 January 1861, 310; *Spirit of the Times,* 29 December 1860, 572; *New York Times,* 24 December 1860, 4, 7.

23. *New York Clipper,* 5 January 1861, 302; 12 January 1861, 311; *New York Times,* 25 December 1860, 4; *Frank Leslie's Illustrated Newspaper,* 12 January 1861, 115.

24. Odell, *Annals of the New York Stage*, 7: 316; *New York Tribune*, 7 January 1861, 7.

25. Henry J. Byron, *Mazeppa* (London: T. H. Lacy, 1865).

26. Hutton, *Curiosities of the American Stage*, 196–99; Byron, *Mazeppa; New York Tribune*, 7 January 1861, 3; *New York Times*, 9 January 1861, 4; *Frank Leslie's Illustrated Newspaper*, 19 January 1861, 131; *American National Biography*, s.v. "John Solomon Rarey," by Sharon E. Creiger; *Spirit of the Times*, 12 January 1861.

27. *New York Times*, 21 January 1861, 5; the *Clipper* of January 19 (318) likewise tells of Joe's problems. Mrs. Cowell mentions Joe's begging to have his second week. Disher, *Cowells*, 228.

28. *Baltimore American and Commercial Advertiser*, 2 February 1861, 4. Baltimore, as well as New York, sported an amateur group of thespians named for Joseph Jefferson.

29. Burrows and Wallace, *Gotham*, 866–67; Nevins and Thomas, eds., *Diary of George Templeton Strong*, 3:101.

30. Bloom, *Joseph Jefferson*, 92; *New York Clipper*, 2 March 1861, 366; *New York Times*, 20 February 1861, 5; Joe mistakenly remembers Margaret's death as occurring in March, an error in line with his general problem with dating throughout his memoir.

31. Bloom, *Joseph Jefferson*, 92–95.

32. Margaret Leech, *Reveille in Washington, 1860–65* (New York: Harper, 1941), 46–50; Henry Watterson, "Joseph Jefferson," *Louisville Courier-Journal*, 15 May 1905, 4.

33. *National Intelligencer*, 22 March 1861, 3.

34. Ibid., 25 March 1861, 3.

35. Leech, *Reveille*, 58–61; *National Intelligencer*, 10 April 1861, 3.

36. *National Intelligencer*, 20 April 1861, 2; 19 April 1861, 3.

37. *New York Clipper*, 4 May 1861, 22; Disher, *Cowells*, 322.

38. *New York Clipper*, 4 May 1861, 22; 11 May 1861, 30; 25 May 1861, 46; Odell, *Annals of New York Stage*, 7:318–19; *Spirit of the Times*, 11 May 1861, 224; 18 May 1861, 240; *New York Times*, 16 May 1861, 5; Disher, *Cowells*, 322.

39. Joseph Jefferson, "Origin of Rip Van Winkle," *Current Literature*, 19 February 1896, 138; Winter, *Life of Jefferson*, 172.

40. Watterson, "Jefferson," *Louisville Courier-Journal*, 15 May 1905, 4; Davis, "At and After the Play," 68.

41. Jefferson, *Autobiography*, 173; "Charles Jefferson Talks of His Famous Father," clipping file, Bourne Historical Center, Bourne, Mass.

42. *New York Times*, 1 June 1861, 5; *New York Clipper*, 18 May 1861, 38.

Chapter Eight. A Mighty Nimrod of Theatrical Touring

1. John Haskell Kemble, *The Panama Route, 1848–1869* (Berkeley: University of California Press, 1943), 96, 153, 156, 160, 218–19.

2. Eric Heyl, *Early American Steamers* (Buffalo: n.p., 1953), 375; Kemble, *Panama Route*, 146–65; *New York Times*, 4 April 1861, 5; *San Francisco Golden Era*, 30 June 1861, 4. Shortly after the Jeffersons' voyage, the *St. Louis* was outfitted with two cannon and enough coal to bypass Acapulco, where Confederate raiders were feared to wait.

3. The description is provided by Richard Henry Dana from his voyage into the bay in 1859, quoted in Oscar Lewis, *This Was San Francisco* (New York: David McKay, 1962), 153.

4. Jefferson, *Autobiography*, 173; *San Francisco Golden Era*, 30 June, 1861, 4, 8. These long and fulsome excerpts of Joe's career carried the telltale fingerprints of press agentry.

5. Lois M. Foster, "Annals of the San Francisco Stage," vol. 1, 1850–1880 (1937), pp. 141–45, unpub. MS, Bancroft Library, University of California–Berkeley; Rodecape, "Tom Maguire, Napoleon of the Stage," *California Historical Society Quarterly* 20 (December 1941): 289; *New York Clipper*, 17 August 1861, 142; Oscar Lewis, *San Francisco: Mission to Metropolis* (Berkeley: Howell-North, 1966), 58–75, 94–107.

6. *New York Clipper*, 3 August 1861, 127; *San Francisco Bulletin*, 9 July 1861, 3; *San Francisco Golden Era*, 14 July 1861, 5.

7. *San Francisco Daily Alta California*, 11 July 1861, 1; 25 July 1861, 1; *San Francisco Golden Era*, 30 June 1861, 3.

8. *San Francisco Daily Alta California*, 11 July 1861, 1; 24 July 1861, 1; *San Francisco Golden Era*, 28 July 1861, 4; Jefferson, *Autobiography*, 173; *San Francisco Bulletin*, 26 July 1861, 3.

9. *San Francisco Bulletin*, 12 July 1861, 3.

10. *San Francisco Golden Era*, 4 August 1861, 5; *San Francisco Daily Alta California*, 3 August 1861, 1.

11. *San Francisco Golden Era*, 18 August 1861, 4.

12. *New York Clipper*, 16 November 1861, 247; 30 November 1861, 263; 7 December 1861, 271.

13. *New York* Clipper 7 December 1861, 271; Ellsler, *Stage Memories*, 120; Bloom, *Joseph Jefferson*, 98.

14. E-mail correspondence with Bill Koiman, National Maritime Museum Library, San Francisco; *Lloyd's Register of British and Foreign Ships*, 1861; *San Francisco Daily Alta California*, 5 November 1861.

15. *San Francisco Daily Placer Times and Transcript*, 24 May 1855, 2. *New York Clipper*, 8 December 1860, 271. I am indebted to Arthur Bloom for bringing this item to my attention. Jefferson mentions in his *Autobiography* (173) that he felt overbilled.

16. Anderson, *Actor's Life*, 287; Basil Greenhill and Ann Giffard, *Traveling by Sea in the Nineteenth Century* (New York: Hastings House, 1974), 12–14; Jefferson, *Autobiography*, 175–76. Jefferson states with great certainty that he left San Francisco on 10 September and arrived in Sydney on 4 November. Both dates are considerably wrong.

17. Robert Hughes, *The Fatal Shore* (New York: Random House, 1986), 87; Jefferson, *Autobiography*, 176–77.

18. *Sydney Mail* 11 January 1862, 4; Hughes, *Fatal Shore*, xiii–xv; Anthony Trollope, *Australia and New Zealand*, 2 vols. (1873; reprint, London: Dawsons, 1968), 1:209, 212; Daniel Bandmann, *An Actor's Tour; or, Seventy Thousand Miles with Shakespeare* (Boston: Cupples, Upham, 1885), 18. The peculiar historical amnesia was abetted by stage censorship. As in England, Australian drama had to be officially approved by the colonial secretary before production. No depiction of a criminal as hero was approved. Further, most native plays that attempted any sort of daring social commentary had to be set in Ruritania or some other exotic location in order that references be suitably veiled. Margaret Williams, *Australia on the Popular Stage, 1829–1929* (Oxford University Press, 1983), 20.

19. Information on the Australian theatre found in Eric Irvin, ed., *Dictionary of the*

Australian Theatre, 1788–1914 (Sydney: Hale and Iremonger, 1985); see also Harold Love, ed., *The Australian Stage: A Documentary History* (Kensington: New South Wales University Press, 1984). E. Daniel Potts and Annette Potts in *Young America and Australian Gold: Americans and the Gold Rush of the 1850s* (St. Lucia: University of Queensland Press, 1974) devote chapter 7 to the American-Australian stage connection.

20. Jefferson, *Autobiography,* 177–78; Joe's son Charley told the story after his father's death about how when Joe asked Simmonds for the funds to rent the theatre, Simmonds admitted that he lost their entire $7,000 stake from the San Francisco run at a card game. Only a timely loan from an American saved the day. Arthur Bloom is properly skeptical of the tale. Jefferson was notoriously careful with his money. Moreover, had such a thing happened, it is inconceivable that he would have missed the chance to make it a choice anecdote for his *Autobiography.* "Charles Jefferson Talks of His Famous Father," clipping, Bourne Historical Center, Bourne, Mass.

21. *Sydney Morning-Herald,* 18 February 1862, 4.

22. "Charles Jefferson Talks of His Famous Father"; *Sydney Morning-Herald,* 24 February 1862, 5; 15 February 1861, 1; 18 February 1861, 4; 13 March 1861, 4; F. C. Brewer, *The Drama and Music in New South Wales* (Sydney: Government Printing Office, 1892), 26.

23. *Sydney Mail* 22 March 1862, 4; Geoffrey Serle, *The Golden Age: A History of the Colony of Victoria, 1851–1861* (Melbourne: Melbourne University Press, 1963), 369–70.

24. Trollope, *Australia and New Zealand,* 2:382–87.

25. *Melbourne Argus,* 27 March 1862, 8; 31 March 1862, 8; 25 April 1862, 6.

26. Jefferson's Melbourne run compiled from the *Argus.* Jefferson, *Autobiography,* 181; "Charles Jefferson Talks of His Famous Father."

27. Love, ed., *Australian Stage,* 83; Elizabeth Webby, ed., *Colonial Voices: Letters, Diaries, Journalism and Other Accounts of Nineteenth-Century Australia* (St. Lucia: University of Queensland Press, 1989), 337.

28. *Melbourne Argus,* 24 May 1862, 6.

29. Ibid., 25 July 1862, 5.

30. Manning Clark, *A History of Australia,* 6 vols. (Melbourne: Melbourne University Press, 1978), 4:86

31. Joe did not stage *London Assurance* during the remainder of his Australian tours, suggesting that it may have lacked appeal. For that matter, there is no record of his ever acting in it again. Meddle exemplifies the many roles Jefferson assumed during a long career that failed to find a permanent place in his repertoire.

32. *Melbourne Argus,* 25 June 1862, 6; Love, ed., *Australian Stage,* 81–82; Irvin, *Dictionary of Australian Theatre,* 270–71.

33. *Melbourne Argus,* 25 August 1862, 6; 26 August 1862, 8; 23 August 1862, 6

34. Ibid., September 6, 1862, 8.

35. Theatrical schedule drawn from the *Argus,* 6 through 27 September.

36. *Melbourne Argus,* 25 September 1862, 5; Irvin, *Dictionary of the Australian Theatre,* 186.

37. Quoted in Lurline Stuart, *James Smith: The Making of a Colonial Culture* (Sydney: Allen and Unwin, 1989), 123–24.

38. Love, *Neild,* passim; Stuart, *James Smith,* chap. 4.

39. Love, *Neild,* 75–77, 94; Jefferson, *Autobiography,* 181.

40. Quoted in Stuart, *James Smith,* 107–8.

41. The two modern biographers of Smith and Neild both judge the accusation to be false. Stuart, *James Smith,* 123–24; Love, *Neild,* 94–100. For all the vitriol spilled in the Neild-Smith incident, years later the two critics renewed their friendship.

42. Joseph Sefton to Joseph Jefferson, 3 December 1889, Performing Arts Museum Archive, the Arts Centre, Melbourne. I am indebted to Gervase Farjeon of London for providing copies of these letters and to Mimi Colligan of Melbourne for her tenacious sleuthing into the background of Buckland. Colligan to McArthur, e-mail correspondence, 2 August 1999.

43. J. M. D. Hardwick, ed., *Emigrant in Motley* (London: Salisbury Square, 1954), 51; Trollope, *Australia and New Zealand,* 1:403–16, 428; Serle, *Golden Age,* 370.

44. *Ballarat Star,* 2 October 1862; 6 October 1862; 14 October 1862. On Ballarat audiences, note the Keans' reaction in Hardwick, *Emigrant in Motley,* 138.

45. Serle, *Golden Age,* 234; Bandmann, *An Actor's Tour,* 21; Trollope, *Australia and New Zealand,* 1:417–28. I also benefited from Harold Love's knowledge of Australian history.

46. *Bendigo Advertiser,* 20 October 1862; 22 October 1862; 28 October 1862; 1 November 1862. Jefferson to Edward A. Sothern, 22 October 1862, Live Oaks Foundation archives, New Iberia, La.

47. *Castlemaine Mount Alexander Mail,* 10 February 1863; 19 February 1863.

48. Jefferson, *Autobiography,* 181–82.

49. Clark, *History of Australia,* 3:99, 440; Weston Bate, "Murndal," *Historic Homesteads of Australia* (Melbourne, 1969), 132–39; Jefferson, *Autobiography,* 182–83.

50. Jefferson, *Autobiography,* 182–92. In his biography of Jefferson, Arthur Bloom interprets his telling of the shepherd's tale as a means of subtly justifying *Rip Van Winkle* to the public.

51. *Melbourne Argus,* 6 April 1863, 8; 13 April 1863, 8; 20 April 1863, 8; 23 April 1863, 8; Bloom, *Joseph Jefferson,* 103.

52. Edward Hudswell birth certificate, Colony of Victoria, 1863. Thanks to Mimi Colligan for her efforts in securing copies of pertinent public documents.

53. Hardwick, *Emigrant in Motley,* 51; Pamela Statham, ed., *The Origins of Australia's Capital Cities* (Cambridge: Cambridge University Press, 1989), 161, 174; Trollope, *Australia and New Zealand,* 2:172–77.

54. Irvin, *Dictionary of the Australian Theatre,* 281–82; *Sydney Morning-Herald,* 10 October 1863; 12 September 1863; 16 September 1863; last *Morning-Herald* quote in Bloom, *Joseph Jefferson,* 103.

55. Hardwick, *Emigrant in Motley,* 44–45; Jefferson, *Autobiography,* 196–201. Kean was not just imagining a lukewarm reception; an editorial in the *Melbourne Argus* scolded local audiences for insufficiently affording the Keans the recognition they deserved (editorial quoted in Hardwick, *Emigrant in Motley,* 82). Michael A. Morrison reminds me that the Keans' determination to maintain their youthful repertory was no more than tragedians would do well into the twentieth century.

56. Jefferson, *Autobiography,* 204; Farjeon, *Portrait of a Family,* 23; Trollope, *Aus-*

tralia and New Zealand, 2:342; Peter Downes, *Shadows on the Stage: Theatre in New Zealand in the First Seventy Years* (Dunedin: John McIndoe, 1975), 54–58.

57. Jefferson, *Autobiography,* 204; Trollope, *Australia and New Zealand,* 2:321–33.

58. Clarence Holt, "Twice Round the World: Recollections of an Old Actor," MS 2244/2/464, National Library of Australia, Canberra. *Otago Daily Times,* 11 January 1864; 12 January 1864; "Clap-trap," in its original meaning was described by critic Leigh Hunt in 1807 as "gradually raising the voice as the speech draws to a conclusion, making an alarming outcry on the last four or five lines, or suddenly dropping them into a tremulous but energetic undertone, and with a vigorous jerk of the right arm, rushing off the stage. All this astonishes the galleries; they are persuaded it must be something very fine, because it is so important and sound intelligible, and they clap for the sake of their own reputation." Quoted in Downes, *Shadows on the Stage,* 60–61.

59. Farjeon, *Portrait of a Family,* 23–24.

60. Trollope, *Australia and New Zealand,* 2:37–39; Hughes, *Fatal Shore,* 398–400; Clark, *History of Australia,* 4:32–33.

61. Bloom, *Joseph Jefferson,* 105; *Launceston Examiner,* 16 February 1864; 18 February 1864; Trollope, *Australia and New Zealand,* 2:50–51; *Hobart Town Mercury,* 29 February 1864; *Canterbury Times,* c. September 1891, 32. I am grateful to Mimi Colligan to bringing this item to my attention.

62. *Hobart Town Mercury,* 2 March 1864; 4 March 1865; Irvin, *Dictionary of Australian Theatre,* 130–31.

63. Background to the play provided in Michael R. Booth, ed., *English Plays of the Nineteenth Century,* vol. 2, *Dramas, 1850–1900* (Oxford: Clarendon Press, 1969), 79–81. The Sydney production is detailed in the *Sydney Morning-Herald,* 2 October 1863; 3 October 1863.

64. Jefferson, *Autobiography,* 195; Michael Booth, *English Plays,* 2:146. The differences between the British and the colonial ticket-of-leave system were stressed by R. Therry in an 1863 work. He faulted the domestic English system for being too lax while the Australian authorities practiced a commendable oversight of their ticket-of-leave clients. *Reminiscences of Thirty Years Residence in New South Wales and Victoria* (London: Simpson Low, 1863), 499–502.

65. Jefferson, *Autobiography,* 196; "Charles Jefferson Talks of His Famous Father"; *Hobart Town Mercury,* 4 April 1864; 5 April 1864.

66. *South Australian Register,* 16 July 1864; 15 July 1864; 2 August 1864.

67. *Sydney Morning Herald,* 17 September 1864; 1 October 1864.

68. *Melbourne Argus,* 25 October, 1864; 25 November 1864; 28 November 1864.

69. *Daylesford Mercury,* 6 March 1865. *The Yankee Teamster* apparently failed. There is no American record of it, suggesting that Jefferson never bothered to bring to stateside with him.

70. Jefferson, *Autobiography,* 202–3.

71. *Melbourne Argus,* 18 March 1865.

72. Brewer, *Drama in New South Wales,* 26.

73. *Sydney Morning Herald,* 14 October 1864; *Melbourne Argus,* 22 April 1865.

Chapter Nine. Mr. Jefferson and Rip Van Winkle

1. Jefferson, *Autobiography*, chap. 10. Charles Burke Jefferson tells an elaborate story of how he and his father were heading home to America until events intervened, causing them to go directly to England. The *Autobiography*, on the other hand, makes no mention of any intention to return home. That, added to newspaper comments in Australia, suggests that Joe intended to go straight to England all along. The Civil War had not quite ended, and though Joe never said so explicitly, he seemed determined to avoid a war-torn America. Moreover, he seemed determined to conquer the London stage. All this would seem poor justification for staying away from his children even longer. Yet one recalls a Victorian paradox: enshrining domestic pleasures even while tolerating years-long separations when work called.

2. Ibid. Jefferson's comments on an American passion play was not mere speculation. A few years before he penned his *Autobiography*, a movement for just this thing had caught the fancy of some theatrical managers. The indifferent American reception to a native passion play production no doubt shaped Joe's observations.

3. Edward H. Sothern, *The Melancholy Tale of "Me": My Remembrances* (New York: Charles Scribner's Sons, 1916), 89–90; Dion Boucicault, "Leaves from a Dramatist's Diary," *North American Review* 149 (1889): 233; Jefferson, *Autobiography*, 225–29; "Charles Jefferson Talks of His Famous Father"; Winter, *Life of Jefferson*, 180–81; Montrose Moses, introduction to *Rip Van Winkle*, in *Representative Plays by American Dramatists, 1856–1911*, 3 vols. (1921; reprint, New York: Benjamin Blom, 1964), 3:24–25. Boucicault's apology for the play is printed in his "The Dramatization of *Rip Van Winkle*," *Critic* 3 (7 April 1888): 159. Boucicault's and Jefferson's recollections of the collaboration differ in spirit. Boucicault recalls Jefferson arriving in London with little notion of what to present, *Rip Van Winkle* having been a failure elsewhere. Nor did he have many ideas as to its remedy until Boucicault brainstormed a substantial refashioning, which Joe at first received unenthusiastically. Joe's success with the play in Australia and his confidence in it casts some doubt on Boucicault's version.

4. Eugénie Paul Jefferson, *Intimate Recollections*, 138; Bloom, *Joseph Jefferson*, 114; Francis Wilson, *Joseph Jefferson: Reminiscences of a Fellow Player* (New York: Charles Scribner's Sons, 1906), 39; Jefferson, *Autobiography*, 227–29.

5. H. Barton Baker, *History of the London Stage and Its Famous Players* (1904; reprint, New York: Benjamin Blom 1969), 434; *Illustrated London News*, 30 September 1865, 319; *Pall Mall Gazette*, 16 September 1865, 11; *Times* (London), 6 September 1865, 12; Jefferson quoted by Ernest Bradlee Watson, "Joseph Jefferson," *Theatre Arts* 13 (June 1929): 426.

6. Mary Farren to Sol Smith, 23 September 1865. Sol Smith Collection, Missouri Historical Society, St. Louis. Henry Adams in his *Education* notes the none-too-subtle disparagement of America, especially surrounding the Laird ram crisis in 1863 (New York: Library of America, 1983), chaps. 9–11; *Times* (London), 6 September 1865, 12; "Mr. Jefferson's Reappearance," *Sunday Times* (London), 7 November 1875, Margaret Farjeon scrapbook, owned by author; Harold Brehm Obee, "A Prompt Script Study of Nineteenth-Century Legitimate Stage Versions of *Rip Van Winkle*" (Ph.D. diss., Ohio

State University, 1961), 10; Boucicault, "Leaves from a Dramatist's Diary," 233; Jefferson to Benjamin Webster, 11 December [1866], letter in possession of Michael Morrison.

7. *Liverpool Mail,* 12 May 1866, 4; 19 May 1866, 5; 16 June 1866, 2; Jefferson, *Autobiography,* 239.

8. Philip Young, "Fallen from Time: The Mythic Rip Van Winkle," *Kenyon Review* 22 (autumn 1960): 547–73; J. P. Thompson, "The Genesis of the Rip Van Winkle Legend," *Harper's New Monthly Magazine* 67 (September 1883): 617–22.

9. The most thorough study of stage versions of *Rip Van Winkle* is Harold Obee's Ph.D. dissertation, "A Prompt Script Study of *Rip Van Winkle.*" I am indebted to his work for much of the following analysis. Other important published studies used here include Moses, introduction to *Rip Van Winkle, Representative Plays,* 3:17–26; Quinn, *History of the American Drama,* 1:324–33; Tom Scanlan, "The Domestication of Rip Van Winkle," *Virginia Quarterly Review* 50 (winter 1974): 51–62; L. Clarke Davis, "At and After the Play: Jefferson and Rip Van Winkle," *Lippincott's* (July 1879): 57–75, Noah Ludlow, *Dramatic Life,* 390–92.

10. There is no biography of Hackett's life, a lacuna in the theatrical literature demanding attention. A good brief modern overview is provided in *American National Biography,* s.v. "James Henry Hackett," by Francis Hodge. See also Charles H. Shattuck's insightful few pages on him in *Shakespeare on the American Stage* (Washington: Folger Shakespeare Library, 1976), 56–62; Vandenhoff quoted in Obee, "Prompt Script Study of *Rip Van Winkle,*" 72.

11. Davis, "At and After the Play," 61; Winter, *Life of Jefferson,* 149–50.

12. Obee, "Prompt Script Study of *Rip Van Winkle,*" 55–59; Rourke, *American Humor,* 77–78.

13. Obee, "Prompt Script Study of *Rip Van Winkle,*" 110–12.

14. Modern readers who bring to the play a transformed sensibility toward marriage relationships may forget how important the shrewish wife and henpecked husband has been in the tradition of American stage and screen humor.

15. Unidentified newspaper clipping, 10 November 1875, Margaret Farjeon scrapbook.

16. Jefferson, *Autobiography,* 341; Jefferson recognized his debt to Boucicault for more than his revision of *Rip Van Winkle.* His first serious role was Caleb Plummer in Boucicault's *The Cricket on the Hearth;* his second, Salem Scudder in *The Octoroon,* was another creation of the Irish master. Wilson, *Joseph Jefferson,* 41. The closest thing to an authorized edition of Jefferson's *Rip Van Winkle* may be the 1896 edition published by Dodd, Mead, *Rip Van Winkle as Played by Joseph Jefferson.* This amply illustrated edition represents the play as it had evolved through thirty years of performance.

17. Jefferson, *Autobiography,* 170–73; Burke edition *Rip* quotation from Moses, ed., *Representative Plays,* 3:52. At the London opening the dwarfs were not completely mute. Critic Henry Morley complained that the play departed from Irving's absolute silence by having the company laugh at his "sly pulls at their flagon." *Journal of a London Playgoer from 1851 to 1866* (London: George Routledge, 1866), 377. Joe at some point took away their voices completely. Tom Scanlan found in the scene an anticipation of early twentieth-century expressionism. This is surely an exaggeration. There is no evidence that later playwrights or moviemakers drew inspiration from the mountain scene. And certainly Jefferson shared no philosophical ground with August Strindberg, Fritz Lang,

Eugene O'Neill, or Elmer Rice. Nonetheless, a viewing of O'Neill's *The Emperor Jones* gives pause. The powerful encounter of Brutus Jones with the imagined spirits of the Caribbean forest and his increasingly desperate monologue reflecting his retreat into madness have a loose affinity to Jefferson's much more psychologically innocent middle act. Scanlan, "Domestication of Rip Van Winkle," 60. A fine general overview of theatrical expressionism is found in J. L. Styan, *Modern Drama in Theory and Practice*, vol. 4, *Expressionism and Epic Theatre* (Cambridge: Cambridge University Press, 1981).

18. Quoted in Moses, ed., *Representative Plays*, 3:23; "Jefferson in 'Rip Van Winkle,'" *Nation* (23 September 1869): 248.

19. Quoted in Moses, ed., *Representative Plays*, 3:25; Wilson, *Joseph Jefferson*, 41. Boucicault quoted in Fawkes, *Dion Boucicault*, 81–82.

20. Obee, "Prompt Script Study of *Rip Van Winkle*," 199; McKenzie, "Acting of Joseph Jefferson," 159.

21. Henry Morley, *Journal of a London Playgoer*, 377–8. Morley wrote the review of *Rip Van Winkle* for the *Examiner*, 23 September 1865; Davis, "At and After the Play," 69; James F. Hoeflinger offers a careful study of the Boucicault-Jefferson version in "The Evolution of a Play: *Rip Van Winkle: As Played by Joseph Jefferson*" (master's thesis, University of North Carolina, 1977).

22. Scanlan, "Domestication of Rip," 55. Marvin Meyers, *The Jacksonian Persuasion: Politics and Beliefs* (Stanford: Stanford University Press, 1957) remains the classic statement of Jacksonian era unease with expansive capitalism.

23. Jefferson once responded to the question of why he did not include a particular crowd-pleasing line in his production. During one of the earliest *Rip Van Winkles*, staged in Cincinnati, an actor interpolated a response to Rip's question, "Who is George Washington?" with the famous quotation, "He was first in war, first in peace, and first in the hearts of his countrymen." This allusion sent the Cincinnati audience into frenzied applause. Why did Jefferson forego it for future productions? "In the first place, they were not the words of the drama; they would be out of place spoken there, and if uttered in that situation, would most assuredly injure the remainder of the scene, if not the whole play. The minds of the audience would fly off on a patriotic rampage, and I should not be able to get them back again to a consideration of the play." This anecdote of Noah Ludlow's suggests the determination of Joe to avoid the pitfall of cheap applause in place of a unified theatrical event. Ludlow, *Dramatic Life*, 391.

24. At least all profanity was gone by the time Jefferson's script was published in 1895. The original Boucicault script never saw publication, so one cannot so with certainty that all was removed in 1865.

25. Scanlan, "Domestication of Rip," 54–55; Bruce McConachie has some useful insights on domesticity on stage in his *Melodramatic Formations*, 166–67.

26. On temperance drama, see Frick, *Theatre, Culture and Temperance Reform in Nineteenth-Century America* (New York: Cambridge University Press, 2003), 60–67, 112–44, 188–92; Michael R. Booth, "The Drunkard's Progress: Nineteenth-Century Temperance Drama," *Dalhousie Review* 44 (1964): 205–12; Meserve, *Heralds of Promise*, 151–54; McConachie, *Melodramatic Formations*, 178–80.

27. "Rip Van Winkle," *Appleton's Journal*, n.s. 4 (February 1878): 146. *Nation* quoted in Bloom, *Joseph Jefferson*, 125; Winter, *Life of Jefferson*, 210.

28. Jefferson, *Autobiography,* 336.

29. Scanlan, "Domestication of Rip," 55–57.

30. My discussion of stage realism is informed by J. L. Styan, *Modern Drama in Theory and Practice,* vol. 1 *Realism and Naturalism* (Cambridge: Cambridge University Press, 1981); William W. Demastes, ed., *Realism and the American Dramatic Tradition* (Tuscaloosa: University of Alabama Press, 1996). See also Lisa Lone-Marker, *David Belasco; Naturalism in the American Theatre* (Princeton: Princeton University Press, 1974).

31. Darwin Reid Payne, *Scenographic Imagination,* 3rd ed. (Carbondale: Southern Illinois University Press, 1993), 37–43; Boucicault quoted in Meisel, *Realizations,* 51; *New York Mirror,* 27 January 1883, 6.

32. Clifford E. Hamar argues for the sophistication of early nineteenth-century spectacle in "Scenery on the Early American Stage," *Theatre Annual* 7 (1948–49): 84–103; Mammen, *Old Stock Company,* 29; Skinner, ed., *One Man in His Time,* 33; Richard Southern, *Changeable Scenery: Its Origin and Development in the British Theatre* (London: Faber and Faber, 1952), 363, 356.

33. Booth, *Victorian Spectacular Theatre,* 1–11; Downer, *Eminent Tragedian,* 224; Richard Southern, *The Seven Ages of the Theatre* (New York: Hill and Wang, 1961), 261; Ernest Bradlee Watson, *Sheridan to Robertson: A Study of the Nineteenth-Century London Stage* (Cambridge: Harvard University Press, 1926), chap. 12.

34. Quotation from Southern, *Changeable Scenery,* 366. Gilbert was speaking of a production featuring one of the Batemans rather than Jefferson's *Rip.* McKenzie, "Acting of Joseph Jefferson," 162–81, offers the best discussion of scenic values in *Rip Van Winkle.* McKenzie's interview with Warren Jefferson, Joe's grandson, provides detail on scenery of the play. Tracks 12, 13, and 14, 1972, New Iberia, Louisiana, compact disc recording in possession of author.

35. Jefferson, *Autobiography,* 336, 338; A. G. Sedgwick, "Jefferson in 'Rip,' " *Nation* 9 (23 September 1869): 247. Jefferson's notions about disabling realism was prompted on one occasion while standing in front of a great fireplace at Edwin Booth's home. Joe admired the fire but reflected that if such a fireplace were in his scene where Gretchen throws him out into the night, all the audience would notice would be the fire. "The fireplace cost $200," Booth boasted. "I would rather pay you $200, than act in front of it," Jefferson rejoined. Jefferson, "Report of Discussion Following Joseph Jefferson's Address on Dramatic Art, September 27, 1901," typescript, American Academy of Arts and Letters, New York City, 24.

36. Jefferson to Daly, 27 January 1889, Augustin Daly Papers, Folger Shakespeare Library.

37. *Hobart Town Mercury,* 2 March 1864; *Sydney Argus,* 7 November 1864; *Pall Mall Gazette* 16 September 1865, 11; *Times* (London), 6 September 1865; *Standard* critic quoted in Bloom, *Joseph Jefferson,* 116; *New York Times,* 15 October 1895, 5.

38. Hunt, *Dramatic Essays,* 1–2.

39. Donald C. Mullin, "Methods and Manners of Traditional Acting," *Educational Theatre Journal* (March 1975): 5–7; Alan S. Downer, "Nature to Advantage Dressed: Eighteenth-Century Acting," *PMLA* 58 (1943):1002–37; Alan S. Downer, "Players and Painted Stage," *PMLA* 61 (1946): 533–35.

40. Aaron Hill, *An Essay on the Art of Acting; in Which the Dramatic Passions are*

Properly Defined and Described, quoted in Downer, "Nature to Advantage Dressed," 1029; Henry Siddons, *Practical Illustrations of Rhetorical Gesture and Action* (London: Sherrod, Neely, and Jones, 1822); Mullin, "Methods and Manners," 6–7.

41. Steiner, *Death of Tragedy,* 133, 128, 238–48.

42. Watson, *Sheridan to Robertson,* 127–28; Downer, "Players and Painted Stage," 549–52.

43. Randall Knoper, *Acting Naturally: Mark Twain in the Culture of Performance,* (Berkeley: University of California Press, 1995), chap. 2. James quote from Allan Wade, ed., *The Scenic Art: Notes on Acting & the Drama, 1872–1901* (New Brunswick, N.J.: Rutgers University Press, 1948), 82.

44. Jefferson, *Autobiography,* 338.

45. Waterman, "Joseph Jefferson as Rip Van Winkle," 375; Richard Watson Gilder, "A Few Words about Joseph Jefferson and His Art," *Christian Union* (4 March 1893): 411.

46. Jefferson's costumes were always immaculately clean, a function of his fastidious nature. William Winter commented on Jefferson's fastidiousness, recalling that Joe allowed that farmers get dirty but "there is a day when he has a bath, and is shaved, has his boots brushed, and wears a clean shirt; and *this is that day.*" Winter (*Other Days,* 77) sees in this an example of Jefferson's idealism — rather than realism — in his approach to acting.

Joe was much interested in stage dress, loving to haunt theatrical wardrobe shops. In later years, when he became almost casually negligent of scenery and props, he remained obsessively careful about the play's costuming. The Rip Van Winkle costume is housed at the archives of Historic Sleepy Hollow, Tarrytown, N.Y. Douglas McKenzie's dissertation, "The Acting of Joseph Jefferson," 188–93, provides the best discussion of Jefferson's costuming.

47. Frederick Wedmore, "Mr. Jefferson," *Academy* (6 November 1875): 490 Stephen Johnson, "Rip Van Winkle," *Drama Review* 26 (spring 1982): 4–20; McKenzie, "Acting of Joseph Jefferson," 227–31; James Huneker, "Joseph Jefferson," *World's Work* (June 1905): 6318; Gilbert Pierce, "A Good-By to Rip Van Winkle," *Atlantic Monthly* 52 (November 1883): 696, 700.

48. Huneker, "Joseph Jefferson," 6318; Love, *James Edward Neil,* 93; Downer, "Players and Painted Stage," 572–73; Otis Skinner, *Footlights and Spotlights* (Indianapolis: Bobbs-Merrill, 1924), 253; Gilder, "A Few Words about Jefferson," 410; Wedmore, "Mr. Jefferson," 490; Sedgwick, "Jefferson in 'Rip,'" 247.

49. Davis, "Among the Comedians," 751.

50. Thomas Postlewait's essay, "From 'Melodrama' to 'Realism,'" 39–60, has recently reminded theatre historians that sharp distinctions between melodrama and realism are unwarranted. Melodramatic elements would always be present in drama perceived as realistic; indeed, the genre of melodrama would not disappear with the nineteenth century. Consequently, it is not surprising that *Rip Van Winkle* should display entangled elements of both.

51. The definition of pathos from Walter Kerr, *The Silent Clowns* (New York: Alfred A. Knopf, 1979), 285. Kerr's is a wonderful study of comedy in the silent movie era.

52. Lowell, "On a Certain Condescension in Foreigners," *Atlantic Monthly* 23 (January, 1869); Jefferson, *Autobiography,* 237–38.

53. Morris Bacheller, "Dean of the American Stage," *Munsey's* 12 (1915): 492–502.

54. Jefferson, *Autobiography*, 239.

Chapter Ten. Bringing the "Sleepy Piece" Home

1. *New York Clipper*, 18 August 1866, 150.

2. Ibid., 25 August 1866, 158; "Berenice Abbott's Changing New York," an exhibition at the Museum of the City of New York, 14 March–21 June 1998.

3. *New York Clipper*, 1 September 1866, 166; Burrows and Wallace, *Gotham*, chaps. 52 and 53.

4. Odell, *Annals of New York Stage*, 8:138; Henderson, *City and the Theatre*, 103–11, 117.

5. *New York Times*, 2 September 1866, 7; *New York Clipper*, 8 September 1866, 174; *New York Daily Tribune*, 5 September 1866, 2.

6. James H. Stoddart, *Recollections*, 140; *New York Times*, 5 September 1866, 5; *New York Clipper*, 15 September 1866, 182.

7. Ibid., *New York Daily Tribune*, 5 September 1866, 2.

8. *New York Clipper*, 22 September 1866, 190.

9. My discussion of *The Black Crook* relies on Odell, *Annals of the New York Stage*, 8:152–55, and Robert G. Allen, *Horrible Prettiness: Burlesque and American Culture* (Chapel Hill: University of North Carolina Press, 1991), 108–17. Quotes from same.

10. Allen, *Horrible Prettiness*, esp. chaps. 1–4. Logan quote from *Before the Footlights and Behind the Scenes*, 586. Odell chronicles the appearance of *The Black Crook* in his *Annals of the New York Stage*, 8:152–55. Allen's interpretation of Thompson's company and Olive Logan's screed should be tempered with the observations of Richard Grant White, who found the "bombs" more refined and winning than he had expected ("As if Venus, in her quality of the goddess of laughter, had come upon the stage," he said of Thompson.). Also, he was surprised at the composition of the audience: "comfortable, middle-aged women from the suburbs, and from the remoter country, their daughters, groups of children, a few professional men, bearing their quality in their faces, some sober, farmer-looking folk, a clergyman or two, apparently, the usual proportion of nondescripts." White, "Age of Burlesque," *Galaxy* 8 (August 1869): 260. Clearly, early female burlesque was not yet the salacious, working-class entertainment that it would be understood to be by the turn of the century.

11. *New York Times*, 5 October 1866, 4; 24 October 1866, 7; *New York Clipper*, 27 October 1866, 230, 238.

12. Durham, ed., *American Theatre Companies*, 210–13; *New York Clipper*, 10 November 1866, 246; 17 November 1866, 255; 24 November 1866, 262; 1 December 1866, 270.

13. Jefferson to John T. Ford, n.d. [c. November 1866], John T. Ford Papers, Manuscript Division, Library of Congress; *National Intelligencer*, 27 November 1866, 2; Bloom, *Joseph Jefferson*, 132–33, 296.

14. Jefferson to Ford, n.d. [c. November 1866], John T. Ford Papers, Manuscript Division, Library of Congress.

15. Jefferson to John T. Ford, n.d. [c. November 1866] John T. Ford Papers, Manu-

script Division, Library of Congress. *National Intelligencer,* 17 December 1866, 2; 18 December 1866, 3; 24 December 1866, 2; 31 December 1866, 2.

16. *Baltimore American and Commercial Advertiser,* 7 January to 9 February 1867.

17. Ibid., 28 January 1867, 2; William Tydeman, ed., *Plays by Tom Robertson* (Cambridge: Cambridge University Press, 1982), 1–19; 85–134. Later in 1867, Jefferson paid Robertson for another play (actually a translation of a French play). First titled *Across the Atlantic,* the drama's lead did not suit Joe, who forfeited his fee to return the vehicle to Robertson. Robertson in turn sold it to E. A. Sothern, who premiered it in London under the name *Home.* Winter, *Life of Jefferson,* 186.

18. *New Orleans Daily Picayune,* 24 February 1867, 2; 26 February 1867, 5; 27 February 1867, 1; 4 March 1867, 2; 5 March 1867, 6; 16 March 1867, 6; 30 March, 1867, 2.

19. Ibid., 3 March, 1867, 3; 16 March 1867, 2.

20. Ibid., 6 July 1867, 102.

21. Bloom, *Joseph Jefferson,* 133–34, 439; *New York Clipper,* 17 August 1867, 130; 10 August 1867, 112.

22. *New York Herald,* 10 September 1867, 6; Bloom, *Joseph Jefferson,* 134–35; *Frank Leslie's Illustrated Magazine,* 28 September 1867, 19; ibid., 21 September 1867, 3; *New York Tribune,* 16 September 1867, 5.

23. *New York Clipper,* 5 October 1867, 206; Bloom, *Joseph Jefferson,* 135.

24. *New York Clipper,* 28 September 1867, 198; 12 October 1867, 214; 19 October 1867, 222; 9 November 1867, 246; 16 November 1867, 254; Laurence Senelick, *The Age and Stage of George L. Fox, 1825–1877* (Hanover, N.H.: University Press of New England, 1988), 135.

25. The standard biography of Fox is the above-cited work of Senelick. A brief sketch of his life, also by Senelick, is found in the *American National Biography.*

26. Senelick, "Fox," *American National Biography;* Senelick, *Fox,* 130–31; 222–23.

27. Arthur Bloom has accomplished a yeoman's feat of tracking Jefferson's tours year by year. See his appendix to *Joseph Jefferson,* 295–378. My references to his movements will frequently draw on this work. *Dictionary of American Biography,* s.v. "James Hubert McVicker," by Edwin Mims, Jr.

28. Donald L. Miller, *City of the Century: The Epic of Chicago and the Making of America* (New York: Simon and Schuster, 1996), 106–142; *Chicago Times,* 4 November 1867, 4; 5 November 1867; 14 November 1867, 4.

29. Jefferson, *Autobiography,* 241; Winter, *Life of Jefferson,* 194.

30. Jefferson, *Autobiography,* 241; Logan, *Before the Footlights,* 458; Watermeier, *Between Actor and Critic,* 183–85.

31. Jefferson to William Winter 9 May [1868], Jefferson Collection, Harry Ransom Humanities Research Center, University of Texas; *New York Clipper,* 18 April 1868, 14.

32. Sarah H. Gordon, *Passage to Union: How the Railroads Transformed American Life, 1829–1929* (Chicago: Ivan R. Dee, 1996), 259; Charles Kean to Mary Kean, 17 January 1866, in Carson, "Letters of Mr. and Mrs. Charles Kean," *Washington University Studies,* 152. Two decades later, after a generation of frustration with railroad rate setting had built up, especially among America's farmers, the Interstate Commerce Commission was empowered by Congress to oversee such matters. The ICC's attempts to

regularize pricing paradoxically hurt theatre managers, who found the discounts they had previously known being banned. The *Mirror* complained that actors' salaries were reduced to offset the managers' higher travel expenses. The cutthroat competition that marked the age of rail expansion was seen in the Baltimore and Ohio's offering two-cent-a-mile rates for companies that traveled under a single ticket, a move that was challenged by the ICC. It was a mark of the theatre industry's increased self-consciousness that an association of theatre managers petitioned the ICC to argue its case for special rates. But the commission refused to grant actors any special consideration, a rebuff bemoaned by the *Mirror.* Rules notwithstanding, managers who knew how to play the system found ways to obtain fare reductions. *New York Mirror,* 22 June 1889, 3; 29 June 1889, 8; 23 November 1889, 2; 1 March 1890, 2. The managers, prodded by *Mirror* editor Harrison Grey Fiske, went on to lobby Congress for alteration of the regulatory law. The issue became moot when a federal judge refused to allow the ICC to enforce the prohibition against group rates for actors. *New York Dramatic Mirror,* 23 August 1890, 2.

33. Bloom, *Joseph Jefferson,* 302; *New York Mirror,* 12 March 1881, 8.

34. John H. White, Jr., *The American Railroad Passenger Car* (Baltimore: Johns Hopkins University Press, 1978), 211, 314–20; *Traveler's Official Railway Guide* (facsimile of 1869 edition, printed by Xerox University Microfilms for National Railway Publication Company), 19; *New York Dramatic Mirror,* 28 June 1890, 2; 26 October 1889, 1; *New York Mirror,* 3 February 1884; 4 June 1881, 2; 30 January 1892, 5; 4 October 1884, 6.

35. John R. Stilgoe, *Metropolitan Corridor: Railroads and the American Scene* (New Haven: Yale University Press, 1983), chaps. 3 and 5.

36. Jefferson, *Autobiography,* 242–43; Bernheim quoted in Peter Davis, "From Stock to Combination: The Panic of 1873 and Its Effects on the American Theatre Industry," *Theatre History Studies* 8 (1988): 1–2.

37. The best discussion of the rise of the combination company system is provided by John Frick, "A Changing Theatre: New York and Beyond," in Don B. Wilmeth and Christopher Bigsby, eds., *The Cambridge History of American Theatre,* vol. 2, *1870–1945* (Cambridge: Cambridge University Press, 1999), 196–232; William R. Reardon and Eugene R. Bristow, "The American Theatre, 1864–1870: An Economic Portrait," *Speech Monographs* 33, no. 4 (November 1966): 438–43; Davis, "From Stock to Combination, " 5–7, argues persuasively for the importance of the Panic of 1873 in the change.

38. McArthur, *Actors and American Culture,* 7–11; see the letters to the editor, *New York Dramatic Mirror,* 27 January 1883, 7.

39. Jefferson, *Autobiography,* 244.

40. *New York Mirror,* 2 May 1885, 8, November 1885, 4. Bloom, *Jefferson,* 129. I am in debt to Arthur Bloom for his thoughts on the developmental nature of Jefferson's touring.

41. Bloom, *Joseph Jefferson,* 306–7; Eugénie Paul Jefferson, *Intimate Recollections,* 175.

42. Bloom, *Joseph Jefferson,* 179–84.

43. Ibid., 184; Gamaliel Bradford, "Joseph Jefferson," *Atlantic Monthly* 129 (January 1922): 89; Jefferson to William Winter, n.d., Jefferson Papers, Harry Ransom Human-

ities Research Center, University of Texas; Jefferson to William Winter, 29 August 1883, Jefferson manuscripts, Historic Hudson Valley, Rockefeller Archive Center, Sleepy Hollow, N.Y.; Jefferson to Ingersoll, 12 June 1890, quoted in Wilson, *Joseph Jefferson*, 208; Skinner, *Footlights and Spotlights*, 254.

44. Skinner, *Footlights and Spotlights*, 253; *American National Biography*, s.v. "Mary Shaw," by Paul Mroczka; Mary Shaw, "The Stage Wisdom of Joseph Jefferson," *Century* 83 (March 1912): 733–35.

45. *New York Clipper*, 21 August 1869, 158.

46. Tracy Davis shows how this process worked in the English theatre at the same time in her *Economics of the British Stage*, 316–21; John Frick, *New York's First Theatrical Center*, (Ann Arbor: UMI Research Press, 1985), 108–114; another recent brief but very useful overview of the theatrical support industries is also by Frick, "A Changing Theatre: New York and Beyond," in Wilmeth and Bigsby, eds., *Cambridge History of American Theatre*, 2:192–232; *New York Dramatic Mirror* gives a short, compelling portrait of Sarony, 12 October 1891, 2.

47. Frick, *First Theatrical Center*, 114–21.

48. Ibid., 122–24.

49. Jefferson to Noah Ludlow 22 May 1868. Ludlow-Field-Maury Collection. Missouri Historical Society, St. Louis; Jefferson to Booth 14 December [1874], Hampden-Booth Theatre Library. The Players; Jefferson to John Ford, 5 April 1891, John T. Ford Papers, Manuscript Division, Library of Congress.

50. Telegram, Jefferson to [?] Bouton, 9 December 1886. Folger Shakespeare Library. Joe had experienced advice for a fellow showman, reminding him of the relative difficulty of "arranging terms with an establishment that is regularly prosperous." Jefferson to Paul [?], 14 November [c. 1869], Special Collections, Hill Memorial Library, Louisiana State University. Arthur Bloom has a fine discussion of Jefferson's financial arrangements in his *Joseph Jefferson*, 137–39.

51. Joseph Francis Daly, *The Life of Augustin Daly* (New York: Macmillan, 1917), 244, 246; Jefferson to Daly, 14 July 1877; 12 September 1877, Folger Shakespeare Library; *New York Times*, 30 October 1877, 5; Arthur Bloom describes the newspaper ads that sought to give *Rip* more legs, including reassurances that shows would end early enough for commuters to catch their trains home. *Joseph Jefferson*, 171, 315; *New York Mirror*, 4 January 1879, 3; Bloom, *Joseph Jefferson*, 176; Edwin Booth to William Winter, February 1879, Folger Shakespeare Library.

52. Several biographies of Edwin Booth, none completely adequate, have appeared. Current works in progress should address this need. A brief and balanced sketch of his life is written by Stephen Archer in *American National Biography*, 8; my discussion of Booth's Theatre relies on Charles H. Shattuck's, *Shakespeare on the American Stage* (Washington, D.C.: Folger Shakespeare Library, 1976), 131–37; Jefferson, *Autobiography*, 283.

53. Shattuck, *Shakespeare on the American Stage*, 134.

54. Lawrence B. Barsness, "Relationship of Stage Lighting Sources and Methods to Acting Styles in Theatres 1850–1915" (master's thesis, University of Oregon, 1950), 9–14, 66–69, 86 (quotations taken from Barsness); Penzel, *Theatre Lighting* (Middletown, Conn.: Wesleyan University Press, 1978), 56–61; Booth, *Victorian Spectacular Theatre*,

24–25. The substitution of electricity for gas brought some regrets from connoisseurs of the stage. Playwright St. John Ervine noted that even when the curtain went up "a veil of sort remained, rising from the fumes of the footlights, a trembling, transparent curtain between us and the players, who thus, although they were near and actual, seemed remote and mysterious." After a brief experiment with electricity at the Lyceum, Henry Irving quickly went back to gas lights. Ellen Terry, his leading lady, had complained of the harshness of electricity compared to the "thick softness of gas." True, the fumes from gas occasionally put actresses into a faint. Yet the olfactory element of gas gave theatre an extra sense that it lost to electricity — and with it a tie to memory. Booth, *Victorian Spectacular Theatre*, 26–27.

55. James, *Old Drury of Philadelphia*, 33–34; Leach, *Bright, Particular Star*, 53–54, 102; Davis, *Economics of British Stage*, 94–95; *New York Dramatic Mirror*, 10 January 1891, 3.

56. Davis, *Economics of British Stage*, 95–98; Henderson, *City and the Theatre*, 137–38; *New York Mirror*, 12 April 1884, 6; *New York Dramatic Mirror*, 14 July 1894, 35; 1 September 1894, 3. The problem of theatre fire was great enough to call forth a considerable literature dealing with the issue.

57. Shattuck, *Shakespeare on American Stage*, 137; Jefferson quote in Bradford, "Joseph Jefferson," 86.

58. *New York Tribune*, 3 August 1869; receipts, Booth Theatre, September 1873, Washington State University Library. My thanks to Arthur Bloom for making copies of these records available to me. Shattuck, *Shakespeare on American Stage*,

59. Oggel, *Letters of Mary Devlin Booth*, xxiii.

Chapter Eleven. A Fellow of Infinite Jest, of Most Excellent Fancy

1. The inspirational literature that drew upon Jefferson is not exhausted by the above examples. B. O. Flower, after the fashion of Carlyle and Emerson, offers up fourteen sketches of individuals from Seneca and Epictatus to Joan of Arc, Henry Clay, Alfred Wallace, Victor Hugo, Edwin Booth, and, of course, Joseph Jefferson. Flower uses Jefferson's life as an exemplary case of overcoming adversity. "It was in the school of poverty and privation that Joe Jefferson mastered the most important lesson of life . . . brought into most intimate connection with people in the humble walks of life, he learned human nature and life as it really is." *Lessons Learned From Other Lives* (Boston: Spectator Publishing, 1889), 79. Logan, *Before the Footlights*, 457; *New York Dramatic Mirror*, 19 July 1890, 3; n.a., "Rip Van Winkle," *Appleton's*, n.s. 4 (February 1878): 146–51; Davis, "At and After the Play"; A. G. Sedgwick, "Jefferson in 'Rip Van Winkle,'" *Nation* (23 September 1869): 247–48; James B. Runnion, "Joseph Jefferson," *Lippincott's* (August 1869): 167–76; Gilbert Pierce, "A Good-By to Rip Van Winkle," *Atlantic Monthly* 52 (November 1883); L. Clarke Davis, "Among the Comedians," *Atlantic Monthly* 19 (June 1867): 750–61; George William Curtis, "Editor's Easy Chair," *Harper's New Monthly* (March 1871): 614–16; Walter R. Houghton, *Kings of Fortune* (Chicago: Davis, 1886). Quote from Winter, *Life of Jefferson*, 12–13, Strong Museum; William Ordway Partridge, "John Rogers, The People's Sculptor," *New England Magazine* 19 (February 1896): 705–21.

2. Moses, ed., *Representative Plays,* 3:22; Obee, "A Prompt Script Study of Rip," 73–93; David Beasley, *Mckee Rankin and the Heyday of American Theater* (Waterloo, Ont.: Wilfred Laurier University Press, 2002), 135, 148–50; *San Francisco Alta California,* 30 September 1868, 6; *New York Clipper,* 8 November 1873, 254; Joseph Keane, *Rip Van Winkle* playbill, 1 January 1877, Robert McWade, *Rip Van Winkle* playbill, Olympic Theatre, 11 November 1873, both in Theatre Archives, Museum of the City of New York: John Howard Wainwright, *Rip Van Winkle: An Original American Grand Opera in Three Acts* (New York: Wardle Corbyn, 1855); J. W. Shannon, *Rip Van Winkle: Grand Romantic Opera in Three Acts* (New York: G. Schirmer, 1882).

3. *Chicago Times,* 4 January 1870, 2. The lawsuit was also reported in the *New York Clipper,* 15 January 1870, 326. My thanks to Arthur Bloom for pointing out this item to me.

4. *New York Times,* 2 September 1873, 5.

5. Davis, "At and After the Play," 70; Pierce, "Good-By to Rip Van Winkle," 695.

6. *New York Mirror,* 14 February 1880, 5.

7. Sarah commiserated with Mrs. William Winter over their respective disappointments in not having daughters in a letter, 22 May 1879, Folger Shakespeare Library.

8. Jefferson to William Winter, 15 March 1869. Jefferson Letters. Harry Ransom Humanities Research Center, University of Texas. Arthur Bloom's research indicates that the actual purchase of the Louisiana estate did not culminate until spring 1870. *Joseph Jefferson,* 443.

9. Davis, "At and After the Play," 73–74; *Frank Leslie's Illustrated Newspaper,* 2 October 1869, 43; Bloom, *Joseph Jefferson,* 143; n.a., *Ho-ho-kus: 1908/1983* (Seventy-fifth Anniversary Committee, 1983), 59, 147.

10. Eugénie Jefferson, *Intimate Recollections,* 79–81.

11. William Hosea Ballou, "Joseph Jefferson at Home," *Cosmopolitan* 7 (June 1889): 121–27; Eugénie Jefferson, *Intimate Recollections,* 59–78; Jefferson to H. H. Furness 28 January (no year), Annenberg Rare Book and Manuscript Library, University of Pennsylvania; Emily Caroline Douglas, unpub. autobiography, vol. 3, 99–100, Douglas Papers, Louisiana State University Library.

12. Bloom, *Joseph Jefferson,* 151–55, 443–44; "Joseph Jefferson's Home in Louisiana," unidentified clipping in possession of author; John Smith Kendall, "Joseph Jefferson in New Orleans," *Louisiana Historical Quarterly* 26 (October 1943): 1156–60; an article commenting on Joe's cattle spread, suggested that if the public tired of *Rip,* Jefferson might star in a new play, "Old Joe, The Cowboy King," *Stage* (13 October 1888): 6.

13. Grace B. Agate, "Joseph Jefferson, Painter of the Teche," *National Historic Magazine,* pp. 23–25, clipping, Live Oaks Garden Foundation, New Iberia, La.; unidentified newspaper clipping, Margaret Farjeon scrapbook, in author's possession; Edwin Booth to William Winter, 10 January 1882, Folger Shakespeare Library. A story was told of how Jefferson gave up hunting on humanitarian grounds while at Orange Island. "Joseph Jefferson as the Spectator Knew Him," *Outlook* 80 (6 May 1905): 17–18. This may be, but a letter from his home at Buzzards Bay in the 1880s suggests that Joe kept a lively interest in hunting.

14. A few of the many examples of journalistic reporting on his private life include Ballou, "Joseph Jefferson at Home," 127; Nathan Haskell Dole took the genre to a higher

level by devoting a complete book to the subject, *Joseph Jefferson at Home* (Boston: Estes and Lauriat, 1898), which was essentially a review of Jefferson's career accompanied by a host of pictures of him at home. Olive Logan's *Before the Footlights* (457–58) contains perhaps the best description of Jefferson's lifestyle as an emerging star. Fishing was more than an avocation for Joe; it was a passion. One of the great attractions of the forty-nine-acre Hohokus estate was its trout ponds, which he kept well stocked for his "fishing rambles" with friends. Jefferson to William Winter, 15 March 1869, Harry Ransom Humanities Research Center, University of Texas; Kendall, "Joseph Jefferson in New Orleans," 1158; churchman's comment in Diary of Charles Todd Quintard, 14 February 1879. Special Collections, Hill Memorial Library, Louisiana State University.

15. On this subject, see Benjamin McArthur's *Actors and American Culture, 1880–1920* (Philadelphia: Temple University Press, 1984), chap. 5.

16. Jefferson, *Autobiography*, 251–53; William Winter provides a useful sketch of Holland's life in his *The Wallet of Time*, 2 vols. (1913; reprint, Freeport, N.Y.: Books for Libraries Press, 1969), 1:38–59; Winter, *Life of Jefferson*, 266. William Winter had sought to organize a benefit for the impecunious Holland in the spring of 1870, soliciting the aid of Jefferson and Booth. But scheduling issues and the reluctance of Augustin Daly to admit that a member of his company might be so impoverished prevented assistance being given the still-breathing Holland and his family. See Edwin Booth to William Winter, 25 April [1870], in Watermeier, *Between Actor and Critic*, 27; I appreciate Don Wilmeth's help with clarifying some details about George Holland's son.

17. Winter, *Wallet of Time*, 1:53–62; *New York Times*, 17 January 1871, 7; Odell, *Annals of New York Stage*, 9:40, 72, 110; Bloom, *Joseph Jefferson*, 160–61; Twain quoted in Thomas Schirer, *Mark Twain and the Theatre* (Nuremberg: H. Carl, 1984), 35.

18. *New York Times*, 19 January 1871, 4; Bloom, *Joseph Jefferson*, 169; *New York Mirror*, 10 January 1885, 10; ibid., 2 February 1889, 6. An Episcopal Actors' Guild brochure, n.d., gives a brief history of the incident and its place in the formation of their organization. See also Zulette M. Catir, *A Parish Guide to the Church of the Transfiguration* (New York: Church of the Transfiguration, 1996) for a broader history of the church. The debate over the "Little Church Around the Corner" incident continued into the 1920s, reinvigorated when a stained-glass window commemorating Jefferson's visit to the church was installed in 1925. Defenders of Sabine asserted that rather than refusing to bury an actor, he had discovered that a wedding had been scheduled for the same hour as the funeral, an explanation that Jefferson misunderstood. Another letter to the editor of the *New York Evening Post* by Holland's grandson insisted that the traditional story was true. Holland said that his father had accompanied Jefferson to the church and clearly heard the exchange. The truth of the encounter is beyond our recall. In any event, its significance lies not in its details but as a symbol of church-stage conflict. Unidentified clipping, William Seymour Theatre Collection, Princeton University Library; *New York Evening Post*, 28 April 1924, Seymour Theatre Collection, Princeton University Library.

19. This history has been masterfully retold by Jonas Barish in his *The Antitheatrical Prejudice* (Berkeley: University of California Press, 1981).

20. John Witherspoon, *A Serious Inquiry into the Nature and Effects of the Stage and a Letter Respecting Play Actors* (New York: Whiting and Watson, 1812); *Distressing Calamity: A Brief Account of the Late Fire at Richmond, Virg., in which the Theatre Was*

Burnt, and Upwards of One Hundred and Sixty Persons, Perished in the Flames (Boston: Repertory Office, 1812); Tocqueville, *Democracy in America*, 492.

21. "The Methodist Amusement Ban," *Literary Digest* 44 (15 June 1912): 1260; Talmage, *Social Dynamite; or, the Wickedness of Modern Society* (Dayton: Historical Pub., 1888), 213; *New York Mirror*, 6 January 1883, 7.

22. *New York Mirror*, 1 December 1883, 6; 28 March 1885, 6; Shinn, "The Theatre as a Place of Amusement," untitled pamphlet in Billy Rose Theatre Collection, New York Public Library at Lincoln Center; Richard Foulkes's *Church and Stage in Victorian England* (Cambridge: Cambridge University Press, 1997) well describes the rapprochement of the two. No equivalent study exists for America.

23. William Winter, who knew Jefferson well, characterized his religious views in *Other Days*, 86, as did Jefferson's daughter-in-law Eugénie Paul Jefferson in her *Intimate Recollections of Joseph Jefferson*, 320–28. The literature on spiritualism and American culture is rich. R. Laurence Moore's *In Search of White Crows: Spiritualism, Parapsychology, and American Culture* (New York: Oxford University Press, 1977) was an early exploration of the subject. Leigh Eric Schmidt's *Hearing Things: Religion, Illusion, and the American Enlightenment* (Cambridge: Harvard University Press, 2000) and Bret E. Carroll's *Spiritualism in Antebellum America* (Bloomington: Indiana University Press, 1997) are two recent fine studies. Russell M. and Clare R. Goldfarb, *Spiritualism and Nineteenth-Century Letters* (Rutherford: Fairleigh Dickinson University Press, 1978) is particularly good on the literary impact of the phenomenon. Neil Harris, *Humbug*, explores the public delight in uncovering hoaxes.

24. Augustus Pitou, *Masters of the Show* (New York: Neale, 1914), 143; Eugénie Jefferson, *Intimate Recollections*, 320–28; Wilson, *Jefferson*, 338–40; Winter, *Other Days*, 79. Jefferson and Booth had a common bond in their interest in spiritualism. In 1874 while in Louisville he and Joe (as Booth confided in mutual friend William Winter) had attended "two or three charming 'seances'—the one just ended was full of genial 'spirits,' who seemed to revel in our society—they led us from 'grave to gay' & back again . . . [Joe will] soon be at Ho-hokus-pokus." Quoted in Watermeier, *Between Actor and Critic*, 47–48. Jefferson found less humor in the prospect that a granddaughter of his, suffering from a serious illness, would be treated by a Christian Science healer. Eugenie Paul Jefferson, from whom we have the fullest statement of her father-in-law's religious affections, insisted to the editor of *Cosmopolitan* magazine that no impression that Joe was a Christian Scientist should be given in any article. Paul to P. Maxwell, n.d., Jefferson miscellaneous file, Louisiana State University Library.

25. Winter, *Other Days*, 73; Walter Leman, *Memories of an Old Actor* (San Francisco: A. Roman, 1886), 206; Farjeon, *Portrait of a Family*, 79–80; *Chicago Record-Herald*, 30 April 1905, Robinson Locke Collection of Dramatic Scrapbooks, vol. 302, New York Public Library for the Performing Arts; Johnson, *Remembered Yesterdays*, 375; Wilson, *Jefferson*, 340; Jefferson poem, "Immortality," reproduced in Eugénie Jefferson, *Intimate Recollections*, 321–23.

26. Unidentified newspaper clippings, Margaret Farjeon scrapbook, in possession of author.

27. "Peter C. Kronfeld, "Glaucoma," in Daniel M. Albert and Diane D. Edwards, *The History of Ophthalmology* (New York: Blackwell, 1996), 203–23; Winter, *Life of Jeffer-*

son, 188; Bloom, *Jefferson,* 162; Sarah Jefferson to Mrs. Winter, 16 June 1872, Folger Shakespeare Library.

28. Joseph Jefferson, unpublished notebook, 17, copy in possession of author.

29. M. A. De Wolfe Howe, *Memories of a Hostess,* (Boston: Atlantic Monthly Press, 1922), 204. Later, unsubstantiated reports, suggest that whatever form of alcohol Jefferson may have imbibed he did not always do so in moderation. Arthur Schlesinger, Jr., tells of traveling to Cape Cod as a college student, where an old-timer told him of once seeing Jefferson and Grover Cleveland getting tipsy and chasing one another around the Sandwich railroad depot. *A Life in the Twentieth Century: Innocent Beginnings* (Boston: Houghton Mifflin, 2000), 116.

30. Booth to Winter, 15 March 1870, Folger Shakespeare Library.

31. Jefferson, *Autobiography,* 258–63.

32. *Times* (London), 3 November 1875, 8; unidentified newspaper clipping, 10 November 1875, "*Rip Van Winkle,*" *World,* 10 November 1875; the last two in Margaret Farjeon scrapbook.

33. Clement Scott, "Joseph Jefferson," *Concordia,* 12 November 1875, Margaret Farjeon scrapbook; "Mr. Jefferson," *Academy* 6 (November 1875): 490.

34. Booth to William Winter, 25 November 1875, in Watermeier, *Between Actor and Critic,* 54.

35. Jefferson's manservant Sam Phillips observed Joe on stage the night his son had died. Eugénie Jefferson, *Intimate Recollections,* 230; Bloom, *Joseph Jefferson,* 168. Jefferson to W. P. Frith, 16 November 1875, Special Collections, Hill Memorial Library, Louisiana State University; Jefferson to Winter, 14 February 1876, Jefferson manuscripts, Historic Hudson Valley, Rockefeller Archive Center.

36. Jefferson to Frith, 16 November 1875; Jefferson, *Autobiography,* 260–62; Edward Walford, *Old and New London,* vol. 5 (London: Cassell, 1879), 494; Stephen Inwood, *A History of London* (New York: Carroll and Graf, 1998), 579, 583.

37. Jefferson to Winter, 29 January 1876, Jefferson manuscripts, Historic Hudson Valley, Rockefeller Archive Center; unidentified newspaper clipping, Margaret Farjeon scrapbook.

38. Bloom, *Joseph Jefferson,* 169.

39. Jefferson to Benjamin Farjeon 27 February 1875. Letter in possession of author. Annabel Farjeon, *Morning Has Broken, A Biography of Eleanor Farjeon* (London: J. Macrae, 1986), 1–13; Bloom, *Joseph Jefferson,* 169.

40. *Manchester Guardian,* 31 May 1876, 5; *Liverpool Mail,* 24 June 1876, 9; unidentified newspaper clipping, Margaret Farjeon scrapbook.

41. *Glasgow Herald,* 23 July, 4; 26 September 1876, 4.

42. Jefferson, *Autobiography,* 280–81; *Dublin Morning News,* 24 October 1876, 3; *Irish Times* (Dublin), 24 October 1876, 4.

43. Bloom, *Joseph Jefferson,* 448; *Frank Leslie's Illustrated Newspaper,* 17 February 1877, 395; Jefferson, *Autobiography,* 270–71.

44. Ibid., 269–70.

45. Jefferson to Stephen Fiske, 26 March 1877. Folger Shakespeare Library; Henry James, *The Tragic Muse* (New York: Library of America, 1989), 830; Bloom, *Joseph Jefferson,* 171; Mowbray Morris, *Essays in Theatrical Criticism* (London: Remington, 1882), 80–81.

46. Henry James, *English Hours* (New York: Weidenfeld and Nicolson, 1989), 108; *Edinburgh Scotsman,* 21 August 1877, 5; *Manchester Guardian,* 4 September 1877, 5; Bloom, *Joseph Jefferson,* 172.

47. Bloom, *Joseph Jefferson,* 173, 175.

48. Ibid., 175, 315–16; *New York Clipper,* 29 June 3 1878, 110; 6 July 1879, 118; 13 July 1878, 126; Booth to William Winter, 14 August 1878, Folger Shakespeare Library.

49. With Mormon country on the horizon, Joe joked with Winter that Mrs. Jefferson "is already quite meek and on her good behavior, fearing I may join 'Brigham's band.'" Jefferson to Winter, 7 July 1878, Harvard Theatre Collection; Bloom, *Joseph Jefferson,* 316. The phenomenon of having trains specially chartered to bring people from outlying regions to see a star was not unique to Jefferson. Edwin Booth's advance man frequently arranged similar accommodations. I am grateful to Arthur Bloom for this insight.

50. Arthur Bloom has painstakingly compiled Jefferson's yearly tours in his *Joseph Jefferson,* 195–366.

51. I discuss the professionalizing impulse in some detail in *Actors and American Culture,* chap. 4.

52. Several years before the founding of The Players, Henry Irving attempted a similar but short-lived club styled The Kinsmen. Formed from the same sort of performing and literary mix that Booth would later invite (e.g., Jefferson, Booth, Barrett, Howells, Twain, etc.), members were given a ceremonial ivory bone (the name and gimmick derived from a line in *Romeo and Juliet*), which they could present at Irving's Lyceum theatre to give them free admission whenever in London. George Parsons Lathrop, "The Literary Movement in New York," *Harper's New Monthly Magazine* 78 (November 1886): 830. Joe also joined the longer-lived Authors' Club, an indication that he felt a kindred vocation with professional writers. Jefferson to Duffield Osborne, 10 January 1894, Harvard Theatre Collection. On the founding of The Players, see McArthur, *Actors and American Culture,* 78–83; Carole Klein, *Gramercy Park: An American Bloomsbury* (Boston: Houghton Mifflin, 1987).

53. Bloom, *Joseph Jefferson,* 209. *New York Dramatic Mirror,* 1 July 1893, 4. Theatrical producer Daniel Frohman tells of Joe's manner of conducting business meetings in an unpublished manuscript (c. 1920) held at the Museum of the City of New York.

54. John Gross has described the English "man of letters" era with great insight in his *The Rise and Fall of the Man of Letters* (New York: Collier Books, 1969).

55. Walt Whitman, "Miserable State of the Stage," *Brooklyn Eagle,* 8 February 1847, quoted in Montrose Moses and John Mason Brown, eds., *The American Theatre as Seen by Its Critics, 1752–1934* (New York: W. W. Norton, 1934), 70–71; Wolter, *Dawning of American Drama,* 18; Tice L. Miller, *Bohemians and Critics: American Theatre Criticism in the Nineteenth Century* (Metuchen, N. J.: Scarecrow Press, 1981) provides the best overview of the century's dramatic criticism. N. Bryllion Fagin, "Poe—Drama Critic," *Theatre Annual* (1945): 23–24; Whitman, quoted in Moses, *American Theatre,* 70.

56. Stephen Fiske, "Playwriting Critics," *New York Dramatic Mirror,* 1 March 1890, 1; Miller, *Bohemians and Critics,* 106, 112–15. Hutton's *Curiosities of the American Stage* (1891), a delightful walk through odd theatrical corners, remains a rewarding work. Along with Matthews he edited *Actors and Actresses of Great Britain and the United States* (1886), a pathbreaking biographical effort. *American National Biography,* s.v. "Brander Matthews," by William J. Hug; *Dictionary of American Biography,* s.v.

"Laurence Hutton," (P.H.B.). The tremendous outpouring of biographies and collections of reviews and essays on the stage toward the end of the nineteenth bespoke both theatre's prominence in American life and the growth of the theatrical "chattering class."

57. Miller, *Bohemians and Critics*, 96; Bernard F. Dukore, ed. *Bernard Shaw: The Drama Observed*, 4 vols. (University Park: Pennsylvania State University Press, 1993).

58. Miller, *Bohemians and Critics*, 12–17, 70–101. Downer quoted in his *American Drama and Its Critics: A Collection of Critical Essays* (Chicago: University of Chicago Press, 1965), xiv; William Winter, *The Actor* (New York: Burt Franklin, 1891), 1–25; Mencken quote in *American National Biography*, s.v. "William Winter," by Walter J. Meserve. Winter, who had both a capacious need and capacity for friendship, had similarly ingratiated himself with Edwin Booth, Richard Mansfield, and several other luminaries. Jefferson to Winter, 4 August 1886, Harry Ransom Humanities Research Center, University of Texas; Jefferson to Winter, 7 October 1875, Folger Shakespeare Library; Jefferson to Winter, 9 April [1872], Ransom Center; Jefferson to Winter, n.d., Huntington Library; Jefferson to Winter, 25 December (no year), Jefferson manuscripts, Historic Hudson Valley, Rockefeller Archive Center; Jefferson to Winter, 22 February 1874, Folger Shakespeare Library; Jefferson to Winter, 30 May 1875, Folger Shakespeare Library. Sarah Jefferson to Lizzie Winter, 7 May 1872, and January 8 1875, both in Folger Shakespeare Library. Toward the close of Joe's English tours, Winter crossed the Atlantic to join Joe on an excursion through Warwickshire countryside. Their short journeys formed the basis for a rather pedestrian travel account by Winter, *The Trip to England* (Boston, 1881), which Jefferson illustrated.

59. On Cushman see Leach, *Bright, Particular Star;* on Twain, see Justin Kaplan, *Mr. Clemens and Mark Twain* (New York: Simon and Schuster, 1966).

60. Gilder, "Few Words about Jefferson," 410; Rosamond Gilder, ed., *The Letters of Richard Watson Gilder* (Boston: Houghton, Mifflin, 1916), 67–69; *American National Biography*, s.v. "Gilder, Richard Watson," by Herbert F. Smith.

61. On at least one occasion Joe was able to provide Gilder an introduction. When Robert Louis Stevenson visited America in 1887, Jefferson, who had made his acquaintance, informed Gilder that the master storyteller would see him. Gilder, ed., *Letters of Gilder*, 145; Robert Underwood Johnson, *Remembered Yesterdays* (Boston: Little, Brown, 1923), 88–93; Morton Sosna, *In Search of the Silent South: Southern Liberals and the Race Issue* (New York: Columbia University Press, 1977), discusses Cable's social critique. Cable quotations from Lucy Leffingwell Cable Bikle, *George W. Cable; His Life and Letters* (New York: Russell and Russell, 1928), 81–82, 100–101. Information on Cable's life found in Arlin Turner, *George W. Cable* (Baton Rouge: Louisiana State University Press, 1966); Louis D. Rubin, Jr., *George W. Cable: The Life and Times of a Southern Heretic* (New York: Pegasus, 1968).

62. *George W. Cable*, 100–101, 106; Jefferson to Cable 28 July 1889, copy in possession of author.

63. Jürgen C. Wolter has compiled a representative selection of criticisms (including Daly's and Boucicault's) in his *The Dawning of American Drama*, 180–92; the *New York Dramatic Mirror* devoted many columns to the disputation over the state of American drama in 1889 and 1890. See especially 2 February 1889, 2; 6 April 1889, 1; 11 May 1889, 1; 6 July 1889, 1;13 July 1889, 1, 2; 27 July 1889, 1; 28 September 1889, 2; 23 November 1889, 1, 2; 7 December 1889, 1; 28 December 1889, 1,13; 1 March 1890, 1.

64. Jefferson, *Autobiography*, 338.

65. First James quotation from Brenda Murphy, *American Realism and American Drama, 1880–1940* (Cambridge: Cambridge University Press, 1987), 50–51; second quotation from James, *Tragic Muse*, 747–48. Howells approached Jefferson in 1880 offering him the leading role in his translation of a Spanish comedy he called *A New Play* (more imaginatively retitled later *Yorick's Love*). Joe demurred, feeling unsuited to the part. He further judged that the play "seems to lack that strong action which the audience of the present day continually demands." Jefferson to Howells, 22 January 1880, Harvard Theatre Collection.

Henry James might seem the least likely candidate to tempt the tragic muse, and indeed his most extended efforts in the 1890s had blatantly mercenary roots. He undertook the theatrical enterprise (much of it in England) with great hopes "to make my fortune" and showed a commendable willingness to rewrite and listen to experienced criticism. But he encountered one disappointment after another. "The Master" had a command of literary dialogue that would seem to have served him well with drama, but his psychological subtleties, intricate turns of plot, and unresolved endings were ill suited to the necessary dramatic transparency. His hauteur did not help. He viewed his theatrical experience as a sort of "artistic slumming expedition," according to biographer Leon Edel. "Forget not that you write for the stupid," James advised a fellow writer. To this dubious end, James proceeded to adapt his novels (notably *The American*) for the stage by discarding their complexity (a partial necessity) and replacing it with a confused amalgam of melodrama and comedy. Reduced to melodramatic formulations and lame comedy, these well-disguised Jamesian products had little in common with his originals save the titles Leon Edel, *Henry James: A Life* (New York: Harper and Row, 1985), 363–86; Murphy, *American Realism,* 56–60.

66. George Arms, Mary Bess Whidden, and Gary Scharnhorst, eds., *Staging Howells: Plays and Correspondence with Lawrence Barrett* (Albuquerque: University of New Mexico Press, 1994), 70–71. Thomas Schirer's *Mark Twain and the Theatre* (Nuremberg: H. Carl, 1984) provides a fine overview of Twain's theatrical efforts.

67. Jefferson to Shewell, 4 March 1884. Huntington Library; *New York Mirror*, 26 July 1884, 6; 16 August 1884, 6; 8 November 1884, 4; 22 November 1884, 2; 22 August 1885, 7; *New York Times,* 18 November 1884, 5. A review of the 1887 production was published in Clement Scott's magazine, *Theatre* (1 August 1887): 102–3. In 1904 Grace Miller White adapted the play into a novel of the same name.

68. Eugénie Jefferson, *Intimate Recollections,* 48; Henry C. Angell, "Records of W. M. Hunt" *Atlantic Monthly* 45 (June 1880): 754.

69. Wilson, *Jefferson,* 308. James explores the singular vocational tug of painting and acting in *The Tragic Muse.*

70. Davis, "At and After the Play," 75; Eugénie Jefferson, *Intimate Recollections,* 55; Jefferson, *Autobiography,* 265; Bloom, *Joseph Jefferson,* 148; Wilson, *Jefferson,* 82, 307. Jefferson himself recognized that his failure early in life to master the drawing of figures limited his possibilities. Wilson, *Jefferson,* 60.

71. Jefferson to Fawcett, 9 November 1893, Harvard Theatre Collection. Winter, *The Trip to England* (Boston: James Osgood, 1881 [orig. pub. 1878]). I am indebted to art historian Jon Carstens for his evaluation of Jefferson's sketches. Jefferson quote on artists' influence from Estill Curtis Pennington, *Subdued Hues: Mood and Scene in Southern*

Landscape Painting, 1865–1925 (Augusta, Ga.: Morris Museum of Art, 1999), 48; Howells, "Life and Letters," *Harper's Weekly* 39 (11 May 1895): 436. Jefferson to Winter, 7 October 1880, Jefferson manuscripts, Historic Hudson Valley, Rockefeller Archive Center.

72. The best study of Jefferson as artist and collector is by M. Elizabeth Boone, "Joseph Jefferson: Actor, Painter and Collector," unpub. paper in possession of author. Arthur Bloom has some fine observations about Jefferson and Corot in his *Joseph Jefferson,* 144–49; on Corot, see "Camille Corot," *GroveArt* online encyclopedia at http://www .groveart.com.

73. Davis, "At and After the Play," 74; Eugénie Jefferson, *Intimate Recollections,* 40; Wilson, *Jefferson,* 226–27; *Deluxe Catalog of the Valuable Paintings Collected by the Late Joseph Jefferson* (New York: American Art Association, 1906), introduction by Charles A. Walker.

74. "Monotypes," *Century* 53 (February 1897): 517; Wilson, *Jefferson,* 86–90; Eugénie Jefferson, *Intimate Recollections,* 56–58.

75. "The Usher" was a pen name for a writer for the *New York Dramatic Mirror,* 1 April 1893, 4.

76. White's portrait of Jefferson now hangs in the clubhouse of The Players. The reproduction appeared as a frontispiece for an article on Jefferson by William Winter in *Harper's New Monthly Magazine* 73 (August 1886): 391–97. Sarah J. Moore, "John White Alexander (1856–1915): In Search of the Decorative" (Ph.D. diss., City University of New York, 1992), 58, 61, 67–71; Sandra Leff, "Essay," in *John White Alexander,* catalog of exhibition at Graham Gallery, 21 October–13 December 1980 (New York: Graham, 1980), 7–18; *American National Biography,* s.v. "John White Alexander," by Martin R. Kalfatovic.

77. Elaine Kilmurray and Richard Ormond, eds., *John Singer Sargent* (Princeton: Princeton University Press, 1998), 32; Richard Ormond, *John Singer Sargent* (New York: Harper and Row, 1970), 32, 43, 249, 74; William Howe Downes, *John S. Sargent: His Life and Work* (London: Thornton Butterworth, 1926), 157; *American National Biography,* s.v. "John Singer Sargent," by Kathleen L. Butler. Homer Fort, "Joe Jefferson and His Favorite Artist," *Leslie's Weekly* (1 May 1902), Robinson Locke Collection of Dramatic Scrapbooks, vol. 302, 33, New York Public Library for the Performing Arts.

78. Wilson, *Joseph Jefferson,* 83, 77.

Chapter Twelve. Are We So Soon Forgot?

1. Ernest Samuels, *Henry Adams* (Cambridge: Harvard University Press, 1989), 370; Wilson, *Jefferson,* 77. Jefferson once approached Laurence Hutton about his legacy. He implored Hutton not make a death mask "to hang with the rest of them in that chamber of horrors of your up-town!" Rather, he hoped that certain things about himself be mentioned, things "which I can't say, and which can't be said by anybody yet!" Joe then volunteered to jot down these burdens and send them to Hutton, but the latter never received them. Hutton, "Recollections of Joseph Jefferson," *Harper's Weekly* 49 (6 May 1905): 663.

2. Watermeier, *Between Actor and Critic,* 281. *New York Mirror,* 13 November

1886, 7; Gilder, ed., *Letters of Richard Gilder,* 167. Wilson, *Jefferson,* 7, 236–37. [The Spectator], "Joseph Jefferson as the Spectator Knew Him," 17. The *Autobiography* ran monthly through the October 1890 issue. It was issued as a volume in late fall 1890.

3. Karl Weintraub provides the most satisfactory explanation of the emerging autobiographical impulse in Western culture in his *The Value of the Individual: Self and Circumstance in Autobiography* (Chicago: University of Chicago Press, 1978); Ronald Moyer, "American Actors, 1886–1910: An Annotated Bibliography of Books Published in the United States in English from 1861 through 1972" (Ph.D. diss., University of Denver, 1974) is an excellent bibliographical guide to biographies and autobiographies of the late nineteenth century.

4. B. R. S. Fone, ed., *An Apology of the Life of Colley Cibber* (Ann Arbor: University of Michigan Press, 1968). Stoddart, *Recollections,* xiii–xiv. Thomas Postlewait, "Autobiography and Theatre History," in Postlewait and Bruce McConachie, eds., *Interpreting the Theatrical Past: Essays in the Historiography of Performance* (Iowa City: University of Iowa Press, 1989), 256–57. Postlewait provides a useful typology of actors' autobiographies as well as other thoughtful insights on the genre. Anna Cora Mowatt, *Autobiography of an Actress* (Boston: Ticknor, Reed, and Fields, 1854); Solomon Franklin Smith, *The Theatrical Apprenticeship and Anecdotal Recollections* (Philadelphia: Carey and Hart, 1842), *The Theatrical Journey—Work and Anecdotal Recollections of Sol. Smith* (Philadelphia: T. B. Peteson, 1854), and *Theatrical Management in the West and South for Thirty Years* (New York: Harper and Brothers,1868). Olive Logan, *Before the Footlights and Behind the Scenes* (1870). Oddly, such stage legends as Charlotte Cushman, Edwin Forrest, Edwin Booth, and Lawrence Barrett failed to pen their own narrative. In Booth's case, the personal agonies of his brother's life, his first wife's death, and his second wife's instability precluded any memoir. The others were perhaps inhibited by a widespread Victorian diffidence toward public discussion of one's private life. Or maybe they simply never got around to it.

5. Carolyn A. Barros, *Autobiography: Narrative of Transformation* (Ann Arbor: University of Michigan Press, 1998), 1; *New York Daily Mirror,* 10 January 1891, 4; "Jefferson as the Spectator Knew Him," 18; Wilson, *Jefferson,* 196–97.

6. Jefferson, *Autobiography,* 69.

7. Howard Helsinger, "Credence and Credibility: The Concern for Honesty in Victorian Autobiography," in George P. Landow, ed., *Approaches to Victorian Autobiography* (Athens, Ohio: Ohio University Press, 1979), 39–40; Charles P. Thompson et al., *Autobiographical Memory: Remembering What and Remembering When* (Mahwah, N.J.: Lawrence Erlbaum, 1996); Robert E. McGlone, "Rescripting a Troubled Past: John Brown's Family and the Harpers Ferry Conspiracy," *Journal of American History* 75 (March 1989): 1182; David Rubin, ed., *Autobiographical Memory* (Cambridge: Cambridge University Press, 1986); Bruce M. Ross, *Remembering the Personal Past* (New York: Oxford University Press, 1991); Twain quote from Henry Nash Smith and William M. Gibson, eds., *Mark Twain–Howells Letters: The Correspondence of Samuel L. Clemens and Willian D. Howells, 1872–1910* (Cambridge: Belknap Press, 1970), 782.

8. On temporal memory, see Thompson, *Autobiographical Memory,* chaps. 1 and 2; Winter, *Other Days,* 76; Jefferson to Booth, 7 October 1886. Hampden-Booth Library, The Players, New York.

9. Dickinson quote in Justin Kaplan, *Walt Whitman, a Life* (New York: Simon and Schuster, 1980), 19.

10. Jefferson, *Autobiography,* 289; Wilson, *Joseph Jefferson,* 231–33; Jefferson to Winter, 5 March 1889. Jefferson Collection, Library of Congress.

11. *New York Dramatic Mirror,* 17 January 1891, 8; ibid., 10 January 1891, 4.

12. James B. Runnion, *Dial* 11 (December 1890): 237–39; *Nation* 51 (13 November 1890): 386; *Critic* 17 (29 November 1890):169.

13. Dreiser, *Sister Carrie,* 101, 40.

14. Wilson, *Joseph Jefferson,* 251; *New York Dramatic Mirror,* 22 November 1890, 3.

15. Wagenknecht, *Merely Players,* 213; Sefton to Jefferson, 3 December 1889, copy in possession of author. I am indebted to Jefferson's great-grandson, Gervase Farjeon, for sharing the Sefton correspondence. Originals in Performing Arts Museum Archive, the Arts Centre, Melbourne, Australia.

16. Jefferson to Sefton, 4 May 1890, copy in author's possession.

17. Ibid.

18. Jefferson to Sefton correspondence, 1890–1904.

19. *New York Times,* 14 December 1885, 1; ibid., 3 January 1885, 6.

20. Bloom, *Joseph Jefferson,* 238–40. Joe purchased half interest in a fishing camp in the remote reaches of New Brunswick where he could angle for salmon on the Miramichi River. Frank H. Risten, "The Salmon of the Sou'west," *Outing* 32 (July 1904): 333–38. I am beholden to Norman DeMerchant for bringing the Canadian property to my attention.

21. Unpub. manuscript (n.a.), Bourne Historical Center, Bourne, Mass.; Eugénie Paul Jefferson, "Joseph Jefferson at Home," *Century* (April 1909): 885; Eugénie Jefferson, *Intimate Recollections,* 32–33.

22. Bloom, *Joseph Jefferson,* 240; Allen Nevins, *Grover Cleveland: A Study in Courage* (New York: Dodd, Mead, 1932), 451–54; undated newspaper clipping, Harvard Theatre Collection; Richard Hofstadter, *The American Political Tradition* (New York: Alfred A. Knopf, 1948), 182. On the actors' rise, see McArthur, *Actors and American Culture,* 157. The story was told of how on the last night of the Democratic Party convention in 1892 Jefferson was at Cleveland's home. Charley kept tab of election results as they were telegraphed in. A famous anecdote from that night, bespeaking Jefferson's political naivete and his love of beauty, has the victorious Cleveland seeking out Jefferson, finding him gazing out over the early morning sunrise. "'Joe,' he said, 'aren't you going to congratulate me?' And Jefferson; 'Ah, I do! Believe me, I do congratulate you. But, good God, if I could paint like that you could be president of a dozen United States and I wouldn't change places with you.'" Gamaliel Bradford, "Joseph Jefferson," *Atlantic Monthly* 129 (January 1922): 92.

23. *Deluxe Catalog of Jefferson Paintings,* introduction; Farjeon, *Intimate Recollections of Joseph Jefferson,* 25–27; Wilson, *Jefferson,* 282. Joe wrote years later that he lost much of his "valued correspondence . . . in a cruel and fatal fire." Jefferson to John Dickey 26 November 1902. Dickey Manuscripts. Lilly Library, Indiana University. Historians can only conjecture how much richer the reconstruction of Jefferson's life would be if such sources had not been lost.

24. William E. Bryant, "Joseph Jefferson at Home," *New England Magazine* 18 (April 1895): 193–205; Eugénie Jefferson, *Intimate Recollections,* 29–30; Wilson, *Jefferson,* 283–84.

25. Eleanor Farjeon tells the family story in a delicate way in her "Joe in Paradise: A Forward," in Jefferson, *"Rip Van Winkle": The Autobiography* (London: Reinhardt and Evans, 1949); Bloom, *Joseph Jefferson,* 172–73.

26. O. B. Stebbins, *"The Rivals,* A Critical History of the Play," *Opera Glass* ((July 1895): 103; Nat C. Goodwin, *Nat Goodwin's Book* (Boston: Richard G Badger, 1914), 44–48.

27. Chicago critic quoted in Bloom, *Joseph Jefferson,* 182.

28. Laura Keene, "Drama," *Fine Arts* (March 1872): 71; J. Rankin Towse, "Joseph Jefferson as 'Caleb Plummer,'" *Century* 5 (January 1884): 476; *New York Times,* 15 October 1895, 5.

29. Jefferson to Winter, 4 January 1887, letter in collection of Don Wilmeth, Brown University. An example of Boucicault's claiming credit for Jefferson's success can be found in his "The Dramatization of 'Rip Van Winkle,'" where he also said that he insisted that Joe would make a hit as Caleb Plummer ("He would not see it"). *Critic* 3 (1883): 158.

30. *New York Dramatic Mirror,* 15 October 1892, 6; 19 July 1890, 3.

31. Ibid., 13 January 1894, 3, 8; 27 January 1894, 10; 17 February 1894, 7.

32. Jefferson to Daly, 17 January 1893; 20 July 1889, both in Folger Shakespeare Library; Bloom, *Jefferson,* 189; John H. Barnes, *Forty Years on the Stage* (New York: Dutton, 1915)), 165. Sam Phillips, Joe's valet for many years, gave several examples of Jefferson's continued support of disabled individuals. Eugénie Jefferson, *Intimate Recollections,* 171–73.

33. Simon, *Actors's Fund,* 156; *New York Dramatic Mirror,* 16 April 1892, 3; 7 May 1892, 6–7.

34. *New York Dramatic Mirror,* 7 May 1892, 6–7; Bloom, *Joseph Jefferson,* 207.

35. Unidentified newspaper clipping, n.d., Robinson Locke Collection of Dramatic Scrapbooks, vol. 301, New York Public Library for the Performing Arts; n.a., "Joseph Jefferson as the Spectator Knew Him," *Outlook,* 18.

36. Jefferson quoted in Bloom, *Joseph Jefferson,* 211.

37. Winter, *Life of Jefferson,* 211–12.

38. On Sheridan and *The Rivals,* see Finian O'Toole, *A Traitor's Kiss: The Life of Richard Brinsley Sheridan, 1751–1816* (New York: Farrar, Straus and Giroux, 1997), esp. 89–99.

39. Bloom, *Joseph Jefferson,* 35, 44–45; McKenzie, "Acting of Joseph Jefferson," 128; Jefferson, *Autobiography,* 296.

40. Jefferson, *Autobiography,* 298; Lawrence Levine, *Highbrow Lowbrow: The Emergence of Cultural Hierarchy in America* (Cambridge: Harvard University Press, 1988), 40–44.

41. Joseph Jefferson, *The Rivals* (n.p.: n.d.), English and American Drama of the Nineteenth Century — American. Microopaque. Readex Microprint (original owned by Museum of City of New York). The original version of Sheridan's play that I consulted is in the *Dramatic Works of Richard Brinsley Sheridan,* Joseph Knight, ed. (London: Henry Froude, Oxford University Press, n.d.).

42. On the new humor of vaudeville, see Albert McLean, Jr., *American Vaudeville as Ritual* (Lexington: University of Kentucky Press, 1965); Henry Jenkins, *What Made Pistachio Nuts: Early Sound Comedy and the Vaudeville Aesthetic* (New York: Columbia University Press, 1992), 78.

43. Winter, *Shadows of the Stage*, 151–58; Stebbins, "*The Rivals*, A Critical History of the Play," 103; *New York Times*, 13 September 1881, 5.

44. Stebbins, "*The Rivals*, A Critical History of the Play," 101–3; Joe told the story of Warren's remark in his *Autobiography*, 297; it was repeated, among other places, in John H. Barnes, *Forty Years on the Stage* (New York: E. P. Dutton, 1915), 166;

45. "Address to Academy of Dramatic Arts," unidentified clipping, Robinson Locke Collection of Dramatic Scrapbooks, vol. 302, New York Public Library for the Performing Arts, (also quoted in Wilson, 111–12); "Report of Discussion following Joseph Jefferson's Address on Dramatic Art, September 27, 1901," typescript, American Academy of Arts and Letters. Jefferson also spoke to the issue of his alterations in his *Autobiography*. "It must be admitted that these were sweeping alterations, and in the event of their failure they were likely to endanger whatever reputation I had acquired as a legitimate comedian. They succeeded, however, and I was only subjected to some slight critical censure from the press and a little quizzing from a few old school members of the profession, who were naturally and honestly shocked at my having taken such unwarrantable liberties with their past hero" (297).

46. Peters, *House of Barrymore*, 97; *New York Mirror*, 17 September 1881, 2; Odell, *Annals*, 14:30, 159; *American National Biography*, s.v. "John Gibbs Gilbert," by Kent Neely. Gilbert took exception with Jefferson's latitude with *The Rivals*. Did that difference of opinion persuade Joe to enter his partnership with William Florence in fall 1889? Or was it simply that he had little choice, given Gilbert's death in June of that year?

47. As with Jefferson, Florence's career was greatly advanced by his earning acclaim on the London stage. Henry P. Goddard, "Players I Have Known — Jefferson and Florence," *Theatre* 7 (April 1907): 100, 102; *New York Dramatic Mirror*, 18 June 1892, 3; 28 November 1892, 3; William Winter, *Wallet of Time*, vol. 1, 233–39.

48. Jefferson to Winter, 5 March 1889, Miscellaneous Manuscripts Collection, Library of Congress; *New York Dramatic Mirror*, 28 November 1891, 3; Bloom, *Joseph Jefferson*, 223.

49. *New York Dramatic Mirror*, 30 March 1889, 1; 28 November 1891, 3; Bloom, *Joseph Jefferson*, 223–27; Shirley Staples, *Male-Female Comedy Teams in American Vaudeville, 1865–1932* (Ann Arbor: MI Research Press, 1968), 20. Jefferson wrote his *Autobiography* before Florence's death, which explains the latter's brief appearances in his memoir.

50. Skinner, *Footlights and Spotlights*, 253.

51. Jefferson-Florence Route 1891–92, printed itinerary in Harvard Theatre Collection. Arthur Bloom has tracked *The Rivals* tours for all three seasons in his *Joseph Jefferson*, 339–45.

52. *New York Dramatic Mirror*, 21 June 1890, 3; MacKenzie, "Acting of Joseph Jefferson," 154; "Autobiographical Sketch of Mrs. John Drew," (second part), 563. Tracy Davis, in his *The Economics of British Stage, 1800–1914* (New York: Cambridge University Press, 2000), notes how the contemporary revolution in color lithography allowed for the production of alluring posters in anticipation of visits by companies such as Jefferson's (pp. 339–40).

53. *New York Dramatic Mirror*, 28 February 1891, 10; same "event of season claim made for Chattanooga, 8 March 1890, 10; Detroit appearance noted in 11 January 1890, 10.

54. Bloom, *Joseph Jefferson*, 226–27; *New York Dramatic Mirror*, 14 December 1889, 9; Skinner, *Footlights and Spotlights*, 253.

55. Their Boston engagement in November gave some indication of the sustained popularity of the tour. *New York Dramatic Mirror*, 7 November 1891, 9.

56. *New York Dramatic Mirror*, 21 November 1891, 3; 28 November 1891, 4–3; Bloom, *Joseph Jefferson*, 234.

57. *American National Biography*, s.v. "Louisa Lane Drew," by Rosemarie K. Bank; Drew gave her in recollections in her "Autobiographical Sketch," *Scribner's* 26 (October 1899): 417–33; (November 1899): 552–69.

58. Barnes, *Forty Years on the Stage*, 191; Jefferson, *Autobiography*, 297.

59. Undated newspaper clipping, Owen Fawcett Collection, University of Tennessee–Knoxville. *New York Dramatic Mirror*, 9 April 1892, 2; 22 October 1892, 7; October 1, 1892, 8.

60. Of the many works dealing with the Chicago World's Fair, James Gilbert's *Perfect Cities: Chicago's Utopias of 1893* (Chicago: University of Chicago Press, 1991) is particularly useful. *New York Dramatic Mirror*, 20 May 1893, 9; 24 June 1893, 9; 1 July 1893, 8; Bloom, *Joseph Jefferson*, 347.

61. *New York Dramatic Mirror*, 1 July 1893, 4; 18 November 1893, 7.

62. The tradition of all-star casts donating their services for a one-night benefit goes well back in the Anglo-American stage. Eminent stars showed their friendship to a fellow player by donating an evening of work in a popular play. The unfortunate George Holland received such in 1870. In 1888 the most acclaimed American benefit (on behalf of Lester Wallack) was staged at the Metropolitan Opera House: a performance of *Hamlet* starring (naturally) Edwin Booth. Jefferson took the low comedy role of first gravedigger. I am indebted to David Rinear for information on this tradition.

63. Wilson's early career was reviewed in a *New York Dramatic Mirror* interview, 29 September 1894, 2. Wilson's own reminiscences were published as *Francis Wilson's Life of Himself* (1924); see also the entry in *American National Biography*, s.v. "Francis Wilson," by Paul Mroczka. The founding of Actors' Equity in 1913 (in which Wilson played a major part) prefigured the founding of the American Association of University Professors in 1915 (John Dewey being Wilson's counterpart in this effort). As dissimilar vocations as acting and university teaching were, adherents of each shared a common sense of powerlessness toward theatrical managers and boards of trustees, respectively. And both sought sanction from the public for a higher degree of professional autonomy: university professors through a series of battles over academic freedom of speech; actors through a highly publicized actors' strike in 1919. See Louis Menand, *The Metaphysical Club* (New York: Straus, Farrar, Giroux, 2001) on academic culture of this age.

64. Jefferson to Board of Directors, 9 December 1893. Hampden-Booth Library, The Players.

65. Wilson's account of *The Rivals* tour was first published in *Scribner's* magazine in 1906 as a means of promoting Scribner's publication of Wilson's *Joseph Jefferson* the same year, "Jefferson and the All-Star Cast in 'The Rivals'" (March 1906): 300–17. It is not clear why Wilson waited until after Jefferson's death to publish his account of the tour. He makes no mention of Jefferson's desire to have him do so.

66. Wilson, *Joseph Jefferson*, 201.

67. Mona Brooks, "Joseph Jefferson's All-Star Tour of *The Rivals,*" *Theatre Southwest* 11 (May 1984): 16–19. Bloom, *Joseph Jefferson,* 258–59. The all-star *Rivals* tour is easily the most-well-documented event in Jefferson's life, partially because of Francis Wilson but also because so many of the other principals left recollections.

68. Bloom, *Joseph Jefferson,* 257; *New York Dramatic Mirror,* 16 May 1896, 15; 23 May 1896, 13.

69. *New York Dramatic Mirror,* 16 May 1896, 10; Charles Edward Russell, *Julia Marlowe: Her Life and Art* (New York: D. Appleton, 1926), 245–47; Goodwin, *Nat Goodwin's Book,* 47. Goodwin's acid (which he dripped throughout his memoirs) appears singularly ungrateful in the light of Jefferson's fondness toward him and that Goodwin would later perform Jefferson's version of *The Rivals* (presumably with his blessing) in Australia. Bloom, *Joseph Jefferson,* 470; Edward H. Sothern, *Julia Marlowe's Story* (New York: Rinehart, 1954), 117–18.

70. Eugénie Jefferson, *Intimate Recollections,* 334–35.

71. "Joe Jefferson's Press Agent Rebuked," unidentified newspaper clipping, Robinson Locke Collection of Dramatic Scrapbooks, vol. 302, New York Public Library for the Performing Arts.

72. On the emergence of actors as social commentators in America, see McArthur, *Actors and American Culture,* esp. chap. 6, from which both quotations are drawn; for a similar phenomenon in England, see Michael Baker, *The Rise of the Victorian Actor* (London: Croom Helm, 1978).

73. Gilder, ed., *Letters of Richard Watson Gilder,* 207. Jefferson's delight in children was apparent in his late-in-life practice of giving away large numbers of one-dollar bills (the equivalent of twenty-dollar bills in twenty-first-century value) to underprivileged children at Christmas parties. See volume 6 of the scrapbooks of the New York Society for the Prevention of Cruelty to Children, NYSPCC archives. I am indebted to Shauna Vey for collecting these references for me. On the child actor labor law issue, see Benjamin McArthur, " 'Forbid Them Not': Child Actor Labor Law and Political Activism in the Theatre," *Theatre Survey* 36 (November 1995): 63–80; Shauna Vey, "Protecting Theatrical Childhoods: The Campaign to Bar Children from Performing Professionally in New York City, 1874–1919" (Ph.D. diss., City University of New York, 1998); *New York Dramatic Mirror,* 7 June 1894, 5. *New York Times,* 30 March 1893, 8. Joe's moment of undiluted political activism advanced the theatre's cause imperceptibly, as managers and the Gerry Society continued to joust well into the twentieth century, until a protocol for the use of children on the New York and touring stages gradually developed.

74. The major works on the evolving business practices of the theatre and rise of the Theatrical Syndicate are Monroe Lippman "The History of the Theatrical Syndicate: Its Effect upon the Theatre in America" (Ph.D. diss., University of Michigan, 1937) and Jack Poggi, *Theater in America: The Impact of Economic Forces, 1870-1967* (New York: Columbia University Press, 1968). A brief overview of these developments is found in McArthur, *Actors and American Culture,* 214–18.

75. *American National Biography,* s.v. "Abraham Lincoln Erlanger," by William Stephenson; *New York Dramatic Mirror,* 2 September 1893, 4; Claudia A. Beach, "Henry Greenwall: Theatre Manager" (Ph.D. diss., Texas Tech University, 1986) 149–50; Wilson, *Joseph Jefferson,* 337.

76. *New York Dramatic Mirror,* 29 August 1896, 12; 28 November 1896, 4; 25 May 1895, 12; 9 December 1893, 9; 11 August 1894, 8. The account of Jefferson's role in suppressing anti-English legislation is given by British actor J. H. Barnes in his *Forty Years on the Stage,* 173–74. The most thorough treatment of the Actors' Society is found in McArthur, *Actors and American Culture,* 105–12.

77. One can gain a sense of Jefferson's benedictory speeches by recalling similar moments from comedians Jackie Gleason and Red Skelton at the close of their television shows. Nat Goodwin describes Joe's curtain speeches in his *Nat Goodwin's Book,* 46. Although Joe determined on a moderate pace to his lecturing, as late as 1897 he wrote his daughter Margaret telling her that he lectured twice the previous week to the Bridgeport, Connecticut, Contemporary Club. Jefferson to Margaret Farjeon, 11 May 1897, letter in possession of Gervase Farjeon. Francis Wilson provides the most complete treatment of Jefferson as public speaker, especially chapter 5 of his *Joseph Jefferson.* His daughter-in-law Eugénie Paul Jefferson also gives a good description in her *Intimate Recollections of Joseph Jefferson.* But Jefferson's various addresses were also widely reported in the contemporary press.

78. Jefferson to Miss Stanford, 24 October 1898. Bryant-Godwin Collection. New York Public Library. *New York Times,* 18 October 1896, 7.

79. Accounts of Jefferson's lectures are scattered throughout the newspapers of the age. See, for example, the Robinson Locke Collection of Dramatic Scrapbooks, vols. 301 and 302, New York Public Library for the Performing Arts. Jefferson's criticism at Yale noted in *New York Dramatic Mirror,* 11 May 1895, 12. Jefferson's desire for a more substantial presence of theatre on college campuses was on the verge of being realized. George Pierce Baker had begun teaching a course on drama at Harvard and would soon offer a workshop in play writing.

80. Bloom, *Joseph Jefferson,* 192; *New York Times,* 5 April 1896, 5; *New York Dramatic Mirror,* 11 April 1896, 14; 17 December 1892, 2; "Jefferson Preaches a Sunday Sermon," unidentified clipping, Robinson Locke Collection of Dramatic Scrapbooks, vol. 302, New York Public Library for the Performing Arts.

81. The National Institute of Arts and Letters was the parent body of the American Academy of Arts and Letters. Joe Jefferson, unpublished notebook, copy in possession of author. Jefferson's dictum about freshness would be elaborated by William Gillette in an influential 1910 essay, "The Illusion of the First Time in Acting," *Illusion of the First Time in Acting* (New York: Dramatic Museum of Columbia University, 1915). Not publicly, but in more private moments when prepping his son Tom to assume Rip's tattered mantle, Jefferson's advice seemed to prefigure Stanislavski's method for approaching a role. "When I begin to waken as Rip Van Winkle I strive to put myself in the mental attitude that would have been his on recovering himself after half a lifetime's slumber. I try to express the uncertainty, the confusion, the hopes and the fears that would crowd the mind of a person passing through such an extraordinary experience." Jefferson's reflections on actor preparation lacked the systematic rigor the Russian master would later bring to bear on acting technique, but his thoughts clearly augur twentieth-century methods. Unidentified clipping, Owen Fawcett scrapbooks, Special Collections, University of Tennessee–Knoxville. Jefferson, *Autobiography,* 324.

82. Wilson, *Jefferson,* 120.

83. Wilson, *Jefferson,* 309; Bloom, *Joseph Jefferson,* 270, 279; Unidentified newspaper clipping, Robinson Locke Collection of Dramatic Scrapbooks, vol. 301, New York Public Library for the Performing Arts.

84. Eugénie Jefferson, *Intimate Recollections,* 147; *New York Times,* 7 December 1896, 5; Mary Shaw, "The Stage Wisdom of Joseph Jefferson," *Century* (March 1912): 736.

85. Bloom, *Joseph Jefferson,* 272; Johnson, *Remembered Yesterdays,* 374. In 1895 Joe admitted to William Winter that his deafness prevented his hearing a stage reading by Agnes Booth. Jefferson to Booth, 9 November 1895, Michael Morrison Collection, New York City. I am indebted to Mr. Morrison for sharing a copy of this letter.

86. Cornelia (Connie) Jefferson Jackson, eight years Joe's junior, had played Tillie Slowboy in Jefferson's productions of *Cricket on the Hearth* for some fifteen years. Notice of her death in unidentified clipping, 8 March 1899, Owen Fawcett scrapbooks, University of Tennessee–Knoxville. Shaw, "Human Side of Joseph Jefferson," 381; Shaw, "Stage Wisdom of Joseph Jefferson," 731.

87. Bloom, *Joseph Jefferson,* 359.

88. Unidentified newspaper clipping, c. 1898, Owen Fawcett scrapbooks, University of Tennessee–Knoxville. Joe's insistence that Tom find his own voice, so to speak, for the role, did not preclude him from writing a detailed critique of his performance, including advice that he keep a glass of lemonade at the wings to wet his lips. This letter and other details on Tom's assumption of the role of Rip in Eugénie Jefferson's *Intimate Recollections of Joseph Jefferson,* chap. 12.

89. Jefferson to Cleveland, 8 January 1897, Cleveland Papers, Library of Congress; Jefferson to Archie, 29 November 1902, Sonneborn Collection of the Joe Jefferson Players, Mobile, Ala.; unidentified newspaper clipping, Owen Fawcett scrapbooks, University of Tennessee–Knoxville; Stuart B. McIver, *Yesterday's Palm Beach* (Miami: E. A. Seemann, 1976), 41.

90. Unidentified newspaper clipping, Owen Fawcett Collection, University of Tennessee–Knoxville.

91. One of many examples of Joe expressing concern for his wife's health in his correspondence can be found in letter to Archie, 20 August 1900, Sonneborn Collection. Joe's reference to Sarah's role in an amateur production made in letter, Jefferson to Mrs. Harcourt, 5 October 1894, Museum of the City of New York.

92. Bradford, "Joseph Jefferson," *Atlantic Monthly* (January 1922): 94.

93. *New York Journal,* 9 November 1890, in Theresa Collins and Lisa Gitelman, *Thomas Edison and Modern America: A Brief History with Documents* (Boston and New York: Bedford/St. Martin's, 2002)), 132. On the history of Berliner, see the fine American Memory Web site of the Library of Congress, http://memory.loc.gov/am mem/berlhtml/berlsp.html. Stephen Fassett, "Generous Joe Jefferson; Celebrated Actor Asked No Fee for His Columbia Recordings," *Hobbies* (December 1945): 31; Jefferson recordings found at Rodgers and Hammerstein Archive of Recorded Sound, New York Public Library at Lincoln Center.

94. For the early history of movies, see Charles Musser, *The Emergence of the Cinema: The American Screen to 1907,* vol. 1 in Charles Harpole, general ed., *History of the American Cinema* (New York: Charles Scribner's Sons, 1990), 148, 150, 340; Stephen

Johnson has done a careful study of the *Rip Van Winkle* in "Evaluating Early Film as a Document of Theatre History: The 1896 Footage of Joseph Jefferson's *Rip Van Winkle*," *Nineteenth Century Theatre* 20 (winter 1992): 101–22.

95. *Rip,* Biograph Films, Paper Film Collection, Library of Congress.

96. Jefferson to Archie, 2 November 1900; 12 January 1901; 25 November 1902, all in Sonneborn Collection.

97. Jefferson to Archie, 10 January 1901; 17 December 1901; 5 May 1902; 20 January 1900, Sonneborn Collection; Wadsworth J. Travers, *History of Beautiful Palm Beach* (Palm Beach: n.p., 1928), 31; Bloom, *Joseph Jefferson,* 473–74.

98. Bloom, *Joseph Jefferson,* 283–84; Farjeon, "Joe in Paradise," xii–xii.

99. Bloom, *Joseph Jefferson,* 285; various newspaper reports of his retirement in Robinson Locke Collection of Dramatic Scrapbooks, vol. 302, New York Public Library for the Performing Arts; Jefferson to Archie, 31 December 1904; 24 March 1905, Sonneborn Collection.

100. Jefferson to Cleveland, 21 March 1905, Cleveland Papers, Library of Congress; "Mourn Jefferson," *New York Globe and Commercial Advertiser* clipping, Robinson Locke Collection Robinson Locke Collection of Dramatic Scrapbooks, vol. 302, New York Public Library for the Performing Arts.

Epilogue

1. "Joseph Jefferson Passes Away," *New York Dramatic News,* 29 April 1905; "Joe Jefferson Succumbs to Long Illness," both clippings in Robinson Locke Collection of Dramatic Scrapbooks, vol. 302, New York Public Library for the Performing Arts; Bloom, *Joseph Jefferson,* 290–91.

2. The Jefferson file at the Bourne Historical Center, Bourne, Mass., and the Robinson Locke Collection of Dramatic Scrapbooks, vol. 302, New York Public Library for the Performing Arts, hold newspaper clippings on the funeral. Arthur Bloom's *Joseph Jefferson* provides more detail, 292–93.

3. The *New York Herald* quote and other critical evaluations are gathered in "Some Estimates of Joseph Jefferson," *Literary Digest,* all clippings in Robinson Locke Collection of Dramatic Scrapbooks, vol. 302, New York Public Library for the Performing Arts. William Winter, "Joseph Jefferson," *Critic* (June 1905).

4. Clayton Hamilton, *Brooklyn Eagle,* 30 April 1905; John Corbin, "Jefferson, Actor and Man," *Sun,* 30 April 1905; James Metcalfe, "Joseph Jefferson," *Theatre* (June 1905), all in Robinson Locke Collection of Dramatic Scrapbooks, vol. 302, New York Public Library for the Performing Arts.

5. Eugénie Paul Jefferson's *Intimate Recollections of Joseph Jefferson* is largely a tribute to her famous father-in-law. But it also contains a chapter about her husband's assumption of the role of Rip, a laudatory and somewhat superfluous addition that suggests an important goal of her book was to forward Tom's career. Gamaliel Bradford, "Joseph Jefferson," *Atlantic Monthly* 129 (January 1922): 84–95; Ernest Bradlee Watson, "Joseph Jefferson," *Theatre Arts* 13 (June 1929): 420–30; Alan Downer, ed., *Autobiography of Joseph Jefferson* (Cambridge: Harvard University Press, 1964); V. M Mironova, *Dzhozef Dzhefferson* (Leningrad, 1982); Joseph Jefferson, *Meng zhong ri yue*

chang (Xianggang, 1974); Gladys Malvern, *Good Troupers All, the Story of Joseph Jefferson* (Philadelphia: Macrae Smith, 1945); Jean Lee Latham, *On Stage Mr. Jefferson* (New York: Harper, 1958). It should also be mentioned that Jefferson's account of Lincoln's assisting his family in Springfield was used as the basis for a television drama, *The Devil's Work* (WNET production, c. 1970). In 2002 Michael Allen Phelps took out a copyright on an updated version of Jefferson's *Rip*. Phelps's claim to originality was in translating the play from "old English to modern English" and making "extensive revisions throughout."

6. Only two of the younger Jeffersons performed under the family name. Joe Jr. acted under the name Joseph Warren. "Through my father's death," Joe Jr. said, "I become Joseph Jefferson." *New York Dramatic Mirror,* undated clipping in possession of author. Neither of the Jefferson girls went on the stage. Thomas Jefferson's obituary in *New York Times,* 2 April 1932, pt. 2, 5 reviews his career, which by the 1910s had moved largely to film. He was a character actor in D. W. Griffith's stock company for a number of years. Moses, *Famous Actor-Families in America,* 84; Hamilton's comment on the limitations of the Jefferson boys as actors in his *Brooklyn Eagle* eulogy is one of several similar observations.

7. On Herbert Farjeon's career, see the online biographical sketch at the University of Bristol theatre collection: http://www.bris.ac.uk/theatrecollection/farjeon.html A useful review of Eleanor's career plus links to information on other family members is at http://www.eldrbarry.net/rabb/farj/farj.htm. It should also be noted that through the line of Joe's Australian son, Joseph Sefton, theatricals continued. His daughter and son-in-law were active on the vaudevillian stage.

8. For recent works on Irving, see Madeleine Bingham and Baroness Clanmorris, *Henry Irving, the Greatest Victorian Actor* (New York: Stein and Day, 1978); Alan Hughes, *Henry Irving, Shakespearean* (Cambridge: Cambridge University Press, 1981).

9. Dade County (Fl.), Probate Records, Register of Will, 1878–1911, microfilm vol. 2, 1904–11, #1870456 (item 2–3); ibid., *Probate Minute Book, 1901–1967,* #1870146 (item 4). Two of Joe's sons died within five years of him. Charley passed away in 1908, just days before Grover Cleveland died. Joseph Warren Jefferson died the next year.

10. Corbin, "Jefferson, Actor and Man," Robinson Locke Collection of Dramatic Scrapbooks, clipping, vol. 302, New York Public Library for the Performing Arts.

11. Charles R. Lyons, *Henrik Ibsen: The Divided Consciousness* (Carbondale: Southern Illinois University Press, 1972); Hjalmar Hjorth Boyesen, *A Commentary on the Works of Henrik Ibsen* (New York: Russell and Russell, 1894); Paul Johnson, *Intellectuals* (New York: Harper and Row, 1988), chap. 4.

12. Levine, *Highbrow, Lowbrow,* chaps. 1 and 2; *New York Times,* 15 October 1895, 5. Some measure of Jefferson's contemporary fame is seen in a June 1903 issue of *The Collector,* a magazine for autograph and historical memorabilia collectors. An autographed letter of Joe's fetched a higher price at auction than a document signed by namesake Thomas Jefferson. My thanks to Michael Morrison for bringing this to my attention.

Index

Page numbers for illustrations are in italics.

Acres, Bob (character in *The Rivals*), 114, 187, 247, 302–3, *303*, 322–26, *322*
acting styles, 233–39, 342–43
actors: and agents, 262; all-star casts, 127–28, 336–37, 417n62; apprenticeship of, 72, 90–91, 92, 260, 290; benefit performances by, 25, 112; British opinion of American actors, 215; child actors, 26–27, 338–39, 365n67; competition among, 105, 106; and contracts, 262–63, 274; and critics, 292–93; helping other actors, 319–20; insincerity and, 64–66; involvement of, in political or social issues, 337–38; Jefferson's role models, 66–70; Jefferson's theory of acting, 342–43, 419n81; and litigation, 157–58, 270–71; marrying other actors, 104; memoirs of, 307, 317–18, 373n36; memorization of parts by, 91–92; natural vs. stylized acting, 233–35; pioneer actors, 30–32; playing to points, 238; professionalization of, 290–91; public readers, 74; relationship of, to audience, 113, 231, 237–38; role entrapment and, 271–72; social and religious antagonism toward, 2, 64–66, 112, 120, 277–80; and spiritualism, 280–81; and stage families, 1–6, 19–20, 91; and temporary nature of fame and success, xiii–xiv, 205, 304, 311, 347–48, 352
Actors Church Alliance, 280
Actor's Fund, 319–20
Actors' Society of America, 290, 340
Addams, Augustus, 19–20, 62, 362n44
Adelaide (Australia), 204–5
Adelphi Theatre (London), 214–17, 232
Aiken, George L., 98
Alabama. *See* Mobile (Alabama)

Aladdin, or the Wonderful Lamp, 125

Albion, 75, 76

alcohol: actors and, 29, 67, 362n44; Jefferson and, 282, 408n29; Rip Van Winkle and, 228–29, 282–83

Alexander, John White, 302–3

Allen, J. H., 117

Allen, Louise, 160

Allen, Viola, 330

all-star casts, 127–28, 336–37, 417n62

American Academy of Dramatic Arts, 342

American Theatre (Bowery Theatre, New York), 25

Anderson, Jane, 33

Anderson, Mary, 10–11

Andreas, A. T., 36

Angle of Repose (Stegner), xvi

Antigone (Sophocles), 96

Apology of the Life of Colley Cibber, An (Cibber), 307

Appleton's Journal, 228

apprenticeship, 72, 90–91, 92, 260, 290

Aram, Matilda (Tilley Buckland), 200, 202, 204, 312

Arch Street Theatre (Philadelphia), 88, 89–90, 92, 96, 326, 330

Arese, Francesco, 15, 18, 29–30

Astor Place riot, 102–3

audiences: children in, 161–62; college students in, 111; desire of, for traditional interpretations, 116; hissing and, 78–79, 231; middle-class, 235; relationship of, to actors, 113, 231, 237–38; rowdiness of, 42, 57–58, 80, 81, 82–83, 111, 112–13; Victorian, xiv, 149–50, 231; violence by, 102–3; women in, 42, 57, 136–37

Augusta (Georgia), 119–20

Australia, 189–212; Adelaide, 204–5, 209–10; gold fields in, 200–203, 210; Melbourne, 193–200, 202, 204, 210, 211–12; Jefferson's outback visit in, 203–4; Sydney, 189–93, 205, 210, 233; Tasmania, 207–9, 233; Winter brothers estate (Victoria), 203

Autobiography of Joseph Jefferson, 305–12; accuracy of, 41, 81–82, 171, 309–10, 366n17, 376n66; on acting, 116, 342–43, 419n81; all-star performance of *The School for Scandal* in, 127–28; on American attitudes toward theatre, 61; on balance and cohesion in theatre, 128; on Charles Burke, 95–96; on Chinese theatre, 211; on combination companies, 256, 257–58; on con artists, 64–65; criticisms of fellow players in, 310; on Edwin Forrest, 129; on English society, 287; on father's death, 54; on first love, Metta, 83–84; itinerant theatricals, 107, 108, 120–21; on Jefferson's childhood, 1, 6–7; on John E. Owens, 86–87; on Julia Dean, 118; on Junius Brutus Booth, 67–68; Lincoln anecdote in, 40–41, 368n32; on Memphis sign-painting contract, 50–51; omissions in, 99, 104, 130, 200, 213, 265; politics in, 380n23; publication of, 306; "Pudding" Stanley anecdote in, 80–81; realism in, 232–33, 236, 398n35; reasons for writing, 305–6; reviews and sales of, 310–11; on *Rip Van Winkle,* 170–71, 216, 222, 310; style and scope of, 307–9; on transiency of success and fame, 205; travel commentaries in, 38–39, 132, 190, 203–4, 213–14, 283, 308–9; on William Don, 111

Baby (MacDonough), 289

Badeau, Adam, 268

Badger, Edward, 83

Bagehot, Walter, 311

Ballarat Star, 201

ballet, 244–46

Baltimore (Maryland): Jefferson family troupe in, 14, 18–20; Jefferson's early performances in, 123–25, 127–28, 172, 177, 179–80; *Rip Van Winkle* in, 247, 248

Baltimore Advertiser, 125

Baltimore Museum (Maryland), 123–25
Banvard, John, 30–31
Barnum's American Museum, 101
Barrie, J. M., 354
Barrymore, Maurice, 326, 330
Bateman, Ellen, 26–27
Bateman, Kate, 26–27, 164
Beaumont, Gustave de, 371n7
Beauty and the Beast, 89
Beecher, Henry Ward, 279–80
Bendigo (Australia), 201–2
Bendigo Advertiser, 202
benefit performances, 25, 112, 193
Berliner, Emile, 347
Bernard, W. Bayle, 218
Bernheim, Alfred, 256
Betty, William, 26
Biograph Company, 347–48
The Black Crook, 244–46
blackfaced entertainers, 11–14, 75, 76,
    97–98, 360n24
Blair, James, 18
Blanche of Brandywine (Lepard), 140
Bloom, Arthur, 258
Boker, George Henry, 158
Booth, Edwin, 268; Actors' Fund Fair
    and, 320; career of, 135, 141, 189,
    264, 267–68; death and memorial of,
    332; and friendship with Jefferson,
    119, 213, 253, 263, 283, 289; Players
    Club and, 290–91; spiritualism of,
    407n24; wives of, 130, 253. *See also*
    Booth's Theatre
Booth, John Wilkes, 67, 113, 129–30,
    213, 382n57
Booth, Junius Brutus, 67–68, 78, 119,
    120
Booth, Michael, 153, 154
Booth's Theatre (New York), 263, 264–
    67, 264
Boston Museum, 121–22
Boston Theatre, 162
Bottom, Nick (character in *A Midsum-
    mer Night's Dream*), 196–97
Boucicault, Dion, 148–49; and American

drama debate, 295–96; and copyright
    protection, 158; on domestic drama,
    221; and *Dot (Cricket on the Hearth),*
    149–50; and first road show, 256; on
    Jefferson and Rip Van Winkle, 318;
    and Keene, 164; and *London Assur-
    ance,* 195–96; and *The Octoroon,*
    155–57, 160; and *The Poor of New
    York,* 154; and *Rip Van Winkle,* 214–
    17; and *Smike (Nicholas Nickleby),*
    152; on stage as picture frame, 231;
    wife of, 123–24, 381n40
Bowery Amphitheater, 101
Bowery b'hoys, 102
Brentano, Agosto, 261
Brewer (New Hampshire), 304
Brierly, Robert (character in *Ticket-of-
    Leave Man*), 208–9
Broadway Journal, 292
Brooklyn Eagle, 292
Brooks, Peter, 153–54
Brougham, John, 127, 167, 169, 243
Brown, John Purdy, 14
Bryant, Dan, 243
Buckstone, J. B., 132
Bulwer-Lytton, Edward, 36, 197–98,
    367n18
Burke, Charles (Jefferson's half-brother),
    95; adult career of, 48, 63–64, 87, 92–
    93, 94–96, 103, 119; childhood and
    adolescence of, 5–6, 14, 33, 38; death
    of, 131; on Jefferson's marriage, 104;
    as Rip Van Winkle, 95, 171, 219, 223
Burke, Joseph, 26, 27
burlesque, 164, 166–69, 175, 216–17
Burton, William E., 89–90, 94, 96
Byrne, Charles A., 292
Byron, Henry, 167, 174

Cable, George Washington, 294–95
Caldwell, James, 55, 56, 58–59
California, 184–89, 288–89
California Theatre, 288–89
canal travel, 33–34
Carey, Henry C., 158

Casimar (character in *Mazeppa*), 21,
    186–87, 206
Castlemaine (Australia), 202–3
censorship, 59–61
Century, 294, 306
Century Publishing Company, 306
Champion (ship), 184–85
Chanfrau, Frank, 101–2, 104, 105, 165,
    243
Chapman, Elizabeth Jefferson. *See*
    Richardson, Elizabeth Chapman
Chapman, Samuel (Jefferson's uncle), 14
Chapman family troupe, 30
Charleston (South Carolina), 108–9,
    117–19
Charleston Courier, 108, 119
Chatterton, F. B., 283–84
Chestnut Street Theatre (Philadelphia), 3,
    88, 122–23, 246
Chevalier, Michael, 52
Chicago (Illinois), 252–53; Jefferson
    family in (1838–40), 34–36; Jefferson
    family troupe in (1839), 42–43; the-
    atre in (1837), 29–30
Chicago Daily American, 42
Chicago Times, 252
child actors, 26–27, 338–39, 365n67
Chinese theatre, 211
cholera, 100
Christy Minstrels, 12
Church of the Transfiguration (Little
    Church Around the Corner), 278, 350,
    351, 406n18
Cibber, Colley, 307
cigar stand, 83, 376n66
Circus and National Theatre (Phila-
    delphia), 92
Civil War: Anglo-American relations dur-
    ing, 216; in Baltimore, 177, 179–80;
    end of, and Lincoln's assassination,
    213; Fort Sumter, 179; Jefferson's
    avoidance of, 181–83; and Lincoln's
    inauguration, 178; memoirs from,
    306–7; *The Octoroon* and, 156, 210;
    reconstruction, 241–42; secession,

    156, 172–73, 177, 178; in Wash-
    ington, D.C., 178, 179
Clapp, Henry, 122, 292
clap-trap, 206, 394n58
Clarke, John Sleeper, 159, 223, 242, 288,
    387n57
Clemens, Samuel (Mark Twain), 182,
    235–36, 278, 294, 296
Cleveland, Grover, 281, 313–14, 315–
    16, 349, 414n22
Colman, George, 114
Columbia (South Carolina), 111
Columbia Record Company, xiii–xiv,
    347
Combe, George, 24
combination companies, 256–60
comedy: classical, 114, 221, 325; come-
    dians as stars, 174, 181; drawing-room
    comedies, 248; *Fashion* as example of,
    74–78. *See also* low comedy
Comstock, Anthony, 11
Confidence-Man, The (Melville), 65
confidence men, 64–65; as stage charac-
    ter, 98–99
Conjugal Lesson, A, 138
Connor, Edmond, 9
Conway Theatre fire, 266
Coppin, George, 191, 200–201
copyright protection, 153, 155, 157,
    158–61, 214, 387n57
Corbin, John, 354
Corot, Camille, 301–2
costume houses, 260, 261
costumes, 22, 65, 132, 343, 399n46
Couldock, Charles, 330
Cowell, Joseph, 18, 58
Cowell, Mrs. Sam, 165
Coyne, J. Sterling, 167–68
Crane, William H., 333
Crayon, Geoffrey, 171
Cricket on the Hearth, The (Dickens),
    148, 149, 195, 318, 331, 385n34
Critic, 311
critics and criticism, 116, 187–88, 198–
    200, 209–10, 291–93

Crow's Nest (Buzzards Bay, Cape Cod), 314–16, *315*, 349

Cushman, Charlotte, 113, 266

Cute, Gumption (character in *Uncle Tom's Cabin*), 98–99

Daily Missouri Republican, 45, 78

Daly, Augustin, 263, 295, 296, 406n16

Daughter of the Regiment (Donizetti), 130

Davenport, E. L., 129, 310, 382n55

Davenport, Fanny, 266

Davis, Clarke, 238

Dean, Julia, 118–19

Deering, William, 109

Denver (Colorado), 289

Devlin, Mary, 130

Dial, 311

Dickens, Charles, 1, 27, 47, 100, 123, 129, 149–50, 152, 162

Dickory (character in *The Spectre Bridegroom*), 97, 138

Dickson, William K. L., 347

Dithmar, Edward, 292

domestic drama, 96, 114, 221, 225, 227

Don, William, 110–12

Dot (Boucicault), 149–51

Downer, Alan, xiv–xv, 293

Drake family troupe, 30

drawing-room comedies, 248

Dreiser, Theodore, xvi, 311

Drew, John, 127

Drew, Mrs. John (Louisa Lane Drew), 326, 328, 330–31, 333

Dublin Morning News, 287

Dubuque (Iowa), 38–39

Dundreary, Lord (character in *Our American Cousin*), 143, 145–46, *145*

Dunlap, William, 3

Durang, Charles, 17

eccentric comedians. *See* low comedy

Ellsler, Fanny, 71

Ellsler, John, 107, 109–12, 116–21

England, 286. *See also* London

equestrian melodrama (horse drama, Hippodrama), 20–22, 126

Erie Canal packet, 33–34

Erlanger, Abraham, 340

European excursion, 131–33

Evangeline (Longfellow), 164

farce, 96–97

Farjeon, Benjamin, 206–7, 285–86, 317, 353

Farjeon, Eleanor, 131, 353

Farjeon, Herbert, 353

Farjeon, Margaret Jefferson (Jefferson's daughter): birth of, 131; childhood of, 170, 272–73, 283; children of, 288, 353; in England, 317, 353; marriage of, 285–86

Farren, Mary, 216

Fashion; or, Life in New York (Mowatt), 74–78

Fifth Avenue Theatre (New York), 263, 343, 344–45

Fisher, Charles, 52

Fisher, Sidney George, 123

Fisher Galleries (Washington), 302

Fiske, Harrison Grey, 161, 261, 290

Fiske, Minnie Maddern, 340, 355

Fiske, Stephen, 263

Flagler, Henry, 345, 349, 350

Florence, Malvina, 327

Florence, William "Billy," 243, 325, 327–31

Flynn, Thomas, 218

Ford, John T., 128–29, 181, 243, 246–47

Ford's Holliday Street Theatre, 172

Forrest, Catherine, 105

Forrest, Edwin, 91, 102–3, 105, 129

Fox, George Washington Lafayette, 251–52

Frank Leslie's Illustrated Magazine, 250

Frank Leslie's Illustrated Newspaper, 150, 164, 174

Franklin Theatre (New York), 25, 101

French, Benjamin Brown, 27
French, Samuel, 261
frontier theatre, 30–32, 81

Galena (Illinois), 37–38
Galveston (Texas), 79–80
Garrick, David, 2–3, 93, 277
gas lights, 265, 266, 403n54
Gentleman's Magazine, The, 89
Germon, Greenbury, 33, 47
Gerry, Elbridge, 339
Gilbert, John, 115, 326–27
Gilbert, W. S., 232
Gilder, Richard Watson, xvi, 294, 306
glaucoma, 281–82
Golightly, Major (character in *Lend Me Five Schillings*), 97, 288, 351
Goodwin, Nat, 317–18, 333, 340
The Governor's Wife, 163
Greville, J. R., 207
Grover, Leonard, 243

Hackett, James H., 72, 219, 270
Hamblin, Thomas, 25
Hamilton, Clayton, 352
Harkins, D. H., 263
Harte, Bret, 296
Hart's company, 81, 82–83
Harvard University, 342
Haymarket Theatre (London), 132, 147, 288
Haymarket Theatre (Melbourne), 198, 202, 205, 211
Haynes, Jack, 83
Hazlitt, William, 19
Heir at Law, The (Sheridan), 114
Herne, James A., 270, 340
Heron, Matilda, 161
Hess Company, 270–71
Hippodrama. *See* equestrian melodrama
Hodgkinson, John, 3
Hofstadter, Richard, 316
Hohokus estate (New Jersey), 273–74, 314
holiday extravaganzas, 124–25

Holland, George, 277–78, 406n16, 406n18
Holliday Street Theatre (Baltimore), 247
Hone, Philip, 20, 32
horse drama. *See* equestrian melodrama
Houghton, George H., 278, 351
Houston (Texas), 79, 80
Howard Athenaeum (Boston), 122
Howells, William Dean, xvi, 296–97, 300–301
humor and pathos, balance of, 151, 171, 195, 233, 239, 243–44, 286, 325, 347
Huneker, James, 237, 238
Hunt, Leigh, 153, 394n58
Hunt, William Morris, 298
Hutton, Laurence, 74–75, 151, 169, 292

Ibsen, Henrik, 354–55
illegitimacy, 313–14
Illinois, 34–36, 37–38, 39–41
Illinois Theatrical Company, 40
immigration and immigrants, 122, 126–27
Ingersoll, David, 17, 18, 22, 24, 29
Ingersoll, Mary-Anne Jefferson, 25. *See* Wright, Mary-Anne Jefferson Ingersoll
Invisible Prince, The (Planché), 165
Iowa, 36, 38–39
Ireland, 286–87
Ireland, Joseph, 14, 17, 94
Irishman stock part, 93, 126–27, 329
Irving, Henry, 332, 353, 409n32, 499n52
Irving, Washington, 170, 171, 217–18, 220, 224–28, 292
Isherwood, Harry, 18–19, 22, 29–30, 37
Item, C. F. (character in *Our Japanese Embassy*), 168–69
Ivanhoe (Scott), 164

James, Henry, 137, 288, 296, 411n65
Japan, 168
Jarrett, Henry C., 123, 125–26
Jefferson, Charles Burke "Charley" (Jefferson's son): birth of, 110; as business manager, 258, 262–63, 297–98, 330; Buzzards Bay home of, 315; and

California-Australia tour, 181, 183, 184, 185, 190, 192–93, 194, 203, 209, 392n20; childhood roles of, 210, 211; children of, 314; and father's death, 350; on father's reaction to Lincoln's assassination, 213; and *The Rivals* tour, 335

Jefferson, Cornelia Burke (Jefferson's mother), 5–6, 6; acting career of, 14, 23–24, 25; and boarding house, 54, 61; death of, 131; health of, 48, 50, 51

Jefferson, Cornelia "Connie" (Jefferson's sister): adult career of, 104–5, 138, 251; birth of, 6; childhood of, 33, 38, 49, 66, 72, 82

Jefferson, Elizabeth. *See* Richardson, Elizabeth Chapman

Jefferson, Frances (Jefferson's daughter), 131

Jefferson, Frank (Jefferson's son), 272–73

Jefferson, Henry (Jefferson's son), 272–73, 283, 284–85

Jefferson, John (Jefferson's uncle), 14, 15, 16–17

Jefferson, Joseph (Jefferson's cousin), 287

Jefferson, Joseph, I (Jefferson's grandfather), 3–5, 4, 14, 15, 16–17, 93, 323

Jefferson, Joseph, II (Jefferson's father), 46; as actor and leader of family company, 5, 17, 23–24, 32–33, 37, 93; death of, 52–53; marriage of, 5–6; as scenic artist, 5, 25, 46, 48, 50–51

Jefferson, Joseph, III, 135, 303, 322; alcohol use of, 282, 408n29; ambition of, 86–87, 90, 107–8, 146–47, 354; as art collector, 301–2, 316; as artist, 298–301, 299, 302, 304; and aversion to risk, 116, 321; and balance of humor and pathos, 151, 171, 195, 233, 239, 243–44, 286, 325, 347; as celebrity, 269–70, 276–77, 287, 317, 337; childhood (*see* Jefferson family troupe); children (*see* Farjeon, Margaret Jefferson; Jefferson, Charles Burke; Jefferson, Frances; Jefferson, Frank; Jefferson, Henry; Jefferson, Josephine; Jefferson, Joseph Warren; Jefferson, Thomas; Jefferson, William Winter; Sefton, Joseph); contributions of, to theatre, 260, 290–91, 318–20, 338–41, 351–52; as dean of the American stage, 337, 338; death and funeral of, 349–51; descriptions of, 88, 134–35, 199; and European excursion (1856), 131–33; family life of (*see* Jefferson homes and family life); father of (*see* Jefferson, Joseph, II); and first love, Metta, 83–84; and fishing, 148, 272, 289, 315; friendships of, 293–95 (*see also* Cleveland, Grover; Ellsler, John; Florence, William "Billy"; Ford, John T.; Sargent, John Singer; Williams, Barney; Wilson, Francis); grandfather of, 3–5, 4; great-grandfather of (*see* Jefferson, Thomas); health of, 148, 181, 188–89, 281–82, 331–32, 343–44; homes of (*see* Jefferson homes and family life); honorary degrees awarded to, 342; marriages of (*see* Jefferson, Margaret "Maggie" Lockyer; Jefferson, Sarah Isabel Warren); mistress of, 200, 202, 204; as one-role actor, 130, 271–72, 320–21, 331; and photography, 302; as playwright and play doctor, 140, 210, 222–30, 297–98, 323–26, 385n34, 414n22; and politics, 338, 414n22; portraits of, 302–4; preference of, for rural quiet, 101; as public speaker, 341–42; recordings and motion pictures of, xiii–xi, 347–48; religious beliefs, 278–79, 280–81; and retirement, 343–49; siblings of (*see* Burke, Charles; Jefferson, Cornelia "Connie"); signature roles of (*see* Acres, Bob; Golightly, Major; Pangloss, Dr.; Plummer, Caleb; Scudder, Salem; Trenchard, Asa); as stage manager, 123, 124–29, 161–62, 164; wealth and investments of, 269, 348, 353–54

Jefferson, Josephine Duff "Josie" (Jefferson's daughter), 152, 283

Jefferson, Joseph Warren (Jefferson's son), 272–73, 283, 315, 330, 335, 350

Jefferson, Margaret (Jefferson's daughter). *See* Farjeon, Margaret Jefferson

Jefferson, Margaret "Maggie" Lockyer (Jefferson's wife), 104–5, 138; career of, 104–5, 117, 148; children of, 126, 131, 138, 148, 152; death of, 177–78; marriage of, 104

Jefferson, Mary-Anne (Jefferson's aunt). *See* Wright, Mary-Anne Jefferson Ingersoll

Jefferson, Sarah Isabel Warren (Jefferson's wife), 253, 272, 283, 285, 316, 346, 353

Jefferson, Thomas (Jefferson's great-grandfather), 2–3, 298

Jefferson, Thomas (Jefferson's son): birth of, 138; at Buzzards Bay, 315; career of, 330, 335, 345, 352–53; childhood of, 283; and father's death, 350

Jefferson, Thomas (U.S. president), 77

Jefferson, William Winter (Jefferson's son), 272–73, 285, 335, 345, 350

Jefferson family troupe (Jefferson's childhood), 2–6; in Baltimore and Washington, 14–20, 22–23; in Chicago, 33–36, 42–43; dividing and recombining of, 18, 22–23, 46–47, 49–50; on Illinois, Iowa, and Missouri tour, 36–41, 43–48; Jefferson's adolescent roles, 66–67, 69, 72, 75, 76, 78–79; Jefferson's childhood appearances, 8, 9, 11–12, 14, 25–26, 27–28, 38, 43, 48, 49; Jefferson's childhood as preparation for stage career, 87–88, 90–91; on Mississippi and Tennessee tour, 62–64; in Mobile, 52–59, 61; in New Orleans, 70–73, 75–77; in New York, 24, 25–26, 32–33; in St. Louis, 77–79; talent of, 28; in Texas and Mexico, 79–84

Jefferson-Florence company, 327–28

Jefferson homes and family life, 182;

advantages of theatrical household, 272–73; Crow's Nest home (Buzzards Bay, Cape Cod), 314–16, 315, 346, 349; English relatives, 240, 287; family as legacy, 352–54; Hohokus estate (New Jersey), 273–74, 314; Louisiana estate (Orange Island), 272, 274–77, 275, 314, 345, 348; New York homes, 152, 241; in Palm Beach, 345–46, 348; Paradise Valley home (Pocono Mountains, Pennsylvania), 147–48, 170, 273; Paris and United Kingdom trip (1875–77), 283–88

Jim Crow, 11, 12

Johnson, Samuel, 113

Jonathan Bradford, 103

Jones, Joseph, 158

Jordan, George, 157, 161

Judith of Geneva, 138

Kean, Charles, 72–73, 78, 205, 254

Kean, Edmund, 67, 68, 102

Kean, Ellen Tree, 72, 73, 78, 205

Keene, Laura, 134, 136–37, 137, 146–47, 157, 159, 164, 318. *See also* Laura Keene's Theatre

Kemble, Frances Anne "Fannie," 15, 19–20

Kemble family, 19–20

Kennedy, John Pendleton, 4

Kerr, John, 218, 219

Lady of Lyons, The (Bulwer-Lytton), 36

Laura Keene's Theatre (New York), 136–47; *1857–58* season of, 137–40; Jefferson's adaptation of *Blanche of Brandywine* (Lepard) at, 140; *Our American Cousin* at, 141–46, 169–70

Laura Keene vs. Wheatley and Clarke, 159, 387n57

Leicester, William, 45, 47

Leighton, Mrs. W. H, 189

Leman, Walter, 19, 48, 67

Lend Me Five Shillings (Morton), 97, 288, 331

Lepard, George, 140
Lesbia (Heron), 161
Leslie, Elsie, 330
Life and Letters of Washington Irving,
 The (Irving), 170, 171
limelight, 265, 266
Lincoln, Abraham, 40–41, 128, 177,
 178, 213, 368n32
Liverpool Mail, 217
Lockyer, Margaret "Maggie." *See* Jeffer-
 son, Margaret "Maggie" Lockyer
Logan, Olive, 245, 253, 307
London: Adelphi Theatre, 214–17, 232;
 Haymarket Theatre, 132, 147, 288;
 Jefferson homes in, 285; Jefferson's
 excursion to (1856), 132; Jefferson's
 reception by elite society, 239–40, 287;
 Lyceum Theatre, 353, 403n54; Prin-
 cess's Theatre, 239, 283–84, 287–88;
 Rip Van Winkle in, 213–17, 216, 232,
 283–84, 285, 287–88
London Assurance (Boucicault), 195–96
London Court Journal, 287
Louisiana. *See* New Orleans
Louisiana estate (Orange Island), 272,
 274–77, 275, 314, 345, 348
low comedy, 93–96; Buckstone and, 132;
 Burke and, 94–96; burlesque, 164,
 166–69, 175, 216–17; farces, 96–97;
 Florence and, 325, 327; humor and
 pathos balance in, 151, 171, 195, 233,
 239, 243–44, 286, 325, 347; as Jefferson family specialty, 3, 17, 72, 93, 95–
 96; Jefferson's mastery of, 138, 187,
 202, 238, 317, 329; Owens and, 86–
 87; Sothern and, 145–46; Warren and,
 122; women in (Matilda Vining
 Wood), 150, 165. *See also* stock
 parts/stock figures
Ludlow, Noah: and feud with Smith,
 369n41; on frontier theatre, 30; on Macready, 69; in Mobile, 55, 56, 57; in New
 Orleans, 71–72, 73, 85–86; and rivalry
 with Caldwell, 58–59; with Samuel
 Drake, 31; in St. Louis, 44–45, 77, 78

Lyceum Theatre (London), 353, 403n54
Lyell, Charles, 71
Lyons, Charles, 173

Macbeth (Shakespeare), 126
MacDonough, Thomas, 289
MacKenzie, Alexander: in Baltimore, 18–
 19; in Chicago, 29–30, 32, 35–36, 42;
 on Illinois, Iowa, and Missouri tour,
 37–40; and Jefferson family troupe,
 17; in Memphis, 50; in Nashville, 62;
 in Washington, 23, 24
MacKenzie-Jefferson company, 17–24,
 37–49, 50–53
Macon (Georgia), 110
Macready, William Charles, 68–70,
 102–3
Maguire, Tom, 186
Mahar, William J., 360n24
Malaprop, Mrs. (character in *The*
 Rivals), 322, 324, 331
Manchester Guardian, 286
Mansfield, Richard, 340
Marble, Dan, 72
Mark Twain (Samuel Clemens), 182,
 235–36, 278, 294, 296
Marlowe, Julia, 333
Marsh troupe of juvenile players, 196
Maryland. *See* Baltimore (Maryland)
Maryland Company of Comedians, 18
Mason, Charles Kemble, 42–43,
 108–9
Massachusetts, 121–22, 162, 334
Matamoros (Mexico), 82–84, 376n66
Mathews, Charles, 310
Matthews, Brander, 292
Mayo, Frank, 271
Mazeppa, 20–22, 126, 174–77, 187
McCann, Dudley, 259
McClure, Mary Ann Meek, 42–43
McVicker, James, 252–53, 263, 281
McVicker's Theatre, 252–53
Melbourne (Australia), 193–200, 202,
 204, 210, 211–12
Melbourne Argus, 194, 198–99

melodrama, 152–57; and acting styles, 235; in *Cricket on the Hearth,* 149; criticism of, 152–53; equestrian, 20–22, 126; in *Lady of Lyons* (Bulwer-Lytton), 36; in *The Octoroon,* 155–57; popularity of, 153–54; in *Rip Van Winkle,* 220–21, 225; visual emphasis in, 154–55
Melville, Herman, 65
Memphis (Tennessee), 50
Memphis American Eagle, 50
Menken, Adah Isaacs, 22
Mestayer, Mrs. Charles, 127
Metcalfe, James, 352
Metropolitan Theatre (San Francisco), 186
Mexican-American War, 79–84, 309–10
Midsummer Night's Dream, A (Shakespeare), 196–97, 250–51
minstrelsy, 11–14, 100, 101, 360n24
Mississippi, 48–49, 62–64
Mississippi River theatricals, 30–32, 36, 38–40, 49–50, 51–52
Missouri, 36, 44–46, 77–79, 336
Mitchell, William, 167
Mobile (Alabama), 52, 54–56, 58–59, 61, 66–70
Mobile Register and Journal, 66, 69
Moncrieff, W. T., 97
Money (Bulwer-Lytton), 197–98
Morris, Mowbray, 288
Morton, John Maddison, 97, 178
Mose the Bowery b'hoy, 102
motion pictures, xiv, 347–48
Mowatt, Anna Cora, 73–78, 79, 307
Murdoch, James E., 32
Mutoscope, xiv
My Neighbor's Wife, 97

Naiad Queen, or the Nymphs of the Rhine!, The, 124–25
Nashville (Tennessee), 48, 62
Nashville Union, 62
Natchez (Mississippi), 48–49
Nation, 228, 238, 311

National Intelligencer, 14, 16, 23, 24, 127, 172, 178, 179, 246
National Theatre (New York), 100, 101–2, 104–6
National Theatre (Washington, D.C.), 126, 128, 246–47
naturalism, 233–35
Neild, James Edward, 198–200
New American Theatre (Mobile), 58–59
New City Theatre (Memphis), 50
New National Theatre (New York), 101–2
New Orleans: Caldwell in, 55, 58–59; Jefferson family in (1845), 70–73; *Rip Van Winkle* in, 248–49; St. Charles Theatre, 59, 71–72, 73, 75–77, 85–87; segregation in theatres in, 57; yellow fever in, 56, 87
New Orleans Daily Picayune, 73, 249
New Richmond Theatre, 173
New St. Charles Theatre (Mobile), 59
New York: American Theatre (Bowery Theatre), 25; *The Black Crook* in, 244–46; Booth's Theatre, 263, 264–67, 264; Broadway, 100–101; Fifth Avenue Theatre, 263, 343, 344–45; Franklin Theatre, 25, 101; Jefferson's first adult appearances in (1849), 99–101, 103–6; Jefferson's premiere as headlined star in (1860), 174–77; Laura Keene's Theatre, 136–47, 169–70; National Theatre, 100, 101–2, 104–6; Niblo's Garden, 32–33, 148, 244; Olympic Theatre, 165, 167, 242–43, 249–51; Park Theatre, 3, 9–10, 19, 25, 74; *Rip Van Winkle* in, 173–74, 242–44, 263, 264, 264, 267, 331; theatre fires in, 266; *1830s* theatre in, 24–25, 32–33; as theatrical capital, 260–62; Union Square, 260–62; Wallack's Theatre, 86; Winter Garden, 148, 155, 160, 161–62, 163–65, 174–77, 180, 267
New York Clipper, 147, 148, 161, 162,

164, 165, 169, 173, 174, 180, 183,
    189, 243, 244, 245, 246, 250
New York Daily Tribune, 243–44
New York Dramatic Mirror, 278, 296,
    302, 318–19, 331, 332, 336, 339
New York Dramatic News, 292
New York Herald, 101, 103, 105, 138,
    156, 249, 340, 351
New York Mirror, 255, 261, 266, 272,
    279, 280, 290, 326
New York Society for the Prevention of
    Cruelty to Children, 339
New York Times, 143, 148, 150, 151,
    152, 160, 170, 174, 177, 181, 183,
    271, 278, 314, 325, 355
New York Tribune, 138, 250, 268
New Zealand, 206–7
Niblo's Garden (New York), 32–33, 148,
    244
Nicholas Nickleby (Dickens), 1, 27, 152
Nicoll, Allardyce, 221
Nimroud (ship), 189–90
Noggs, Newman (character in *Smike*), 152
North Carolina, 111–12, 117
Nott, Josiah, 56, 371n6

Octoroon, The (Boucicault), 152, 155–
    57, 158, 160, 205, 210, 217
Odell, George C. D., 24, 104, 141, 168,
    270, 326–27
Ohio River theatricals, 30–32
Oliver Twist (Dickens), 123, 162
Ollapod, Dr. (character in *The Poor Gen-
    tleman*), 114
Olympic Theatre (New York), 165, 167,
    242–43, 249–51
O'Neill, James, 271, 340
Opera House (San Francisco), 186, 188,
    189
Orange Island. *See* Louisiana estate
    (Orange Island)
Otago Daily Times, 206, 207
Our American Cousin (Taylor), 141–46,
    158, 159, 169–70, 187, 194–95,
    387n57

Our Japanese Embassy, 168–69
Ours (Robertson), 248
Owens, John E., 86–87, 94, 214,
    242

Pall Mall Gazette, 216, 233
Palm Beach (Florida), 345–46, 348
Panama crossing, 185
Pangloss, Dr. (character in *The Heir at
    Law*), 114–16, 115, 138, 304
Panic of 1837, 32, 34
Panic of 1857, 135, 139
Panic of 1873, 257, 263, 268
Panic of 1893, 319
pantomime, 124, 234, 237, 251
Paradise Valley home (Pocono Moun-
    tains, Pennsylvania), 147–48, 170,
    273
Paris, 132, 283
Park Theatre (New York), 3, 9–10, 19,
    25, 74
pathos: defined, 239. *See also* humor and
    pathos, balance of
Paulding, James Kirke, 153
Paul Pry, 169
Payne, John Howard, 26
Peale's Philadelphia Museum (Phila-
    delphia), 90, 92
Pekin (Illinois), 39–40
Peru, 213–14
Peter Pan, 354
Phelps, Samuel, 132
Philadelphia: 1820s theatre in, 3–5; Arch
    Street Theatre, 88, 89–90, 92, 96, 326,
    330; Chestnut Street Theatre, 3, 88,
    122–23, 246; Circus and National
    Theatre, 92; Jefferson's childhood in,
    7; Jefferson's early adult career in, 88–
    99; Peale's Philadelphia Museum, 90,
    92; *Rip Van Winkle* in, 246, 249; Wal-
    nut Street Theatre, 5, 88
phonographs, 347
Planché, J. R., 124, 165, 239
Players Club, 290–91
playing to points, 238

playwrights: and acting styles, 235; and copyright protection, 153, 155, 157, 158–61, 214, 387n57; and Revolutionary War plays, 140; Shakespeare as most revised playwright, 323; and true American drama debate, 295–98

Plummer, Caleb (character in *Cricket on the Hearth, Dot*), 149–51, 151, 195, 318

Poe, Edgar Allan, 74, 292

Poor Gentleman, The (Colman), 114

Poor of New York, The (Boucicault), 154

Potter, John, 48, 50

Power, Tyrone, 23, 48, 57, 127

Prince of Wales Opera House (Sydney), 205

Princess's Theatre (London), 239, 283–84, 287–88

Princess Theatre (New Zealand), 206

proscenium stage, 230–31

public readers, 74

Puritanism, 279

Quadroon, The (Reid), 155, 160

Quincy (Illinois), 39

race/racism: blackfaced entertainers, 11–14, 75, 76, 97–98, 360n24; New Orleans race relations, 71; in *The Octoroon*, 155–57; and Palm Beach cakewalk, 346; segregation in theatres, 56–57, 371n7; *Uncle Tom's Cabin* (Stowe) and, 60, 97–99, 358n18

railroads, 116–17, 125–26, 254–55, 256, 288, 328, 334, 401n32

Rankin, McKee, 270

Rarey, John, 175

Reade, Charles, 239

realism: and acting styles, 233–36, 343; critics and, 292; Jefferson on, 232–33, 296, 343; *Rip Van Winkle* and, 217, 230–37; in stage design, scenery, and props, 230–32, 237

Regular Fix, A (Maddison), 178

Reid, Mayne, 155, 160

religion and theatre, 40–41, 60, 277–80

Reuling, George, 282

Revolutionary War plays, 140

Rialto Theatre (Chicago), 35–36, 42

Rice, Dan, 32

Rice, Thomas D., 11, 12

Richard III (Shakespeare), 21, 26–27, 80, 83, 120, 167–68

Richardson, Elizabeth Chapman (Jefferson's aunt), 14, 16, 18, 23, 24, 25, 52, 58, 361n27

Richmond (Virginia), 129–30, 172–73

Richmond Enquirer, 129, 172–73

Rip Van Winkle, 215, 227, 229; in Australia, 192, 194, 209–10, 233; in Baltimore, 247, 248; Burke as Rip, 95, 171, 219, 223; burlesque version of, 216–17; casting of, 259–60; in Chicago, 252–53; comedy in, 221–22; conflicted message of, 229–30; Dutch accent in, 237; enduring appeal of, 239; in England, 214–17, 216, 232, 283–84, 285, 286, 287–88; folk tale roots of, 217–18; Gulf Coast tour of, 248–49; Hackett as Rip, 219; illusion in, 236–37; in Ireland, 286–87; Irving's tale, 217–18, 219–20; Jefferson-Boucicault version of, 214, 222–30; Jefferson's appropriation of Rip, 170–71; Jefferson's children and grandchildren in, 273, 314, 345, 349; Jefferson's style in, 237–39; as melodrama, 220–21, 225, 239; mid-Atlantic tour of (1866–67), 246–48; mountain scene in, 222–23; music in, 224; in New Orleans, 248–49; in New York, 242–44, 249–50, 263, 264, 264, 267, 332; and Peter Pan comparison, 354; political and social issues in, 225–26; realism in, 217, 230–36; recordings and motion pictures of, 237, 347–48; in Richmond, 172; Rip impostors, 270–71; as role entrapment, 271–72, 320–21; in San Francisco, 188; in Scotland, 286; sets and costumes in, 237;

stage history of, 218–19; tours of, to smaller communities (1871–72), 258–60; transcontinental tours of, 288–89; Victorian sentiments and, 226–29, 247–48; in Washington, D.C., 178–79, 246–47, 247–48

Rivals, The (Sheridan), 321–31; acclaim and criticism of, 187, 326–27, 329; all-star tour of (1896), 332–37; burlesque in, 324–25; cast of, 330–31, 333, 335; in Charleston, 114; Jefferson's redaction of, 323–26; Sherman's original story, 321–23; tours of (1889–92), 327–31; in Washington, D.C., 247

Robertson, Agnes, 123–24, 126, 150, 160, 381n40

Robertson, Tom, 239, 248

Robson, Frederick, 132

romanticism, 26, 153, 170, 217, 221, 230, 292, 293

Rourke, Constance, 11, 13, 360n24

Royal Princess's Theatre (Melbourne), 193–98, *197*

Royal Street Theatre (Mobile), 52, 55, 57

Royal Victoria Theatre (Sydney), 191

Sabine, Lorenzo, 277–78, 406n18

St. Charles Theatre (New Orleans), 59, 71–72, 73, 75–77, 85–87

St. Louis (Missouri), 44–46, 77–79, 336

St. Louis (ship), 185

St. Louis Theatre, 44–45

San Francisco (California), 184–85, 185–89, 288–89

San Francisco Bulletin, 187, 188

San Francisco Daily Alta California, 188, 270

Sangamo Journal, 40, 41, 43

Sardou, Victorien, 235

Sargent, John Singer, 298, 302, 303–4, 350

Sarony, Napoleon, 261

Savannah (Georgia), 108, 110–11

Savannah Morning News, 111

scenery, 231–32

School for Scandal, The (Sheridan), 127–28

Scotland, 286

Scott, Clement, 284

Scott, James, 49

Scott, Walter, 164

Scribe, Eugène, 235

Scudder, Salem (character in *The Octoroon*), 155–56, 217

Sea of Ice, or a Mother's Prayer, 139

Sedgwick, A. G., 232

Sefton, John, 32–33, 107

Sefton, Joseph (Jefferson's son), 204, 312–13, 353

segregation, 56–57, 371n7

Serious Inquiry into the Nature and Effects of the Stage, A (Witherspoon), 279

Seth the Yankee (character in *Blanche of Brandywine*), 140

Shadows of a Great City (Jefferson, Shewell), 297–98

Shakespeare, William: *Macbeth,* 126; *A Midsummer Night's Dream,* 196–97, 250–51; as most revised playwright, 167–68, 323; *Richard III,* 21, 26–27, 80, 83, 120, 167–68

Shaw, Mary, 260

Sheepface (character in *The Village Lawyer*), 173

Sheridan, Richard Brinsley, 114, 321

Shewell, L. B., 297

Shinn, G. W., 280

showboat theatre, 30–31

Simmonds, James, 190, 191, 194, 199

Simpson, Edward, 25

Sketch-Book of Geoffrey Crayon, Gent., The (Irving), 170–71, 217

Skinner, Otis, 93, 238, 329, 330

Smike (Boucicault), 152

Smith, George Frederic, 27

Smith, H. S., 108–9

Smith, James, 194, 195, 198–200, 211

Smith, Sol: and feud with Ludlow, 369n41; on frontier theatre, 32, 307, 366n5; in Mobile, 55, 56, 57; in New Orleans, 71–72, 73, 75–77, 85; and rivalry with Caldwell, 58–59; in St. Louis, 44–45, 77
Snow-bound (Whittier), 248
Society for the Prevention of Vice, 11
Sothern, Edward A., 141, 142, 143, 144–46, 214
South Australian Register, 209–10
South Carolina, 108–9, 111, 117–19
Spectre Bridegroom, The; or, A Ghost in Spite of Himself (Moncrieff), 97, 138
Spirit of the Times, 52, 55, 70, 137, 138, 140, 141, 146, 156, 158, 165, 168, 169, 173, 180
spiritualism, 280–81, 407n24
spotlights, 265
Springfield (Illinois), 40–41, 43
Springfield (Massachusetts), 334
stage design, 230–31
stage families, 1–2, 19–20, 91
stage managing, 123, 124–29, 161–62, 164
Standard, 233
Stanley, "Pudding," 80–81
Star Theatre, 331
steamship travel, 34, 48, 51–52, 62–63
Stegner, Wallace, xvi
Steiner, George, 153, 235
stock company system, 90–93, 113, 256–57
stock parts/stock figures, 93–94, 126–27, 140, 154, 221, 329; Gumption Cute (character in *Uncle Tom's Cabin*) as, 98–99, 221, 329. *See also* Yankee stock figure
Stoddart, James H., 161
Stowe, Harriet Beecher, 97–98
Strong, George Templeton, 100
Stuart, Mary, 57
Stuart, William, 148, 160
stylized acting, 233–35
Sullivan, Barry, 196, 197–98

Swedenborg, Emanual, 280
Sydney-Morning Herald, 192, 205

Taber, Robert, 333
tableaux vivants (living pictures), 9–11
Talmage, Thomas De Witt, 279
Tasmania, 207–9, 233
Taylor, Benjamin T., 36
Taylor, Tom, 141, 143, 147, 159, 208, 387n57
Taylor, Zachary, 81, 82
temperance plays, 228
Tennessee, 50, 62
Terry, Ellen, 2, 353
Texas, 79–84
theatre: American attitudes toward, 2, 60, 61, 277–80; burlesque, 164, 166–69, 175, 216–17; censorship of, 59–61; and combination companies, 256–60; and death of tragedy, 153–54, 166, 235; drama debate, 295–97; equestrian melodrama, 20–22; farce, 96–97; frontier theatre, 30–32, 81; golden age of the American Stage, xvi–xvii; holiday extravaganzas, 124–25; immorality of, 35; Jefferson's career and the evolution of, xv, 351–56; Jefferson's metaphor of, 128; and litigation, 157–61; minstrelsy, 11–14, 100, 101, 360n24; monopoly in, 59, 339–41; New York as center of, 260–62; and political and social issues, 60–61, 98, 225–26; stock company system, 90–93, 113, 256–57; tableaux vivants, 9–11; as tradition-bound, 234–35, 258; vaudeville, 9–10, 32–33, 257
Theatre, 284
theatre critics. *See* critics and criticism
theatre managers, 136, 262–63, 265
Theatre Royal (Australia), 201
theatres: and agents, 262; backstage rules in, 122; comfort of, 118; and contracts, 108–9, 262–63, 274, 339–41; design of, 198; fires in, 5, 35, 56, 266; lighting in, 265, 403n54; and munici-

pal licensing, 35, 40–41, 60; Saturday matinees in, 161–62; scenery and props in, 231–32; segregation in, 56–57, 371n7; and stage design, 230–31; and stage lighting, 16; violence in, 57–58, 102–3

theatrical agents, 262

theatrical printers, 261

Theatrical Syndicate, 59, 339–41

Thomas, Elizabeth, 121

Thompson, Denman, 271

Thorne, James, 49

Ticket-of-Leave Man (Taylor), 208–9

Times (London), 233, 288

Titus, Master, 27, 365n67

Tocqueville, Alexis de, 18, 35, 57, 60–61, 279

Towse, John Ranken, 292

tragedy, death of, 153–54, 166, 235

Tree, Ellen. *See* Kean, Ellen Tree

Trenchard, Asa (character in *Our American Cousin*), 142, *142*, 143–44, 187, 207–8

Trollope, Anthony, 193, 201–2, 239

Trueman, Adam (character in *Fashion*), 75, 77

tuberculosis, 148, 181, 188–89

Uncle Tom's Cabin (Stowe), 60, 97–99, 358n18

Union Square (New York), 260–62

United States transcontinental tours, 288–89

Vandenhoff, George, 69, 219

Vanderbilt, Cornelius, 184–85

Varieties Theatre (New Orleans), 248–49

variety shows, 161–62

vaudeville, 9–10, 32–33, 257

Vicksburg (Mississippi), 49

Vicksburg Daily Whig, 49

Victorian era: and alcohol use, 228–29; and hypocrisy, 200; idleness as sin in, 227–28; importance of propriety in, 195; Jefferson as representative of, xvi;

and profanity, 226; sentimentality of, 226–27, 227, 239; and sincerity, 64–66; theatre as window to values of, xiv–xv; use of euphemism in, 122

Village Lawyer, The (Lyons), 173

Virginia Minstrels, 12

Vogel, Julius, 207

Walhalla Theatre, 101

Wallack, James, Sr., 67

Wallack, James W., Jr., 85–86, 96, 136, 141, 161, 169

Wallack's Theatre (New York), 86

Walnut Street Theatre (Philadelphia), 5, 88

Warren, William, 3, 20, 33, 121–22, 326

Warren, William, Jr., 38, 122

Washington, D.C.: in *1831*, 15; in *1860*, 171–72; and Civil War, 178, 179; Jefferson family troupe in (Jefferson's childhood), 8, 9, 14–15, *15*–18; National Theatre, 126–28, 246–48; *Rip Van Winkle* in, 178–79, 246–47, 247–48; *The Rivals* all-star tour in, 336; showing of Jefferson's art in, 302

Washington Theatre (Washington, D.C.), 8, 9, 14–15, *15*–18, 20

Washington Times, 302

Waterman, Arthur, 171

Watkins, Harry, 21–22, 27, 73, 106

Watterson, Henry, 181, 352

Waverly, Charles, 260

Webster, Benjamin, 214, 215–16

Wedmore, Frederick, 237, 238

Wemyss, Francis, 67

Wemyss, Frederick, 4

Werner (Byron), 68, 69

Westward migration, 30–32

Wheatley, William, 159, 244, 246, 387n57

Whitman, Walt, 100, 292

Whittier, John Greenleaf, 248

Wilde, Oscar, 99

Williams, Barney, 105, 126, 127

Wilmington Daily Journal, 117

Wilson, Francis, 298, 304, 311, 333–34, 352, 414n63

Winter, Samuel Pratt, 203, 244

Winter, William: on Burke and Burton, 95; and friendship with Jefferson, 293, 300; on George Holland, 278, 406n16; on Jefferson, xiv, 181, 325; on *Rip Van Winkle,* 171, 228, 250; on theatrical memoirs, 307

Winter Garden (New York), 148, 155, 160, 161–62, 163–65, 174–77, 180, 267

Witherspoon, John, 279

Wittke, Carl, 360n24

Wood, Mrs. John (Matilda Vining Wood), 150–51, 163, 164, 165, 166, 168, 175, 180

Wood, William B., 3, 27

Wright, Mary-Anne Jefferson Ingersoll (Jefferson's aunt), 17, 24, 25, 29–30, 43, 45, 47

Yale University, 342

Yankee stock figure, 94, 210; Asa Trenchard (*Our American Cousin*), 142, *142,* 143–44, 187, 207–8; Bob Acres (*The Rivals*), 114, 187, 247, 302–3, *303,* 322–26, *322;* C. F. Item (*Our Japanese Embassy*), 168–69; Fox as, 251; Gumption Cute (character in *Uncle Tom's Cabin*), 98–99; Salem Scudder (*The Octoroon*), 155–56, 217; Seth (*Blanche of Brandywine*), 140

Yankee Teamster, The (Jefferson), 210

yellow fever, 52–53, 56, 87, 371n6

Yosemite National Park, 289